Chrysler
Cirrus
Dodge Stratus
Plymouth
Breeze
Automotive Repair Manual

by Marc M Scribner
and John H Haynes
Member of the Guild of Motoring Writers

Models covered:
Chrysler Cirrus, Dodge Stratus and Plymouth Breeze
1995 through 1998

ABCDE
FGHIJ
KLMNO
PQ

Haynes Publishing Group
Sparkford Nr Yeovil
Somerset BA22 7JJ England

Haynes North America, Inc
861 Lawrence Drive
Newbury Park
California 91320 USA

Acknowledgments

We are grateful to the Chrysler Corporation for providing technical information and certain illustrations. Wiring diagrams produced exclusively for Haynes North America, Inc. by Valley Forge Technical Communications.

A book in the Haynes Automotive Repair Manual Series

Printed in the U.S.A.

ISBN 1 56392 296 7

Library of Congress Catalog Card Number 98-85028

Contents

Haynes mechanic, author and photographer with 1996 Chrysler Cirrus

About this manual

Its purpose

The purpose of this manual is to help you get the best value from your vehicle. It can do so in several ways. It can help you decide what work must be done, even if you choose to have it done by a dealer service department or a repair shop; it provides information and procedures for routine maintenance and servicing; and it offers diagnostic and repair procedures to follow when trouble occurs.

We hope you use the manual to tackle the work yourself. For many simpler jobs, doing it yourself may be quicker than arranging an appointment to get the vehicle into a shop and making the trips to leave it and pick it up. More importantly, a lot of money can be saved by avoiding the expense the shop must pass on to you to cover its labor and overhead costs. An added benefit is the sense of satisfaction and accomplishment that you feel after doing the job yourself.

Using the manual

The manual is divided into Chapters. Each Chapter is divided into numbered Sections, which are headed in bold type between horizontal lines. Each Section consists of consecutively numbered paragraphs.

At the beginning of each numbered Section you will be referred to any illustrations which apply to the procedures in that Section. The reference numbers used in illustration captions pinpoint the pertinent Section and the Step within that Section. That is, illustration 3.2 means the illustration refers to Section 3 and Step (or paragraph) 2 within that Section.

Procedures, once described in the text, are not normally repeated. When it's necessary to refer to another Chapter, the reference will be given as Chapter and Section number. Cross references given without use of the word "Chapter" apply to Sections and/or paragraphs in the same Chapter. For example, "see Section 8" means in the same Chapter.

References to the left or right side of the vehicle assume you are sitting in the driver's seat, facing forward.

Even though we have prepared this manual with extreme care, neither the publisher nor the author can accept responsibility for any errors in, or omissions from, the information given.

NOTE

A **Note** provides information necessary to properly complete a procedure or information which will make the procedure easier to understand.

CAUTION

A **Caution** provides a special procedure or special steps which must be taken while completing the procedure where the Caution is found. Not heeding a Caution can result in damage to the assembly being worked on.

WARNING

A **Warning** provides a special procedure or special steps which must be taken while completing the procedure where the Warning is found. Not heeding a Warning can result in personal injury.

Introduction to the Chrysler Cirrus, Dodge Stratus and Plymouth Breeze

The Chrysler Cirrus, Dodge Stratus and Plymouth Breeze models are four-door sedan type body styles. They feature transversely mounted engines which were offered in three displacements; a 2.0 liter in-line four-cylinder engine with a Single Overhead-Camshaft (SOHC), a 2.4 liter in-line four-cylinder engine with a Dual Overhead-Camshaft (DOHC) and the 60-degree V6 six-cylinder engine with Single Overhead-Camshafts (SOHC) (one over each cylinder head).

All models are equipped with an electronically controlled multi-port electronic fuel injection system.

The engine transmits power to the front wheels through either a five-speed manual transaxle or a four-speed automatic transaxle via independent driveaxles.

All models feature an all steel unibody design and independent front and rear suspension. The front suspension incorporates a shock absorber/coil spring assembly with upper and lower control arms, while the rear suspension utilizes a shock absorber/coil spring assembly and upper control arm in combination with a trailing arm and lateral links.

The standard power rack and pinion steering unit is mounted behind the engine on the front suspension crossmember. An electronically controlled variable-assist speed-proportional power steering was available as an option, which provided maximum power steering at low vehicle speeds.

All models are equipped with power assisted front disc and rear drum brakes with an Anti-lock Brake System (ABS) available as an option.

Vehicle identification numbers

Modifications are a continuing and unpublicized process in vehicle manufacturing. Since spare parts manuals and lists are compiled on a numerical basis, the individual vehicle numbers are essential to correctly identify the component required.

Vehicle Identification Number (VIN)

This very important identification number is located on a plate attached to the dashboard inside the windshield on the driver's side of the vehicle **(see illustration)**. The VIN also appears on the Vehicle Certifi-

cate of Title and Registration. It contains information such as where and when the vehicle was manufactured, the model year and the body style.

VIN engine and model year codes

Two particularly important pieces of information found in the VIN are the engine code and the model year code. Counting from the left, the engine code letter designation is the 8th digit and the model year code designation is the 10th digit.

On the models covered by this manual the engine codes are:

C.......................... 2.0L 4-cyl SOHC
H.......................... 2.5L V6 SOHC
X.......................... 2.4L 4-cyl DOHC

On the models covered by this manual the model year codes are:

S...........................1995
T 1996
V 1997
W...........................1998

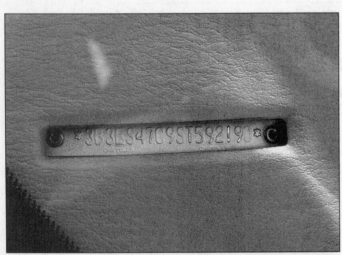

The Vehicle Identification Number (VIN) is stamped into a metal plate fastened to the dashboard on the driver's side - it's visible through the windshield

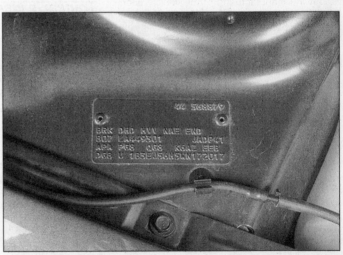

The Body Code Plate is mounted to the right hand shock tower in the engine compartment

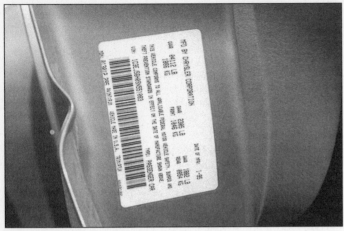

The Vehicle Safety Certification label is affixed to the rear edge of the driver's door

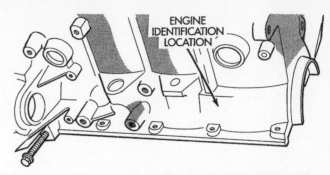

On 2.0L four-cylinder engines, the engine identification number is stamped on the left rear of the engine block (behind the starter motor)

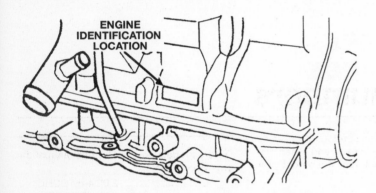

2.4L four-cylinder engine identification number locations

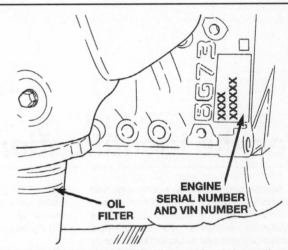

On V6 engines, the engine identification number is located on the rear of the engine block just below the cylinder head

Body Code Plate

The Body Code Plate is a stamped metal plate attached to the driver's side shock tower in the engine compartment (see illustration). It contains more specific information about the manufacturing of the vehicle such as the paint code, trim code and vehicle order number, as well as the VIN.

Vehicle Safety Certification label

The Vehicle Safety Certification label is attached to the driver's side door end (see illustration). The label contains the name of the manufacturer, the month and year of production, the Gross Vehicle Weight Rating (GVWR), the Gross Axle Weight Rating (GAWR) and the certification statement.

Engine identification numbers

The 2.0L and 2.4L four-cylinder engine

identification numbers can be found stamped on a machined pad on the left rear of the engine block. 2.5L V6 engine identification is located on the rear of the engine block just below the cylinder head (see illustrations).

Transaxle identification numbers

The transaxle identification information can be found on a bar code label located on the front of the transaxle (see illustration).

Vehicle Emissions Control Information (VECI) label

The emissions control information label is found under the hood, normally on the radiator support or the bottom side of the hood. This label contains information on the emissions control equipment installed on the vehicle, as well as tune-up specifications (see Chapter 6 for more information).

The transaxle identification number can be found on the side of the case (as shown) or the top of the bell housing

Buying parts

Replacement parts are available from many sources, which generally fall into one of two categories - authorized dealer parts departments and independent retail auto parts stores. Our advice concerning these parts is as follows:

Retail auto parts stores: Good auto parts stores will stock frequently needed components which wear out relatively fast, such as clutch components, exhaust systems, brake parts, tune-up parts, etc. These stores often supply new or reconditioned parts on an exchange basis, which can save a considerable amount of money. Discount auto parts stores are often very good places to buy materials and parts needed for general vehicle maintenance such as oil, grease, filters, spark plugs, belts, touch-up paint, bulbs, etc. They also usually sell tools and general accessories, have convenient hours, charge lower prices and can often be found not far from home.

Authorized dealer parts department: This is the best source for parts which are unique to the vehicle and not generally available elsewhere (such as major engine parts, transmission parts, trim pieces, etc.).

Warranty information: If the vehicle is still covered under warranty, be sure that any replacement parts purchased - regardless of the source - do not invalidate the warranty!

To be sure of obtaining the correct parts, have engine and chassis numbers available and, if possible, take the old parts along for positive identification.

Maintenance techniques, tools and working facilities

Maintenance techniques

There are a number of techniques involved in maintenance and repair that will be referred to throughout this manual. Application of these techniques will enable the home mechanic to be more efficient, better organized and capable of performing the various tasks properly, which will ensure that the repair job is thorough and complete.

Fasteners

Fasteners are nuts, bolts, studs and screws used to hold two or more parts together. There are a few things to keep in mind when working with fasteners. Almost all of them use a locking device of some type, either a lockwasher, locknut, locking tab or thread adhesive. All threaded fasteners should be clean and straight, with undamaged threads and undamaged corners on the hex head where the wrench fits. Develop the habit of replacing all damaged nuts and bolts with new ones. Special locknuts with nylon or fiber inserts can only be used once. If they are removed, they lose their locking ability and must be replaced with new ones.

Rusted nuts and bolts should be treated with a penetrating fluid to ease removal and prevent breakage. Some mechanics use turpentine in a spout-type oil can, which works quite well. After applying the rust penetrant, let it work for a few minutes before trying to loosen the nut or bolt. Badly rusted fasteners may have to be chiseled or sawed off or removed with a special nut breaker, available at tool stores.

If a bolt or stud breaks off in an assembly, it can be drilled and removed with a special tool commonly available for this purpose.

Most automotive machine shops can perform this task, as well as other repair procedures, such as the repair of threaded holes that have been stripped out.

Flat washers and lockwashers, when removed from an assembly, should always be replaced exactly as removed. Replace any damaged washers with new ones. Never use a lockwasher on any soft metal surface (such as aluminum), thin sheet metal or plastic.

Grade 1 or 2   Grade 5   Grade 8

Bolt strength marking (standard/SAE/USS; bottom - metric)

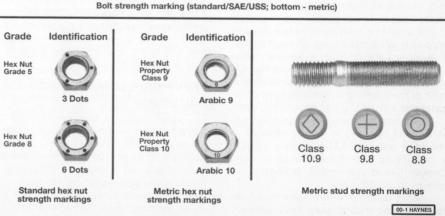

Grade	Identification
Hex Nut Grade 5	3 Dots
Hex Nut Grade 8	6 Dots

Standard hex nut strength markings

Grade	Identification
Hex Nut Property Class 9	Arabic 9
Hex Nut Property Class 10	Arabic 10

Metric hex nut strength markings

Class 10.9   Class 9.8   Class 8.8

Metric stud strength markings

00-1 HAYNES

Fastener sizes

For a number of reasons, automobile manufacturers are making wider and wider use of metric fasteners. Therefore, it is important to be able to tell the difference between standard (sometimes called U.S. or SAE) and metric hardware, since they cannot be interchanged.

All bolts, whether standard or metric, are sized according to diameter, thread pitch and length. For example, a standard 1/2 - 13 x 1 bolt is 1/2 inch in diameter, has 13 threads per inch and is 1 inch long. An M12 - 1.75 x 25 metric bolt is 12 mm in diameter, has a thread pitch of 1.75 mm (the distance between threads) and is 25 mm long. The two bolts are nearly identical, and easily confused, but they are not interchangeable.

In addition to the differences in diameter, thread pitch and length, metric and standard bolts can also be distinguished by examining the bolt heads. To begin with, the distance across the flats on a standard bolt head is measured in inches, while the same dimension on a metric bolt is sized in millimeters (the same is true for nuts). As a result, a standard wrench should not be used on a metric bolt and a metric wrench should not be used on a standard bolt. Also, most standard bolts have slashes radiating out from the center of the head to denote the grade or strength of the bolt, which is an indication of the amount of torque that can be applied to it. The greater the number of slashes, the greater the strength of the bolt. Grades 0 through 5 are commonly used on automobiles. Metric bolts have a property class (grade) number, rather than a slash, molded into their heads to indicate bolt strength. In this case, the higher the number, the stronger the bolt. Property class numbers 8.8, 9.8 and 10.9 are commonly used on automobiles.

Strength markings can also be used to distinguish standard hex nuts from metric hex nuts. Many standard nuts have dots stamped into one side, while metric nuts are marked with a number. The greater the number of dots, or the higher the number, the greater the strength of the nut.

Metric studs are also marked on their ends according to property class (grade). Larger studs are numbered (the same as metric bolts), while smaller studs carry a geometric code to denote grade.

It should be noted that many fasteners, especially Grades 0 through 2, have no distinguishing marks on them. When such is the case, the only way to determine whether it is standard or metric is to measure the thread pitch or compare it to a known fastener of the same size.

Standard fasteners are often referred to as SAE, as opposed to metric. However, it should be noted that SAE technically refers to a non-metric fine thread fastener only. Coarse thread non-metric fasteners are referred to as USS sizes.

Since fasteners of the same size (both standard and metric) may have different

Metric thread sizes	Ft-lbs	Nm
M-6	6 to 9	9 to 12
M-8	14 to 21	19 to 28
M-10	28 to 40	38 to 54
M-12	50 to 71	68 to 96
M-14	80 to 140	109 to 154
Pipe thread sizes		
1/8	5 to 8	7 to 10
1/4	12 to 18	17 to 24
3/8	22 to 33	30 to 44
1/2	25 to 35	34 to 47
U.S. thread sizes		
1/4 - 20	6 to 9	9 to 12
5/16 - 18	12 to 18	17 to 24
5/16 - 24	14 to 20	19 to 27
3/8 - 16	22 to 32	30 to 43
3/8 - 24	27 to 38	37 to 51
7/16 - 14	40 to 55	55 to 74
7/16 - 20	40 to 60	55 to 81
1/2 - 13	55 to 80	75 to 108

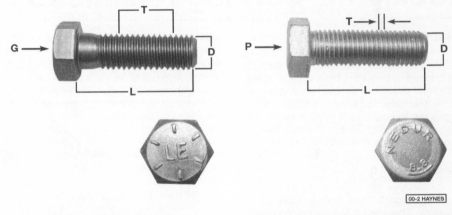

Standard (SAE and USS) bolt dimensions/grade marks

G   Grade marks (bolt strength)
L   Length (in inches)
T   Thread pitch (number of threads per inch)
D   Nominal diameter (in inches)

Metric bolt dimensions/grade marks

P   Property class (bolt strength)
L   Length (in millimeters)
T   Thread pitch (distance between threads in millimeters)
D   Diameter

strength ratings, be sure to reinstall any bolts, studs or nuts removed from your vehicle in their original locations. Also, when replacing a fastener with a new one, make sure that the new one has a strength rating equal to or greater than the original.

Tightening sequences and procedures

Most threaded fasteners should be tightened to a specific torque value (torque is the twisting force applied to a threaded component such as a nut or bolt). Overtightening the fastener can weaken it and cause it to break, while undertightening can cause it to eventually come loose. Bolts, screws and studs, depending on the material they are

made of and their thread diameters, have specific torque values, many of which are noted in the Specifications at the beginning of each Chapter. Be sure to follow the torque recommendations closely. For fasteners not assigned a specific torque, a general torque value chart is presented here as a guide. These torque values are for dry (unlubricated) fasteners threaded into steel or cast iron (not aluminum). As was previously mentioned, the size and grade of a fastener determine the amount of torque that can safely be applied to it. The figures listed here are approximate for Grade 2 and Grade 3 fasteners. Higher grades can tolerate higher torque values.

Fasteners laid out in a pattern, such as cylinder head bolts, oil pan bolts, differential cover bolts, etc., must be loosened or tight-

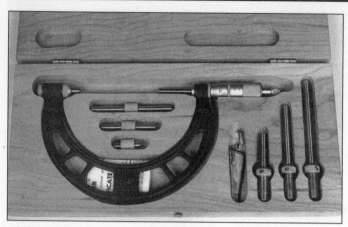

Micrometer set

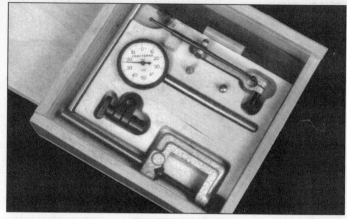

Dial indicator set

ened in sequence to avoid warping the component. This sequence will normally be shown in the appropriate Chapter. If a specific pattern is not given, the following procedures can be used to prevent warping.

Initially, the bolts or nuts should be assembled finger-tight only. Next, they should be tightened one full turn each, in a criss-cross or diagonal pattern. After each one has been tightened one full turn, return to the first one and tighten them all one-half turn, following the same pattern. Finally, tighten each of them one-quarter turn at a time until each fastener has been tightened to the proper torque. To loosen and remove the fasteners, the procedure would be reversed.

Component disassembly

Component disassembly should be done with care and purpose to help ensure that the parts go back together properly. Always keep track of the sequence in which parts are removed. Make note of special characteristics or marks on parts that can be installed more than one way, such as a grooved thrust washer on a shaft. It is a good idea to lay the disassembled parts out on a clean surface in the order that they were removed. It may also be helpful to make sketches or take instant photos of components before removal.

When removing fasteners from a component, keep track of their locations. Sometimes threading a bolt back in a part, or putting the washers and nut back on a stud, can prevent mix-ups later. If nuts and bolts cannot be returned to their original locations, they should be kept in a compartmented box or a series of small boxes. A cupcake or muffin tin is ideal for this purpose, since each cavity can hold the bolts and nuts from a particular area (i.e. oil pan bolts, valve cover bolts, engine mount bolts, etc.). A pan of this type is especially helpful when working on assemblies with very small parts, such as the carburetor, alternator, valve train or interior dash and trim pieces. The cavities can be marked with paint or tape to identify the contents.

Whenever wiring looms, harnesses or connectors are separated, it is a good idea to identify the two halves with numbered pieces of masking tape so they can be easily reconnected.

Gasket sealing surfaces

Throughout any vehicle, gaskets are used to seal the mating surfaces between two parts and keep lubricants, fluids, vacuum or pressure contained in an assembly.

Many times these gaskets are coated with a liquid or paste-type gasket sealing compound before assembly. Age, heat and pressure can sometimes cause the two parts to stick together so tightly that they are very difficult to separate. Often, the assembly can be loosened by striking it with a soft-face hammer near the mating surfaces. A regular hammer can be used if a block of wood is placed between the hammer and the part. Do not hammer on cast parts or parts that could be easily damaged. With any particularly stubborn part, always recheck to make sure that every fastener has been removed.

Avoid using a screwdriver or bar to pry apart an assembly, as they can easily mar the gasket sealing surfaces of the parts, which must remain smooth. If prying is absolutely necessary, use an old broom handle, but keep in mind that extra clean up will be necessary if the wood splinters.

After the parts are separated, the old gasket must be carefully scraped off and the gasket surfaces cleaned. Stubborn gasket material can be soaked with rust penetrant or treated with a special chemical to soften it so it can be easily scraped off. A scraper can be fashioned from a piece of copper tubing by flattening and sharpening one end. Copper is recommended because it is usually softer than the surfaces to be scraped, which reduces the chance of gouging the part. Some gaskets can be removed with a wire brush, but regardless of the method used, the mating surfaces must be left clean and smooth. If for some reason the gasket surface is gouged, then a gasket sealer thick enough to fill scratches will have to be used during reassembly of the components. For most applications, a non-drying (or semi-drying) gasket sealer should be used.

Hose removal tips

Warning: *If the vehicle is equipped with air conditioning, do not disconnect any of the A/C hoses without first having the system depressurized by a dealer service department or a service station.*

Hose removal precautions closely parallel gasket removal precautions. Avoid scratching or gouging the surface that the hose mates against or the connection may leak. This is especially true for radiator hoses. Because of various chemical reactions, the rubber in hoses can bond itself to the metal spigot that the hose fits over. To remove a hose, first loosen the hose clamps that secure it to the spigot. Then, with slip-joint pliers, grab the hose at the clamp and rotate it around the spigot. Work it back and forth until it is completely free, then pull it off. Silicone or other lubricants will ease removal if they can be applied between the hose and the outside of the spigot. Apply the same lubricant to the inside of the hose and the outside of the spigot to simplify installation.

As a last resort (and if the hose is to be replaced with a new one anyway) the rubber can be slit with a knife and the hose peeled from the spigot. If this must be done, be careful that the metal connection is not damaged.

If a hose clamp is broken or damaged, do not reuse it. Wire-type clamps usually weaken with age, so it is a good idea to replace them with screw-type clamps whenever a hose is removed.

Tools

A selection of good tools is a basic requirement for anyone who plans to maintain and repair his or her own vehicle. For the owner who has few tools, the initial investment might seem high, but when compared to the spiraling costs of professional auto maintenance and repair, it is a wise one.

To help the owner decide which tools are needed to perform the tasks detailed in this manual, the following tool lists are offered: *Maintenance and minor repair, Repair/overhaul* and *Special.*

The newcomer to practical mechanics

Dial caliper

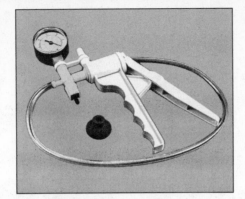

Hand-operated vacuum pump

Timing light

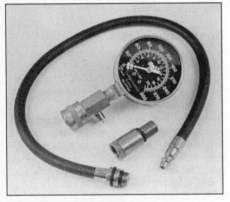

Compression gauge with spark plug
hole adapter

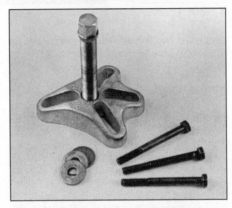

Damper/steering wheel puller

General purpose puller

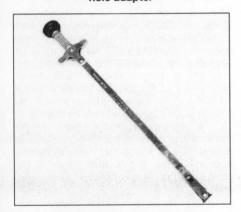

Hydraulic lifter removal tool

Valve spring compressor

Valve spring compressor

Ridge reamer

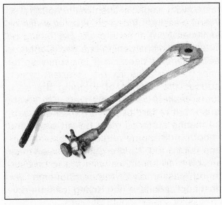

Piston ring groove cleaning tool

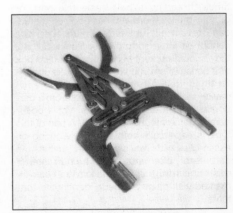

Ring removal/installation tool

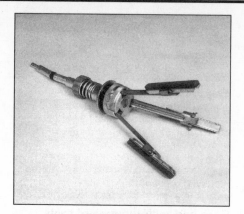

Ring compressor

Brake hold-down spring tool

Brake cylinder hone

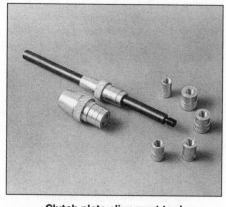

Clutch plate alignment tool

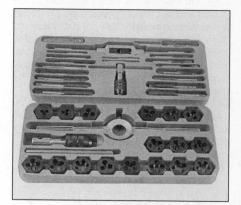

Tap and die set

should start off with the *maintenance and minor repair* tool kit, which is adequate for the simpler jobs performed on a vehicle. Then, as confidence and experience grow, the owner can tackle more difficult tasks, buying additional tools as they are needed. Eventually the basic kit will be expanded into the *repair and overhaul* tool set. Over a period of time, the experienced do-it-yourselfer will assemble a tool set complete enough for most repair and overhaul procedures and will add tools from the special category when it is felt that the expense is justified by the frequency of use.

Maintenance and minor repair tool kit

The tools in this list should be considered the minimum required for performance of routine maintenance, servicing and minor repair work. We recommend the purchase of combination wrenches (box-end and open-end combined in one wrench). While more expensive than open end wrenches, they offer the advantages of both types of wrench.

Combination wrench set (1/4-inch to
*   1 inch or 6 mm to 19 mm)*
Adjustable wrench, 8 inch
Spark plug wrench with rubber insert
Spark plug gap adjusting tool
Feeler gauge set
Brake bleeder wrench
Standard screwdriver (5/16-inch x
*   6 inch)*

Phillips screwdriver (No. 2 x 6 inch)
Combination pliers - 6 inch
Hacksaw and assortment of blades
Tire pressure gauge
Grease gun
Oil can
Fine emery cloth
Wire brush
Battery post and cable cleaning tool
Oil filter wrench
Funnel (medium size)
Safety goggles
Jackstands (2)
Drain pan

Note: *If basic tune-ups are going to be part of routine maintenance, it will be necessary to purchase a good quality stroboscopic timing light and combination tachometer/dwell meter. Although they are included in the list of special tools, it is mentioned here because they are absolutely necessary for tuning most vehicles properly.*

Repair and overhaul tool set

These tools are essential for anyone who plans to perform major repairs and are in addition to those in the maintenance and minor repair tool kit. Included is a comprehensive set of sockets which, though expensive, are invaluable because of their versatility, especially when various extensions and drives are available. We recommend the 1/2-inch drive over the 3/8-inch drive. Although the larger drive is bulky and more expensive, but

it has the capacity of accepting a very wide range of large sockets. Ideally, however, the mechanic should have a 3/8-inch drive set and a 1/2-inch drive set.

Socket set(s)
Reversible ratchet
Extension - 10 inch
Universal joint
Torque wrench (same size drive as
*   sockets)*
Ball peen hammer - 8 ounce
Soft-face hammer (plastic/rubber)
Standard screwdriver (1/4-inch x 6 inch)
Standard screwdriver (stubby -
*   5/16-inch)*
Phillips screwdriver (No. 3 x 8 inch)
Phillips screwdriver (stubby - No. 2)
Pliers - vise grip
Pliers - lineman's
Pliers - needle nose
Pliers - snap-ring (internal and external)
Cold chisel - 1/2-inch
Scribe
Scraper (made from flattened copper
*   tubing)*
Centerpunch
Pin punches (1/16, 1/8, 3/16-inch)
Steel rule/straightedge - 12 inch
Allen wrench set (1/8 to 3/8-inch or
*   4 mm to 10 mm)*
A selection of files
Wire brush (large)
Jackstands (second set)
Jack (scissor or hydraulic type)

Note: *Another tool which is often useful is an electric drill with a chuck capacity of 3/8-inch and a set of good quality drill bits.*

Special tools

The tools in this list include those which are not used regularly, are expensive to buy, or which need to be used in accordance with their manufacturer's instructions. Unless these tools will be used frequently, it is not very economical to purchase many of them. A consideration would be to split the cost and use between yourself and a friend or friends. In addition, most of these tools can be obtained from a tool rental shop on a temporary basis.

This list primarily contains only those tools and instruments widely available to the public, and not those special tools produced by the vehicle manufacturer for distribution to dealer service departments. Occasionally, references to the manufacturer's special tools are included in the text of this manual. Generally, an alternative method of doing the job without the special tool is offered. However, sometimes there is no alternative to their use. Where this is the case, and the tool cannot be purchased or borrowed, the work should be turned over to the dealer service department or an automotive repair shop.

Valve spring compressor
Piston ring groove cleaning tool
Piston ring compressor
Piston ring installation tool
Cylinder compression gauge
Cylinder ridge reamer
Cylinder surfacing hone
Cylinder bore gauge
Micrometers and/or dial calipers
Hydraulic lifter removal tool
Balljoint separator
Universal-type puller
Impact screwdriver
Dial indicator set
Stroboscopic timing light (inductive pick-up)
Hand operated vacuum/pressure pump
Tachometer/dwell meter
Universal electrical multimeter
Cable hoist
Brake spring removal and installation tools
Floor jack

Buying tools

For the do-it-yourselfer who is just starting to get involved in vehicle maintenance and repair, there are a number of options available when purchasing tools. If maintenance and minor repair is the extent of the work to be done, the purchase of individual tools is satisfactory. If, on the other hand, extensive work is planned, it would be a good idea to purchase a modest tool set from one of the large retail chain stores. A set can usually be bought at a substantial savings over the individual tool prices, and they often come with a tool box. As additional tools are

needed, add-on sets, individual tools and a larger tool box can be purchased to expand the tool selection. Building a tool set gradually allows the cost of the tools to be spread over a longer period of time and gives the mechanic the freedom to choose only those tools that will actually be used.

Tool stores will often be the only source of some of the special tools that are needed, but regardless of where tools are bought, try to avoid cheap ones, especially when buying screwdrivers and sockets, because they won't last very long. The expense involved in replacing cheap tools will eventually be greater than the initial cost of quality tools.

Care and maintenance of tools

Good tools are expensive, so it makes sense to treat them with respect. Keep them clean and in usable condition and store them properly when not in use. Always wipe off any dirt, grease or metal chips before putting them away. Never leave tools lying around in the work area. Upon completion of a job, always check closely under the hood for tools that may have been left there so they won't get lost during a test drive.

Some tools, such as screwdrivers, pliers, wrenches and sockets, can be hung on a panel mounted on the garage or workshop wall, while others should be kept in a tool box or tray. Measuring instruments, gauges, meters, etc. must be carefully stored where they cannot be damaged by weather or impact from other tools.

When tools are used with care and stored properly, they will last a very long time. Even with the best of care, though, tools will wear out if used frequently. When a tool is damaged or worn out, replace it. Subsequent jobs will be safer and more enjoyable if you do.

How to repair damaged threads

Sometimes, the internal threads of a nut or bolt hole can become stripped, usually from overtightening. Stripping threads is an all-too-common occurrence, especially when working with aluminum parts, because aluminum is so soft that it easily strips out.

Usually, external or internal threads are only partially stripped. After they've been cleaned up with a tap or die, they'll still work. Sometimes, however, threads are badly damaged. When this happens, you've got three choices:

1) *Drill and tap the hole to the next suitable oversize and install a larger diameter bolt, screw or stud.*
2) *Drill and tap the hole to accept a threaded plug, then drill and tap the plug to the original screw size. You can also buy a plug already threaded to the original size. Then you simply drill a hole to the specified size, then run the threaded plug into the hole with a bolt and jam*

nut. Once the plug is fully seated, remove the jam nut and bolt.
3) *The third method uses a patented thread repair kit like Heli-Coil or Slimsert. These easy-to-use kits are designed to repair damaged threads in straight-through holes and blind holes. Both are available as kits which can handle a variety of sizes and thread patterns. Drill the hole, then tap it with the special included tap. Install the Heli-Coil and the hole is back to its original diameter and thread pitch.*

Regardless of which method you use, be sure to proceed calmly and carefully. A little impatience or carelessness during one of these relatively simple procedures can ruin your whole day's work and cost you a bundle if you wreck an expensive part.

Working facilities

Not to be overlooked when discussing tools is the workshop. If anything more than routine maintenance is to be carried out, some sort of suitable work area is essential.

It is understood, and appreciated, that many home mechanics do not have a good workshop or garage available, and end up removing an engine or doing major repairs outside. It is recommended, however, that the overhaul or repair be completed under the cover of a roof.

A clean, flat workbench or table of comfortable working height is an absolute necessity. The workbench should be equipped with a vise that has a jaw opening of at least four inches.

As mentioned previously, some clean, dry storage space is also required for tools, as well as the lubricants, fluids, cleaning solvents, etc. which soon become necessary.

Sometimes waste oil and fluids, drained from the engine or cooling system during normal maintenance or repairs, present a disposal problem. To avoid pouring them on the ground or into a sewage system, pour the used fluids into large containers, seal them with caps and take them to an authorized disposal site or recycling center. Plastic jugs, such as old antifreeze containers, are ideal for this purpose.

Always keep a supply of old newspapers and clean rags available. Old towels are excellent for mopping up spills. Many mechanics use rolls of paper towels for most work because they are readily available and disposable. To help keep the area under the vehicle clean, a large cardboard box can be cut open and flattened to protect the garage or shop floor.

Whenever working over a painted surface, such as when leaning over a fender to service something under the hood, always cover it with an old blanket or bedspread to protect the finish. Vinyl covered pads, made especially for this purpose, are available at auto parts stores.

Booster battery (jump) starting

Observe these precautions when using a booster battery to start a vehicle:

a) *Before connecting the booster battery, make sure the ignition switch is in the OFF position.*
b) *Turn off the lights, heater and other electrical loads.*
c) *Your eyes should be shielded. Safety goggles are a good idea.*
d) *Make sure the booster battery is the same voltage as the dead one in the vehicle.*
e) *The two vehicles MUST NOT TOUCH each other!*
f) *Make sure the transaxle is in Neutral (manual) or Park (automatic).*
g) *If the booster battery is not a maintenance-free type, remove the vent caps and lay a cloth over the vent holes.*

The battery on these vehicles is located inside the wheel well of the left front fender. Due to the lack of accessibility, remote battery connections are provided inside the engine compartment for jump-starting and easy battery disconnection **(see illustration)**.

Connect the red colored jumper cable to the positive (+) terminal of booster battery and the other end to the positive (+) remote terminal inside the engine compartment. Then connect one end of the black colored jumper cable to the negative (-) terminal of the booster battery and other end of the cable to the negative (-) remote terminal.

Start the engine using the booster battery, then, with the engine running at idle speed, disconnect the jumper cables in the reverse order of connection.

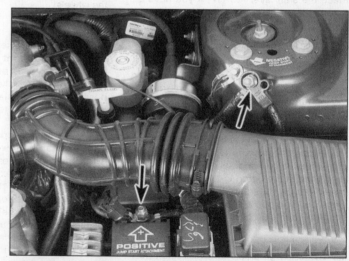

The remote battery terminals (arrows) are located in the engine compartment and well marked - when connecting jumper cables connect the cable to the positive terminal first, then the negative terminal

Jacking and towing

Jacking

Warning: *The jack supplied with the vehicle should only be used for changing a tire or placing jackstands under the frame. Never work under the vehicle or start the engine while this jack is being used as the only means of support.*

The vehicle should be on level ground. Place the shift lever in Park, if you have an automatic, or Reverse if you have a manual transaxle. Block the wheel diagonally opposite the wheel being changed. Set the parking brake.

Remove the spare tire and jack from stowage. Remove the wheel cover and trim ring (if so equipped) with the tapered end of the lug nut wrench by inserting and twisting the handle and then prying against the back of the wheel cover. Loosen the wheel lug nuts about 1/4-to-1/2 turn each.

Place the scissors-type jack under the side of the vehicle and adjust the jack height until it fits in the notch in the vertical rocker panel flange nearest the wheel to be changed. There is a front and rear jacking point on each side of the vehicle **(see illustration)**.

Turn the jack handle clockwise until the tire clears the ground. Remove the lug nuts and pull the wheel off. Replace it with the spare.

Install the lug nuts with the beveled edges facing in. Tighten them snugly. Don't attempt to tighten them completely until the vehicle is lowered or it could slip off the jack. Turn the jack handle counterclockwise to lower the vehicle. Remove the jack and tighten the lug nuts in a diagonal pattern.

Install the cover (and trim ring, if used) and be sure it's snapped into place all the way around.

Stow the tire, jack and wrench. Unblock the wheels.

Towing

As a general rule, the vehicle should be towed with the front (drive) wheels off the ground. If they can't be raised, place them on a dolly. The ignition key must be in the ACC position, since the steering lock mechanism isn't strong enough to hold the front wheels straight while towing.

Vehicles equipped with an automatic transaxle can be towed from the front only with all four wheels on the ground, provided that speeds don't exceed 25 mph and the distance is not over 15 miles. Before towing, check the transmission fluid level (see Chapter 1). If the level is below the HOT line on the dipstick, add fluid or use a towing dolly.

Caution: *Never tow a vehicle with an automatic transaxle from the rear with the front wheels on the ground.*

When towing a vehicle equipped with a manual transaxle with all four wheels on the ground, be sure to place the shift lever in

The jack fits over the rocker panel flange (there are two jacking points on each side of the vehicle, indicated by a notch in the rocker panel flange)

Neutral and release the parking brake.

Equipment specifically designed for towing should be used. It should be attached to the main structural members of the vehicle, not the bumpers, brackets or suspension.

Safety is a major consideration when towing and all applicable state and local laws must be obeyed. A safety chain system must be used at all times.

Automotive chemicals and lubricants

A number of automotive chemicals and lubricants are available for use during vehicle maintenance and repair. They include a wide variety of products ranging from cleaning solvents and degreasers to lubricants and protective sprays for rubber, plastic and vinyl.

Cleaners

Carburetor cleaner and choke cleaner is a strong solvent for gum, varnish and carbon. Most carburetor cleaners leave a dry-type lubricant film which will not harden or gum up. Because of this film it is not recommended for use on electrical components.

Brake system cleaner is used to remove grease and brake fluid from the brake system, where clean surfaces are absolutely necessary. It leaves no residue and often eliminates brake squeal caused by contaminants.

Electrical cleaner removes oxidation, corrosion and carbon deposits from electrical contacts, restoring full current flow. It can also be used to clean spark plugs, carburetor jets, voltage regulators and other parts where an oil-free surface is desired.

Demoisturants remove water and moisture from electrical components such as alternators, voltage regulators, electrical connectors and fuse blocks. They are non-conductive, non-corrosive and non-flammable.

Degreasers are heavy-duty solvents used to remove grease from the outside of the engine and from chassis components. They can be sprayed or brushed on and, depending on the type, are rinsed off either with water or solvent.

Lubricants

Motor oil is the lubricant formulated for use in engines. It normally contains a wide variety of additives to prevent corrosion and reduce foaming and wear. Motor oil comes in various weights (viscosity ratings) from 0 to 50. The recommended weight of the oil depends on the season, temperature and the demands on the engine. Light oil is used in cold climates and under light load conditions. Heavy oil is used in hot climates and where high loads are encountered. Multi-viscosity oils are designed to have characteristics of both light and heavy oils and are available in a number of weights from 5W-20 to 20W-50.

Gear oil is designed to be used in differentials, manual transmissions and other areas where high-temperature lubrication is required.

Chassis and wheel bearing grease is a heavy grease used where increased loads and friction are encountered, such as for wheel bearings, balljoints, tie-rod ends and universal joints.

High-temperature wheel bearing grease is designed to withstand the extreme temperatures encountered by wheel bearings in disc brake equipped vehicles. It usually contains molybdenum disulfide (moly), which is a dry-type lubricant.

White grease is a heavy grease for metal-to-metal applications where water is a problem. White grease stays soft under both low and high temperatures (usually from -100 to +190-degrees F), and will not wash off or dilute in the presence of water.

Assembly lube is a special extreme pressure lubricant, usually containing moly, used to lubricate high-load parts (such as main and rod bearings and cam lobes) for initial start-up of a new engine. The assembly lube lubricates the parts without being squeezed out or washed away until the engine oiling system begins to function.

Silicone lubricants are used to protect rubber, plastic, vinyl and nylon parts.

Graphite lubricants are used where oils cannot be used due to contamination problems, such as in locks. The dry graphite will lubricate metal parts while remaining uncontaminated by dirt, water, oil or acids. It is electrically conductive and will not foul electrical contacts in locks such as the ignition switch.

Moly penetrants loosen and lubricate frozen, rusted and corroded fasteners and prevent future rusting or freezing.

Heat-sink grease is a special electrically non-conductive grease that is used for mounting electronic ignition modules where it is essential that heat is transferred away from the module.

Sealants

RTV sealant is one of the most widely used gasket compounds. Made from silicone, RTV is air curing, it seals, bonds, waterproofs, fills surface irregularities, remains flexible, doesn't shrink, is relatively easy to remove, and is used as a supplementary sealer with almost all low and medium temperature gaskets.

Anaerobic sealant is much like RTV in that it can be used either to seal gaskets or to form gaskets by itself. It remains flexible, is solvent resistant and fills surface imperfections. The difference between an anaerobic sealant and an RTV-type sealant is in the curing. RTV cures when exposed to air, while an anaerobic sealant cures only in the absence of air. This means that an anaerobic sealant cures only after the assembly of parts, sealing them together.

Thread and pipe sealant is used for sealing hydraulic and pneumatic fittings and vacuum lines. It is usually made from a Teflon compound, and comes in a spray, a paint-on liquid and as a wrap-around tape.

Chemicals

Anti-seize compound prevents seizing, galling, cold welding, rust and corrosion in fasteners. High-temperature ant-seize, usually made with copper and graphite lubricants, is used for exhaust system and exhaust manifold bolts.

Anaerobic locking compounds are used to keep fasteners from vibrating or working loose and cure only after installation, in the absence of air. Medium strength locking compound is used for small nuts, bolts and screws that may be removed later. High-strength locking compound is for large nuts, bolts and studs which aren't removed on a regular basis.

Oil additives range from viscosity index improvers to chemical treatments that claim to reduce internal engine friction. It should be noted that most oil manufacturers caution against using additives with their oils.

Gas additives perform several functions, depending on their chemical makeup. They usually contain solvents that help dissolve gum and varnish that build up on carburetor, fuel injection and intake parts. They also serve to break down carbon deposits that form on the inside surfaces of the combustion chambers. Some additives contain upper cylinder lubricants for valves and piston rings, and others contain chemicals to remove condensation from the gas tank.

Miscellaneous

Brake fluid is specially formulated hydraulic fluid that can withstand the heat and pressure encountered in brake systems. Care must be taken so this fluid does not come in contact with painted surfaces or plastics. An opened container should always be resealed to prevent contamination by water or dirt.

Weatherstrip adhesive is used to bond weatherstripping around doors, windows and trunk lids. It is sometimes used to attach trim pieces.

Undercoating is a petroleum-based, tar-like substance that is designed to protect metal surfaces on the underside of the vehicle from corrosion. It also acts as a sound-deadening agent by insulating the bottom of the vehicle.

Waxes and polishes are used to help protect painted and plated surfaces from the weather. Different types of paint may require the use of different types of wax and polish. Some polishes utilize a chemical or abrasive cleaner to help remove the top layer of oxidized (dull) paint on older vehicles. In recent years many non-wax polishes that contain a wide variety of chemicals such as polymers and silicones have been introduced. These non-wax polishes are usually easier to apply and last longer than conventional waxes and polishes.

Conversion factors

Length (distance)

Inches (in)	X	25.4	= Millimetres (mm)	X 0.0394	= Inches (in)
Feet (ft)	X	0.305	= Metres (m)	X 3.281	= Feet (ft)
Miles	X	1.609	= Kilometres (km)	X 0.621	= Miles

Volume (capacity)

Cubic inches (cu in; in³)	X	16.387	= Cubic centimetres (cc; cm³)	X 0.061	= Cubic inches (cu in; in³)
Imperial pints (Imp pt)	X	0.568	= Litres (l)	X 1.76	= Imperial pints (Imp pt)
Imperial quarts (Imp qt)	X	1.137	= Litres (l)	X 0.88	= Imperial quarts (Imp qt)
Imperial quarts (Imp qt)	X	1.201	= US quarts (US qt)	X 0.833	= Imperial quarts (Imp qt)
US quarts (US qt)	X	0.946	= Litres (l)	X 1.057	= US quarts (US qt)
Imperial gallons (Imp gal)	X	4.546	= Litres (l)	X 0.22	= Imperial gallons (Imp gal)
Imperial gallons (Imp gal)	X	1.201	= US gallons (US gal)	X 0.833	= Imperial gallons (Imp gal)
US gallons (US gal)	X	3.785	= Litres (l)	X 0.264	= US gallons (US gal)

Mass (weight)

Ounces (oz)	X	28.35	= Grams (g)	X 0.035	= Ounces (oz)
Pounds (lb)	X	0.454	= Kilograms (kg)	X 2.205	= Pounds (lb)

Force

Ounces-force (ozf; oz)	X	0.278	= Newtons (N)	X 3.6	= Ounces-force (ozf; oz)
Pounds-force (lbf; lb)	X	4.448	= Newtons (N)	X 0.225	= Pounds-force (lbf; lb)
Newtons (N)	X	0.1	= Kilograms-force (kgf; kg)	X 9.81	= Newtons (N)

Pressure

Pounds-force per square inch (psi; lbf/in²; lb/in²)	X	0.070	= Kilograms-force per square centimetre (kgf/cm²; kg/cm²)	X 14.223	= Pounds-force per square inch (psi; lbf/in²; lb/in²)
Pounds-force per square inch (psi; lbf/in²; lb/in²)	X	0.068	= Atmospheres (atm)	X 14.696	= Pounds-force per square inch (psi; lbf/in²; lb/in²)
Pounds-force per square inch (psi; lbf/in²; lb/in²)	X	0.069	= Bars	X 14.5	= Pounds-force per square inch (psi; lbf/in²; lb/in²)
Pounds-force per square inch (psi; lbf/in²; lb/in²)	X	6.895	= Kilopascals (kPa)	X 0.145	= Pounds-force per square inch (psi; lbf/in²; lb/in²)
Kilopascals (kPa)	X	0.01	= Kilograms-force per square centimetre (kgf/cm²; kg/cm²)	X 98.1	= Kilopascals (kPa)

Torque (moment of force)

Pounds-force inches (lbf in; lb in)	X	1.152	= Kilograms-force centimetre (kgf cm; kg cm)	X 0.868	= Pounds-force inches (lbf in; lb in)
Pounds-force inches (lbf in; lb in)	X	0.113	= Newton metres (Nm)	X 8.85	= Pounds-force inches (lbf in; lb in)
Pounds-force inches (lbf in; lb in)	X	0.083	= Pounds-force feet (lbf ft; lb ft)	X 12	= Pounds-force inches (lbf in; lb in)
Pounds-force feet (lbf ft; lb ft)	X	0.138	= Kilograms-force metres (kgf m; kg m)	X 7.233	= Pounds-force feet (lbf ft; lb ft)
Pounds-force feet (lbf ft; lb ft)	X	1.356	= Newton metres (Nm)	X 0.738	= Pounds-force feet (lbf ft; lb ft)
Newton metres (Nm)	X	0.102	= Kilograms-force metres (kgf m; kg m)	X 9.804	= Newton metres (Nm)

Vacuum

Inches mercury (in. Hg)	X	3.377	= Kilopascals (kPa)	X 0.2961	= Inches mercury
Inches mercury (in. Hg)	X	25.4	= Millimeters mercury (mm Hg)	X 0.0394	= Inches mercury

Power

Horsepower (hp)	X	745.7	= Watts (W)	X 0.0013	= Horsepower (hp)

Velocity (speed)

Miles per hour (miles/hr; mph)	X	1.609	= Kilometres per hour (km/hr; kph)	X 0.621	= Miles per hour (miles/hr; mph)

Fuel consumption*

Miles per gallon, Imperial (mpg)	X	0.354	= Kilometres per litre (km/l)	X 2.825	= Miles per gallon, Imperial (mpg)
Miles per gallon, US (mpg)	X	0.425	= Kilometres per litre (km/l)	X 2.352	= Miles per gallon, US (mpg)

Temperature

Degrees Fahrenheit = (°C x 1.8) + 32

Degrees Celsius (Degrees Centigrade; °C) = (°F - 32) x 0.56

*It is common practice to convert from miles per gallon (mpg) to litres/100 kilometres (l/100km),
where mpg (Imperial) x l/100 km = 282 and mpg (US) x l/100 km = 235

Safety first!

Regardless of how enthusiastic you may be about getting on with the job at hand, take the time to ensure that your safety is not jeopardized. A moment's lack of attention can result in an accident, as can failure to observe certain simple safety precautions. The possibility of an accident will always exist, and the following points should not be considered a comprehensive list of all dangers. Rather, they are intended to make you aware of the risks and to encourage a safety conscious approach to all work you carry out on your vehicle.

Essential DOs and DON'Ts

DON'T rely on a jack when working under the vehicle. Always use approved jackstands to support the weight of the vehicle and place them under the recommended lift or support points.

DON'T attempt to loosen extremely tight fasteners (i.e. wheel lug nuts) while the vehicle is on a jack - it may fall.

DON'T start the engine without first making sure that the transmission is in Neutral (or Park where applicable) and the parking brake is set.

DON'T remove the radiator cap from a hot cooling system - let it cool or cover it with a cloth and release the pressure gradually.

DON'T attempt to drain the engine oil until you are sure it has cooled to the point that it will not burn you.

DON'T touch any part of the engine or exhaust system until it has cooled sufficiently to avoid burns.

DON'T siphon toxic liquids such as gasoline, antifreeze and brake fluid by mouth, or allow them to remain on your skin.

DON'T inhale brake lining dust - it is potentially hazardous (see *Asbestos* below).

DON'T allow spilled oil or grease to remain on the floor - wipe it up before someone slips on it.

DON'T use loose fitting wrenches or other tools which may slip and cause injury.

DON'T push on wrenches when loosening or tightening nuts or bolts. Always try to pull the wrench toward you. If the situation calls for pushing the wrench away, push with an open hand to avoid scraped knuckles if the wrench should slip.

DON'T attempt to lift a heavy component alone - get someone to help you.

DON'T rush or take unsafe shortcuts to finish a job.

DON'T allow children or animals in or around the vehicle while you are working on it.

DO wear eye protection when using power tools such as a drill, sander, bench grinder, etc. and when working under a vehicle.

DO keep loose clothing and long hair well out of the way of moving parts.

DO make sure that any hoist used has a safe working load rating adequate for the job.

DO get someone to check on you periodically when working alone on a vehicle.

DO carry out work in a logical sequence and make sure that everything is correctly assembled and tightened.

DO keep chemicals and fluids tightly capped and out of the reach of children and pets.

DO remember that your vehicle's safety affects that of yourself and others. If in doubt on any point, get professional advice.

Asbestos

Certain friction, insulating, sealing, and other products - such as brake linings, brake bands, clutch linings, torque converters, gaskets, etc. - may contain asbestos. Extreme care must be taken to avoid inhalation of dust from such products, since it is hazardous to health. If in doubt, assume that they do contain asbestos.

Fire

Remember at all times that gasoline is highly flammable. Never smoke or have any kind of open flame around when working on a vehicle. But the risk does not end there. A spark caused by an electrical short circuit, by two metal surfaces contacting each other, or even by static electricity built up in your body under certain conditions, can ignite gasoline vapors, which in a confined space are highly explosive. Do not, under any circumstances, use gasoline for cleaning parts. Use an approved safety solvent.

Always disconnect the battery ground (-) cable at the battery before working on any part of the fuel system or electrical system. Never risk spilling fuel on a hot engine or exhaust component. It is strongly recommended that a fire extinguisher suitable for use on fuel and electrical fires be kept handy in the garage or workshop at all times. Never try to extinguish a fuel or electrical fire with water.

Fumes

Certain fumes are highly toxic and can quickly cause unconsciousness and even death if inhaled to any extent. Gasoline vapor falls into this category, as do the vapors from some cleaning solvents. Any draining or pouring of such volatile fluids should be done in a well ventilated area.

When using cleaning fluids and solvents, read the instructions on the container carefully. Never use materials from unmarked containers.

Never run the engine in an enclosed space, such as a garage. Exhaust fumes contain carbon monoxide, which is extremely poisonous. If you need to run the engine, always do so in the open air, or at least have the rear of the vehicle outside the work area.

If you are fortunate enough to have the use of an inspection pit, never drain or pour gasoline and never run the engine while the vehicle is over the pit. The fumes, being heavier than air, will concentrate in the pit with possibly lethal results.

The battery

Never create a spark or allow a bare light bulb near a battery. They normally give off a certain amount of hydrogen gas, which is highly explosive.

Always disconnect the battery ground (-) cable at the battery before working on the fuel or electrical systems.

If possible, loosen the filler caps or cover when charging the battery from an external source (this does not apply to sealed or maintenance-free batteries). Do not charge at an excessive rate or the battery may burst.

Take care when adding water to a non maintenance-free battery and when carrying a battery. The electrolyte, even when diluted, is very corrosive and should not be allowed to contact clothing or skin.

Always wear eye protection when cleaning the battery to prevent the caustic deposits from entering your eyes.

Household current

When using an electric power tool, inspection light, etc., which operates on household current, always make sure that the tool is correctly connected to its plug and that, where necessary, it is properly grounded. Do not use such items in damp conditions and, again, do not create a spark or apply excessive heat in the vicinity of fuel or fuel vapor.

Secondary ignition system voltage

A severe electric shock can result from touching certain parts of the ignition system (such as the spark plug wires) when the engine is running or being cranked, particularly if components are damp or the insulation is defective. In the case of an electronic ignition system, the secondary system voltage is much higher and could prove fatal.

Troubleshooting

Contents

This section provides an easy reference guide to the more common problems which may occur during the operation of your vehicle. These problems and their possible causes are grouped under headings denoting various components or systems, such as Engine, Cooling system, etc. They also refer you to the chapter and/or section which deals with the problem.

Remember that successful troubleshooting is not a mysterious art practiced only by professional mechanics. It is simply the result of the right knowledge combined with an intelligent, systematic approach to the problem. Always work by a process of elimination, starting with the simplest solution and working through to the most complex - and never overlook the obvious. Anyone can run the gas tank dry or leave the lights on overnight, so don't assume that you are exempt from such oversights.

Finally, always establish a clear idea of why a problem has occurred and take steps to ensure that it doesn't happen again. If the electrical system fails because of a poor connection, check the other connections in the system to make sure that they don't fail as well. If a particular fuse continues to blow, find out why - don't just replace one fuse after another. Remember, failure of a small component can often be indicative of potential failure or incorrect functioning of a more important component or system.

Engine

1 Engine will not rotate when attempting to start

1　Battery terminal connections loose or corroded (Chapters 1 and 5).
2　Battery discharged or faulty (Chapter 1).
3　Automatic transaxle not completely engaged in Park (Chapter 7B) or clutch pedal not completely depressed (Chapter 8).
4　Broken, loose or disconnected wiring in the starting circuit (Chapters 5 and 12).
5　Starter motor pinion jammed in flywheel ring gear (Chapter 5).
6　Starter solenoid faulty (Chapter 5).
7　Starter motor faulty (Chapter 5).
8　Ignition switch faulty (Chapter 12).
9　Starter pinion or flywheel teeth worn or broken (Chapter 5).
10　Defective fusible link (see Chapter 12).

2 Engine rotates but will not start

1　Fuel tank empty.
2　Battery discharged (engine rotates slowly) (Chapter 5).
3　Battery terminal connections loose or corroded (Chapters 1 and 5).
4　Leaking fuel injector(s), faulty fuel pump, pressure regulator, etc. (Chapter 4).

5　Broken or stripped timing belt (Chapter 2).
6　Ignition components damp or damaged (Chapter 5).
7　Worn, faulty or incorrectly gapped spark plugs (Chapter 1).
8　Broken, loose or disconnected wiring in the starting circuit (Chapter 5).
9　Broken, loose or disconnected wires at the ignition coil(s) or faulty coil(s) (Chapter 5).
10　Defective crankshaft sensor, camshaft sensor or PCM (see Chapter 6).

3 Engine hard to start when cold

1　Battery discharged or low (Chapter 1).
2　Malfunctioning fuel system (Chapter 4).
3　Faulty coolant temperature sensor or intake air temperature sensor (Chapter 6).
4　Fuel injector(s) leaking (Chapter 4).
5　Faulty ignition system (Chapter 5).
6　Defective MAP sensor (see Chapter 6).

4 Engine hard to start when hot

1　Air filter clogged (Chapter 1).
2　Fuel not reaching the fuel injection system (Chapter 4).
3　Corroded battery connections, especially ground (Chapters 1 and 5).
4　Faulty coolant temperature sensor or intake air temperature sensor (Chapter 6).

5 Starter motor noisy or excessively rough in engagement

1　Pinion or flywheel gear teeth worn or broken (Chapter 5).
2　Starter motor mounting bolts loose or missing (Chapter 5).

6 Engine starts but stops immediately

1　Loose or faulty electrical connections at ignition coil (Chapter 5).
2　Insufficient fuel reaching the fuel injector(s) (Chapters 4).
3　Vacuum leak at the gasket between the intake manifold/plenum and throttle body (Chapter 4).
4　Fault in the engine control system (Chapter 6).
5　Intake air leaks, broken vacuum lines (see Chapter 4).

7 Oil puddle under engine

1　Oil pan gasket and/or oil pan drain bolt washer leaking (Chapter 2).
2　Oil pressure sending unit leaking (Chapter 2).

3　Oil filter or adapter block leaking (Chapter 1).
4　Valve cover(s) leaking (Chapter 2).
5　Engine oil seals leaking (Chapter 2).

8 Engine lopes while idling or idles erratically

1　Vacuum leakage (Chapters 2 and 4).
2　Leaking EGR valve or EGR vacuum lines (Chapter 6).
3　Air filter clogged (Chapter 1).
4　Fuel pump not delivering sufficient fuel to the fuel injection system (Chapter 4).
5　Leaking head gasket (Chapter 2).
6　Timing belt and/or pulleys worn (Chapter 2).
7　Camshaft lobes worn (Chapter 2).

9 Engine misses at idle speed

1　Spark plugs worn or not gapped properly (Chapter 1).
2　Faulty spark plug wires (Chapter 1).
3　Vacuum leaks (Chapters 2 and 4).
4　Faulty ignition coil(s) (Chapter 5).
5　Uneven or low compression (Chapter 2).
6　Faulty fuel injector(s) (Chapter 4).

10 Engine misses throughout driving speed range

1　Fuel filter clogged and/or impurities in the fuel system (Chapter 4).
2　Low fuel output at the fuel injector(s) (Chapter 4).
3　Faulty or incorrectly gapped spark plugs (Chapter 1).
4　Defective spark plug wires (Chapters 1 or 5).
5　Faulty emission system components (Chapter 6).
6　Low or uneven cylinder compression pressures (Chapter 2).
7　Burned valves (Chapter 2).
8　Weak or faulty ignition system (Chapter 5).
9　Vacuum leak in fuel injection system, throttle body, intake manifold or vacuum hoses (Chapter 4).

11 Engine stumbles on acceleration

1　Spark plugs fouled (Chapter 1).
2　Problem with fuel injection system (Chapter 4).
3　Fuel filter clogged (Chapter 4).
4　Fault in the engine control system (Chapter 6).
5　Intake manifold air leak (Chapters 2 and 4).
6　EGR system malfunction (Chapter 6).

12 Engine surges while holding accelerator steady

1   Intake air leak (Chapter 4).
2   Fuel pump or fuel pressure regulator faulty (Chapter 4).
3   Problem with fuel injection system (Chapter 4).
4   Problem with the emissions control system (Chapter 6).

13 Engine stalls

1   Idle speed incorrect (Chapter 1).
2   Fuel filter clogged and/or water and impurities in the fuel system (Chapter 4).
3   Ignition components damp or damaged (Chapter 5).
4   Faulty emissions system components (Chapter 6).
5   Faulty or incorrectly gapped spark plugs (Chapter 1).
6   Faulty spark plug wires (Chapter 1).
7   Vacuum leak in the fuel injection system, intake manifold or vacuum hoses (Chapters 2 and 4).

14 Engine lacks power

1   Worn camshaft lobes (Chapter 2).
2   Burned valves or incorrect valve timing (Chapter 2).
3   Faulty spark plug wires or faulty coil(s) (Chapters 1 and 5).
4   Faulty or incorrectly gapped spark plugs (Chapter 1).
5   Problem with the fuel injection system (Chapter 4).
6   Plugged air filter (Chapter 1).
7   Brakes binding (Chapter 9).
8   Automatic transaxle fluid level incorrect (Chapter 1).
9   Clutch slipping (Chapter 8).
10   Fuel filter clogged and/or impurities in the fuel system (Chapter 4).
11   Emission control system not functioning properly (Chapter 6).
12   Low or uneven cylinder compression pressures (Chapter 2).
13   Restricted exhaust system or catalytic converter (Chapter 4).

15 Engine backfires

1   Emission control system not functioning properly (Chapter 6).
2   Faulty spark plug wires or coil(s) (Chapter 5).
3   Problem with the fuel injection system (Chapter 4).
4   Vacuum leak at fuel injector(s), intake manifold or vacuum hoses (Chapters 2 and 4).
5   Burned valves or incorrect valve timing (Chapter 2).

16 Pinging or knocking engine sounds during acceleration or uphill

1   Incorrect grade of fuel.
2   Problem with the engine control system (Chapter 6).
3   Fuel injection system faulty (Chapter 4).
4   Improper or damaged spark plugs or wires (Chapter 1).
5   EGR valve not functioning (Chapter 6).
6   Vacuum leak (Chapters 2 and 4).

17 Engine runs with oil pressure light on

1   Low oil level (Chapter 1).
2   Idle rpm below specification (Chapter 1).
3   Short in wiring circuit (Chapter 12).
4   Faulty oil pressure sender (Chapter 2).
5   Worn engine bearings and/or oil pump (Chapter 2).

18 Engine diesels (continues to run) after switching off

1   Idle speed too high (Chapter 1).
2   Excessive engine operating temperature (Chapter 3).
3   Excessive carbon deposits on valves and pistons (see Chapter 2).

Engine electrical system

19 Alternator light fails to come on when key is turned on

1   Warning light bulb defective (Chapter 12).
2   Fault in the printed circuit, dash wiring or bulb holder (Chapter 12).

20 Alternator light fails to go out

1   Faulty alternator or charging circuit (Chapter 5).
2   Alternator drivebelt defective or out of adjustment (Chapter 1).
3   Alternator voltage regulator fault (Chapter 5).

21 Battery will not hold a charge

1   Alternator drivebelt defective or not adjusted properly (slipping) (Chapter 1).
2   Battery electrolyte level low (not applicable on maintenance-free batteries) (Chapter 1).
3   Battery terminals loose or corroded (Chapters 1 and 5).
4   Alternator not charging properly (Chapter 5).
5   Loose, broken or faulty wiring in the charging circuit (Chapter 5).
6   Short in vehicle wiring (Chapter 12).
7   Internally defective battery (Chapters 1 and 5).

Fuel and emissions systems

22 CHECK ENGINE light remains on or is flashing

1   Light remains on:
a)   Fuel filler cap (gas cap) is not seated or tightened properly.
b)   On-Board Diagnostic (OBD-II) computer has detected an emissions or fuel injection component fault (Chapter 6).
2   Light is flashing:
If the CHECK ENGINE light is flashing, severe catalytic converter damage has occurred and engine power loss will soon result. Take the vehicle to your nearest dealer service department or other qualified shop for immediate repair.

23 Excessive fuel consumption

1   Dirty or clogged air filter element (Chapter 1).
2   Emissions system not functioning properly (Chapter 6).
3   Fuel injection system not functioning properly (Chapter 4).
4   Low tire pressure or incorrect tire size (Chapter 1).
5   Dragging brakes (Chapter 9).

24 Fuel leakage and/or fuel odor

1   Leaking fuel feed or return line (Chapters 1 and 4).
2   Fuel tank overfilled.
3   Evaporative canister filter clogged (Chapters 1 and 6).
4   Problem with fuel injection system (Chapter 4).

Cooling system

25 Overheating

1   Insufficient coolant in system (Chapter 1).
2   Water pump defective (Chapter 3).
3   Radiator core blocked or grille restricted (Chapter 3).
4   Thermostat faulty (Chapter 3).
5   Electric cooling fan inoperative or blades broken (Chapter 3).

6   Radiator cap not maintaining proper pressure (Chapter 3).

26 Overcooling

1   Faulty thermostat (Chapter 3).
2   Inaccurate temperature gauge sending unit (Chapter 3).

27 External coolant leakage

1   Deteriorated/damaged hoses; loose clamps (Chapters 1 and 3).
2   Water pump defective (Chapter 3).
3   Leakage from radiator core or coolant reservoir (Chapter 3).
4   Engine drain or water jacket core plugs leaking (Chapter 2).

28 Internal coolant leakage

1   Leaking cylinder head gasket (Chapter 2).
2   Cracked cylinder bore or cylinder head (Chapter 2).

29 Coolant loss

1   Too much coolant in system (Chapter 1).
2   Coolant boiling away because of overheating (Chapter 3).
3   Internal or external leakage (Chapter 3).
4   Faulty pressure cap (Chapter 3).

30 Poor coolant circulation

1   Inoperative water pump (Chapter 3).
2   Restriction in cooling system (Chapters 1 and 3).
3   Thermostat sticking (Chapter 3).

Clutch

31 Pedal travels to floor - no pressure or very little resistance

1   Broken or disconnected clutch cable (Chapter 8).
2   Broken release bearing or fork (Chapter 8).

32 Unable to select gears

1   Faulty transaxle (Chapter 7).
2   Faulty clutch disc or pressure plate (Chapter 8).
3   Faulty release lever or release bearing (Chapter 8).
4   Faulty shift lever assembly or rods (Chapter 8).

33 Clutch slips (engine speed increases with no increase in vehicle speed)

1   Clutch plate worn (Chapter 8).
2   Clutch plate is oil soaked by leaking rear main seal (Chapter 8).
3   Clutch plate not seated (Chapter 8).
4   Warped pressure plate or flywheel (Chapter 8).
5   Weak clutch diaphragm springs (Chapter 8).
6   Clutch plate overheated. Allow to cool.
7   Faulty clutch self-adjusting mechanism (Chapter 8).

34 Grabbing (chattering) as clutch is engaged

1   Oil on clutch plate lining, burned or glazed facings (Chapter 8).
2   Worn or loose engine or transaxle mounts (Chapters 2 and 7).
3   Worn splines on clutch plate hub (Chapter 8).
4   Warped pressure plate (Chapter 8).
5   Burned or smeared resin on pressure plate (Chapter 8).

35 Transaxle rattling (clicking)

1   Release fork loose (Chapter 8).
2   Low engine idle speed (Chapter 1).

36 Noise in clutch area

1   Faulty throw-out bearing (Chapter 8).

37 Clutch pedal stays on floor

1   Broken release bearing or fork (Chapter 8).
2   Broken or disconnected clutch cable (Chapter 8).

38 High pedal effort

1   Binding clutch cable (Chapter 8).
2   Pressure plate faulty (Chapter 8).

Manual transaxle

39 Knocking noise at low speeds

1   Worn driveaxle constant velocity (CV) joints (Chapter 8).
2   Worn side gear shaft counterbore in differential case (Chapter 7A).*

40 Noise most pronounced when turning

1   Differential gear noise (Chapter 7A).*

41 Clunk on acceleration or deceleration

1   Loose engine or transaxle mounts (Chapters 2 and 7A).
2   Worn differential pinion shaft in case.*
3   Worn side gear shaft counterbore in differential case (Chapter 7A).*
4   Worn or damaged driveaxle inboard CV joints (Chapter 8).

42 Clicking noise in turns

1   Worn or damaged outboard CV joint (Chapter 8).

43 Vibration

1   Rough wheel bearing (Chapters 1 and 10).
2   Damaged driveaxle (Chapter 8).
3   Out of round tires (Chapter 1).
4   Tire out of balance (Chapters 1 and 10).
5   Worn CV joint (Chapter 8).

44 Noisy in Neutral with engine running

1   Damaged input gear bearing (Chapter 7A).*
2   Damaged clutch release bearing (Chapter 8).

45 Noisy in one particular gear

1   Damaged or worn constant mesh gears (Chapter 7A).*
2   Damaged or worn synchronizers (Chapter 7A).*
3   Bent reverse fork (Chapter 7A).*
4   Damaged fourth speed gear or output gear (Chapter 7A).*
5   Worn or damaged reverse idler gear or idler bushing (Chapter 7A).*

46 Noisy in all gears

1   Insufficient lubricant (Chapters 1 and 7A).
2   Damaged or worn bearings (Chapter 7A).*
3   Worn or damaged input gear shaft and/or output gear shaft (Chapter 7A).*

47 Slips out of gear

1 Worn or improperly adjusted linkage (Chapter 7A).
2 Transaxle loose on engine (Chapter 7A).
3 Shift linkage does not work freely, binds (Chapter 7A).
4 Input gear bearing retainer broken or loose (Chapter 7A).*
5 Dirt between clutch cover and engine housing (Chapter 7A).
6 Worn shift fork (Chapter 7A).*

48 Leaks lubricant

1 Driveshaft seals worn (Chapter 7A).
2 Excessive amount of lubricant in transaxle (Chapters 1 and 7A).
3 Loose or broken input gear shaft bearing retainer (Chapter 7A).*
4 Input gear bearing retainer O-ring and/or lip seal damaged (Chapter 7A).*
5 Vehicle speed sensor O-ring leaking (Chapter 7A).

49 Hard to shift

1 Shift linkage loose or worn (Chapter 7A).
2 Crossover cable out of adjustment.

Although the corrective action necessary to remedy the symptoms described is beyond the scope of this manual, the above information should be helpful in isolating the cause of the condition so that the owner can communicate clearly with a professional mechanic.

Automatic transaxle

Note: *Due to the complexity of the automatic transaxle, it is difficult for the home mechanic to properly diagnose and service this component. For problems other than the following, the vehicle should be taken to a dealer service department or other qualified transmission shop.*

50 Fluid leakage

1 Automatic transaxle fluid is a deep red color. Fluid leaks should not be confused with engine oil, which can easily be blown onto the transaxle by air flow.
2 To pinpoint a leak, first remove all built-up dirt and grime from the transaxle housing with degreasing agents and/or steam cleaning. Then drive the vehicle at low speeds so air flow will not blow the leak far from its source. Raise the vehicle and determine where the leak is coming from. Common areas of leakage are:
   a) *Pan (Chapters 1 and 7)*
   b) *Dipstick tube (Chapters 1 and 7).*
   c) *Transaxle oil cooler lines (Chapter 7).*
   d) *Speed sensor (Chapter 7).*
   e) *Driveaxle oil seals (Chapter 7).*

51 Transaxle fluid brown or has a burned smell

1 Transaxle fluid overheated - change fluid and filter (Chapter 1).

52 General shift mechanism problems

1 Chapter 7, Part B, deals with checking and adjusting the shift linkage on automatic transaxles. Common problems which may be attributed to poorly adjusted linkage are:
   a) *Engine starting in gears other than Park or Neutral.*
   b) *Indicator on shifter pointing to a gear other than the one actually being used.*
   c) *Vehicle moves when in Park.*
2 Refer to Chapter 7B for the shift linkage adjustment procedure.

53 Transaxle will not downshift with accelerator pedal pressed to the floor

1 The transaxle is electronically controlled. This type of problem - which is caused by a malfunction in the Transmission Control Module (TCM), a sensor or solenoid, or the circuit itself - is beyond the scope of this manual. Have the problem diagnosed by a dealer service department or other qualified automatic transmission shop.

54 Engine will start in gears other than Park or Neutral

1 Neutral start switch out of adjustment or malfunctioning (Chapter 7B).

55 Transaxle slips, shifts roughly, is noisy or has no drive in forward or reverse gears

1 There are many probable causes for the above problems, but the home mechanic should be concerned with only one possibility - fluid level. Before taking the vehicle to a repair shop, check the level and condition of the fluid and/or filter as described in Chapter 1. Correct the fluid level as necessary or change the fluid and filter if needed. If the problem persists, have a professional diagnose the cause.

Driveaxles

56 Clicking noise in turns

1 Worn or damaged outboard CV joint (Chapter 8).

57 Shudder or vibration during acceleration

1 Excessive toe-in (Chapter 10).
2 Incorrect spring heights (Chapter 10).
3 Worn or damaged inboard or outboard CV joints (Chapter 8).
4 Sticking inboard CV joint assembly (Chapter 8).

58 Vibration at highway speeds

1 Out of balance front wheels and/or tires (Chapters 1 and 10).
2 Out of round front tires (Chapters 1 and 10).
3 Worn CV joint(s) (Chapter 8).

Brakes

Note: *Before assuming that a brake problem exists, make sure that:*
   a) *The tires are in good condition and properly inflated (Chapter 1).*
   b) *The front end alignment is correct (Chapter 10).*
   c) *The vehicle is not loaded with weight in an unequal manner.*

59 Vehicle pulls to one side during braking

1 Incorrect tire pressures (Chapter 1).
2 Front end out of alignment (have the front end aligned).
3 Front tire sizes or tread types not matched to one another.
4 Restricted brake lines or hoses (Chapter 9).
5 Malfunctioning/leaking brake cylinder or caliper assembly (Chapter 9).
6 Loose suspension parts (Chapter 10).
7 Loose calipers (Chapter 9).
8 Excessive wear of brake shoe or pad material or disc/drum on one side.

60 Noise (high-pitched squeal when the brakes are applied)

1 Front disc brake pads worn out. The noise comes from the wear sensor rubbing

against the disc (does not apply to all vehicles). Replace pads with new ones immediately (Chapter 9).

61 Brake roughness or chatter (pedal pulsates)

1 Excessive lateral runout (Chapter 9).
2 Uneven pad wear (Chapter 9).
3 Defective disc (Chapter 9).
4 If the vehicle is equipped with an anti-lock brake system (ABS), brake pedal pulsation and associated noises are normal when severe braking is required.

62 Excessive brake pedal effort required to stop vehicle

1 Malfunctioning power brake booster (Chapter 9).
2 Partial system failure (Chapter 9).
3 Excessively worn pads or shoes (Chapter 9).
4 Piston in caliper or wheel cylinder stuck or sluggish (Chapter 9).
5 Brake pads or shoes contaminated with oil or grease (Chapter 9).
6 Brake disc grooved and/or glazed (Chapter 1).
7 New pads or shoes installed and not yet seated. It will take a while for the new material to seat against the disc or drum.

63 Excessive brake pedal travel

1 Partial brake system failure (Chapter 9).
2 Insufficient fluid in master cylinder (Chapters 1 and 9).
3 Air trapped in system (Chapters 1 and 9).

64 Dragging brakes

1 Incorrect adjustment of brake light switch (Chapter 9).
2 Master cylinder pistons not returning correctly (Chapter 9).
3 Restricted brakes lines or hoses (Chapters 1 and 9).
4 Incorrect parking brake adjustment (Chapter 9).

65 Grabbing or uneven braking action

1 Malfunction of proportioning valve (Chapter 9).
2 Malfunction of power brake booster unit (Chapter 9).
3 Binding brake pedal mechanism (Chapter 9).

66 Brake pedal feels spongy when depressed

1 Air in hydraulic lines (Chapter 9).
2 Master cylinder mounting bolts loose (Chapter 9).
3 Master cylinder defective (Chapter 9).

67 Brake pedal travels to the floor with little resistance

1 Little or no fluid in the master cylinder reservoir caused by leaking caliper piston(s) (Chapter 9).
2 Loose, damaged or disconnected brake lines (Chapter 9).

68 Parking brake does not hold

1 Parking brake cables improperly adjusted (Chapters 1 and 9).

Suspension and steering systems

Note: *Before attempting to diagnose suspension and steering system problems, perform the following preliminary checks:*

a) *Tires for wrong pressure and uneven wear.*
b) *Steering universal joints from the column to the rack and pinion for loose connectors or wear.*
c) *Front and rear suspension and the rack and pinion assembly for loose or damaged parts.*
d) *Out-of-round or out-of-balance tires, bent rims and loose and/or rough wheel bearings.*

69 Vehicle pulls to one side

1 Mismatched or uneven tires (Chapter 10).
2 Broken or sagging coil springs (Chapter 10).
3 Wheel alignment out-of-specification (Chapter 10).
4 Front brake dragging (Chapter 9).

70 Abnormal or excessive tire wear

1 Wheel alignment out-of-specification (Chapter 10).
2 Sagging or broken coil springs (Chapter 10).
3 Tire out-of-balance (Chapter 10).
4 Worn shock absorber (Chapter 10).
5 Overloaded vehicle.
6 Tires not rotated regularly.

71 Wheel makes a thumping noise

1 Blister or bump on tire (Chapter 10).
2 Faulty shock absorber(s) (Chapter 10).

72 Shimmy, shake or vibration

1 Tire or wheel out-of-balance or out-of-round (Chapter 10).
2 Loose or worn wheel bearings (Chapters 1, 8 and 10).
3 Worn tie-rod ends (Chapter 10).
4 Worn lower balljoints (Chapters 1 and 10).
5 Excessive wheel runout (Chapter 10).
6 Blister or bump on tire (Chapter 10).

73 Hard steering

1 Lack of lubrication at balljoints, tie-rod ends and rack and pinion assembly (Chapter 10).
2 Low power steering fluid level (Chapter 1).
3 Faulty power steering pump (Chapter 10).
4 Front wheel alignment out-of-specifications (Chapter 10).
5 Low tire pressure(s) (Chapters 1 and 10).

74 Poor returnability of steering to center

1 Lack of lubrication at balljoints and tie-rod ends (Chapter 10).
2 Binding in balljoints (Chapter 10).
3 Binding in steering column (Chapter 10).
4 Lack of lubricant in steering gear assembly (Chapter 10).
5 Front wheel alignment out-of-specifications (Chapter 10).

75 Abnormal noise at the front end

1 Lack of lubrication at balljoints and tie-rod ends (Chapters 1 and 10).
2 Damaged strut mounting (Chapter 10).
3 Worn control arm bushings or tie-rod ends (Chapter 10).
4 Loose stabilizer bar (Chapter 10).
5 Loose wheel nuts (Chapters 1 and 10).
6 Loose suspension bolts (Chapter 10)

76 Wander or poor steering stability

1 Mismatched or unevenly worn tires (Chapter 10).
2 Lack of lubrication at balljoints and tie-rod ends (Chapters 1 and 10).
3 Bad shock absorber(s) (Chapter 10).
4 Loose stabilizer bar (Chapter 10).

5   Broken or sagging coil springs (Chapter 10).
6   Wheels out of alignment (Chapter 10).

77   Erratic steering when braking

1   Wheel bearings worn (Chapter 10).
2   Broken or sagging coil springs (Chapter 10).
3   Leaking wheel cylinder or caliper (Chapter 10).
4   Warped rotors or drums (Chapter 10).

78   Excessive pitching and/or rolling around corners or during braking

1   Loose stabilizer bar (Chapter 10).
2   Worn shock absorbers or mountings (Chapter 10).
3   Broken or sagging coil springs (Chapter 10).
4   Overloaded vehicle.

79   Suspension bottoms

1   Overloaded vehicle.
2   Worn shock absorbers (Chapter 10).

3   Incorrect, broken or sagging coil springs (Chapter 10).

80   Cupped tires

1   Front wheel or rear wheel alignment out-of-specifications (Chapter 10).
2   Worn shock absorbers (Chapter 10).
3   Wheel bearings worn (Chapter 10).
4   Excessive tire or wheel runout (Chapter 10).
5   Worn balljoints (Chapter 10).

81   Excessive tire wear on outside edge

1   Inflation pressures incorrect (Chapter 1).
2   Excessive speed during turns.
3   Front end alignment incorrect (excessive toe-in). Have professionally aligned.
4   Suspension arm bent or twisted (Chapter 10).

82   Excessive tire wear on inside edge

1   Inflation pressures incorrect (Chapter 1).

2   Front end alignment incorrect (toe-out). Have professionally aligned.
3   Loose or damaged steering components (Chapter 10).

83   Tire tread worn in one place

1   Tires out-of-balance.
2   Damaged or buckled wheel. Inspect and replace if necessary.
3   Defective tire (Chapter 1).

84   Excessive play or looseness in steering system

1   Wheel bearing(s) worn (Chapter 10).
2   Tie-rod end loose (Chapter 10).
3   Steering gear loose (Chapter 10).
4   Worn or loose steering intermediate shaft (Chapter 10).

85   Rattling or clicking noise in steering gear

1   Steering gear loose (Chapter 10).
2   Steering gear defective.

Notes

Chapter 1
Tune-up and routine maintenance

Contents

Specifications

Recommended lubricants and fluids

Engine oil

Type .... API Certified, SG, SG/CD, SH, or SH/CD multi-grade and fuel efficient oil

Viscosity .... See accompanying chart

Manual transaxle lubricant .... Mopar manual transaxle fluid type MS 9417 or equivalent

Automatic transaxle fluid .... Mopar automatic transaxle fluid ATF type 7176 or equivalent

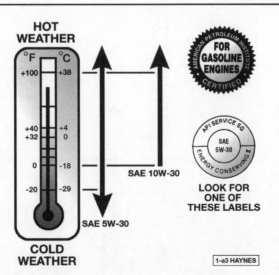

Engine oil viscosity chart - For best fuel economy and cold starting, select the lowest SAE viscosity grade for the expected temperature range

HOT WEATHER

SAE 10W-30

SAE 5W-30

COLD WEATHER

FOR GASOLINE ENGINES

LOOK FOR ONE OF THESE LABELS

1-a3 HAYNES

Recommended lubricants and fluids

Power steering fluid .... Mopar power steering fluid or equivalent
Brake fluid.. DOT 3 brake fluid
Engine coolant .... 50/50 mixture of ethylene glycol-based antifreeze and water
Parking brake mechanism grease .... White lithium-based grease NLGI no. 2
Chassis lubrication grease .... NLGI no. 2 LB grease
Hood, door and trunk hinge lubricant... Engine oil
Hood latch, door hinge and check spring grease .... NLGI no. 2 multi-purpose grease
Key lock cylinder lubricant.. Graphite spray
Door latch striker lubricant .... Mopar Door Ease no. 3744859 or equivalent

Capacities*

Engine oil (including filter)
　V6 and 2.0L four-cylinder engines .... 4.5 quarts
　2.4L four-cylinder engine .... 5.0 quarts
Fuel tank .... 16 gallons
Automatic transaxle
　Dry fill (including torque converter) .... 9.1 quarts
　Drain and refill .... 4.0 quarts
Manual transaxle .... 2.2 quarts
Cooling system
　2.0L four-cylinder engine .... 8.5 quarts
　2.4L four-cylinder engine .... 9.0 quarts
　V6 engine.. 10.5 quarts
All capacities approximate. Add as necessary to bring to appropriate level.

Brakes

Disc brake pad wear limit .... 1/8 inch
Drum brake shoe wear limit... 1/16 inch

Ignition system

Spark plug type
　2.0L four-cylinder engine .... Champion RCY9C or equivalent
　2.4L four-cylinder engine .... Champion RC12YC5 or equivalent
　V6 engine.. Champion RC10PYP4 or equivalent
Spark plug gap
　2.0L four-cylinder engine .... 0.033 to 0.038 inch
　2.4L four-cylinder engine .... 0.048 to 0.053 inch
　V6 .... 0.038 to 0.043 inch
Spark plug wire resistance
　Four-cylinder engines
　　Wire numbers 1 and 4.. 3,500 to 4,900 ohms
　　Wire numbers 2 and 3.. 2,950 to 4,100 ohms
　V6 engine
　　Minimum .... 250 ohms per inch (3,000 ohms per foot)
　　Maximum .... 560 ohms per inch (6,700 ohms per foot)
Firing order
　Four-cylinder engines... 1-3-4-2
　V6 engine.. 1-2-3-4-5-6

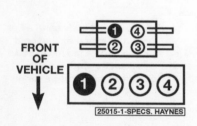

Four-cylinder engine cylinder numbering and coil terminal locations

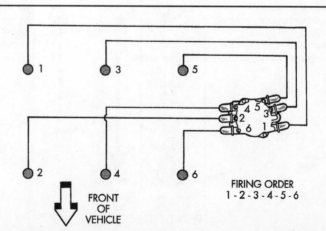

V6 engine cylinder numbering and distributor cap terminal locations

FRONT OF VEHICLE

FIRING ORDER
1 - 2 - 3 - 4 - 5 - 6

Torque specifications

	Ft-lbs (unless otherwise indicated)
Automatic transaxle oil pan bolts	165 in-lbs
Engine oil pan drain plug	25
Manual transaxle drain plug	22
Spark plugs...	20
Wheel lug nuts	80 to 110

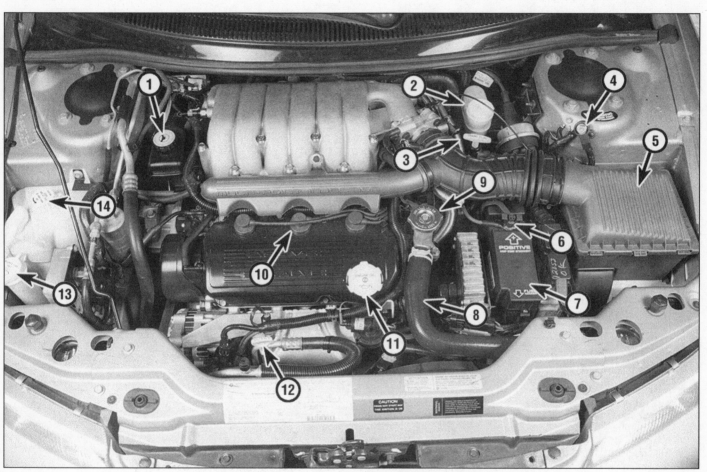

Typical engine compartment layout (V6 engine shown)

1	Power steering fluid reservoir	8	Upper radiator hose
2	Brake fluid reservoir	9	Engine coolant pressure/filler cap
3	Transmission fluid dipstick	10	Spark plug boot
4	Battery negative remote terminal	11	Engine oil filler cap
5	Air filter housing	12	Engine oil dipstick
6	Battery positive remote terminal	13	Windshield washer reservoir
7	Power Distribution Center (PDC) - fuses and relays	14	Engine coolant reservoir

Typical engine compartment underside components (V6 engine shown)

1   Air conditioning compressor
2   Engine oil drain plug
3   Engine oil filter
4   Exhaust crossover pipe
5   Starter motor
6   Automatic transaxle fluid pan
7   Driveaxle inner CV joint boot
8   Front suspension crossmember
9   Battery location (inside fenderwell)
10   Driveaxle outer CV joint boot
11   Front brake caliper
12   Front stabilizer bar
13   Catalytic converter
14   Shock absorber lower mount
15   Front suspension lower control arm

Typical rear underside components

1   Rear suspension upper control arm
2   Rear stabilizer bar
3   Lateral links
4   Fuel tank drain plug
5   Fuel tank retaining straps
6   Rear suspension crossmember
7   Muffler
8   Coil/shock absorber assembly
9   Trailing arm

1 Chrysler Cirrus, Dodge Stratus, and Plymouth Breeze maintenance schedule

The following maintenance intervals are based on the assumption that the vehicle owner will be doing the maintenance or service work, as opposed to having a dealer service department do the work. Although the time/mileage intervals are loosely based on factory recommendations, most have been shortened to ensure, for example, that such items as lubricants and fluids are checked/changed at intervals that promote maximum engine/driveline service life. Also, subject to the preference of the individual owner interested in keeping his or her vehicle in peak condition at all times, and with the vehicle's ultimate resale in mind, many of the maintenance procedures may be performed more often than recommended in the following schedule. We encourage such owner initiative.

When the vehicle is new it should be serviced initially by a factory authorized dealer service department to protect the factory warranty. In many cases the initial maintenance check is done at no cost to the owner (check with your dealer service department for more information).

Every 250 miles or weekly, whichever comes first

Check the engine oil level; add oil as necessary (see Section 4)
Check the engine coolant level; add coolant as necessary (see Section 4)
Check the windshield washer fluid level (see Section 4)
Check the brake fluid level (see Section 4)
Check the tires and tire pressures (see Section 5)
Check the automatic transaxle fluid level (see Section 6)
Check the power steering fluid level (see Section 7)
Check the operation of all lights
Check the horn operation

Every 7500 miles or 6 months, whichever comes first

Change the engine oil and filter (see Section 8)*
Check and clean the battery and terminals (see Section 9)
Check the manual transaxle fluid level (see Section 16)
Check the cooling system hoses and connections for leaks and damage (see Section 10)
Check the condition of all vacuum hoses and connections (see Section 11)
Check the wiper blade condition (see Section 12)
Rotate the tires (see Section 13)
Check for free play in the steering linkage and ball joints (see Section 14)
Check the CV joints and front suspension components (see Section 14)
Check the driveaxle boots (see Section 17)
Check the exhaust pipes and hangers (see Section 15)
Inspect brake hoses (see Section 11)

Every 15,000 miles or 12 months, whichever comes first

All items listed above, plus:
Check the brake system (see Section 18)

Check the fuel system hoses and connections for leaks and damage (see Section 19)
Check the drivebelts and adjust if necessary (see Section 20)

Every 30,000 miles or 24 months, whichever comes first

All items listed above, plus:
Lubricate the front and rear suspension and steering ball joints (see Section 21)*
Replace the air filter element (see Section 22)*
Change the automatic transaxle fluid and filter (see Section 23)*
Change the manual transaxle lubricant (see Section 24)*
Check the fuel evaporative emission system hoses (see Section 26)
Replace the spark plugs (four-cylinder engines) (see Section 27)
Check the spark plug wires (see Section 29)
Drain and replace the engine coolant (see Section 25)

Every 60,000 miles or 48 months, whichever comes first

All items listed above, plus:
Check and replace, if necessary, the PCV valve (see Section 28)*
Replace drivebelts (see Section 20)
Replace spark plug wires (four-cylinder engines) (see Section 29)

Every 100,000 miles or 84 months, whichever comes first

Replace the spark plugs (V6 engine) (see Section 27)*
Replace the spark plug wires, distributor cap and rotor (V6 engine) (see Section 29)*
Replace the timing belt (see Chapter 2)

This item is affected by "severe" operating conditions as described below. If the vehicle in question is operated under "severe" conditions, perform all maintenance procedures marked with an asterisk (*) at the intervals specified by the mileage headings below.

Consider the conditions "severe" if most driving is done . . .
In dusty areas
Towing a trailer
Idling for extended periods and/or low-speed operation
When outside temperatures remain below freezing and most trips are less than four miles
In heavy city traffic where outside temperatures regularly reach 90-degrees F or higher

Maintenance schedule (continued)

Every 3000 miles

Change the engine oil and filter (see Section 8)

Every 15,000 miles

Check and replace, if necessary, the air filter element (see Section 22)
Change the automatic transaxle fluid and filter (see Section 23)
Change the manual transaxle lubricant (see Section 24)
Lubricate the front and rear suspension and steering ball joints (see Section 21)

Every 30,000 miles

Check and replace, if necessary, the PCV valve (see Section 28)

Every 75,000 miles

Replace the spark plugs (V6 engine) (see Section 27)
Replace the spark plug wires (V6 engine) (see Section 29)

2   Introduction

This Chapter is designed to help the home mechanic maintain the Chrysler Cirrus, Dodge Stratus and Plymouth Breeze models with the goals of maximum performance, economy, safety and reliability in mind.

Included is a master maintenance schedule, followed by procedures dealing specifically with each item on the schedule. Visual checks, adjustments, component replacement and other helpful items are included. Refer to the accompanying illustrations of the engine compartment and the underside of the vehicle for the locations of various components.

Adhering to the mileage/time maintenance schedule and following the step-by-step procedures, which is simply a preventive maintenance program, will result in maximum reliability and vehicle service life. Keep in mind that it's a comprehensive program - maintaining some items but not others at the specified intervals will not produce the same results.

As you service the vehicle, you'll discover that many of the procedures can - and should - be grouped together because of the nature of the particular procedure you're performing or because of the close proximity of two otherwise unrelated components to one another.

For example, if the vehicle is raised, you should inspect the exhaust, suspension, steering and fuel systems while you're under the vehicle. When you're rotating the tires, it makes good sense to check the brakes, since the wheels are already removed. Finally, let's suppose you have to borrow or rent a torque wrench. Even if you only need it to tighten the spark plugs, you might as well check the torque of as many critical fasteners as time allows.

The first step in this maintenance program is to prepare yourself before the actual work begins. Read through all the procedures you're planning to do, then gather up all the parts and tools needed. If it looks like you might run into problems during a particular job, seek advice from a mechanic or an experienced do-it-yourselfer.

3   Tune-up general information

The term "tune-up" is used in this manual to represent a combination of individual operations rather than one specific procedure.

If, from the time the vehicle is new, the routine maintenance schedule is followed closely and frequent checks are made of fluid levels and high wear items, as suggested throughout this manual, the engine will be kept in relatively good running condition and the need for additional work will be minimized.

More likely than not, however, there will be times when the engine is running poorly due to lack of regular maintenance. This is even more likely if a used vehicle, which hasn't received regular and frequent maintenance checks, is purchased. In such cases, an engine tune-up will be needed outside of the regular routine maintenance intervals.

The first step in any tune-up or diagnostic procedure to help correct a poor running engine is a cylinder compression check. A compression check (see Chapter 2, Part C) will help determine the condition of internal engine components and should be used as a guide for tune-up and repair procedures. For instance, if a compression check indicates serious internal engine wear, a conventional tune-up will not improve the performance of the engine and would be a waste of time and money. Because of its importance, the compression check should be done by someone with the right equipment and the knowledge to use it properly.

The following procedures are those most often needed to bring a generally poor running engine back into a proper state of tune:

Minor tune-up

Check all engine related fluids (see Section 4)

Clean, inspect and test the battery (see Section 9)
Replace the spark plugs (see Section 27)
Inspect the spark plug wires (see Section 29)
Check and adjust the drivebelts (see Section 20)
Check the air filter (see Section 22)
Check the PCV valve (see Section 28)
Check all underhood hoses (see Section 11)
Service the cooling system (see Section 25)

Major tune-up

All items listed under Minor tune-up plus . . .
Replace the air filter (see Section 22)
Check the fuel system (see Section 19)
Check the charging system (see Chapter 5)

4   Fluid level checks (every 250 miles or weekly)

Note: *The following are fluid level checks to be done on a 250 mile or weekly basis. Additional fluid level checks can be found in specific maintenance procedures which follow. Regardless of the intervals, develop the habit of checking under the vehicle periodically for evidence of fluid leaks.*

1   Fluids are an essential part of the lubrication, cooling, brake and window washer systems. Because the fluids gradually become depleted and/or contaminated during normal operation of the vehicle, they must be replenished periodically. See *Recommended lubricants and fluids* at the beginning of this Chapter before adding fluid to any of the following components. **Note:** *The vehicle must be on level ground when fluid levels are checked.*

Engine oil

Refer to illustrations 4.2a, 4.2b, 4.4 and 4.5
2   The engine oil level is checked with a

4.2a The engine oil dipstick is located at the front left (passenger's) side of the engine (four-cylinder engine shown)

4.2b Engine oil dipstick location - V6 engine

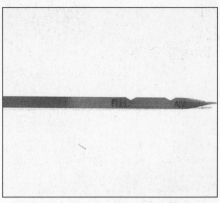

4.4 The oil level should be between the notches on the dipstick - if it isn't, add enough oil to bring the level up to or near the upper notch (do not overfill)

1

dipstick which is located on the side of the engine facing the front of the vehicle **(see illustrations)**. The dipstick extends through a tube and into the oil pan at the bottom of the engine.

3   The oil level should be checked before the vehicle has been driven, or about 15 minutes after the engine has been shut off. If the oil is checked immediately after driving the vehicle, some of the oil will remain in the upper engine components, resulting in an inaccurate reading on the dipstick.

4   Pull the dipstick out of the tube and wipe all the oil off the end with a clean rag or paper towel. Insert the clean dipstick all the way back into the tube, then pull it out again. Note the oil level at the end of the dipstick. Add oil as necessary to bring the oil level to the second notch in the dipstick **(see illustration)**.

5   Oil is added to the engine after removing a cap located on the valve cover **(see illustration)**. The cap will be marked "Engine oil". Use a funnel to reduce spills as the oil is added.

6   Don't allow the level to drop below the lower notch on the dipstick or engine damage may occur. On the other hand, don't overfill the engine by adding too much oil - it may result in oil aeration and loss of oil pressure and also could result in oil fouled spark plugs, oil leaks or seal failures.

7   Checking the oil level is an important preventive maintenance step. A consistently low oil level indicates oil leakage through damaged seals, defective gaskets or past worn rings or valve guides. If the oil looks milky in color or has water droplets in it, the block or head may be cracked and leaking coolant is entering the crankcase. The engine should be checked immediately. The condition of the oil should also be checked. Each time you check the oil level, slide your thumb and index finger up the dipstick before wiping off the oil. If you see small dirt or metal particles clinging to the dipstick, the oil should be changed **(see Section 8)**.

4.5 Turn the oil filler cap counterclockwise to remove it (four-cylinder engine shown)

Engine coolant

Refer to illustrations 4.9 and 4.10

Warning: *Do not allow coolant (antifreeze) to come in contact with your skin or painted surfaces of the vehicle. Flush contaminated areas immediately with plenty of water. Don't store new coolant or leave old coolant lying around where it's accessible to children or pets - they're attracted by its sweet smell. Ingestion of even a small amount of coolant can be fatal! Wipe up garage floor and drip pan spills immediately. Keep antifreeze containers covered and repair cooling system leaks as soon as they are noticed. Check with local authorities about the disposal of used antifreeze. Many communities have collection centers which will see that antifreeze is disposed of properly.*

8   All vehicles covered by this manual are equipped with a pressurized coolant recovery system. A coolant reservoir (expansion tank) is attached to the engine compartment firewall on the right (passenger's) side is connected by a hose to the engine coolant system filler neck. As the engine warms up, the system pressure increases causing some

4.9 With the engine COLD, remove the engine coolant pressure cap - the coolant level should be up to the pressure cap seat inside the filler neck

coolant to escape through a valve in the radiator cap and travel through the hose and into the coolant reservoir. As the engine cools, the coolant in the reservoir is automatically drawn back into the cooling system via the vacuum created by the contracting coolant. This recovery type system maintains the maximum amount of coolant available at all times.

9   **Warning:** *Never remove the pressure cap on the filler neck to add coolant while the engine is warm! If the cap feels even slightly warm, wrap a towel or rag around the cap and open it very slowly.* With the engine cold, remove the coolant system filler cap **(see illustration)**. The coolant level should be up to the pressure cap seat inside the filler neck. If it is low, add a mixture of high-quality antifreeze/coolant and water in the ratio specified on the antifreeze container or in this Chapter's Specification Section to bring it up to the correct level.

10   The coolant level in the recovery tank should be checked while the engine is at normal operating temperature. Simply note the fluid level in the reservoir - it should be at or

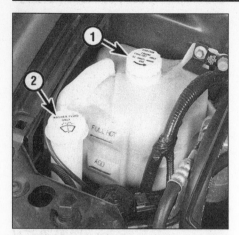

4.10 Engine coolant (1) and windshield washer (2) reservoirs

4.17 The brake fluid level, indicated on the translucent white plastic brake fluid reservoir, should be kept at the FULL mark (arrow)

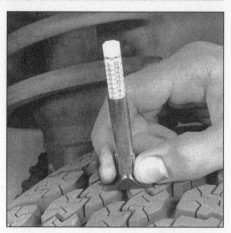

5.2 Use a tire tread depth indicator to monitor tire wear - they are available at auto parts stores or service stations and are relatively inexpensive

close to the FULL HOT mark when the engine is at normal operating temperature **(see illustration)**.

11   If only a small amount of coolant is required to bring the system up to the proper level, ordinary tap water may be used. However, to maintain the proper antifreeze/water mixture in the system, a blend of high-quality antifreeze/coolant and water in the ratio specified on the antifreeze container or in this Chapter's Specification Section should be added.

12   As the coolant level is checked, note the condition of the coolant as well. It should be relatively clean and the color of new antifreeze. If it's brown or rust colored, the system should be drained, flushed and refilled (see Section 25).

13   If the coolant level drops consistently, there is a leak in the system. Check the radiator, hoses, filler cap, drain plugs and water pump (see Section 25). If no leaks are noted, have the filler cap and coolant system pressure tested by your dealer service department or other qualified service station.

Windshield washer fluid

14   The fluid for the windshield washer system is stored in a plastic reservoir. The reservoir level should be maintained about one inch below the filler cap. The reservoir is accessible after opening the hood and is located on the right (passenger's) side of the engine compartment next to the coolant recovery tank **(see illustration 4.10)**.

15   In milder climates, plain water can be used in the reservoir, but it should be kept no more than two-thirds full to allow for expansion if the water freezes. In colder climates, use windshield washer system antifreeze, available at any auto parts store, to lower the freezing point of the fluid. Mix the antifreeze with water in accordance with the manufacturer's directions on the container. **Caution:** *DO NOT use cooling system antifreeze - it will damage the vehicle's paint. To help prevent icing in cold weather, warm the windshield with the defroster before using the washer.*

Brake fluid

Refer to illustration 4.17

16   The brake fluid reservoir is located on top of the brake master cylinder on the driver's side of the engine compartment near the firewall.

17   The brake fluid level should be maintained at the FULL mark on the reservoir **(see illustration)**.

18   If additional fluid is necessary to bring the level up, use a rag to clean all dirt off the top of the reservoir. If any foreign matter enters the reservoir when the cap is removed, blockage in the brake system lines can occur. Also, make sure all painted surfaces around the master cylinder are covered, since brake fluid will ruin paint. Carefully pour new, clean brake fluid obtained from a sealed container into the master cylinder. Be careful not to spill the fluid on painted surfaces. Be sure the specified fluid is used; mixing different types of brake fluid can cause damage to the system. See *Recommended lubricants and fluids* at the beginning of this Chapter or your owner's manual.

19   At this time the fluid and the master cylinder should be inspected for contamination. Normally the brake hydraulic system won't need periodic draining and refilling, but if rust deposits, dirt particles or water droplets are observed in the fluid, the system should be dismantled, cleaned and refilled with fresh fluid. Over time brake fluid will absorb moisture from the air. The moisture in the fluid then produces rust in the system and lowers the fluid boiling point increasing the possibility of premature brake failure. Normal brake fluid is clear in color. If the brake fluid is dark brown in color or is over three years old, its a good idea to flush the system and refill it with new fluid.

20   Reinstall the brake fluid reservoir cap.

21   The brake fluid in the master cylinder will drop slightly as the brake shoes and pads at each wheel wear down during normal operation. If the master cylinder requires repeated replenishing to maintain the correct level, there is a leak in the brake system which should be corrected immediately. Check all brake lines and connections, along with the wheel cylinders and vacuum booster (see Section 18 and Chapter 9 for more information).

22   If you discover that the reservoir is empty or nearly empty, the brake system should be thoroughly inspected, refilled and then bled (see Chapter 9).

---

5   Tire and tire pressure checks (every 250 miles or weekly)

Refer to illustrations 5.2, 5.3, 5.4a, 5.4b and 5.8

1   Periodic inspection of the tires may spare you the inconvenience of being stranded with a flat tire. It can also provide you with vital information regarding possible problems in the steering and suspension systems before major damage occurs.

2   The original tires on this vehicle are equipped with 1/2-inch wide bands that will appear when tread depth reaches 1/16-inch, but they don't appear until the tires are worn out. Tread wear can be monitored with a simple, inexpensive device known as a tread depth indicator **(see illustration)**.

3   Note any abnormal tread wear **(see illustration)**. Tread pattern irregularities such as cupping, flat spots and more wear on one side than the other are indications of front end alignment and/or balance problems. If any of these conditions are noted, take the vehicle to a tire shop or service station to correct the problem.

4   Look closely for cuts, punctures and embedded nails or tacks. Sometimes a tire will hold air pressure for a short time or leak down very slowly after a nail has embedded itself in the tread. If a slow leak persists, check the valve stem core to make sure it's tight **(see illustration)**. Examine the tread for

CUPPING

Cupping may be caused by:

- **Underinflation and/or mechanical irregularities such as out-of-balance condition of wheel and/or tire, and bent or damaged wheel.**
- **Loose or worn steering tie-rod or steering idler arm.**
- **Loose, damaged or worn front suspension parts.**

UNDERINFLATION

5.4a If a tire loses air on a steady basis, check the valve core first to make sure it's snug (special inexpensive wrenches are commonly available at auto parts stores)

INCORRECT TOE-IN OR EXTREME CAMBER   **OVERINFLATION**   **FEATHERING DUE TO MISALIGNMENT**

5.3 This chart will help you determine the condition of the tires, the probable cause(s) of abnormal wear and the corrective action necessary

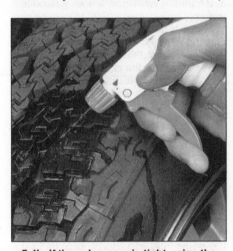

5.4b If the valve core is tight, raise the corner of the vehicle with the low tire and spray a soapy water solution onto the tread as the tire is turned slowly - leaks will cause small bubbles to appear

an object that may have embedded itself in the tire or for a "plug" that may have begun to leak (radial tire punctures are repaired with a plug that's installed in a puncture). If a puncture is suspected, it can be easily verified by spraying a solution of soapy water onto the puncture area **(see illustration)**. The soapy solution will bubble if there's a leak. Unless the puncture is unusually large, a tire shop or service station can usually repair the tire.

5   Carefully inspect the inner sidewall of each tire for evidence of brake fluid leakage. If you see any, inspect the brakes immediately.

6   Correct air pressure adds miles to the life span of the tires, improves mileage and enhances overall ride quality. Tire pressure cannot be accurately estimated by looking at a tire, especially if it's a radial. A tire pressure gauge is essential. Keep an accurate gauge in the vehicle. The pressure gauges attached to the nozzles of air hoses at gas stations are often inaccurate.

7   Always check tire pressure when the tires are cold. Cold, in this case, means the vehicle has not been driven over a mile in the three hours preceding a tire pressure check. A pressure rise of four to eight pounds is not uncommon once the tires are warm.

8   Unscrew the valve cap protruding from the wheel or hubcap and push the gauge firmly onto the valve stem **(see illustration)**. Compare the reading on the gauge to the recommended tire pressure shown on the placard on the driver's side door pillar. Be sure to reinstall the valve cap to keep dirt and moisture out of the valve stem mechanism. Check all four tires and, if necessary, add enough air to bring them up to the recommended pressure.

9   Don't forget to keep the spare tire inflated to the specified pressure (refer to your owner's manual or the tire sidewall). Note that the pressure recommended for the compact spare is higher than for the tires on the vehicle.

6   Automatic transaxle - fluid level check (every 250 miles or weekly)

Refer to illustration 6.4

1   The fluid inside the transaxle should be at normal operating temperature to get an accurate reading on the dipstick. This is done by driving the vehicle for several miles, making frequent starts and stops to allow the

5.8 To extend the life of the tires, check the air pressure at least once a week with an accurate gauge (don't forget the spare!)

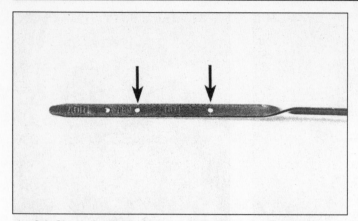

6.4 Check the fluid with the transaxle at normal operating temperature - the level should be kept in the HOT range, between the two upper holes (arrows)

7.2 The power steering reservoir is located on the right (passenger's) side rear of the engine compartment (2.5L engine shown)

transaxle to shift through all gears.

2   Park the vehicle on a level surface and apply the parking brake. With the engine running, apply the brakes and place the gear selector lever momentarily in Reverse, then Drive and repeat the sequence again ending with the gear selector in the Park position.

3   With the engine still running, locate the transaxle fluid dipstick near the brake fluid reservoir. The dipstick has a "T" handle and is identified as "TRANS FLUID". Remove the dipstick and wipe the fluid from the end with a clean rag.

4   Insert the dipstick back into the transaxle until the cap seats completely. Remove the dipstick again and note the fluid level on the end. The level should be in the area marked Hot (between the two upper holes in the dipstick) **(see illustration)**. If the fluid isn't hot (temperature approximately 100-degrees F), the level should be in the area marked Warm (between the two lower holes).

5   If the fluid level is at or below the ADD mark on the dipstick, add just enough of the specified fluid (see *Recommended lubricants and fluids* at the beginning of this Chapter) to raise the level to within the marks indicated for the appropriate temperature. Fluid should be slowly added into the dipstick tube, using a funnel to prevent spills.

6   DO NOT overfill the transaxle. Never allow the fluid level to go above the upper hole on the dipstick - it could cause internal transaxle damage. The best way to prevent overfilling is to add fluid a little at a time, driving the vehicle and checking the level between additions.

7   Use only transaxle fluid specified by the manufacturer. This information can be found in the *Recommended lubricants and fluids* Section at the beginning of this Chapter or in your owner's manual.

8   The condition of the fluid should also be checked along with the level. If it's a dark reddish-brown color, or if it smells burned, it should be changed. If you're in doubt about the condition of the fluid, purchase some new fluid and compare the two for color and odor.

7   Power steering fluid level check (every 250 miles or weekly)

Refer to illustrations 7.2 and 7.5

1   Unlike manual steering, the power steering system relies on hydraulic fluid which may, over a period of time require replenishing.

2   The fluid reservoir for the power steering pump is located at the rear of the engine compartment on the right (passenger's) side **(see illustration)**.

3   The power steering fluid level can be checked with the engine either hot or cold.

4   With the engine off, use a rag to clean the reservoir cap and the area around the cap. This will help prevent foreign material from falling into the reservoir when the cap is removed.

5   Turn and pull out the reservoir cap, which has a dipstick attached to it. Wipe the fluid at the bottom of the dipstick with a clean rag. Reinstall the cap to get a fluid level reading. Remove the cap again and note the fluid level. It should be at the appropriate mark on the dipstick in relation to the engine temperature **(see illustration)**.

6   If additional fluid is required, pour the specified type fluid (see *Recommended lubricants and fluids* at the beginning of this Chapter or your owner's manual) directly into the reservoir using a funnel to prevent spills. DO NOT use automatic transmission fluid!

7   If the reservoir requires frequent topping up, all power steering hoses, hose connections, the power steering pump and the steering gear should be carefully examined for leaks.

8   Engine oil and filter change (every 7500 miles or 6 months)

Refer to illustrations 8.3, 8.8, 8.13 and 8.18

1   Frequent oil changes are the most important preventive maintenance procedures that can be performed by the home

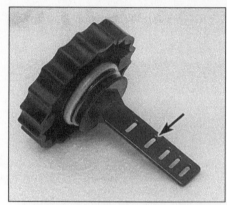

7.5 The power steering fluid dipstick on most models is marked on both sides for checking the fluid level (the arrow is pointing to the COLD level mark)

mechanic. When engine oil ages, it gets diluted and contaminated, which ultimately leads to premature engine wear.

2   Although some sources recommend oil filter changes every other oil change, a new filter should be installed every time the oil is changed.

3   Gather together all necessary tools and materials before beginning this procedure **(see illustration)**. **Note:** *To avoid rounding off the corners of the drain plug, use a box-end type wrench or socket. In addition, you should have plenty of clean rags and newspapers handy to mop up any spills.*

4   Raise the front of the vehicle and support it securely on jackstands. **Warning:** *Never work under a vehicle that is supported only by a jack!*

5   If this is your first oil change on the vehicle, familiarize yourself with the locations of the oil drain plug and the oil filter. Since the engine and exhaust components will be warm during the actual work, it's a good idea to figure out any potential problems beforehand.

6   Allow the engine to warm up to normal operating temperature. If oil or tools are needed, use the warm-up time to gather

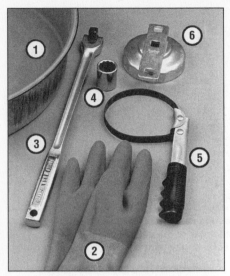

8.8 To avoid rounding off the corners, use the correct size box-end wrench or a socket to remove the engine oil drain plug

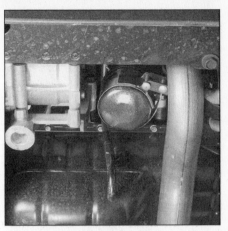

8.13 Removing the oil filter (V6 engine shown)

8.3 These tools are required when changing the engine oil and filter

1 **Drain pan** - It should be fairly shallow in depth, but wide to prevent spills and capable of holding at least 5 quarts
2 **Rubber gloves** - When removing the drain plug and filter, you will get oil on your hands (the gloves will prevent burns)
3 **Breaker bar** - Sometimes the oil drain plug is tight, and a long breaker bar is needed to loosen it
4 **Socket** - To be used with the breaker bar or a ratchet (must be the correct size to fit the drain plug - six-point preferred)
5 **Filter wrench** - This is a metal band-type wrench, which requires clearance around the filter to be effective
6 **Filter wrench** - This type fits on the bottom of the filter and can be turned with a ratchet or breaker bar (different size wrenches are available for different types of filters)

everything necessary for the job. The correct type of oil to buy for your application can be found in the *Recommended lubricants and fluids* Section at the beginning of this Chapter or your owner's manual.

7 Move all necessary tools, rags and newspapers under the vehicle. Place a drain pan capable of holding at least 5 quarts under the drain plug. Keep in mind that the oil will initially flow from the engine with some force, so position the pan accordingly.
8 Being careful not to touch any of the hot exhaust components, use the breaker bar and socket or box-end wrench to remove the drain plug **(see illustration)**. Depending on how hot the oil is, you may want to wear gloves while unscrewing the plug the final few turns.
9 Allow the oil to drain into the pan. It may be necessary to move the pan further under the engine as the oil flow reduces to a trickle.
10 After all the oil has completely drained, clean the plug thoroughly with a rag. Small

8.18 Lubricate the oil filter gasket with clean engine oil before installing the filter on the engine

metal particles may cling to it and would immediately contaminate the new oil.
11 Clean the area around the drain plug opening and reinstall the plug. Tighten it to the torque given in this Chapter's Specifications.
12 Next, carefully move the drain pan into position under the oil filter.
13 Now use the filter wrench to loosen the oil filter in a counterclockwise direction **(see illustration)**.
14 Sometimes the oil filter is on so tight it cannot be loosened, or it's positioned in an area inaccessible with a conventional filter wrench. Other type of tools, which fit over the end of the filter and turned with a ratchet or breaker bar, are available and may be better suited for removing the filter. If the filter is extremely tight, position the filter wrench near the threaded end of the filter, close to the engine.
15 Completely unscrew the old filter. Be careful, it's full of oil. Empty the old oil inside the filter into the drain pan. **Note:** *To make removing a vertically installed filter a little less messy, a paper or plastic cup placed over the*

filter will catch the oil that will drain as it is unscrewed.
16 Compare the old filter with the new one to make sure they're identical.
17 Use a clean rag to remove all oil, dirt and sludge from the area where the oil filter seals on the engine. Check the old filter to make sure the rubber gasket isn't stuck to the engine mounting surface.
18 Apply a light coat of clean engine oil to the rubber gasket on the new oil filter **(see illustration)**.
19 Install the new filter on the engine hand-tight plus 1/4 turn more. Do not overtighten.
20 Remove all tools and materials from under the vehicle, being careful not to spill the oil in the drain pan. Lower the vehicle.
21 Working inside the engine compartment, locate and remove the oil filler cap from the engine valve cover **(see illustration 4.5)**.
22 Using a funnel to prevent spills, pour the specified type and amount of new oil required (see Specification Section in the beginning of this Chapter) into the engine. Wait a few minutes to allow the oil to drain down to the pan, then check the level on the dipstick (see Section 4 if necessary). If the oil level is at or above the first notch on the dipstick, start the engine and allow the new oil to circulate.
23 Run the engine for only about a minute, then shut it off. Immediately look under the vehicle and check for leaks at the oil pan drain plug and around the oil filter. If either one is leaking, tighten it with a bit more force.
24 With the new oil circulated and the filter now completely full, wait about ten minutes for the oil to drain back down into the pan then recheck the oil level on the dipstick. If necessary, add enough oil to bring the level to the second notch on the dipstick. DO NOT overfill!
25 During the first few trips after an oil change, make it a point to check for leaks and keep a close watch on the oil level.
26 The old oil drained from the engine cannot be reused in its present state and should be disposed of properly. Oil reclamation centers, auto repair shops and gas stations will

9.1 Tools and materials required for battery maintenance. Note: *Items 4 through 7 do not apply to "side" post batteries.*

1   ***Face shield/safety goggles*** - *When removing corrosion with a brush, the acidic particles can easily fly up into your eyes*
2   ***Baking soda*** - *A solution of baking soda and water can be used to neutralize corrosion*
3   ***Petroleum jelly*** - *A layer of this on the battery posts will help prevent corrosion*
4   ***Battery post/cable cleaner*** - *This wire brush cleaning tool will remove all traces of corrosion from the battery posts and cable clamps*
5   ***Treated felt washers*** - *Placing one of these on each post, directly under the cable clamps, will help prevent corrosion*
6   ***Puller*** - *Sometimes the cable clamps are very difficult to pull off the posts, even after the nut/bolt has been completely loosened. This tool pulls the clamp straight up and off the post without damage*
7   ***Battery post/cable cleaner*** - *Here is another cleaning tool which is a slightly different version of Number 4 above, but it does the same thing*
8   ***Rubber gloves*** - *Another safety item to consider when servicing the battery; remember that's acid inside the battery!*

normally accept used oil. After the oil has cooled, it should be drained into sealable containers (plastic bottles with screw-on tops are preferred) for transport to a disposal site.

9   Battery - check, maintenance and charging (every 7,500 miles or 6 months)

Warning: *Certain precautions must be followed when checking and servicing the battery. Hydrogen gas, which is highly explosive,*

9.6a Use a side terminal battery brush (available at most auto parts stores) to clean up the terminal contact area

is produced by the battery. Keep lighted tobacco, open flames, bare light bulbs or other possible sources of ignition away from the battery. Furthermore, the electrolyte inside the battery is sulfuric acid which is highly corrosive and can burn your skin and cause severe injury to your eyes. Always wear eye protection! It will also destroy clothing and ruin painted surfaces.*

Servicing

Refer to illustrations 9.1, 9.6a and 9.6b

1   A routine preventive maintenance program for the battery in your vehicle is the only way to ensure quick and reliable starts. But before performing any battery maintenance, make sure that you have the proper equipment necessary to work safely around the battery **(see illustration)**.
2   Before servicing the battery, always turn the engine and all accessories off and disconnect the cable from the negative terminal of the battery.
3   The battery on these vehicles is located inside the wheel well of the left front fender.
4   Remove the battery from the vehicle (see Chapter 5).
5   Inspect the external condition of the battery. Check the battery case for cracks or other damage.
6   Clean the battery terminals and cable connections thoroughly with a wire brush or a terminal cleaner and a solution of warm water and baking soda **(see illustrations)**. Wash the terminals and the top of the battery case with the same solution but make sure that the solution doesn't get into the battery. When cleaning the cables, terminals and battery top, wear safety goggles and rubber gloves to prevent any solution from coming in contact with your eyes or hands. Wear old clothes too - even diluted, sulfuric acid splashed onto clothes will burn holes in them. Thoroughly wash all cleaned areas with plain water.
7   Inspect the battery carrier. If it's dirty or covered with corrosion, clean it with the same solution of warm water and baking

9.6b The side terminal battery brush includes a special ring-type portion used to clean the battery cable sealing recess around the terminal

soda and rinse it with clean water.
8   If the battery is a maintenance-type, it has removable cell caps which allow you to add water (use distilled water only) to the battery when the electrolyte level gets low.
9   If you are not sure what type of battery you have (some maintenance-types have recessed cell caps that resemble maintenance-free batteries), one simple way to confirm your type of battery is to look for a built-in hydrometer. Most maintenance-free batteries have built-in hydrometers that indicate the state of charge by the color displayed in the hydrometer window since measuring the specific gravity of the electrolyte is not possible. Also check for cut-outs near the cell caps - if the caps can be removed, cut-outs are usually provided to assist with prying off the caps.
10   If your battery is a maintenance-type, remove the cell caps and check the level of the electrolyte. It should be up the split-ring inside the battery. If the level is low, add distilled water (distilled water is mineral-free, tap water contains minerals that will shorten the life of your battery) to bring the electrolyte up to the proper level.
11   Next, check the entire length of each battery cable for cracks, worn insulation and frayed conductors. Replace the cable(s) if necessary.
12   Install the battery (see Chapter 5).

Charging

Warning: *The battery produces hydrogen gas, which is highly explosive. Never create a spark, smoke or light a match around the battery. Always charge the battery in a ventilated area.*

13   The battery on these vehicles is located inside the wheel well of the left front fender.
14   Remove the battery from the vehicle (see Chapter 5).
15   On maintenance-type batteries, remove the cell caps. Make sure the electrolyte level is OK before beginning to charge the battery. Cover the holes with a clean cloth to prevent

Check for a soft area indicating the hose has deteriorated inside.

Overtightening the clamp on a hardened hose will damage the hose and cause a leak.

Check each hose for swelling and oil-soaked ends. Cracks and breaks can be located by squeezing the hose.

10.4a Hoses, like drivebelts, have a habit of failing at the worst possible time - to prevent the inconvenience of a blown radiator or heater hose, inspect them carefully as shown here

spattering electrolyte.

16   On batteries with the terminals located on the side, install bolts (with the appropriate thread size and pitch) in the terminals so the charger can be attached.

17   Connect the battery charger leads to the battery posts (positive to positive, negative to negative), then plug in the charger. Make sure it is set at 12 volts if it has a selector switch. If the battery charger does not have a built-in timer, its a good idea to use one in case you forget - you won't over charge the battery.

18   If you're using a charger with a rate higher than two amps, check the battery regularly during charging to make sure it doesn't overheat. If you're using a trickle charger, you can safely let the battery charge overnight after you've checked it regularly for the first couple of hours.

19   If the battery has removable cell caps,

10.4b Squeeze the hoses to locate cracks or breaks that may cause leaks

measure the specific gravity with a hydrometer every hour during the last few hours of the charging cycle. Hydrometers are available inexpensively from auto parts stores - follow the instructions that come with the hydrometer. Consider the battery charged when there's no change in the specific gravity reading for two hours and the electrolyte in the cells is outgassing (bubbling) freely. The specific gravity reading from each cell should be very close to the others. If not, the battery probably has a bad cell(s).

20   Most batteries with sealed tops have built-in hydrometers on the top that indicate the state of charge by the color displayed in the hydrometer window. Normally, a bright-colored hydrometer indicates a full charge and a dark hydrometer indicates the battery still needs charging. Check the battery manufacturer's instructions to be sure you know what the colors mean. **Note:** *It may be necessary to jiggle the battery to bring the test indicator fluid into view.*

21   If the battery has a sealed top and does not have a built-in hydrometer, you can hook up a voltmeter across the battery terminals to check the charge. A fully charged battery should read approximately 12.6 volts or higher.

22   Further information on the battery and jump starting can be found in Chapter 5 and at the front of this manual, respectively.

10   Cooling system - check (every 7,500 miles or 6 months)

Refer to illustrations 10.4a and 10.4b
Warning: *The electric cooling fan(s) on these models can activate at any time the ignition switch is in the ON position. Make sure the ignition is OFF when working in the vicinity of the fan(s).*

1   Many major engine failures can be attributed to a faulty cooling system. If the vehicle is equipped with an automatic transaxle, a transmission fluid cooler is incorporated inside the radiator side tank.

2   The cooling system should be checked with the engine cold. Do this before the vehicle is driven for the day or after it has been shut off for three or four hours and the upper radiator hose feels cool to the touch.

3   Remove the coolant system pressure cap **(see illustration 4.9)** and thoroughly clean the cap with water. Also clean the filler neck. All traces of corrosion and gum should be removed.

4   Carefully check the upper and lower radiator hoses along with the smaller diameter heater hoses. Inspect the entire length of each hose, replacing any that are cracked, swollen or deteriorated **(see illustration)**. Cracks may become more apparent when a hose is squeezed **(see illustration)**.

5   Also check that all hose connections are tight. If the vehicle came equipped with spring-type hose clamps which loose their tension over time, replace them with the more reliable screw-type clamps when new hoses are installed. A leak in the cooling system will usually show up as white or rust-colored deposits on the areas adjoining the leak.

6   Use compressed air, water or a soft brush to remove bugs, leaves, and other debris from the front of the radiator or air conditioning condenser. Be careful not to damage the delicate cooling fins, or cut yourself on them.

7   Finally, have the cap and system pressure tested. If you do not have a pressure tester available, most gas stations and repair shops will do this for a minimal charge.

11   Underhood hose - check and replacement (every 7,500 miles or 6 months)

Warning: *Replacement of air conditioning hoses must be left to a dealer service department or air conditioning shop equipped to depressurize the system safely. Never remove air conditioning components or hoses until the system has been depressurized.*

General

1   High temperatures under the hood can cause the deterioration of the rubber and plastic hoses used for engine, accessory and emission systems operation. Periodic inspection should be made for cracks, loose clamps, material hardening and leaks.

2   Information specific to the cooling system hoses can be found in Section 10.

3   Some hoses use clamps to secure the hoses to fittings. Where clamps are used, check to be sure they haven't lost their tension, allowing the hose to leak. Where clamps are not used, make sure the hose hasn't expanded and/or hardened where it slips over the fitting, allowing it to leak.

Vacuum hoses

4   It's quite common for vacuum hoses, especially those in the emissions system, to be color coded or identified by colored

1

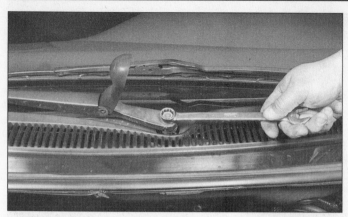

12.3 Lift the cover and check the mounting nut for tightness

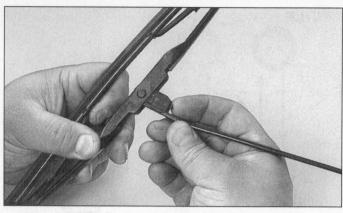

12.5a Depress the release lever and . . .

stripes molded into the hose. Various systems require hoses with different wall thickness, collapse resistance and temperature resistance. When replacing hoses, make sure the new ones are made of the same material as the original.

5   Often the only effective way to check a hose is to remove it completely from the vehicle. Where more than one hose is removed, be sure to label the hoses and their attaching points to insure proper reattachment.

6   When checking vacuum hoses, be sure to include any plastic T-fittings in the check. Check the fittings for cracks and the hose where it fits over the fitting for enlargement, which could cause leakage.

7   A small piece of vacuum hose (1/4-inch inside diameter) can be used as a stethoscope to detect vacuum leaks. Hold one end of the hose to your ear and probe around vacuum hoses and fittings, listening for the "hissing" sound characteristic of a vacuum leak. **Warning:** *When probing with the vacuum hose stethoscope, be careful not to allow your body or the hose to come into contact with moving engine components such as the drivebelt, cooling fan, etc.*

Fuel hose

Warning: *Gasoline is extremely flammable, so take extra precautions when you work on any part of the fuel system. Don't smoke or allow open flames or bare light bulbs near the work area, and don't work in a garage where a natural gas-type appliance (such as a water heater or clothes dryer) with a pilot light is present. If you spill any fuel on your skin, rinse it off immediately with soap and water. When you perform any kind of work on the fuel system, wear safety glasses and have a Class B type fire extinguisher on hand. Before working on any part of the fuel system, relieve the fuel system pressure (see Chapter 4).*

8   Check all rubber fuel hoses for damage and deterioration. Check especially for cracks in areas where the hose bends and just before clamping points, such as where a hose attaches to the fuel injection system.

9   High quality fuel line, specifically designed for fuel injection systems, should be used for fuel line replacement. **Warning:**

Never use vacuum line, clear plastic tubing or water hose for fuel lines.

Brake hoses

10   The hoses used to connect the brake calipers or wheel cylinders to the metal lines are subject to extreme working conditions. They must endure high hydraulic pressures, heat and still maintain flexibility. The brake hoses typically can be inspected without removing the wheels. Carefully examine each hose for leakage, cracks, bulging, delamination and damage. If any damage is found, the hose must be replaced immediately (see Chapter 9).

Fuel and brake system metal lines

11   Sections of metal line are often used for fuel line between the fuel tank and fuel injection system. Check carefully to be sure the line has not been bent and crimped and that cracks have not started in the line.

12   If a section of metal fuel line must be replaced, only seamless steel tubing should be used, since copper and aluminum tubing do not have the strength necessary to withstand normal engine operating vibration.

13   Check the metal brake lines where they enter the master cylinder and brake proportioning or ABS unit (if equipped) for cracks in the lines or loose fittings. Any sign of brake fluid leakage calls for an immediate thorough inspection of the brake system.

---

12   Windshield wiper blade - inspection and replacement (every 7,500 miles or 6 months)

Refer to illustrations 12.3, 12.5a and 12.5b

1   The windshield wiper blade elements should be checked periodically for cracks and deterioration.

2   Road film can build up on the wiper blades and affect their efficiency, so they should be washed regularly with a mild detergent solution.

3   The action of the wiping mechanism can

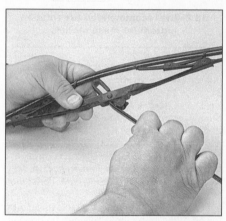

12.5b . . . slide the wiper element down out of the hook in the end of the arm

loosen the wiper arm retaining nuts, so they should be checked and tightened at the same time the wiper blades are checked **(see illustration)**.

4   Lift the wiper blade assembly away from the windshield.

5   Press the release lever and slide the blade assembly out of the hook in the end of the wiper arm **(see illustrations)**. Carefully rest the wiper arm on the windshield.

6   The rubber element is secured to the blade assembly at one end of the blade element channel. Compress the locking feature on the element so it clears the tangs on the blade assembly channel claw and then slide the element out of the frame.

7   Installation is the reverse of removal. Make sure the rubber element and blade assembly are securely attached.

---

13   Tire rotation (every 7,500 miles or 6 months)

Refer to illustration 13.2

1   The tires should be rotated at the specified intervals and whenever uneven wear is noticed. Since the vehicle will be raised and the tires removed, this is a good time to check the brakes also (see Section 18).

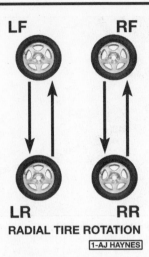

RADIAL TIRE ROTATION

1-AJ HAYNES

13.2 The recommended tire rotation pattern for these models

14.5 Checking the steering rack tie-rod boot for damage

14.10 Checking the wheel bearing freeplay

2   Radial tires must be rotated in a specific pattern **(see illustration)**.

3   See the information in *Jacking and towing* at the front of this manual for the proper procedures to follow when raising the vehicle and changing a tire; however, if the brakes are to be checked, don't apply the parking brake as stated. Make sure the tires are blocked to prevent the vehicle from rolling. **Note:** *Prior to raising the vehicle, loosen all lug nuts a quarter turn.*

4   Preferably, the entire vehicle should be raised at the same time. This can be done on a hoist or by jacking up each corner of the vehicle and lowering it onto jackstands. Always use jackstands and make sure the vehicle is safely supported. **Warning:** *Never work under a vehicle that is supported only by a jack!*

5   After the tire rotation, check and adjust the tire pressures as necessary and tighten the wheel lug nuts to the torque listed in this Chapter's Specifications.

14 Steering and suspension - check (every 7,500 miles or 6 months)

Refer to illustrations 14.5 and 14.10

1   Whenever the vehicle is raised for service it is a good idea to visually check the suspension and steering components for wear and damage.

2   Indications of wear and damage include excessive play in the steering wheel before the front wheels react, excessive lean around corners, body movement over rough roads or binding at some point as the steering wheel is turned.

3   Before the vehicle is raised for inspection, test the shock absorbers by pushing down to rock the vehicle at each corner. If it does not come back to a level position within one or two bounces, the shocks are worn and should be replaced (see Chapter 10). As you perform this procedure, check for

squeaks and unusual noises from the suspension components. Check the shock absorbers for fluid leakage.

4   Raise the vehicle and support it securely on jackstands. **Warning:** *Never work under a vehicle that is supported only by a jack!*

5   Working under the vehicle, check for loose bolts, cracked, broken or disconnected parts and deteriorated rubber bushings on all suspension and steering components (shocks, springs, control arms, etc.). Look for grease or fluid leaking from around the steering gear input shaft and tie-rod boots **(see illustration)**. Check the power steering hoses, cooler and connections for leaks.

6   Have an assistant turn the steering wheel from side-to-side and check the steering components for free movement, chafing and binding. If the wheels don't respond closely to the movement of the steering wheel, determine where the slack is located.

7   Check the tie-rod ends and ball joints for wear. They are designed not to have any free play. Using a pry bar or other method, attempt to create movement (up/down and side-to-side) in the tie-rod ends and ball joints. If any movement is seen or felt, a worn balljoint is indicated. To service the tie-rod ends and ball joints see Chapter 10.

8   Next, have an assistant grasp the tire at the sides and pivot the tire in an in-and-out motion (left-to-right) while you are touching the tie-rod end. If any looseness is felt, suspect a loose tie-rod stud nut, worn out tie-rod stud or a widened hole in the steering knuckle boss. If the latter problem exists, the steering knuckle should be renewed along with the tie-rod (see Chapter 10).

9   Check the rear suspension ball joints for wear as described in Step 7. Inspect the trailing arms and lateral links for damage, looseness or worn bushings. If replacement is necessary, see Chapter 10.

10   Check each wheel bearing for excessive free play by grasping the wheel at the top and bottom, then pivot the wheel on the spindle **(see illustration)**. The free play should be minimal, zero (no play) to approximately 1/16 inch. Next, spin the wheel and listen for a

grinding noise or roughness in the bearings. Don't mistake light brake drag for a wheel bearing problem. **Note:** *The wheel bearings, front and rear, are integral with the wheel hubs. They are "lubricated for life" and are not serviceable.* If the hub/wheel bearing assembly has excessive play or they feel rough or noisy, replace them (see Chapter 10).

15 Exhaust system - check (every 7,500 or 6 months)

Refer to illustration 15.3

Note: *Perform the following procedure with the engine cold.*

1   Raise the vehicle and support it securely on jackstands. **Warning:** *Never work under a vehicle that is supported only by a jack!*

2   With the engine cold (at least three hours after the vehicle has been driven), check the complete exhaust system from its starting point at the engine to the end of the tailpipe.

3   Check the pipes and connections for signs of leakage and/or corrosion indicating a potential failure. Make sure that all brackets and hangers are in good condition and tight **(see illustration)**.

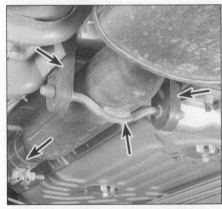

15.3 Check the exhaust system connections, clamps, mounting bolts, brackets and hangers for damage (arrows)

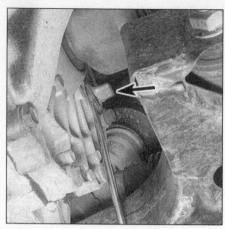

16.4 Pry the rubber plug from the oil fill hole on the side of the transaxle housing

17.3 Check each driveaxle inner and outer boot for cracks and/or leaking grease

18.5 Measure the thickness of the brake pad from the metal backing to the brake disc - note the inner pad generally wears faster than the outer pad so measure both of them

4   At the same time, inspect the underside of the body for holes, corrosion and open seams which may allow exhaust gases to enter the passenger compartment. Seal all body openings with silicone sealant or body putty.

5   Rattles and other noises can often be traced to the exhaust system, especially the mounts and hangers. Try to move the pipes, muffler and catalytic converter. If the components can come into contact with the body, secure the exhaust system with new mounts.

6   This is also an ideal time to check the running condition of the engine by inspecting the very end of the tailpipe. The exhaust deposits here are an indication of the engine's state-of-tune. If the pipe is black and sooty or coated with white deposits, the engine may be in need of a tune-up (including a thorough fuel injection system inspection).

16   Manual transaxle - lubricant level check (every 7500 miles or 6 months)

Refer to illustration 16.4

1   Manual transaxles do not have a fluid dipstick. The lubricant level is checked by removing a rubber plug from the side of the transaxle case. The lubricant level should be checked with the engine cold and the vehicle level.

2   Raise the vehicle and support it securely on jackstands in a level position. **Warning:** *Never work under a vehicle that is supported only by a jack!*

3   Locate the rubber plug on the left (driver's) side of the transaxle differential near the driveaxle shaft. Use a rag to clean it and the surrounding area. It may be necessary to remove the left inner fenderwell cover for access to the plug. Place a drain pan under the transaxle.

4   Using pliers or a large screwdriver, remove the plug **(see illustration)**. If oil begins to run out, let it find its own level (presuming the vehicle is relatively level). If oil

does not run out, insert your finger to feel the lubricant level. It should be within 3/16 of the bottom of the plug hole.

5   If the transaxle requires additional lubricant, use a funnel with a rubber tube or a syringe to pour or squeeze the recommended lubricant into the plug hole to restore the level. If you overfill it, let the fluid run out until it is level with the plug hole. **Caution:** *Use only the specified transaxle lubricant - see* Recommended lubricants and fluids *at the beginning of this Chapter or your owner's manual.* **Note:** *Most auto parts stores sell pumps that screw into the oil containers which make this job much easier and less messy.*

6   Push the plug securely back into the transaxle and lower the vehicle. Test drive it and check for leaks.

17   Driveaxle boot - check (every 7,500 miles or 6 months)

Refer to illustration 17.3

1   If the driveaxle boots are damaged, letting grease out and water in, serious not to mention costly damage can occur to the CV joints. The boots should be inspected very carefully at the recommended intervals or anytime the vehicle is raised.

2   Raise the front of the vehicle and support it securely on jackstands. **Warning:** *Never work under a vehicle that is supported only by a jack!*

3   Place the transaxle in Neutral. While rotating the wheels, inspect the four driveaxle boots (two on each driveaxle) very carefully for cracks, tears, holes, deteriorated rubber and loose or missing clamps **(see illustration)**. If the boots are dirty, wipe them clean before beginning the inspection.

4   If damage or deterioration is evident, replace the boots and check the CV joints for damage (see Chapter 8).

5   Place the transaxle in Park or in-gear as applicable and lower the vehicle.

18   Brake system - check (every 15,000 miles or 12 months)

Warning: *Dust created by the brake system may contain asbestos, which is harmful to your health. Never blow it out with compressed air and don't inhale any of it. An approved filtering mask should be worn when working on brakes. Do not, under any circumstances, use petroleum-based solvents to clean brake parts. Use brake system cleaner only!*

1   The brakes should be inspected every time the wheels are removed or whenever a defect is suspected. Indications of a potential brake system problem include the vehicle pulling to one side when the brake pedal is depressed, noises coming from the brakes when they are applied, excessive brake pedal travel, a pulsating pedal and leakage of fluid, usually seen on the inside of the tire or wheel. **Note:** *It is normal for a vehicle equipped with an Anti-lock Brake System (ABS) to exhibit brake pedal pulsation's during severe braking conditions.*

Disc brakes

Refer to illustrations 18.5

2   Disc brakes can be visually checked without removing any parts except the wheels. Remove the hub caps (if applicable) and loosen the front wheel lug nuts a quarter turn each.

3   Raise the front of the vehicle and place it securely on jackstands. **Warning:** *Never work under a vehicle that is supported only by a jack!*

4   Remove the front wheels. Now visible is the disc brake caliper which contains the pads. There is an outer brake pad and an inner pad. Both must be checked for wear. **Note:** *Usually the inner pad wears faster than the outer pad.*

5   Measure the pad thickness at each end of the caliper **(see illustration)** and through the inspection hole in the caliper body. Compare the measurement with the limit given in

18.14 If the lining is bonded to the brake shoe, measure the lining thickness from the outer surface to the metal shoe, as shown here: if the lining is riveted to the shoe, measure from the lining outer surface to the rivet head

18.17 Pry the boot away from the cylinder and check for fluid leakage

this Chapter's Specifications, if any brake pad thickness is less than specified, then all brake pads must be replaced (see Chapter 9).

6   If you're in doubt as to the exact pad thickness or quality, remove them for measurement and further inspection (see Chapter 9).

7   Before installing the wheels, check the brake hoses for leakage and damage (cracks, leaks, chafed areas, etc.). Replace the hoses or fittings as necessary (see Chapter 9).

8   Check the disc for score marks, wear and burned spots. If any of these conditions exist, the disc should be removed for servicing or replacement (see Chapter 9).

9   Install the front wheels, lower the vehicle and tighten the wheel lug nuts to the torque given in this Chapter's Specifications.

Drum brakes

Refer to illustrations 18.14 and 18.17

10   Remove the hub caps (if applicable) and loosen the wheel lug nuts a quarter turn each.

11   Raise the rear of the vehicle and support it securely on jackstands. **Warning:** *Never work under a vehicle that is supported only by a jack!* Block the front wheels to prevent the vehicle from rolling, however, do not apply the parking brake or it will lock the drums in place. Remove the rear wheels.

12   Remove the brake drum as described in Chapter 9.

13   With the drum removed, carefully clean off any accumulations of dirt and dust using brake system cleaner. **Warning:** *DO NOT blow the dust out with compressed air and don't inhale any of it (it may contain asbestos, which is harmful to your health).*

14   Measure the thickness of the lining material on both leading and trailing brake shoes **(see illustration)**. Compare the measurement with the limit given in this Chapter's Specifications, if any brake shoe thickness is less than specified, then all brake shoes must be replaced (see Chapter 9).

15   Inspect the brake shoes for uneven wear patterns, cracks, glazing and delamination and replace if necessary. If the shoes have been saturated with brake fluid, oil or grease,

this also necessitates replacement (see Chapter 9).

16   Make sure all the brake assembly springs are connected and in good condition.

17   Check the brake wheel cylinder for signs of fluid leakage. Carefully pry back the rubber dust boots on the wheel cylinder **(see illustration)**. Any leakage here is an indication that the wheel cylinders must be overhauled immediately (see Chapter 9). Also, check all hoses and connections for signs of leakage.

18   Wipe the inside of the drum with a clean rag and denatured alcohol or brake cleaner. Again, be careful not to breathe the dangerous asbestos dust.

19   Inspect the inside of the drum for cracks, score marks, deep scratches and "hard spots" which will appear as small discolored areas. If imperfections cannot be removed with fine emery cloth, the drum must be taken to an automotive machine shop for resurfacing.

20   Repeat the procedure for the remaining wheel.

21   Install the wheels, lower the vehicle and tighten the wheel lug nuts to the torque given in this Chapter's Specifications.

Parking brake

22   The easiest, and perhaps most obvious, method of periodically checking the operation of the parking brake assembly is to park the vehicle on a steep hill with the parking brake set and the transmission in Neutral. If the parking brake cannot prevent the vehicle from rolling, it needs adjustment (see Chapter 9).

19   Fuel system hoses and connections - check (every 15,000 miles or 12 months)

Refer to illustration 19.5

Warning: *Gasoline is extremely flammable, so take extra precautions when you work on any part of the fuel system. Don't smoke or allow open flames or bare light bulbs near the work area, and don't work in a garage where a natural gas-type appliance (such as a water*

heater or clothes dryer) with a pilot light is present. If you spill any fuel on your skin, rinse it off immediately with soap and water. When you perform any kind of work on the fuel system, wear safety glasses and have a Class B type fire extinguisher on hand.

1   If the smell of gasoline is noticed while driving, or after the vehicle has been parked in the sun, the fuel system and evaporative emissions system (see Section 26) should be thoroughly inspected immediately.

2   The fuel system is under pressure even when the engine is off. Consequently, the fuel system must be depressurized before servicing the system (see Chapter 4). Even after depressurization, if any fuel lines are disconnected for servicing, be prepared to catch some fuel as it spills out. Plug all disconnected fuel lines immediately to prevent the tank from emptying itself.

3   Remove the gas tank filler cap and check for damage, corrosion and a proper sealing imprint on the gasket. Replace the cap with a new one if necessary.

4   Raise the vehicle and support it securely on jackstands. **Warning:** Never work under a vehicle that is supported only by a jack!

5   Inspect the gas tank and filler neck for punctures, cracks and other damage. The hose connection between the filler neck and the tank is especially critical **(see illustra-**

19.5 Fuel filler neck-to-tank hose (arrow)

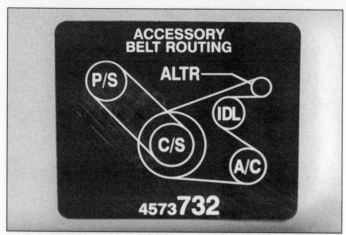

20.2 A drivebelt routing diagram is mounted under the hood

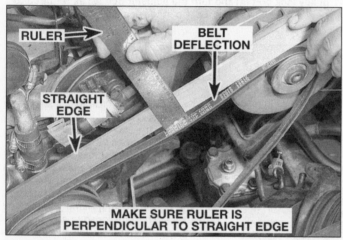

20.4 Measuring drivebelt deflection with a straightedge and ruler

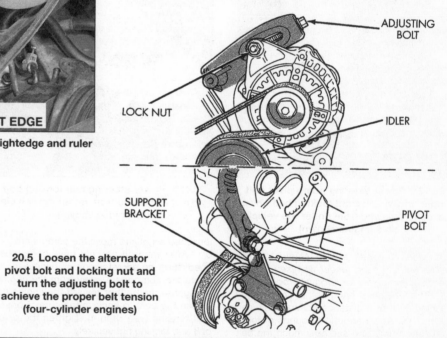

ACCEPTABLE

Cracks Running Across "V" Portions of Belt

1/2"

Missing Two or More Adjacent Ribs 1/2" or longer

UNACCEPTABLE

Cracks Running Parallel to "V" Portions of Belt

20.3 Here are some of the more common problems associated with drivebelts (check the belts very carefully to prevent an untimely breakdown)

20.5 Loosen the alternator pivot bolt and locking nut and turn the adjusting bolt to achieve the proper belt tension (four-cylinder engines)

tion). Sometimes the filler neck hose will leak due to loose clamps or deteriorated rubber; problems a home mechanic can usually rectify.

6   Carefully inspect all rubber hoses and metal lines leading to-and-from the fuel tank. Check for loose connections, deteriorated hoses, crimped lines and damage of any kind. Follow the lines up to the front of the vehicle, carefully inspecting them all the way. Repair or replace damaged sections as necessary (see Chapter 4).

20   Drivebelt - check, adjustment and replacement (every 15,000 miles or 12 months)

Warning: *The electric cooling fan(s) on these models can activate at any time the ignition switch is in the ON position. Make sure the ignition is OFF when working in the vicinity of the fan(s).*

Check

Refer to illustrations 20.2, 20.3 and 20.4

1   The drivebelts located at the front of the engine, play an important role in the opera-

tion of the vehicle and its components. Due to their function and material makeup, the belts are prone to failure after a period of time and should be inspected and adjusted periodically to prevent major damage.

2   The number of belts used depends on the engine accessories. All engines equipped with power steering and/or air conditioning are equipped with two drivebelts **(see illustration)**. One drivebelt drives the alternator and air conditioning compressor while the other belt drives the power steering pump.

3   With the engine off, open the hood and locate the drivebelts at the front of the engine. Using a flashlight, check each belt for

separation of the adhesive rubber on both sides of the core, core separation from the belt side, a severed core, separation of the ribs from the adhesive rubber, cracking or separation of the ribs, and torn or worn ribs or cracks in the inner ridges of the ribs **(see illustration)**. Also check for fraying and glazing, which gives the belt a shiny appearance. Both sides of the belt should be inspected, which means you will have to twist the belt to check the underside. Use your fingers to feel the belt where you can't see it. If any of the above conditions are evident, replace the belt(s). **Note:** *On V6 engines, a better drivebelt inspection can be made by removing the*

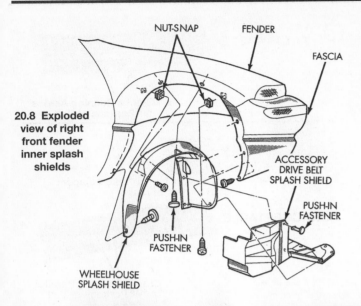

20.8 Exploded view of right front fender inner splash shields

NUT-SNAP   FENDER

FASCIA

ACCESSORY DRIVE BELT SPLASH SHIELD

PUSH-IN FASTENER

PUSH-IN FASTENER

WHEELHOUSE SPLASH SHIELD

20.9 To adjust the alternator drivebelt tension, loosen the idler pulley lock bolt (A) and turn the adjuster bolt (B) as required to achieve the proper belt tension (V6 engine)

20.12a Power steering pump pivot bolt (upper arrow) and front locking bolt (lower arrow) as viewed from under the vehicle (V6 engine shown)

20.12b Power steering rear locking bolt (arrow) as viewed from under the vehicle (V6 engine shown)

accessory drivebelt splash shield located inside the right hand fender well (see Adjustment Section below for removal procedures).

4   The tension of each belt is checked by pushing on it at a distance halfway between the pulleys. Apply about 10 pounds of force with your thumb and see how much the belt moves down (deflects). Measure the deflection with a ruler **(see illustration)**. The belt should deflect about 1/4-inch if the distance between pulleys is between 7 and 11 inches and around 1/2-inch if the distance is between 12 and 16 inches.

Adjustment

Alternator and air conditioning compressor drivebelt

Four-cylinder engines

Refer to illustration 20.5

5   Loosen the alternator locking nut and pivot bolt **(see illustration)**. Both must be

loosened slightly to move the component.

6   After the bolt and nut have been loosened, turn the adjuster bolt as necessary to move the component away from the engine (to tighten the belt) or toward the engine (to loosen the belt) to achieve the correct drivebelt tension (see Step 4). Tighten the pivot bolt and locking nut securely.

V6 engine

Refer to illustrations 20.8 and 20.9

7   Raise the front of the vehicle and support it securely on jackstands. Remove the right front wheel. **Warning:** *Never work under a vehicle that is only supported by a jack!*

8   Remove the screw and push-in fasteners securing the accessory drivebelt splash shield to the fender and frame rail, respectively **(see illustration)**.

9   Loosen the idler pulley lock bolt then turn the adjuster bolt **(see illustration)** as required to achieve the correct drivebelt tension (see Step 4). Tighten the idler pulley lock bolt securely after adjustment.

Power steering drivebelt

Refer to illustrations 20.12a and 20.12b

10   Raise the front of the vehicle and support it securely on jackstands. **Warning:** *Never work under a vehicle that is supported only by a jack!*

11   Remove the accessory drivebelt splash shield **(see illustration 20.8)**.

12   Working under the vehicle, loosen the power steering pump pivot and locking bolts (front and rear) **(see illustrations)**. The power steering pump should now be free to move.

13   The power steering pump is equipped with a square hole designed to accept a 1/2-inch square drive breaker bar to assist with adjusting the drivebelt tension.

14   Position the power steering pump as required to achieve the correct drivebelt tension (see Step 4). Tighten the pivot and locking bolts securely.

15   Install the accessory drivebelt splash shield and lower the vehicle.

Replacement

Refer to illustration 20.18

16   To replace a drivebelt, follow the above procedures for drivebelt adjustment except loosen the adjustment enough to allow you to slip the drivebelt off the crankshaft pulley and remove it. If you are replacing the alternator and A/C compressor drivebelt, you must remove the power steering drivebelt first because of the way they are arranged on the crankshaft pulley. Because both drivebelts tend to wear out equally, its a good idea to replace both belts at the same time. As they are removed, identify each belt as to it's appropriate drive function (PS or ALT-A/C) so the replacement belts can be installed in their proper positions.

17   Take the old drivebelts with you when you go to the auto parts store in order to make a direct comparison for length, width and design.

18   Install the new drivebelts. Make sure they are routed correctly and properly seated

CORRECT

WRONG   WRONG

20.18 When installing the V-ribbed drivebelt, make sure it is centered on each pulley - it must not overlap either edge

21.1 Materials required for chassis and body lubrication

1   *Engine oil - Light engine oil in a can like this can be used for door and hood hinges*
2   *Graphite spray - Used to lubricate lock cylinders*
3   *Grease - Grease, in a variety of types and weights, is available for use in a grease gun. Check the Specifications for your requirements*
4   *Grease gun - A common grease gun, shown here with a detachable hose and nozzle, is needed for chassis lubrication. After use, clean it thoroughly*

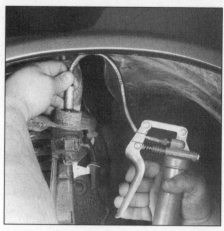

21.5 Greasing the front suspension upper control arm ball joint

in each pulley **(see illustration)**.
19   Adjust the respective drivebelts as described earlier in this Section. After the drivebelts have been in service for approximately ten (10) hours, check the drivebelt tension again and adjust if necessary as new drivebelts tend to stretch after initial installation.

21   Chassis lubrication (every 30,000 miles or 24 months)

Refer to illustrations 21.1 and 21.5
1   A grease gun and a cartridge filled with the proper grease (see *Recommended lubricants and fluids*), graphite spray and an oil can filled with engine oil will be required to lubricate the chassis components **(see illustration)**.
2   Raise the vehicle and support it securely on jackstands. **Warning:** *Never work under a vehicle that is supported only by a jack!*
3   Before beginning, force a little grease out of the nozzle to remove any dirt from the end of the gun. Wipe the nozzle clean with a rag.
4   Armed with the grease gun and plenty of clean rags, begin lubricating the components. **Note:** *The tie-rod ends and front suspension lower control arm ball joints are not serviceable.*
5   Wipe the grease fitting clean and push the nozzle firmly over it. Operate the lever on the grease gun to force grease into the fitting until it oozes out of the joint between the two components **(see illustration)**. If grease escapes around the grease gun nozzle, the fitting is clogged or the nozzle is not completely seated on the fitting. Reattach the gun nozzle to the fitting and try again. If necessary, replace the fitting with a new one.
6   Lubricate the sliding contact and pivot points of the parking brake cable along with the cable guides and levers. This can be done by smearing some of the chassis grease onto the cable and related parts with your fingers. Be careful of frayed wires!
7   Lower the vehicle to the ground.
8   Open the hood and smear a little chassis grease on the hood latch mechanism and

striker. Have an assistant pull the hood release lever from inside the vehicle as you lubricate the cable at the latch.
9   Lubricate all the hinges (door, hood, trunk, etc.) with the recommended lubricant (see *Recommended lubricants and fluids* at the beginning of this Chapter) to keep them in proper working order.
10   The key lock cylinders can be lubricated with spray-type graphite or silicone lubricant which is available at auto parts stores.
11   Lubricate the door weather-stripping with silicone spray. This will reduce chafing and retard wear.

22.2 To remove the air cleaner top cover, release the 2 latches (arrows), lift the cover and disengage it from the locking lugs on the opposite side

12   Some components should not be lubricated for the following reasons. Some are permanently lubricated, some lubricants will cause component failure or the lubricants will be detrimental to the components operating characteristics. Do not lubricate the following: air pump, generator bearings, drivebelts, drivebelt idler pulley, front wheel bearings, rubber bushings, starter motor bearings, suspension strut bearings, throttle control cable, throttle linkage ball bearings and water pump bearings.

22   Air filter - replacement (every 30,000 miles or 24 months)

Refer to illustrations 22.2 and 22.3
1   The air filter element is located in a housing on the driver's side of the engine compartment.
2   Unclip the 2 latches securing the top cover of the air cleaner housing **(see illustration)**. Lift the latching side of the cover and disengage it from the locking lugs on the opposite side.
3   Position the cover out of the way and

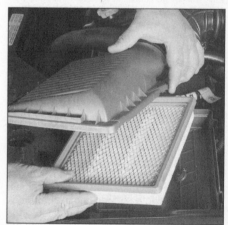

22.3 With the cover positioned out of the way, remove the air filter element from the housing

23.4 To drain the transaxle fluid, first loosen the bolts, then remove all the bolts except for 2 on the high side and 2 on the low side - after breaking the pan seal, remove the 2 bolts on the lower side and let the pan hang down to drain further

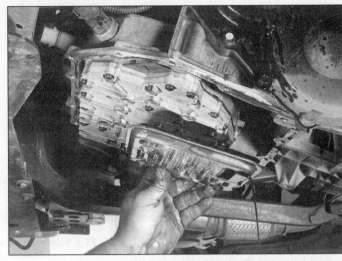

23.5a Remove the transaxle fluid filter . . .

remove the air filter element **(see illustration)**.

4   Inspect the inside of the air cleaner housing, top and bottom, for dirt, debris or damage. If necessary, clean the inside of the housing with a rag or shop vacuum as applicable. If the air cleaner housing is damaged and requires replacement, refer to Chapter 4.

5   Place the new filter element in position (metal screen up), install the top cover and secure it with the retaining latches.

23 Automatic transaxle - fluid and filter change (every 30,000 miles or 24 months)

Refer to illustrations 23.4, 23.5a and 23.5b

1   The automatic transaxle fluid and filter should be changed and the magnet cleaned at the recommended intervals.

2   Raise the front of the vehicle and support it securely on jackstands. **Warning:** *Never work under a vehicle that is supported only by a jack!* Extract the two push-in fasteners and remove the transaxle splash shield.

3   Since the transaxle drain pan does not have a drain plug, this procedure can get a bit messy, so you should have plenty of clean rags and newspapers handy to mop up any spills that may occur. If the drain pan you're using isn't very large in diameter, place it on a piece of plastic such as a trash bag to catch any splashing oil.

4   Position a container capable of holding at least 5 quarts under the transaxle oil pan. Loosen only the pan bolts. Remove the bolts on each side of the pan leaving two bolts loosely in place on the upper and lower sides of the pan **(see illustration)**. Tap the corners of the pan using a soft-faced mallet to break the seal and allow the fluid to drain into the container (the remaining bolts will prevent the pan from completely separating from the transaxle). Remove the 2 bolts from the lower side of the pan and let it hang down to drain

further. After the pan has finished draining, remove the remaining bolts and detach the pan.

5   Remove the filter and O-ring seal **(see illustrations)**.

6   Carefully remove all traces of old sealant from the pan, transaxle body (be careful not to nick or gouge the sealing surfaces) and the bolts.

7   Clean the pan and the magnet located inside the pan with a clean, lint-free cloth moistened with solvent. Don't forget to place the magnet back in its proper location at the bottom of the pan.

8   Fit the new filter, with a new O-ring installed, in place on the transaxle valve body.

9   Apply a 1/8-inch bead of Mopar RTV sealant (or equivalent) to the pan sealing surface (stay on the inboard side of the bolt holes) and to the underside of each bolt head.

10   Position the pan on the transaxle and install the bolts. Tighten them to the torque listed in this Chapter's Specifications following a criss-cross pattern. Work up to the final torque in three or four steps. Allow the RTV sealant time to dry according to the manufacturer's instructions.

11   Install the transaxle splash shield and secure it with the two push-in fasteners.

12   Lower the vehicle and add four quarts of the specified fluid (see *Recommended lubricants and fluids* at the beginning of this Chapter) to the transaxle (see Section 6 if necessary). Start the engine and allow it to idle for at least two minutes while checking for leakage around the pan.

13   With the engine running and the brakes applied, move the shift lever through each of the gear positions and ending in Park. Check the fluid level on the dipstick. The level should be just up to the ADD mark. If necessary, add more fluid (a little at a time) until the level is just at the ADD mark (be careful not to overfill it).

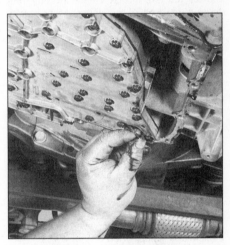

23.5b . . . and O-ring seal

14   Drive the vehicle until it reaches normal operating temperature. Recheck the fluid level and add as necessary until the fluid reaches the HOT range on the dipstick (see Section 6).

15   The old oil cannot be reused in its present state and should be disposed of properly. Oil reclamation centers, auto repair shops and gas stations will normally accept used oil. It should be placed into sealable containers (plastic bottles with screw-on tops are preferred) for transport to a disposal site.

24 Manual transaxle - lubricant change (every 30,000 or 24 months)

Refer to illustrations 24.2a and 24.2b

1   Raise the vehicle and support it securely on jackstands in a level position. **Warning:** *Never work under a vehicle that is supported only by a jack!*

2   Using a box-end wrench or socket to prevent rounding off the plug wrenching flats,

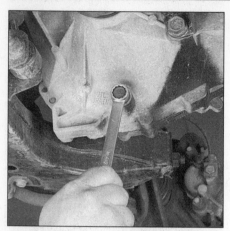

24.2a To avoid rounding off the corners, use the correct size box-end wrench or a socket to remove the manual transaxle oil drain plug . . .

24.2b . . . and drain the fluid

25.5 The drain fitting (arrow) is located at the bottom of the radiator on the right hand side (radiator removed for clarity)

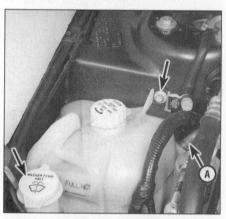

25.11 To remove the coolant reservoir, disconnect the hose (A) and remove the 2 mounting bolts (arrows)

remove the drain plug. Drain the fluid into a suitable container capable of holding at least 4 quarts **(see illustrations)**.

3   After the fluid has completely drained, install the drain plug and tighten it to the torque given in this Chapter's Specifications.

4   Fill the transaxle with the recommended lubricant (see Section 16).

5   The old oil cannot be reused in its present state and should be disposed of properly. Oil reclamation centers, auto repair shops and gas stations will normally accept used oil. It should be placed into sealable containers (plastic bottles with screw-on tops are preferred) for transport to a disposal site.

25 Cooling system - servicing (draining, flushing and refilling) (every 30,000 miles or 24 months)

Warning 1: *Do not allow coolant (antifreeze) to come in contact with your skin or painted surfaces of the vehicle. Flush contaminated areas immediately with plenty of water. Do not store new coolant or leave old coolant lying around where it's accessible to children or pets - they're attracted by its sweet smell. Ingestion of even a small amount of coolant can be fatal! Wipe up garage floor and drip pan spills immediately. Keep antifreeze containers covered and repair cooling system leaks as soon as they're noticed. Check with local authorities about the disposal of used antifreeze. Many communities have collection centers which will see that antifreeze is disposed of properly.*

Warning 2: *The electric cooling fan(s) on these models can activate at any time the ignition switch is in the ON position. Make sure the ignition is OFF when working in the vicinity of the fan(s).*

1   Periodically, the cooling system should be drained, flushed and refilled to replenish the coolant (antifreeze) mixture and prevent formation of rust and corrosion, which can

impair the performance of the cooling system and cause engine damage. When the cooling system is serviced, all hoses and the radiator cap should be checked and replaced, if necessary.

Draining

Refer to illustration 25.5

2   At the same time the cooling system is serviced, all hoses and the radiator (pressure) cap should be inspected, tested and replaced if faulty (see Section 10).

3   With the engine cold, remove the pressure cap and set the heater control to maximum heat.

4   Move a large container capable of holding at least 10 quarts under the radiator drain fitting to catch the coolant mixture as it's drained.

5   Open the drain fitting located at the bottom of the radiator **(see illustration)**. On vehicles equipped with the V6 engine, the drain fitting cannot be reached by hand. To open the drain fitting, use a universal joint and socket attached to a long extension. Allow the coolant to completely drain out.

Flushing

Refer to illustration 25.11

6   Remove the thermostat housing and the thermostat (see Chapter 3).

7   Disconnect the lower hose from the radiator (see Chapter 3 if necessary).

8   Place a garden hose in the upper radiator hose (to flush radiator) and then the thermostat opening in the engine block (to flush engine block and heater core). Flush the system until the water runs clear out of the radiator and lower radiator hose respectively.

9   In severe cases of contamination or clogging of the radiator, remove it (see Chapter 3) and reverse flush it. This involves inserting the hose in the bottom radiator outlet to allow the clean water to run against the normal flow, draining out through the top. A radiator repair shop should be consulted if further cleaning or repair is necessary.

10   When the coolant is regularly drained and the system refilled with the correct

coolant mixture there should be no need to employ chemical cleaners or descalers.

11   Disconnect the coolant reservoir hose, remove the reservoir from the vehicle and flush it with clean water **(see illustration)**. Inspect it for damage and replace if necessary.

Refilling

12   Install the thermostat, the thermostat housing and connect the radiator hose (see Chapter 3).

13   Connect the lower radiator hose (see Chapter 3 if necessary).

14   Install the coolant reservoir, reconnect the hose and close the radiator drain fitting.

15   Add the correct mixture of high-quality antifreeze/coolant and water in the ratio specified on the antifreeze container or in this Chapter's Specifications through the filler neck until it reaches the pressure cap seat.

16   Add the same coolant mixture to the reservoir until it the level is between the FULL and ADD marks.

17   Run the engine until normal operating temperature is reached and with the engine

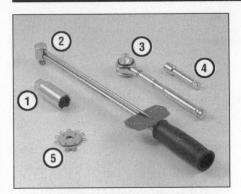

27.2 Tools required for changing spark plugs

1 **Spark plug socket** - *This will have special padding inside to protect the spark plug's porcelain insulator*
2 **Torque wrench** - *Although not mandatory, using this tool is the best way to ensure the plugs are tightened properly*
3 **Ratchet** - *Standard hand tool to fit the spark plug socket*
4 **Extension** - *Depending on model and accessories, you may need special extensions and universal joints to reach one or more of the plugs*
5 **Spark plug gap gauge** - *This gauge for checking the gap comes in a variety of styles. Make sure the gap for your engine is included*

idling, add coolant up to the correct level. Install the pressure cap.

18 Always refill the system with the specified mixture of coolant and water. See Chapter 3 for more information on antifreeze mixtures.

19 Keep a close watch on the coolant level and the various cooling system hoses during the first few miles of driving and check for any coolant leaks. Tighten the hose clamps and add more coolant mixture as necessary.

26 Evaporative emissions control system - check (every 30,000 miles or 24 months)

1 The function of the evaporative emissions control system is to prevent fuel vapors from escaping the fuel system and being released into the atmosphere. Vapors from the fuel tank are temporarily stored in a charcoal canister. The Powertrain Control Module (PCM) monitors the system and allows the vapors to be drawn into the intake manifold when the engine reaches normal operating temperature.

2 The charcoal canister on 1995 through 1997 models is mounted to a bracket behind the right front bumper fascia adjacent to the windshield washer reservoir. On 1998 models, it's located on top of the fuel tank. The canisters are maintenance-free and should last the life of the vehicle.

27.5a Spark plug manufacturers recommend using a wire-type gauge when checking the gap - if the wire does not slide between the electrodes with a slight drag, adjustment is required

3 The most common symptom of a fault in the evaporative emissions system is a strong fuel odor in the engine compartment or raw fuel leaking from the canister. These indications are usually more prevalent in hot temperatures. All systems except for those installed on 1995 models are pressurized by a Leak Detection Pump (LDP). If normal system pressure cannot be achieved by the LDP, which indicates a leak, the PCM will store the appropriate fault code and illuminate the CHECK ENGINE light on the instrument panel. The most common cause of system pressure loss is a loose or poor sealing gas cap.

4 For more information and replacement procedures see Chapter 6.

27 Spark plugs - check and replacement (see Maintenance schedule for intervals)

Refer to illustrations 27.2, 27.5a and 27.5b

All models

1 The spark plugs are located in the cylinder head.

2 In most cases the tools necessary for spark plug replacement include a spark plug socket which fits onto a ratchet (this special socket is padded inside to protect the porcelain insulators on the new plugs and hold them in place), various extensions and a feeler gauge to check and adjust the spark plug gap **(see illustration)**. A special plug wire removal tool is available for separating the wire boot from the spark plug, but it isn't absolutely necessary. Since these engines are equipped with an aluminum cylinder head(s), a torque wrench should be used when tightening the spark plugs.

3 The best approach when replacing the spark plugs is to purchase the new spark

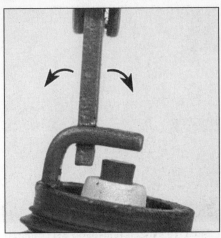

27.5b To change the gap, bend the side electrode only, as indicated by the arrows, and be very careful not to crack or chip the porcelain insulator surrounding the center electrode

plugs beforehand, adjust them to the proper gap and then replace each plug one at a time. When buying the new spark plugs, be sure to obtain the correct plug for your specific engine. This information can be found in the Specification Section at the front of this Chapter, in your owner's manual or on the Vehicle Emissions Control Information (VECI) label located under the hood. If differences exist between the sources, purchase the spark plug type specified on the VECI label as it was printed for your specific engine.

4 Allow the engine to cool completely before attempting to remove any of the plugs. During this cooling off time, each of the new spark plugs can be inspected for defects and the gaps can be checked.

5 The gap is checked by inserting the proper thickness gauge between the electrodes at the tip of the plug **(see illustration)**. The gap between the electrodes should be as specified on the VECI label in the engine compartment or as listed in this Chapter's Specifications. The wire should touch each of the electrodes. If the gap is incorrect, use the adjuster on the thickness gauge body to bend the curved side electrode slightly until the proper gap is obtained **(see illustration)**. Also, at this time check for cracks in the spark plug body (if any are found, the plug must not be used). If the side electrode is not exactly over the center one, use the adjuster to align the two.

6 Cover the fender to prevent damage to the paint, fender covers are available from auto parts stores but an old blanket will work just fine.

Four-cylinder engines

Refer to illustrations 27.7a and 27.7b

7 **Note:** *Due to the short length of the spark plug wire, always disconnect the spark plug wire from the ignition coil pack first. Dis-connect the spark plug wire from any retaining clips. With the engine cool, disconnect*

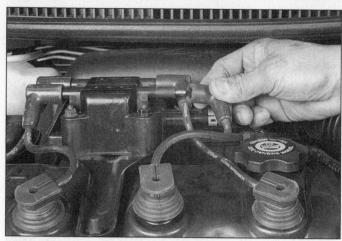

27.7a Pull on the spark plug wire boot and twist it back-and-forth while pulling it from the ignition coil pack

27.7b Use a twisting motion to free the boot and then pull it from the valve cover

27.12 Use a ratchet and extension to remove the spark plugs

27.14 Apply a thin coat of anti-seize compound to the spark plug threads - DO NOT get any on the electrodes!

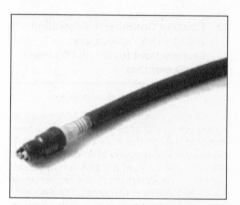

27.15 A length of 3/8-inch ID rubber hose will save time and prevent damaged threads when installing the spark plugs

one of the spark plug wires from the ignition coil pack **(see illustration)**. Pull only on the boot at the end of the wire; don't pull on the wire. Using a twisting motion, loosen the boot/wire at the valve cover, then withdraw the boot/wire from the valve cover **(see illustration)**.

V6 engine

Note: *On V6 models, the manufacturer recommends replacing the spark plugs, spark plug wires, distributor cap and rotor at the same time. Refer to Section 29 for spark plug wire, distributor cap and rotor replacement.*

8   Remove the upper intake manifold (see Chapter 2B).

9   To prevent dirt or other foreign debris from entering the engine, place clean rags into the openings in the lower intake manifold.

10   Detach any clips securing the spark plug wires. Using a twisting motion, loosen the boot/wire at the valve cover, then withdraw the boot/wire from the valve cover **(see illustration 27.7b)**.

All models

Refer to illustrations 27.12, 27.14 and 27.15

11   If compressed air is available, use it to blow any dirt or foreign material away from the spark plug area. **Warning:** *Use proper eye protection!* A common bicycle pump will also work. The idea here is to eliminate the possibility of material falling into the cylinder through the spark plug hole as the spark plug is removed.

12   Place the spark plug socket over the plug and remove it from the engine by turning it in a counterclockwise direction **(see illustration)**.

13   Compare the spark plug with the chart on the inside back cover of this manual to get an indication of the overall running condition of the engine.

14   It's a good idea to lightly coat the threads of the spark plugs with an anti-seize compound **(see illustration)** to insure that the spark plugs do not seize in the aluminum cylinder head. Be careful not to get any of the anti-seize compound on the plug electrodes!

15   It's often difficult to insert spark plugs into their holes without cross-threading them. To avoid this possibility, fit a piece of 3/8-inch ID rubber hose over the end of the spark plug **(see illustration)**. The flexible hose acts as a universal joint to help align the plug with the plug hole. Should the plug begin to cross-thread, the hose will slip on the spark plug, preventing thread damage. Install the spark plug and tighten it to the torque listed in this Chapter's Specifications.

16   Attach the plug wire to the new spark plug, again using a twisting motion on the boot until it is firmly seated on the end of the spark plug. On four-cylinder engines, attach the other end to the ignition coil pack. Attach the spark plug wire to any retaining clips to secure the wires in their proper location on the valve cover.

17   Follow the above procedure for the remaining spark plugs, replacing them one at a time to prevent mixing up the spark plug wires.

18   On V6 models, replace the spark plug wires, distributor cap and rotor (see Section 29). Remove the rags from the lower intake manifold and install the upper intake manifold (see Chapter 2B).

28.2a The PCV valve (arrow) is located in a hose leading from the valve cover to the intake manifold (four-cylinder engines)

28.2b Removing the PCV valve from the valve cover (V6 engine)

1

28 Positive Crankcase Ventilation (PCV) valve - check and replacement (every 60,000 miles or 48 months)

Refer to illustrations 28.2a and 28.2b

1   The PCV valve controls the amount of crankcase vapors allowed to enter the intake manifold. Inside the PCV valve is a spring loaded valve that opens in relation to intake manifold vacuum, which allows crankcase vapors to be drawn from the valve cover back into the engine combustion chamber.

2   The PCV valve on four-cylinder engines is located in the rubber hose connected to the intake manifold plenum and the valve cover **(see illustration)**. On V6 models, its located in the front of the left-bank valve cover **(see illustration)**.

3   To check the operation of the PCV valve, disconnect the valve from the valve cover or hose that leads to the valve cover, depending on your particular application.

4   Start the engine. A hissing sound should be heard coming from the PCV valve. Place your finger over the valve opening - there should be vacuum present. If there's no vacuum at the valve, check for a plugged hose, plenum port or valve. Replace any plugged or deteriorated hoses.

5   Check the spring-loaded valve located inside for freedom of movement by using a small screwdriver or equivalent to push the valve off its seat and see it returns to the fully seated position. If the valve is sluggish or the inside of the valve is contaminated with gum and carbon deposits, the valve must be replaced.

6   To replace the valve, disconnect it from the intake manifold hose and valve cover or valve cover hose as applicable.

7   When purchasing a replacement PCV valve, make sure it's for your particular vehicle and engine size. Compare the old valve with the new one to make sure they're the same.

8   Installation is the reverse of removal. Make sure the new PCV valve is installed with the closed end (plunger seat) towards the valve cover.

29 Spark plug wires, distributor cap and rotor - check and replacement (see Maintenance schedule for intervals)

Note: *Distributor cap and rotor replacement applies to V6 engines only.*

All models

1   The spark plug wires should be checked at the recommended intervals or whenever new spark plugs are installed.

2   Begin this procedure by making a visual check of the spark plug wires while the engine is running. In a darkened garage (make sure there is adequate ventilation) or at night while using a flashlight, start the engine and observe each plug wire. Be careful not to come into contact with any moving engine parts. If possible, use an insulated or non-conductive object to wiggle each wire. If there is a break in the wire, you will see arcing or a small blue spark coming from the damaged area. Secondary ignition voltage increases with engine speed and sometimes a damaged wire will not produce an arc at idle speed. Have an assistant press the accelerator pedal to raise the engine speed to approximately 2000 rpm. Check the spark plug wires for arcing as stated previously. If arcing is noticed, replace all spark plug wires.

Four-cylinder engines

3   Perform the following checks with the engine OFF. The wires should be inspected one at a time to prevent mixing up the order which is essential for proper engine operation. **Note:** *Due to the short length of the spark plug wire, always disconnect the spark plug wire from the ignition coil pack first.*

4   With the engine cool, disconnect the spark plug wire from the ignition coil pack. Pull only on the boot at the end of the wire; don't pull on the wire itself. Use a twisting motion to free the boot/wire from the coil. Disconnect the same spark plug wire from the spark plug, using the same twisting method while pulling on the boot. Disconnect the spark plug wire from any retaining clips as necessary and remove it from the engine.

5   Check inside the boot for corrosion, which will look like a white, crusty powder (don't mistake the white dielectric grease used on some plug wire boots for corrosion protection).

6   Now push the wire and boot back onto the end of the spark plug. It should be a tight fit on the plug end. If not, remove the wire and use a pair of pliers to carefully crimp the metal connector inside the wire boot until the fit is snug.

7   Now push the wire and boot back into the end of the ignition coil terminal. It should be a tight fit in the terminal. If not, remove the wire and use a pair of pliers to carefully crimp the metal connector inside the wire boot until the fit is snug.

8   Now, using a cloth, clean each wire along its entire length. Remove all built-up dirt and grease. As this is done, inspect for burned areas, cracks and any other form of damage. Bend the wires in several places to ensure that the conductive material inside hasn't hardened. Repeat the procedure for the remaining wires.

9   If new spark plug wires are required, purchase a complete set for your particular engine. The terminals and rubber boots should already be installed on the wires. Replace the wires one at a time to avoid mixing up the firing order and make sure the terminals are securely seated on the coil pack and the spark plugs.

10   Attach the plug wire to the new spark plug and to the ignition coil pack using a twisting motion on the boot until it is firmly seated. Attach the spark plug wire to any retaining clips to keep the wires in their proper location on the valve cover.

V6 engine

Refer to illustration 29.15

Note: *On V6 engines, the manufacturer recommends replacing the spark plugs, spark plug wires, distributor cap and rotor at the same time.*

11   Remove the upper intake manifold (see Chapter 2B).

12   To prevent dirt or other foreign debris from entering the engine, place duct tape over the openings of the lower intake manifold.

13   Remove the EGR tube from the EGR valve (see Chapter 6 if necessary).

14   Disconnect one spark plug wire from the distributor cap. Pull only on the boot at the end of the wire; don't pull on the wire itself. Use a twisting motion to free the boot/wire from the distributor. Install the removed wire into the new distributor cap in the exact same location. Repeat this procedure until all spark plug wires are installed in the new cap.

15   Loosen the 2 screws and remove the old distributor cap **(see illustration)**. Remove the rotor.

16   Install the new rotor and distributor cap (with spark plug wires attached).

17   Replace the spark plugs as described in Section 27, except do not reattach the spark plug wires to the retaining clips.

18   Replace the spark plug wires one at a time to avoid mixing up the firing order and make sure the terminals are securely seated on the distributor cap and the spark plugs. Install the plug wires using a twisting motion

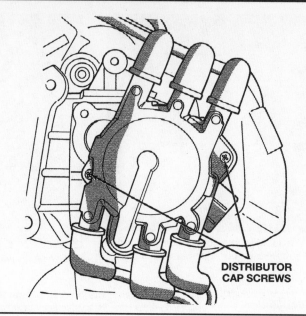

29.15 Distributor cap retaining screw locations (V6 engines only)

DISTRIBUTOR CAP SCREWS

on the boot until it is firmly seated. Attach the spark plug wire to any retaining clips as required.

19   Using a new gasket, install the EGR tube onto the EGR valve (see Chapter 6). Tighten the bolts to the torque given in the Specification Section of Chapter 6.

20   Remove the duct tape from the lower intake manifold.

21   Install the upper intake manifold (see Chapter 2B).

30   Fuel filter - replacement

1   The manufacturer does not suggest periodic fuel filter replacement on JA series models. See Chapter 4 if the fuel filter requires replacement due to a fuel restriction or fuel contamination problem.

Chapter 2 Part A
Four-cylinder engines

Contents

Specifications

General

Bore	3.445 inches
Stroke	
2.0L	3.268 inches
2.4L	3.976 inches
Compression ratio	
2.0L	9.8:1
2.4L	9.4:1
Compression pressure	170 to 225 psi
Displacement	
2.0L	122 cubic inches
2.4L	148 cubic inches
Firing order	1-3-4-2
Oil pressure	
At idle speed	4 psi (minimum)
At 3000 rpm	25 to 80 psi

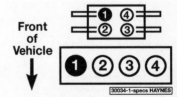

Cylinder numbering and coil
terminal locations

Camshaft

Bearing journal diameter
  2.0L
    No. 1 .... 1.619 to 1.6199 inches
    No. 2 .... 1.634 to 1.635 inches
    No. 3 .... 1.650 to 1.651 inches
    No. 4 .... 1.666 to 1.668 inches
    No. 5 .... 1.682 to 1.6829 inches
  2.4L .... 1.021 to 1.022 inches
Bearing bore diameter
  2.0L
    No. 1 .... 1.622 to 1.6228 inches
    No. 2 .... 1.637 to 1.638 inches
    No. 3 .... 1.653 to 1.654 inches
    No. 4 .... 1.669 to 1.670 inches
    No. 5 .... 1.685 to 1.6858 inches
  2.4L .... 1.024 to 1.025 inches
Bearing clearance .... 0.0027 to 0.003 inch
Endplay
  2.0L .... 0.0059 inch
  2.4L .... 0.002 to 0.006 inch
Lobe lift
  2.0L
    Intake .... 0.307 inch
    Exhaust .... 0.277 inch
  2.4L
    Intake .... 0.324 inch
    Exhaust .... 0.256 inch

Cylinder head

Head gasket surface warpage limit .... 0.004 inch maximum
Exhaust manifold mounting surface warpage limit .... 0.006 inch maximum (per foot)

Intake and exhaust manifolds

Warpage limit .... 0.006 inch maximum (per foot)

Rocker arm shaft assemblies (2.0L engine only)

Rocker arm shaft diameter .... 0.786 to 0.7867 inch
Rocker arm inside diameter... 0.787 to 0.788 inch
Rocker arm-to-shaft clearance.. 0.0006 to 0.0021 inch
Rocker arm shaft retainer width
  Intake... 1.12 inches
  Exhaust
    No. 1 and No. 5.. 1.14 inches
    No. 2, No. 3 and No. 4.. 1.59 inches

Oil pump

Cover warpage limit... 0.003 inch
Inner rotor thickness
  2.0L .... 0.301 inch (minimum)
  2.4L .... 0.370 inch (minimum)
Outer rotor thickness
  2.0L .... 0.301 inch (minimum)
  2.4L .... 0.370 inch (minimum)
Outer rotor diameter .... 3.148 inch (minimum)
Rotor-to-pump cover clearance .... 0.004 inch
Outer rotor-to-housing clearance.. 0.015 inch (maximum)
Inner rotor-to-outer rotor lobe clearance.............................. 0.008 inch (maximum)
Pressure relief spring free length .... 2.39 inches (approximate)

Torque specifications   **Ft-lbs (unless otherwise indicated)**

Camshaft bearing cap bolts
  M6 bolts .... 105 in-lbs
  M8 bolts .... 250 in-lbs
Camshaft position sensor bolts
  2.0L .... 85 in-lbs
  2.4L 20

Torque specifications (continued)

Ft-lbs (unless otherwise indicated)

Camshaft sprocket/pulley bolt	
2.0L	85
2.4L	75
Crankshaft damper bolt	100 to 105
Cylinder head bolts	
Step 1	25
Step 2	50
Step 3	50
Step 4	Tighten an additional 1/4 turn (90-degrees)
Engine mounting bracket bolts	30 to 45
Exhaust manifold-to-cylinder head bolts	200 in-lbs
Exhaust manifold-to-exhaust pipe bolts	20
Exhaust manifold heat shield bolts	105 in-lbs
Front engine mount strut and structural collar bolts (1998 2.4L engine only) **(see illustration 13.16)**	
Bolts 1 through 3	75
Bolts 4 through 8	45
Driveplate-to-crankshaft bolts	70
Intake manifold bolts	
2.0L (plastic manifold)	105 in-lbs
2.4L (aluminum manifold)	200 in-lbs
Oil filter adapter fastener	60
Oil pan bolts	105 in-lbs
Oil pan-to-transaxle structural collar bolts (1997 2.4L and 1998 2.0L engines only)	
Step 1 (collar-to-oil pan bolts)	30 in-lbs
Step 2 (collar-to-transaxle bolts)	80
Step 3 (collar-to-oil pan bolts)	40
Oil pump	
Attaching bolts	250 in-lbs
Cover screws	105 in-lbs
Pick-up tube bolt	250 in-lbs
Relief valve cap bolt	30
Rocker arm shaft bolts (2.0L)	250 in-lbs
Thermostat housing bolts	200 in-lbs
Timing belt	
Cover bolts	
2.0L	105 in-lbs
2.4L	
Outer-to-inner attaching bolts	40 in-lbs
Inner cover-to-head/oil pump bolts	105 in-lbs
Tensioner bolts	
Mechanical type	250 in-lbs
Hydraulic type	
Tensioner pulley assembly plate bolts	23
Tensioner unit bolts	23
Tensioner pulley bolt	30
Timing belt idler pulley bolt (2.4L)	45
Valve cover bolts	105 in-lbs
Water pump mounting bolt	105 in-lbs

Refer to Part C for additional torque specifications

2A

3.6a Remove the valve cover mounting bolts . . .

3.6b . . . and lift the cover and gasket off the cylinder head

1   General information

This Part of Chapter 2 is devoted to in-vehicle engine repair procedures on models equipped with 2.0 liter and 2.4 liter four-cylinder engines. Information concerning engine removal and installation and engine block and cylinder head overhaul can be found in Part C of this Chapter.

The following repair procedures are based on the assumption that the engine is installed in the vehicle. If the engine has been removed from the vehicle and mounted on a stand, many of the steps outlined in this Part of Chapter 2 will not apply.

The Specification Section included in this Part of Chapter 2 apply only to the procedures contained in this Part. Part C of Chapter 2 contains the Specification Section necessary for cylinder head and engine block rebuilding.

There are two four-cylinder engines installed in the models covered in this manual; the 2.0L Single Overhead Camshaft (SOHC) engine and the 2.4L Double Overhead Camshaft (DOHC) engine. The main difference between the 2.0 liter and 2.4 liter engines, besides the obvious engine displacement, is the incorporation of two balance shafts installed below the crankshaft of the 2.4L engine. For service information on the balance shafts refer to Part C of this Chapter.

2   Repair operations possible with the engine in the vehicle

Many major repair operations can be accomplished without removing the engine from the vehicle.

Clean the engine compartment and the exterior of the engine with some type of degreaser before any work is done. It will make the job easier and help keep dirt out of the internal areas of the engine.

Depending on the components involved, it may be helpful to remove the hood to improve access to the engine as repairs are performed (refer to Chapter 11 if necessary). Cover the fenders to prevent damage to the paint. Special pads are available, but an old bedspread or blanket will also work.

If vacuum, exhaust, oil or coolant leaks develop, indicating a need for gasket or seal replacement, the repairs can generally be made with the engine in the vehicle. The intake and exhaust manifold gaskets, oil pan gasket, camshaft and crankshaft oil seals and cylinder head gasket are all accessible with the engine in place.

Exterior engine components, such as the intake and exhaust manifolds, the oil pan, the oil pump, the water pump, the starter motor, the alternator, the distributor and the fuel system components can be removed for repair with the engine in place.

Since the camshaft(s) and cylinder head can be removed without pulling the engine, valve component servicing can also be accomplished with the engine in the vehicle. Replacement of the timing belt and sprockets is also possible with the engine in the vehicle.

In extreme cases caused by a lack of necessary equipment, repair or replacement of piston rings, pistons, connecting rods and rod bearings is possible with the engine in the vehicle. However, this practice is not recommended because of the cleaning and preparation work that must be done to the components involved.

3   Valve cover - removal and installation

Removal

Refer to illustrations 3.6a and 3.6b

1   Disconnect the negative battery cable from the ground stud on the left shock tower (see Chapter 5, Section 1).

2   Remove the ignition coil pack from the valve cover (see Chapter 5).

3   Remove the spark plug wires (see Chapter 1).

4   On 2.4L engines, disconnect the ground strap from the valve cover.

5   Clearly label and then disconnect any emission hoses and electrical cables which connect to or cross over the valve cover.

6   Remove the valve cover bolts and lift the cover off **(see illustrations)**. If the cover sticks to the cylinder head, tap on it with a soft-face hammer or place a wood block against the cover and tap on the wood with a hammer. **Caution:** *If you have to pry between the valve cover and the cylinder head, be extremely careful not to gouge or nick the gasket surfaces of either part. A leak could develop after reassembly.*

7   Remove the valve cover gasket, 1/2 round seal (2.4L engines) and spark plug tube seals. Thoroughly clean the valve cover and remove all traces of old gasket material. Gasket removal solvents are available from auto parts stores and may prove helpful. After cleaning the surfaces, degrease them with a rag soaked in lacquer thinner or acetone.

Installation

Refer to illustrations 3.8 and 3.9

8   Install the new spark plug tube seals **(see illustration)**.

9   Install a new gasket on the cover, using RTV sealant to hold it in place **(see illustration)**.

3.8 Install new spark plug tube seals and make sure they are properly seated in the cover

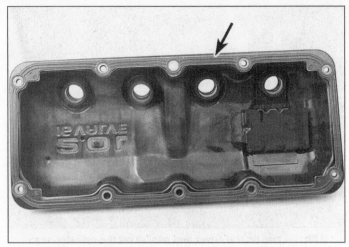

3.9 Apply a light coat of RTV sealant onto the cover sealing surfaces and install the new gasket (arrow)

3.16 After applying a small amount of Loctite No. 271 (or equivalent) to the lower end of the tube(s) (arrows), install it and carefully tap the tube into place until its fully seated in the cylinder head (2.0L engine only)

2A

10   On 2.4L engines, install the half-round seal, apply anaerobic RTV sealant to the camshaft cap corners and at the top edges of the half-round seal.

11   Place the cover on the engine and install the cover bolts. Tighten the valve cover bolts in three steps to the torque listed in this Chapter's Specifications using a criss-cross pattern, starting in the middle of the cover and working outwards.

12   The remaining installation steps are the reverse of removal. When installation is complete, start the engine and check for oil leaks.

Spark plug tube replacement (2.0L engine only)

Refer to illustration 3.16

13   Remove the valve cover (see above).

14   Grasp spark plug tube with locking pliers, carefully twist back and forth and remove the tube from cylinder head.

15   Clean the locking agent from the tube end and the receptacle in cylinder head with solvent and dry.

16   Apply approximately 1/8 inch wide strip of Loctite sealer No. 271, or equivalent, around the lower end of the tube and install the tube into the cylinder head. Carefully tap the tube into the receptacle with a soft face mallet or wood block. Tap the tube in until it is fully seated in the cylinder head **(see illustration)**.

17   Allow the Loctite to cure according to the manufacturer's instructions.

18   Install the valve cover (see above).

---

4   Intake manifold - removal, inspection and installation

Warning: *Allow the engine to cool completely before beginning this procedure.*

Removal

Refer to illustrations 4.4a, 4.4b, 4.8, 4.11a and 4.11b

1   Relieve the fuel system pressure (see Chapter 4).

2   Disconnect the negative battery cable from the ground stud on the left shock tower (see Chapter 5, Section 1).

3   Remove the air cleaner assembly (see Chapter 4).

4   Clearly label and disconnect all vacuum hoses, wires, brackets and emission hoses which run to the fuel injection system, throttle body and intake manifold **(see illustrations)**.

5   Remove the fuel rail and injector assembly (see Chapter 4).

6   Remove the throttle body (see Chapter 4).

7   Remove the transaxle-to-throttle body support bracket fasteners and loosen (only) the fastener on the transaxle side. Be sure to disconnect any electrical connections that are fastened to the support bracket before trying to move the parts out of the way.

8   Remove the EGR tube **(see illustration)**.

9   On 2.0L engines, remove the water inlet tube support-to-intake manifold fastener.

10   On 2.4L engines, remove the intake manifold support bracket located on the driver's side of the manifold.

4.4a Disconnect the PCV valve hose from the intake manifold fitting (2.0L engine shown)

4.4b Disconnect the power brake booster vacuum hose from the intake manifold (2.0L engine shown)

4.8 Remove the mounting bolts from the EGR tube (arrows) at the intake manifold and EGR valve (shown) and remove the tube

4.11a Remove the intake manifold mounting bolts in a criss-cross pattern . . .

4.11b . . . then remove the intake manifold from the cylinder head

11   Unbolt the intake manifold and remove it from the engine **(see illustrations)**. If it sticks, lightly tap the manifold with a soft-face hammer or carefully pry it from the head. **Caution:** *On 2.4L engines, do not pry between gasket sealing surfaces or tap on any fuel injector boss. On 2.0L engines, the intake manifold is made of plastic. Although it's pretty strong, it's not very impact resistant so use caution when tapping on it.*

Inspection

Refer to illustration 4.13

12   On 2.4L engines, remove intake manifold gasket by carefully scraping all traces of gasket material from both the cylinder head and the intake manifold. **Caution:** *The cylinder head and intake manifold are made of aluminum and are easily nicked or gouged. Don't damage the gasket surfaces or a leak may result after the work is complete. Gasket removal solvents are available from auto parts stores and may prove helpful.*

13   On 2.0L engines, remove the O-ring seal gaskets on the intake and throttle body ports **(see illustration)**. **Caution:** *The intake manifold is made of plastic and can be easily dam-*

aged, *don't scrape too hard when removing any dirt or residue.* Examine the intake manifold for evidence of cracks and other damage. Replace if any are found.

14   Using a straightedge and feeler gauge, check the intake manifold mating surface for warpage. Check the intake manifold surface on the cylinder head also. If the warpage on any surface exceeds the limits listed in this Chapter's Specifications, the intake manifold and/or cylinder head must be replaced or resurfaced by an automotive machine shop.

Installation

Refer to illustrations 4.15a and 4.15b

Note: *On 2.0L engines whenever the intake manifold is removed, the manufacturer recommends using new bolts and washers for installation.*

15   Install the intake manifold, using a new gasket or O-rings as applicable. Tighten the bolts in three stages, in the sequence shown **(see illustrations)**, to the torque listed in this Chapter's Specifications.

16   The remaining installation steps are the reverse of removal.

5   Exhaust manifold - removal, inspection and installation

Warning: *Allow the engine to cool completely before beginning this procedure.*

Removal

Refer to illustrations 5.3, 5.4, 5.5 and 5.6

1   Disconnect the negative battery cable from the ground stud on the left shock tower (see Chapter 5, Section 1).

2   Set the parking brake and block the rear wheels. Raise the front of the vehicle and support it securely on jackstands.

3   Working under the vehicle, apply penetrating oil to the exhaust pipe-to-manifold fasteners to make removal easier. Remove the fasteners securing the exhaust pipe to the exhaust manifold and separate them **(see illustration)**. Remove the seal ring (2.0L) or gasket (2.4L) as applicable.

4   Disconnect the wiring harness from the upstream oxygen sensor **(see illustration)**.

5   Remove the bolts that secure the heat shield to the exhaust manifold and remove the heat shield **(see illustration)**.

4.13 On 2.0L engines, remove the O-ring seal gaskets (arrows) on the throttle body and intake ports

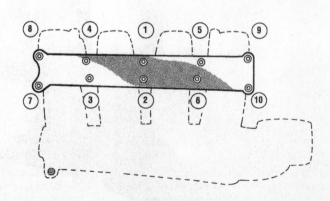

4.15a Intake manifold bolt tightening sequence (2.0L engine)

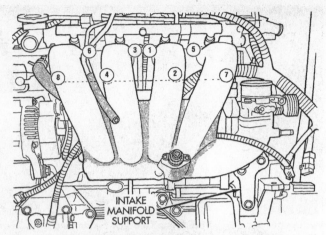

4.15b Intake manifold bolt tightening sequence (2.4L engine)

5.3 Using a box wrench on the nuts and a socket on the bolt, remove the shoulder bolts, springs and nuts securing the exhaust pipe to the exhaust manifold

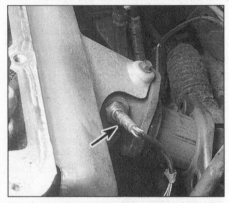

5.4 Follow the harness from the upstream oxygen sensor (arrow) and disconnect it at the connector

6   Remove the exhaust manifold mounting bolts and remove the exhaust manifold **(see illustration). Note:** *The exhaust pipe may have to be removed from the vehicle to facilitate manifold removal (see Chapter 4 if necessary).*

Inspection

7   Using a wire brush, clean the exhaust manifold bolts, replacing any that exhibit thread damage.

8   Using a scraper, remove all traces of gasket material from the exhaust flange mating surfaces and inspect them for wear and cracks. **Caution:** *When removing gasket material, be very careful not to scratch or gouge the sealing surface. Any damage to the surface may a leak after reassembly. Gasket removal solvents are available from auto parts stores and may prove helpful.*

9   Using a straightedge and feeler gauge, check the exhaust manifold-to-cylinder head mating surface for warpage. Check the surface on the cylinder head also. If the warpage exceeds the limits listed in this Chapter's Specifications, the exhaust manifold and/or cylinder head must be replaced or resurfaced by an automotive machine shop.

Installation

10   Apply Loctite No. 271 to the mounting bolt threads prior to installation.
11   Install the new gasket (use no sealant), manifold and bolts. Tighten the bolts in three stages, working from the center out, to the torque listed in this Chapter's Specifications.
12   The remaining installation steps are the reverse of removal. Install a new gasket or seal ring (as applicable) between the exhaust manifold and exhaust pipe.
13   Run the engine and check for exhaust leaks.

6   Timing belt - removal, inspection and installation

Caution: *If the timing belt failed with the engine operating, damage to the valves may have occurred. Perform an engine compression check after belt replacement to determine if any valve damage is present.*

Removal

Refer to illustrations 6.4, 6.5, 6.8a, 6.8b, 6.9a, 6.9b, 6.11 and 6.12
Caution: *Do not turn the crankshaft or camshaft(s) after the timing belt has been removed, as this will damage the valves from contact with the pistons. Do not try to turn the crankshaft with the camshaft(s) sprocket bolt(s) and do not rotate the crankshaft counterclockwise.*

5.5 Remove the exhaust manifold heat shield mounting bolts (arrows) and remove the heat shield

5.6 Remove the exhaust manifold mounting bolts (arrows) and separate the exhaust manifold from the cylinder head

1   Position the number one piston at Top Dead Center (see Chapter 2C).
2   Disconnect the negative battery cable from the ground stud on the left shock tower (see Chapter 5, Section 1).
3   Remove the drivebelts (see Chapter 1).
4   Loosen the large bolt in the center of the crankshaft damper pulley. It might be very tight, to break it loose insert a large screwdriver or bar through the opening in the pulley to keep the pulley stationary and loosen the bolt with a socket and breaker bar **(see illustration)**.
5   Install a 3-jaw puller onto the damper pulley and remove the pulley from the crankshaft **(see illustration)**. Use the proper insert to keep the puller from damaging the crankshaft bolt threads. If the pulley is difficult to remove, tap the center bolt of the puller with a brass mallet to break it loose. **Caution:** *Do not use a puller that has jaws which grip the outer diameter of the damper as the damper and hub may separate. Use only the type shown in the illustration.*
6   After removing the crankshaft pulley, reinstall the crankshaft bolt using an appropriate spacer (this will enable you to turn the crankshaft later).
7   Remove the right (passenger side) engine mount and the mounting bracket from the engine (see Section 17). **Note:** *Make sure the engine is supported with a floor jack placed under the oil pan. Place a wood block on the jack head to prevent the floor jack from denting or damaging the oil pan.*
8   Remove the timing belt outer cover(s) **(see illustrations)**.
9   Make sure the camshaft sprocket(s) and crankshaft timing marks align before remov-

6.4 Insert a large screwdriver or bar through the opening in the crankshaft pulley and wedge it against the engine block, then loosen the bolt with a socket and breaker bar

ing the timing belt **(see illustrations)**. If necessary, align the timing marks by rotating the crankshaft - clockwise only! **Note:** *If you plan to reuse the timing belt, paint an arrow on it to indicate the direction of rotation (clockwise).*
10   Two different types of timing belt tensioners were incorporated on these engines, hydraulic and mechanical. The hydraulic tensioner is easily recognizable by the sealed hydraulic unit which maintains constant pressure on the timing belt tensioner pulley. The mechanical type has a built-in spring inside the pulley which supplies clockwise tension to the belt.
11   On engines equipped with a hydraulic tensioner, loosen, then remove the timing

6.5 Install a 3-jaw puller onto the damper pulley, position the center post of the puller on the crankshaft end (use the proper insert to keep from damaging the crankshaft threads), and remove the pulley from the crankshaft

belt tensioner mounting bolts **(see illustration)** and remove the tensioner. **Note:** *The tensioner piston will extend when the assembly is removed.*
12   On engines equipped with a mechanical tensioner, insert an 8 mm (2.0L engine) or 6 mm (2.4L engine) Allen wrench in the hexagon fitting in the tensioner pulley. Insert the long end of a 3 mm Allen wrench (or 1/8 inch drill bit) into the small hole on the pulley. While applying light pressure to the Allen wrench or drill bit, rotate the tensioner pulley counterclockwise until the Allen wrench or drill bit slides into the locking hole **(see illustration)**.

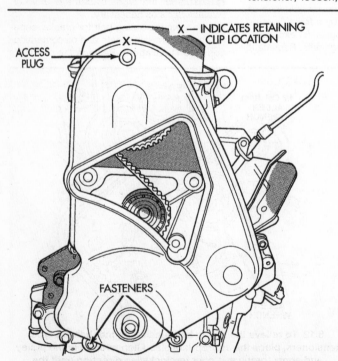

6.8a Remove the two lower bolts and upper clip retaining the timing belt outer cover to the engine (2.0L SOHC engine)

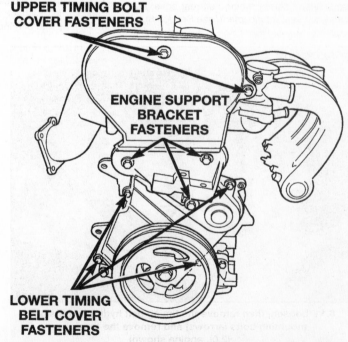

6.8b Timing belt outer cover fastener locations (2.4L engine)

2A

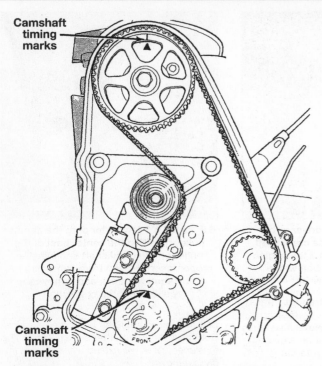

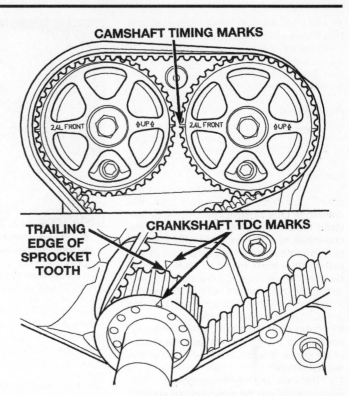

6.9a Before removing the timing belt, make sure the camshaft sprocket and crankshaft timing marks align with their respective marks - rotate the engine (clockwise only as viewed from the crankshaft end) as required to align both sets of timing marks (2.0L engine timing marks)

6.9b 2.4L engine timing marks - The crankshaft sprocket timing mark is on the trailing edge of the sprocket tooth

13 Carefully slip the timing belt off the sprockets and set it aside. If you plan to reuse the timing belt, store it in a plastic bag - do not allow the belt to come in contact with any type of oil or water as this will greatly shorten belt life.

14 If it's necessary to remove the camshaft sprocket(s), and/or timing belt rear cover (for camshaft seal replacement, see Section 8).

Inspection

Refer to illustration 6.18

15 Inspect the crankshaft front oil seal for leaks and replace it if necessary (see Section 7).

16 Inspect the water pump for evidence of leakage (usually indicated by a trail of wet or dried coolant). Check the pulley for excessive radial play and bearing roughness. Replace if

necessary (see Chapter 3).

17 Rotate the tensioner pulley and idler pulley (2.4L engines) by hand and move them side-to-side to detect bearing roughness and excess play. Visually inspect all timing belt sprockets for any signs of damage or wear. Replace parts as necessary.

18 Inspect the timing belt for cracks, separation, wear, missing teeth and oil contamination **(see illustration)**. Replace the belt if it's

6.11 Loosen, then remove the timing belt hydraulic tensioner mounting bolts (arrows) and remove the tensioner (2.0L engine shown)

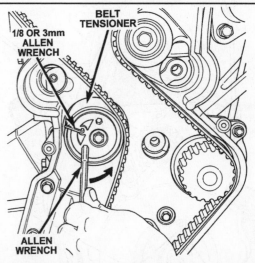

6.12 To relieve the timing belt tension on mechanical type tensioners, place the appropriate size Allen wrench in the pulley and apply torque in a counterclockwise direction until the retaining pin holes align and insert a 3mm Allen wrench or 1/8 inch drill bit to hold the pulley in place

in questionable condition or the engine mileage is close to that referenced in the *Maintenance Schedule* (see Chapter 1).

19   If equipped, check the hydraulic tensioner for leaks or any other obvious damage, replace if necessary.

Installation

2.0L engine

Refer to illustrations 6.21a, 6.21b and 6.21c

20   Confirm that the camshaft sprocket timing marks are aligned **(see illustration 6.9a)**. Reposition as required.

21   Position the crankshaft timing belt sprocket as follows **(see illustrations):**

a) *Initially align the TDC mark on the sprocket with the arrow on the oil pump housing.*

b) *Then back it off counterclockwise 3 teeth BTDC.*

c) *Rotate the crankshaft sprocket clockwise to 1/2-tooth before the arrow mark on the oil pump housing.*

22   Install the timing belt as follows; first place the belt onto the crankshaft sprocket, maintaining tension on the belt, wrap it around the water pump sprocket, camshaft sprocket and the tensioner pulley.

23   To take the slack out of the timing belt, rotate the crankshaft timing sprocket clockwise to align the timing marks (TDC), make sure the camshaft sprocket timing marks remain aligned.

2.4L engine

Refer to illustration 6.25

24   Confirm that the timing marks on the camshaft sprockets are aligned **(see illustration 6.9b)**.

25   Rotate the exhaust camshaft sprocket clockwise so the timing mark is 1/2 tooth below the intake camshaft timing mark as shown **(see illustration)**.

26   Next, align the crankshaft sprocket timing mark with the arrow mark on the oil pump housing **(see illustration 6.9b)**.

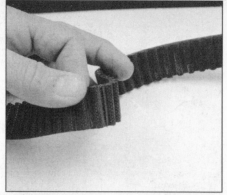

6.18 Carefully inspect the timing belt - bending it backwards will often make wear or damage more apparent

27   Install the timing belt as follows; first place the belt onto the crankshaft sprocket, maintaining tension on the belt, wrap it around the water pump sprocket, idler pulley, camshaft sprockets and the tensioner pulley. To take up the belt slack, rotate the exhaust camshaft counterclockwise until the timing marks on both sprockets align.

Engines with a mechanical tensioner

28   On engines equipped with a mechanical tensioner, pull the retaining pin from the tensioner pulley.

29   Using the bolt in the center of the crankshaft sprocket, turn the crankshaft clockwise two complete revolutions. **Caution:** *If you feel resistance while turning the crankshaft - STOP, the valves may be hitting the pistons from incorrect valve timing. Stop and re-check the valve timing.* **Note:** *The camshaft and crankshaft sprocket marks will align every two revolutions of the crankshaft.*

30   Recheck the alignment of the timing marks **(see illustrations 6.9a and 6.9b)**. If the marks do not align properly, loosen the tensioner, slip the belt off the camshaft

6.21a On 2.0L engines, use a box-end wrench or socket to rotate the crankshaft timing sprocket until the TDC mark on the sprocket is aligned with the arrow on the oil pump housing (arrow) . . .

6.21b . . . then back it off counterclockwise 3 teeth BTDC (arrows)

sprocket, realign the marks, reinstall the belt, and check the alignment again.

31   The remaining installation steps are the reverse of removal. Tighten the crankshaft pulley bolt to the torque listed in this Chapter's Specifications. Start the engine and road test the vehicle.

6.21c Rotate the crankshaft timing sprocket clockwise to 1/2-tooth BTDC (arrows)

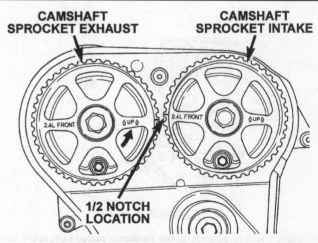

6.25 Before installing the timing belt, rotate the exhaust camshaft sprocket clockwise so the timing mark is 1/2 tooth below the timing mark on the intake camshaft sprocket

6.32a The hydraulic tensioner piston (arrow) must be compressed into the tensioner housing prior to installation

6.32b Place the tensioner in a vise with the hole (arrow) facing up. Compress the piston with the vise and insert a 5/64 inch Allen wrench or drill bit through the hole to keep the piston retracted for installation

2A

Engines with a hydraulic tensioner

Refer to illustrations 6.32a, 6.32b and 6.34

32   On engines equipped with a hydraulic tensioner, the piston must be compressed into the tensioner housing prior to installation. Place the tensioner in a vise with the pin holes facing up. Slowly compress the tensioner, then install a 5/64-inch Allen wrench or drill bit through the body to retain the piston in this position **(see illustrations)**. Remove the tensioner from the vise.

33   Install the tensioner assembly - except don't tighten the bolts at this time.

34   Have an assistant place a torque wrench on the center bolt of the tensioner pulley and apply 250 in-lbs of torque in a clockwise direction. With the torque applied to the tensioner pulley, move the tensioner up against the tensioner pulley bracket and tighten the tensioner bolts to the torque listed in this Chapter's Specifications **(see illustration)**. Remove the torque wrench.

35   Pull the Allen wrench or drill bit from the

tensioner. The timing belt tension is correct when the pin can be withdrawn and reinserted easily. Verify that the timing marks on the camshaft sprocket(s) and crankshaft sprocket are still aligned at TDC.

36   Using the bolt in the center of the crankshaft sprocket, turn the crankshaft clockwise two complete revolutions. **Caution:** *If you feel resistance while turning the crankshaft - STOP, the valves may be hitting the pistons from incorrect valve timing. Stop and re-check the valve timing.* **Note:** *The camshaft and crankshaft sprocket marks will align every two revolutions of the crankshaft.* Recheck the alignment of the timing marks **(see illustrations 6.9a and 6.9b)**. If the marks do not align properly, loosen the tensioner, slip the belt off the camshaft sprocket(s), realign the marks, reinstall the belt, and check the alignment again.

37   After crankshaft rotation, recheck the timing belt tension by inserting the retaining pin (5/64-inch Allen wrench or drill bit) back into the tensioner. If the retaining pin cannot

be inserted and withdrawn freely, readjust the timing belt tension and repeat Steps 34 through 37.

38   The remaining installation steps are the reverse of removal. Tighten the crankshaft pulley bolt to the torque listed in this Chapter's Specifications.

39   Start the engine and road test the vehicle.

7   Crankshaft front oil seal - replacement

Refer to illustrations 7.2, 7.3, 7.5 and 7.6
Caution: *Do not rotate the camshaft(s) or crankshaft when the timing belt is removed or damage to the engine may occur.*

1   Remove the timing belt (see Section 6).

2   Remove the crankshaft timing belt sprocket from the crankshaft with a bolt-type gear puller **(see illustration)**. Remove the Woodruff key from the crankshaft keyway.

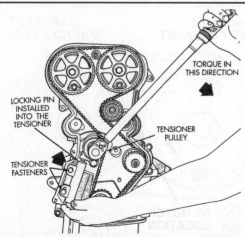

6.34 Using a torque wrench on the tensioner pulley bolt, apply 250 inch-lbs of torque as shown, move the hydraulic tensioner up against the tensioner pulley bracket and tighten the tensioner mounting bolts to the torque listed in this Chapter's Specifications

7.2 Attach a bolt-type gear puller to the crankshaft sprocket and remove the sprocket from the crankshaft

7.3 Using a screwdriver, very carefully pry the front crankshaft seal from it's bore

7.5 Lubricate the new front crankshaft seal with engine oil and using a hammer and socket, drive the seal into the bore until it's flush with the oil pump housing

7.6 Position the crankshaft sprocket with the word FRONT (arrow) facing out and install it onto the crankshaft

8.4a Remove the hydraulic tensioner pulley/plate assembly mounting bolts (arrows) . . .

8.4b . . . and then remove the pulley and bracket assembly (2.0L engine)

8.7 Remove the rear timing belt cover

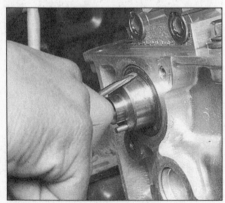

8.8 Carefully pry the camshaft seal out of the bore - DO NOT nick or scratch the camshaft or seal bore

3   Wrap the tip of a small screwdriver with tape. Working from below the right inner fender, use the screwdriver to carefully pry the seal out of its bore **(see illustration)**. Take care to prevent damaging the oil pump assembly, the crankshaft and the seal bore.

4   Thoroughly clean and inspect the seal bore and sealing surface on the crankshaft. Minor imperfections can be removed with emery cloth. If there is a groove worn in the crankshaft sealing surface (from contact with the seal), installing a new seal will probably not stop the leak.

5   Lubricate the new seal with engine oil and using a hammer and the appropriate size socket, drive the seal into the bore until it's flush with the oil pump housing. **(see illustration)**.

6   Install the Woodruff key and the crankshaft timing belt sprocket with the word FRONT facing out onto the crankshaft **(see illustration)**.

7   The remaining installation steps are the reverse of removal. Tighten the crankshaft pulley bolt to the torque listed in this Chapter's Specifications.

8   Start the engine and check for oil leaks.

8   Camshaft oil seal - replacement

Refer to illustrations 8.4a, 8.4b, 8.7, 8.8, 8.10a, 8.10b and 8.12

Caution: *Do not rotate the camshaft(s) or crankshaft when the timing belt is removed or damage to the engine may occur.*

1   Remove the timing belt (see Section 6).

2   Rotate the crankshaft counterclockwise until the crankshaft sprocket is three teeth BTDC **(see illustration 6.21b)**. This will prevent engine damage if the camshaft sprocket is inadvertently rotated during sprocket bolt removal.

3   While holding the camshaft sprocket, remove the camshaft sprocket bolt. Then, using two large screwdrivers, lever the sprocket off the camshaft. **Note:** *To hold the camshaft/sprocket while loosening the bolt, a strap-type damper/pulley holder tool is recommended and is available at most auto parts stores. If the strap wrench is unavailable, remove the valve cover to access the wrenching flats on the camshaft (2.4L engines only).*

4   On 2.0L engines, remove the 2 bolts securing the tensioner pulley bracket to the engine block and remove the pulley and bracket assembly **(see illustrations)**. Do not attempt to loosen the center bolt on the pulley or the pulley pivot bolt, remove the pulley and bracket together.

5   On 2.4L engines, remove the idler pulley.

6   On 2.0L engines equipped with a hydraulic timing belt tensioner, remove the tensioner pulley.

7   Remove the bolts securing the rear cover to the engine block and cylinder head. Remove the rear cover **(see illustration)**.

8   Carefully pry out the camshaft oil seal using a small screwdriver **(see illustration)**. Don't scratch the bore or damage the camshaft in the process (if the camshaft is damaged, the new seal will end up leaking).

8.10a Using a hammer and socket, gently tap the new seal into place with the spring side facing inward

8.10b If space is limited and you can't use a hammer and socket to install the seal, a seal installer can be made from a section of pipe (of appropriate diameter), a bolt and washer. Place the pipe over the seal and press it into place by tightening the bolt

8.12 When installing a camshaft sprocket, make sure the pin in the camshaft is aligned with the hole in the sprocket (arrows)

9   Clean the bore and coat the outer edge of the new seal with engine oil or multi-purpose grease. Also lubricate the seal lip.

10   Using a socket with an outside diameter slightly smaller than the outside diameter of the seal and a hammer **(see illustration)**, carefully drive the new seal into the cylinder head until it's flush with the face of the cylinder head. If a socket isn't available, a short section of pipe will also work. **Note:** *If engine location makes it difficult to use a hammer to install the camshaft seal, fabricate a seal installation tool from a piece of pipe cut to the appropriate length, a bolt and a large washer* **(see illustration)**. *Place the section of pipe over the seal and thread the bolt into the camshaft. The seal can now be pressed into the bore by tightening the bolt.*

11   Install the rear timing belt cover, tensioner pulley/bracket, idler pulley and tensioner pulley as applicable.

12   Install the camshaft sprocket, aligning the pin in the camshaft with the hole in the sprocket **(see illustration)**. Use an appropriate tool to hold the camshaft sprocket while tightening the sprocket bolt to the torque listed in this Chapter's Specifications.

13   Reinstall the timing belt (see Section 6).

14   Run the engine and check for oil leaks.

9   Rocker arm and hydraulic valve lash adjuster - removal, inspection and installation

Removal

2.0L engine

Refer to illustration 9.6

1   Position the number one piston at Top Dead Center (see Chapter 2C).

2   Disconnect the negative battery cable from the ground stud on the left shock tower (see Chapter 5, Section 1).

3   Remove the valve cover (see Section 3).

4   Prior to removing the rocker arm shafts, mark the front shaft (intake manifold side) as the intake rocker arm shaft and the rear shaft (exhaust manifold side) as the exhaust. **Caution:** *Do not interchange the rocker arms onto a different shaft as this could lead to premature wear.*

5   Loosen the rocker arm shaft bolts 1/4-

turn at a time each, until the valve spring pressure is relieved, in the *reverse* order of the tightening sequence **(see illustration 9.20)**. Completely loosen the bolts, but do not remove them, since leaving them in place will prevent the assembly from falling apart when it is lifted off the cylinder head.

6   Lift the rocker arms and shaft assemblies from the cylinder head and set them on the workbench **(see illustration)**. **Note:** *The hydraulic valve lash adjusters may become dislodged from the rocker arms during shaft removal. If required, secure the adjusters in place using electrical tape.*

7   Disassemble the rocker arm shaft components. **Caution:** *Before disassembly, mark the rocker arm shafts, rocker arms, shaft retainers and plastic shaft spacers (intake only) so all the parts can be reassembled in their original locations. To keep the rocker arms and related parts in order, it's a good idea to remove them and put them onto two lengths of wire (such as unbent coat hangers) in the same order as they're removed, marking each wire (which simulates the rocker shaft) as to which end would be the front of the engine.*

2A

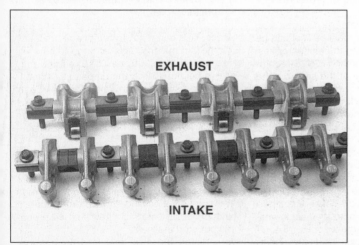

9.6 Intake and exhaust rocker arms and shaft assemblies (2.0L engine)

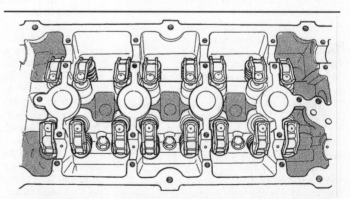

9.9 On 2.4L engines, once the camshafts have been removed, the rocker arms and hydraulic valve lash adjusters (located below the rocker arm can be removed) - be sure to keep the rocker arms and lash adjusters in order so they can be returned to their original locations

2.4L engine

Refer to illustration 9.9

8   Remove both camshafts (see Section 10).

9   Once the camshafts have been removed, the rocker arms (a.k.a. cam followers) can be lifted off **(see illustration)**. **Caution:** *Each rocker arm and valve lash adjuster must be placed back in it's original location, so mark them or place them in a marked container (such as an egg carton or cupcake tray) so they won't get mixed up.*

10   Remove the rocker arms and hydraulic valve lash adjusters from the cylinder head.

Inspection

2.0L engine

Refer to illustration 9.11

Note: *The valve lash adjuster is an integral part of each rocker arm and cannot be replaced separately.*

11   Visually check the rocker arms for wear **(see illustration)**. Replace them if evidence of wear or damage is found.

12   Inspect each lash adjuster carefully for signs of wear and damage, particularly on the surface that contacts the valve tip. Since the lash adjusters frequently become clogged, we recommend replacing the rocker arm/lash adjuster assembly if you're concerned about their condition or if the engine is exhibiting valve "tapping" noises.

13   Check all the rocker shaft components. Look for worn or scored shafts, etc. and replace any parts found to be damaged or worn excessively.

2.4L engine

Refer to illustration 9.14

14   Visually check the rocker arm tip, roller and lash adjuster pocket for wear **(see illustration)**. Replace them if evidence of wear or damage is found.

15   Inspect each adjuster carefully for signs of wear and damage, particularly on the ball tip that contacts the rocker arm. Since the lash adjusters frequently become clogged, we recommend replacing them if you're concerned about their condition or if the engine is exhibiting valve "tapping" noises.

Installation

2.0L engine

Refer to illustrations 9.18, 9.19 and 9.20

16   Prior to installation, the lash adjusters must be partially full of engine oil - indicated by little or no plunger action when the adjuster is depressed. If there's excessive plunger travel, place the rocker arm assembly into clean engine oil and pump the plunger until the plunger travel is eliminated. **Note:** *If the plunger still travels within the rocker arm when full of oil it's defective and the rocker arm assembly must be replaced.*

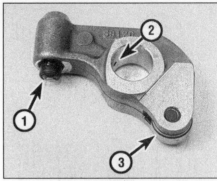

9.11 2.0L engine rocker arm/valve lash adjuster assembly (intake rocker arm shown)

1   *Hydraulic valve lash adjuster*
2   *Rocker shaft bore*
3   *Roller*

17   When assembling the rocker arms on the shaft assembly, make sure they're reinstalled in their original locations.

18   On the intake rocker arm shaft, make sure the plastic spacers are installed on the shaft in the correct locations **(see illustration)**.

19   Install the rocker arm assemblies with the notch in each rocker arm shaft located at the timing belt end of the engine and facing UP **(see illustration)**.

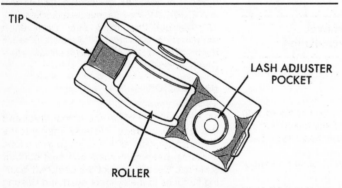

9.14 2.4L engine rocker arm

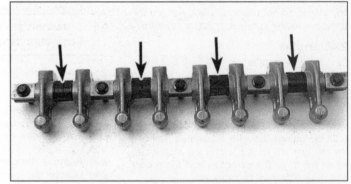

9.18 Intake rocker arm plastic spacer locations (arrows) (2.0L engine)

9.19 Both rocker arm shafts must be installed with the notches (arrows) facing UP and at the timing belt end of the engine

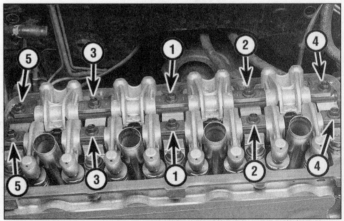

9.20 Rocker arm shaft bolt tightening sequence (2.0L engine)

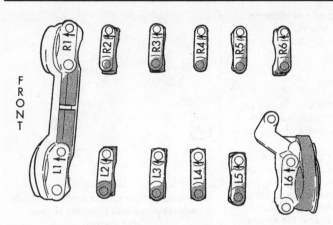

10.7 2.4L engine camshaft bearing cap location numbers - they must be reinstalled in their original locations

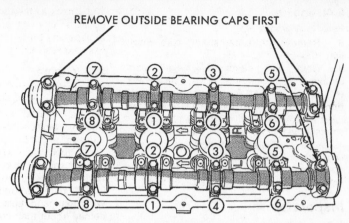

10.8 Remove the outside bearing caps first, then loosen the remaining bearing cap bolts in the sequence shown 1/4 turn at a time until they can be unscrewed by hand (2.4L engine)

20 Tighten the rocker arm bolts in sequence shown **(see illustration)** using 3 steps to reach the torque listed in this Chapter's Specifications.

21 The remaining installation steps are the reverse of removal. Run the engine and check for oil leaks and proper operation.

22 When re-starting the engine after replacing the rocker arm/lash adjusters, the adjusters will normally make "tapping" noises. After warm-up, slowly raise the speed of the engine from idle to 3,000 rpm and back to idle over a one minute period. If the adjuster(s) do not become silent, replace the defective rocker arm/lash adjuster assembly.

2.4L engine

23 Prior to installation, the lash adjusters must be partially full of engine oil - indicated by little or no plunger action when the adjuster is depressed. If there's excessive plunger travel, place the rocker arm assembly into clean engine oil and pump the plunger until the plunger travel is eliminated. **Note:** *If the plunger still travels within the rocker arm when full of oil it's defective and the rocker arm assembly must be replaced.*

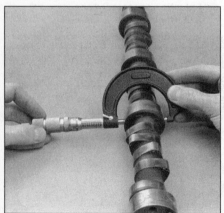

10.12 Measure the camshaft bearing journal diameters with a micrometer and compare the measurements to the dimensions given in this Chapter's Specifications

24 Install the hydraulic lash adjusters and rocker arms back in their proper locations on the cylinder head.

25 Install the camshafts (see Section 10).

26 When re-starting the engine after replacing the rocker arm/lash adjusters, the adjusters will normally make "tapping" noises. After warm-up, slowly raise the speed of the engine from idle to 3,000 rpm and back to idle over a one minute period. If the adjuster(s) do not become silent, replace the defective lash adjuster assembly.

10 Camshaft(s) - removal, inspection and installation

Removal

2.0L engine

Note: *The camshaft cannot be removed with the cylinder head installed in the vehicle.*

1 Remove the cylinder head (see Section 12).

2 Remove the camshaft position sensor (see Chapter 6).

3 Carefully withdraw the camshaft from the opening in the rear of the cylinder head. **Caution:** *Don't damage the camshaft lobes or bearing journals during removal and installation through the opening in the cylinder head.*

4 Remove the camshaft front seal from the cylinder head.

2.4L engine

Refer to illustrations 10.7 and 10.8

5 Remove the timing belt (see Section 6).

6 Remove the camshaft sprockets and the rear timing belt cover (see section 8).

7 The camshaft bearing caps are identified with their numbered location in the cylinder head **(see illustration)**.

8 Remove the outside bearing caps at each end of the camshafts first. Remove the remaining camshaft bearing caps, loosening the bolts a little at a time to prevent distorting the camshaft(s) by loosening the caps in the

sequence shown **(see illustration)**. Once the bearing caps have all been loosened enough for removal, they may still be difficult to remove. Using the bearing cap bolts for extra leverage, move the cap back and forth to loosen the cap from the cylinder head. If they are still difficult to remove you can tap them gently with a soft face mallet so they can be lifted off. **Caution:** *Store them in order so they can be returned to their original locations, with the same side facing forward.*

9 Carefully lift the camshafts out of the cylinder head. Mark the camshafts INTAKE and EXHAUST, they cannot be mixed-up.

10 Remove the front seal from each camshaft. **Note:** *Now is a good time to inspect the rocker arms and lash adjusters (see Section 9).*

Inspection

Refer to illustration 10.12

11 Thoroughly clean the camshaft(s) and the gasket surface. Visually inspect the camshaft for wear and/or damage to the lobe surfaces, bearing journals and seal contact surfaces. Visually inspect the camshaft bearing surfaces in the cylinder head and bearing caps (2.4L engines) for scoring and other damage.

12 Measure the camshaft bearing journal diameters **(see illustration)**. Measure the inside diameter of the camshaft bearing surfaces in the cylinder head, using a telescoping gauge (on 2.4L engines, temporarily install the bearing caps). Subtract the journal measurement from the bearing measurement to obtain the camshaft bearing oil clearance. Compare this clearance with the value listed in this Chapter's Specifications. Replace worn components as required.

13 Replace the camshaft if it fails any of the above inspections. **Note:** *If the lobes are worn, replace the rocker arms and lash adjusters along with the camshaft. Cylinder head replacement may be necessary if the camshaft bearing surfaces in the head are damaged or excessively worn.*

14 Clean and inspect the cylinder head as described in Part C of this Chapter.

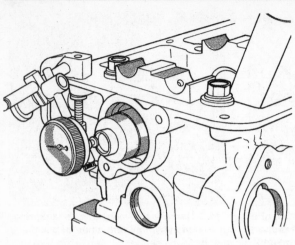

10.18 Measure the camshaft endplay with a dial indicator positioned on the sprocket end of the camshaft as shown

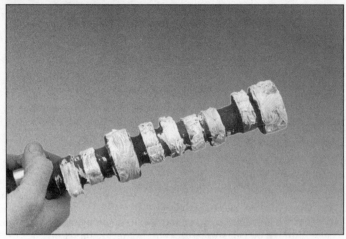

10.20 Prior to installing the camshaft, lubricate the bearing journals, thrust surfaces and lobes with assembly lube or clean engine oil

Camshaft endplay measurement

Refer to illustration 10.18

15   Lubricate the camshaft(s) and cylinder head bearing journals with clean engine oil.

16   On 2.0L engines, carefully insert the camshaft into the cylinder head and install the camshaft position sensor. Tighten the bolts to the torque listed in this Chapter's Specifications.

17   On 2.4L engines, place the camshaft in it's respective place in the cylinder head. **Note:** *Do not install the rocker arms for this check.* Install the rear bearing cap and tighten the bolts to the torque listed in this Chapter's Specifications.

18   Install a dial indicator set up on the cylinder head and place the indicator tip on the camshaft at the sprocket end **(see illustration)**.

19   Using a screwdriver, carefully pry the camshaft fully to the rear (toward the camshaft position sensor) until it stops. Zero the dial indicator and pry the camshaft fully to the front (toward the dial indicator end). The amount of indicator travel is the camshaft endplay. Compare the endplay measurement with the tolerance given in this Chapter's Specification Section. If the endplay is exces-

sive, check the camshaft and cylinder head bearing journals for wear and replace as necessary.

Installation

2.0L engine

Refer to illustration 10.20

20   Very carefully clean the camshaft and bearing journals. Liberally coat the journals, lobes and thrust portions of the camshaft with assembly lube or clean engine oil **(see illustration)**.

21   Carefully install the camshaft in the cylinder head.

22   Install a new camshaft oil seal (see Section 8).

23   Install the camshaft position sensor (see Chapter 6).

24   Install the cylinder head (see Section 12).

25   Install the rocker arm shaft assembly (see Section 9).

2.4L engine

Refer to illustrations 10.29 and 10.30

26   If removed, install the valve lash adjusters and rocker arms (see Section 9).

27   Clean the camshaft and bearing journals and caps. Liberally coat the journals, lobes

and thrust portions of the camshaft with assembly lube or engine oil **(see illustration 10.20)**.

28   Carefully install the camshafts in the cylinder head in their correct location. Temporarily install the camshaft sprockets and rotate the camshafts so their timing marks align **(see illustration 6.9b)**. Make sure the crankshaft is positioned with the crankshaft sprocket timing mark at three teeth BTDC **(see illustration 6.21b)**. **Caution:** *If the pistons are at TDC when tightening the camshaft bearing caps, damage to the engine may occur.*

29   Install the bearing caps, except for the No. 1 and No. 6 (left side) end caps **(see illustration 10.7)**. Tighten the bolts in 3 progressive steps in the sequence shown to the torque listed in this Chapter's Specifications **(see illustration)**.

30   Apply a small bead of anaerobic sealant (approximately 1/8 inch) to the No. 1 and No. 6 (left side) bearing caps **(see illustration)**. Install the bearing caps and tighten the bolts to the torque listed in this Chapter's Specifications.

31   Install new camshaft oil seals (see Section 8).

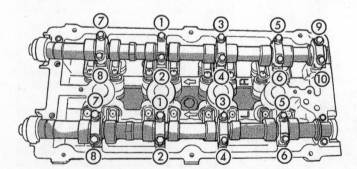

10.29 Tighten the camshaft bearing caps progressing in 3 equal steps in the sequence shown until the torque value given in this Chapter's Specifications has been reached (2.4L engine)

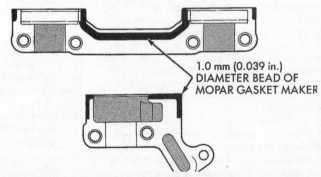

FRONT CAM CAP (#1L/1R)

1.0 mm (0.039 in.) DIAMETER BEAD OF MOPAR GASKET MAKER

10.30 Apply a small bead of anaerobic sealant to the No. 1 and left side No. 6 bearing caps as shown

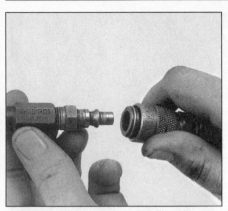

11.4 This is what the air hose adapter that threads into the spark plug hole looks like - they're usually available from auto parts stores

11.7 Use needle-nose pliers (shown) or a small magnet to remove the valve keepers - be careful not to drop them down into the engine!

11.8 Remove the valve guide seal/spring seat assembly with a pair of pliers

32   Install the timing belt, covers and related components (see Section 6).
33   Run the engine while checking for oil leaks.

11   Valve springs, retainers and seals - replacement

Refer to illustrations 11.4, 11.7, 11.8, 11.13 and 11.15

Note: *Broken valve springs and defective valve stem seals can be replaced without removing the cylinder heads. Two special tools and a compressed air source are normally required to perform this operation, so read through this Section carefully and rent or buy the tools before attempting the job.*

1   Remove the valve cover (see Section 3).
2   Remove the spark plug from the cylinder which has the defective component. If all of the valve stem seals are being replaced, all of the spark plugs should be removed.
3   Turn the crankshaft until the piston in the affected cylinder is at top dead center on the compression stroke (refer to Chapter 2C). If you're replacing all of the valve stem seals, begin with cylinder number one and work on the valves for one cylinder at a time. Move from cylinder-to-cylinder following the firing order sequence (see this Chapter's Specifications).
4   Thread an adapter into the spark plug hole **(see illustration)** and connect an air hose from a compressed air source to it. Most auto parts stores can supply the air hose adapter. **Note:** *Many cylinder compression gauges utilize a screw-in fitting that may work with your air hose quick-disconnect fitting. On 2.0L engines, the spark plug tubes may need to be removed to facilitate adapter installation.*
5   Remove the rocker arms (see Section 9).
6   Apply compressed air to the cylinder. **Warning:** *The piston may be forced down by compressed air, causing the crankshaft to turn suddenly. If the wrench used when positioning the number one piston at TDC is still attached to the crankshaft bolt, it could cause*

damage or injury when the crankshaft moves.
7   Stuff clean shop rags into the cylinder head holes above and below the valves to prevent parts and tools from falling into the engine, then use a valve spring compressor to compress the spring. Remove the keepers with small needle-nose pliers or a magnet **(see illustration).**
8   Remove the spring retainer and valve spring, then remove the valve guide seal/spring seat assembly **(see illustration).** **Caution:** *If air pressure fails to hold the valve in the closed position during this operation, the valve face and/or seat is probably damaged. If so, the cylinder head will have to be removed for additional repair operations.*
9   Wrap a rubber band or tape around the top of the valve stem so the valve won't fall into the combustion chamber, then release the air pressure.
10   Inspect the valve stem for damage. Rotate the valve in the guide and check the end for eccentric movement, which would indicate that the valve is bent and needs to be replaced.
11   Move the valve up-and-down in the guide and make sure it doesn't bind. If the valve stem binds, either the valve is bent or the guide is damaged. In either case, the

head will have to be removed for repair.
12   Pull up on the valve stem to close the valve, reapply air pressure to the cylinder to retain the valve in the closed position, then remove the tape or rubber band from the valve stem.
13   Lubricate the valve stem with engine oil and install a new valve guide seal/spring seat assembly. Tap into place with deep socket **(see illustration).**
14   Install the spring in position over the valve.
15   Install the valve spring retainer. Compress the valve spring and carefully position the keepers in the groove. Apply a small dab of grease to the inside of each keeper to hold it in place if necessary **(see illustration).**
16   Remove the pressure from the spring tool and make sure the keepers are seated.
17   Disconnect the air hose and remove the adapter from the spark plug hole.
18   If applicable, install the spark plug tubes (2.0L engines only, see Section 3).
19   Install the rocker arms (see Section 9).
20   Install the spark plug(s) and connect the wire(s).
21   Install the valve cover (see Section 3).
22   Start and run the engine, then check for oil leaks and unusual sounds coming from the valve cover area.

2A

11.13 Gently tap the new seal into place with a hammer and a deep socket

11.15 Apply a small dab of grease to each keeper before installation to hold it in place on the valve stem until the spring is released

12.4 Cover the intake ports with duct tape (arrow) to keep out debris before removing the cylinder head (2.0L engine shown)

12.15a Carefully lift the cylinder head straight up and place the head on wood blocks to prevent damage to the sealing surfaces (2.0L engine shown)

12 Cylinder head - removal and installation

Caution: *Allow the engine to cool completely before beginning this procedure.*

Removal

Refer to illustrations 12.4, 12.15a, 12.15b and 12.16

1   Position the number one piston at Top Dead Center (see Chapter 2C).
2   Disconnect the negative battery cable from the ground stud on the left shock tower (see Chapter 5, Section 1).
3   Drain the cooling system and remove the spark plugs (see Chapter 1).
4   Remove the intake manifold (see Section 4). Cover the intake ports on the manifold and cylinder head with duct tape to keep out foreign debris and contamination **(see illustration)**.

5   Remove the bolts securing the power steering reservoir and hoses to the cylinder head and position them out of the way (see Chapter 10 if necessary).
6   Remove the exhaust manifold (see Section 5). **Note:** *The exhaust manifold is easier to remove after the cylinder head is removed, if possible leave it attached.*
7   Disconnect the upper radiator hose from the thermostat housing (see Chapter 3 if necessary).
8   Disconnect the electrical connector from the camshaft position sensor (see Chapter 5).
9   Remove the timing belt (see Section 6).
10   Remove camshaft sprocket(s) and rear timing belt cover (see Section 8).
11   On 2.0L engines, remove rocker arm shaft assemblies (see Section 9).
12   On 2.4L engines, remove the camshafts, rocker arms and valve lash adjusters (see Section 9).
13   Remove the EGR valve from the cylinder

head (see Chapter 6).
14   Loosen the cylinder head bolts, 1/4-turn at a time, in the *reverse* order of the tightening sequence **(see illustrations 12.21a or 12.21b)** until they can be removed by hand. **Note:** *Mark the locations of the different length bolts so they can be reinstalled in their original locations.*
15   Carefully lift the cylinder head **(see illustration)** straight up and place the head on wood blocks to prevent damage to the sealing surfaces. If the head sticks to the engine block, dislodge it by placing a wood block against the head casting and tapping the wood with a hammer or by prying the head with a prybar placed carefully on a casting protrusion **(see illustration)**. **Note:** *Cylinder head disassembly and inspection procedures are covered in Chapter 2, Part C. It's also a good idea to have the head checked for warpage, even if you're just replacing the gasket.*

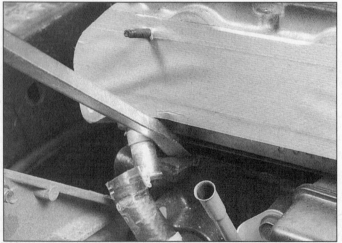

12.15b If the head is stuck to the engine block, dislodge it by placing a wood block against the head casting and tapping the wood with a hammer or by prying the head with a prybar placed carefully on a casting protrusion

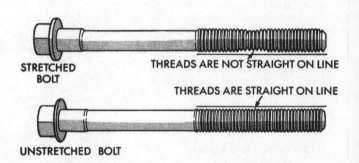

12.16 Place a precision straightedge along the cylinder head bolt thread profile as shown, if any part of the bolt threads are not on the straightedge, the bolt must be replaced

12.21a Cylinder head bolt tightening sequence - 2.0L engine

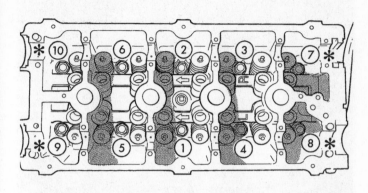

12.21b Cylinder head bolt tightening sequence - 2.4L engine

2A

16   Remove all traces of old gasket material from the block and head. **Caution:** *The cylinder head is aluminum, be very careful not to gouge the sealing surfaces.* Special gasket removal solvents that soften gaskets and make removal much easier are available at auto parts stores. When working on the block, place clean shop rags into the cylinders to help keep out debris. Use a vacuum to remove any contamination from the engine. Use a tap of the correct size to chase the threads in the engine block. Clean and inspect all threaded fasteners for damage. Inspect the cylinder head bolt threads for "necking," where the diameter of threads narrow due to bolt stretching **(see illustration)**. If any cylinder head bolt exhibits damage or necking, it must be replaced. **Note:** *If further disassembly of the cylinder head is required, refer to Part C of this Chapter.*

17   Refer to Part C of this Chapter for cleaning and inspection of the cylinder head.

Installation

Refer to illustrations 12.21a and 12.21b

18   On 2.0L engines, install the camshaft if removed (see Section 10).

19   Place a new gasket and the cylinder head in position on the engine block.

20   Apply clean engine oil to the cylinder head bolt threads and install them back in their original locations (noted in Step 14).

21   Tighten the cylinder head bolts in the sequence shown **(see illustrations)** progressing in 3 stages to the torque listed in this Chapter's Specifications. After the third pass, tighten the bolts in the proper sequence, an additional 90-degrees (1/4-turn) more. **Note:** *A torque wrench is not required for the 1/4-turn procedure. Before performing the final pass, mark the bolts in relation to the cylinder head and place another mark 90-degrees clockwise from the starting mark.*

22   Install the rocker arms and hydraulic valve lash adjusters (see Section 9).

23   On 2.4L engines, install the rear timing belt cover, camshafts and camshaft sprockets (see Section 10).

24   ON 2.0L engines, install the rear timing belt cover and camshaft sprocket (see Section 10).

25   Install the timing belt (see Section 6). After installation, slowly rotate the crankshaft by hand clockwise through two complete revolutions. Recheck the camshaft timing marks.

26   Reinstall the remaining components in the reverse order of removal.

27   Be sure to refill the cooling system and check all fluid levels (see Chapter 1 if necessary).

28   Start the engine and run it until normal operating temperature is reached. Check for leaks and proper operation.

13   Oil pan - removal and installation

Removal

Refer to illustrations 13.7, 13.10a, 13.10b, 13.11a and 13.11b

1   Disconnect the negative battery cable from the ground stud on the left shock tower (see Chapter 5, Section 1).

2   Raise the vehicle and support it securely on jackstands.

3   Remove the accessory drivebelt splash shield (see Chapter 1).

4   Drain the engine oil (see Chapter 1).

5   Remove the transmission support bracket.

6   Remove the front engine mount and strut (see Section 17). **Note:** *On 2.4L engines, it may be necessary to remove the engine support module, if equipped.*

7   If equipped, remove the transaxle-to-oil pan structural collar **(see illustration)**.

8   On 2.0L engines, remove the transaxle inspection cover.

9   On 2.0L engines, equipped with air conditioning, remove the oil filter and adapter.

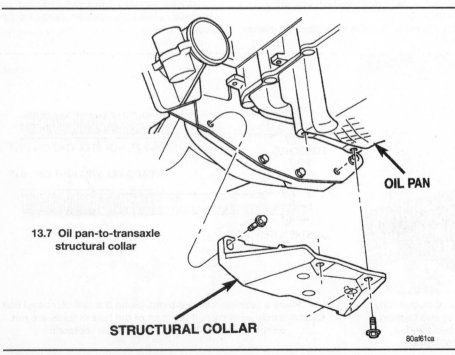

13.7 Oil pan-to-transaxle structural collar

OIL PAN

STRUCTURAL COLLAR

80af61ca

13.10a If the oil pan is stuck to the block, tap it with a soft faced mallet to break it loose

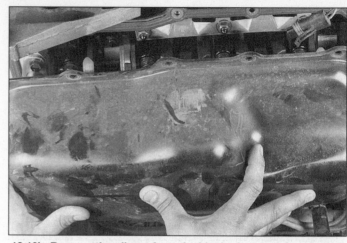

13.10b Remove the oil pan from the block - be careful not to spill any residual oil that may be inside

10   Using a criss-cross pattern, loosen and remove the mounting bolts, then lower the oil pan from the vehicle. **Note:** *On models equipped with an engine support module (see Section 17), separate the oil pan from the engine block enough to facilitate oil pump pickup tube removal. If the pan is stuck, tap it with a soft-face hammer* **(see illustrations)** *or place a wood block against the pan and tap the wood block with a hammer.* **Caution:** *If you're wedging something between the oil pan and the engine block to separate the two, be extremely careful not to gouge or nick the gasket surface of either part; an oil leak could result.*

11   Remove the oil pump pick-up tube and screen assembly **(see illustration)**. Remove the O-ring seal from the oil pick-up tube and discard **(see illustration)**. Thoroughly clean the tube and screen. On vehicles equipped with an engine support module, the oil pan can now be removed from the engine.

12   Thoroughly clean the sealing surfaces on the oil pan and block. Use a scraper to remove all traces of old gasket material. Gasket removal solvents are available at auto parts stores and may prove helpful. Check the oil pan sealing surface for distortion.

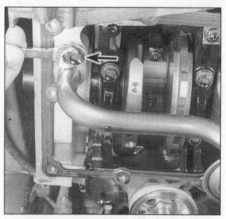

13.11a Unscrew the bolt (arrow) and remove the oil pump pick-up tube assembly - clean both the tube and screen thoroughly and inspect for damage or foreign debris

Straighten or replace as necessary. After cleaning and straightening (if necessary), wipe the gasket surfaces of the pan and block clean with a rag soaked in lacquer thinner or acetone.

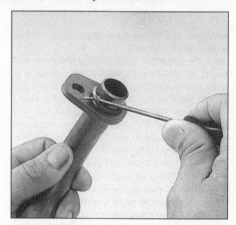

13.11b Removing the O-ring seal from the oil pump pick-up tube

Installation

Refer to illustrations 13.14 and 13.16

13   Install a new O-ring onto the oil pick-up tube and install it onto the oil pump housing. Tighten the bolt to the torque listed in this Chapter's Specifications.

14   Apply a 1/8-inch bead of RTV sealant at the cylinder block-to-oil pump assembly joint

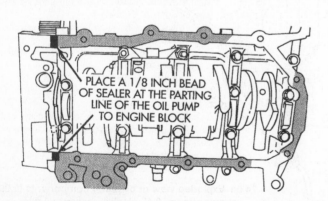

PLACE A 1/8 INCH BEAD OF SEALER AT THE PARTING LINE OF THE OIL PUMP TO ENGINE BLOCK

13.14 Apply a 1/8-inch bead of RTV sealant to the cylinder block-to-oil pump assembly joint on the oil pan flange

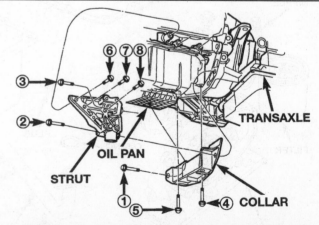

TRANSAXLE

OIL PAN

STRUT

COLLAR

13.16 Front engine mount strut and structural collar bolt identification - 1998 2.4L engine

14.5a Remove the oil pump assembly mounting bolts (arrows) and separate the assembly from the engine block (2.0L engine shown)

14.5b If the pump will not come off by hand, tap it gently with a soft-faced hammer or pry gently on a casting protrusion

at the oil pan flange **(see illustration)**. Install a new oil pan gasket.

15   Place the oil pan into position and install the bolts finger tight. Working side-to-side from the center out, tighten the bolts to the torque listed in this Chapter's Specifications.

16   When installing the front engine mount strut and collar on 1998 2.4L engines, install all bolts hand tight, then tighten the bolts in the order shown to the torque listed in this Chapter's Specifications **(see illustration)**.

17   On 1997 2.4L and 1998 2.0L engines, install the oil pan-to-transaxle structural collar and tighten the bolts in three steps to the torque listed in this Chapter's Specifications.

18   The remaining installation steps are the reverse of removal.

19   Refill the crankcase with the proper quantity and grade of oil (see *Recommended lubricants and fluids* Section in Chapter 1).

20   Run the engine and check for leaks. Road test the vehicle and check for leaks again.

---

14   Oil pump - removal, inspection and installation

Note: *The oil pump pressure relief valve can be serviced without removing the oil pan and oil pick-up tube.*

Removal

Refer to illustrations 14.5a, 14.5b, 14.6a, 14.6b, 14.6c, 14.6d, 14.8 and 14.9

1   Disconnect the negative battery cable from the ground stud on the left shock tower (see Chapter 5, Section 1).

2   Remove the oil pan and pick-up tube assembly (see Section 13).

3   Remove the timing belt (see Section 6) and crankshaft sprocket (see Section 7).

4   On 2.4L engines, remove the oil filter.

5   Remove the bolts and detach the oil pump assembly from the engine **(see illustration)**. **Caution:** *If the pump doesn't come off by hand, tap it gently with a soft-faced hammer or pry on a casting boss* **(see illustration)**.

6   Unscrew the mounting screws and remove the rotor assembly cover from the oil pump housing. Withdraw the inner and outer rotors from the body **(see illustrations)**. **Caution:** *Be very careful with these components. Close tolerances are critical in creating the correct oil pressure. Any nicks or other damage will require replacement of the complete pump assembly.*

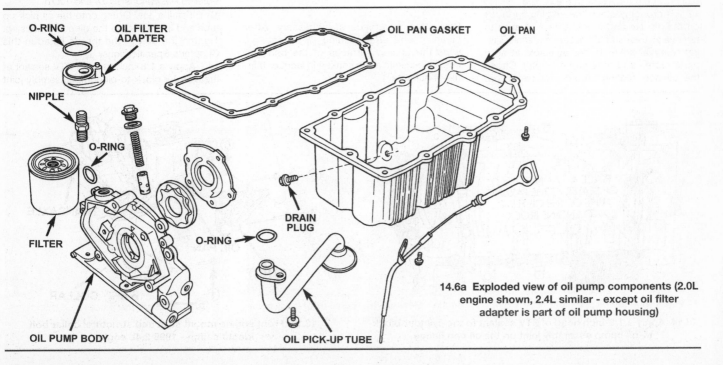

14.6a Exploded view of oil pump components (2.0L engine shown, 2.4L similar - except oil filter adapter is part of oil pump housing)

O-RING · OIL FILTER ADAPTER · OIL PAN GASKET · OIL PAN · NIPPLE · O-RING · FILTER · O-RING · DRAIN PLUG · OIL PUMP BODY · OIL PICK-UP TUBE

14.6b Remove the rotor cover mounting screws (arrows) . . .

14.6c . . . and lift off the rotor cover

7   Using a hammer and brass drift, carefully remove the crankshaft front seal from the oil pump housing and discard it.
8   Remove the O-ring seal from the oil pump housing discharge port and discard it **(see illustration)**.
9   Disassemble the relief valve assembly, taking note of the way the relief valve piston

is installed. Unscrew the cap bolt and remove the bolt, washer, spring and relief valve **(see illustration)**.

Inspection

Refer to illustrations 14.12a, 14.12b, 14.12c, 14.12d and 14.12e
10   Clean all components including the

block surfaces and oil pan with solvent, then inspect all surfaces for excessive wear and/or damage.
11   Inspect the oil pressure relief valve piston sliding surface and valve spring for damage. If either the spring or the valve is damaged, they must be replaced as a set. Measure the relief valve spring free length

14.6d Exploded view of oil pump assembly

A   Rotor cover
B   Outer rotor
C   Inner rotor
D   Oil pump body

14.8 Remove the discharge port O-ring seal from the oil pump body - apply clean engine oil to the new seal at installation

14.9 Remove the oil pressure relief valve cap bolt from the oil pump body and withdraw the spring and the relief valve piston

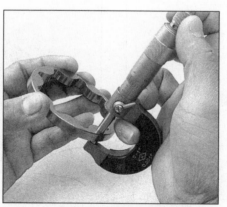

14.12a Measure the outer rotor thickness at 4 locations equally spaced

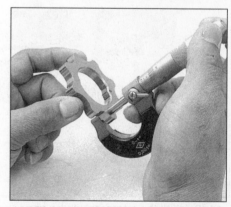

14.12b Measure the inner rotor thickness at 4 locations equally spaced

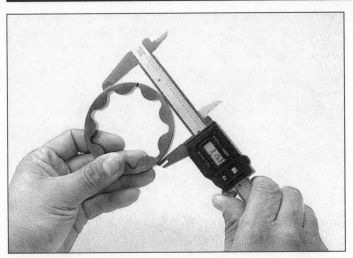

14.12c Measure the outer rotor's outer diameter at 4 locations equally spaced

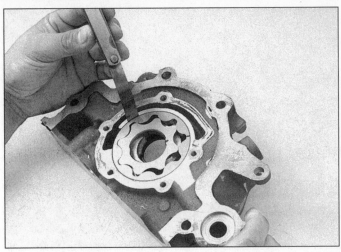

14.12d Use a flat feeler gauge to measure the outer rotor-to-oil pump body clearance at 4 locations equally spaced

and compare it with the dimension given in this Chapter's Specifications. Replace the spring if its out of tolerance by more than 1/8 of an inch.

12 Check the oil pump rotor dimensions and clearances with a micrometer or vernier calipers and a feeler gauge **(see illustrations)** and compare the results to the tolerances given in this Chapter's Specifications. Replace both rotors if any dimension is out of tolerance.

Installation

Refer to illustration 14.16

13 Lubricate the relief valve piston, piston bore and spring with clean engine oil. Install the relief valve piston into the bore with the grooved end going in first followed by the spring and cap bolt. Tighten the cap bolt to the torque listed in this Chapter's Specifications. **Note:** *If the relief valve piston is installed incorrectly, serious engine damage could occur.*

14 Lubricate the oil pump rotor recess in the housing and the inner and outer rotors with clean engine oil and install both rotors in the body. If the inner rotor has a chamfer, install it so the chamfer is facing the rotor cover. Next, fill the rotor cavity with clean engine oil and install the cover. Tighten the cover screws to the torque listed in this Chapter's Specifications.

15 Install a new O-ring in the oil discharge passage.

16 Apply anaerobic sealant to the oil pump body sealing surface **(see illustration)**, and position the pump assembly on the block aligning the inner rotor and crankshaft drive flats. Tighten the oil pump attaching bolts to the torque listed in this Chapter's Specifications.

17 Install the new crankshaft front seal into the oil pump housing (see Section 7).

18 Install the crankshaft sprocket (see Section 7) and timing belt (see Section 6).

19 Install the oil pump pick-up tube assembly and oil pan (see Section 13).

20 Install a new oil filter (see Chapter 1). Lower the vehicle.

21 Fill the crankcase with the proper quantity and grade of oil (see *Recommended lubricants and fluids* Section in Chapter 1).

22 Connect the negative battery cable to the ground stud on the left shock tower.

23 After the sealant has cured per the manufacturer's directions, start the engine and check for leaks.

15 Driveplate - removal and installation

Removal

Refer to illustrations 15.5 and 15.6

1 Raise the vehicle and support it securely on jackstands.

14.12e With the rotors installed, place a precision straightedge across the rotor cover surface and measure the clearance between the rotors and the rotor cover surface at 4 locations equally spaced

14.16 Apply a bead of anaerobic sealant to the oil pump housing sealing surface as shown

15.5 Match-mark the position of the driveplate and backing plate to the crankshaft and using an appropriate tool to hold the driveplate, remove the bolts

15.6 Remove the driveplate from the crankshaft

2   Remove the transaxle assembly (see Chapter 7).
3   On vehicles equipped with a manual transaxle, now is a good time to check/replace the modular clutch assembly (see Chapter 8).
4   To ensure correct alignment during reinstallation, match-mark the driveplate and backing plate to the crankshaft so they can be reassembled in the same position.
5   Remove the bolts that secure the flywheel or driveplate to the crankshaft **(see illustration)**. A special tool is available a most auto parts stores to hold the driveplate while loosening the bolts, if the tool is not available wedge a screwdriver in the starter ring gear teeth to jam the driveplate.
6   Remove the driveplate from the crankshaft **(see illustration)**.
7   Clean the driveplate to remove any

grease and oil. Inspect it for cracks, distortion and missing or excessively worn ring gear teeth. Replace if necessary.
8   Clean and inspect the mating surfaces of the driveplate and the crankshaft.
9   If the crankshaft rear main seal is leaking, replace it before reinstalling the driveplate (see Section 16).

Installation

10   Position the driveplate and backing plate against the crankshaft. Align the previously applied match marks. Before installing the bolts, apply thread locking compound to the threads.
11   Hold the driveplate with the special holding tool, or wedge a screwdriver in the starter ring gear teeth to keep the driveplate from turning. Tighten the bolts to the torque

listed in this Chapter's Specifications.
12   The remaining installation steps are the reverse of the removal.

16   Rear main oil seal - replacement

Refer to illustrations 16.3 and 16.5

1   The one-piece rear main oil seal is pressed into a bore machined into the rear main bearing cap and engine block.
2   Remove the transaxle, modular clutch assembly (if equipped) and driveplate (see Section 15).
3   **Note:** *Observe that the oil seal is installed flush with the outer surface of the block.* Pry out the old seal with a 3/16-inch flat blade screwdriver **(see illustration)**. **Caution:** *To prevent an oil leak, be very careful*

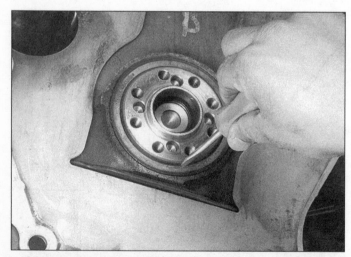

16.3 Using a 3/16 inch flat blade screwdriver, very carefully pry the crankshaft rear main seal out of it's bore - DO NOT nick or scratch the sealing surfaces on the crankshaft or seal bore

16.5 Position the new seal with the words THIS SIDE OUT facing away from the rear of the engine. Install this seal DRY! DO NOT lubricate! Gently and evenly drive the seal into the cylinder block until it is FLUSH with the outer surface of the block. DO NOT drive it past flush or there will be an oil leak - the seal must be FLUSH!

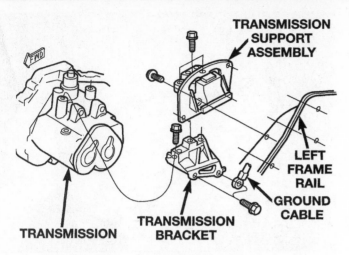

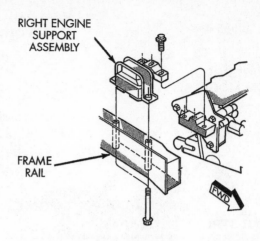

17.9a Typical left engine mount (passenger's side)

17.9b Typical right engine mount (driver's side)

not to scratch or otherwise damage the crankshaft sealing surface or the seal bore in the engine block.

4   Clean the crankshaft and seal bore in the block thoroughly and de-grease the areas by wiping them with a rag soaked in lacquer thinner or acetone. DO NOT lubricate the lip or outer diameter of the new seal - it must be installed as it comes from the manufacturer - DRY.

5   Position the new seal onto the crankshaft. **Note:** *When installing the new seal, if so marked, the words THIS SIDE OUT on the seal must face out, toward the rear of the engine.* Using an appropriate size driver and pilot tool, drive the seal into the cylinder block until it is flush with the outer surface of the block. If the seal is driven in past flush, there will be an oil leak. Check that the seal is flush **(see illustration)**.

6   The remaining installation steps are the reverse of removal.

17   Engine mounts - check and replacement

1   Engine mounts seldom require attention, but broken or deteriorated mounts should be replaced immediately or the added strain placed on the driveline components may cause damage or accelerated wear.

Check

2   During the check, the engine must be raised slightly to remove the weight from the mounts.

3   Raise the vehicle and support it securely on jackstands, then position a jack under the engine oil pan. Place a large wood block between the jack head and the oil pan to prevent oil pan damage, then carefully raise the engine just enough to take the weight off the mounts. **Warning:** *DO NOT place any part of your body under the engine when it's sup-*

ported only by a jack!

4   Check the mounts to see if the rubber is cracked, hardened or separated from the metal backing. Sometimes the rubber will split right down the center.

5   Check for relative movement between the mount plates and the engine or frame (use a large screwdriver or pry bar to attempt to move the mounts). If movement is noted, lower the engine and tighten the mount fasteners.

6   Rubber preservative may be applied to the mounts to help slow deterioration.

Replacement

Refer to illustrations 17.9a, 17.9b, 17.9c, 17.9d, 17.9e and 17.9f

7   Raise the front of the vehicle and support it securely on jackstands.

8   Place a floor jack under the engine (with a wood block between the jack head and oil pan) and raise the engine slightly to relieve

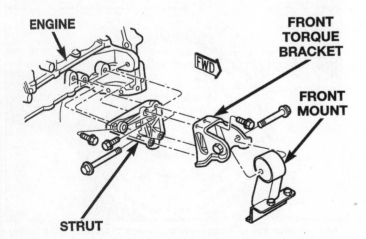

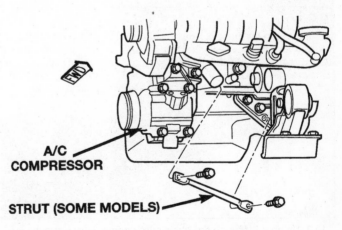

17.9c Typical front engine mount

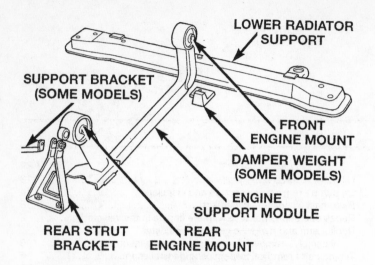

17.9d Typical engine support module (front and rear lower mounts - 1995 through 1997 models)

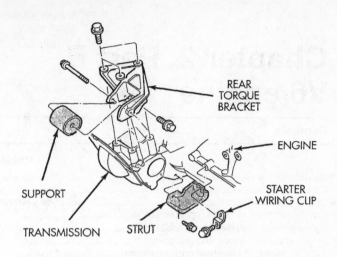

17.9e Typical 2.0L rear engine mount

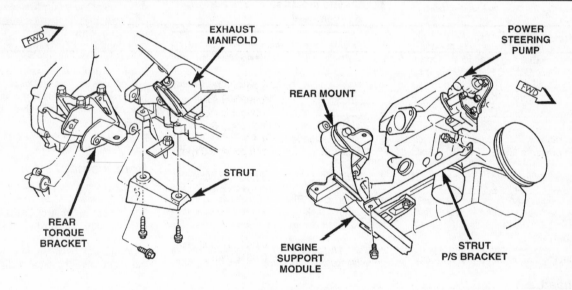

17.9f Typical 2.4L rear engine mount

the weight from the mounts. **Note:** *On 1995 to 1997 models, the front engine mount (engine support module) is attached to the lower radiator support. When removing the engine support module, the radiator and air conditioning* condenser *(if equipped) must be supported.*
9   Remove the fasteners and detach the mount from the frame and engine **(see illustrations)**. **Caution:** *Do not disconnect more than one mount at a time, except during* engine/transaxle removal.
10   Installation is the reverse of removal. Use thread locking compound on the mounting bolts and be sure to tighten them securely.

Chapter 2 Part B
V6 engine

Contents

2B

Specifications

General
Bore	3.29 inches
Stroke	2.992 inches
Displacement	152 cubic inches (2.5 liters)
Firing order	1-2-3-4-5-6
Compression ratio	9.4:1
Compression pressure	178 psi @ 250 rpm
Oil pressure	
At idle speed	6 psi (minimum)
At 3000 rpm	35 to 75 psi

Camshaft
Endplay	
Standard	0.004 to 0.008 inch
Service limit	0.0016 inch

Cylinder head
Cylinder head gasket surface warpage limit	0.008 inch

Intake and exhaust manifolds
Intake manifold warpage limit	0.008 inch
Exhaust manifold warpage limit	0.012 inch

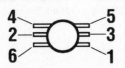

Cylinder numbering
and spark plug wire
terminal locations

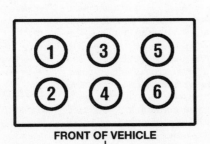

FRONT OF VEHICLE

Oil pump

Inner rotor-to-outer rotor lobe clearance..	0.003 to 0.007 inch
Outer rotor-to-housing clearance	
Standard..	0.004 to 0.007 inch
Service limit...	0.0138 inch
Rotor-to-cover clearance (end clearance)...	0.0015 to 0.0035 inch

Torque specifications

	Ft-lbs (unless otherwise indicated)
Camshaft sprocket bolt	65
Camshaft thrust case bolts..	108 in-lbs
Crankshaft damper/pulley bolt	134
Crankshaft rear main seal retainer bolts	97 in-lbs
Cylinder head bolts	80
EGR tube bolts	95 in-lbs
Engine mounting bracket bolts..	33
Exhaust manifold-to-cylinder head nuts..	33
Exhaust manifold-to-exhaust pipe nuts	21
Exhaust manifold heat shield bolts..	115 in-lbs
Driveplate-to-crankshaft bolts...	70
Intake manifold	
Upper intake manifold bolts	160 in-lbs
Lower intake manifold bolts	185 in-lbs
Oil filter adapter bolts	17
Oil pan bolts	53 in-lbs
Oil pump	
Attaching bolts	
M8 bolts	10
M10 bolts	30
Cover bolts	88 in-lbs
Pick-up tube bolts	168 in-lbs
Relief valve cap bolt	30
Rocker arm shaft bolts	23
Thermostat housing bolts...	168 in-lbs
Timing belt	
Cover bolts	105 in-lbs
Tensioner arm assembly bolt	33
Tensioner pulley bolt	35
Valve cover bolts	88 in-lbs
Water pump mounting bolt..	17

Refer to Part C for additional torque specifications

1   General information

This Part of Chapter 2 is devoted to in-vehicle engine repair procedures. Information concerning engine removal and installation and engine block and cylinder head overhaul can be found in Part C of this Chapter.

The following repair procedures are based on the assumption that the engine is installed in the vehicle. If the engine has been removed from the vehicle and mounted on a stand, many of the steps outlined in this Part of Chapter 2 will not apply.

The Specifications included in this Part of Chapter 2 apply only to the procedures contained in this Part. Part C of Chapter 2 contains the Specifications necessary for cylinder head and engine block rebuilding.

2   Repair operations possible with the engine in the vehicle

Many major repair operations can be accomplished without removing the engine from the vehicle.

Clean the engine compartment and the exterior of the engine with some type of degreaser before any work is performed. It will make the job easier and help keep dirt out of the internal areas of the engine.

Depending on the components involved, it may be helpful to remove the hood to improve access to the engine as repairs are performed (refer to Chapter 11 if necessary). Cover the fenders to prevent damage to the paint. Special pads are available, but an old bedspread or blanket will also work.

If vacuum, exhaust, oil or coolant leaks develop, indicating a need for gasket or seal replacement, the repairs can generally be made with the engine in the vehicle. The intake and exhaust manifold gaskets, oil pan gasket, camshaft and crankshaft oil seals and cylinder head gasket are all accessible with the engine in place.

Exterior engine components, such as the intake and exhaust manifolds, the oil pan, the oil pump, the water pump, the starter motor, the alternator, the distributor and the fuel system components can be removed for repair with the engine in place.

Since the camshafts and cylinder head can be removed without pulling the engine, valve component servicing can also be accomplished with the engine in the vehicle. Replacement of the timing belt and sprockets is also possible with the engine in the vehicle.

In extreme cases caused by a lack of necessary equipment, repair or replacement of piston rings, pistons, connecting rods and rod bearings is possible with the engine in the vehicle. However, this practice is not recommended because of the cleaning and preparation work that must be done to the components involved.

3   Valve cover - removal and installation

Removal

Refer to illustrations 3.6 and 3.7

1   Disconnect the negative battery cable from the ground stud on the left shock tower (see Chapter 5, Section 1).

2   Remove the air cleaner assembly (see Chapter 4).

3.6 Valve cover mounting bolts (arrows)

3.7 Remove and replace the seal from each spark plug tube

2B

3   If removing the rear valve cover (near the firewall), remove the upper intake manifold (see Section 4).

4   Clearly label then remove the spark plug wires from the valve cover (see Chapter 1 if necessary).

5   Clearly label and then disconnect any emission hoses and electrical cables which connect to or cross over the valve cover.

6   Remove the valve cover bolts and lift off the cover (see illustration). If the cover sticks to the cylinder head, tap on it with a soft-face hammer or place a wood block against the cover and tap on the wood with a hammer. Caution: *If you have to pry between the valve cover and the cylinder head, be extremely careful not to gouge or nick the gasket surfaces of either part. A leak could develop after reassembly.*

7   Remove the spark plug tube seals. Even if they look OK, they should be replaced (see illustration).

8   Thoroughly clean the valve cover and remove all traces of old gasket material. Gasket removal solvents are available from auto parts stores and may prove helpful. After

cleaning the surfaces, degrease them with a rag soaked in lacquer thinner or acetone.

Installation

9   Install the new spark plug seals onto the tubes.

10   Install a new gasket on the cover, using anaerobic RTV sealant to hold it in place.

11   Tighten the valve cover bolts in 3 steps to the torque listed in this Chapter's Specifications using a criss-cross pattern starting in the middle of the cover and working outwards.

12   The remaining installation steps are the reverse of removal. When complete, run the engine and check for oil leaks.

Spark plug tube replacement

13   Remove the applicable valve cover (see above).

14   Grasp spark plug tube with locking pliers, carefully twist back and forth and remove the tube from cylinder head.

15   Clean the locking agent from the tube and the recess in cylinder head with solvent, and dry thoroughly.

16   Apply a small amount of Loctite No. 271, or equivalent, around the lower end of the tube and install the tube into the cylinder head. Carefully tap the tube into the recess with a wood block and mallet until it is fully seated in the cylinder head.

4   Intake manifold - removal and installation

Upper intake manifold

Removal

Refer to illustrations 4.3a, 4.3b, 4.5, 4.6, 4.7a and 4.7b

1   Disconnect the negative battery cable from the ground stud on the left shock tower (see Chapter 5, Section 1).

2   Remove the air filter inlet duct from the throttle body (see Chapter 4 if necessary).

3   Clearly label and disconnect all hoses, wires, brackets and emission lines which attach to the intake manifold (see illustrations).

4   Disconnect the accelerator cable and

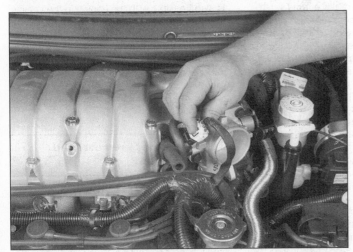

4.3a Disconnect the throttle position sensor connector

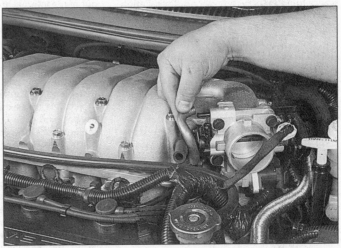

4.3b Disconnect the purge vacuum hose from the throttle body fitting

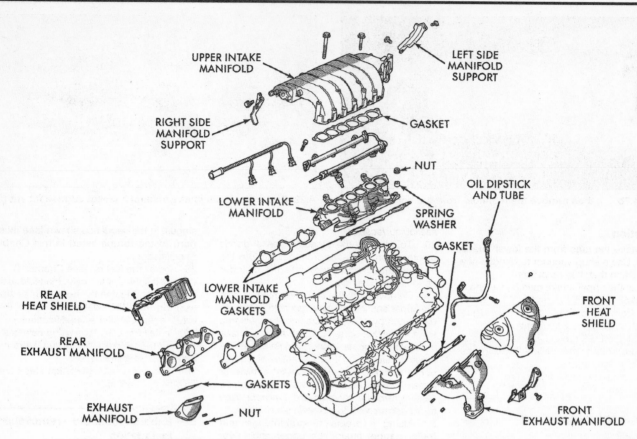

4.5 Exploded view of V6 engine intake and exhaust system components

cruise control cable (if applicable) from the throttle body (see Chapter 4 if necessary).

5   Remove the bolts securing the upper intake manifold to the right and left side support brackets **(see illustration)**.

6   Remove the EGR tube **(see illustration)**.

7   Loosen the upper intake manifold bolts in a criss-cross pattern 1/4 turn at a time until they can be removed by hand. Remove the upper intake manifold from the engine **(see illustrations)**. If it sticks, tap the manifold with a soft-face hammer or carefully pry it

from the lower intake manifold. **Caution:** *Do not pry between gasket sealing surfaces.*

8   To minimize the chance of gasket debris or other contamination from getting into the engine, place clean rags into the lower intake manifold passages.

9   Remove all traces of gasket material from both the upper and lower intake manifold by carefully scraping them using a suitable gasket scraper. **Caution:** *The intake manifold components are made of aluminum and are easily nicked or gouged. Do not dam-*

age the gasket surfaces or a leak may result after the work is complete. Gasket removal solvents are available from auto parts stores and may prove helpful.

10   Using a precision straightedge and feeler gauge, check the upper and lower intake manifold mating surfaces for warpage **(see illustration 4.22)**. If the warpage on any surface exceeds the limits listed in this Chapter's Specifications, the discrepant intake manifold must be replaced or resurfaced by an automotive machine shop.

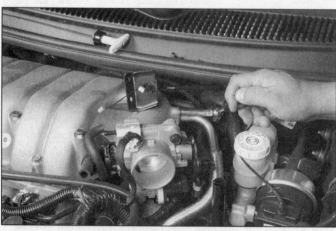

4.6 Remove the EGR tube

4.7a Starting in the center and working outwards, remove the upper intake manifold mounting bolts in a criss-cross pattern . . .

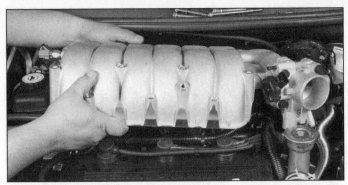

4.7b . . . then remove the manifold from the engine

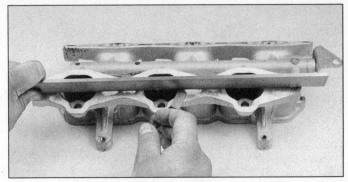

4.22 Check the lower intake manifold gasket surface for warpage

Installation

11   Remove the rags from the lower intake manifold. Use a shop vacuum to remove any contamination that may be present.

12   Install the upper intake manifold, using a new gasket. Tighten the bolts in 3 stages, working from the center out, to the torque listed in this Chapter's Specifications.

13   Install the EGR tube using new gaskets. Tighten the bolts to the torque listed in this Chapter's Specifications.

14   The remaining installation steps are the reverse of removal.

Lower intake manifold

Removal

Refer to illustration 4.22

15   Perform the fuel pressure relief procedure (see Chapter 4).

16   Remove the upper intake manifold (see above).

17   Remove the fuel rail and injector assembly (see Chapter 4).

18   Loosen the intake manifold nuts in the *reverse* order of the tightening sequence **(see illustration 4.24)**, 1/4 turn at a time until they can be removed by hand. Remove the washers.

19   Remove the lower intake manifold from the engine. If it sticks, tap the manifold with a soft-face hammer or carefully pry it from the heads. **Caution:** *Do not pry between gasket*

sealing surfaces.

20   To minimize the chance of gasket debris or other contamination from getting into the engine, place clean rags into the cylinder head intake passages.

21   Remove all traces of gasket material from the upper and lower intake manifold and cylinder heads by carefully scraping them using a suitable gasket scraper. **Caution:** *The intake manifold components and cylinder heads are made of aluminum and are easily nicked or gouged. Do not damage the gasket surfaces or a leak may result after the work is complete. Gasket removal solvents are available from auto parts stores and may prove helpful.*

22   Using a precision straightedge and feeler gauge, check the upper and lower intake manifold gasket surfaces for warpage **(see illustration)**. Check the gasket surface on the cylinder head also. If the warpage on any surface exceeds the limits listed in this Chapter's Specifications, the discrepant component must be replaced or resurfaced by an automotive machine shop.

Installation

Refer to illustration 4.24

23   Remove the rags from the cylinder head intake passages. Use a shop vacuum to remove any contamination that may be present.

24   Install the lower intake manifold, using new gaskets. Tighten the nuts in three

stages, in the sequence shown **(see illustration)** to the torque listed in this Chapter's Specifications.

25   Install the fuel rail (see Chapter 4).

26   Install the upper intake manifold, using a new gasket. Tighten the bolts in three stages, working from the center out, to the torque listed in this Chapter's Specifications.

27   Install the EGR tube using new gaskets. Tighten the bolts to the torque listed in this Chapter's Specifications.

28   The remaining installation steps are the reverse of removal.

---

5   Exhaust manifold - removal and installation

Warning: *Allow the engine to cool completely before beginning this procedure.*

Note: *This procedure can be used to remove one or both of the exhaust manifolds as required.*

Removal

Refer to illustrations 5.3, 5.8 and 5.9

1   Disconnect the negative battery cable from the ground stud on the left shock tower (see Chapter 5, Section 1).

2   Raise the vehicle and support it securely on jackstands.

3   Remove the exhaust manifold heat shield(s) **(see illustration)**. Before attempting

2B

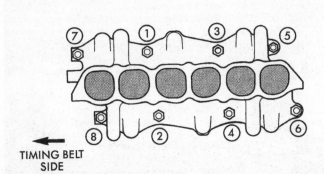

4.24 Lower intake manifold nut tightening sequence

TIMING BELT SIDE

5.3 Exhaust manifold heat shield bolts (arrows) (front exhaust manifold shown) - the upper alternator bracket must be removed to extract the upper left heat shield bolt

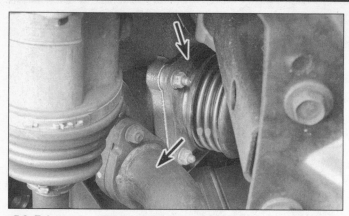

5.8 Exhaust manifold-to-exhaust system joint (upper arrow) and cross-over pipe (lower arrow)

5.9 Exhaust manifold mounting nuts (arrows) (front manifold shown, heat shield removed)

to remove the rear manifold heat shield, disconnect the oxygen sensor wiring harness at the connector. In order to remove the front manifold heat shield, the alternator upper bracket must be removed.

4   To make removal easier, apply penetrating oil to the exhaust manifold and manifold-to-pipe fasteners.

5   Working under the vehicle, remove the exhaust manifold cross-pipe.

6   Disconnect the oxygen sensor wiring harness at the connector.

7   If you are removing the rear exhaust manifold (near the firewall), remove the power steering pump bracket (see Chapter 10).

8   If you are removing the rear exhaust manifold (near the firewall), detach the exhaust system from the manifold **(see illustration)**. **Note:** *It may be necessary to remove, or partially remove, the exhaust system to facilitate rear manifold removal (see Chapter 4 if necessary).*

9   Unscrew the mounting nuts, remove the exhaust manifold and gasket **(see illustration)**.

10   Using a wire brush, clean the exhaust manifold studs, replacing any that show thread damage.

11   Using a scraper, remove all traces of gasket material from the exhaust manifold, cylinder head, and exhaust pipe mating surfaces and inspect them for wear and cracks. **Caution:** *When removing gasket material from any surface, especially aluminum, be very careful not to scratch or gouge the gasket surface. Any damage to the surface may a leak after reassembly. Gasket removal solvents are available from auto parts stores and may prove helpful.*

12   Using a precision straightedge and feeler gauge, check the exhaust manifold gasket surfaces for warpage. Check the surface on the cylinder head also. If the warpage on any surface exceeds the limits listed in this Chapter's Specifications, the exhaust manifold and/or cylinder head must be replaced or resurfaced by an automotive machine shop.

Installation

13   Install the new exhaust gasket(s) onto

6.4a To keep the crankshaft from turning, insert a large screwdriver or bar through the opening in the damper/pulley and wedge it against the engine block, then loosen the bolt with a socket and breaker bar

the cylinder head.

14   Apply Loctite No. 271 to the exhaust manifold mounting stud threads.

15   Install the manifold, washers and nuts. Tighten the nuts in three stages, working from the center out, to the torque listed in this Chapter's Specifications.

16   The remaining installation steps are the reverse of removal. Install a new gasket(s) between the exhaust manifold and exhaust pipe(s). Tighten the nuts to the torque listed in this Chapter's Specifications.

17   Run the engine and check for exhaust leaks.

6   Timing belt - removal, inspection and installation

Caution: *If the timing belt failed with the engine operating, damage to the valves may have occurred. Perform an engine compression check after belt replacement to determine if any valve damage is present.*

6.4b Remove the damper/pulley from the crankshaft

Removal

Refer to illustrations 6.4a, 6.4b, 6.6, 6.7, 6.11a, 6.11b, 6.12 and 6.13

Caution: *Do not turn the crankshaft or camshafts after the timing belt has been removed, as this will damage the valves from contact with the pistons. Do not try to turn the crankshaft with the camshaft sprocket bolt(s) and do not rotate the crankshaft counterclockwise as viewed from the timing belt end of the engine.*

Note: *In order to perform this procedure, a special tool is required to properly tension the timing belt. The manufacturers tool number is "MD 998767" and may be available from a dealership parts department or directly from Miller Special Tools (phone no. 800-801-5420).*

1   Position the number one piston at Top Dead Center (see Chapter 2C).

2   Disconnect the negative battery cable from the ground stud on the left shock tower (see Chapter 5, Section 1).

3   Remove the drivebelts (see Chapter 1).

4   Loosen the large bolt in the center of the crankshaft damper/pulley. It might be very tight, to break it loose insert a large screwdriver or bar through the opening in the pulley to keep the crankshaft stationary, then

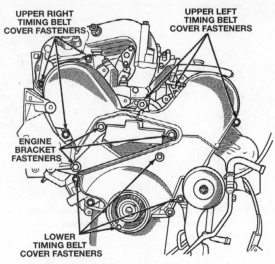

6.6 Timing belt cover bolt locations

6.7 Remove the bolts (arrows) that attach the timing belt lower cover to the engine

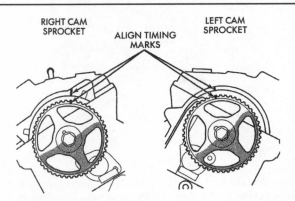

6.11a Verify that the camshaft sprocket timing marks are aligned with their respective marks on the rear timing belt covers

6.11b Crankshaft timing belt sprocket and oil pump housing timing marks (arrows)

2B

loosen the bolt with a socket and breaker bar. Remove the bolt, washer and damper/pulley from the crankshaft **(see illustrations)**.

5 After removing the crankshaft pulley, reinstall the crankshaft bolt using an appropriate spacer (this will enable you to turn the crankshaft later).

6 Remove the upper-left timing belt cover **(see illustration)**.

7 Remove the lower timing belt cover **(see illustration)**.

8 Detach the power steering pump bracket from the engine (see Chapter 10 if necessary).

9 Remove the upper-right timing belt cover **(see illustration 6.6)**.

10 Remove the right (passenger side) engine mount and the mounting bracket from the engine (see Section 17). **Note:** *Make sure the engine is supported with a floor jack placed under the oil pan. Place a wood block on the jack head to prevent the floor jack from denting or damaging the oil pan.*

11 Make sure the timing marks on the crankshaft sprocket and camshaft sprockets align with their respective marks before removing the timing belt **(see illustrations)**.

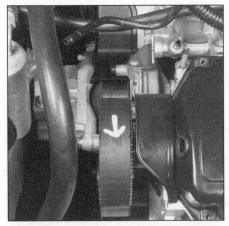

6.12 Paint an arrow on the timing belt in the direction of rotation (clockwise) so it may be reinstalled in the same direction

12 If you plan to reuse the timing belt, paint an arrow on it to indicate the direction of rotation (clockwise) **(see illustration)**.

13 Loosen the timing belt tensioner mounting bolts and then remove the tensioner **(see illustration)**. **Note:** *The tensioner piston will*

6.13 Timing belt tensioner mounting bolts (arrows)

extend when the assembly is removed.

14 Carefully slip the timing belt off the sprockets and set it aside. If you plan to reuse the timing belt, place it in a plastic bag - do not allow the belt to come in contact with any type of oil or water as this will greatly shorten belt life.

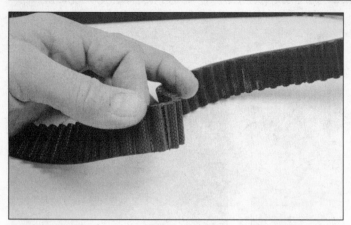

6.18 Carefully inspect the timing belt for damage or wear - bending it backwards will often make defects more apparent

6.22 Binder clips (arrows) can be used to retain the timing belt in position on the camshaft sprockets during installation

6.24 Using a vise (lined with soft-jaws), compress the timing belt tensioner piston until the holes in the housing and piston align. Then place a small Allen wrench (arrow) or drill bit, through the holes to keep the piston in position for installation

6.25 Using special tool MD 998767 attached to a torque wrench, apply 39 in-lbs of torque (in a counterclockwise direction) to the tensioner pulley, then move the tensioner unit up against the tensioner pulley bracket and tighten the tensioner mounting bolts to the torque listed in this Chapter's Specifications

Inspection

Refer to illustration 6.18

15   With the timing belt covers removed, now is a good time to inspect the front crankshaft and camshaft seals for leakage. If leakage is evident, replace the them (see Section 7 and 8, respectively).

16   Inspect the water pump for evidence of leakage (usually indicated by a trail of wet or dried coolant). Check the pulley for excessive radial play and bearing roughness. Replace if necessary (see Chapter 3).

17   Rotate the tensioner pulley and idler pulley by hand and move them side-to-side to detect bearing roughness and/or excessive play. Visually inspect all timing belt sprockets for any signs of damage or wear. Replace as necessary.

18   Inspect the timing belt for cracks, separation, wear, missing teeth and oil contamination **(see illustration)**. Replace the belt if it's in questionable condition or the engine mileage is close to that referenced in the *Maintenance Schedule* (see Chapter 1).

19   Check the timing belt tensioner unit for leaks or any other obvious damage, replace if necessary.

Installation

Refer to illustrations 6.22, 6.24, 6.25 and 6.27

20   Confirm that the timing marks on both camshaft sprockets are aligned with their respective marks on the rear timing belt covers **(see illustration 6.11a)**. Reposition the camshafts if required. **Caution:** *If it is necessary to rotate the camshafts to align the timing marks, first rotate the crankshaft slightly counterclockwise (three notches on the sprocket) to ensure the valves do not contact the pistons.*

21   Position the crankshaft sprocket with the timing marks aligned **(see illustration 6.11b)**.

22   Install the timing belt as follows; first place the belt onto the right camshaft sprocket (the one towards the rear of the vehicle) and clamp it to the sprocket, while maintaining tension on the belt, wrap it under the water pump pulley and place it onto the left sprocket camshaft sprocket. Secure the timing belt to the left camshaft sprocket **(see illustration)**. Continue to wrap the timing belt over the idler pulley, around the crankshaft sprocket and finishing with the tensioner pulley. Remove the clamps from the camshaft

sprockets.

23   Make sure the timing belt is tight between the left camshaft sprocket and the crankshaft sprocket, all the slack is at the tensioner pulley and all the timing marks are aligned.

24   Before installation, the timing belt tensioner piston must be compressed into the tensioner housing. Place the tensioner in a vise so the surface with the pin hole is facing up. Slowly compress the tensioner using the vise, then install an appropriate size Allen wrench or drill bit through the body and into the piston to retain the piston in this position **(see illustration)**. Remove the tensioner from the vise.

25   Using the special tool "MD 998767" engaged in the tensioner pulley, have an assistant apply 39 in-lbs of torque in a counterclockwise direction **(see illustration)**.

26   With the torque applied to the tensioner pulley, install the tensioner assembly. Move the tensioner up against the tensioner pulley bracket and tighten the mounting bolts to the torque listed in this Chapter's Specifications. Remove the torque wrench and special tool from the tensioner pulley.

6.27 If the timing belt tension is set correctly, the tensioner piston retaining pin (arrow) (an Allen wrench in this case) can be removed and installed easily

7.2 After removing the timing belt sprocket, remove the Woodruff key (arrow) from the crankshaft

7.3 Using a hooked tool or screwdriver, carefully pry the crankshaft front seal out of its bore - DO NOT nick or scratch the crankshaft or seal bore

27   Remove the Allen wrench or drill bit retaining the piston from the tensioner. The timing belt tension is correct when the tensioner piston retaining pin (Allen wrench or drill bit) can be withdrawn and reinserted easily **(see illustration)**. Verify that the timing marks on the camshaft sprockets and crankshaft sprocket are still aligned with their respective timing marks **(see illustrations 6.11a and 6.11b)**.
28   Using the bolt in the center of the crankshaft sprocket, slowly turn the crankshaft clockwise two complete revolutions. **Caution:** *If you feel strong resistance while turning the crankshaft - STOP, the valves may be hitting the pistons from incorrect valve timing. Stop and re-check the valve timing.* **Note:** *The camshafts and crankshaft sprocket marks will align every two revolutions of the crankshaft.* Recheck the alignment of the timing marks **(see illustrations 6.11a and 6.11b)**. If the marks do not align properly, remove the timing belt tensioner, slip the belt off the camshaft sprockets, realign the marks, reinstall the belt and tensioner, then check the alignment again.
29   After crankshaft rotation, recheck the timing belt tension by inserting the tensioner piston retaining pin (Allen wrench or drill bit) back into the tensioner. If the retaining pin cannot be inserted and withdrawn freely, readjust the timing belt tension and repeat Steps 24 through 29.
30   The remaining installation steps are the reverse of removal. Tighten the crankshaft damper/pulley bolt to the torque listed in this Chapter's Specifications.

7   Crankshaft front oil seal - replacement

Refer to illustrations 7.2, 7.3 and 7.5
Caution: *Do not rotate the camshafts or crankshaft when the timing belt is removed or damage to the engine may occur.*

1   Remove the timing belt (see Section 6).
2   Remove the crankshaft timing belt sprocket using a gear puller. Remove the Woodruff key from the crankshaft keyway **(see illustration)**.
3   Wrap the tip of a small screwdriver with vinyl tape. Carefully use the screwdriver to pry the seal out of its bore **(see illustration)**. Take care to prevent damaging the oil pump assembly, the crankshaft and the seal bore.
4   Thoroughly clean and inspect the seal bore and sealing surface on the crankshaft. Minor imperfections can be removed with fine emery cloth. If there is a groove worn in the crankshaft sealing surface (from contact with the seal), installing a new seal will probably not stop the leak.
5   Lubricate the new seal with engine oil and using a hammer and the appropriate size socket, drive the seal into the bore until it's flush with the oil pump housing **(see illustration)**.
6   Install the Woodruff key into the slot in the crankshaft. Place the crankshaft timing belt sprocket onto the crankshaft with the timing belt retaining lip facing inward (toward the engine).
7   The remaining installation steps are the reverse of removal. Tighten the crankshaft pulley bolt to the torque listed in this Chapter's Specifications.
8   Start the engine and check for oil leaks.

8   Camshaft oil seal - replacement

Refer to illustrations 8.3, 8.4, 8.6a and 8.6b
Caution: *Do not rotate the camshafts or crankshaft when the timing belt is removed or damage to the engine may occur.*
1   Remove the timing belt (see Section 6).
2   Rotate the crankshaft counterclockwise until the crankshaft sprocket is three notches BTDC. This will prevent engine damage if the camshaft sprocket is inadvertently rotated during removal.
3   While keeping the camshaft from rotat-

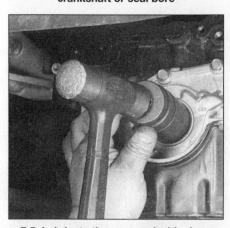

7.5 Lubricate the new seal with clean engine oil and drive it into place using a hammer and socket

8.3 To hold the camshaft while removing the sprocket bolt, use an old piece of timing belt wrapped around the sprocket and a chain wrench as shown

ing, remove the camshaft sprocket bolt. Then using two large screwdrivers, lever the sprocket off the camshaft. **Note:** *A strap-type damper/pulley holder tool is available at most auto parts stores and is recommended for*

2B

8.4 Using a hooked tool or screwdriver, carefully pry the camshaft seal out of the bore - DO NOT nick or scratch the camshaft or seal bore

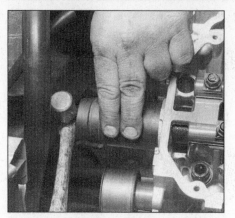

8.6a Using a hammer and the appropriate size socket, drive the camshaft seal into the bore until it is flush with the cylinder head

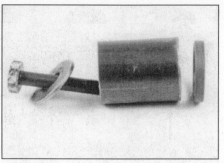

8.6b If the space is too confined to use a hammer to drive the seal in place, fabricate a tool using a bolt, washer and section of pipe. Place the section of pipe over the seal and thread the bolt into the camshaft to press the seal into the bore

this procedure, however, if you are not going to reuse the old timing belt, you can wrap a piece of it around the sprocket and use a chain wrench to hold the sprocket in place as shown **(see illustration)**.

4   Carefully pry out the camshaft oil seal using a small hooked tool or screwdriver **(see illustration)**. Don't scratch the bore or damage the camshaft in the process (if the camshaft is damaged, the new seal will end up leaking).

5   Clean the bore and coat the outer edge of the new seal with engine oil or multi-purpose grease. Also lubricate the seal lip.

6   Using a socket with an outside diameter slightly smaller than the outside diameter of the seal and a hammer **(see illustration)**, carefully drive the new seal into the cylinder head until it's flush with the face of the cylinder head. If a socket isn't available, a short section of pipe will also work. **Note:** If engine location makes it difficult to use a hammer to install the camshaft seal, fabricate a seal installation tool from a piece of pipe cut to the appropriate length, a bolt and a large washer **(see illustration)**. Place the section of pipe over the seal and thread the bolt into the camshaft. The seal can now be pressed into the bore by tightening the bolt.

7   Install the camshaft sprocket, aligning the pin in the camshaft with the hole in the sprocket. Using an appropriate tool to hold the camshaft sprocket, tighten the camshaft sprocket bolt to the torque listed in this Chapter's Specifications.

8   Install the timing belt (see Section 6).

9   Run the engine and check for oil leaks.

9   Rocker arm and hydraulic valve lash adjuster assembly - removal, inspection and installation

Removal

1   Disconnect the negative battery cable from the ground stud on the left shock tower

(see Chapter 5, Section 1).

2   Position the number one piston at Top Dead Center (see Chapter 2C).

3   Remove the valve cover(s) as required (see Section 3).

4   Prior to removing the rocker arm shafts, identify each rocker arm and shaft as to its proper location (cylinder number and intake or exhaust). **Caution:** Do not interchange the rocker arms onto a different shaft or shaft assemblies onto a different location as this could lead to premature wear.

5   Loosen the rocker arm shaft bolts 1/4-turn at a time, until they can be loosened by hand, in the reverse order of the tightening sequence **(see illustration 9.17)**. Completely loosen the bolts, but do not remove them, leaving them in place will prevent the assembly from falling apart when it is lifted off the cylinder head.

6   Lift the rocker arms and shaft assemblies from the cylinder head and set them on the workbench. **Note:** The hydraulic valve lash adjusters may become dislodged from the rocker arms during shaft removal. If required, secure the adjusters in place with vinyl tape.

7   Disassemble the rocker arm shaft components paying close attention to their positions. **Note:** To keep the rocker arms and related parts in order, it's a good idea to remove them and put them onto two lengths of wire (such as unbent coat hangers) in the same order as they're removed, marking each wire (which simulates the rocker shaft) as to which end would be the front of the engine.

Inspection

Refer to illustration 9.8

Note: The valve lash adjuster is an integral part of each rocker arm and cannot be replaced separately. If defective, both must be replaced.

8   Visually check the rocker arms for excessive wear or damage **(see illustration)**. Replace them if evidence of wear or damage is found.

9   Inspect each lash adjuster carefully for

signs of wear and damage, particularly on the surface that contacts the valve tip. Use a small diameter wire to check the oil holes for restrictions.

10   Since the lash adjusters frequently become clogged, we recommend replacing the rocker arm/lash adjuster assembly if you're concerned about their condition or if the engine is exhibiting valve "tapping" noises.

11   Inspect all rocker arm shaft components. Look for cracks, worn or scored surfaces or other damage. Replace any parts found to be damaged or worn excessively.

Installation

Refer to illustrations 9.14 and 9.17

12   Prior to installation, the lash adjusters must be partially full of engine oil - indicated by little or no plunger action when the adjuster is depressed. If there's excessive plunger travel, place the rocker arm assembly into clean engine oil and pump the plunger until the plunger travel is eliminated. **Note:** If the plunger still travels within the rocker arm when full of oil it's defective and the rocker arm assembly must be replaced.

13   Install the rocker arms (and springs - intake shafts only) onto the shafts, making sure they are reinstalled in their original locations.

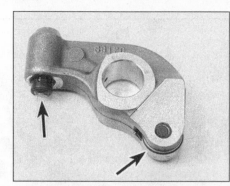

9.8 Visually inspect the hydraulic lash adjuster and roller (arrows) for damage and excessive play - check the rocker arm shaft bore for score marks or excessive wear

9.14 The intake rocker arm shaft springs (arrows) must be installed as shown

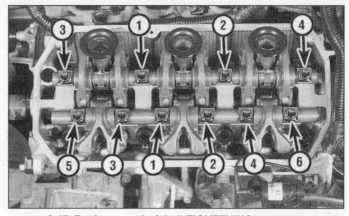

9.17 Rocker arm shaft bolt TIGHTENING sequence

14 On the intake rocker arm shafts, make sure that the springs are installed on the shaft in the correct locations (see illustration).

15 On the right (rear) cylinder head, install the rocker arm assemblies with the flat at the end of each rocker arm shaft located at the timing belt end of the engine and positioned toward their respective valves.

16 On the left (front) cylinder head, install the rocker arm assemblies with the flat at the end of each rocker arm shaft located at the transaxle end of the engine and positioned toward their respective valves.

17 Tighten the rocker arm shaft bolts in sequence shown (see illustration) in three steps to the torque listed in this Chapter's Specifications.

18 The remaining installation steps are the reverse of removal. Run the engine and check for oil leaks and proper operation.

19 When re-starting the engine after replacing the rocker arm/lash adjusters, the adjusters will normally make "tapping" noises due to air in the lubrication system. To bleed air from the lash adjusters, start the engine and allow it to reach operating temperature, slowly raise the speed of the engine from idle to 3,000 rpm and back to idle over a one minute period. If, after several attempts, the adjuster(s) do not become silent, replace the defective rocker arm/lash adjuster assembly.

10 Camshafts - removal, inspection and installation

Note: *The camshaft(s) cannot be removed with the cylinder head(s) installed on the engine.*

Removal

Refer to illustration 10.5

1 Remove the rocker arm shaft assemblies (see Section 9).

2 If you are removing the camshaft in the right (rear) cylinder head, remove the distributor (see Chapter 5).

3 Remove the cylinder head (see Section 12).

4 On the right cylinder head, carefully withdraw the camshaft from the distributor opening in the rear of the cylinder head. **Caution:** *Do not damage the camshaft lobes or bearing journals during removal.* **Note:** *If you are removing both camshafts, identify each one as it is removed from the cylinder head so that it may be installed back in it's original location.*

5 On the left (front) cylinder head, remove the thrust case from the rear of the cylinder head and withdraw the camshaft (see illustration). **Caution:** *Do not damage the camshaft lobes or bearing journals during removal.*

6 Remove the camshaft seal(s) from the cylinder head(s) (see Section 8 if necessary).

Inspection

Refer to illustration 10.10

7 Using a suitable scraper, remove all traces of gasket material from all gasket surfaces. **Caution:** *When removing gasket material from any surface, especially aluminum, be very careful not to scratch or gouge the gasket surface. Any damage to the surface may a leak after reassembly. Gasket removal solvents are available from auto parts stores and may prove helpful.*

8 Thoroughly clean the camshaft(s) with a rag soaked in lacquer thinner or acetone. Visually inspect the camshaft(s) for wear and/or damage to the lobe surfaces, bearing journals and seal contact surfaces. Visually inspect the camshaft bearing surfaces in the cylinder head(s) for scoring and other damage. Cylinder head replacement may be necessary if the camshaft bearing surfaces in the head are damaged or excessively worn.

9 Replace any component that fails the above inspections.

10 Using a micrometer, check the camshaft lobes for excessive wear by measuring the center of the lobe (the area the rocker arm roller rides on) and comparing it with the edges of the lobes (the area the rocker arm

2B

10.5 On the left (front) cylinder head, remove the thrust cover and carefully withdraw the camshaft

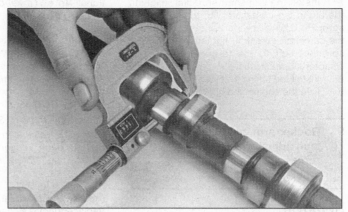

10.10 Check the camshaft lobes for wear with a micrometer

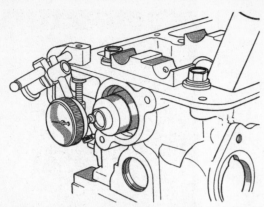

10.13 Measure the camshaft endplay with a dial indicator positioned on the sprocket end of the camshaft as shown

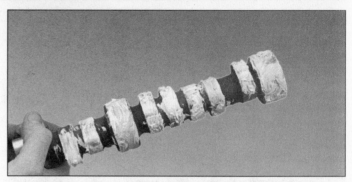

10.15 Prior to installing the camshaft, lubricate the bearing journals, thrust surfaces and lobes with engine assembly lube or clean engine oil

11.5 This is what the air hose adapter that threads into the spark plug hole looks like - they're readily available from auto parts stores

11.7 Use a small magnet (shown) or needle-nose pliers to remove the valve spring keepers - be careful not to drop them down into the engine!

roller does not ride on) **(see illustration)**. If any wear is indicated, check the corresponding rocker arm, replace the camshaft and rocker arms if necessary.

Camshaft endplay measurement

Refer to illustration 10.13

11   Lubricate the camshaft(s) and cylinder head bearing journals with clean engine oil.

12   Carefully insert the camshaft into the cylinder head and install the thrust case or distributor as applicable. Tighten the bolts to the torque listed in this Chapter's Specifications.

13   Install a dial indicator set up on the cylinder head and place the indicator tip on the camshaft at the sprocket end **(see illustration)**.

14   Using a screwdriver, carefully pry the camshaft to the rear of the cylinder head until it stops. Zero the dial indicator and pry the camshaft forward. The amount of indicator travel is the camshaft endplay. Compare the endplay measurement with the tolerance listed in this Chapter's Specifications. If the endplay is excessive, check the camshaft and cylinder head thrust bearing surfaces for wear and replace components as necessary.

Installation

Refer to illustration 10.15

15   Very carefully clean the camshaft and

bearing journals. Liberally coat the bearing journals, lobes and thrust bearing surfaces of the camshaft with engine assembly lube or engine oil **(see illustration)**.

16   Carefully insert the camshaft into the cylinder head. On the left side cylinder head, install the thrust case, using a new O-ring, and tighten the bolts to the torque listed in this Chapter's Specifications.

17   Install a new camshaft oil seal in the cylinder head (see Section 8).

18   Inspect the cylinder head bolts and install the cylinder head(s) (see Section 12). Torque the cylinder head bolts as described in Section 12.

19   If removed, install the distributor using a new O-ring (see Chapter 5). Tighten the mounting nuts to the torque listed in the Chapter 5 Specifications.

20   The remaining installation steps are the reverse of removal. Start the engine and check for leaks and proper operation.

11   Valve springs, retainers and seals - replacement

Refer to illustrations 11.5, 11.7, 11.8, 11.13 and 11.15

Note: *Broken valve springs and defective*

valve stem seals can be replaced without removing the cylinder heads. Two special tools and a compressed air source are normally required to perform this operation, so read through this Section carefully and rent or buy the tools before beginning the job.

1   Remove the appropriate valve cover (see Section 3).

2   Remove the rocker arm assemblies (see Section 9).

3   Remove the spark plugs from that head (see Chapter 1 if necessary).

4   Turn the crankshaft until the piston in the affected cylinder is at Top Dead Center on the compression stroke (refer to Chapter 2C). If you're replacing all of the valve stem seals, begin with cylinder number one and work on the valves for one cylinder at a time. Move from cylinder-to-cylinder following the firing order sequence (see this Chapter's Specifications).

5   Thread an adapter into the spark plug hole **(see illustration)** and connect an air hose from a compressed air source to it. Most auto parts stores can supply the air hose adapter. **Note:** *Many cylinder compression gauges utilize a screw-in fitting that may work with your air hose quick-disconnect fitting.*

6   Apply compressed air to the cylinder. **Warning:** *The piston may be forced down by*

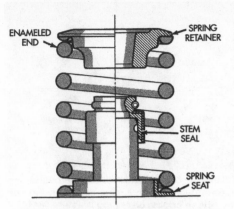

11.8 Cut-away view of the valve seal and spring components

11.13 Gently tap the new seal onto the valve guide with a hammer and deep socket

11.15 Apply a small dab of grease to each keeper before installation to hold it in place on the valve stem until the spring is released

compressed air, causing the crankshaft to turn suddenly. If the wrench used when positioning the number one piston at TDC is still attached to the crankshaft pulley bolt, it could cause damage or injury when the crankshaft moves.

7   Stuff clean shop rags into the cylinder head holes above and below the valves to prevent parts and tools from falling into the engine, then use a valve spring compressor tool to compress the spring. Remove the keepers with small needle-nose pliers or a magnet **(see illustration)**.

8   Remove the spring retainer and valve spring. Next, using pliers remove the valve guide seal and then lift off spring seat **(see illustration)**. **Caution:** *If air pressure fails to hold the valve in the closed position during this operation, the valve face and/or seat is probably damaged. If so, the cylinder head will have to be removed for additional repair operations.*

9   Wrap a rubber band or tape around the top of the valve stem so the valve won't fall into the combustion chamber, then release the air pressure.

10   Inspect the valve stem for damage. Rotate the valve in the guide and check the end for eccentric movement, which would indicate that the valve is bent.

11   Move the valve up-and-down in the guide and make sure it doesn't bind. If the valve stem binds, either the valve is bent or the guide is damaged. In either case, the head will have to be removed for repair.

12   Pull up on the valve stem to close the valve, reapply air pressure to the cylinder to retain the valve in the closed position, then remove the tape or rubber band from the valve stem.

13   Install the valve spring seat. Lubricate the valve stem with clean engine oil and place the new valve guide seal. Tap it into place with deep socket **(see illustration)**.

14   Install the spring in position over the valve.

15   Install the valve spring retainer. Compress the valve spring and carefully position the keepers in the groove. Apply a small dab of grease to the inside of each keeper to hold

it in place if necessary **(see illustration)**.

16   Remove the pressure from the spring tool and make sure the keepers are seated.

17   Disconnect the air hose and remove the adapter from the spark plug hole. Repeat the procedure for any other defective valves.

18   Install the rocker arm assemblies (see Section 9).

19   Install the spark plug and connect the wire(s).

20   Install the valve cover (see Section 3).

21   Start and run the engine, then check for oil leaks and unusual sounds coming from the valve cover area.

12   Cylinder head - removal and installation

Caution: *Allow the engine to cool completely before beginning this procedure.*

Removal

Refer to illustrations 12.11, 12.18, 12.19a and 12.19b

1   Disconnect the negative battery cable from the ground stud on the left shock tower (see Chapter 5, Section 1).

2   Position the number one piston at Top Dead Center (see Chapter 2C).

3   Remove the upper and lower intake manifolds (see Section 4).

4   Drain the cooling system, remove the spark plugs and spark plug wires (see Chapter 1). **Note:** *Leave the plug wires attached to the distributor cap.*

5   If you are removing the right (rear) cylinder head, remove the distributor (see Chapter 5).

6   Remove the thermostat housing from the rear of the cylinder heads (see Chapter 3).

7   Remove rocker arm shaft assemblies (see Section 9).

8   If you are removing the right (rear) cylinder head, remove the bolts securing the power steering reservoir and hoses to the cylinder head and position them out of the

way (see Chapter 10).

9   Disconnect the power steering pump bracket from the engine (see Chapter 10).

10   Remove the exhaust manifold(s) (see Section 5).

11   If you are removing the left (front) cylinder head, remove the EGR solenoid/transducer assembly and EGR valve from the rear of the cylinder head **(see illustration)**.

12   Remove the timing belt (see Section 6).

13   Remove camshaft sprocket(s) (see Section 8).

14   Clearly label and disconnect any hoses, lines, brackets or electrical connections that may interfere with cylinder head removal.

15   Loosen the cylinder head bolts, 1/4-turn at a time, in the *reverse* order of the tightening sequence **(see illustration 12.24)** until they can be removed by hand.

16   Carefully lift the cylinder head straight up and place it on wood blocks to prevent damage to the sealing surfaces. If the head sticks to the engine block, dislodge it by placing a wood block against the head cast-

12.11 EGR solenoid/transducer assembly (upper arrow) and EGR valve (lower arrow) - remove the EGR solenoid/transducer and engine lifting bracket as an assembly

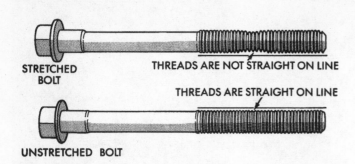

12.18 Place a precision straightedge along the cylinder head bolt thread profile as shown, if any part of the bolt threads are not on the straightedge, the bolt is stretched and must be replaced

12.19a Checking the cylinder head-to-engine block gasket surface for warpage

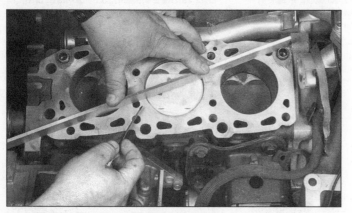

12.19b Checking the engine block head gasket surface for warpage

12.22 When installing the head gasket onto the block, make sure all passages in the block align with the holes in the gasket

ing and tapping the wood with a hammer or by prying the head with a prybar placed carefully on a casting protrusion. **Note:** *If further disassembly of the cylinder head is required, refer to Part C of this Chapter.*

17   Remove all traces of old gasket material from the block and head. Special gasket removal solvents that soften gaskets and make removal much easier are available at auto parts stores. **Caution:** *The cylinder head is aluminum, be very careful not to gouge the sealing surfaces.* When working on the block, place clean shop rags into the cylinders to help keep out debris. Use a vacuum to remove any contamination from the engine. Use a tap of the correct size to chase the threads in the engine block. Clean and inspect all threaded fasteners for damage.

18   Inspect the cylinder head bolt threads for "necking," where the diameter of threads narrow due to bolt stretching **(see illustration)**. If any cylinder head bolt exhibits damage or necking, it must be replaced.

19   Using a precision straightedge and feeler gauge, check all gasket surfaces for warpage **(see illustrations)**. If the warpage on any surface exceeds the limits listed in this Chapter's Specifications, the discrepant component must be replaced or resurfaced by an automotive machine shop.

20   Refer to Part C of this Chapter for cleaning and inspection of the cylinder head.

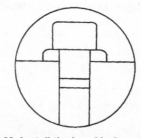

12.23 Install the head bolt washers as shown

Installation

Refer to illustrations 12.22, 12.23 and 12.24

21   Install the camshaft(s) if removed (see Section 10).

22   Place a new gasket on the engine block **(see illustration)**. Use no sealer unless indicated by the gasket manufacturer. Note any directions printed on the gasket such as "Front" or "This side up." Place the cylinder head(s) in position on the engine block.

23   Install the washers onto the cylinder head bolts as shown **(see illustration)**. Apply clean engine oil to the cylinder head bolt threads and install them into the cylinder head.

24   Tighten the cylinder head bolts in the sequence shown **(see illustration)** progress-

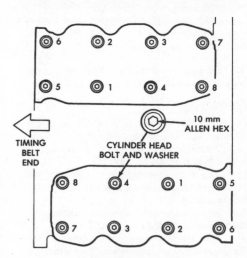

12.24 Cylinder head bolt TIGHTENING sequence

ing in three stages to the torque listed in this Chapter's Specifications.

25   The remaining installation steps are the reverse of removal.

26   Refill the cooling system and check all fluid levels (see Chapter 1 if necessary).

27   Start the engine and let it run until normal operating temperature is reached. Check for leaks and proper operation.

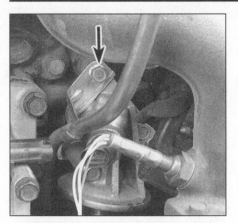

13.5 Engine oil dipstick tube mounting bolt (arrow) - exhaust manifold heat shield removed for clarity

13.10 If the pan is stuck, tap it with a soft-face hammer or place a wood block against the pan and tap the wood block with a hammer to jar it loose

13.11a Lower the front of the oil pan to access the oil pump pick-up tube and remove the mounting bolts . . .

2B

13.11b . . . then remove the oil pump pick up tube from the pump body

13.12 With the oil pump pick up tube removed, the oil pan can then be withdrawn over the engine support module (arrow)

13 Oil pan - removal and installation

Removal

Refer to illustrations 13.5, 13.10, 13.11a, 13.11b, 13.12, 13.13a and 13.13b

1   Disconnect the negative battery cable from the ground stud on the left shock tower (see Chapter 5, Section 1).
2   Raise the vehicle and support it securely on jackstands.
3   Remove the accessory drivebelt splash shield (see Chapter 1).
4   Drain the engine oil (see Chapter 1).
5   Remove the dipstick tube **(see illustration)**.
6   Remove the starter motor (see Chapter 5).
7   Remove the engine-to-transmission support brackets.
8   Remove the exhaust manifold crossover pipe (see Section 5).
9   Remove the transaxle inspection cover.
10   Remove the mounting bolts and separate the oil pan from the engine block enough to facilitate oil pump pickup tube removal. If the pan is stuck, tap it with a soft-face hammer **(see illustration)** or place a wood block

13.13a Thoroughly clean the oil pan and engine block gasket surfaces with a scraper to remove all traces of old gasket material

against the pan and tap the wood block with a hammer. **Caution:** *If you're wedging something between the oil pan and the engine block to separate them, be extremely careful not to gouge or nick the gasket surface of either part; an oil leak could result.*
11   Remove the oil pump pickup tube and

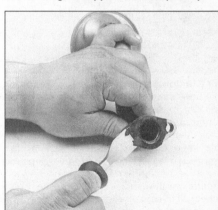

13.13b Remove the old gasket from the oil pump pick up tube

screen assembly **(see illustrations)**.
12   Remove the oil pan from the vehicle **(see illustration)**.
13   Thoroughly clean all gasket sealing surfaces. Use a scraper to remove all traces of old gasket material **(see illustrations)**. Gasket removal solvents are available at auto parts stores and may prove helpful. Check the oil pan sealing surface for distortion.

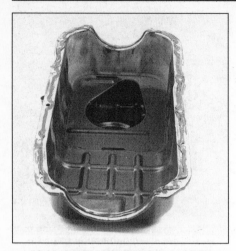

13.14 Apply a 1/8-inch bead of RTV sealant to the oil pan sealing surface as shown - stay on the inside of the bolt holes

Straighten or replace as necessary. After cleaning and straightening (if necessary), wipe the gasket surfaces of the pan and block clean with a rag soaked in lacquer thinner or acetone.

Installation

Refer to illustration 13.14

14   Apply a 1/8-inch bead of RTV sealant to the oil pan as shown **(see illustration)**. Also apply a light coating of RTV sealant to the underside of the oil pan bolt heads.

15   Place the oil pan into position under the engine block and install the oil pump pick-up tube. Tighten the bolts to the torque listed in this Chapter's Specifications.

16   Place the oil pan against the engine block and install the bolts. Working from the center and proceeding outward in a criss-cross pattern, tighten the oil pan bolts to the torque listed in this Chapter's Specifications.

17   The remaining installation steps are the reverse of removal.

18   Lower the vehicle and fill the crankcase with the proper quantity and grade of engine oil (see *Recommended lubricants and fluids* at the beginning of Chapter 1) and run the engine, checking for leaks. Road test the vehicle and check for leaks again.

14   Oil pump - removal, inspection and installation

Removal

Refer to illustrations 14.7, 14.8, 14.9 and 14.10

1   Disconnect the negative battery cable from the ground stud on the left shock tower (see Chapter 5, Section 1).

2   Raise the vehicle and support it securely on jackstands.

3   Remove the drivebelts (see Chapter 1).

4   Remove the timing belt (see Section 6) and crankshaft sprocket and Woodruff key (see Section 7).

5   Remove the oil pan (see Section 13).

6   If equipped, remove the air conditioning compressor bracket from the engine and position it out of the way.

7   Remove the bolts and detach the oil pump assembly from the engine **(see illustration)**. **Caution:** *If the pump doesn't come off by hand, tap it gently with a soft-faced hammer or pry on a casting boss.*

8   Remove the oil filter passage O-ring

14.7 Remove the oil pump assembly mounting bolts (arrows) and detach it from the engine - bolt (A) also secures the air conditioning compressor bracket (if equipped)

14.8 The oil filter passage O-ring seals (arrows) may remained attached to the engine block

14.9 Remove the rotor cover mounting screws (arrows)

14.10 The alignment mark has worn off the inner rotor on this oil pump; in this case we'll use a permanent marker to match-mark the rotors for reinstallation - oil pressure relief cap bolt (A)

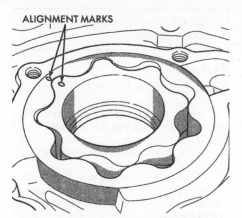

14.16a Install the rotors into the oil pump body with the match marks aligned

14.16b Use a feeler gauge to measure the inner rotor-to-outer rotor lobe clearance

14.16c Measuring the outer rotor-to-pump body clearance

seals and discard them. They may stick to the engine block as shown **(see illustration)** or remain in the oil pump housing.

9 Remove the oil pump rotor cover **(see illustration)**.

10 New rotors are manufactured with arrows on them which are aligned at installation. If both arrows are not clearly visible **(see illustration)**, use a permanent marker to match-mark the rotors so they can be installed back in their original position. Remove the inner and outer rotor from the body. **Caution:** *Be very careful with these components. Close tolerances are critical in creating the correct oil pressure. Any nicks or other damage will require replacement of the complete pump assembly.*

11 Using a hammer and drift, carefully and evenly drive the crankshaft front seal from the oil pump housing and discard it.

12 Disassemble the oil pressure relief valve assembly, taking note of the way the relief valve piston is installed. Unscrew the cap bolt and remove the bolt, washer, spring and relief valve **(see illustration 14.10)**.

13 Thoroughly clean all gasket sealing surfaces. Use a scraper to remove all traces of old gasket material. Gasket removal solvents

are available at auto parts stores and may prove helpful. Check the oil pan sealing surface for distortion. Straighten or replace as necessary. After removing the residual gasket material, wipe the gasket surfaces of the oil pan and block clean with a rag soaked in lacquer thinner or acetone.

Inspection

Refer to illustrations 14.16a, 14.16b, 14.16c, and 14.16d

14 Clean all oil pump components with solvent and inspect them for excessive wear and/or damage. Replace as required. **Note:** *If either rotor is damaged, they must be replaced as a set.*

15 Inspect the oil pressure relief valve piston sliding surface and valve spring for damage. **Note:** *If either the spring or the valve is damaged, they must be replaced as a set.*

16 Install the rotors into the pump housing with the match-marks aligned **(see illustration)**. Check the oil pump rotor clearances using a precision straightedge and feeler gauges **(see illustrations)**. Compare the results to the tolerances listed in this Chapter's Specifications. Replace both rotors if any clearance is out of tolerance.

Installation

Refer to illustration 14.19

17 Lubricate the relief valve piston, piston bore and spring with clean engine oil. Install the relief valve piston into the bore maintaining original orientation followed by the spring and cap bolt. Tighten the cap bolt to the torque listed in this Chapter's Specifications. **Note:** *If the relief valve piston is installed incorrectly, serious engine damage could occur.*

18 Lubricate the oil pump rotor recess in the housing and the inner and outer rotors with clean engine oil. Install the rotors into the pump housing with the match-marks aligned **(see illustration 14.16a)**. Next, fill the rotor cavity with clean engine oil and install the cover. Tighten the cover screws to the torque listed in this Chapter's Specifications.

19 Install new O-ring seals in the oil pump passages located on the pump body **(see illustration)**. If necessary, apply a light coating of grease on the O-rings to hold them in place.

20 Install the new crankshaft front seal into the oil pump housing (see Section 7).

21 Apply a 1/8 inch bead of anaerobic sealant to the oil pump body sealing surface,

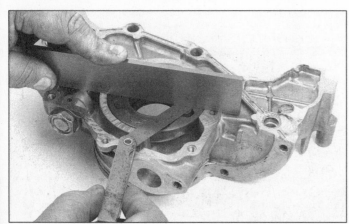

14.16d Place a precision straightedge over the rotors and measure the clearance between the rotors and the straightedge to determine the rotor-to-cover clearance

14.19 Install new O-ring seals on the oil filter passages (arrows)

15.5 Remove the flywheel/driveplate from the crankshaft

16.3 Carefully pry the crankshaft seal out of the bore - DO NOT nick or scratch the crankshaft or seal bore

and position the pump assembly on the block aligning the inner rotor and crankshaft drive flats. Install the mounting bolts.

22   If equipped, install the air conditioning bracket onto the engine (one bolt secures both the air conditioning bracket and the oil pump housing).

23   Tighten the oil pump attaching bolts **(see illustration 14.7)** to the torque listed in this Chapter's Specifications.

24   Install the Woodruff key, crankshaft timing belt sprocket (see Section 7) and timing belt (see Section 6).

25   Install the oil pan (see Section 13).

26   If applicable, install a new oil filter (see Chapter 1).

27   The remaining installation steps are the reverse of removal.

28   Lower the vehicle and fill the crankcase with the proper quantity and grade of oil (see *Recommended lubricants and fluids* Section in Chapter 1).

29   Connect the negative battery cable to the ground stud.

30   After the sealant has cured per the manufacturer's directions, start the engine and check for leaks.

15   Driveplate - removal and installation

Removal

Refer to illustration 15.5

1   Raise the vehicle and support it securely on jackstands.

2   Remove the transaxle assembly (see Chapter 7).

3   To ensure correct alignment during reinstallation, match-mark the backing plate and driveplate to the crankshaft before removal.

4   Remove the bolts securing the driveplate to the crankshaft. A tool is available a most auto parts stores to hold the driveplate while loosening the bolts, if the tool is not available, wedge a screwdriver in the ring gear teeth to jam the driveplate.

5   Remove the driveplate from the crankshaft **(see illustration)**.

6   Clean the driveplate to remove any

grease and oil. Inspect it for cracks, distortion and missing or excessively worn ring gear teeth. Replace if necessary.

7   Clean and inspect the mating surfaces of the driveplate and the crankshaft. Check the crankshaft rear main seal for leakage; if leakage is evident replace it before reinstalling the driveplate (see Section 16).

Installation

8   Position the driveplate and backing plate against the crankshaft. Align the previously applied match marks. Before installing the bolts, apply thread locking compound to the threads.

9   Hold the driveplate with the special holding tool, or wedge a screwdriver in the ring gear teeth to keep the driveplate from turning as you tighten the bolts to the torque listed in this Chapter's Specifications.

10   The remaining installation steps are the reverse of removal.

16   Rear main oil seal - replacement

Refer to illustrations 16.3, 16.6 and 16.12

1   The crankshaft rear main oil seal is pressed into a retainer and bolted to the rear of the engine block.

2   Remove the driveplate (see Section 15).

3   The crankshaft rear main oil seal can be renewed without removing the oil pan or seal retainer. However, this method is NOT recommended because the lip of the seal is quite stiff and it's possible to cock the seal in the retainer bore or damage it during installation. If you want to take the chance, carefully and evenly pry out the old seal using a 3/16 flat blade screwdriver - do not to damage the crankshaft sealing surface **(see illustration)**. Apply a light coating of clean engine oil to the crankshaft seal journal and the lip of the new seal then carefully tap the new seal into place using a hammer and socket. The seal lip is stiff, so carefully work it onto the seal journal of the crankshaft with a smooth object like the rounded end of a socket extension as you tap the seal into place **(see illustration 16.12)**. Don't force it or you may damage the seal.

16.6 With the seal retainer supported on wood blocks, use a hammer and drift to drive the seal out of the retainer

4   The following method is recommended and requires removal of the oil pan (see Section 13).

5   Remove the mounting bolts from the crankshaft rear seal retainer and separate the retainer from the engine block.

6   Using a hammer and drift, carefully drive the old seal out of the retainer and discard it **(see illustration)**.

7   Thoroughly clean all gasket sealing surfaces. Use a scraper to remove all traces of old gasket material. Gasket removal solvents are available at auto parts stores and may prove helpful. Check the oil pan sealing surface for distortion. Straighten or replace as necessary. After removing the residual gasket material, wipe the gasket surfaces clean using a rag soaked in lacquer thinner or acetone.

8   Thoroughly clean and inspect the seal bore and sealing surface on the crankshaft. Minor imperfections can be removed with fine emery cloth. If there is a groove worn in the crankshaft sealing surface (from contact with the seal), installing a new seal will probably not stop the leak.

9   Install the new seal into the retainer using a socket (or block of wood) and a hammer. Drive it in until it's flush with the retainer.

16.12 Using a rounded object like a socket extension, carefully work the seal onto the crankshaft

17.9a Front engine mount (arrow) - exhaust manifold removed for clarity

10   Apply a 1/8 inch bead of RTV sealant to the retainer gasket sealing surface.

11   Lubricate the lip of the new seal and the crankshaft sealing surface with a light coat of clean engine oil.

12   Place the seal retainer in position on the engine block and install the mounting bolts. The seal lip is stiff, so carefully work it onto the seal journal of the crankshaft with a smooth object like the rounded end of a socket extension as you tap the seal into place **(see illustration)**. Don't force it or you may damage the seal. Tighten the bolts to the torque listed in this Chapter's Specifications.

13   Install the oil pan (see Section 13).

14   The remaining installation steps are the reverse of removal.

17   Engine mounts - check and replacement

1   Engine mounts seldom require attention, but broken or deteriorated mounts should be replaced immediately or the added strain placed on the driveline components may cause damage or wear.

Check

2   During the check, the engine must be raised slightly to relieve the weight from the mounts.

3   Raise the vehicle and support it securely on jackstands, then position a jack under the engine oil pan. Place a large wood block between the jack head and the oil pan to prevent oil pan damage, then carefully raise the engine just enough to take the weight off the mounts. **Warning:** *DO NOT place any part of your body under the engine when it's supported only by a jack!*

4   Inspect the mounts to see if the rubber is cracked, hardened or separated from the metal backing. Sometimes the rubber will split right down the center.

5   Check for relative movement between the mount plates and the engine or frame (use a large screwdriver or pry bar to attempt to move the mounts). If movement is noted, lower the engine and tighten the mount fasteners.

6   Rubber preservative may be applied to the mounts to slow deterioration.

Replacement

Refer to illustrations 17.9a, 17.9b, 17.9c 17.9d and 17.9e

7   Disconnect the negative battery cable from the ground stud on the left shock tower (see Chapter 5, Section 1). Raise the vehicle

17.9b Rear engine mount - exhaust crossover pipe removed for clarity

and support it securely on jackstands.

8   Place a floor jack under the engine (with a wood block between the jack head and oil pan) and raise the engine slightly to relieve the weight from the mount to be replaced. **Note:** *On 1995 through 1997 models, the lower front engine mount (engine support module) is attached to the lower radiator support. When removing the engine support module, the radiator and air conditioning condenser (if equipped) must be supported.*

9   Remove the fasteners and detach the

17.9c Engine support module (arrow) - connects front and rear engine mounts (1995 through 1997 models)

17.9d Right-side engine mount (arrow)

mount from the frame and engine **(see illustrations)**. **Caution:** *Do not disconnect more than one mount at a time, except during engine/transaxle removal.*

10   Installation is the reverse of removal. Use thread locking compound on the mount bolts and be sure to tighten them securely.

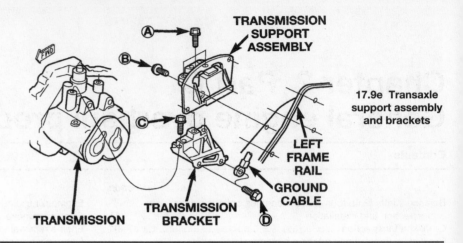

17.9e Transaxle support assembly and brackets

Chapter 2 Part C
General engine overhaul procedures

Contents

Specifications

Four-cylinder engines

General

Bore	3.4446 to 3.4452 inches
Stroke	
2.0L	3.268 inches
2.4L	3.976 inches
Displacement	
2.0L	122 cubic inches
2.4L	148 cubic inches
Compression ratio	
2.0L	9.8:1
2.4L	9.4:1
Compression pressure	170 to 225 psi
Firing order	1-3-4-2
Oil pressure	
At idle speed	4 psi (minimum)
At 3000 rpm	25 to 80 psi
Cylinder head warpage	
Head gasket surface	0.004 inch maximum
Intake/exhaust manifold mounting surfaces	0.006 inch maximum

Valves and related components

Face angle	
2.0L	45 to 45-1/2 degrees
2.4L	44-1/2 to 45 degrees
Seat angle	45 degrees
Valve margin width	
2.0L	
Intake	0.0452 to 0.0582 inch
Exhaust	0.058 to 0.071 inch
2.4L	
Intake	0.050 to 0.063 inch
Exhaust	0.038 to 0.051 inch

Four-cylinder engines (continued)

Valves and related components

Valve spring	
Out of square limit	1/16 inch
Free length (approximate)	
2.0L	1.747 inches
2.4L	1.905 inches
Installed height	
2.0L	1.580 inches
2.4L	1.496 inches
Valve stem diameter	
Intake	0.234 to 0.235 inch
Exhaust	0.233 to 0.234 inch
Valve stem-to-guide clearance	
Intake	0.0018 to 0.0025 inch
Exhaust	0.0029 to 0.0037 inch
Valve stem tip-to-spring seat surface height (valve installed - 2.0L only)	
1995 and 1996	
Intake	1.891 inches
Exhaust	1.889 inches
1997 and 1998	
Intake	1.77 to 1.81 inches
Exhaust	1.71 to 1.75 inches

Crankshaft and connecting rods

Crankshaft connecting rod journal	
Diameter	
2.0L	1.8894 to 1.8900 inches
2.4L	1.967 to 1.9685 inches
Taper and Out-of-round limit	0.0001 inch (maximum)
Connecting rod bearing oil clearance	0.001 to 0.0025 inch
Connecting rod endplay (side clearance)	0.005 to 0.015 inch
Crankshaft main bearing journal	
Diameter	
2.0L	2.0469 to 2.0475 inches
2.4L	2.3610 to 2.3625 inches
Taper and out-of-round limits	0.0001 inch
Crankshaft main bearing oil clearance	0.008 to 0.0024 inch
Crankshaft end play	0.0035 to 0.0094 inch

Engine block

Cylinder bore diameter	3.4446 to 3.4452 inches
Cylinder taper and out-of-round limits	0.002 inch

Pistons and piston rings

Piston diameter (nominal)*	3.4434 to 3.4441 inches
Piston-to-bore clearance*	
2.0L	
1995	0.0002 to 0.0015 inch
1996 to 1998	0.0004 to 0.0017 inch
2.4L	0.0009 to 0.0022 inch
Piston ring side clearance	
2.0L	
Both compression rings	0.0010 to 0.0026 inch
Oil ring (pack)	0.0002 to 0.0070 inch
2.4L	
Both compression rings	0.0011 to 0.0031 inch
Oil ring (pack)	0.0004 to 0.0070 inch
Piston ring end gap	
2.0L	
Number 1 (top) compression ring	0.009 to 0.020 inch
Number 2 compression ring	0.019 to 0.031 inch
Oil control ring (side rails)	0.009 to 0.026 inch
2.4L	
Number 1 (top) compression ring	0.0098 to 0.020 inch
Number 2 compression ring	0.009 to 0.018 inch
Oil control ring (side rails)	0.0098 to 0.025 inch

Measured 11/16-inch up from the bottom of the piston skirt on 2.0L engines and 9/16-inch up from the bottom of the piston skirt on 2.4L engines.

Torque specifications**

	Ft-lbs (unless otherwise indicated)
Balance shaft carrier-to-engine bolts	40
Balance shaft chain tensioner and guide fasteners	105 in-lbs
Balance shaft gear cover stud (double-ended)	105 in-lbs
Balance shaft rear cover bolts	105 in-lbs
Balance shaft sprocket bolts	250 in-lbs
Main bearing cap assembly bolts	
2.0L	
Main cap bolts (M11)	60
Bedplate bolts (M8)	22
2.4L	
Main cap bolts (M11)	
Step 1	30
Step 2	Tighten an additional 90-degrees (1/4 turn)
Bedplate bolts (M8)	250 in-lbs
Connecting rod cap bolts	
Step 1	20
Step 2	Tighten an additional 90-degrees (1/4 turn)

Note: *Refer to Chapter 2 Part A for additional torque specifications.*

V6 engine

General

Bore	3.29 inches
Stroke	2.992 inches
Displacement	152 cubic inches (2.5 liters)
Firing order	1-2-3-4-5-6
Compression ratio	9.4:1
Compression pressure	178 psi @ 250 rpm
Oil pressure	
At idle speed	6 psi (minimum)
At 3000 rpm	35 to 75 psi

Valves and related components

Face angle	45 to 45-1/2 degrees
Seat angle	44 to 44-1/2 degrees
Valve margin width	
Intake	
Standard	0.039 inch
Service limit	0.019 inch
Exhaust	
Standard	0.047 inch
Service limit	0.028 inch
Valve stem diameter	0.236 inch
Valve stem-to-guide clearance	
Intake	
Standard	0.0008 to 0.0020 inch
Service limit	0.004 inch
Exhaust	
Standard	0.0016 to 0.0028 inch
Service limit	0.006 inch
Valve spring	
Free length (approximate)	2.01 inches
Service limit	1.97 inches
Installed height	1.74 inches

Crankshaft and connecting rods

Crankshaft connecting rod journal	
Diameter	1.968 to 1.969 inches
Out-of-round limit	0.001 inch (maximum)
Taper limit	0.0002 inch (maximum)
Connecting rod bearing oil clearance	
1995 through 1997	0.0008 to 0.0028 inch
1998	0.0006 to 0.0018 inch
Connecting rod endplay (side clearance)	
Standard	0.004 to 0.010 inch
Service limit	0.016 inch

V6 engine (continued)

Crankshaft and connecting rods

Crankshaft main bearing journal
    Diameter .... 2.361 to 2.362 inches
    taper and out-of-round limits .... 0.0001 inch
Crankshaft end play
    Standard .... 0.002 to 0.010 inch
    Service limit .... 0.012 inch
Crankshaft main bearing oil clearance
    Standard .... 0.0008 to 0.0016 inch
    Service limit .... 0.0039 inch

Engine block

Cylinder bore diameter .... 3.29 inches
Flatness of top surface .... 0.002 inch
    Service limit .... 0.004 inch

Pistons and piston rings

Piston diameter (nominal)* .... 3.29 inches
Piston-to-bore clearance .... 0.0008 to 0.0016 inch
Piston ring side clearance
    Number 1 (top) compression ring
        Standard .... 0.0012 to 0.0028 inch
        Service limit .... 0.004 inch
    Number 2 compression ring
        Standard .... 0.0007 to 0.0024 inch
        Service limit .... 0.004 inch
    Oil control ring .... Loose fit
Piston ring end gap
    Number 1 (top) compression ring
        Standard .... 0.010 to 0.016 inch
        Service limit .... 0.031 inch
    Number 2 compression ring
        Standard .... 0.016 to 0.022 inch
        Service limit .... 0.031 inch
    Oil control ring (side rails)
        Standard .... 0.006 to 0.019 inch
        Service limit .... 0.039 inch

Measured 0.080 inch up from the bottom of the piston skirt.

Torque specifications**

Ft-lbs (unless otherwise indicated)

Main bearing cap bolts 69
Connecting rod cap nuts 38

****Note:** *Refer to Part B of this Chapter for additional torque specifications.*

1   General information

Included in this portion of Chapter 2 are the general overhaul procedures for the cylinder head and internal engine components. The information ranges from advice concerning preparation for an overhaul and the purchase of replacement parts to detailed, step-by-step procedures covering removal and installation of internal engine components and the inspection of parts.

The following Sections have been written based on the assumption that the engine has been removed from the vehicle. For information concerning in-vehicle engine repair, as well as removal and installation of the external components necessary for the overhaul, see the applicable Part of this Chapter. For information on determining models and engine numbers, refer to the Vehicle Identification Numbers at the beginning of this manual.

The Specifications included in this Part are only those necessary for the inspection and overhaul procedures which follow. Refer to Part A or B for additional Specifications as applicable.

2   Engine overhaul - general information

It's not always easy to determine when, or if, an engine should be completely overhauled, as a number of factors must be considered.

High mileage is not necessarily an indication that an overhaul is needed, while low mileage doesn't preclude the need for an overhaul. Frequency of servicing is probably the most important consideration. An engine that's had regular and frequent oil and filter changes, as well as other required maintenance, will most likely give many thousands of miles of reliable service. Conversely, a neglected engine may require an overhaul very early in its life.

Excessive oil consumption is an indication that piston rings, valve seals and/or valve guides are in need of attention. Make sure that oil leaks aren't responsible before deciding that the rings and/or guides are bad. Perform a compression check to determine the extent of the work required (see Section 4).

Check the oil pressure with a gauge installed in place of the oil pressure sending unit, located under the exhaust manifold in front of the transaxle bell housing, and compare the pressure to the pressure listed in this Chapter's Specifications. If it's extremely low, the bearings and/or oil pump are probably worn out.

Loss of power, rough running, knocking

or metallic engine noises, excessive valve train noise and high fuel consumption rates may also point to the need for an overhaul, especially if they're all present at the same time. If a complete tune-up doesn't remedy the situation, major mechanical work is the only solution.

An engine overhaul involves restoring the internal parts to the specifications of a new engine. During an overhaul, the piston rings are replaced and the cylinder walls are reconditioned (rebored and/or honed). If a re-bore is done by an automotive machine shop, new oversize pistons will also be installed. The main bearings, connecting rod bearings and camshaft bearings are generally replaced with new ones and, if necessary, the crankshaft may be reground to restore the journals. Generally, the valves are serviced as well, since they're usually in less-than-perfect condition at this point. While the engine is being overhauled, other components, such as the distributor, starter and alternator, can be rebuilt as well. The end result should be a like-new engine that will give many trouble free miles. **Note:** *Critical cooling system components such as the hoses, drivebelts, thermostat and water pump MUST be replaced with new parts when an engine is overhauled. The radiator should be checked carefully to ensure that it isn't clogged or leaking (see Chapter 3). Also, we don't recommend overhauling the oil pump - always install a new one when an engine is rebuilt.*

Before beginning the engine overhaul, read through the entire procedure to familiarize yourself with the scope and requirements of the job. Overhauling an engine isn't difficult, but it is time consuming. Plan on the vehicle being tied up for a minimum of two weeks, especially if parts must be taken to an automotive machine shop for repair or reconditioning. Check on availability of parts and make sure that any necessary special tools and equipment are obtained in advance. Most work can be done with typical hand tools, although a number of precision measuring tools are required for inspecting parts to determine if they must be replaced. Often an automotive machine shop will handle the inspection of parts and offer advice concerning reconditioning and replacement. **Note:** *Always wait until the engine has been completely disassembled and all components, especially the engine block, have been inspected before deciding what service and repair operations must be performed by an automotive machine shop. Since the block's condition will be the major factor to consider when determining whether to overhaul the original engine or buy a rebuilt one, never purchase parts or have machine work done on other components until the block has been thoroughly inspected. As a general rule, time is the primary cost of an overhaul, so it doesn't pay to install worn or sub-standard parts.*

As a final note, to ensure maximum life and minimum trouble from a rebuilt engine, everything must be assembled with care in a spotlessly clean environment.

3 Top Dead Center (TDC) for number one piston - locating

Note: *The crankshaft timing marks on these engines aren't visible until after the timing belt cover(s) have been removed.*

1   Top Dead Center (TDC) is the highest point in the cylinder that each piston reaches as it travels up-and-down when the crankshaft rotates. Each piston reaches TDC on the compression stroke and again on the exhaust stroke, but TDC generally refers to the piston position on the compression stroke. The cast-in timing mark on the crankshaft timing belt sprocket installed on the front of the crankshaft is referenced to the number 1 piston. When the mark on the crankshaft timing belt sprocket is aligned with the cast-in timing mark on the oil pump housing and the timing marks on the camshaft sprockets align with their respective marks (see Section 6 of the appropriate Part of this Chapter), the number 1 piston is at TDC on the compression stroke.

2   In order to bring any piston to TDC, the crankshaft must be rotated manually. When looking at the front of the engine (drivebelt end), normal crankshaft rotation is clockwise. DO NOT rotate the engine counterclockwise as the crankshaft timing belt sprocket may jump a tooth, requiring timing belt removal.

3   The preferred method is to turn the crankshaft with a large socket and breaker bar attached to the crankshaft damper/pulley bolt that is threaded into the front of the crankshaft.

4   Remove all (accessible) spark plugs as this will make it easier to rotate the engine by hand (see Chapter 1 if necessary). **Note:** *On V6 engines, the spark plugs for cylinders 1, 3 and 5 are located under the upper intake manifold and not easily accessible. Unless they are required to be removed, depending on what procedure you are performing, leave them installed.*

5   Disconnect the battery cable from the remote negative battery terminal.

6   Remove the accessory drivebelt splash shield (see Chapter 1) to gain access to the crankshaft damper/pulley bolt.

Four-cylinder engines

Refer to illustration 3.9

7   Install a compression gauge (screw-in type with a hose) in the number 1 cylinder spark plug hole. Place the gauge dial where you can see it while turning the crankshaft damper/pulley bolt. **Note:** *On 4 cylinder engines the number 1 cylinder is located at the front (drivebelt end) of the engine.*

8   Rotate the crankshaft clockwise until you see compression building up on the gauge - indicating you are on the compression stroke.

9   On 2.0L engines, remove the access hole plug on the timing belt cover **(see illustration)**. Slowly turn the crankshaft until the camshaft sprocket timing mark is visible

through the access hole. Using a flashlight, look inside the access hole to locate the camshaft timing mark on the timing belt rear cover. Slowly rotate the crankshaft clockwise as required until the timing mark on the camshaft sprocket aligns with the arrow on the timing belt rear cover. The crankshaft is now located at number 1 piston TDC on the compression stroke. **Note:** *If you turn the crankshaft too far, it will be necessary to rotate the crankshaft clockwise 1-3/4 turns to approach the compression stroke again.*

10   On 2.4L engines, remove the timing belt upper cover (see Chapter 2A, Section 6). Rotate the crankshaft clockwise until the camshaft sprocket timing marks are aligned **(see illustration 6.9b in Chapter 2 Part A)**. The crankshaft is now located at number 1 piston TDC on the compression stroke. **Note:** *If you turn the crankshaft too far, it will be necessary to rotate the crankshaft clockwise approximately 1-3/4 turns to approach the compression stroke again.*

11   After the number 1 piston has been positioned at TDC on the compression stroke, TDC for the remaining pistons can be located by turning the crankshaft exactly 180 degrees (1/2 turn) from that position, following the spark plug firing order; i.e. the first 180 degree rotation from number 1 piston TDC will bring the number 3 cylinder piston to TDC on it's compression stroke, another 180 degree rotation will bring the number 4 cylinder piston to TDC on it's compression stroke, etc.

V6 engine

Note: *This method assumes that the upper intake manifold is installed, making the number 1 spark plug inaccessible.*

12   Install a compression gauge (screw-in type with a hose) in the number 6 cylinder spark plug hole. Place the gauge dial where you can see it while turning the crankshaft damper/pulley bolt. **Note:** *The number six*

3.9 2.0L four-cylinder models have an access hole in the front timing belt cover so you can see the camshaft timing marks without removing the cover

cylinder is located at the rear (transaxle end) of the left cylinder bank (refer to the Specifications in Chapter 1, if necessary).

13   Rotate the crankshaft clockwise until you see compression building up on the gauge - indicating you are on the compression stroke.

14   Remove the upper left timing belt cover **(see illustration 6.6 in Chapter 2 Part B)**. **Note:** *If the number 6 piston is near TDC, the camshaft timing mark should be approximately 60 degrees counterclockwise of the timing mark on the valve cover.*

15   Rotate the crankshaft clockwise until the timing mark on the left camshaft sprocket lines up with the timing mark on the valve cover **(see illustration 6.11a in Chapter 2 Part B)**. The crankshaft is now located at number 1 piston TDC on the compression stroke. **Note:** *If you turn the crankshaft too far, it will be necessary to rotate the crankshaft clockwise approximately 1-3/4 turns to approach the compression stroke again.*

16   After the number 1 piston has been positioned at TDC on the compression stroke, TDC for the remaining pistons can be located by turning the crankshaft exactly 120 degrees from that position, following the spark plug firing order; i.e. the first 120 degree rotation from number 1 piston TDC will bring the number 2 cylinder piston to TDC on it's compression stroke, another 120 degree rotation will bring the number 3 cylinder piston to TDC on it's compression stroke, etc.

4   Compression check

Note: *On V6 engines it is necessary to remove the upper intake manifold to access the right bank of spark plugs, refer to Part B of this Chapter.*

1   A compression check will tell you the mechanical condition of the upper end (pistons, rings, valves, head gasket) of your engine. Specifically, it can tell you if the compression is low due to leakage caused by worn piston rings, defective valves and seats or a blown head gasket. **Note:** *The engine must be at normal operating temperature and the battery must be fully charged for this check to be accurate.*

2   Begin by cleaning the area around the spark plugs before you remove them (compressed air should be used, if available, otherwise a small brush or even a bicycle tire pump will work). The idea is to prevent dirt from getting into the cylinders as the compression check is being performed.

3   Remove all of the spark plugs from the engine (Chapter 1).

4   Block the throttle wide open.

5   Disable the ignition by disconnecting the primary (low voltage) wire electrical connector from the ignition coil pack (four-cylinder engines) or the disconnecting the 2 pin connector from the distributor (V6 engine) (see Chapter 5).

6   Install the compression gauge in the number one spark plug hole.

7   Crank the engine over at least seven compression strokes and watch the gauge. The compression should build up quickly in a healthy engine. Low compression on the first stroke, followed by gradually increasing pressure on successive strokes, indicates worn piston rings. A low compression reading on the first stroke, which doesn't build up during successive strokes, indicates leaking valves or a blown head gasket (a cracked head could also be the cause). Deposits on the undersides of the valve heads can also cause low compression. Record the highest gauge reading obtained.

8   Repeat the procedure for the remaining cylinders and compare the results to the Specifications in this Chapter.

9   Add some engine oil (about three squirts from a plunger-type oil can) to each cylinder, through the spark plug hole, and repeat the test recording the results.

10   If the compression increases after the oil is added, the piston rings are definitely worn. If the compression doesn't increase significantly, the leakage is occurring at the valves or head gasket. Leakage past the valves may be caused by burned valve seat(s), and/or faces or warped, cracked or bent valve(s).

11   If two adjacent cylinders have equally low compression, there's a strong possibility that the head gasket between them is blown. The appearance of coolant in the combustion chambers or the crankcase would verify this condition.

12   If one cylinder is 20 percent lower than the others, and the engine has a slightly rough idle, a worn exhaust lobe on the camshaft could be the cause.

13   If the compression is unusually high, the combustion chambers are probably coated with carbon deposits. If that's the case, the cylinder head should be removed and decarbonized.

14   If compression is way down or varies greatly between cylinders, it would be a good idea to have a leak-down test performed by an automotive repair shop. This test will pinpoint exactly where the leakage is occurring and determine how severe it is.

5   Vacuum gauge diagnostic checks

Refer to illustration 5.6

1   A vacuum gauge provides valuable information about what is going on in the engine at a low-cost. You can check for worn rings or cylinder walls, leaking head or intake manifold gaskets, restricted exhaust, stuck or burned valves, weak valve springs, improper ignition or valve timing and ignition problems.

2   Unfortunately, vacuum gauge readings are easy to misinterpret, so they should be used in conjunction with other tests to confirm the diagnosis.

3   Both the absolute readings and the rate of needle movement are important for accurate interpretation. Most gauges measure vacuum in inches of mercury (in-Hg). The following references to vacuum assume the diagnosis is being performed at sea level. As elevation increases (or atmospheric pressure decreases), the reading will decrease. For every 1,000 foot increase in elevation above approximately 2000 feet, the gauge readings will decrease about one inch of mercury.

4   Connect the vacuum gauge directly to intake manifold vacuum, not to ported (throttle-body) vacuum. Be sure no hoses are left disconnected during the test or false readings will result.

5   Before you begin the test, allow the engine to warm up completely. Block the wheels and set the parking brake. With the transmission in neutral (or Park, on automatics), start the engine and allow it to run at normal idle speed. **Warning:** *Carefully inspect the fan blades for cracks or damage before starting the engine. Keep your hands and the vacuum tester clear of the fan and do not stand in front of the vehicle or in line with the fans when the engine is running.*

6   Read the vacuum gauge; an average, healthy engine should normally produce about 17 to 22 inches of vacuum with a fairly steady needle. Refer to the following vacuum gauge readings and what they indicate about the engines condition **(see illustration)**.

7   A low steady reading usually indicates a leaking gasket between the intake manifold and throttle body, a leaky vacuum hose, late ignition timing or incorrect camshaft timing. Check ignition timing with a timing light and eliminate all other possible causes, utilizing the tests provided in this Chapter before you remove the timing belt cover to check the timing marks.

8   If the reading is 3 to 8 inches below normal and it fluctuates at that low reading, suspect an intake manifold gasket leak at an intake port or a faulty injector.

9   If the needle has regular drops of about 2 to 4 inches at a steady rate the valves are probably leaking. Perform a compression or leak-down test to confirm this.

4   An irregular drop or down-flick of the needle can be caused by a sticking valve or an ignition misfire. Perform a compression or leak-down test. Check the condition of the spark plugs and compare them to the chart on the back cover of this manual.

10   A rapid vibration of about 4 in-Hg vibration at idle combined with exhaust smoke indicates worn valve guides. Perform a leak-down test to confirm this. If the rapid vibration occurs with an increase in engine speed, check for a leaking intake manifold gasket or head gasket, weak valve springs, burned valves or ignition misfire.

11   A slight fluctuation, say 1 inch up-and-down, may mean ignition problems. Check all the usual tune-up items and, if necessary, run the engine on an ignition system analyzer.

12   If there is a large fluctuation, perform a compression or leak-down test to look for a weak or dead cylinder or a blown head gasket.

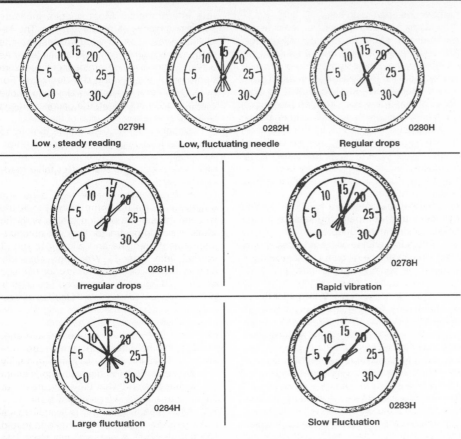

Low , steady reading	Low, fluctuating needle	Regular drops
0279H	0282H	0280H

Irregular drops	Rapid vibration
0281H	0278H

Large fluctuation	Slow Fluctuation
0284H	0283H

5.6 Typical vacuum gauge diagnostic readings

13   If the needle moves slowly through a wide range, check for a clogged PCV system, inoperative or clogged fuel injector(s), throttle body or intake manifold gasket or vacuum hose leaks.

14   Check for a slow return after revving the engine by quickly snapping the throttle open until the engine reaches about 2,500 rpm and let it shut. Normally the reading should drop to near zero, rise above normal idle reading (about 5 in-Hg over) and then return to the previous idle reading. If the vacuum returns slowly and doesn't peak when the throttle is snapped shut, the rings may be worn. If there is a long delay, look for a restricted exhaust system (often the muffler or catalytic converter). An easy way to check this is to temporarily disconnect the exhaust ahead of the suspected part and repeat the test.

6   Engine removal - methods and precautions

If you've decided that an engine must be removed for overhaul or major repair work, several preliminary steps should be taken.

Locating a suitable place to work is extremely important. Adequate work space, along with storage space for the vehicle, will be needed. If a shop or garage isn't available, at the very least a flat, level, clean work surface made of concrete or asphalt is required.

Cleaning the engine compartment and engine before beginning the removal procedure will help keep tools clean and organized.

An engine hoist or A-frame will also be necessary. Make sure the equipment is rated in excess of the combined weight of the engine and accessories. Safety is of primary importance, considering the potential hazards involved in lifting the engine out of the vehicle.

If the engine is being removed by a novice, a helper should be available. Advice and aid from someone more experienced would also be helpful. There are many instances when one person cannot simultaneously perform.all of the operations required when lifting the engine out of the vehicle.

Plan the operation ahead of time. Arrange for, or obtain all of the tools and equipment you'll need prior to beginning the job. Some of the equipment necessary to perform engine removal and installation safely and with relative ease are (in addition to an engine hoist) a heavy duty floor jack, complete sets of wrenches and sockets as described in the front of this manual, wooden blocks and plenty of rags and cleaning solvent for mopping up spilled oil, coolant and gasoline. If the hoist must be rented, make sure that you arrange for it in advance and perform all of the operations possible without

it beforehand. This will save you time and money.

Plan for the vehicle to be out of use for quite a while. A machine shop will be required to perform some of the work which the do-it-yourselfer can't accomplish without special equipment. These shops often have a busy schedule, so it would be a good idea to consult them before removing the engine in order to accurately estimate the amount of time required to rebuild or repair components that may need work.

Always be extremely careful when removing and installing the engine. Serious injury can result from careless actions. Plan ahead, take your time and a job of this nature, although major, can be accomplished successfully.

7   Engine - removal and installation

Note 1: *Read through the entire Section before beginning this procedure. The engine and transaxle are removed from the vehicle as an assembly and separated once outside of the vehicle.*
Note 2: *The engine/transaxle assembly is designed to be removed from the underside of the vehicle. This manual assumes that the do-it-yourselfer is performing the job at home and is removing the engine without the use of a vehicle lift.*
Warning: *These models have airbags. Always disable the airbag system and wait 2 minutes before working in the vicinity of the impact sensors, steering column or instrument panel to avoid the possibility of accidental deployment of the airbags, which could cause personal injury (see Chapter 12).*

Removal

Refer to illustration 7.10
1   If the vehicle is equipped with air conditioning, have the system discharged by a dealer service department or automotive air conditioning service facility.
2   Place protective covers on the front fenders and cowl. Special fender covers are available, but an old bedspread or blanket will also work.
3   Remove the hood (see Chapter 11).
4   Perform the fuel system pressure relief procedure (see Chapter 4).
5   Disconnect the negative battery cable from the ground stud on the left shock tower (see Chapter 5, Section 1).
6   Remove the air cleaner assembly (see Chapter 4).
7   Raise the vehicle and support it securely on jackstands. Drain the cooling system, engine oil and transaxle fluid (see Chapter 1).
8   Remove the engine cooling fans, radiator and air conditioning condenser unit (if equipped) (see Chapter 3).
9   Remove the front bumper fascia and reinforcement bar (see Chapter 11).
10   Carefully label, then disconnect all vacuum lines, coolant and emissions hoses, wire

2C

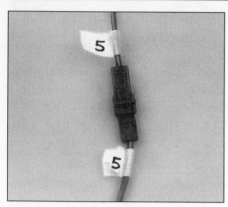

7.10 Label both ends of each wire or vacuum connection before separating them

harness connectors and brackets connected to the engine. Masking tape and felt-tip pens work well for marking items **(see illustration)**. If necessary, take instant photos or sketch the locations to ensure correct location at installation.

11   Detach the Powertrain Control Module (PCM), Power Distribution Center (PDC) and Transmission Control Module (TCM) (if equipped) from their mountings and position them out of the way. **Caution:** *The PCM and TCM are Electro-Static Discharge (ESD) sensitive electronic devices, meaning a static discharge from your body could possibly damage internal electrical components. Make sure to properly ground yourself and the control modules before handling them. Avoid touching the electrical terminals unless absolutely necessary.*

12   Disconnect the fuel line from the fuel injection system (see Chapter 4). Cap the fittings to prevent leakage and contamination.

13   Detach the accelerator cable and cruise control cable (if equipped) (see Chapter 4).

14   If equipped, remove the oil pan-to-transaxle structural collar (see Chapter 2A).

15   On manual transaxle equipped models, detach the shift cables (see Chapter 7A) and the clutch release cable (see Chapter 8).

16   On automatic transaxle equipped vehicles, detach the shift control cable and oil cooler lines from the transaxle (see Chapter 7B). After removing the oil cooler lines, plug the ends to prevent leakage and contamination.

17   Clearly label and disconnect all electrical connections and ground straps (where applicable) from the transaxle.

18   Remove the driveaxles from the transaxle (see Chapter 8). Stuff clean rags into the transaxle openings to prevent leakage and contamination.

19   Remove the bellhousing lower cover, match-mark the torque converter or modular clutch assembly (as applicable) to the driveplate and remove the four bolts (refer to the appropriate Part of Chapter 7).

20   Disconnect the exhaust system from the exhaust manifold (see Chapter 4).

21   On V6 models, remove the cross-over tube connecting the exhaust manifolds (see Chapter 2B).

22   Remove the drivebelts (see Chapter 1).

23   If equipped, remove the air conditioning compressor (see Chapter 3).

24   Detach the power steering pump, reservoir and the power steering lines (mounted to the rear cylinder head) from the brackets without disconnecting the hoses and position them out of the way.

25   Remove the through-bolt from the rear engine mount (refer to the appropriate Part of Chapter 2).

26   Disconnect the ground straps from the engine.

27   Lower the vehicle.

28   Attach a chain or an engine lifting fixture to the engine lifting brackets (or to bolts which are securely mounted in the cast iron block or accessory mounting bracket) and attach the hoist. Take up the slack until there is tension on the chain to support the engine/transaxle assembly. **Warning:** *Attaching the engine lifting chain to a bolt or stud located in an aluminum component (such as the cylinder head) may not provide the necessary strength to support the weight of the engine/transaxle assembly during removal.*

29   Support the transaxle with a floor jack. Place a block of wood on the jack pad to protect the transaxle. **Warning:** *Do not place any part of your body under the engine/transaxle when it's supported only by a hoist or other lifting device.*

30   Remove the mount through-bolts on all of the engine or transaxle mounts (refer to the appropriate Part of Chapter 2).

31   Confirm that all of the cables, hoses, wires and other items are disconnected from the engine/transaxle.

32   Carefully push the transaxle down, or adjust the engine lifting fixture to position the engine slightly higher than the transaxle, while lifting the engine up to clear obstructions.

33   Lift the engine and transaxle high enough to clear the front of the vehicle and slowly move the hoist away.

34   Lower the hoist and set the transaxle on blocks - leave the hoist hooked to the engine.

35   With the transaxle securely supported, remove the transaxle-to-engine bolts and separate the engine from the transaxle (refer to Chapter 7 if necessary).

36   Remove the driveplate (refer to the appropriate Part of Chapter 2) and then remove the engine rear plate. Mount the engine on an engine stand.

Installation

37   Before installing the engine assembly, inspect the engine/transaxle mounts. If they're worn or damaged, replace them.

38   On manual transaxle equipped models, inspect the modular clutch assembly (see Chapter 8) and apply a very small amount of high temperature grease to the transaxle input shaft splines.

39   On automatic transaxle equipped vehicles, inspect the torque converter/input shaft seal.

40   Carefully mate the transaxle to the engine following the procedure outlined in Chapter 7. **Caution:** *Do not use the bolts to force the engine and transaxle into alignment. It may crack or damage major components.*

41   Install the transaxle-to-engine bolts and tighten them to the torque listed in the Specifications of Chapter 7.

42   Attach the hoist to the engine and carefully lower the engine/transaxle assembly into the vehicle.

43   Install the engine/transaxle mount bolts and tighten them securely.

44   The remaining installation steps are the reverse of removal.

45   After lowering the vehicle, add coolant, engine oil, power steering and transmission fluid/lubricant as needed (see Chapter 1).

46   Run the engine and check for proper operation and leaks. Shut off the engine and recheck the fluid levels. **Note:** *If the engine has just been rebuilt, see Section 27 for break-in procedures.*

8   Engine rebuilding alternatives

The do-it-yourselfer is faced with a number of options when performing an engine overhaul. The decision to replace the engine block, piston/connecting rod assemblies and crankshaft depends on a number of factors, with the number one consideration being the condition of the block. Other considerations are cost, access to machine shop facilities, parts availability, time required to complete the project and the extent of prior mechanical experience on the part of the do-it-yourselfer.

Some of the rebuilding alternatives include:

Individual parts - If the inspection procedures reveal that the engine block and most engine components are in reusable condition, purchasing individual parts may be the most economical alternative. The block, crankshaft and piston/connecting rod assemblies should all be inspected carefully. Even if the block shows little wear, the cylinder bores should be surface honed.

Short block - A short block consists of an engine block with a crankshaft and piston/connecting rod assemblies already installed. All new bearings are incorporated and all clearances will be correct. The existing camshaft, valve train components, cylinder head(s) and external parts can be bolted to the short block with little or no machine shop work necessary.

Long block - A long block consists of a short block plus an oil pump, oil pan, cylinder head, rocker arm cover, camshaft(s) and valve train components, timing sprockets and timing covers. All components are installed with new bearings, seals and gaskets incorporated throughout. The installation of manifolds and external parts is all that's necessary.

Give careful thought to which alternative is best for you and discuss the situation with local automotive machine shops, auto parts dealers and experienced rebuilders before ordering or purchasing replacement parts.

9 Engine overhaul - disassembly sequence

Refer to illustrations 9.5a, 9.5b and 9.5c

1   It's much easier to disassemble and work on the engine if it's mounted on a portable engine stand. A stand can often be rented quite cheaply from an equipment rental yard. Before the engine is mounted on a stand, the driveplate must be removed from the engine.

2   If a stand isn't available, it's possible to disassemble the engine with it blocked up on the floor. Be extra careful not to tip or drop the engine when working without a stand.

3   If you're going to obtain a rebuilt engine, all external components must be removed from the old engine first, to be transferred to the replacement engine, just as they will if you're doing a complete engine overhaul yourself. These include but are not limited too:

> Air conditioning compressor and
>> brackets
> Alternator and brackets
> Coil pack or distributor, spark plug wires
>> and spark plugs
> Driveplate
> Electronic engine control components
> Emissions control components
> Engine mounts
> Fuel injection components
> Intake and exhaust manifolds
> Oil filter (and adapter if equipped)
> Power steering pump and brackets
> Thermostat cover, thermostat and
>> housing
> Water pump

Note: *When removing the external components from the engine, pay close attention to details that may be helpful or important during installation. Note the installed position of gaskets, seals, spacers, pins, brackets, washers, bolts and other small items.*

4   If you're obtaining a short block, which consists of the engine block, crankshaft, pistons and connecting rods all assembled, then the cylinder head, oil pan and oil pump will have to be removed as well. See Engine rebuilding alternatives for additional information regarding the different possibilities to be considered.

5   If you're planning a complete overhaul, the engine must be disassembled and the internal components removed in the general following order **(see illustrations)**:

> Intake and exhaust manifolds
> Valve cover
> Rocker arms and shafts (SOHC engine)
> Timing belt covers
> Timing belt and sprockets
> Camshaft(s)
> Rocker arms and hydraulic lash
>> adjusters (DOHC engines)

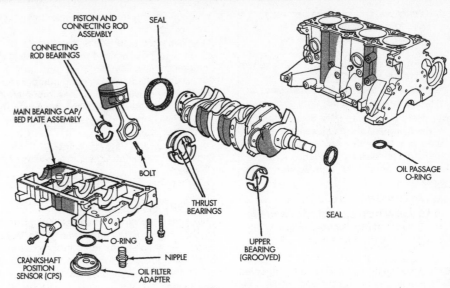

9.5a Engine block components - 2.0L four-cylinder

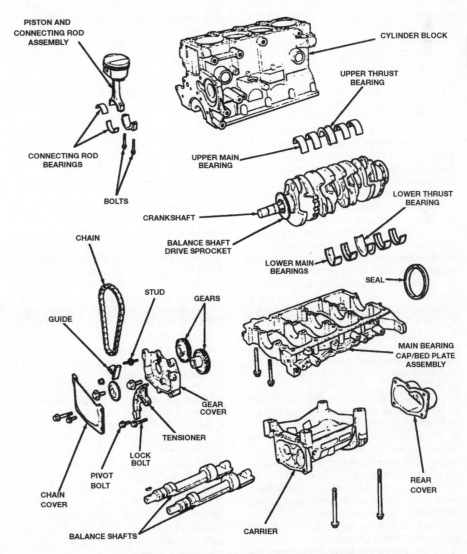

9.5b Engine block components - 2.4L four-cylinder

2C

Water pump
Cylinder head(s)
Oil pan and oil pickup tube
Oil pump
Balance shaft carrier (2.4L four-cylinder engine)
Piston/connecting rod assemblies
Crankshaft

6   Before beginning the disassembly and overhaul procedures, make sure the following items are available. Also, refer to *Engine overhaul - reassembly sequence* for a list of tools and materials needed for engine reassembly.

Common hand tools
Small cardboard boxes or plastic bags for storing parts
Gasket scraper
Ridge reamer
Micrometers
Telescoping gauges
Dial indicator set
Valve spring compressor
Cylinder surfacing hone
Piston ring groove cleaning tool
Electric drill motor
Tap and die set
Wire brushes
Oil gallery brushes
Cleaning solvent

---

10   Cylinder head - disassembly

Refer to illustrations 10.2, 10.3, 10.4a, 10.4b and 10.4c

Note: *New and rebuilt cylinder heads are commonly available for most engines at dealerships and auto parts stores. Due to the fact that some specialized tools are necessary for the disassembly and inspection procedures, and replacement parts may not be readily available, it may be more practical and economical for the home mechanic to purchase a replacement head rather than taking the time to disassemble, inspect and recondition the original.*

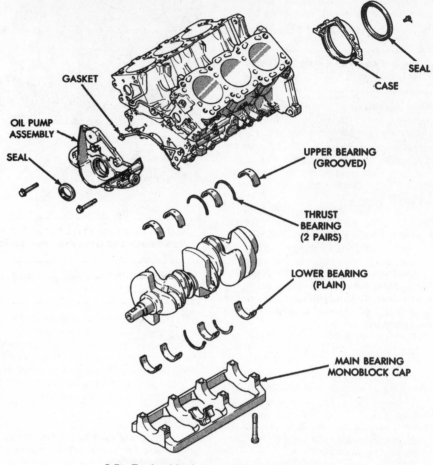

9.5c Engine block components - V6 engine

1   Cylinder head disassembly involves removal of the intake and exhaust valves and related components. If they're still in place, remove the rocker arm shafts and camshaft, on the SOHC engine (refer to the appropriate Part of Chapter 2) or the bearing caps, camshafts, rocker arms and lash adjusters, on the DOHC engine (see Chapter 2A). Label the parts or store them separately so they can be reinstalled in their original locations.

2   Before the valves are removed, arrange to label and store them, along with their related components, so they can be kept separate and reinstalled in the same valve guides they are removed from **(see illustration)**.

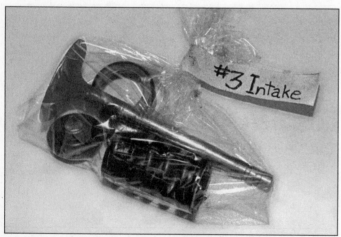

10.2 A small plastic bag with an appropriate label can be used to store the valvetrain components so they don't get mixed up

10.3 After compressing the valve spring, use a magnet (shown) or needle-nose pliers to extract the valve keepers - a valve spring compressor adapter, such as the one shown, will be needed to compress the valve spring on this type of cylinder head

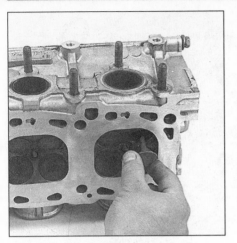

10.4a Remove the valve from the cylinder head . . .

10.4b . . . then use pliers to remove the valve stem seal from the valve guide

3   Compress the springs on the first valve with a spring compressor and remove the keepers **(see illustration)**. Carefully release the valve spring compressor and remove the retainer and the spring.

4   Pull the valve out of the head, then remove the valve stem seal with pliers and withdraw spring seat from the guide **(see illustrations)**. **Note:** *On the four-cylinder engines the valve stem seal and spring seat are an assembly.* If the valve binds in the guide (won't pull through), push it back into the head and deburr the area around the keeper groove and step tip with a fine file or whetstone **(see illustration)**.

5   Repeat the procedure for the remaining valves. Remember to keep all the parts for each valve together so they can be reinstalled in the same locations.

6   Once the valves and related components have been removed and stored in an organized manner, the head should be thoroughly cleaned and inspected. If a complete engine overhaul is being performed, finish the engine disassembly procedures before beginning the cylinder head cleaning and inspection process.

11 Cylinder head - cleaning and inspection

1   Thorough cleaning of the cylinder head and related valvetrain components, followed by a detailed inspection, will enable you to decide how much valve service work must be performed during the engine overhaul. **Note:** *If the engine was severely overheated, the cylinder head is probably warped.*

Cleaning

2   Scrape all traces of old gasket material and sealing compound off the head gasket, intake manifold and exhaust manifold sealing surfaces. **Caution:** *The cylinder head is aluminum, be very careful not to gouge the sealing surfaces.* Special gasket removal solvents that soften gaskets and make removal much easier are available at auto parts stores.

3   Remove all built-up scale from the coolant passages.

4   Run a stiff wire brush through the various holes to remove deposits that may have formed in them.

5   Run an appropriate size tap into each of the threaded holes to remove corrosion and thread sealant that may be present. If compressed air is available, use it to clear the holes of debris produced by this operation. **Warning:** *Wear eye protection when using compressed air!*

6   Clean the cylinder head with solvent and dry it thoroughly. Compressed air will speed the drying process and ensure that all holes and recessed areas are clean. **Note:** *Decarbonizing chemicals are available and may prove very useful when cleaning cylinder heads and valve train components. They are very caustic and should be used with caution. Be sure to follow the instructions on the container.*

7   Clean the rocker arms hydraulic lash adjusters, spacers and shafts with solvent. **Note:** *The lash adjusters and rocker arms on SOHC engines are precision assemblies, be careful not to mix-up parts when cleaning.* Dry all parts thoroughly (don't mix them up during the cleaning process). Compressed air will speed the drying process and can be used to clean out the oil passages. **Warning:** *Wear eye protection when using compressed air!*

8   Clean all the valve springs, spring seats, keepers and retainers with solvent and dry them thoroughly. Clean the components one valve at a time to avoid mixing up the parts.

9   Scrape off any heavy deposits that may have formed on the valves, then use a motorized wire brush to remove deposits from the valve heads and stems. **Warning:** *Wear eye protection when using a motorized wire brush!* Again, make sure the valves don't get mixed up.

Inspection

Note: *Be sure to perform all of the following inspection procedures before concluding that machine shop work is required. Make a list of the items that need attention.*

Cylinder head

Refer to illustrations 11.10, 11.11 and 11.13

10   Inspect the head very carefully for cracks, evidence of coolant leakage and

10.4c If the valve stem won't pass through the guide, chances are its because of a burr or raised material on the end of the valve stem. Use a fine file or whetstone to deburr the valve stem as required

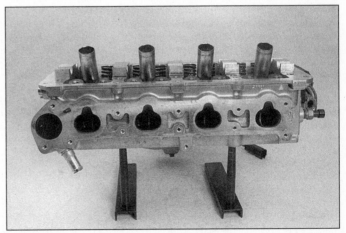

11.10 Inspect the cylinder head internal passages for cracks or other defects

2C

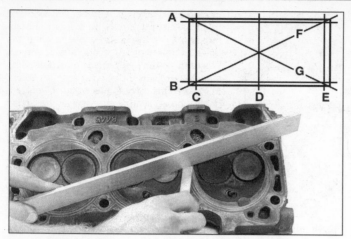

11.11 Measure the cylinder head gasket surface(s) flatness and compare to the limits listed in this Chapter's Specifications

11.13 Checking valve stem-to-guide clearance - remember to divide the measurement by 2 to obtain the correct dimension

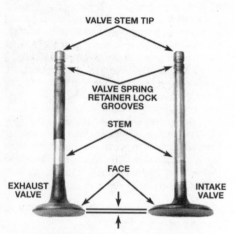

11.15 Carefully inspect the areas indicated for wear or damage

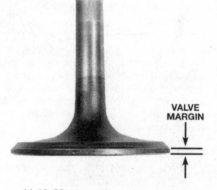

11.16 Measure the valve margin of each valve

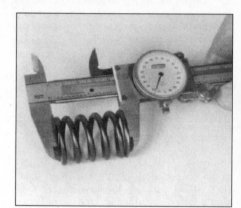

11.17 Measuring the valve spring free length

11.18 Check each valve spring for squareness

other damage **(see illustration)**. If cracks are found, check with an automotive machine shop concerning repair. If repair isn't possible, a new cylinder head must be obtained.

11   Using a straightedge and feeler gauge, check the head gasket mating surface **(see illustration)**. Check the intake and exhaust manifold surfaces on the cylinder head also. If the warpage on any of the surfaces exceeds the limits listed in this Chapter's Specifications, they can be resurfaced at an automotive machine shop.

12   Examine the valve seats in each of the combustion chambers. If they're pitted, cracked or burned, the head will require valve service that's beyond the scope of the home mechanic.

13   Check the valve stem-to-guide clearance, using a clamping dial indicator base attached securely to the head, by measuring the lateral movement of the valve stem inside the valve guide **(see illustration)**. The valve must be in the guide and approximately 1/16-inch off the seat. The total valve stem movement indicated by the gauge needle must be divided by two to obtain the actual clearance.

14   After this is done, if there's still some

doubt regarding the condition of the valve guides they should be checked by an automotive machine shop (the cost should be minimal).

Valves

Refer to illustrations 11.15 and 11.16

15   Carefully inspect each valve face for uneven wear, deformation, cracks, pits and burned areas **(see illustration)**. Check the valve stem for scuffing and galling and the neck for cracks. Rotate the valve and check for any obvious indication that it's bent. Look for pits and excessive wear on the end of the stem. The presence of any of these conditions indicates the need for valve service by an automotive machine shop.

16   Measure the margin width on each valve **(see illustration)**. Any valve with a margin narrower than listed in this Chapter's Specifications will have to be replaced.

Valve components

Refer to illustrations 11.17 and 11.18

17   Check each valve spring for wear (on the ends) and pits. Measure the free length **(see illustration)** and compare it to the value listed in this Chapter's Specifications. Any springs that are shorter than specified have sagged and should not be reused. The ten-

sion of all springs should be checked with a special fixture before deciding that they're suitable for use in a rebuilt engine (take the springs to an automotive machine shop for this check).

18   Stand each spring on a flat surface and check it for squareness **(see illustration)**. If any of the springs are distorted or sagged, replace all of them with new parts.

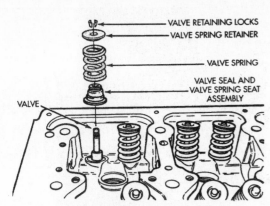

13.4a On four-cylinder models, the valve seal and spring seat are an assembly

- VALVE RETAINING LOCKS
- VALVE SPRING RETAINER
- VALVE SPRING
- VALVE SEAL AND VALVE SPRING SEAT ASSEMBLY
- VALVE

13.4b Install the valve stem seal using an appropriate size socket and hammer

19   Check the spring retainers and keepers for obvious wear and cracks. Any questionable parts should be replaced with new ones, as extensive damage will occur if they fail during engine operation.

Rocker arm components

20   Refer to the appropriate Part of Chapter 2 for the rocker arm and hydraulic lash adjusters inspection procedures.
21   Any damaged or excessively worn parts must be replaced with new ones.
22   If the inspection process indicates that the valve components are in generally poor condition and worn beyond the limits specified, which is usually the case in an engine that's being overhauled, reassemble the valves in the cylinder head and refer to Section 12 for valve servicing recommendations.

12   Valves - servicing

1   Because of the complex nature of the job and the special tools and equipment needed, servicing of the valves, the valve seats and the valve guides, commonly known as a valve job, should be performed by an experienced professional.
2   The home mechanic can remove and disassemble the head, do the initial cleaning and inspection, then reassemble and deliver it to a dealer service department or an automotive machine shop for the actual service work. Doing the inspection will enable you to see what condition the head and valvetrain components are in and will ensure that you know what work and new parts are required when dealing with an automotive machine shop.
3   The dealer service department, or automotive machine shop, will remove the valves and springs, recondition or replace the valves and valve seats, recondition the valve guides, check and replace the valve springs, spring retainers and keepers (as necessary), replace the valve seals with new ones, reassemble the valve components and make sure the installed spring height is correct. The cylinder head gasket surface will also be resurfaced if

13.6a Install the spring over the valve guide and onto the seat . . .

it's warped.
4   After the valve job has been performed by a professional, the head will be in like-new condition. When the head is returned, be sure to clean it again before installing it on the engine to remove any metal particles and abrasive grit that may still be present from the valve service or head resurfacing operations (which happens frequently). Use compressed air, if available, to blow out all the oil holes and passages.

13   Cylinder head - reassembly

Refer to illustrations 13.4a, 13.4b, 13.6a, 13.6b, 13.7 and 13.9

1   Regardless of whether or not the head was sent to an automotive repair shop for valve servicing, make sure it's clean before beginning reassembly.
2   If the head was sent out for valve servicing, the valves and related components will already be in place. Begin the reassembly procedure with Step 8.
3   If the valve faces or seats have been ground on a 2.0L four-cylinder engine, measure the valve stem tip-to-spring seat surface height (without spring or seat installed) (see

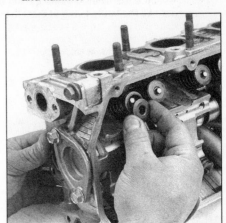

13.6b . . . and place the retainer onto the spring

illustration 13.9 Dimension "A"). If the dimension is greater than the tolerance listed in this Chapter's Specifications, grind the valve stem as required to achieve the correct dimension.
4   Install the spring seats and new valve stem seals (V6 engines) or the new valve seal/spring seat assembly (four-cylinder engines) onto each of the valve guides (see illustration). Note: *On V6 engines, install the silver colored valve stem seals onto the intake valve guides and the black colored valve stem seals onto the exhaust valve guides.* Using a hammer and a deep socket or seal installation tool, gently tap each valve stem seal/spring seat assembly into place until it's completely seated on the guide (see illustration). Don't twist or cock the seals during installation or they won't seal properly on the valve stems.
5   Beginning at one end of the head, apply moly-based grease or clean engine oil to the valve stem and install the first valve.
6   Install spring over the valve guide and set the spring and retainer in place (see illustrations). Note: *On V6 engines, install the valve springs with the enameled end up.*
7   Compress the spring with a valve spring compressor and carefully install the keepers in the upper groove, then slowly release the

2C

13.7 Apply a small dab of grease to each keeper as shown here - it will hold them in place on the valve stem as the spring is released

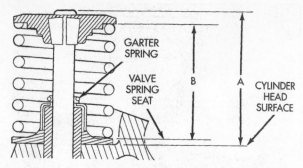

13.9 Valve stem tip-to-spring seat surface (Dimension "A" - 2.0L four-cylinder engines only) and installed spring height (Dimension "B" - all engines)

compressor and make sure the keepers seat properly. Apply a small dab of grease to each keeper to hold it in place if necessary **(see illustration)**.

8   Repeat the procedure for the remaining

14.1 Before you try to remove the pistons, use a ridge reamer to remove the raised material (ridge) from the top of the cylinders

valves. Be sure to return the components to their original locations - don't mix them up!

9   Measure the installed valve spring height (Dimension "B") with a vernier or dial caliper **(see illustration)**. If the head was sent out for service work, the installed height should be correct, but don't automatically assume that it is. If the height is greater than listed in this Chapter's Specifications, shims can be added under the spring seat to correct it. **Caution:** *Do not shim the springs to the point where the installed height is less than specified.*

10   Refer to the appropriate Part of this Chapter for the procedure to install the camshaft(s) and rocker arms.

14   Pistons and connecting rods - removal

Refer to illustrations 14.1, 14.3 14.4 and 14.6
Note: *Prior to removing the piston/connecting rod assemblies, remove the cylinder head and oil pan by referring to the appropriate Part of this Chapter.*

1   Use your fingernail to feel if a ridge has formed at the upper limit of ring travel (about 1/4-inch down from the top of each cylinder). If carbon deposits or cylinder wear have produced ridges, they must be completely removed with a special tool **(see illustration)**.

Follow the manufacturer's instructions provided with the tool. Failure to remove the ridges before attempting to remove the piston/connecting rod assemblies may result in piston breakage.

2   After the cylinder ridges have been removed, turn the engine so the crankshaft is facing up.

3   Before the main bearing cap assembly and connecting rods are removed, check the connecting rod endplay with feeler gauges. Slide them between the first connecting rod and the crankshaft throw until the play is removed **(see illustration)**. The endplay is equal to the thickness of the feeler gauge(s). If the endplay exceeds the service limit, new connecting rods will be required. If new rods (or a new crankshaft) are installed, the endplay may fall under the minimum listed in this Chapter's Specifications (if it does, the rods will have to be machined to restore it - consult an automotive machine shop for advice if necessary). Repeat the procedure for the remaining connecting rods.

4   Check the connecting rods and caps for identification marks **(see illustration)**. If they aren't plainly marked, use a small center-punch to make the appropriate number of indentations on each rod and cap (1, 2, 3, etc., depending on the cylinder they're associated with).

5   Loosen each of the connecting rod cap nuts or bolts 1/2-turn at a time until they can

14.3 Checking the connecting rod endplay (side clearance)

14.4 If the connecting rods and caps are not identified, use a center punch or numbered impression stamps to mark the caps to the rods by cylinder number (No. 4 connecting rod shown)

14.6 On V6 engines, place a section of plastic or rubber hose over the connecting rod studs to prevent damaging the crankshaft journals during piston/rod removal

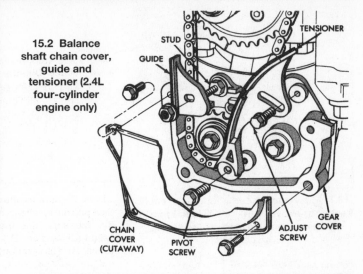

15.2 Balance shaft chain cover, guide and tensioner (2.4L four-cylinder engine only)

be removed by hand. Remove the number one connecting rod cap and bearing insert. Don't drop the bearing insert out of the cap.

6   If you are removing the rods from a V6 engine, slip a short length of plastic or rubber hose over each connecting rod stud to protect the crankshaft journal and cylinder wall as the rod is removed **(see illustration)**.

7   Remove the bearing insert and push the connecting rod/piston assembly out through the top of the engine. Use a wooden or plastic hammer handle to push on the upper bearing surface in the connecting rod. If resistance is felt, double-check to make sure that all of the ridge was removed from the cylinder.

8   Repeat the procedure for the remaining cylinders. **Note:** *On four-cylinder engines, new connecting rod bolts must be installed when the engine is reassembled.*

9   After removal, reassemble the connecting rod caps and bearing inserts in their respective connecting rods and install the cap bolts finger tight. Leaving the old bearing inserts in place until reassembly will help prevent the connecting rod bearing surfaces from being accidentally nicked or gouged.

10   Don't separate the pistons from the connecting rods (see Section 20 for additional information).

15 Balance shafts (2.4L four-cylinder engine only) - removal, inspection and installation

Note: *This procedure assumes that the engine has been removed from the vehicle and the driveplate, timing belt, oil pan and oil pump have also been removed (see Chapter 2, Part A).*

Removal

Refer to illustrations 15.2, 15.4, 15.5 and 15.6

1   The balance shafts are installed in a carrier that is mounted to the main bearing cap assembly on the lower part of the engine block **(see illustration 9.5b)**. The shafts are

interconnected through two gears which rotate them in opposite directions. These gears are driven by a chain from the crankshaft and they are designed to rotate at a 2:1 ratio with the crankshaft (one turn of the crankshaft equals two turns of the balance shafts). This motion will counterbalance certain reciprocating masses within the engine.

2   Remove the chain cover, guide and tensioner from the engine block **(see illustration)**.

3   While keeping the crankshaft from rotating, remove the balance shaft bolts. **Caution:** *If the rocker arm shaft assemblies have not been removed, DO NOT rotate the crankshaft as valve damage could occur.* **Note:** *A block of wood placed tightly between the engine block and the crankshaft counterbalance will prevent crankshaft rotation.*

4   Remove the balance shaft chain sprocket, chain and crankshaft chain sprocket **(see illustration)**. Use two prybars to work the sprocket back and forth until it is free from the crankshaft. **Note:** *The carrier assembly may be removed from the main bearing cap assembly at this time, if balance shaft removal is not required.*

5   Remove the special stud (double-ended)

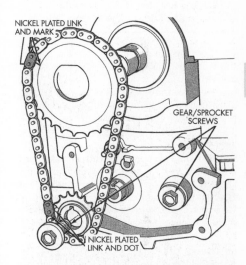

15.4 Balance shaft chain, crankshaft and balance shaft sprockets assembly details

from the gear cover. Then remove the gear cover and balance shaft drive and driven gears **(see illustration)**.

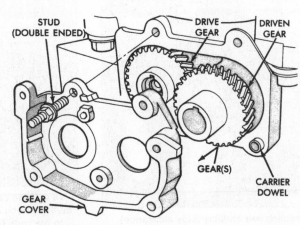

15.5 Remove the double ended stud and separate the gear cover from the balance shaft carrier

2C

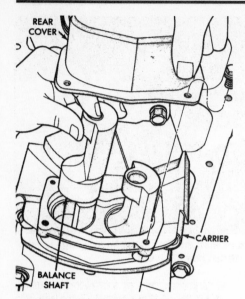

15.6 Remove the rear cover from the carrier and withdraw the balance shafts

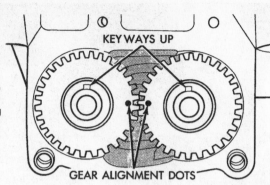

15.12 After gear installation, the balance shaft keyways should be parallel and facing the crankshaft, and the gear alignment marks should be together as shown

6   Remove the rear cover from the carrier and withdraw the balance shafts (see illustration).

7   Remove the bolts that retain the carrier to the main bearing cap assembly, and separate the carrier from the engine.

Inspection

8   Clean all components with solvent and dry thoroughly. Inspect all components for damage and wear. Pay special attention to the chain, sprocket and gear teeth and the bearing surfaces of the carrier and balance shafts. Replace defective parts as necessary.

Installation

Refer to illustrations 15.12 and 15.15

9   Install the balance shaft carrier onto the main bearing cap assembly and tighten the bolts to the torque listed in this Chapter's Specifications.

10   Lubricate the balance shafts with clean engine oil and insert them into the carrier.

11   Install the rear cover and tighten the bolts to the torque listed in this Chapter's Specifications.

12   Rotate the balance shafts until both shaft keyways are parallel and facing toward the crankshaft. Install the short hub drive gear on the sprocket driven shaft and the long hub gear on the gear driven shaft. After installation, the timing marks (dots) should be together and the keyways positioned as shown (see illustration).

13   Install the gear cover and tighten the double-ended stud to the torque listed in this Chapter's Specifications.

14   Install the sprocket onto the crankshaft with the timing mark facing out, be careful

not to cock the sprocket as its being installed.

15   Position the crankshaft so the timing mark on the chain sprocket is aligned with the parting line on the left side of the number 1 main bearing cap as shown (see illustration).

16   Place the chain onto the crankshaft sprocket so that the nickel plated link of the chain is located at the timing mark on the crankshaft sprocket (see illustration 15.15).

17   Install the balance shaft sprocket into the chain so that the timing mark on the sprocket (yellow dot) mates with the nickel plated link on the chain (8 links from the upper nickel plated link) (see illustration 15.15).

18   Slide the balance shaft sprocket onto the balance shaft. If the sprocket is difficult to install on the balance shaft, it may be necessary to loosen the rear cover and push the balance shaft slightly out of the carrier to facilitate sprocket installation. **Note:** *The timing mark on the balance shaft sprocket and*

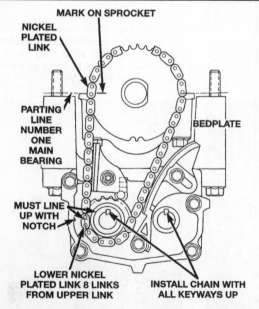

15.15 The timing mark on the crankshaft sprocket, nickel plated links, notch and the yellow dot on balance shaft sprocket must be aligned for correct timing

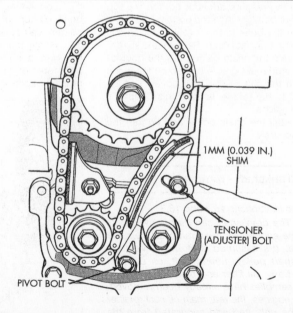

15.20 With the shim in place, apply approximately 5.5 to 6.5 lbs of pressure to the chain tensioner and then tighten the bolt to the torque listed in this Chapter's Specifications

16.1 Checking the crankshaft endplay using a dial indicator

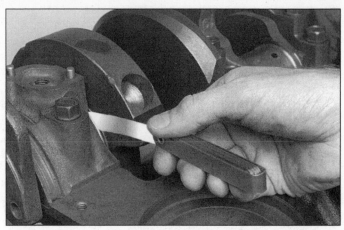

16.3 Checking the crankshaft endplay using feeler gauges at the thrust bearing journal

the nickel plated link should align with the notch on the side of the gear cover (see illustration 15.15).

19   Install the balance shaft bolts. While keeping the crankshaft from rotating, tighten the balance shaft bolts to the torque listed in this Chapter's Specifications. **Note:** *A block of wood placed tightly between the engine block and the crankshaft counterbalance will prevent crankshaft rotation.*

Chain tensioning

Refer to illustration 15.20

20   Install the chain tensioner loosely. Place a 0.039 x 2.75 inch shim (a feeler gauge cut to the appropriate size can be used) between the tensioner and the chain (see illustration). Push the tensioner up against the chain. Apply firm pressure (approximately 5.5 to 6.5 lbs) directly behind the adjustment slot to remove the slack.

21   With pressure applied, tighten the top tensioner bolt first then the bottom pivot bolt. Tighten the bolts to the torque listed in this Chapter's Specifications. Remove the shim.

22   Place the chain guide onto the double-ended stud making sure the tab on the guide fits into the slot on the gear cover. Tighten the nut to the torque listed in this Chapter's Specifications.

23   Install the chain cover and tighten the bolts securely.

16   Crankshaft - removal

Refer to illustrations 16.1 and 16.3

Note: *The crankshaft can be removed only after the engine has been removed from the vehicle. It's assumed that the driveplate, crankshaft pulley, timing belt, oil pan, oil pump body, oil filter and piston/connecting rod assemblies have already been removed. On V6 engines, the rear main oil seal retainer must be unbolted and separated from the block before proceeding with crankshaft removal.*

1   Before the crankshaft is removed, mea-

sure the endplay. Mount a dial indicator with the indicator in line with the crankshaft and just touching the end of the crankshaft as shown (see illustration).

2   Pry the crankshaft all the way to the rear and zero the dial indicator. Next, pry the crankshaft to the front as far as possible and check the reading on the dial indicator. The distance traveled is the endplay. If it's greater than the tolerance listed in this Chapter's Specifications, check the crankshaft thrust surfaces for wear after its removed. If no wear is evident, new main bearings should correct the endplay.

3   If a dial indicator isn't available, feeler gauges can be used. Gently pry the crankshaft all the way to the front of the engine. Slip feeler gauges between the crankshaft and the front face of the thrust bearing or washer to determine the clearance (see illustration).

4   Loosen the main bearing cap assembly bolts 1/4-turn at a time each, until they can be removed by hand.

5   Gently tap the main bearing cap assembly with a soft-face hammer around the perimeter of the assembly. Pull the main bearing cap assembly straight up and off the

cylinder block. On 2.0L four-cylinder engines, remove the oil filter passage O-ring seal and the three main bearing cap assembly locating dowels. Try not to drop the bearing inserts if they come out with the assembly.

6   Carefully lift the crankshaft out of the engine. It may be a good idea to have an assistant available, since the crankshaft is quite heavy and awkward to handle. With the bearing inserts in place inside the engine block and main bearing caps, reinstall the main bearing cap assembly onto engine block and tighten the bolts finger tight. Make sure you install the main bearing cap assembly on V6 models with the arrow facing the front (timing belt end) of the engine.

17   Engine block - cleaning

Refer to illustrations 17.1a, 17.1b, 17.8 and 17.10

1   Remove the core plugs from the engine block. To do this, knock one side of the plugs into the block with a hammer and a punch, then grasp them with large pliers and pull them out (see illustrations).

17.1a Use a hammer and a large punch to knock the core plugs sideways in their bores . . .

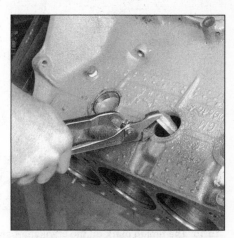

17.1b . . . then pull the core plugs out with pliers

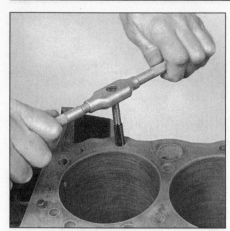

17.8 All bolt holes in the block, particularly the main bearing cap and head bolt holes, should be cleaned and restored with the appropriate tap (be sure to remove the debris from the holes after this operation)

2   Using a gasket scraper, remove all traces of gasket material from the engine block. Be very careful not to nick or gouge the gasket sealing surfaces.

3   Remove the main bearing cap assembly and separate the bearing inserts from the caps and the engine block. **Note:** *The upper bearings are equipped with the oil groove and hole, the thrust bearing is in the No. 3 (center) location.* Tag the bearings, indicating which cylinder they were removed from, then set them aside.

4   Remove all of the threaded oil gallery plugs from the block. The plugs are usually very tight - they may have to be drilled out and the holes retapped. Use new plugs when the engine is reassembled.

5   If the engine is extremely dirty it should be taken to an automotive machine shop for cleaning.

6   After the block is returned, clean all oil holes and oil galleries one more time. Brushes specifically designed for this purpose are available at most auto parts stores. Flush the passages with warm water until the water runs clear, dry the block thoroughly and wipe all machined surfaces with a light, rust preventive oil. If you have access to compressed air, use it to speed the drying process and to blow out all the oil holes and galleries. **Warning:** *Wear eye protection when using compressed air!*

7   If the block isn't extremely dirty or slugged up, you can do an adequate cleaning job with hot soapy water and a stiff brush. Take plenty of time and do a thorough job. Regardless of the cleaning method used, be sure to clean all oil holes and galleries very thoroughly, dry the block completely and coat all machined surfaces with light oil.

8   The threaded holes in the block must be clean to ensure accurate torque readings during reassembly. Run the proper size tap into each of the holes to remove rust, corrosion, thread sealant or sludge and restore

17.10 A large 1/2 drive socket on an extension can be used to drive the new core plugs into the block

damaged threads **(see illustration)**. If possible, use compressed air to clear the holes of debris produced by this operation. Now is a good time to clean the threads on the head bolts and the main bearing cap bolts as well.

9   Reinstall the bearing inserts in their correct locations and place the main bearing cap assembly onto the engine block. Tighten the bolts finger tight.

10   After coating the sealing surfaces of the new core plugs with Permatex No. 2 sealant (or equivalent), install them in the engine block **(see illustration)**. Make sure they're driven in straight and seated properly or leakage could result. Special tools are available for this purpose, but a large socket, with an outside diameter that will just slip into the core plug, a 1/2-inch drive extension and a hammer will work just as well.

11   Apply non-hardening sealant (such as Permatex No. 2 or Teflon pipe sealant) to the

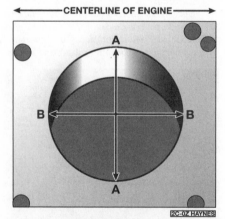

18.4a Measure the diameter of each cylinder at a right angle to the engine centerline (A) and parallel to the engine centerline (B) - the cylinder out-of-round is the difference between (A) and (B); the cylinder taper is the difference between (A) and (B) at the top of the cylinder and (A) and (B) at the bottom of the cylinder

new oil gallery plugs and thread them into the holes in the block. Make sure they're tightened securely.

12   If the engine isn't going to be reassembled right away, cover it with a large plastic trash bag to keep it clean.

18   Engine block - inspection

Refer to illustrations 18.4a, 18.4b. 18.4c, 18.4d and 18.8

1   Before the block is inspected, it must be cleaned as described in Section 17.

2   Visually check the block for cracks, rust and corrosion. Look for stripped threads in the threaded holes. It's also a good idea to have the block checked for hidden cracks by an automotive machine shop that has the special equipment to do this type of work. If defects are found, have the block repaired, if possible, or replaced. **Note:** *If the engine block requires machining, be sure to send the main bearing cap assembly along with the block.*

3   Check the cylinder bores for scuffing and scoring.

4   Check the cylinders for taper and out-of-round conditions as follows **(see illustrations)**:

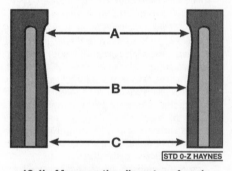

18.4b Measure the diameter of each cylinder just under the wear ridge (A), at the center (B) and the bottom (C)

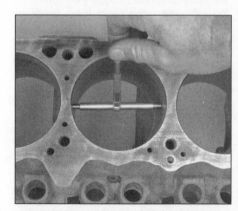

18.4c The ability to "feel" when the telescoping gauge is at the correct point will be developed over time, so work slowly and repeat the check until you're satisfied that the measurement is accurate

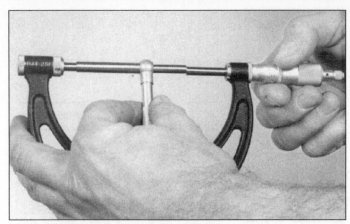

18.4d To determine the diameter, the telescoping gauge is then measured with a micrometer

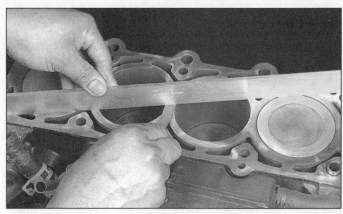

18.8 Check the cylinder block head gasket surface for warpage by placing a precision straightedge across the surface and trying to slip a feeler gauge between the block and straightedge

a) *Measure the diameter of each cylinder at the top (just under the ridge area), center and bottom of the cylinder bore, parallel to the crankshaft axis.*

b) *Next, measure each cylinder's diameter at the same three locations perpendicular to the crankshaft axis.*

c) *The taper of each cylinder is the difference between the bore diameter at the top of the cylinder and the diameter at the bottom. The out-of-round specification is the difference between the parallel and perpendicular measurements. Compare the results to the tolerance listed in this Chapter's Specifications.*

5   Repeat the procedure for the remaining cylinders.

6   If the cylinder walls are badly scuffed or scored, or if they're out-of-round or tapered beyond the limits listed in this Chapter's Specifications, have the engine block rebored and honed at an automotive machine shop. If a rebore is performed, oversize pistons and rings will be required.

7   If the cylinders are in reasonably good condition and not worn to the outside of the limits, and if the piston-to-cylinder bore clearances are acceptable, then they don't have to be rebored. Honing is all that's necessary (see Section 19).

8   Using a precision straightedge and a feeler gauge, check the block deck (the surface that mates with the cylinder head) for distortion **(see illustration)**. If it's distorted beyond the tolerance listed in this Chapter's Specifications, it can usually be resurfaced by an automotive machine shop.

19   Cylinder honing

Refer to illustrations 19.3a and 19.3b

1   Prior to engine reassembly, the cylinder bores must be honed so the new piston rings will seat correctly and provide the best possible combustion chamber seal. **Note:** *If you don't have the tools or don't want to tackle the honing operation, most automotive*

machine shops will do it for a reasonable fee.

2   Before honing the cylinders, install the main bearing cap assembly and tighten the bolts to the torque listed in this Chapter's Specifications following the recommended tightening sequence **(see illustrations 25.13a, 25.13b and 25.13c)**. Make sure you install the main bearing cap assembly on V6 models with the arrow facing the front (timing belt end) of the engine.

3   Two types of cylinder hones are commonly available - the flex hone or "bottle brush" type and the more traditional surfacing hone with spring-loaded stones. Both will do the job, but for the less experienced mechanic the "bottle brush" hone will probably be easier to use. You'll also need some kerosene or honing oil, rags and an electric drill motor. Proceed as follows:

a) *Mount the hone in the drill motor, compress the stones and slip it into the first cylinder* **(see illustration)**. *Be sure to wear safety goggles or a face shield!*

b) *Lubricate the cylinder with plenty of honing oil, turn on the drill and move the hone up-and-down in the cylinder at a pace that will produce a fine crosshatch pattern on the cylinder walls* **(see illus-**

tration). *Ideally, the crosshatch lines should intersect at approximately a 60-degree angle. Be sure to use plenty of lubricant and don't take off any more material than is absolutely necessary to produce the desired finish.* **Note:** *Piston ring manufacturers may specify a smaller crosshatch angle than the traditional 60-degrees - read and follow any instructions included with the new rings.*

c) *Don't withdraw the hone from the cylinder while it's running. Instead, shut off the drill and continue moving the hone up-and-down in the cylinder until it comes to a complete stop, then compress the stones and withdraw the hone. If you're using a "bottle brush" type hone, stop the drill motor, then turn the chuck in the normal direction of rotation while withdrawing the hone from the cylinder.*

d) *Wipe the oil out of the cylinder and repeat the procedure for the remaining cylinders.*

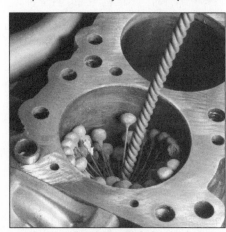

19.3a A "bottle brush" type hone will generally produce the best results in most applications

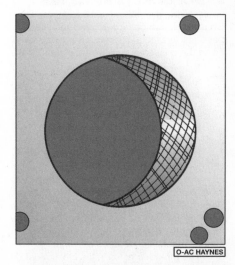

19.3b The honing procedure should produce a smooth crosshatch pattern with the lines intersecting at approximately 60 degree angles

2C

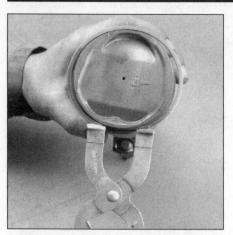

20.2 Use a piston ring removal tool (shown) to remove the rings from the pistons

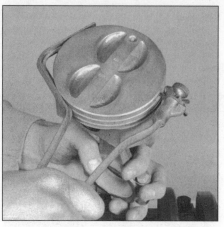

20.4a The piston ring grooves can be cleaned using a special tool like this one . . .

20.4b . . . or a short piece of an old compression ring

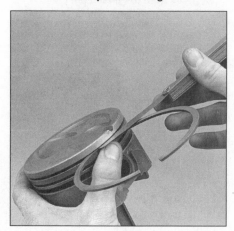

20.10 Checking the piston ring side clearance

4   After the honing job is complete, chamfer the top edges of the cylinder bores with a small file so the rings won't catch when the pistons are installed. Be very careful not to nick the cylinder walls with the end of the file.

5   The entire engine block must be washed again very thoroughly with warm, soapy water to remove all traces of the abrasive grit produced during the honing operation. **Note:** *The bores can be considered clean when a lint-free white cloth - dampened with clean engine oil - used to wipe them out doesn't pick up any more honing residue, which will show up as gray areas on the cloth. Be sure to run a brush through all oil holes and galleries and flush them with running water.*

6   After rinsing, dry the block and apply a coat of light rust preventive oil or Vaseline to all machined surfaces. Wrap the block in a plastic trash bag to keep it clean and set it aside until reassembly.

20   Pistons and connecting rods - inspection

Refer to illustrations 20.2, 20.4a, 20.4b, 20.10 and 20.11

1   Before the inspection process can be carried out, the piston/connecting rod assemblies must be cleaned and the original piston rings removed from the pistons. **Note:** *Always use new piston rings when the engine is reassembled.*

2   Using a piston ring removal tool **(see illustration)**, carefully remove the rings from the pistons. Be careful not to nick or gouge the pistons in the process.

3   Scrape all traces of carbon from the top of the piston. A hand-held wire brush or a piece of fine emery cloth can be used once the majority of the deposits have been scraped away. Do not, under any circumstances, use a wire brush mounted in a drill motor to remove deposits from the pistons. The piston material is soft and may be eroded away by the wire brush.

4   Use a piston ring groove cleaning tool to remove carbon deposits from the ring grooves. If a tool isn't available, a piece broken off the old ring will do the job. Be very careful to remove only the carbon deposits - don't remove any metal and do not nick or scratch the sides of the ring grooves **(see illustrations)**.

5   Once the deposits have been removed, clean the piston/rod assemblies with solvent and dry them with compressed air (if available). Make sure the oil return holes in the back sides of the ring grooves are free from obstructions.

6   If the pistons and cylinder walls aren't damaged or worn excessively, and if the engine block is not rebored, new pistons won't be necessary. Normal piston wear appears as even, vertical wear on the piston thrust surfaces and slight looseness of the top ring in its groove. However, new piston rings should always be installed when an engine is rebuilt.

7   Carefully inspect each piston for cracks around the skirt, at the pin bosses and at the ring lands.

8   Look for scoring and scuffing on the thrust faces of the skirt, holes in the piston crown and burned areas at the edge of the crown. If the skirt is scored or scuffed, the engine may have been suffering from overheating and/or abnormal combustion, which caused excessively high operating temperatures. The cooling and lubrication systems should be checked thoroughly. A hole in the piston crown is an indication that abnormal combustion (pre-ignition) was occurring. Burned areas at the edge of the piston crown are usually evidence of spark knock (detonation). If any of the above problems exist, the causes must be corrected or the damage will occur again. The causes may include intake air leaks, incorrect fuel/air mixture, incorrect ignition timing and EGR system malfunctions.

9   Corrosion of the piston, in the form of small pits, indicates that coolant is leaking into the combustion chamber and/or the crankcase. Again, the cause must be corrected or the problem may persist in the

rebuilt engine.

10   Measure the piston ring side clearance by laying a new piston ring in each ring groove and slipping a feeler gauge in beside it **(see illustration)**. Check the clearance at three or four locations around each groove. Be sure to use the correct ring for each groove - they are different. If the side clearance is greater than specified, new pistons must be installed. If new pistons are installed, repeat this step with the new pistons and rings.

11   Check the piston-to-bore clearance by measuring the cylinder bore (see Section 18) and the piston diameter. Make sure the pistons and bores are correctly matched. Measure the piston across the skirt 11/16-inch (2.0L four-cylinder), 9/16-inch (2.4L four-cylinder) or 0.080 inch (V6 engine) above the bottom of the piston, at a 90-degree angle to the piston pin **(see illustration)**. Subtract the piston diameter from the bore diameter to obtain the piston-to-bore clearance. If it's greater than the limit listed in this Chapter's Specifications, the block must be rebored and new pistons and rings installed.

12   Check the piston-to-rod clearance by twisting the piston and rod in opposite directions. Any noticeable play indicates exces-

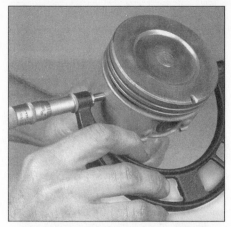

20.11 Measure the piston diameter 90 degrees from the piston pin and the specified distance from the bottom of the piston skirt

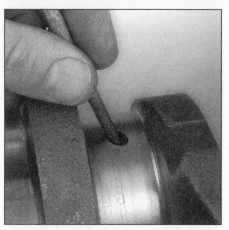

21.1 Using a fine file, break the edge on the crankshaft journal oil passages so sharp edges won't gouge or scratch the new bearings

21.2 Use a wire or stiff bristle brush to clean the crankshaft oil passages - be sure to flush them with solvent after this operation

21.4 An easy way to check the surface finish on the bearing journals is to rub a penny over the bearing surface - if the copper transfers to the crankshaft, the surface is too rough and must be reground by an automotive machine shop

21.7 Measure the diameter of each bearing journal at several locations to determine if it's excessively worn or taper and out-of-round conditions exist

sive wear, which must be corrected. The piston/connecting rod assemblies should be taken to an automotive machine shop to have the pistons and rods resized and new pins installed.

13   If the pistons must be removed from the connecting rods for any reason, they should be taken to an automotive machine shop for disassembly. While at the automotive machine shop, have the connecting rods checked for bend and twist, since automotive machine shops have special equipment specifically used for this purpose. **Note:** *Unless new pistons and/or connecting rods must be installed, do not disassemble the pistons and connecting rods.*

14   Inspect the connecting rods for cracks and other damage. Temporarily remove the rod caps, lift out the old bearing inserts, wipe the rod and cap bearing surfaces clean and inspect them for nicks, gouges and scratches. After checking the rods, replace the old bearings, slip the caps into place and tighten the nuts (or bolts as applicable) finger tight. **Note:** *If the engine is being rebuilt*

because of a connecting rod knock, always install new rods.

21   Crankshaft - inspection

Refer to illustration 21.1, 21.2, 21.4 and 21.7

1   Remove all burrs from the crankshaft oil holes with a stone, file or scraper **(see illustration)**.

2   Clean the crankshaft with solvent and dry it with compressed air (if available). Be sure to clean the oil holes with a stiff brush and flush them with solvent **(see illustration)**. **Warning:** *If compressed air is used always wear eye protection to prevent solvents or debris from causing an injury to your eyes.*

3   Check the main and connecting rod bearing journals for uneven wear, scoring, pits and cracks.

4   Rub a penny across each journal several times. If a journal picks up copper from the penny, it's too rough and must be reground **(see illustration)**.

5   Remove all burrs from the crankshaft oil

holes with a stone, file or scraper.

6   Check the rest of the crankshaft for cracks and other damage. It should be magnafluxed to reveal hidden cracks - an automotive machine shop will handle the procedure.

7   Using a micrometer, measure the diameter of the main bearing and connecting rod journals and compare the results to the tolerances listed in this Chapter's Specifications **(see illustration)**. By measuring the diameter at a number of points around each journal's circumference, you'll be able to determine whether or not the journal is out-of-round. Take the measurement at each end of the journal, near the crank throws, to determine if the journal is tapered.

8   If the crankshaft journals are damaged, tapered, out-of-round or worn beyond the limits listed in this Chapter's Specifications, the crankshaft must be reground by an automotive machine shop. Be sure to obtain and install the correct size bearing inserts if the crankshaft is reconditioned.

9   Check the oil seal journals at each end

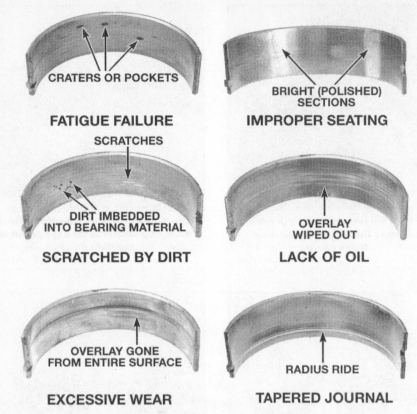

22.1 Typical bearing wear patterns and probable causes

of the crankshaft for wear and damage. If the seal has worn a groove in the journal, or if it's nicked or scratched, the new seal may leak when the engine is reassembled . In some cases, an automotive machine shop may be able to repair the journal by pressing on a thin sleeve. If repair isn't feasible, a new or different crankshaft must be installed.

10   Refer to Section 22 and examine the main and rod bearing inserts.

22   Main and connecting rod bearings - inspection

Refer to illustration 22.1

1   Even though the main and connecting rod bearings should be replaced with new ones during the engine overhaul, the old bearings should be retained for close examination, as they may reveal valuable information about the condition of the engine **(see illustration)**.

2   Bearing failure occurs because of lack of lubrication, the presence of dirt or other foreign particles, overloading the engine and corrosion. Regardless of the cause of bearing failure, it must be corrected before the engine is reassembled to prevent it from happening again.

3   When examining the bearings, remove them from the engine block, the main bearing caps, the connecting rods and the rod caps and lay them out on a clean surface in the same general position as their location in the engine. This will enable you to match any bearing problems with the corresponding crankshaft journal.

4   Dirt and other foreign particles get into the engine in a variety of ways. It may be left in the engine during assembly, or it may pass through filters or the PCV system. It may get into the oil, and from there into the bearings. Metal chips from machining operations and normal engine wear are often present. Abrasives are sometimes left in engine components after reconditioning, especially when parts are not thoroughly cleaned using the proper cleaning methods. Whatever the source, these foreign objects often end up embedded in the soft bearing material and are easily recognized. Large particles will not embed in the bearing and will score or gouge the bearing and journal. The best prevention for this cause of bearing failure is to clean all parts thoroughly and keep everything spotlessly clean during engine assembly. Frequent and regular engine oil and filter changes are also recommended.

5   Lack of lubrication (or lubrication breakdown) has a number of interrelated causes. Excessive heat (which thins the oil), overloading (which squeezes the oil from the bearing face) and oil leakage or throw off (from excessive bearing clearances, worn oil pump or high engine speeds) all contribute to lubrication breakdown. Blocked oil passages, which usually are the result of misaligned oil

holes in a bearing shell, will also oil starve a bearing and destroy it. When lack of lubrication is the cause of bearing failure, the bearing material is wiped or extruded from the steel backing of the bearing. Temperatures may increase to the point where the steel backing turns blue from overheating.

6   Driving habits can have a definite effect on bearing life. Full throttle, low speed operation (lugging the engine) puts very high loads on bearings, which tends to squeeze out the oil film. These loads cause the bearings to flex, which produces fine cracks in the bearing face (fatigue failure). Eventually the bearing material will loosen in pieces and tear away from the steel backing. Short trip driving leads to corrosion of bearings because insufficient engine heat is produced to drive off the condensed water and corrosive gases. These products collect in the engine oil, forming acid and sludge. As the oil is carried to the engine bearings, the acid attacks and corrodes the bearing material.

7   Incorrect bearing installation during engine assembly will lead to bearing failure as well. Tight fitting bearings leave insufficient bearing oil clearance and will result in oil starvation. Dirt or foreign particles trapped behind a bearing insert result in high spots on the bearing which lead to failure.

23   Engine overhaul - reassembly sequence

1   Before beginning engine reassembly, make sure you have all the necessary new parts, gaskets and seals as well as the following items on hand:

> *Common hand tools*
> *A 1/2-inch drive torque wrench*
> *Piston ring installation tool*
> *Piston ring compressor*
> *Plastigage set*
> *Feeler gauges*
> *A fine-tooth file*
> *New engine oil*
> *Engine assembly lube or moly-base*
>   *grease*
> *Gasket sealants (anaerobic and RTV*
>   *type)*
> *Thread locking compound*

2   In order to save time and avoid problems, engine reassembly should be performed in the following general order:

> *Piston rings installed on pistons*
> *Crankshaft and main bearings*
> *Piston/connecting rod assemblies*
> *Rear main oil seal*
> *Balance shaft carrier (2.4L four-cylinder)*
> *Front case and oil pump assembly*
> *Oil pan*
> *Cylinder head(s) assembly*
> *Water pump*
> *Timing belt and sprockets*
> *Timing belt cover(s)*
> *Rocker arm cover(s)*
> *Intake and exhaust manifolds*
> *Driveplate*

24.3 Install the piston ring into the cylinder then push it down into position using a piston so the ring will be square in the cylinder

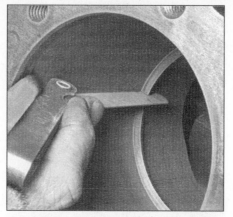

24.4 With the ring square in the cylinder, measure the ring end gap with a feeler gauge

24.5 If the ring end gap is too small, clamp a file in a vise as shown and file the piston ring ends - be sure to remove all raised material

24 Piston rings - installation

Refer to illustrations 24.3, 24.4, 24.5, 24.9a, 24.9b, 24.11 and 24.12

1   Before installing the new piston rings, the ring end gaps must be checked. It's assumed that the piston ring side clearance has been checked and verified correct (see Section 20).

2   Lay out the piston/connecting rod assemblies and the new ring sets so the ring sets will be matched with the same piston and cylinder during the end gap measurement and engine assembly.

3   Insert the top (number one) ring into the first cylinder and square it up with the cylinder walls by pushing it in with the top of the piston **(see illustration)**. The ring should be near the bottom of the cylinder, at the lower limit of ring travel.

4   To measure the end gap, slip feeler gauges between the ends of the ring until a gauge equal to the gap width is found **(see illustration)**. The feeler gauge should slide between the ring ends with a slight amount of drag. Compare the measurement to the tolerance listed in this Chapter's Specifications. If the gap is larger or smaller than specified, double-check to make sure you have the correct rings before proceeding.

5   If the gap is too small, it must be enlarged or the ring ends may come in contact with each other during engine operation, which can cause serious damage to the engine. The end gap can be increased by filing the ring ends very carefully with a fine file. Mount the file in a vise equipped with soft jaws, slip the ring over the file with the ends contacting the file face and slowly move the ring to remove material from the ends. When performing this operation, file only by pushing the ring from the outside end of the file towards the vise **(see illustration)**.

6   Excess end gap isn't critical unless it's greater than the limit listed in this Chapter's Specifications. Again, double-check to make sure you have the correct ring type and that

24.9a Installing the spacer/expander in the oil ring groove

you are referencing the correct section and category of specifications.

7   Repeat the procedure for each ring that will be installed in the first cylinder and for each ring in the remaining cylinders. Remember to keep rings, pistons and cylinders matched up.

8   Once the ring end gaps have been checked/corrected, the rings can be installed on the pistons.

9   The oil control ring (lowest one on the piston) is usually installed first. It's composed of three separate components. Slip the spacer/expander into the groove **(see illustration)**. If an anti-rotation tang is used, make sure it's inserted into the drilled hole in the ring groove. Next, install the upper side rail in the same manner **(see illustration)**. Don't use a piston ring installation tool on the oil ring side rails, as they may be damaged. Instead, place one end of the side rail into the groove between the spacer/expander and the ring land, hold it firmly in place and slide a finger around the piston while pushing the rail into the groove. Finally, install the lower side rail.

10   After the three oil ring components have been installed, check to make sure that both the upper and lower side rails can be rotated smoothly inside the ring grooves.

24.9b DO NOT use a piston ring installation tool when installing the oil control side rails

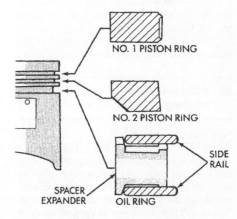

24.11 Piston ring assembly details

11   The number two (middle) ring is installed next. It's usually stamped with a mark which must face up, toward the top of the piston. Do not mix up the top and middle rings, as they have different cross-sections **(see illustration)**. **Note:** *Always follow the instructions printed on the ring package or box - different manufacturers may require different approaches.*

24.12 Use a piston ring installation tool to install the 2nd and top rings - be sure the directional mark on the piston ring(s) is facing toward the top of the piston

12   Use a piston ring installation tool and make sure the identification mark is facing the top of the piston, then slip the ring into the middle groove on the piston **(see illustration)**. Don't expand the ring any more than necessary to slide it over the piston.

13   Install the number one (top) ring in the same manner. Make sure the mark is facing up. Be careful not to confuse the number one and number two rings **(see illustration 24.11)**.

14   Repeat the procedure for the remaining pistons and rings.

25   Crankshaft installation and main bearing oil clearance check

1   Crankshaft installation is the first step in engine reassembly. It's assumed at this point that the engine block and crankshaft have

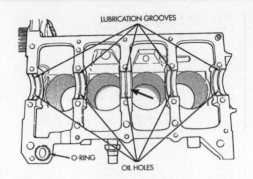

25.5a On four-cylinder engines, install the upper bearings (with grooves and holes) into the engine block. Be sure to align the oil holes and install the thrust bearing in the center bearing position (arrow)

25.5b Main bearing installation details - four-cylinder engines

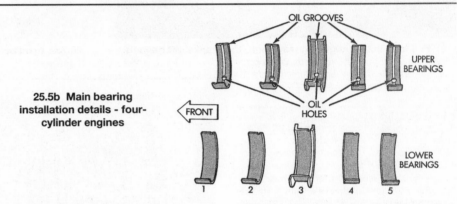

been cleaned, inspected and repaired or reconditioned.
2   Position the engine block with the bottom facing up.
3   Remove the mounting bolts and lift off the main bearing cap assembly.
4   If they're still in place, remove the original bearing inserts from the block and the main bearing cap assembly. Wipe the bearing surfaces of the block and main bearing cap assembly with a clean, lint-free cloth. They must be kept spotlessly clean. This is critical for determining the correct bearing oil clearance.

Main bearing oil clearance check

Refer to illustrations 25.5a, 25.5b, 25.5c, 25.11, 25.13a, 25.13b, 25.13c and 25.15

5   Without mixing them up, clean the back sides of the new upper main bearing inserts (with grooves and oil holes) and lay one in each main bearing saddle in the block. Each upper bearing has an oil groove and oil hole in it. **Caution:** *The oil holes in the block must line up with the oil holes in the upper bearing inserts.* The thrust bearing insert or thrust washers (V6 engine) must be installed in the No. 3 bearing position **(see illustrations)**. V6 engines have two two-piece thrust washers which are installed on each side of the No. 3 bearing. Install the thrust washers with the grooved side toward the crankshaft (plain sides should be facing each other). Install the thrust washers so that one set has a tab located in the block and the other set's tab is in the main bearing cap assembly. Clean the back sides of the lower main bearing inserts (without grooves) and lay them in the corresponding location in the main bearing cap assembly. Make sure the tab on the bearing insert fits into the recess in the block or main bearing cap assembly. **Caution:** *Do not hammer the bearing insert into place and don't nick or gouge the bearing faces. DO NOT apply any lubrication at this time.*
6   Clean the faces of the bearing inserts in the block and the crankshaft main bearing journals with a clean, lint-free cloth.
7   Check or clean the oil holes in the crankshaft, as any dirt here can go only one way - straight through the new bearings.
8   Once you're certain the crankshaft is

25.5c Crankshaft main bearing and thrust washer arrangement - V6 engine

25.11 Place the Plastigage (arrow) onto the crankshaft bearing journal as shown

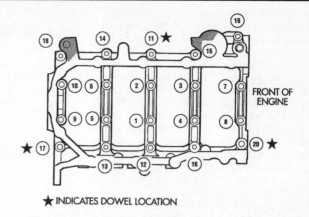

★ INDICATES DOWEL LOCATION

25.13a Main bearing cap assembly bolt tightening sequence - 2.0L four-cylinder engine

clean, carefully lay it in position in the cylinder block.

9   Before the crankshaft can be permanently installed, the main bearing oil clearance must be checked. **Note:** *On four-cylinder engines, the crankshaft position sensor must be removed prior to main bearing oil clearance check* (see Chapter 6 if necessary).

10   On 2.0L four-cylinder engines, make sure the three locating dowels are in place on the cylinder block. This is necessary for proper alignment of the main bearing cap assembly to the cylinder block and crankshaft.

11   Cut several pieces of the appropriate size Plastigage (they must be slightly shorter than the width of the main bearing journal) and place one piece on each crankshaft main bearing journal, parallel with the journal axis as shown **(see illustration)**.

12   Clean the faces of the bearing inserts in the main bearing cap assembly. Hold the bearing inserts in place and install the assembly onto the crankshaft and cylinder block.

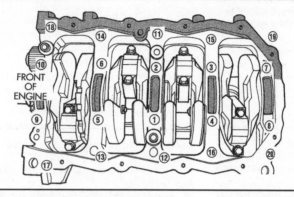

25.13b Main bearing cap assembly bolt tightening sequence - 2.4L four-cylinder engine

2C

DO NOT disturb the Plastigage. Make sure you install the main bearing cap assembly on V6 models with the arrow facing the front (timing belt end) of the engine.

13   Apply clean engine oil to all bolt threads prior to installation, then install all bolts finger-tight. Tighten main bearing cap assembly bolts in the sequence shown **(see illustrations)** progressing in three steps, to the

torque listed in this Chapter's Specifications. DO NOT rotate the crankshaft at any time during this operation.

14   Remove the bolts in the *reverse* order of the tightening sequence and carefully lift the main bearing cap assembly straight up and off the block. Do not disturb the Plastigage or rotate the crankshaft. If the main bearing cap assembly is difficult to remove, tap it gently from side-to-side with a soft-face hammer to loosen it.

15   Compare the width of the crushed Plastigage on each journal to the scale printed on

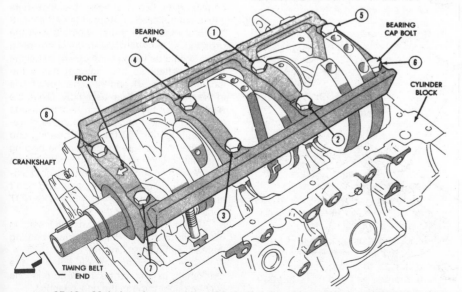

25.13c Main bearing cap assembly bolt tightening sequence - V6 engine

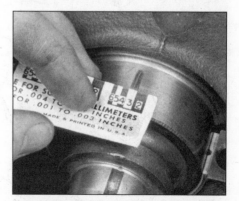

25.15 Use the scale on the Plastigage package to determine the bearing oil clearance - be sure to measure the widest part of the Plastigage and use the correct scale; it comes with both standard and metric scales

the Plastigage envelope to determine the main bearing oil clearance (see illustration). Check the tolerance listed in this Chapter's Specifications to make sure it's acceptable.

16   If the clearance is not as specified, the bearing inserts may be the wrong size (which means different ones will be required). Before deciding if different inserts are needed, make sure that no dirt or oil was between the bearing inserts and the cap assembly or block when the clearance was measured. If the Plastigage was wider at one end than the other, the crankshaft journal may be tapered (refer to Section 21). If the clearance still exceeds the limit specified, the bearing insert(s) will have to be replaced with an undersize bearing insert(s). **Caution:** *When installing a new crankshaft always install a standard bearing insert set.*

17   Carefully scrape all traces of the Plastigage material off the main bearing journals and/or the bearing insert faces. Be sure to remove all residue from the oil holes. Use your fingernail or the edge of a plastic card - don't nick or scratch the bearing faces.

Final installation

Refer to illustration 25.21

18   Carefully lift the crankshaft out of the cylinder block.

19   Clean the bearing insert faces in the cylinder block, then apply a thin, uniform layer of moly-base grease or engine assembly lube to each of the bearing surfaces. Be sure to coat the thrust faces as well as the journal face of the thrust bearing. **Caution:** *Be sure to install the thrust bearing inserts or thrust washers (V6 engine) in the No. 3 journal* (see illustrations 25.5a, 25.5b and 25.5c).

20   On 2.0L four-cylinder engines, install a new oil filter passage O-ring seal and make sure the three locating dowels are in place on the cylinder block. The dowels are necessary for proper alignment of the main bearing cap assembly to the cylinder block and crankshaft.

21   On four-cylinder engines, clean the main bearing cap assembly-to-cylinder block mating surfaces. They must be free of any oil residue. Apply a 1/16-inch bead of anaerobic sealer (Mopar Torque Cure Gasket Maker, or equivalent) to the cylinder block as shown (see illustration). **Caution:** *Use ONLY anaerobic sealant meeting the manufacturers specifications or engine damage may occur.*

22   Make sure the crankshaft journals are clean, then lay the crankshaft back in place in the cylinder block.

23   Clean the bearing insert faces in the main bearing cap assembly, then apply the same lubricant to them. **Caution:** *On four-cylinder engines, DO NOT get any lubricant on the main bearing cap assembly-to-cylinder block mating surfaces as it will inhibit the sealing ability of the anaerobic sealant.*

24   Hold the bearing inserts in place and install the main bearing cap assembly onto the crankshaft and cylinder block. On four-cylinder engines, push the assembly down

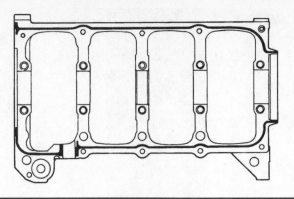

25.21 On four-cylinder engines, apply a 1/16-inch bead of anaerobic sealer (Mopar Torque Cure Gasket Maker, or equivalent) to the engine block as shown

until it contacts the locating dowels.

25   Prior to installation, apply clean engine oil to all bolt threads wiping off any excess, then install all bolts finger-tight. On 2.0L four-cylinder engines, install baffle studs in positions 12, 13 and 16 (see illustration 25.13a).

26   On 2.0L four-cylinder engines, tighten the main bearing cap assembly as follows (see illustration 25.13a):

a) *Tighten bolts 11, 17 and 20 until the assembly contacts the engine block.*

b) *Tighten bolts 1 through 10 in the sequence shown, in 3 steps to the torque listed in this Chapter's Specifications.*

c) *Tighten bolts 11 through 20 in the sequence shown to the torque listed in this Chapter's Specifications.*

27   On 2.4L four-cylinder engines, tighten the main bearing cap assembly as follows (see illustration 25.13b):

a) *Tighten bolts 11, 17 and 20 until the assembly contacts the engine block.*

b) *To ensure correct thrust bearing alignment, rotate the crankshaft until the No. 4 piston is at TDC.*

c) *Carefully pry the crankshaft all the way towards the rear of the block and then towards the front of the block.*

d) *Wedge an appropriate tool such as a block of wood, between the engine block and the crankshaft counterweight to hold the crankshaft in the most forward position. DO NOT drive the wedge between the main bearing cap assembly and the crankshaft.*

e) *Tighten bolts 1 through 10 in the sequence shown, in 3 steps to the torque listed in this Chapter's Specifications - except DO NOT tighten the bolts the additional 1/4-turn.*

f) *Remove the wedge and tighten bolts 1 through 10 in the sequence shown, the additional 1/4-turn.*

g) *Tighten bolts 11 through 20 in the sequence shown to the torque listed in this Chapter's Specifications.*

28   On V6 engines, tighten the main bearing cap assembly bolts in the sequence shown (see illustration 25.13c) progressing in three steps, to the torque listed in this Chapter's Specifications.

29   After tightening the main bearing cap

assembly, tap the ends of the crankshaft forward and backward with a lead or brass hammer to seat the main bearing and crankshaft thrust surfaces.

30   Rotate the crankshaft a number of times by hand to check for any obvious binding. It should rotate with a running torque of 50 in-lbs or less. If the running torque is too high, correct the problem at this time.

31   Recheck the crankshaft endplay with a feeler gauge or a dial indicator as described in Section 16. The endplay should be correct if the crankshaft thrust faces aren't worn or damaged and new bearings have been installed.

32   Refer to the appropriate Part of Chapter 2 and install the new rear main oil seal.

26   Pistons and connecting rods - installation and rod bearing oil clearance check

1   Before installing the piston/connecting rod assemblies, the cylinder walls must be perfectly clean, the top edge of each cylinder bore must be chamfered, and the crankshaft must be in place.

2   Remove the cap from the end of the number one connecting rod (refer to the marks made during removal). Remove the original bearing inserts and wipe the bearing surfaces of the connecting rod and cap with a clean, lint-free cloth. They must be kept spotlessly clean.

Connecting rod bearing oil clearance check

Refer to illustrations 26.6, 26.11, 26.13 and 26.14 and 26.17

3   Clean the back side of the new upper bearing insert, then lay it in place in the connecting rod. Make sure the tab on the bearing fits into the recess in the rod. Don't hammer the bearing insert into place and be very careful not to nick or gouge the bearing face. Don't lubricate the bearing at this time.

4   Clean the back side of the other bearing insert and install it in the rod cap. Again, make sure the tab on the bearing fits into the recess in the cap, and don't apply any lubricant. It's critically important that the mating surfaces of the bearing and connecting rod

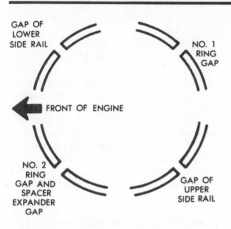

26.6 Position the piston ring end gaps as shown

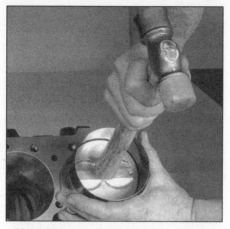

26.11 Use a plastic or wooden hammer handle to push the piston into the cylinder

26.13 Place Plastigage on each connecting rod bearing journal parallel to the crankshaft centerline

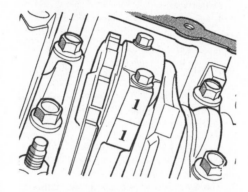

26.14 Install the connecting rod cap making sure the cap and rod identification numbers match

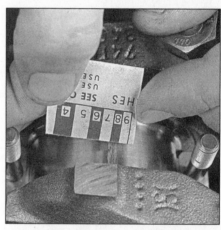

26.17 Use the scale on the Plastigage package to determine the bearing oil clearance - be sure to measure the widest part of the Plastigage and use the correct scale; it comes with both standard and metric scales

2C

are perfectly clean and oil free when they're assembled.

5   On V6 engines, slip a short section of plastic or rubber hose over the connecting rod studs to avoid damaging the cylinder wall or crankshaft journal **(see illustration 14.6)**.

6   Position the piston ring gaps at 90-degree intervals around the piston as shown **(see illustration)**.

7   Lubricate the piston and rings with clean engine oil and attach a piston ring compressor to the piston. Leave the skirt protruding about 1/4-inch to guide the piston into the cylinder. The rings must be compressed until they're flush with the piston.

8   Rotate the crankshaft until the number one connecting rod journal is at BDC (bottom dead center) and apply a liberal coat of engine oil to the cylinder walls.

9   With the weight designation mark, or arrow, on top of the piston facing the front (timing belt end) of the engine, gently insert the piston/connecting rod assembly into the number one cylinder bore and rest the bottom edge of the ring compressor on the engine block. **Note:** *The connecting rod also has a mark on it that must face the front (timing belt end) of the engine if it faces the opposite direction, the piston and connecting rod have been assembled improperly.*

10   Tap the top edge of the ring compressor to make sure it's contacting the block around its entire circumference.

11   Gently tap on the top of the piston with the end of a wooden or plastic hammer handle **(see illustration)** while guiding the end of the connecting rod into place on the crankshaft journal. The piston rings may try to pop out of the ring compressor just before entering the cylinder bore, so keep some downward pressure on the ring compressor. Work slowly, and if any resistance is felt as the piston enters the cylinder, stop immediately. Find out what's hanging up and fix it before proceeding. Do not, for any reason, force the piston into the cylinder - you might break a ring and/or the piston.

12   Once the piston/connecting rod assembly is installed, the connecting rod bearing oil

clearance must be checked before the rod cap is permanently installed.

13   Cut a piece of the appropriate size Plastigage slightly shorter than the width of the connecting rod bearing and lay it in place on the number one connecting rod journal, parallel with the journal axis **(see illustration)**.

14   Clean the connecting rod cap bearing face and install the rod cap. Make sure the mating mark on the cap is on the same side as the mark on the connecting rod **(see illustration)**. **Note:** *Check to make sure the identification mark on the connecting rod faces toward the front (timing belt) end of the engine.*

15   Install the old rod bolts or nuts, at this time, and tighten them to the torque listed in this Chapter's Specifications, working up to it in three steps. **Note:** *Use a thin-wall socket to avoid erroneous torque readings that can result if the socket is wedged between the rod cap and the bolt or nut. If the socket tends to wedge itself between the fastener and the cap, lift up on it slightly until it no longer contacts the cap. DO NOT rotate the crankshaft at any time during this operation.*

16   Remove the fasteners and detach the rod cap, being very careful not to disturb the Plastigage. Discard the cap bolts at this time

as they cannot be reused. **Note:** *On four-cylinder engines, new connecting rod bolts must be installed.*

17   Compare the width of the crushed Plastigage to the scale printed on the Plastigage envelope to obtain the oil clearance **(see illustration)**. Compare it to the tolerance listed in this Chapter's Specifications to make sure the clearance is acceptable.

18   If the clearance is not as specified, the bearing inserts may be the wrong size (which means different ones will be required). Before deciding that different inserts are needed, make sure that no dirt or oil was between the bearing inserts and the connecting rod or cap when the clearance was measured. Also, recheck the journal diameter. If the Plastigage was wider at one end than the other, the journal may be tapered (refer to Section 21). If the clearance still exceeds the limit specified, the bearing will have to be replaced with an undersize bearing. **Caution:** *When installing a new crankshaft always use a standard size bearing.*

Final installation

19   Carefully scrape all traces of the Plastigage material off the rod journal and/or bearing face. Be very careful not to scratch the bearing - use your fingernail or the edge of a plastic card.

20   Make sure the bearing faces are perfectly clean, then apply a uniform layer of clean moly-base grease or engine assembly lube to both of them. You'll have to push the piston into the cylinder to expose the face of the bearing insert in the connecting rod.

21   **Caution:** *On four-cylinder engines, new connecting rod cap bolts must be installed at this time. DO NOT reuse the old bolts as they have stretched and cannot be reused.* Slide the connecting rod back into place on the journal, install the rod cap, install new bolts and tighten the bolts to the torque listed in this Chapter's Specifications. Again, work up to the torque in three steps.

22   Repeat the entire procedure for the remaining pistons/connecting rods.

23   The important points to remember are:

  a) *Keep the back sides of the bearing inserts and the insides of the connecting rods and caps perfectly clean when assembling them.*

  b) *Make sure you have the correct piston/rod assembly for each cylinder.*

  c) *The mark on the piston must face the front (timing belt end) of the engine.*

  d) *Lubricate the cylinder walls liberally with clean oil.*

  e) *Lubricate the bearing faces when installing the rod caps after the oil clearance has been checked.*

24   After all the piston/connecting rod assemblies have been properly installed, rotate the crankshaft a number of times by hand to check for any obvious binding.

25   As a final step, the connecting rod endplay must be checked. Refer to Section 14 for this procedure.

26   Compare the measured endplay to the tolerance listed in this Chapter's Specifications to make sure it's acceptable. If it was correct before disassembly and the original crankshaft and rods were reinstalled, it should still be correct. If new rods or a new crankshaft were installed, the endplay may be inadequate. If so, the rods will have to be removed and taken to an automotive machine shop for resizing.

27   Initial start-up and break-in after overhaul

Warning: *Have a fire extinguisher handy when starting the engine for the first time.*

1   Once the engine has been installed in the vehicle, double-check the engine oil and coolant levels. Add transaxle fluid as needed.

2   With the spark plugs out of the engine and the ignition system disabled (disconnect the primary [low voltage] electrical connector from the coil pack or distributor see Chapter 5), crank the engine until the oil pressure light goes out. **Caution:** *Do not crank the engine for more than 15 seconds at a time, as starter motor could over-heat and damage could occur.*

3   Install the spark plugs, hook up the plug wires and restore the ignition system functions.

4   Start the engine. It may take a few moments for the fuel system to build up pressure, but the engine should start without a great deal of effort. **Note:** *If backfiring occurs through the throttle body, recheck the valve timing and spark plug wire locations.*

5   After the engine starts, it should be allowed to warm up to normal operating temperature. Try to keep the engine speed at approximately 2000 rpm. While the engine is warming up, make a thorough check for fuel, oil and coolant leaks. Check the automatic transaxle fluid level (if so equipped).

6   Shut the engine off and recheck the engine oil and coolant levels.

7   Drive the vehicle to an area with minimum traffic, accelerate from 30 to 50 mph, then allow the vehicle to slow to 30 mph with the throttle closed. Repeat the procedure 10 or 12 times. This will load the piston rings and cause them to seat properly against the cylinder walls. Check again for oil and coolant leaks.

8   Drive the vehicle gently for the first 500 miles (no sustained high speeds) and keep a constant check on the oil level. It is not unusual for an engine to use oil during the break-in period.

9   At approximately 500 to 600 miles, change the oil and filter.

10   For the next few hundred miles, drive the vehicle normally. Do not pamper it or abuse it.

11   After 2000 miles, change the oil and filter again and consider the engine broken in.

Chapter 3
Cooling, heating and air conditioning systems

Contents

Specifications

General

Radiator cap pressure rating	14 to 18 psi
Thermostat rating (opening temperature)	195 degrees F
Cooling system capacity	See Chapter 1
Refrigerant capacity	28 ounces

Torque specifications

Ft-lbs (unless otherwise indicated)

Thermostat housing bolts/nuts	
Four-cylinder engines	110 in-lbs
V6 engine	168 in-lbs
Water pump mounting bolts	
Four-cylinder engines	105 in-lbs
V6 engine	17

1   General information

Engine cooling system

All vehicles covered by this manual employ a pressurized engine cooling system with thermostatically controlled coolant circulation. An impeller-type water pump mounted on the front of the engine pumps coolant through the engine. The pump mounts directly on the engine block. The coolant flows around the combustion chambers and toward the rear of the engine. Cast-in coolant passages direct coolant near the intake ports, exhaust ports, and spark plug areas.

A wax pellet-type thermostat is located in a housing near the front of the engine. During warm-up, the closed thermostat prevents coolant from circulating through the radiator. As the engine nears normal operating temperature, the thermostat opens and allows hot coolant to travel through the radiator, where it's cooled before returning to the engine.

The cooling system is sealed by a pressure-type cap, which raises the boiling point of the coolant and increases the cooling efficiency of the system. If the system pressure exceeds the cap pressure relief value, the excess pressure in the system forces the spring-loaded valve inside the cap off its seat and allows the coolant to escape through the overflow tube into a coolant reservoir. When the system cools the excess coolant is automatically drawn from the reservoir back into the radiator.

The coolant reservoir does double duty as both the point at which fresh coolant is added to the cooling system to maintain the proper fluid level and as a holding tank for overheated coolant. This type of cooling system is known as a closed design because coolant that escapes past the pressure cap is saved and reused.

Heating system

The heating system consists of a blower fan and heater core located in the heater housing, with hoses connecting the heater core to the engine cooling system. Hot engine coolant is circulated through the heater core. When the heater mode on the heater/air conditioning control panel on the instrument panel is activated, a flap door opens to expose the heater core to the passenger compartment. A fan switch on the control panel activates the blower motor, which forces air through the core, heating the air.

Air conditioning system

The air conditioning system consists of a condenser mounted in front of the radiator, an evaporator mounted adjacent to the heater core, a compressor mounted on the engine, receiver/drier which contains a high pressure relief valve and the plumbing connecting all of the above components.

A blower fan forces the warmer air of the passenger compartment through the evaporator core, transferring the heat from the air to the refrigerant (sort of a "radiator in reverse"). The liquid refrigerant boils off into low pressure vapor, taking the heat with it when it leaves the evaporator.

3

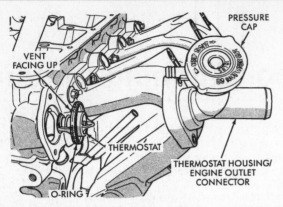

3.10a Thermostat installation details - 2.0L four-cylinder engine

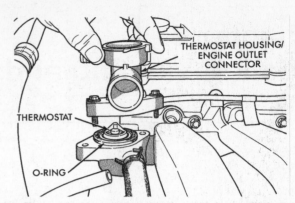

3.10b Thermostat installation details - 2.4L four-cylinder engine

2   Antifreeze - general information

Warning: *Do not allow antifreeze to come in contact with your skin or painted surfaces of the vehicle. Rinse off spills immediately with plenty of water. Antifreeze is highly toxic if ingested. Never leave antifreeze lying around in an open container or in puddles on the floor; children and pets are attracted by it's sweet smell and may drink it. Antifreeze is also flammable, so don't store or use it near open flames. Check with local authorities about disposing of used antifreeze. Many communities have collection centers which will see that antifreeze is disposed of safely. Never dump used anti-freeze on the ground or into drains.*
Note: *Non-Toxic coolant is available at local auto parts stores. Although the coolant is non-toxic when fresh, proper disposal is still required.*

The cooling system should be filled with a water/ethylene glycol based antifreeze solution, which will prevent freezing down to at least 20 degrees F, or lower if local climate requires it. It also provides protection against corrosion and increases the coolant boiling point.

The cooling system should be drained, flushed and refilled at the specified intervals (see Chapter 1). Old or contaminated antifreeze solutions are likely to cause damage and encourage the formation of rust and scale in the system. Use distilled water with the antifreeze.

Before adding antifreeze, check all hose connections, because antifreeze tends to leak through very minute openings. Engines don't normally consume coolant, so if the level goes down, find the cause and correct it.

The exact mixture of antifreeze-to-water which you should use depends on the relative weather conditions. The mixture should contain at least 50 percent antifreeze, but should never contain more than 70 percent antifreeze. Consult the mixture ratio chart on the antifreeze container before adding coolant. Hydrometers are available at most auto parts stores to test the coolant. Use antifreeze that meets the vehicle manufacturer's specifications.

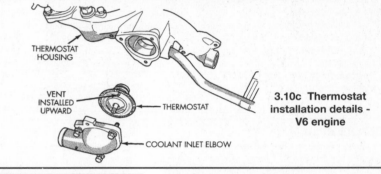

3.10c Thermostat installation details - V6 engine

3   Thermostat - check and replacement

Warning: *Do not remove the coolant tank cap, drain the coolant or replace the thermostat until the engine has cooled completely.*

Check

1   Before assuming the thermostat is to blame for a cooling system problem, check the coolant level, drivebelt tension (see Chapter 1) and temperature gauge operation.
2   If the engine seems to be taking a long time to warm up (based on heater output or temperature gauge operation), the thermostat is probably stuck open. Replace the thermostat with a new one.
3   If the engine runs hot, use your hand to check the temperature of the upper radiator hose. If the hose isn't hot, but the engine is, the thermostat is probably stuck closed, preventing the coolant inside the engine from escaping to the radiator. Replace the thermostat. **Caution:** *Don't drive the vehicle without a thermostat. The computer may stay in open loop and emissions and fuel economy will suffer.*
4   If the upper radiator hose is hot, it means that the coolant is flowing and the thermostat is open. Consult the Troubleshooting Section at the front of this manual for cooling system diagnosis.

Replacement

Refer to illustrations 3.10a, 3.10b and 3.10c
5   Disconnect the negative battery cable from the ground stud on the left shock tower

(see Chapter 5, section 1).
6   Drain the cooling system (see Chapter 1). If the coolant is relatively new or in good condition, save it and reuse it.
7   Follow the upper radiator hose to the engine to locate the thermostat housing.
8   Loosen the hose clamp, then detach the hose from the fitting. If it's stuck, grasp it near the end with a pair of adjustable pliers and twist it to break the seal, then pull it off. If the hose is old or deteriorated, cut it off and install a new one.
9   If the outer surface of the large fitting that mates with the hose is deteriorated (corroded, pitted, etc.) it may be damaged further by hose removal. If it is, the thermostat housing cover will have to be replaced.
10   Remove the fasteners and detach the housing cover **(see illustrations)**. If the cover is stuck, tap it with a soft-face hammer to jar it loose. Be prepared for some coolant to spill as the gasket seal is broken.
11   Note how it's installed (which end is facing up), then remove the thermostat.
12   Remove all traces of old gasket material and sealant from the housing and cover with a gasket scraper.
13   Using a new O-ring, install the thermostat on the housing, spring-end facing into the engine block and the vent facing up. Install a new gasket (if equipped) and place it on the thermostat housing, lining up the bolt holes.
14   Install the cover and fasteners. Tighten the fasteners to the torque listed in this Chapter's Specifications.
15   Reattach the hose to the fitting and tighten the hose clamp securely.
16   Refill the cooling system (see Chapter 1).

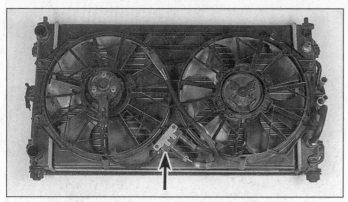

4.1a The high-speed and low-speed fans are mounted in one housing, with a harness connecting them to the RFI module (arrow)

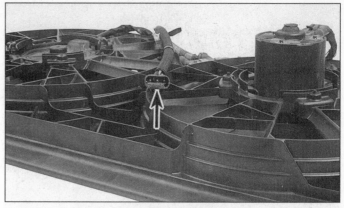

4.1b Disconnect the fan connector (arrow) and try operating the fan with a fused battery-voltage jumper wire and a ground wire

17 Start the engine and allow it to reach normal operating temperature, then check for leaks and proper thermostat operation (as described in Steps 2 through 4). See Chapter 1 for cooling system air-bleeding procedure.

4 Engine cooling fans and circuit - check and replacement

Warning: *To avoid possible injury or damage, DO NOT operate the engine with a damaged fan. Do not attempt to repair fan blades - replace a damaged fan with a new one.*
Note: *Always be sure to check for blown fuses before attempting to diagnose an electrical circuit problem.*

Check

Refer to illustrations 4.1a, 4.1b, 4.3, and 4.4
1 If the engine is overheating and the cooling fan is not coming on, unplug the electrical connector at the motor and use fused jumper wires to connect the fan directly to the battery. If the fan still doesn't work, replace the motor. test each motor separately. They are connected to an RFI module (Radio Frequency Interference), with the low-speed motor having a two-pin connector and

a three-pin connector on the high-speed fan **(see illustrations)**.
2 If the motor is OK, but the cooling fan doesn't come on when the engine gets hot, the fault may be in the coolant temperature sensor in the thermostat housing, the fan relays, the engine control computer or the wiring which connects the components.
3 The engine coolant temperature sensor is located in the thermostat housing and varies resistance with temperature to signal the PCM **(see illustration)**. A test for checking the sensor is found in Chapter 6.
4 Remove the fan relays (one low-speed and one high-speed relay) from the Power Distribution Center. Using an ohmmeter, measure the resistance between terminals A and C of the relay **(see illustration)**, it should read approximately 75 ohms. Check for continuity between terminals B and D, there should be no continuity. Using fused jumper wires, apply battery voltage (+) to terminal A and ground (-) terminal C; the relay should "click" and continuity should be indicated between terminals B and D.
5 Carefully check all wiring and connections (wiring diagrams are included at the end of Chapter 12). If no obvious problems are found, further diagnosis should be done by a dealer service department or repair shop with the proper diagnostic equipment.

4.3 The coolant temperature sensor (arrow) is located at the front of the engine, next to the thermostat

Replacement

Refer to illustrations 4.7, 4.8a, 4.8b, 4.9 and 4.10
6 Disconnect the negative battery cable from the ground stud on the left shock tower (see Chapter 5, Section 1). Disconnect the fan motor electrical connector **(see illustration 4.1a)**.
7 Remove the upper radiator crossmember, either detaching the four bolts and laying

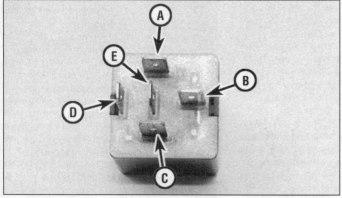

4.4 Cooling fan relay terminal guide - there should be continuity between A and C, and no continuity between B and D unless battery power is applied to A and ground applied to C

4.7 Remove the four bolts and the isolators on the upper radiator crossmember (arrows) - if necessary, remove the bolts securing the shroud and remove the shroud

4.8a Remove the fan shroud mounting bolts (arrows)

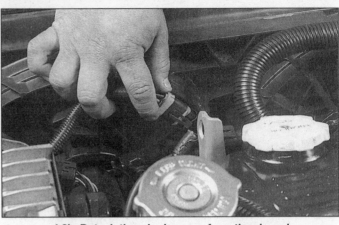

4.8b Detach the wire harness from the shroud

it aside, or also removing the two bolts to the latch and removing the crossmember entirely **(see illustration)**.

8   Remove the fan shroud mounting bolts, detach the clips at the top and bottom of the shroud with a small screwdriver, detach the wire harness clips from the shroud, then carefully lift the fan assembly out of the engine compartment **(see illustrations)**. **Note:** *It is easier to remove the fan assembly if the upper radiator hose is disconnected first from the radiator.*

9   To detach the fan blade from the motor, remove the nut or retaining clip from the motor shaft **(see illustration)**. Remove the fan blade from the motor.

10   To detach the motor from the shroud, remove the retaining nuts or screws **(see illustration)**. Remove the motor from the shroud.

11   Installation is the reverse of removal. **Note:** *When reinstalling the fan assembly, make sure the rubber air shields around the assembly are still in place - without them, the cooling system may not work efficiently.*

---

5   Radiator and coolant reservoir - removal and installation

---

Warning: *Wait until the engine is completely cool before beginning this procedure.*

Radiator

Removal

Refer to illustration 5.6

1   Disconnect the negative battery cable from the ground stud on the left shock tower (see Chapter 5, Section 1).

2   Drain the cooling system (see Chapter 1). If the coolant is relatively new and in good condition, save it and reuse it.

3   Remove the upper radiator crossmember and cooling fan assembly (see Section 4).

4   Disconnect the overflow hose from the radiator filler neck.

5   Loosen the hose clamps, then detach the upper and lower coolant hoses from the radiator. If they're stuck, grasp each hose

4.9 The fan blade is retained to the motor with either a nut or a clip (arrow)

near the end with a pair of adjustable pliers and twist it to break the seal, then pull it off - be careful not to distort the radiator fittings! If the hoses are old or deteriorated, cut them off and install new ones.

6   Disconnect and plug the transmission fluid cooler lines **(see illustration)**.

7   Remove the two upper radiator-to-body mounting bolts. At this point, if the vehicle is equipped with air conditioning, there are two ways to remove the radiator. If the condenser is staying in the vehicle, remove the four condenser-to-radiator mounting screws (accessible through the lower openings in the front of the body) and the one screw in the air conditioning line on the passenger side, and the radiator can be pulled up. **Note:** *Make sure the rubber radiator insulators (they fit on the bottom of the radiator and into sockets in the body) remain in place in the body for proper reinstallation of the radiator.*

8   If the condenser is being removed (and the air conditioning system has already been evacuated of refrigerant), disconnect the condenser lines (see Section 15) and remove the radiator and condenser as a unit, separating the two components outside of the vehicle where the fasteners are easier to get at. **Warning:** *The air conditioning system is under high pressure. Do not loosen any hose*

4.10 To remove the fan motor from the shroud, remove the three screws (arrows)

fittings or remove any components until after the system has been discharged by a dealer service department or service station. Always wear eye protection when disconnecting air conditioning system fittings.

9   Carefully lift out the radiator. Don't spill coolant on the vehicle or scratch the paint.

10   Check the radiator for leaks and damage. If it needs repair, have a radiator shop or

5.6 Detach the transmission cooler lines

5.18 Remove the mounting bolt and remove the coolant reservoir from the vehicle for cleaning or replacement

[d]ealer service department perform the work, [a]s special techniques are required.
[1] Remove bugs and dirt from the radiator [w]ith compressed air and a soft brush (don't [b]end the cooling fins).

Installation

2 Inspect the radiator mounts for deterioration and ensure they are clean of dirt or [g]ravel when the radiator is installed.
[3] Installation is the reverse of the removal [p]rocedure. Make sure the radiator is properly [s]eated on the lower mounting insulators [b]efore fastening the top brackets.
[4] After installation, fill the cooling system [w]ith the proper mixture of antifreeze and [w]ater (see Chapter 1).
[5] Start the engine and check for leaks. [A]llow the engine to reach normal operating [t]emperature, indicated by the upper radiator [h]ose becoming hot. Recheck the coolant [l]evel and add more if required.
[6] If you're working on an automatic [t]ransaxle equipped vehicle, check and add [fl]uid as needed.

Coolant reservoir

Refer to illustration 5.18
[7] Detach the hoses at the reservoir. Plug

the hoses to prevent leakage.
18 Remove the reservoir retaining bolt and lift the reservoir out of the engine compartment **(see illustration)**.
19 Installation is the reverse of removal. While the reservoir is off the vehicle, it should be cleaned with soapy water and a brush to remove any deposits inside.

---

6 Water pump - check

1 A failure in the water pump can cause serious engine damage due to overheating.
2 There are three ways to check the operation of the water pump while it's installed on the engine. If the pump is defective, it should be replaced with a new or rebuilt unit.
3 Water pumps are equipped with weep or vent holes. If a failure occurs in the pump seal, coolant will leak from the hole. In most cases you'll need a flashlight to find the hole on the water pump from underneath to check for leaks. **Note:** *Some small black staining around the weep hole is normal. If the stain is heavy brown or actual coolant is evident, replace the pump.*
4 If the water pump shaft bearings fail there may be a howling sound at the front of the engine while it's running. With the engine off, shaft wear can be felt if the water pump pulley is rocked up-and-down. Don't mistake drivebelt slippage, which causes a squealing sound, for water pump bearing failure.
5 A quick water pump performance check is to put the heater on. If the pump is failing, it won't be able to efficiently circulate hot water all the way to the heater core as it should.

---

7 Water pump - replacement

Four-cylinder engines

Refer to illustration 7.12
1 Disconnect the negative battery cable from the ground stud on the left shock tower (see Chapter 5, Section 1).
2 Raise the vehicle and support it securely

on jackstands.
3 Remove the right inner splash shield (see Chapter 11).
4 Remove the drivebelts (see Chapter 1).
5 Drain the cooling system (see Chapter 1).
6 Using a floorjack (with a wood block placed between the jackhead and the oil pan to prevent engine damage), support the engine from underneath and remove the right engine mount.
7 Remove the power steering pump bracket bolts and move the power steering pump and bracket aside. The power steering lines do not have to be disconnected.
8 Remove the right engine mount bracket (see Chapter 2).
9 Remove the timing belt (see Chapter 2).
10 Remove the inner timing belt cover (see Chapter 2).
11 Remove the bolts attaching the water pump to the engine block and remove the pump.
12 Install a new O-ring in the water pump body groove **(see illustration)**.
13 Installation is the reversal of removal. Tighten the mounting bolts to the torque listed in this Chapter's specifications.
14 Reinstall the pulleys and drive belts and check for tension (see Chapter 1).
15 Refill the cooling system (see Chapter 1). Run the engine and check for leaks.

V6 engine

Refer to illustrations 7.18 and 7.21
16 Disconnect the negative battery cable from the ground stud on the left shock tower (see Chapter 5, Section 1). Remove the drivebelts and drain the cooling system (see Chapter 1).
17 Refer to Chapter 2, Part B and remove the crankshaft damper/pulley, timing belt covers and timing belt.
18 Remove the water pump mounting bolts **(see illustration)**.
19 Separate the pump from the water inlet pipe and remove the pump.
20 Clean all the gasket and O-ring surfaces on the pump and the water pipe inlet tube.
21 Install a new O-ring on the water inlet

3

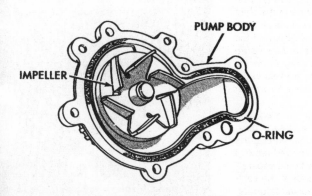

7.12 Install a new O-ring onto the water pump

7.18 Remove the water pump bolts (arrows) - V6 engine

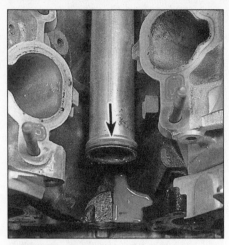

7.21 Install a new O-ring on the water inlet pipe (arrow)

pipe **(see illustration)**. Wet the O-ring with water to facilitate assembly.

22   Install a new gasket on the water pump and install the inlet opening over the water pipe. Press the water pipe into the pump housing.

23   Install the water pump mounting bolts and tighten the bolts to the torque listed in this Chapter's specifications.

24   Install the timing belt (see Chapter 2B).

25   The remainder of installation is the reverse of removal.

26   Refill the cooling system (see Chapter 1) and operate the engine to check for leaks.

---

8   Coolant temperature sending unit - check and replacement

Warning: *Wait until the engine is completely cool before beginning this procedure.*

Check

1   The coolant temperature indicator system is composed of a light or temperature gauge mounted in the dash and a coolant temperature sending unit mounted on the engine **(see illustration 4.3)**. On the models covered by this manual, there is only one coolant temperature sensor, which functions as indicator to both the PCM and the instrument panel.

2   If an overheating indication occurs, check the coolant level in the system and then make sure the wiring between the light or gauge and the sending unit is secure and all fuses are intact.

3   When the ignition switch is turned on and the starter motor is turning, the indicator light (if equipped) should be on (overheated engine indication).

4   If the light is not on, the bulb may be burned out, the ignition switch may be faulty or the circuit may be open.

5   As soon as the engine starts, the light should go out and remain out unless the engine overheats. Failure of the light to go

out may be due to a grounded wire between the light and the sending unit, a defective sending unit or a faulty ignition switch. See Chapter 6 for a diagnostic check of the coolant temperature switch. Check the coolant to make sure it's the proper type. **Note:** *Plain water may have too low a boiling point to activate the sending unit.*

Replacement

Warning: *Wait until the engine is completely cool before beginning this procedure.*

6   Disconnect the electrical connector from the sensor.

7   Wrap the threads of the new sensor with Teflon tape to prevent leaks.

8   Unscrew the sensor. Be prepared for some coolant spillage (read the Warning in Section 2).

9   Install the sensor and tighten it securely.

10   Connect the electrical connector.

11   Check the coolant level after the replacement unit has been installed and top up the system, if necessary (see Chapter 1). Check now for proper operation of the gauge and sending unit. Observe the system for leaks after operation.

---

9   Blower motor and circuit - check and replacement

Warning: *These models are equipped with airbags, always disable the airbag system before working in the vicinity of the impact sensors, steering column or instrument panel to avoid the possibility of accidental deployment of the airbag, which could cause personal injury (see Chapter 12).*

Check

Refer to illustrations 9.3 and 9.7

1   Check the fuse and all connections in the circuit for looseness and corrosion. Make sure the battery is fully charged.

2   Remove the lower right dash insulator panel (below the glove box) for access to the blower motor. **Note:** *When reinstalling this panel, be sure the left end fits properly into its recess in the ducting.*

3   Using suitable probes, backprobe the blower motor electrical connector at the resistor and connect the positive probe of the voltmeter to the dark blue wire and the negative probe to the black wire **(see illustration)**.

4   With the transmission in Park, the parking brake securely set, turn the ignition switch On. It isn't necessary to start the vehicle.

5   Move the blower switch through each of its positions and note the voltage readings. Changes in voltage indicate that the motor speeds will also vary as the switch is moved to the different positions.

6   If there is voltage present, but the blower motor does not operate, the blower motor is probably faulty. Disconnect the blower motor connector and hook one side to a chassis ground and the other to a fused

source of battery voltage. If the blower doesn't operate, it is faulty.

7   If voltage was not present at the blower motor at all speeds, and the motor itself tested OK, the problem is in the blower motor resistor, the blower switch in the control panel assembly or the related wiring. To check the resistor, remove the two screws and remove the resistor from the heater housing. Using an ohmmeter, check for continuity across each of the resistor terminals **(see illustration)**. If an open circuit is indicated, replace the resistor assembly. To test the blower switch, refer to Section 11, remove the control panel assembly and check for continuity through the switch in each position. Refer to the wiring diagrams at the end of Chapter 12 to determine the correct terminals for testing.

Replacement

Refer to illustration 9.11

8   Disconnect the battery negative cable from the ground stud on the left shock tower (see Chapter 5, Section 1).

9   Detach the panel underneath the right

9.3 Using suitable probes, backprobe the blower harness plug (twisted pair of wires) at the blower motor resistor block - connect a voltmeter to the dark blue wire (+) and black wire (-), voltage should vary as the blower switch is moved through each position

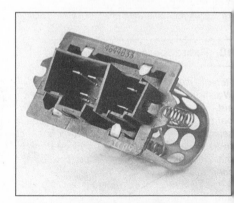

9.7 To test the blower resistor, check for continuity at each of the resistor terminals

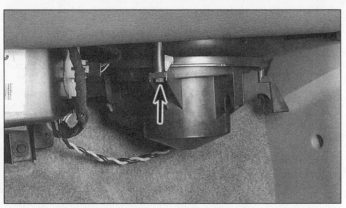

9.11 Remove the screws retaining the blower motor to the heater housing (arrow)

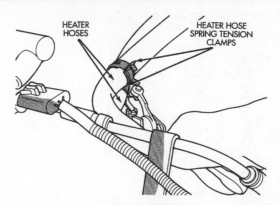

10.2 Disconnect the heater hoses at the firewall

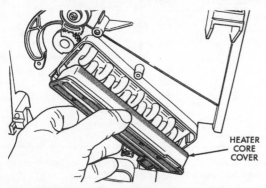

10.6 Remove the heater core cover

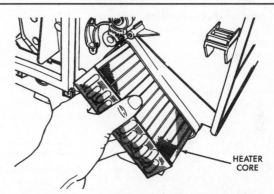

10.7 Withdraw the heater core from the housing

3

end of the dash. It has four fasteners, all of them facing up - two screws in front (side toward the passenger seat) and two sheet metal nuts on the backside (toward the firewall).

10   Disconnect the wiring connector at the blower motor resistor.

11   Remove the screws retaining the blower motor to the heater housing **(see illustration)**.

12   Lower the blower motor from the housing.

13   The fan is balanced with the blower motor, and is available only as an assembly. If the fan is damaged, both fan and blower motor must be replaced.

14   Installation is the reverse of removal.

10   Heater core - replacement

Refer to illustrations 10.2, 10.6 and 10.7
Warning: *These models are equipped with airbags, always disable the airbag system before working in the vicinity of the impact sensors, steering column or instrument panel to avoid the possibility of accidental deployment of the airbag, which could cause personal injury (see Chapter 12).*

1   Drain the cooling system (see Chapter 1) and disconnect the negative battery cable from the ground stud on the left shock tower (see Chapter 5, Section 1).

2   Disconnect the heater hoses at the fire-wall **(see illustration)**. **Note:** *On V6 models, it may be necessary to remove the upper intake manifold to access the heater hoses (see Chapter 2B).*

3   Refer to Chapter 11 and remove the radio/air conditioning control panel bezel, the instrument panel bezel and end covers and the knee bolster.

4   Remove the center console from the vehicle (see Chapter 11).

5   Remove two screws at the lower right side support beam, the bolt for the instrument panel support at the A-pillar and remove the right side instrument panel support strut.

6   Remove the heater core cover screws and the cover **(see illustration)**.

TRIM BEZEL

11.2 Remove the radio/control module bezel

7   Withdraw the heater core from the housing **(see illustration)**.

8   If the heater core has been leaking, clean the coolant from the heater/air conditioning housing. **Note:** *If a significant amount of coolant has leaked into the housing, it is recommended that the complete heater/air conditioning housing be removed from the vehicle, disassembled and thoroughly cleaned (see Section 16).*

9   Installation is the reverse of removal. Be sure to refill the cooling system (see Chapter 1).

11   Heater/air conditioner control assembly - removal, check and installation

Warning: *These models are equipped with airbags, always disable the airbag system before working in the vicinity of the impact sensors, steering column or instrument panel to avoid the possibility of accidental deployment of the airbag, which could cause personal injury (see Chapter 12).*

Removal

Refer to illustrations 11.2, 11.3 and 11.7

1   Disconnect the negative battery cable from the ground stud on the left shock tower (see Chapter 5, Section 1).

2   Remove the trim bezel from the instrument panel **(see illustration)**.

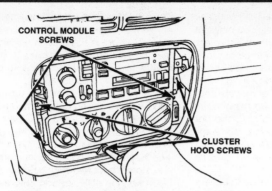

11.3 Remove the cluster hood screws and the control module screws

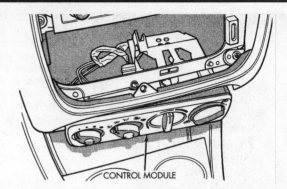

11.7 Lower the control module into the cubby bin opening

3   Remove the three cluster hood screws from the trim bezel opening **(see illustration)**.

4   Pry up the cluster hood bezel a few inches to expose the cubby bin screws.

5   Disconnect the wiring and remove the cubby bin.

6   Remove the control module screws **(see illustration 11.3)**.

7   Lower the control module into the cubby bin opening **(see illustration)** and disconnect the wiring harness from the rear of the control module.

8   Release the cable clips from the top of the control module. Retain the clips for further use. Disconnect the temperature control and the recirculation control cables.

9   Remove the control module.

Check

Refer to illustration 11.11

10   Remove the control module (see Steps above).

11   Using an ohmmeter, measure the resistance between terminals 5 and 8 of the control module 8-way connector **(see illustration)**. Turn the control module to each position and check the resistance as follows:

a) *PANEL = 828 to 856 ohms*
b) *BI-LEVEL = 1280 to 1300 ohms*
c) *FLOOR = 2300 to 2358 ohms*
d) *MIX = 5200 to 5300 ohms*
e) *DEFROST = 99 to 100 K-ohms*

12   If any resistance is not correct, replace the control module.

13   If the resistance's are correct, check for blown fuses, damaged wiring, bad connections, defective Body Control Module (BCM) or bulkhead connector. Refer to the wiring diagrams at the end of Chapter 12, if necessary.

14   Further testing of the system can be accomplished with the use of a special scan tool; see a dealer or other qualified repair shop.

Installation

15   Installation is the reverse of removal. If necessary, adjust the cables as follows:

a) *Attach the cable to the control module lever.*
b) *Rotate the knob fully counterclockwise.*

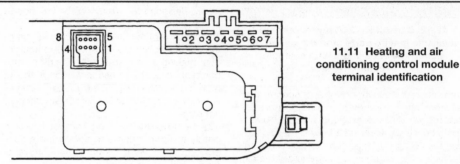

11.11 Heating and air conditioning control module terminal identification

c) *Pull the cable housing away from the cable end to remove all freeplay and clip the cable housing to the control module.*
d) *Verify the knob travels through its full range.*

12   Air conditioning and heating system - check and maintenance

Warning: *The air conditioning system is under high pressure. Do not loosen any hose fittings or remove any components until after the system has been discharged by a dealer service department or air conditioning service station. Always wear eye protection when disconnecting air conditioning system fittings.*

1   The following maintenance checks should be performed on a regular basis to ensure the air conditioner continues to operate at peak efficiency.

a) *Check the compressor drivebelt. If it's worn or deteriorated, replace it (see Chapter 1).*
b) *Check the drivebelt tension and, if necessary, adjust it (see Chapter 1).*
c) *Check the system hoses. Look for cracks, bubbles, hard spots and deterioration. Inspect the hoses and all fittings for oil bubbles and seepage. If there's any evidence of wear, damage or leaks, replace the hose(s).*
d) *Inspect the condenser fins for leaves, bugs and other debris. Use a "fin comb" or compressed air to clean the condenser.*
e) *Make sure the system has the correct refrigerant charge.*

f) *Check the evaporator housing drain tube for blockage.*

2   It's a good idea to operate the system for about 10 minutes at least once a month, particularly during the winter. Long term non-use can cause hardening, and subsequent failure, of the seals.

3   Because of the complexity of the air conditioning system and the special equipment necessary to service it, in-depth troubleshooting and repairs are not included in this manual (refer to the *Haynes Automotive Heating and Air Conditioning Repair Manual*). However, simple checks and component replacement procedures are provided in this Chapter.

4   The most common cause of poor cooling is simply a low system refrigerant charge. If a noticeable drop in cool air output occurs, the following quick check will help you determine if the refrigerant level is low.

Checking the refrigerant charge

5   Warm the engine up to normal operating temperature.

6   Place the air conditioning temperature selector at the coldest setting and the blower at the highest setting. Open the doors (to make sure the air conditioning system does not cycle off as soon as it cools the passenger compartment).

7   With the compressor engaged - the clutch will make an audible click and the center of the clutch will rotate - note the temperature of the compressor inlet and discharge lines. If the compressor discharge line feels warm and the compressor inlet pipe feels cool, the system is properly charged.

8   Place a thermometer in the dashboard

12.12 Cans of R-134A refrigerant are available in auto parts stores that can be added to your system with a simple recharging kit

vent nearest the evaporator and operate the system until the indicated temperature is around 40 to 45 degrees F. If the ambient (outside) air temperature is very high, say 110 degrees F, the duct air temperature may be as high as 60 degrees F, but generally the air conditioning is 30-50 degrees F cooler than the ambient air. **Note:** *Humidity of the ambient air also affects the cooling capacity of the system. Higher ambient humidity lowers the effectiveness of the air conditioning system.*

Adding refrigerant

Refer to illustration 12.12

9   Buy an automotive charging kit at an auto parts store. A charging kit includes a 14-ounce can of refrigerant, a tap valve and a short section of hose that can be attached between the tap valve and the system low side service valve. Because one can of refrigerant may not be sufficient to bring the system charge up to the proper level, it's a good idea to buy an additional can. Make sure that one of the cans contains red refrigerant dye.

If the system is leaking, the red dye will leak out with the refrigerant and help you pinpoint the location of the leak. **Caution:** *There are two types of refrigerant used in automotive systems; R-12 - which has been widely used on earlier models and the more environmentally-friendly R-134a used in all models covered by this manual. These two refrigerants (and their appropriate refrigerant oils) are not compatible and must never be mixed or components will be damaged. Use only R-134a refrigerant in the models covered by this manual.*

10   Hook up the charging kit by following the manufacturer's instructions. **Warning:** *DO NOT hook the charging kit hose to the system high side! The fittings on the charging kit are designed to fit only on the low side of the system.*

11   Back off the valve handle on the charging kit and screw the kit onto the refrigerant can, making sure first that the O-ring or rubber seal inside the threaded portion of the kit is in place. **Warning:** *Wear protective eyewear when dealing with pressurized refrigerant cans.*

12   Remove the dust cap from the low-side charging connection and attach the quick-connect fitting on the kit hose **(see illustration)**.

13   Warm up the engine and turn on the air conditioner. Keep the charging kit hose away from the fan and other moving parts. **Note:** *The charging process requires the compressor to be running.*

14   Turn the valve handle on the kit until the stem pierces the can, then back the handle out to release the refrigerant. You should be able to hear the rush of gas. Add refrigerant to the low side of the system until both the receiver-drier surface and the evaporator inlet pipe feel about the same temperature. Allow stabilization time between each addition.

15   If you have an accurate thermometer, you can place it in the center air conditioning duct inside the vehicle and keep track of the "conditioned" air temperature. A charged system that is working properly should cool

down to approximately 40 degrees F. If the ambient (outside) air temperature is very high, say 110 degrees F, the duct air temperature may be as high as 60 degrees F, but generally the air conditioning is 30 to 40 degrees F cooler than the ambient air.

16   When the can is empty, turn the valve handle to the closed position and release the connection from the low-side port. Replace the dust cap. **Warning:** *Never add more than two cans of refrigerant to the system.*

17   Remove the charging kit from the can and store the kit for future use with the piercing valve in the UP position, to prevent inadvertently piercing the can on the next use.

13   Air conditioning compressor - removal and installation

Warning: *The air conditioning system is under high pressure. DO NOT disassemble any part of the system (hoses, compressor, line fittings, etc.) until after the system has been evacuated and the refrigerant recovered by a dealer service department or air conditioning service station.*

Note: *The filter-drier/receiver-drier (see Section 14) should be replaced whenever the compressor is replaced.*

Removal

Refer to illustrations 13.3, 13.5 and 13.6

1   Have the system discharged (see the **Warning** at the beginning of this Section).

2   Disconnect the negative battery cable from the ground stud on the left shock tower (see Chapter 5, Section 1).

3   Unplug the electrical connector from the compressor clutch **(see illustration)**.

4   Remove the drivebelt (see Chapter 1).

5   Disconnect the refrigerant lines from the compressor **(see illustration)**. Plug the open fittings to prevent entry of dirt and moisture.

6   Unbolt the compressor from the mounting bracket **(see illustration)** and lift it out of the vehicle.

3

13.3 Unplug the electrical connector (arrow) from the compressor clutch

13.5 Remove the retaining bolts, detach and plug the refrigerant lines at the compressor

13.6 To detach the compressor from its mounting bracket, remove these bolts (arrows)

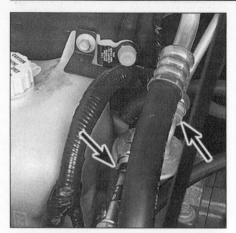

14.4 Using a back-up wrench to prevent damage to the fittings, disconnect the refrigerant lines (arrows) from the receiver-drier

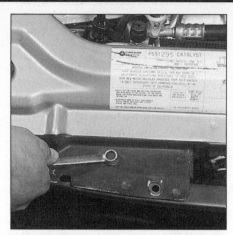

15.4 Remove the upper radiator support crossmember

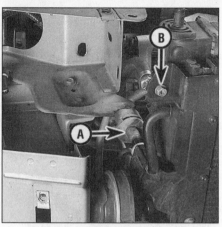

15.5 Using the appropriate quick-connect coupling tool, disconnect the air conditioner condenser lines (A) from the condenser and remove the mounting bolts (B)

Installation

7   If a new compressor is being installed, pour out the oil from the old compressor into a graduated container and add that amount of new refrigerant oil to the new compressor. Also follow any directions included with the new compressor.

8   The clutch may have to be transferred from the original to the new compressor.

9   Installation is the reverse of removal. Replace all O-rings with new ones specifically made for use with R-134a refrigerant and lubricate them with R-134a-compatible refrigerant oil.

10   Have the system evacuated, recharged and leak tested by the shop that discharged it.

14   Air conditioning receiver-drier - removal and installation

Warning: *The air conditioning system is under high pressure. DO NOT disassemble any part of the system (hose, compressor, line fittings, etc.) until after the system has been evacuated and the refrigerant recovered by a dealer service department or air conditioning service station.*

Caution: *Replacement filter-drier/receiver-drier units are so effective at absorbing moisture that they can quickly saturate upon exposure to the atmosphere. When installing a new unit, have all tools and supplies ready for quick reassembly to avoid having the system open any longer than necessary.*

Removal

Refer to illustration 14.4

1   The receiver-drier acts as a reservoir for the system refrigerant. It's located on the right side of the engine compartment, next to the radiator and condenser.

2   Have the system discharged (see the **Warning** at the beginning of this Section).

3   Disconnect the negative battery cable from the ground stud on the left shock tower

(see Chapter 5, Section 1).

4   Disconnect the refrigerant lines from the receiver-drier **(see illustration)**. Use a back-up wrench to prevent twisting the tubing where it joins the condenser.

5   Plug the open fittings to prevent entry of dirt and moisture.

6   Remove the bracket bolt at the base of the receiver/drier. Spread the aluminum clamp and remove the receiver/drier.

Installation

7   Installation is the reverse of removal. If a new receiver-drier is being installed add one ounce of refrigerant oil to it before installation.

8   Take the vehicle back to the shop that discharged it. Have the system evacuated, recharged and leak tested.

15   Air conditioning condenser - removal and installation

Warning: *The air conditioning system is under high pressure. Do not loosen any hose fittings or remove any components until after the system has been discharged by a dealer service department or air conditioning service station. Always wear eye protection when disconnecting air conditioning system components.*

Note: *The receiver-drier should be replaced whenever the condenser is replaced (see section 14).*

Removal

Refer to illustrations 15.4 and 15.5

1   Have the system discharged (see the **Warning** at the beginning of this Section).

2   Disconnect the negative battery cable from the ground stud on the left shock tower (see Chapter 5, Section 1).

3   Remove the radiator grille (see Chapter 11).

4   Remove the upper radiator support crossmember **(see illustration)**.

5   Using the appropriate quick-connect

coupling tools (available at auto parts stores), disconnect and cap the air conditioning lines at the condenser **(see illustration)**.

6   Remove the radiator fan module mounts.

7   Remove the condenser line support bracket.

8   Remove the condenser mounting bolts **(see illustration 15.5)**.

9   Remove the condenser from the vehicle.

Installation

10   Installation is the reverse of removal. If a new condenser is being installed add one ounce of refrigerant oil to it before installation.

11   Take the vehicle back to the shop that discharged it. Have the system evacuated, recharged and leak tested.

16   Air conditioning evaporator and expansion valve - removal and installation

Warning 1: *These models are equipped with airbags, always disable the airbag system before working in the vicinity of the impact sensors, steering column or instrument panel to avoid the possibility of accidental deployment of the airbag, which could cause personal injury (see Chapter 12).*

Warning 2: *The air conditioning system is under high pressure. Do not loosen any hose fittings or remove any components until after the system has been discharged by a dealer service department or air conditioning service station. Always wear eye protection when disconnecting air conditioning system components.*

Note: *Evaporator removal on these models is a difficult undertaking for the home mechanic. It can be done, but it requires discharging the air conditioning system, disconnecting the passenger airbag system and a great many wiring connectors under the dash and removing the complete instrument panel assembly.*

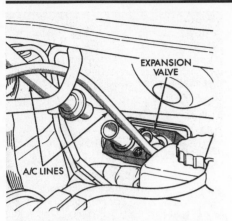

16.3 Disconnect and cap the refrigerant lines from the expansion valve

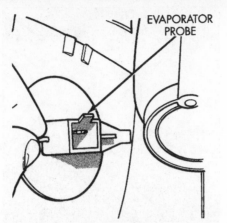

16.15 Remove the evaporator probe from the evaporator core

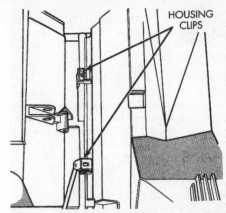

16.17 Remove the clips retaining the two housing sections

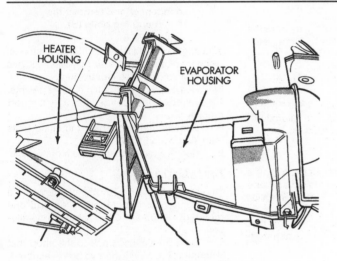

16.18a Pull the two sections apart . . .

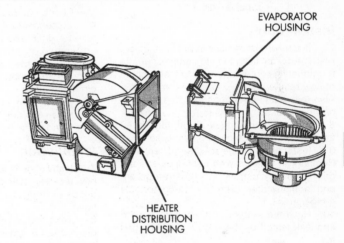

16.18b . . . and separate the heater housing from the evaporator housing

The air conditioning evaporator is contained in a two-piece housing which must be removed from under the dash and separated into two halves.

Expansion valve

Note: *The expansion valve can be replaced without removing the evaporator from the vehicle or removed along with the evaporator.*

Removal

Refer to illustration 16.3

1   Have the system discharged (see the **Warning** at the beginning of this Section).

2   Disconnect the negative battery cable from the ground stud on the left shock tower (see Chapter 5, Section 1).

3   Remove the security clips from expansion valve refrigerant line quick-connect fittings. Using the appropriate quick-connect coupling tools (available at auto parts stores), disconnect and cap the air conditioning lines at the expansion valve **(see illustration)**.

4   Remove the retaining bolts and separate the expansion valve from the evaporator.

Installation

5   Installation is the reverse of removal. Install new O-ring seals on the expansion valve and lubricate them with R-134a-compatible refrigerant oil prior to installation.

6   Take the vehicle back to the shop that discharged it. Have the system evacuated, recharged and leak tested.

Evaporator

Removal

Refer to illustrations 16.15, 16.17, 16.18a, 16.18b and 16.20

7   Have the system discharged (see the **Warning** at the beginning of this Section).

8   Disconnect the negative battery cable from the ground stud on the left shock tower (see Chapter 5, Section 1).

9   Drain the cooling system. Disconnect the heater hoses from the heater core at the firewall (see Section 10). Cap the heater core fittings to prevent spilling coolant on the interior when the housing is removed.

10   Disconnect and cap the refrigerant lines from the expansion valve (see above).

11   Refer to Chapter 11 and remove the complete instrument panel assembly.

12   Remove the center air distribution ducts from the heater/air conditioning housing.

13   Disconnect any wiring harness connectors attached to the housing.

14   Remove the bolts securing the heater/air conditioning housing to the bulkhead and carefully remove the housing from the vehicle.

15   Using a screwdriver, pry the locking tab off the evaporator probe. Twist the evaporator probe access cover 1/4-turn clockwise and remove the cover. Carefully withdraw the evaporator probe from the evaporator core **(see illustration)**.

16   Remove the recirculating door inlet cover.

17   Remove the clips retaining the housing sections together **(see illustration)**.

18   Separate the evaporator housing from the heater/distribution housing **(see illustrations)**.

19   Remove the seal around the evaporator

3

tube inlet.

20   Remove the evaporator housing upper cover **(see illustration)**.

21   Withdraw the evaporator core from the housing.

Installation

Note: *When installing a new evaporator, always use a new gasket on the expansion valve* **(see illustration)** *and reinstall the temperature sensor from the old core into the new core before installation.*

22   Installation is the reverse of removal. If a new evaporator is being installed, add one ounce of new, R-134a-compatible refrigerant oil into it prior to installation.

23   Take the vehicle back to the shop that discharged it. Have the system evacuated, recharged and leak tested.

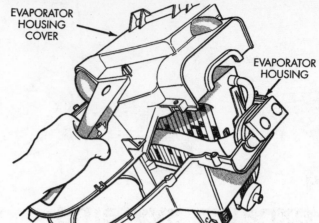

EVAPORATOR HOUSING COVER

EVAPORATOR HOUSING

16.20 Remove the evaporator housing upper cover

Chapter 4
Fuel and exhaust systems

Contents

Specifications

General

Fuel pressure	47 to 51 psi
Fuel injector resistance (approximate)	12 to 15 ohms @ 68-degrees F
Fuel level sending unit resistance (approximate)	
Full position	50 ohms (minimum)
Empty position	1040 to 1060 ohms

Torque specifications

Ft-lbs (unless otherwise indicated)

Fuel rail mounting bolts	
Four-cylinder engines	200 in-lbs
V6 engine	106 in-lbs
Fuel tank drain plug	32 in-lbs
Fuel tank strap bolts	44
Idle Air Control motor-to-throttle body screws	25 in-lbs
Throttle body mounting bolts	
Four-cylinder engines	200 in-lbs
V6 engine	250 in-lbs

1 General information

The vehicles covered by this manual are equipped with a sequential Multi-Port Fuel Injection (MPFI) system. This system uses timed impulses to sequentially inject the fuel directly into the intake ports of each cylinder. The injectors are controlled by the Powertrain Control Module (PCM). The PCM monitors various engine parameters and delivers the exact amount of fuel, in the correct sequence, to the intake ports. It also controls the engine idle speed via the idle air control motor which is mounted to the throttle body.

All models are equipped with an electric fuel pump which is located inside the fuel tank. It is necessary to remove the fuel tank to gain access to the fuel pump. The fuel level sending unit is an integral component of the fuel pump and it must be removed from the fuel tank in the same manner. These vehicles are equipped with a "returnless" fuel system. In this system the fuel pressure regulator is part of the fuel pump/fuel level sending unit and also located inside the fuel tank. Regulated fuel is sent to the fuel rail and excess fuel is bled off directly into the fuel tank.

The exhaust system consists of the exhaust manifold(s), a catalytic converter, an exhaust pipe and a muffler. Each of these components is replaceable. For further information regarding the catalytic converter, refer to Chapter 6.

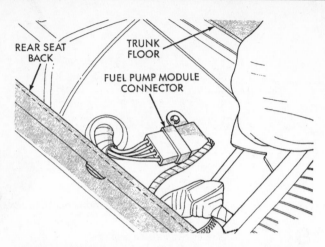

2.3 The fuel pump module electrical connector is located in the trunk, under the mat near the base of the left shock tower

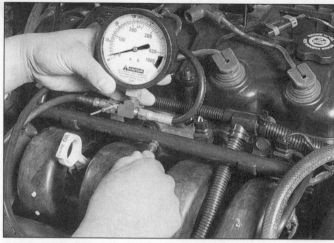

3.4 On four-cylinder engines, connect a fuel pressure gauge to the fuel rail at the test port

2   Fuel pressure relief procedure

Refer to illustration 2.3

Warning: *Gasoline is extremely flammable, so take extra precautions when you work on any part of the fuel system. Don't smoke or allow open flames or bare light bulbs near the work area, and don't work in a garage where a natural gas-type appliance (such as a water heater or a clothes dryer) with a pilot light is present. Since gasoline is carcinogenic, wear latex gloves when there's a possibility of being exposed to fuel, and if you spill any on your skin, rinse it off immediately with soap and water. Mop up any spills immediately and do not store fuel-soaked rags where they could ignite. The fuel system is under constant pressure, so, if any fuel lines are to be disconnected, the pressure must be relieved first. When you perform any kind of work on the fuel system, wear safety glasses and have a Class B type fire extinguisher on hand.*

1   Remove the fuel filler cap to relieve the fuel tank pressure.

2   Working inside the trunk, fold back the trunk mat near the base of the left shock tower.

3   Locate the fuel pump electrical connector and disconnect it from the wiring harness **(see illustration)**.

4   Next, start the engine and allow it to run until it stops. This should only take a few seconds. Crank the engine again, to ensure the fuel pressure is completely relieved. Before working on any part of the fuel system, disconnect the negative battery cable from the ground stud on the left shock tower (see Chapter 5, Section 1).

5   Even after the fuel pressure has been relieved, always lay a shop towel over any fuel connection that is to be separated to absorb the residual fuel that will leak out.

6   When you are finished working on the fuel system, reconnect fuel pump electrical connector to the wiring harness. Turn the ignition key to the ON position a few times to pressurize the system and check the serviced area for leaks.

7   Install the fuel filler cap and tighten it securely. **Note:** *If the fuel filler cap seal allows the fuel tank pressure to escape because of a damaged seal or it has not been tightened sufficiently, the CHECK ENGINE light will illuminate on the instrument panel.*

3   Fuel pump/fuel pressure regulator - check

Warning: *Gasoline is extremely flammable, so take extra precautions when you work on any part of the fuel system (see the **Warning** in Section 2).*

Note 1: *These vehicles are equipped with a "returnless" fuel system in which the fuel pressure regulator is part of the fuel pump module and located inside the fuel tank.*

Note 2: *The fuel pump will operate as long as the engine is cranking or running and the PCM is receiving ignition reference pulses from the electronic ignition system. If there are no reference pulses, the fuel pump will shut off after approximately 1 second.*

Note 3: *To perform the fuel pressure check, you will need to obtain a fuel pressure gauge and adapter set (fuel line fittings). On V6 engines, the fuel supply line is not equipped with a fuel pressure test port (Schrader valve fitting). A special fuel pressure test adapter (factory tool No. 6539 or equivalent) must be installed between the fuel supply line and the fuel rail.*

Preliminary check

Note: *On all models, the fuel pump is located inside the fuel tank (see Section 7).*

1   If you suspect insufficient fuel delivery, first inspect all fuel lines to ensure that the problem is not simply a leak in a line.

2   Set the parking brake and remove the fuel filler cap. Have an assistant turn the ignition switch to the ON position while you listen at the fuel filler neck opening. You should hear a "whirring" sound, lasting for a couple of seconds. Start the engine. The whirring sound should now be continuous (although harder to hear with the engine running). If there is no sound, either the fuel pump fuses, fuel pump, fuel pump relay, automatic shutdown (ASD) relay or related circuits are defective (proceed to Step 15).

System pressure check

Refer to illustrations 3.4 and 3.5

3   Perform the fuel pressure relief procedure (see Section 2).

4   On four-cylinder engines, remove the cap from the fuel pressure test port (Schrader valve fitting) on the fuel rail and attach a fuel pressure gauge **(see illustration)**.

5   On V6 engines, the fuel supply line is not equipped with a fuel pressure test port (Schrader valve fitting). A special fuel pressure test adapter (factory tool No. 6539 or equivalent) must be installed between the fuel supply line and the fuel rail. Disconnect the fuel supply line from the fuel rail (see Section 4) and install the fuel pressure test adapter between the supply line and the fuel rail **(see illustration)**. Attach a fuel pressure gauge to the test adapter fitting.

6   Start the engine and observe the pressure reading on the gauge. Compare it with the pressure listed in this Chapter's Specifications.

7   If the fuel pressure is higher than specified, check for a kinked or restricted fuel line between the fuel filter and fuel pump module. If the line is OK, replace the fuel pressure regulator (see Section 14).

8   If the fuel pressure is lower than specified, replace the fuel filter (see Section 15) and perform the pressure check again. If it's still low, remove the fuel pump module (see Section 7) and inspect the fuel inlet strainer for obstructions. If it's clogged, replace the strainer. If the strainer is OK, replace the fuel pump.

9   If there is no fuel pressure, check the fuel pump, ASD and fuel pump relays as outlined below.

10   Next, verify that the system holds pressure. Note the fuel pressure with the engine

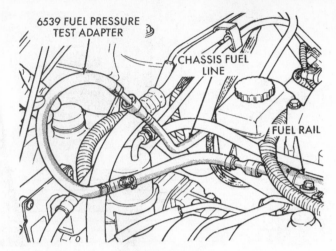

3.5 On V6 engines, a special fuel pressure test adapter must be installed between the fuel supply line and the fuel rail

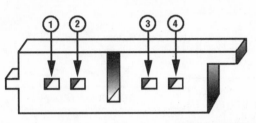

25015-4-3.17 HAYNES

3.17 Fuel pump module electrical connector (body harness side)

1   Fuel pump (positive feed)
2   Fuel level sending unit (signal)
3   Fuel pump (ground)
4   Fuel level sending unit (ground)

running, then turn off the engine and observe the reading on the fuel pressure gauge. The fuel pressure should remain constant for a minimum of one minute. A drop of more than 5 psi in one minute indicates an unacceptable leak in the system. If the pressure drop is unacceptable, first visually inspect the system for obvious leaks, especially at the quick-connect fittings.

11   If there aren't any obvious leaks, the fuel is escaping either from one or more of the fuel injectors or the fuel pressure regulator.

12   On four-cylinder engines, to perform the following check it is necessary to install the special fuel pressure test adapter (factory tool No. 6539 or equivalent) between the fuel rail and the fuel supply line. Perform the fuel relief procedure (see Section 2) and install the adapter and gauge set-up.

13   To determine where the fuel system is leaking, pressurize the fuel system. With the engine OFF, isolate the fuel injectors by pinching off the rubber hose on the special fuel pressure test adapter (factory tool No. 6539 or equivalent) between the fuel pressure gauge and the fuel supply line. Observe the

reading on the fuel pressure gauge. If the fuel pressure bleeds down there is a leak at one or more of the injectors. Refer to Section 16 for further testing and replacement procedures.

14   If the pressure remains constant, the fuel injectors are OK and the fuel pressure regulator must be replaced (see Section 14). After the pressure tests are complete, perform the fuel pressure relief procedure (see Section 2), remove the fuel pressure gauge and adapter (if used) and assemble the quick-connect fittings (see Section 4).

Component checks

Note: *The fuel pressure regulator check is part of the system pressure check (see above).*

Fuel pump

Refer to illustration 3.17

15   If you cannot hear the fuel pump operate when energized (refer to preliminary check above), use a test light or voltmeter to verify the pump is receiving battery voltage.

16   Working inside the trunk, fold back the trunk mat near the base of the left shock

tower. Locate the fuel pump 4-pin electrical connector and disconnect it **(see illustration 2.3).**

17   Connect a test light or voltmeter to the fuel pump positive feed and ground terminals of the electrical connector **(see illustration).**

18   Have an assistant crank the engine - battery voltage should be present at the electrical connector. If voltage is present, replace the fuel pump. If voltage is not present, check the ASD and fuel pump relays (see below).

ASD and fuel pump relays

Refer to illustrations 3.20a, 3.20b, 3.21a, 3.21b, 3.23, 3.24 and 3.25

Note: *The Automatic Shutdown (ASD) relay and the fuel pump relay must both be tested to insure proper fuel pump operation. Testing procedures for the ASD relay and the fuel pump relay are identical.*

19   To access the relay box where the ASD relay is located, remove air cleaner assembly (see Section 9).

20   To test a relay, first remove it from its location in the engine compartment Power Distribution Center (PDC) **(see illustrations).**

4

3.20a The Automatic Shutdown relay (arrow) is located in the Power Distribution Center under the square cover

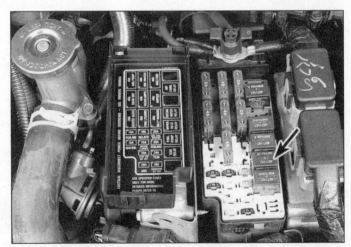

3.20b The fuel pump relay (arrow) is located in the Power Distribution Center under the rectangular cover

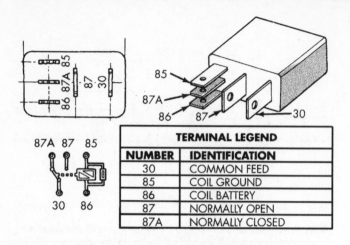

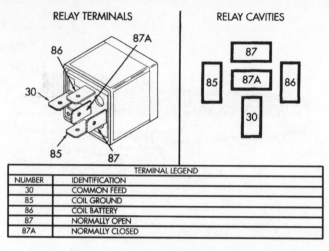

TERMINAL LEGEND	
NUMBER	IDENTIFICATION
30	COMMON FEED
85	COIL GROUND
86	COIL BATTERY
87	NORMALLY OPEN
87A	NORMALLY CLOSED

3.21a ASD and fuel pump relay terminal identification (rectangle type)

TERMINAL LEGEND	
NUMBER	IDENTIFICATION
30	COMMON FEED
85	COIL GROUND
86	COIL BATTERY
87	NORMALLY OPEN
87A	NORMALLY CLOSED

3.21b ASD and fuel pump relay terminal identification (square type)

21　Verify that there is battery voltage at the terminal in the PDC that corresponds with terminal 30 of the relay **(see illustrations)**. This terminal should have voltage present at all times. Now check the terminal in the PDC that corresponds with terminal 86 on the relay - it should have voltage present only with the ignition key in the ON position.

22　If there is no voltage, check the fuel pump fuses in cavities 8 and 10 in the PDC. If voltage is not present at the fuse, check the wiring and connectors to the PDC for a short, broken wire or a bad connection.

23　Next, check relay operation by connecting the probes of an ohmmeter to terminals 86 and 85 and measure the resistance. There should be approximately 75 ohms resistance **(see illustration)**.

24　Now connect the ohmmeter probes to terminals 30 and 87A and check for continuity. Continuity should be present **(see illustration)**.

25　Check for continuity between terminals 30 and 87 **(see illustration)**. There should be no continuity.

26　Next, with the ohmmeter still connected to relay terminals 87 and 30, use jumper

wires to connect the relay to the battery. Connect the battery positive terminal to relay terminal 86 and the battery negative terminal to relay terminal 85. Continuity should exist between terminals 87 and 30 when terminals 86 and 85 are energized. If continuity is not present, replace the relay.

4　Quick-connect fittings and fuel lines - disassembly, assembly and replacement

---

Warning: *Gasoline is extremely flammable, so take extra precautions when you work on any part of the fuel system (see the* **Warning** *in Section 2).*

General information

1　Always perform the fuel pressure relief procedure (see Section 2) before servicing fuel lines or fittings.

2　The fuel supply and vapor lines extend from the fuel tank to the engine compartment. The lines are constructed of steel, plastic and rubber. They are secured to the underbody with clips and brackets. These lines should be

inspected for leaks, kinks and dents anytime the vehicle is raised for service.

3　If evidence of dirt is found in the fuel system or fuel filter during service, the affected line should be disconnected and blown out. Check the fuel inlet strainer on the fuel pump module for blockage or contamination (see Section 14).

Quick-connect fittings

4　Chrysler uses three different types of quick-connect fittings to join various fuel lines and components. The first type uses a single-tab retainer, the second type a two-tab retainer and the third type incorporates a plastic retainer ring (usually black in color) which connects/disconnects much like a common compressed air hose fitting. Some are equipped with safety latch clips. The fittings are equipped with non-serviceable O-ring seals located in the female part of the fitting. In the event the fitting or tubing becomes damaged or develops a leak, replace the entire fuel line/quick-connect fitting as an assembly. Always use original equipment parts, or parts that meet or exceed the original equipment standards.

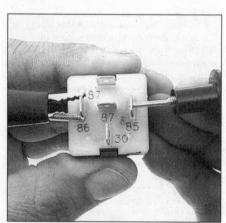

3.23 Measure the resistance between terminals 86 and 85 - it should be approximately 75 ohms

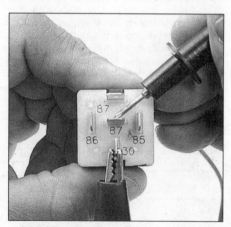

3.24 Measure the resistance between terminals 30 and 87A - continuity should be present

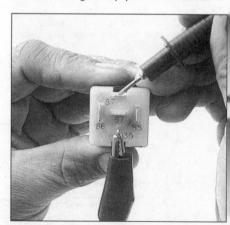

3.25 Check for continuity between terminals 30 and 87 - there should be no continuity

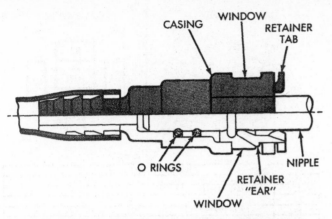

4.5a Cross-sectional view of a two-tab quick-connect fuel line fitting

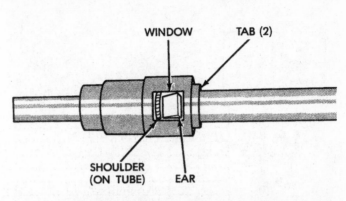

4.5b When properly assembled, the tab ear and shoulder on the male fitting should be visible in the window

Single and two-tab retainer fittings

Disassembly

Refer to illustrations 4.5a, 4.5b, 4.9a and 4.9b

5   These quick-connect fittings have one or 2 windows (depending on type) located in the side(s) of the female fitting. When the male fitting is inserted into the female, the tab(s) on the male engage in the window(s) and lock the fitting together **(see illustrations)**.

6   Perform the fuel pressure relief procedure (see Section 2).

7   Remove all fasteners, brackets or clips securing the lines as applicable.

8   Clean the area around the fitting to remove dirt and foreign debris.

9   Depress the retaining tab(s) on the quick-connect fitting and pull it apart **(see illustrations)**. **Note:** *The retaining tabs and shoulder should remain on the metal fuel line after separation.*

Assembly

10   Clean the male part of the fitting and lightly lubricate it with clean engine oil.

11   Position the retaining tab ears on the tube so they align with the windows in the female fitting and push them together. You should hear the fitting snap into place as the retaining tab ears lock into the windows.

12   Verify the fitting is properly fastened by trying to pull the lines apart.

13   Secure the fuel line using any clips or brackets as applicable.

14   Pressurize the system and check for leaks.

4.9a Depress the plastic tabs on the male fitting . . .

Plastic retainer ring fittings

Disassembly

Refer to illustration 4.18

15   Perform the fuel pressure relief procedure (see Section 2).

16   Remove all fasteners, brackets or clips securing the lines as applicable.

17   Clean the area around the fitting to remove dirt and foreign debris.

18   Grasp the male line and push it in (towards the fitting). While applying pressure on the male line, press the plastic retainer ring into the female fitting and then pull the male line from the female fitting **(see illustration)**. **Note:** *The plastic retainer ring must be pushed*

4.9b . . . and separate the fitting - to assemble it, lubricate the male end with a small amount of clean engine oil, then push the fitting together until it locks into place - tug on it to ensure the connection is secure

into the female fitting squarely! If it gets cocked, the fitting will be difficult to separate. If necessary, use an open-end wrench applied to the plastic retainer to assist in evenly pressing it into the female fitting. The plastic retainer ring should remain attached to the female fitting after separation.

Assembly

19   Clean the male part of the fitting and lightly lubricate it with clean engine oil.

20   Insert the male end into the female and push them together **(see illustration 4.18)**. You should hear the retainer ring snap into

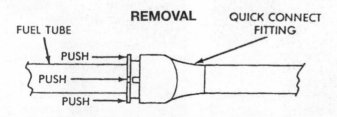

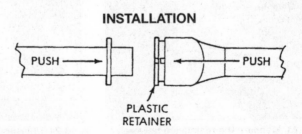

4.18 Plastic retainer ring type quick-connect fitting removal and installation

5.6 Fuel tank drain plug (arrow)

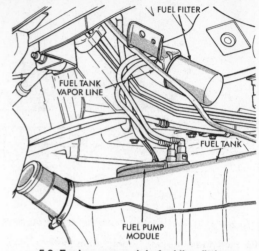

5.9 Fuel pump module fuel line fittings

place as it locks the fitting together. Make sure the retainer ring is fully extended after assembly.

21   Verify the fitting is properly fastened by trying to pull the lines apart.

22   Secure the fuel line using any clips or brackets as applicable.

23   Pressurize the system and check for leaks.

Fuel lines - replacement
Steel tubing

24   If replacement of a metal line is required, disassemble the applicable quick-connect fittings as described above and remove the line from the vehicle. If the quick-connect fitting is damaged or leaks, replace the affected section of fuel line/quick-connect fittings as an assembly.

25   If the quick-connect fittings are acceptable, a new piece of steel tubing may be spliced-in to replace a damaged section by flaring the tubing ends and joining them with a union. Use tubing that meets or exceeds original equipment standards. Do not use copper or aluminum tubing to replace steel tubing. These materials cannot withstand normal vehicle vibration. Do not use a rubber hose to replace a damaged section of steel tubing!

26   When installing the replacement section into the line, assemble the quick-connect fittings first, then tighten the unions. **Warning:** *Metal lines must never be allowed to rub against other components or each other. A minimum of 1/4-inch clearance must be maintained to prevent contact unless it is properly secured.*

27   After replacing the line or section, pressurize the system and check for leaks.

Plastic lines

28   If replacement of a plastic line is required, disassemble the applicable quick-connect fittings as described above and remove the line from the vehicle. The plastic lines used on these vehicles are not serviceable. If replacement is required, the affected section of fuel line/quick-connect fittings

must be replaced as an assembly.

29   Install the new line onto the vehicle and assemble the quick-connect fittings as applicable (see above). Secure the line to the vehicle as required. **Warning:** *Plastic lines must never be allowed to rub against other components or each other. A minimum of 1/4-inch clearance must be maintained to prevent contact unless it is properly secured. Do not route plastic fuel lines within four inches of any part of the exhaust system or within ten inches of the catalytic converter.*

30   After replacing the line, pressurize the system and check for leaks.

Rubber hoses

Warning: *Fuel-injected vehicles use specially constructed hoses. Only use hoses marked EFM/EFI. Replace with only original equipment hoses, or hoses that meet or exceed original equipment standards. Others may have a lower fatigue threshold.*

31   Perform the fuel pressure relief procedure (see Section 2).

32   Loosen the clamps securing the hose and remove it from the vehicle.

33   Installation is the reverse of removal. **Warning:** *Do not route rubber fuel hoses within four inches of any part of the exhaust system or within ten inches of the catalytic converter. Rubber hoses must never be allowed to rub against other components or each other. A minimum of 1/4-inch clearance must be maintained to prevent contact with other components unless it is properly secured.*

34   After replacing the hose, pressurize the system and check for leaks.

5   Fuel tank - removal and installation

Warning: *Gasoline is extremely flammable, so take extra precautions when you work on any part of the fuel system (see the **Warning** in Section 2).*

Removal
Refer to illustrations 5.6 and 5.9

1   Remove the fuel tank filler cap to relieve fuel tank pressure.

2   Perform the fuel pressure relief procedure (see Section 2).

3   Disconnect the negative battery cable from the ground stud on the left shock tower (see Chapter 5, Section 1).

4   Working inside the trunk, fold back the trunk mat near the base of the left shock tower. Locate the fuel pump wiring harness 4-pin connector and disconnect it from the wiring harness **(see illustration 2.3)**. Follow the fuel pump wiring to the grommet at the base of the rear seat. Push the grommet through the floorpan and feed the wiring and 4-pin connector through the hole.

5   Raise the vehicle and support it securely on jackstands.

6   Position an approved gasoline container under the fuel tank drain plug. If necessary, use a funnel to prevent spilling fuel. **Warning:** *The fuel tank capacity is 16 gallons. Unless the fuel tank is almost empty, be prepared to collect a significant amount of fuel. Do not leave the fuel tank draining operation unattended. Be prepared to replace the drain plug in case the fuel tank capacity exceeds the container capacity.* Remove the drain plug **(see illustration)** and allow the fuel to exit the fuel tank.

7   After the fuel has finished draining, replace the drain plug and tighten it to the torque listed in this Chapter's Specifications. **Warning:** *There will be approximately 1 to 2 gallons of fuel remaining inside the tank.*

8   Loosen the clamp and detach the filler neck hose from the fuel tank. **Warning:** *There may be fuel inside the filler neck and hose, protect yourself accordingly.*

9   Disconnect the quick-connect fuel line fittings (see Section 4 if necessary) from the fuel pump module **(see illustration)**.

10   At the rear of the fuel tank, detach the vapor hose from the rollover valve.

11   Support the fuel tank with a floor jack.

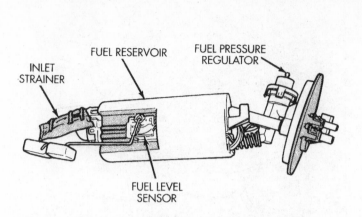

INLET STRAINER

FUEL RESERVOIR

FUEL PRESSURE REGULATOR

FUEL LEVEL SENSOR

7.6a Fuel pump module - component identification

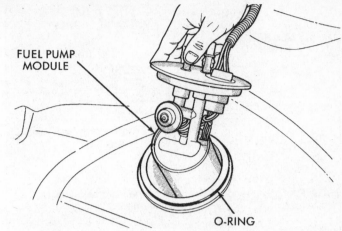

FUEL PUMP MODULE

O-RING

7.6b When removing the fuel pump module from the fuel tank, slightly angle the module to avoid damaging the fuel level sending unit float arm

Place a piece of wood between the jack head and the fuel tank to protect the tank.

12   Remove the fuel tank strap bolts and straps.

13   On 1998 models, slightly lower the fuel tank and detach the EVAP canister purge line. Remove the hoses from the EVAP canister (see Chapter 6 if necessary) and disconnect the electrical connector from the Leak Detection Pump (LDP). **Note:** *Before disconnecting any lines or hoses, clearly label the hose and fitting so they can be reinstalled in their proper locations.*

14   Slightly lower the fuel tank and then slide it forward to allow the filler neck to clear the rear suspension crossmember. Remove the tank from the vehicle.

Installation

15   Installation is the reverse of removal. However, before installing the fuel tank, tie a length of string or wire to the fuel pump module wiring harness and route it through the hole in the trunk floorpan. Once the fuel tank is securely in position, pull the string to access the wiring harness.

16   Tighten the fuel tank strap bolts to the torque listed in this Chapter's Specifications.

6   Fuel tank cleaning and repair - general information

Warning: *Gasoline is extremely flammable, so take extra precautions when you work on any part of the fuel system. (See the* **Warning** *in Section 2).*

1   The fuel tank on these vehicles is made of plastic and is not repairable.

2   If the fuel tank is removed from the vehicle, do not place it in an area where sparks or open flames could ignite the fuel vapors escaping from the tank. Be especially careful inside a garage where a natural gas-type appliance is located, because the pilot light could cause an explosion.

7   Fuel pump module - removal and installation

Warning 1: *Gasoline is extremely flammable, so take extra precautions when you work on any part of the fuel system (see the* **Warning** *in Section 2).*

Warning 2: *The fuel reservoir in the fuel pump module does not empty when the fuel tank is drained. This fuel will drain out when the fuel pump module is removed from the fuel tank - protect yourself accordingly.*

Caution: *Be sure to change the fuel pump module O-ring seal whenever the assembly is removed for service.*

Note: *The fuel pump module consists of the following components; fuel pump, fuel pressure regulator, fuel inlet strainer and fuel level sending unit.*

Removal

Refer to illustrations 7.6a and 7.6b

1   Perform the fuel pressure relief procedure (see Section 2).

2   Disconnect the negative cable from the remote battery terminal.

3   Remove the fuel tank from the vehicle (see Section 5).

4   Clean the top of the fuel tank around the fuel pump module to remove any dirt or debris.

5   Using a large pair of pliers, remove the fuel pump module ring nut. **Caution:** *Do not apply too much pressure on the ring nut during removal or damage may result.*

6   Remove the fuel pump module from the tank (**see illustrations**). Angle the assembly slightly to avoid damaging the fuel level sending unit float arm. Remove and discard the O-ring seal.

7   The electric fuel pump is not serviceable. In the event of failure, the complete assembly must be replaced. The only serviceable parts on the fuel pump module are the fuel inlet strainer, fuel pressure regulator and the fuel level sending unit.

8   For service procedures on the fuel pressure regulator and inlet strainer refer to Section 14.

9   For service procedures on the fuel level sending unit refer to Section 8.

Installation

10   Clean sealing area on the fuel tank. Obtain the new fuel pump module O-ring seal. Lightly lubricate the O-ring seal with clean engine oil and install it on the fuel tank opening.

11   Carefully insert the fuel pump module into the fuel tank. Align the tab on the fuel pump module with the notch in the fuel tank.

12   While holding the fuel pump module in place, install the ring nut, tightening it securely. **Caution:** *Over-tightening the ring nut may result in a leak.*

13   The remaining installation steps are the reverse of removal.

8   Fuel level sending unit - check and replacement

Warning: *Gasoline is extremely flammable, so take extra precautions when you work on any part of the fuel system (see the* **Warning** *in Section 2).*

Note: *The fuel pump module consists of the following components; fuel pump, fuel pressure regulator, fuel inlet strainer and fuel level sending unit.*

Check

Refer to illustrations 8.3, 8.9 and 8.10

In-vehicle

1   Begin this procedure with the fuel tank completely full.

2   Working inside the trunk, fold back the trunk mat near the base of the left shock tower. Locate the fuel pump wiring harness 4-pin connector and disconnect it from the wiring harness (**see illustration 2.3**).

4

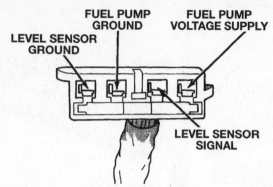

LEVEL SENSOR GROUND

FUEL PUMP GROUND

FUEL PUMP VOLTAGE SUPPLY

LEVEL SENSOR SIGNAL

8.3 Fuel pump module electrical connector (fuel pump side) terminal identification

1   Fuel level sending unit (ground)
2   Fuel pump (ground)
3   Fuel level sending unit (signal)
4   Fuel pump (positive feed)

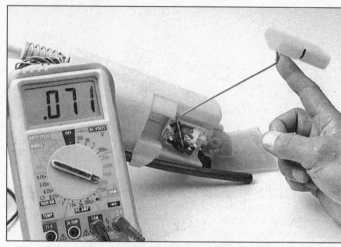

8.9 Measuring the resistance of the fuel level sending unit with the float arm in the FULL position

8.10 Measuring the resistance of the fuel level sending unit with the float arm in the EMPTY position

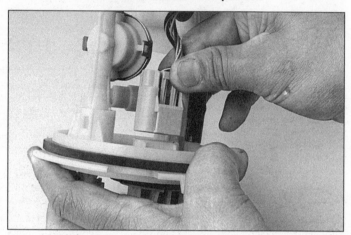

8.13 Disconnect the electrical connector from the base of the fuel pump module flange

3   Connect the probes of an ohmmeter to the fuel level sending unit terminals of the fuel pump module electrical connector and measure the resistance **(see illustration)**. Compare the measured resistance to the value listed in this Chapter's Specifications. If the resistance is less than specified, replace the fuel level sending unit.

4   Next, drive the vehicle until the fuel tank is nearly empty or drain the fuel tank via the drain plug into a container approved to hold gasoline (see Section 5).

5   With the fuel tank empty, check the resistance again **(see illustration 8.3)**. Compare the measured resistance to the value listed in this Chapter's Specifications. If the resistance is out of tolerance, replace the fuel level sending unit.

Removed from vehicle

6   A more thorough check of the fuel level sending unit can be performed with the sending unit removed from the vehicle.

7   Remove the fuel pump module (see Section 7).

8   Connect the probes of an ohmmeter to the fuel level sending unit terminals of the fuel pump module electrical connector **(see illustration 8.3)**.

9   First, check the resistance of the sending unit with the float arm in the FULL position **(see illustration)**. Compare the measured resistance to the value listed in this Chapter's Specifications. If the resistance is less than specified, replace the fuel level sending unit.

10   Next, while observing the ohmmeter, slowly lower the float arm to the EMPTY position. The ohmmeter should register a smooth change in resistance value from the FULL to EMPTY position **(see illustration)**. Compare the measured resistance to the value listed in this Chapter's Specifications. If the resistance is out of tolerance or the ohmmeter exhibited fluctuation during the transition from FULL to EMPTY, replace the fuel level sending unit.

Replacement

Refer to illustrations 8.13, 8.14, 8.15 and 8.17

11   Perform the fuel pressure relief procedure (see Section 2).

12   Remove the fuel pump module (see Section 7).

13   Disconnect the fuel level sensor/fuel pump electrical connector from the base of the fuel pump module flange **(see illustration)**.

14   Use needle-nose pliers to remove the blue locking wedge **(see illustration)**.

15   Use a small screwdriver or needle-nose pliers to lift the connector locking finger away from the fuel level sending unit wire terminals and then withdraw them from the module

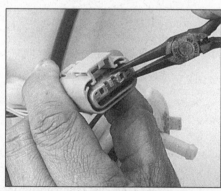

8.14 Use needle-nose pliers and carefully remove the blue locking wedge

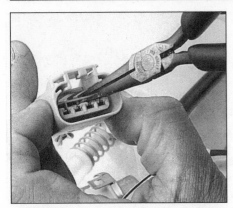

8.15 Use a small screwdriver, or needle-nose pliers, and lift the locking fingers away from the terminals, then carefully remove the terminals from the connector

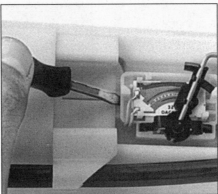

8.17 Using a screwdriver, pry the sensor down slightly to disengage the locking feature

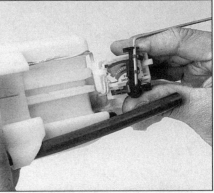

8.19 Place the wires into the groove on the backside of the sending unit, then while guiding the wires, slide the sending unit up the channel until it snaps into place - tug on it to ensure it's locked into place

20   Install the wire terminals into the module connector in their proper locations (see illustration).

21   Install the blue locking wedge into the module connector.

22   Verify the wire terminals are properly installed in the module connector by gently pulling on the wires.

23   Connect the fuel level sensor/fuel pump electrical connector to the base of the fuel pump module flange.

24   The remaining installation steps are the reverse of removal.

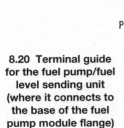

8.20 Terminal guide for the fuel pump/fuel level sending unit (where it connects to the base of the fuel pump module flange)

PUMP GROUND

LEVEL SENSOR GROUND

FUEL PUMP SUPPLY

LEVEL SENSOR SIGNAL

9   Air cleaner assembly - removal and installation

Removal

Refer to illustrations 9.1a, 9.1b, 9.2, 9.4a and 9.4b

1   On the 2.0L four-cylinder engine and the V6 engine, remove the air inlet resonator-to-manifold bolts (see illustrations).

electrical connector (see illustration).

16   If necessary, use factory tool No. C-4334 or equivalent to remove the fuel level sending unit terminals from the module connector.

17   To remove the sending unit, insert a screwdriver between the module fuel reservoir and the top of the level sensor as shown and pry the sensor down slightly (see illustration).

18   While guiding the sensor wires through the module fuel reservoir opening, slide the sensor out of the channel.

Installation

Refer to illustrations 8.19 and 8.20

19   Place the wires into the guide groove on the back side of the sending unit, route them through the module fuel reservoir and then slide the sensor up the channel until it snaps into place (see illustration).

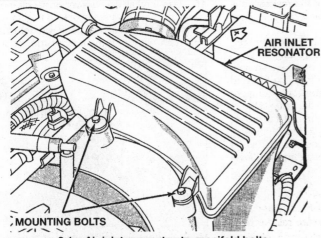

9.1a Air inlet resonator-to-manifold bolts (2.0L four-cylinder engine only)

AIR INLET RESONATOR

MOUNTING BOLTS

9.1b Removing the air inlet resonator bolt (V6 engine)

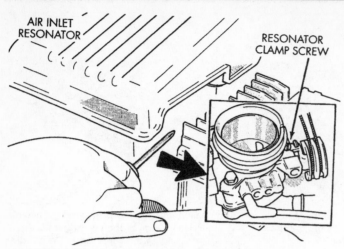

**9.2 Four-cylinder engines - air inlet resonator clamp
at the throttle body**

**9.4a Loosening the air duct clamp at the air filter housing
(V6 engine shown, others similar)**

2   On four-cylinder engines, loosen the clamp and detach the air inlet resonator from the throttle body **(see illustration)**.

3   On four-cylinder engines, loosen the air duct clamp at the air cleaner housing and remove the air ducting with air inlet resonator attached.

4   On V6 engines, loosen the air duct clamps at the air cleaner housing and throttle body **(see illustrations)** then remove the air ducting with air inlet resonator attached.

Installation

5   Installation is the reverse of removal.

Air filter housing

Removal

Refer to illustration 9.8

6   Loosen the air duct clamp and detach it from the air cleaner top cover **(see illustration 9.4a)**.

7   Remove the air filter top cover and filter element (see Chapter 1 if necessary).

8   Remove the three bolts securing the air filter lower housing to the inner fender panel **(see illustration)**.

9   Detach the air inlet duct at the front of

the housing and remove it from the engine compartment.

Installation

10   Installation is the reverse of removal. Make sure the lower housing is free of dirt and contamination prior to installation.

10   Accelerator cable - replacement

Refer to illustrations 10.2, 10.3, 10.4, 10.5 and 10.6

1   On four-cylinder engines, remove the air cleaner assembly (see Section 9).

2   Rotate the throttle valve cam to the full throttle position and disconnect the accelerator cable from the slot in the throttle valve cam **(see illustration)**.

3   On four-cylinder engines, compress the cable retaining tabs and push the accelerator cable out of the bracket **(see illustration)**.

4   On V6 engines, compress the cable retaining tab and slide the cable out of the side of the bracket **(see illustration)**.

5   Disconnect the accelerator cable from the bracket on the firewall **(see illustration)**.

6   At the accelerator pedal arm inside the

vehicle, use pliers to compress the cable retainer clips, then push the cable retainer out of the accelerator pedal arm. Next, slide the cable out of the slot in the accelerator pedal arm **(see illustration)**.

7   Push the cable through the firewall into the engine compartment and remove it from the vehicle.

8   Installation is the reverse of removal.

11   Fuel injection system - general information

The sequential Multi-Port Fuel Injection (MPFI) system consists of three sub-systems: air intake, engine control and fuel delivery. The MPFI system is controlled by the Powertrain Control Module (PCM) which uses the information from various sensors to determine the proper air/fuel ratio under all operating conditions.

The fuel injection system, emissions and engine control systems work together to provide maximum performance, fuel economy and the lowest exhaust emissions. For complete information on the emissions and engine control system, refer to Chapter 6.

**9.4b Loosening the air duct clamp at
the throttle body (V6 engine)**

**9.8 Remove the three bolts then remove
the air filter lower housing from
the fender panel**

**10.2 Disconnecting the accelerator cable
from the throttle lever at the throttle body
(V6 engine shown)**

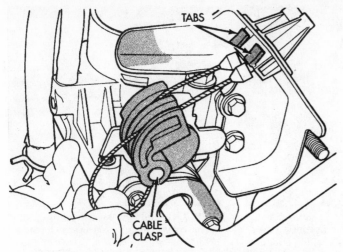

10.3 On four-cylinder engines, after detaching the cable from the throttle lever, compress the tab on the cable outer housing and push it through the bracket

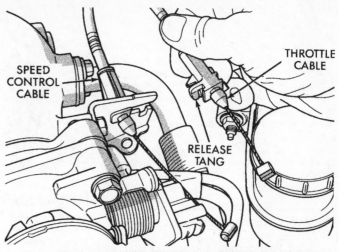

10.4 On V6 engines, compress the retaining tab on the cable housing and slide the cable from the bracket

Air intake system

The air intake system consists of the air filter, the air ducts, air inlet resonator, the throttle body, the idle control system and the intake manifold.

The engine idle speed is controlled by the PCM via the Idle Air Control (IAC) motor. The IAC motor regulates the flow of air allowed to by-pass the throttle valve in the throttle body thereby increasing engine speed. The PCM uses information from various sensors to determine the correct amount of airflow required to maintain the proper engine speed during engine warm-up and when a load is placed on the engine, such as engaging the air conditioning compressor, low speed steering or when an automatic transaxle is placed in gear.

Engine control system

For information on the engine control system, refer to Chapter 6.

Fuel delivery system

The fuel delivery system consists of the following components: an electric fuel pump, a fuel pressure regulator, an in-line fuel filter, the fuel rail, the fuel injectors, various metal and plastic lines, the Automatic Shutdown (ASD) relay and the fuel pump relay.

The fuel pump and fuel pressure regulator are located inside the fuel tank. Fuel is drawn through the fuel inlet strainer into the pump, pumped past the fuel pressure regulator, then through the fuel filter and delivered to the injectors.

The fuel pressure regulator maintains a constant fuel pressure to the injectors. Excess fuel is released back into the fuel tank through the fuel pressure regulator. This system is called a "returnless" system.

The fuel rail supplies the regulated fuel to each electronically controlled fuel injector. The injectors are solenoid types consisting of a solenoid, plunger, needle valve and housing. When the PCM sends a voltage signal to the fuel injector, the needle valve raises off its seat and lets metered fuel enter the intake

4

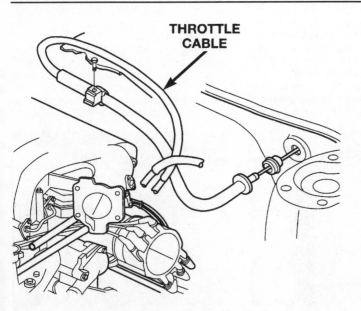

10.5 Accelerator cable bracket at firewall (V6 engine shown, typical routing for all models)

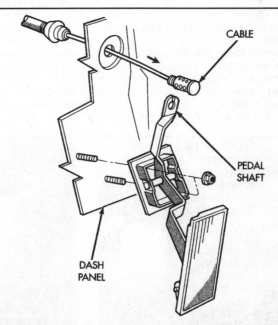

10.6 Use pliers to compress the cable retainer tabs and push the cable retainer from the accelerator pedal arm, then remove the cable through the slot in the pedal arm and remove the cable from inside the engine compartment

manifold. The injection quantity is determined by the length of time which current is supplied to the injector.

The Automatic Shutdown (ASD) and the fuel pump relays are located in the Power Distribution Center, which is located in the engine compartment on the left (driver's) side. The ASD relay connects battery voltage to the fuel injectors and the ignition coil while the fuel pump relay connects battery voltage only to the fuel pump. If the PCM senses there is NO signal from the camshaft or crankshaft sensors while the ignition key is RUN or cranking, the PCM will de-energize both relays in approximately one second.

12 Fuel injection system - general check

Refer to illustration 12.6

Warning: *Gasoline is extremely flammable, so take extra precautions when you work on any part of the fuel system) see the* **Warning** *in Section 2).*

Note: *The following procedure is based on the assumption that the fuel pump/pressure is acceptable (see Section 3).*

1   Visually check all electrical connectors that are related to the system. Check ground wire connections on the intake manifold and engine for tightness. Loose connectors and poor grounds can cause many problems that resemble more serious component malfunctions.

2   Check to see that the battery is fully charged, as the PCM and information sensors depend on proper battery voltage in order to operate correctly.

3   Check the air filter element - a dirty or partially blocked filter will severely impede performance and economy (see Chapter 1).

4   Check the air intake ducts for cracks or loose connections. Also check the condition of all vacuum hoses connected to the intake manifold. Make sure they fit tightly on the vacuum ports and are free from cracks or other defects.

5   Remove the air intake duct (V6 engine) or air inlet resonator (four-cylinder engines) from the throttle body and inspect for dirt, carbon or other residue build-up around the throttle valve and Idle Air Control by-pass port. If the throttle body is dirty, clean it with a spray-type carburetor cleaner and a toothbrush or clean rag. **Note:** *If the throttle body cannot be cleaned properly while installed on the vehicle, remove it* (see Section 13).

6   With the engine running, place an automotive stethoscope against each injector, one at a time, and listen for a clicking sound, indicating operation **(see illustration)**. If you don't have a stethoscope, place the tip of a screwdriver against the injector and listen through the handle. **Note:** *On V6 engines, the air inlet resonator must be removed to access the left bank of fuel injectors. The right bank of fuel injectors CANNOT be checked using this procedure, as they are covered by the upper intake manifold.*

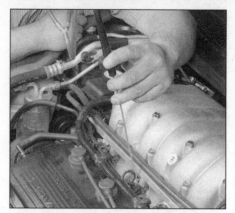

12.6 Use a stethoscope to determine if the injectors are working properly - they should make a steady clicking sound that rises and falls with engine speed changes (V6 engine shown)

7   Individual component checks can be found in their appropriate Sections.

13 Throttle body - check, removal and installation

Check

1   Remove the air cleaner assembly (see Section 9).

2   Verify the accelerator cable, cruise control cable (if equipped) and throttle valve operate smoothly without binding or sticking.

3   Inspect the throttle bore, throttle valve, IAC by-pass port and canister purge vacuum port for carbon deposits. If carbon build-up is present, remove the throttle body from the vehicle (see below) and remove the IAC motor (see Section 17). Clean the throttle body and IAC motor pintle with a spray-type carburetor cleaner and a toothbrush.

4   If the throttle valve does not operate freely after cleaning, replace the throttle body.

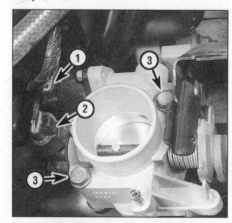

13.10a Four-cylinder engine IAC, TPS and throttle body bolts

1   *Idle Air Control motor*
2   *Throttle Position Sensor*
3   *Throttle body bolts*

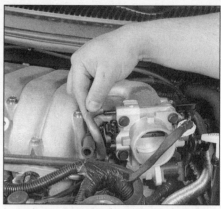

13.7 Disconnect the canister purge control vacuum hose from the throttle body (V6 engine shown, others similar)

Removal

Refer to illustrations 13.7, 13.10a, 13.10b and 13.11

Warning: *Wait until the engine is completely cool before beginning this procedure.*

5   Disconnect the negative battery cable from the ground stud on the left shock tower.

6   Remove the air cleaner assembly (see Section 9).

7   Disconnect the canister purge vacuum hose from the throttle body **(see illustration)**.

8   Detach the accelerator cable and cruise control cable (if equipped), from the throttle valve lever (see Section 10).

9   On four-cylinder engines, remove the accelerator and cruise control cable bracket and position the bracket (with cable) out of the way.

10   Disconnect the TPS and IAC sensor connectors from the throttle body, remove the mounting bolts and then withdraw the throttle body and gasket from the manifold **(see illustrations)**.

11   The throttle body O-ring seal on 2.0L four-cylinder engines is reusable **(see illustration)**. Remove it from the manifold and

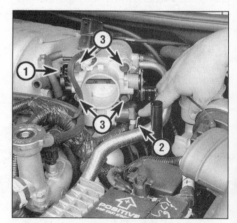

13.10b V6 engine IAC, TPS and throttle body bolts

1   *Throttle Position Sensor*
2   *Idle Air Control motor*
3   *Throttle body bolts*

inspect it for hardness and cracks. If visual inspection does not reveal any defects, the O-ring seal may be reused.

12 On all other models, remove all traces of gasket material from the throttle body and manifold.

13 If necessary, clean the throttle body as outlined in Step 3.

Installation

14 Install the throttle body with a new gasket (2.0L four-cylinder engines may reuse the O-ring seal) onto the intake manifold.

15 Tighten the throttle body mounting bolts to the torque listed in this Chapter's Specifications.

16 The remaining installation steps are the reverse of removal. After installation, check to see that the throttle body operates freely.

---

14 Fuel pressure regulator and fuel inlet strainer - replacement

Warning: *Gasoline is extremely flammable, so take extra precautions when you work on any part of the fuel system (see the **Warning** in Section 2).*
Note: *The fuel pump module consists of the following components; fuel pump, fuel pressure regulator, fuel inlet strainer and fuel level sending unit.*

Fuel pressure regulator

Replacement

Refer to illustrations 14.3a, 14.3b and 14.4

1 Perform the fuel pressure relief procedure (see Section 2).

2 Remove the fuel pump module (see Section 7).

3 Spread the tabs on the pressure regulator retainer and remove the retainer, then carefully pry the pressure regulator out of the fuel pump module housing **(see illustrations)**. Ensure that both upper and lower O-ring seals come out with the regulator. Dis-

13.11 On 2.0L four-cylinder engines, the throttle body O-ring gasket (arrow) is reusable

card the old O-ring seals.

4 Apply a light coat of clean engine oil to the new O-ring seals and install them in the receptacle in the fuel pump module **(see illustration)**. Ensure they are properly seated.

5 Install the new pressure regulator into the fuel pump module.

6 Install the regulator retainer and fold the retainer tangs over the tabs on the fuel pump module. Make sure the retainer is securely attached.

7 Install the fuel pump module (see Section 7).

Fuel inlet strainer

Replacement

Refer to illustration 14.10

8 Perform the fuel pressure relief procedure (see Section 2).

9 Remove the fuel pump module (see Section 7).

10 Using a flat-blade screwdriver, pry the tangs on the fuel inlet strainer away from the tabs on the fuel pump reservoir and remove the strainer and O-ring seal **(see illustration)**.

11 Before installing the new O-ring seal, apply a light coating of clean engine oil to the

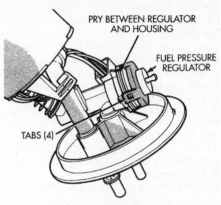

14.3a Spread the four tabs and remove the retainer

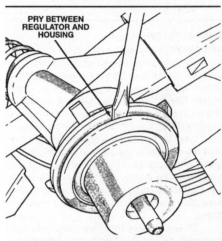

14.3b Using a screwdriver, carefully pry the fuel pressure regulator out of the fuel pump module

O-ring seal and install it in onto the fuel pump reservoir.

12 Install the fuel inlet strainer onto the fuel pump reservoir and make sure it is securely locked in place.

13 Install the fuel pump module (see Section 7).

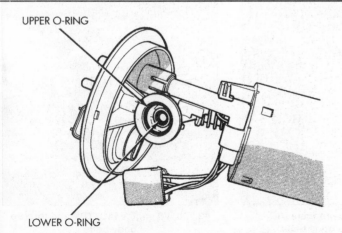

14.4 Apply a light coating of clean engine oil to the new O-ring seals and install them into the fuel pump module

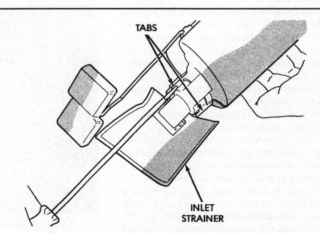

14.10 To remove the inlet strainer, use a screwdriver to pry the retaining tabs away from the fuel pump module and then detach the strainer

15   Fuel filter - removal and installation

Warning: *Gasoline is extremely flammable, so take extra precautions when you work on any part of the fuel system (see the Warning in Section 2).*

Removal

Refer to illustration 15.1

1   The in-line fuel filter mounts to the frame above the rear of the fuel tank, near the filler neck **(see illustration)**.

2   Remove the fuel tank filler cap to relieve fuel tank pressure.

3   Perform the fuel pressure relief procedure (see Section 2).

4   Disconnect the negative battery cable from the ground stud on the left shock tower (see Chapter 5, Section 1).

5   Working inside the trunk, fold back the trunk mat near the base of the left shock tower. Locate the fuel pump wiring harness 4-pin connector and disconnect it from the wiring harness **(see illustration 2.3)**. Follow the fuel pump wiring to the grommet at the base of the rear seat. Tie a length of string to the fuel pump wiring harness and secure the other end somewhere in the trunk (this will allow you to easily retrieve the wiring harness). Push the grommet through the floorpan and feed the wiring and 4 pin connector through the hole.

6   Raise the vehicle and support it securely on jackstands.

7   Position an approved gasoline container under the fuel tank drain plug. If necessary, use a funnel to prevent spilling fuel. **Warning:** *The fuel tank capacity is 16 gallons. Unless the fuel tank is almost empty, be prepared to collect a significant amount of fuel. Do not leave the fuel tank draining operation unattended. Be prepared to replace the drain plug in case the fuel tank capacity exceeds the container capacity.* Remove the drain plug **(see illustration 5.6)** and drain the fuel into the container.

8   After the fuel has finished draining, reinstall the drain plug and tighten it to the torque listed in this Chapter's Specifications.

9   Support the fuel tank with a floor jack. Place a piece of wood between the jack head and the fuel tank to protect the tank.

10   Remove the driver's side fuel tank strap (the long strap).

11   Loosen, but do not remove, the passenger side fuel tank strap so the fuel tank filler neck just touches the rear suspension crossmember. **Caution:** *Do not let the weight of the fuel tank rest on the filler neck! Support it with the jack at all times.*

12   Label and disconnect the quick-connect fuel line fittings (see Section 4 if necessary) connecting the fuel filter to the fuel system.

13   Detach the fuel filter from its mounting and remove it from the vehicle.

Installation

14   Installation is the reverse of removal.

15.1 The fuel filter (arrow) is tucked up behind the fuel tank and mounted to the frame above the rear suspension crossmember

15   Assemble the fuel line quick-connect fittings as described in Section 4. Verify the fittings are securely assembled by trying to pull them apart. **Note:** *The fuel filter larger line fitting attaches to the fuel pump module "supply" port and the smaller fitting attaches to the "return" port.*

16   Tighten the fuel tank strap bolts to the torque given in this Chapter's Specifications.

17   Pressurize the system and check for leaks.

16   Fuel rail and injectors - check, removal and installation

Warning: *Gasoline is extremely flammable, so take extra precautions when you work on any part of the fuel system (see the Warning in Section 2).*

Fuel injector operation check

Refer to illustrations 16.6 and 16.7

1   Start the engine and allow it warm up to normal operating temperature.

2   Remove the air cleaner assembly (see Section 9).

3   If the vehicle is not equipped with a tachometer, connect one to the engine in accordance with the tool manufacturer's instructions.

4   Make sure all test equipment is positioned away from the drivebelts and cooling fans, then start the engine. With the engine idling, detach each fuel injector electrical connector one-at-a-time, and note the rpm change on the tachometer, then reconnect the injector. **Note:** *On V6 engines, this test can only be applied to the left bank of fuel injectors and only after removing the air inlet resonator (see Section 9). If the rpm change is approximately the same for each cylinder, the injectors are operating correctly. If disconnecting a particular injector fails to*

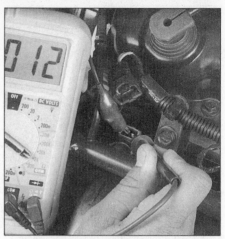

16.6 Measure the resistance of each injector. It should be approximately 12 ohms

change the engine rpm, proceed to the next Step. If the fuel injectors are operating properly, check the ignition system (see Chapter 5), condition of the spark plugs and wires (see Chapter 1) and, if necessary, perform a compression check (see Chapter 2C) to determine the cause of the dead cylinder.

5   On V6 engines, remove the upper intake manifold (see Chapter 2B).

6   Disconnect the injector electrical connectors and using an ohmmeter, measure the resistance of each injector **(see illustration)**. Compare the measured resistance to the value given this Chapter's Specifications. If the resistance is not within specifications, replace the injector.

7   If the resistance is as specified, connect a special injector harness test light (commonly known as a "noid light" which is available at most auto parts stores) to the injector electrical connector **(see illustration)**. If the light flashes, the injector is receiving voltage. If there is no voltage, check the ASD relay operation (see Section 3). If the ASD relay is OK, check the injector wiring circuit for a short, a break in the wire or a bad connection (see Chapter 12 if necessary).

8   With the electrical connector removed from the injector, use a fused jumper wire to connect one terminal of the injector to the positive remote terminal of the battery near the Power Distribution Center (PDC). Attach another jumper wire to the other terminal on the fuel injector. Make sure the jumper wires are properly insulated from each other! Using the grounded jumper wire, quickly connect and disconnect it to a solid ground on the engine. **Note:** *Do not subject the fuel injector to battery voltage any longer than necessary.* Each time the injector is energized and de-energized, the injector should make an audible "clicking" sound. If no sound is heard, replace the injector. Repeat the test for each injector.

9   If the fuel injectors are operating properly, install all removed components in the reverse order of removal.

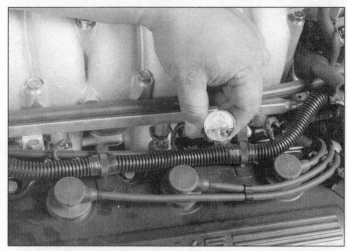

16.7 Install a "noid" light (available at most auto part stores) into each injector electrical connector and confirm that it illuminates when the engine is cranking or running

16.21a Disconnecting the fuel supply line quick-connect fitting at the fuel rail (four-cylinder engine shown)

Fuel injector leak check

Warning: *Wear eye protection during this check.*

Note: *After identifying that a fuel injector is leaking (see Section 3), use the following procedure to determine which one (or more) of the fuel injectors is defective.*

10 Perform the fuel pressure relief procedure (see Section 2).

11 Remove the fuel rail and injector assembly from the intake manifold as described below, however, do not disconnect the fuel supply line or the fuel injectors from the fuel rail.

12 With the fuel rail resting on the intake manifold (injectors nozzles exposed), place some clean shop rags under the fuel injectors to catch the fuel that will leak out of the defective injector(s).

13 Attach the fuel pump module electrical connector to the wiring harness and the battery negative cable to the remote battery terminal.

14 Turn the ignition key to the ON position (engine OFF) several times to pressurize the fuel system. **Warning:** *Do not crank the engine over.* With the system under pressure, inspect each injector for fuel leaking out of the nozzle. Label the faulty injector(s).

15 Next, relieve the fuel pressure via a faulty fuel injector by using a small Phillips head screwdriver (or equivalent) to push the injector pintle off its seat to release the fuel pressure through the injector nozzle. Wrap a dry shop rag around the faulty injector to catch the fuel as it escapes.

16 Once the fuel pressure has been relieved, detach the fuel supply line quick-connect fitting from the fuel rail (see Section 4 if necessary) and replace the faulty fuel injector(s) (see below).

Removal

Refer to illustrations 16.21a, 16.21b, 16.24a, 16.24b, 16.25a, 16.25b, 16.25c, 16.26a, 16.26b and 16.26c

17 Perform the fuel pressure relief procedure (see Section 2).

18 Disconnect the negative battery cable from the ground stud on the left shock tower (see Chapter 5, Section 1).

19 Remove the air cleaner assembly (see Section 9).

20 On V6 engines, remove the upper intake manifold (see Chapter 2B).

21 Detach the fuel supply line quick-connector fitting (see Section 4 if necessary) from the fuel rail **(see illustrations)**.

22 Disconnect the wiring harness electrical connectors from the fuel injectors. Clearly label and remove any vacuum hoses or electrical wiring that will interfere with the fuel rail removal.

23 Clean the injector-to-manifold area using compressed air (a can of compressed-gas duster like those used to blow out electrical components will work just as well) or spray-type carburetor cleaner to remove any dirt or debris from around the injectors.

24 Remove the fuel rail mounting bolts **(see illustrations)**.

25 Remove the fuel rail assembly (with the fuel injectors attached) from the engine **(see**

4

16.21b Disconnecting the fuel supply line quick-connect fitting at the fuel rail (V6 engine shown)

16.24a Fuel rail mounting bolts (arrows) (four-cylinder engines)

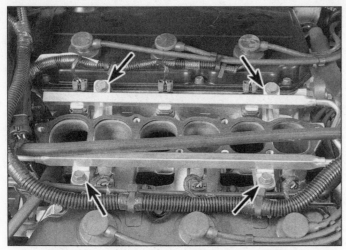

16.24b Fuel rail mounting bolts (arrows) (V6 engine)

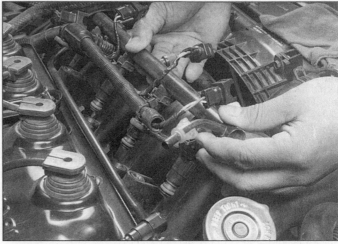

16.25a Removing the fuel rail/injectors (four-cylinder engines)

16.25b Removing the fuel rail/injectors (V6 engine)

16.25c On V6 engines, these plastic spacers must be installed between the fuel rail and the lower intake manifold

illustrations). **Note:** *On V6 engines, there are spacers located between the fuel rail and the lower intake manifold, if they become dislodged, make sure you reinstall them* **(see illustration).**

26   Remove the retaining clips and withdraw the injectors from the fuel rail **(see illustrations).** Remove the O-ring seals and discard them **(see illustration). Note:** *Whether you're replacing an injector or a bad O-ring*

seal, it's standard practice to replace all O-ring seals at this time.
27   On V6 engines, clean and inspect the upper-to-lower manifold gasket surfaces (see Chapter 2B).

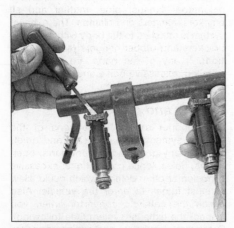

16.26a Using a screwdriver or pliers, remove the injector retaining clip securing the injector to the fuel rail . . .

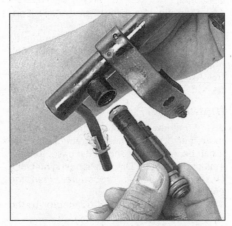

16.26b . . . then withdraw the injector from the fuel rail

16.26c Remove the old O-ring seals from the fuel injector and discard them

Installation

28   Apply a light coating of clean engine oil to the new O-ring seals and carefully install them onto the injectors.

29   Insert each injector into its corresponding bore in the fuel rail. Position the electrical terminals appropriately and secure the fuel injectors to the fuel rail with the retaining clips.

30   On V6 engines, make sure the fuel rail spacers are installed **(see illustration 16.25c)**.

31   Apply a light coating of clean engine oil to the injector-to-manifold O-ring seals and install the injector/fuel rail assembly onto the intake manifold. Make sure the injectors are fully seated, then tighten the fuel rail mounting bolts to the torque listed in this Chapter's Specifications.

32   Connect the fuel supply line quick-connect fitting to the fuel rail (see Section 4).

33   Attach the fuel pump module electrical connector to the wiring harness and the battery negative cable to the ground stud on the left shock tower.

34   Turn the ignition key to the ON position (engine OFF) several times to pressurize the fuel system. Inspect the fuel rail and injectors for leaks. If leakage is evident, perform the fuel pressure relief procedure (see Section 2) and rectify the problem. **Warning:** *On V6 engines, before performing the fuel relief procedure, disconnect the spark plug wires from the spark plugs and make sure all loose objects or rags have been removed from inside or around the lower intake manifold ports.*

35   The remaining installation steps are the reverse of removal. On V6 engines, make sure to install a new upper intake manifold gasket and tighten the upper intake manifold bolts to the torque listed in the Chapter 2B Specifications.

17   Idle Air Control (IAC) motor - check and replacement

General description

The engine idle speed is controlled by the PCM via the Idle Air Control motor. The IAC motor regulates the flow of air allowed to by-pass the throttle valve in the throttle body thereby increasing engine speed. The PCM uses information from various sensors to determine the correct amount of airflow required to maintain the proper engine speed during engine warm-up and when a load is placed on the engine, such as engaging the air conditioning compressor, low speed steering or when an automatic transaxle is placed in gear.

Check

1   Run the engine until it reaches normal operating temperature, then shut off the engine.

2   Locate a vacuum fitting on the intake manifold. Remove the hose from the fitting and attach a vacuum gauge in its place. Position the vacuum gauge so you can see it from inside the vehicle.

3   If the vehicle is not equipped with a tachometer, connect one to the engine per the manufacturer's instructions and place it so you can see the meter from inside the vehicle.

4   Inside the vehicle, start the engine and note the reading on the vacuum gauge and the engine speed on the tachometer.

5   If the vehicle is equipped with an automatic transaxle, apply the brakes and place the transaxle in DRIVE. If the vehicle is equipped with air conditioning, turn it on. If the vehicle does not have either of the previously mentioned options, turn the steering wheel all the way to the left and hold it in there. Observe the reading on the vacuum gauge. It should drop slightly as the IAC motor opens the throttle by-pass airway. The engine speed should drop momentarily and then rise to the previously noted rpm. If the vacuum reading remains the same and the engine speed drops, turn off the engine and proceed to the next step.

6   Remove the air cleaner assembly (see Section 9) and inspect the by-pass airway for obstructions or carbon build-up, clean if necessary.

7   If the by-pass airway appears to be clear, remove the IAC motor from the throttle body (see below).

8   Next, turn the ignition key to the ON position (engine OFF). **Note:** *Perform this check when the engine is completely COLD.*

9   While observing the IAC pintle, attach the electrical connector to the IAC motor. The IAC pintle should retract. If it doesn't, use a voltmeter or a test light to verify voltage is present at the RED wire terminal in the female connector. If voltage is present, replace the IAC motor. If no voltage is present, check for a blown fuse. If a fuse was blown, replace it and see if it blows again. If it does, check the circuit for a short (see Chapter 12).

Removal

10   Remove the air cleaner assembly (see Section 9).

11   Remove the throttle body (see Section 13).

12   Remove the IAC motor from the throttle body **(see illustrations 13.10a and 13.10b)**. Make sure the O-ring seal is removed with the IAC motor, if not, retrieve it from the throttle body orifice.

Installation

13   If the new IAC motor pintle is protruding more than 1 inch, it must be retracted before it can be installed. If this is the case, turn the ignition key to the ON position (engine OFF). **Note:** *Perform this procedure when the engine is completely COLD.*

14   Attach the electrical connector to the IAC motor, the pintle will retract.

15   With the pintle retracted and the O-ring seal in place, carefully install the IAC motor into the throttle body and secure it with the

18.1 Inspect the exhaust system mounting brackets, clamps and rubber hangers for damage or improper installation

mounting screws. Tighten the screws to the torque given in this Chapter's Specifications. **Note:** *The ignition key may be turned OFF after the IAC motor is installed on the throttle body.*

16   Install the throttle body (see Section 13). Tighten the throttle body bolts to the torque listed in this Chapter's Specifications.

17   Install the air cleaner assembly (see Section 9).

18   Exhaust system servicing - general information

Refer to illustration 18.1

Warning: *Inspection and repair of exhaust system components should be done only after enough time has elapsed after driving the vehicle to allow the system components to cool completely. Also, when working under the vehicle, make sure it is securely supported on jackstands.*

1   The exhaust system consists of the exhaust manifold, the catalytic converter, the resonator, exhaust pipe, muffler and all brackets, hangers and clamps. The exhaust system is attached to the body with mounting brackets and rubber hangers **(see illustration)**. If any of the parts are improperly installed, excessive noise and vibration will be transmitted to the body.

Muffler and pipes

2   Conduct regular inspections of the exhaust system to keep it safe and quiet. Look for any damaged or bent parts, open seams, holes, loose connections, excessive corrosion or other defects which could allow exhaust fumes to enter the vehicle. Also check the catalytic converter when you inspect the exhaust system (see following). Deteriorated exhaust system components should not be repaired; they should be replaced with new parts.

3   Before trying to disassemble any exhaust components, spray the fasteners with a penetrating oil to help ease removal. If the exhaust system components are extremely corroded or rusted together, welding equipment will probably be required to remove them. The convenient way to accomplish this is to have a muffler repair shop remove the corroded sections with a cutting torch. If, however, you want to save money by doing it yourself (and you don't have a welding outfit with a cutting torch), simply cut off the old components with a hacksaw. If you have compressed air, special pneumatic cutting chisels can also be used. If you decide to tackle the job at home, be sure to wear safety goggles to protect your eyes from metal chips and work gloves to protect your hands.

4   Here are some simple guidelines to follow when repairing the exhaust system:

a) *Work from the back to the front when removing exhaust system components.*

b) *Apply penetrating oil to the exhaust system component fasteners to make them easier to remove.*

c) *Use new gaskets, hangers and clamps when installing exhaust systems components.*

d) *Apply anti-seize compound to the threads of all exhaust system fasteners at reassembly.*

e) *Be sure to allow sufficient clearance between newly installed parts and all points on the underbody to avoid overheating the floor pan and possibly damaging the interior carpet and insulation. Pay particularly close attention to the catalytic converter and heat shield.*

Catalytic converter

Warning: *The converter gets extremely hot during operation, and can remain very hot for hours after the engine has been turned off. Make sure it has cooled down before you touch it.*

Note: *See Chapter 6 for more information on the catalytic converter.*

5   Periodically inspect the heat shield for cracks, dents and loose or missing fasteners.

6   Remove the heat shield and inspect the converter for cracks or other damage.

7   If the converter must be replaced, detach the exhaust system from the exhaust manifold. Loosen the rear band clamp at the resonator and separate the converter from the exhaust system.

8   Installation is the reverse of removal. Be sure to use new gaskets and tighten the fasteners securely.

Chapter 5
Engine electrical systems

Contents

Specifications

General

Battery voltage	12 volts (approximate)
Engine firing order	
Four-cylinder engines	1-3-4-2
V6 engine	1-2-3-4-5-6
Ignition timing	Not adjustable

Ignition system

Ignition coil resistance (approximate, at 70 to 80-degrees F)	
Four-cylinder engines	
Primary resistance	0.51 to 0.61 ohms
Secondary resistance	11,000 to 13,500 ohms
V6 engine	
Primary resistance	0.6 to 0.8 ohms
Secondary resistance	12,000 to 18,000 ohms
Spark plug wire resistance (approximate)	
Four-cylinder engines	
Wires 1 and 4	3,500 to 4,900 ohms
Wires 2 and 3	2,950 to 4,100 ohms
V6 engine	
Minimum	250 ohms per inch (3,000 ohms per foot)
Maximum	560 ohms per inch (6,700 ohms per foot)

Torque specifications

Distributor hold-down nuts	108 in-lbs
Starter motor mounting bolts	40 ft-lbs

5

1   General information, precautions and battery disconnection

General information

The engine electrical systems include all ignition, charging and starting components. Because of their engine-related functions, these components are discussed separately from body electrical devices such as the lights, the instruments, etc. (which are included in Chapter 12).

Precautions

Always observe the following precautions when working on the electrical system:

(a) *Be extremely careful when servicing engine electrical components. They are easily damaged if checked, connected or handled improperly.*

(b) *Never leave the ignition switched on for long periods of time when the engine is not running.*

(c) *Don't disconnect the battery cables while the engine is running.*

(d) *Maintain correct polarity when connecting battery cables from another vehicle during jump starting - see the "Booster battery (jump) starting" section at the front of this manual.*

(e) *Always disconnect the negative cable first, and reconnect it last, or the battery may be shorted by the tool being used to loosen the cable clamps.*

It's also a good idea to review the safety-related information regarding the engine electrical systems located in the *"Safety first!"* section at the front of this manual, before beginning any operation included in this Chapter.

Battery disconnection

Refer to illustrations 1.4a and 1.4b

The battery on these vehicles is located behind the left fender, in front of the left front wheel. Since the battery terminals cannot be easily accessed, the manufacturer has provided a remote ground terminal on the left shock tower and also a remote positive terminal for jump starting purposes. To disconnect the battery for service procedures requiring power to be cut from the vehicle, remove the nut and detach the negative cable from the ground stud on the strut tower, then press the hole in the side of the cable insulator over the stud **(see illustrations)**. This will isolate the cable end and prevent it from accidentally coming into contact with ground.

Several systems on the vehicle require battery power to be available at all times, either to ensure their continued operation (such as the clock) or to maintain control unit memories (such as that in the engine management system's Powertrain Control Module [PCM]) which would be wiped out if the battery were to be disconnected. Therefore, whenever the battery is to be disconnected,

1.4a To disconnect battery power from the vehicle, remove the nut from the ground stud on the left strut tower (arrow) . . .

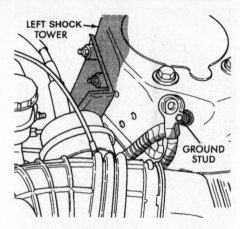

1.4b . . . then detach the cable and push the hole in the cable insulator over the stud

first note the following to ensure that there are no unforeseen consequences of this action:

(a) *First, on any vehicle with central locking, it is a wise precaution to remove the key from the ignition and to keep it with you, so that it does not get locked in if the central locking should engage accidentally when the battery is reconnected!*

(b) *The engine management system's PCM will lose the information stored in its memory when the battery is disconnected. This includes idling and operating values, and any fault codes detected (see Chapter 6). Whenever the battery is disconnected, the information relating to idle speed control and other operating values will have to be re-programmed into the unit's memory. The PCM does this by itself, but until then, there may be surging, hesitation, erratic idle and a generally inferior level of performance. To allow the PCM to relearn these values, start the engine and run it as close to idle speed as possible until it reaches its normal operating temperature, then run it for approximately two minutes at 1200 rpm. Next, drive the vehicle as far as necessary - approximately 5 miles of varied driving conditions is usually sufficient - to complete the relearning process.*

Devices known as "memory-savers" can be used to avoid some of the above problems. Precise details vary according to the device used. Typically, it is plugged into the cigarette lighter, and is connected by its own wires to a spare battery; the vehicle's own battery is then disconnected from the electrical system, leaving the "memory-saver" to pass sufficient current to maintain audio unit security codes and PCM memory values, and also to run permanently live circuits such as the clock, all the while isolating the battery in the event of a short-circuit occurring while

work is carried out.

Warning: *Some of these devices allow a considerable amount of current to pass, which can mean that many of the vehicle's systems are still operational when the main battery is disconnected. If a "memory-saver" is used, ensure that the circuit concerned is actually "dead" before carrying out any work on it!*

2   Battery - emergency jump starting

Refer to the *Booster battery (jump) starting* procedure at the front of this manual.

3   Battery cables - check and replacement

1   Periodically inspect the entire length of each battery cable for damage, cracked or burned insulation and corrosion. Poor battery cable connections can cause starting problems and decreased engine performance.

2   Check the cable-to-terminal connections at the ends of the cables for cracks, loose wire strands and corrosion. The presence of white, fluffy deposits under the insulation at the cable terminal connection at the battery is a sign that the cable is corroded and should be replaced. Check the terminals for distortion, missing mounting bolts and corrosion.

3   When removing the cables, always disconnect the negative cable first and hook it up last or the battery may be shorted by the tool used to loosen the cables. Even if only the positive cable is being replaced, be sure to disconnect the negative cable from the ground terminal on the left shock tower first!

4   Disconnect the old cables from the battery (see Section 4), then trace each of them to their remote terminals and detach them. Note the routing of each cable to ensure correct installation.

5   Check the cables that connect the

4.3 Removing the battery cover/splash shield from the left front wheel well

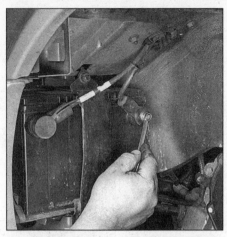

4.4 Always disconnect the negative battery cable first and attach it last!

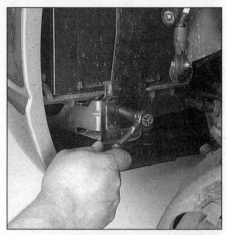

4.5a Removing the battery strap and hold-down bracket bolt

4.5b Removing the battery strap upper nut

4.7 Position the cables out of the way and slide the battery out of the fenderwell - be careful, it's heavy!

5

starter solenoid and ground terminals to the remote terminals. If they require replacement, note the routing of each cable to ensure correct installation and detach them.

6   If you are replacing a cable, take it along with you when purchasing a new one. It is vitally important that you replace it with an identical part. Cables have characteristics that make them easy to identify: positive cables are usually red and larger in cross-section; ground cables are usually black and smaller in cross-section.

7   Clean all connections with a wire brush to remove rust, oxidation and corrosion. Apply a light coat of petroleum jelly or grease to all fastener threads to prevent future corrosion.

8   Attach the cable to it's proper connection and tighten the mounting fastener securely. Apply a light coat of petroleum jelly or grease to the connection to seal it and help prevent future corrosion.

9   Before connecting a new cable to the battery, make sure that it reaches the battery without having to be stretched.

10   Connect the positive cable first, followed by the negative cable.

4   Battery - removal and installation

Refer to illustrations 4.3, 4.4, 4.5a, 4.5b and 4.7

Warning: *Certain precautions must be followed when checking and servicing the battery. Hydrogen gas, which is highly explosive, is produced by the battery. Keep lighted tobacco, open flames, bare light bulbs or other possible sources of ignition away from the battery. Furthermore, the electrolyte inside the battery is sulfuric acid which is highly corrosive and can burn your skin and cause severe injury to your eyes. Always wear eye protection! It will also destroy clothing and ruin painted surfaces.*

Note: *The battery on these vehicles is located inside the fenderwell of the left front fender and can be removed without removing the wheel. However, removing the wheel makes the job much easier.*

1   Disconnect the negative battery cable from the ground stud on the left shock tower (see Section 1).

2   Loosen the left front wheel lug nuts, raise the vehicle and support it securely on

jackstands. Remove the wheel.

3   Remove the battery cover/splash shield from the wheel well by turning the four plastic fasteners 1/4-turn counterclockwise **(see illustration)**.

4   Using a box-end wrench, disconnect the negative cable from the battery first, then the positive cable **(see illustration)**.

5   Remove the bolt and nut securing the battery strap and hold-down bracket, then remove the them **(see illustrations)**.

6   Vehicles manufactured with the cold weather package option (Alaska, Canada and northern USA) are equipped with a battery blanket heater. If equipped, disconnect the blanket heater electrical connector.

7   Remove the battery from the vehicle **(see illustration)**. Be careful - it's heavy.

Note: *Battery handling tools are available at most auto parts stores for a reasonable price. They make it easier to remove and carry the battery.*

8   If equipped, remove the battery blanket heater from around the battery.

9   While the battery is removed, inspect the tray, strap, hold-down bracket and related fasteners for corrosion or damage.

10   If corrosion is evident on the battery

6.4b Distributor terminal identification

1   *Camshaft position sensor terminals*
2   *Coil primary terminals*
3   *Coil secondary terminal (hi-tension tower)*

6.4a Distributor cap and rotor - V6 engine only

1   Coil terminal   3   Rotor
2   Rotor button

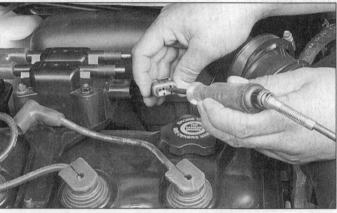

6.6 Using a calibrated ignition tester to visually verify spark is reaching the spark plugs - If the engine starts during this check, do not let it run more than 1 minute or damage to the catalytic converter may occur

6.9 On four-cylinder engines, connect a test light between the coil electrical connector center terminal and one of the outer terminals. Crank the engine. The test light should blink on-and-off

tray, unscrew the mounting bolts and remove it. Use baking soda/water solution to clean corroded parts to prevent further oxidation. Repaint parts as necessary using rust resistant paint.

11   Clean and service the battery and cables (see Chapter 1).

12   If you are replacing the battery, make sure you purchase one that is identical to yours, with the same dimensions, amperage rating, cold cranking amps rating, etc. Make sure it is fully charged prior to installation in the vehicle.

13   Installation is the reverse of removal. Make sure you install the negative cable last.

14   After connecting the cables to the battery, apply a light coating of petroleum jelly or grease to the connections to help prevent corrosion.

15   Tighten the wheel lug nuts to the torque given in the Chapter 1 Specifications.

5   Ignition system - general information

All models are equipped with an electronic ignition system. The ignition system consists of the ignition switch, the battery, the coil, the primary (low voltage) and secondary (high voltage) wiring circuits, the igni-

tion wires and spark plugs, the camshaft position sensor, the crankshaft position sensor and the Powertrain Control Module (PCM). The PCM controls the ignition timing and spark advance characteristics for the engine. The ignition timing is not adjustable.

The crankshaft sensor and camshaft sensor generate voltage pulses that are sent to the PCM. The PCM then determines the crankshaft position, injector sequence and ignition timing. The PCM supplies battery voltage to the ignition coil through the Automatic Shutdown Relay (ASD). The PCM also controls the ground circuit for the coil.

If the PCM does not receive a signal from the crankshaft or camshaft position sensors, the PCM signals the ASD relay and fuel pump relay to shut down the ignition and fuel delivery systems respectively. Refer to Chapter 6 for testing and replacement procedures for the crankshaft and camshaft sensors.

On four-cylinder engines, the secondary ignition system is controlled by energizing the coil drivers in the proper firing order. On V6 engines, a conventional type distributor with a rotor is used to send the ignition voltage to the proper cylinder in the firing order. On V6 engines, the ignition coil and camshaft position sensor are part of the distributor, which is located on the rear of the engine on the right side (rear) cylinder head and driven by the camshaft (see Section 8).

6   Ignition system - check

Refer to illustrations 6.4a, 6.4b, 6.6 and 6.9

Warning: *Because of the very high voltage generated by the ignition system (approximately 40,000 volts), extreme care should be taken whenever an operation is performed involving ignition components. This not only includes the coil and spark plug wires, but related items connected to the system as well, such as the electrical connectors, tachometer and any test equipment.*

1   With the ignition switch turned to the "ON" position, a glowing instrument panel "Battery" light or "Oil Pressure" light is a basic check for battery voltage supply to the ignition system and PCM.

2   First, check all ignition wiring connections for tightness, cuts, corrosion or any other signs of a bad connection.

3   Check the condition of the spark plug wires (see Chapter 1). Using an ohmmeter, measure the resistance of each spark plug wire and compare the measured value to the resistance value listed in this Chapter's Specifications. A bad spark plug wire or poor connection at the spark plug or coil (four-cylinder engines) or distributor cap (V6 engine) could also result in a misfire.

4   On V6 engines, remove the distributor cap and rotor (see Steps 7 thru 10 in Sec-

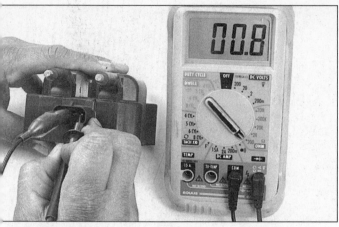

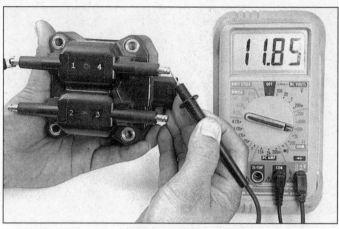

7.4 Test each coil's primary resistance by connecting one probe of the ohmmeter to the center terminal and the other probe to each end terminal. The primary resistance of each coil should be within specifications

7.5 Checking the secondary resistance of coil "1" - repeat the test for coil "2". The secondary resistance of each coil should be within specifications

tion 7). Inspect the cap and rotor for moisture, cracks, erosion, carbon tracks, worn rotor button or other damage **(see illustration)**. Remove one spark plug wire at a time from the cap (so they don't get mixed up) and check the terminals inside the cap for corrosion, which will appear as a white crusty powder (slight corrosion can be removed with a screwdriver or round wire brush). On the distributor cap, use an ohmmeter to measure the resistance between the rotor button and the coil terminal. The resistance should be approximately 5,000 ohms. On the distributor, inspect the coil hi-tension tower for cracks, carbon tracks or corrosion **(see illustration)**. If the coil is found to be defective, the entire distributor must be replaced. If the cap or rotor is defective and the ignition components (including spark plugs) have been in service for more than 60,000 miles, the manufacturer recommends replacing all ignition components at the same time.

5   If the engine turns over but won't start, disconnect the number 1 spark plug wire (four-cylinder engines) or the number 2 spark plug wire (V6 engines) (see Chapter 1 if necessary) and install a calibrated ignition tester (available at most auto parts stores). Make sure the tester is designed for Chrysler electronic ignition systems if a universal tester is not available.

6   Connect the clip of the tester to a bolt or metal bracket located on the engine **(see illustration)**. Note: *If an ignition tester is not available, a good spark plug with the gap set to the maximum tolerance can also be used. Ground the threaded portion of the spark plug to the engine. Crank the engine while observing the ignition tester - if bright blue, well defined sparks occur, sufficient voltage is reaching the spark plug to fire it.* **Caution:** *If the engine starts, do not run the engine for longer than one minute during this test - the raw fuel escaping from the cylinder being tested may cause damage to the catalytic converter.*

7   On four-cylinder engines, perform this check at the number 2 spark plug location also. This will check the other ignition coil

inside the coil pack. **Note:** *It is not necessary to perform this check at another location on V6 engines because that system uses a single coil.*

8   If spark is present, the coil is firing, however, the spark plugs themselves may be fouled or damaged, so remove and check them (see Chapter 1) or install new ones.

9   If no spark or intermittent sparks occur, disconnect the coil electrical connector **(see illustration)** and connect a test light to the center terminal of the coil electrical connector and one of the outer terminals on four-cylinder engines or across both harness terminals on V6 engines **(see illustration 6.4b).**

10   With the test light placed where you can see it from the driver's seat, crank the engine and watch the test light. It should flash on-and-off while the engine is cranking. If the test light does not blink, check the wiring harness for damage or a short. If the wiring is OK, check the operation of the Automatic Shutdown (ASD) relay (see Chapter 4). If necessary, check the operation of the camshaft and crankshaft position sensors (see Chapter 6). If the ASD relay and cam/crank sensors check out OK, have the PCM diagnosed by a dealer service department or other qualified repair shop.

11   If voltage is present (light blinks), check the ignition coil (see Section 7) and replace it if necessary.

12   If these checks do not identify the problem, further diagnosis should be performed by a dealer service department or other qualified repair shop.

7   Ignition coil - check and replacement

Check

Four-cylinder engines

Refer to illustrations 7.4 and 7.5

1   Located inside the coil pack are two individual ignition coils. Coil "1" supplies volt-

age for cylinders 1 and 4, while coil "2" supplies voltage for cylinders 2 and 3.

2   Clearly label the spark plug wires and detach them from the coil pack.

3   Disconnect the primary wiring electrical connector from the coil pack.

4   Measure the each coil primary resistance; connect an ohmmeter between the center terminal (B+) and one of the outer terminals and note the resistance **(see illustration)**. Repeat the check with the probe connected to the other outer terminal. Compare the measured resistances with the coil primary resistance value listed in this Chapter's Specifications. Replace the coil if the primary resistance is out of tolerance.

5   Next, measure the secondary resistance of each coil; connect an ohmmeter between spark plug wire terminals 1 and 4 and note the resistance **(see illustration)**. Repeat the check on terminals 2 and 3. Compare the measured resistances with the secondary resistance value listed in this Chapter's Specifications. Replace the coil if the secondary resistance is out of tolerance.

6   Install the spark plug wires in their proper locations and connect the primary wiring electrical connector.

V6 engine

7   Remove the air cleaner assembly (see Chapter 4).

8   Remove the EGR tube (see Chapter 6).

9   Label each spark plug wire to it's location in the distributor cap and then disconnect them.

10   Loosen the 2 screws and remove the distributor cap.

11   Disconnect the primary wiring electrical connector (two-pin) from the distributor **(see illustration 6.4b).**

12   Measure the coil primary resistance; connect an ohmmeter across the terminals of the two-pin connector on the distributor and note the resistance. Compare the measured resistance with the coil primary resistance value listed in this Chapter's Specifications. If the coil primary resistance is out of tolerance,

5

7.17 After disconnecting the wiring harness electrical connector, remove the coil pack mounting nuts and lift the coil from the valve cover

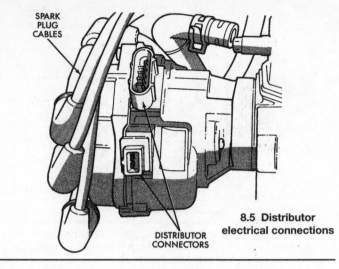

8.5 Distributor electrical connections

the entire distributor must be replaced - the coil is not serviceable.

13   Measure the coil secondary resistance; using an ohmmeter, measure the resistance between the coil hi-tension tower terminal and each terminal of the two-pin connector. Compare the measured resistances with the secondary resistance value listed in this Chapter's Specifications. If the coil secondary resistance is out of tolerance, the entire distributor must be replaced - the coil is not serviceable.

14   Install the distributor cap and related components in the reverse order of removal.

Replacement

Four-cylinder engines

Refer to illustration 7.17

15   Label the spark plug wires and detach them from the coil pack.

16   Disconnect the primary wiring electrical connector from the coil pack.

17   Remove the coil pack mounting nuts **(see illustration)** and lift the coil pack from the mounting bracket on the valve cover.

18   Installation is the reverse of removal.

V6 engine

19   The ignition coil on V6 engines is not serviceable. If the coil is defective, replace the distributor assembly (see Section 8).

8   Distributor (V6 engine only) - removal and installation

Removal

Refer to illustrations 8.5 and 8.8

1   Disconnect the negative battery cable from the ground stud on the left shock tower.

2   Remove the air cleaner assembly (see Chapter 4).

3   Remove the EGR tube (see Chapter 6).

4   Clean the area around and then remove the transaxle fluid dipstick tube. To prevent foreign debris from entering the transaxle, cover the dipstick hole in the transaxle with

duct tape or equivalent.

5   Disconnect the electrical connectors from the distributor **(see illustration)**.

6   Label each spark plug wire to it's location in the distributor cap and then disconnect them.

7   Remove the spark plug wire routing bracket from the distributor.

8   Loosen the two screws and remove the distributor cap **(see illustration)**.

9   Using a felt tip pen and/or a piece of tape, match-mark the rotor tip to the distributor body.

10   Remove the two nuts and washers securing the distributor and withdraw it from the cylinder head.

Installation

11   Inspect the distributor O-ring seal for hardness, cracks, swelling or other damage and replace it if necessary.

12   Install the rotor onto the distributor shaft.

13   Apply a light coat of clean engine oil to the distributor O-ring seal and carefully insert the distributor into the cylinder head with the rotor aligned with the previously applied match-mark. Make sure the distributor is fully seated in the cylinder head and secure with the two nuts and washers. Tighten the distributor hold-down nuts to the torque given in this Chapter's Specifications.

14   If engine was rotated while the distributor was removed, proceed as follows:

a) *Rotate the engine to Top Dead Center for number 1 piston (see Chapter 2C).*

b) *Using an ohmmeter, perform a continuity test on the distributor cap to identify the location of the number 1 terminal inside the cap and mark it's location on the outside of the cap.*

c) *Place the cap onto the distributor and place another mark on the distributor body in line with the number 1 terminal mark on the cap. Remove the cap.*

d) *Perform Steps 11 thru 13. After installation, use the distributor cap to make sure the rotor is pointed at the number 1 terminal.*

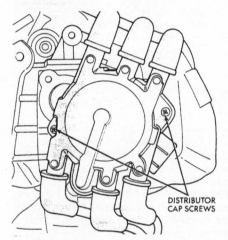

8.8 Distributor cap mounting screws

15   The remaining installation steps are the reverse of removal with the following additions:

a) *Check and replace if necessary, the transaxle dipstick tube O-ring seal. Apply a light coat of clean transaxle fluid to the seal before installation.*

b) *Use new gaskets on the EGR tube and tighten the bolts to the torque listed in the Specification Section of Chapter 6.*

9   Charging system - general information and precautions

The charging system includes the alternator, a charge indicator light, the battery, the Powertrain Control Module (PCM), the ASD relay, a fusible link and the wiring between all the components. The charging system supplies electrical power to maintain the battery at its full charge capacity. The alternator is driven by a drivebelt on the front of the engine.

The Electronic Voltage Regulator (EVR) within the PCM varies the battery charge rate

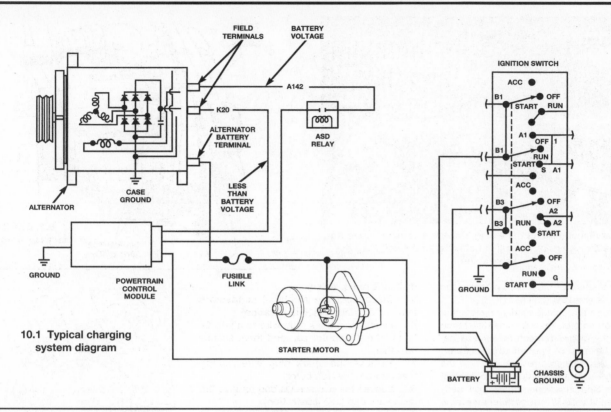

10.1 Typical charging system diagram

in accordance with driving conditions. Depending on electric load, vehicle speed, engine coolant temperature, battery temperature sensor, accessories (air conditioning system, radio, cruise control etc.) and the intake air temperature, the PCM will adjust the amount of voltage generated, creating less load on the engine.

The purpose of the voltage regulator is to limit the alternator's voltage to a preset value. This prevents power surges, circuit overloads, etc., during peak voltage output. Since the EVR is contained within the PCM, the PCM must be replaced in the event of EVR failure.

Four-cylinder models are equipped with a Nippondenso type alternator and V6 models use a Mitsubishi (MELCO) alternator. Both types have a rating of 90 amperes. The alternator is not serviceable and therefore must be replaced as a unit in the event of failure.

The charging system doesn't ordinarily require periodic maintenance. However, the drivebelt, battery, wires and connections should be inspected at the intervals outlined in Chapter 1.

The dashboard warning light should illuminate when the ignition key is turned to ON, but it should go off immediately after the engine is started. If it remains on, there is a malfunction in the charging system which must be diagnosed (see Section 10).

Be very careful when making electrical circuit connections to a vehicle equipped with an alternator and note the following:

a) *When reconnecting wires to the alternator from the battery, be sure to note the polarity.*

b) *Never start the engine with a battery charger connected.*

c) *Before using arc welding equipment to repair any part of the vehicle, disconnect the wiring from the alternator and the cables from the battery.*

d) *Always disconnect both battery cables before using a battery charger.*

e) *The alternator is turned by an engine drivebelt which could cause serious injury if your hands, hair or clothes become entangled in it with the engine running.*

f) *Because the alternator is connected directly to the battery, it could arc or cause a fire if overloaded or shorted out.*

g) *Wrap a plastic bag over the alternator and secure it with rubber bands before steam cleaning the engine.*

10 Charging system - check

Refer to illustrations 10.1 and 10.2

Note: *These vehicles are equipped with an On Board Diagnostic (OBD-II) system that is useful for detecting charging system problems. Refer to Chapter 6 for the trouble code extracting procedures.*

1   If a malfunction occurs in the charging circuit **(see illustration)**, do not immediately assume that the alternator is causing the problem. First check the following items:

a) *The battery cables where they connect to the battery and at the remote terminals. Make sure the connections are clean and tight (see Section 3).*

b) *Check the alternator wiring connections; make sure they are clean and tight.*

c) *Check the battery voltage. If its less than 12 volts, charge the battery (see Chapter 1).*

d) *Check the drivebelt condition and tension (see Chapter 1).*

e) *Check the alternator mounting bolts for tightness.*

f) *Run the engine and check the alternator for abnormal noise.*

2   Check the battery temperature sensor. Remove the front bumper (see Chapter 11). Locate the battery temperature sensor on the driver's side of the front bumper bar **(see illustration)**. Disconnect the electrical connector from the sensor. Using an ohmmeter, measure the resistance between the sensor electrical terminals. With the air temperature at approximately 75 to 80-degrees F, the

10.2 Battery temperature sensor (arrow) - front bumper removed

5

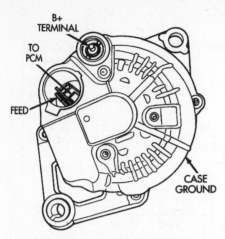

11.6 Alternator electrical connections - four-cylinder engines

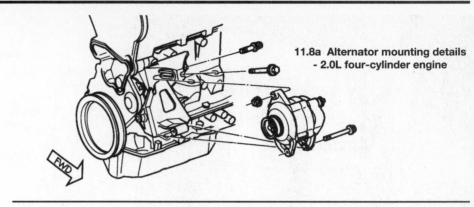

11.8a Alternator mounting details - 2.0L four-cylinder engine

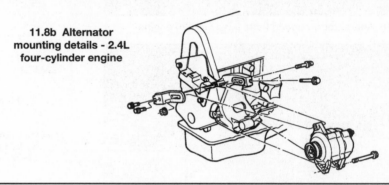

11.8b Alternator mounting details - 2.4L four-cylinder engine

resistance should be 9,000 to 11,000 ohms. If the resistance is out of tolerance, replace the sensor.

3   Using a voltmeter, check the battery voltage with the engine off. It should be approximately 12 volts.

4   Start the engine and check the battery voltage again. If the system is operating properly, the voltage should increase to a value between 13 to 15 volts.

5   If the indicated voltage reading is less or more than the specified charging voltage, have the PCM diagnosed at a dealer service department or other qualified repair shop. The voltage regulator on these models is contained within the PCM and it cannot be removed or serviced in any way.

6   Due to the special equipment necessary to test the PCM and alternator, it is recommended that if a fault is suspected, the vehicle be taken to a dealer service department or other qualified repair shop with the proper equipment. Because of this, the home mechanic should limit maintenance to checking connections and the inspection and replacement of the alternator itself. As a general rule, when the battery is in good condition and all electrical connections are clean and tight, if the charging voltage is low, the alternator is faulty. If the charging voltage is high, the voltage regulator is the problem.

11   Alternator - removal and installation

General information

1   If you are replacing the alternator, take the old one with you when purchasing a replacement unit. Make sure the new/rebuilt unit looks identical to the old alternator. Look at the terminals - they should be the same in number, size and location as the terminals on the old alternator. Finally, look at the identification numbers - they will be stamped into the housing or printed on a tag attached to the housing. Make sure the numbers are the

same on both the old and new alternators.

2   Many new/rebuilt alternators do not have a pulley installed, so you may have to switch the pulley from the old unit to the new/rebuilt one. When buying an alternator, find out the shop's policy regarding pulleys; some shops will perform this service free of charge.

Four-cylinder engines

Removal

Refer to illustrations 11.6, 11.8a and 11.8b

3   Disconnect the negative battery cable from the ground stud on the left shock tower (see Section 1).

4   On 1995 to 1997 models with 2.4L engines equipped with anti-lock brakes, disconnect the electrical connector and remove the two lower plate mounting bolts securing the Controller Anti-lock Brakes (CAB) and withdraw it from the vehicle (see Chapter 9).

5   On 2.4L engines, remove the engine coolant reservoir (see Chapter 3).

6   Disconnect the electrical connector and B+ cable from the alternator (**see illustration**).

7   Loosen the drivebelt adjustment bolts and nut, then detach the alternator drivebelt (see Chapter 1).

8   Remove the pivot bolt and spacer (**see illustrations**).

9   While supporting the alternator, remove the T-bolt, adjustment nut and bolt, then separate the alternator from the bracket. Maneuver it toward the passenger side of the vehicle and remove it from the engine compartment. **Note:** *On 2.4L engines equipped with air conditioning, slide the alternator under the air conditioning lines.*

Installation

10   Installation is the reverse of removal.

11   After the alternator is installed, adjust the drivebelt tension (see Chapter 1).

12   Check the charging voltage to verify proper operation of the alternator (see Section 10).

V6 engine

Removal

Refer to illustrations 11.14, 11.16 and 11.18

13   Disconnect the negative battery cable from the ground stud on the left shock tower (see Section 1).

14   Disconnect the electrical connector and B+ cable from the alternator (**see illustration**).

11.14 Alternator electrical connections (arrows) - V6 engine

11.16 Alternator mounting bolts (arrows) - V6 engine

11.18 Alternator upper bracket mounting bolts (arrows) - V6 engine

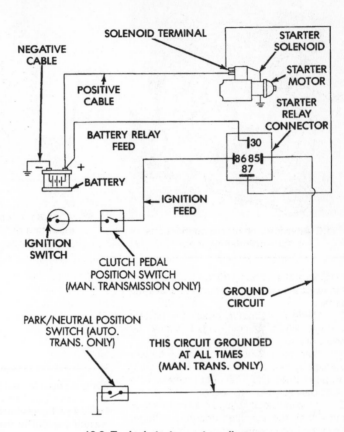

12.2 Typical starter system diagram

15 Remove the drivebelt from the alternator (see Chapter 1).
16 Loosen the upper and lower mounting bolts **(see illustration)**.
17 Remove the lower mounting bolt and spacer - be careful not to drop the spacer or nut.
18 While supporting the alternator, remove the two bolts securing the alternator upper bracket to the cylinder head **(see illustration)** and then remove the bracket and the alternator.
19 Remove the upper mounting bolt and separate the bracket from the alternator.

Installation

20 Installation is the reverse of removal.
21 After the alternator is installed, adjust the drivebelt tension (see Chapter 1).
22 Check the charging voltage to verify proper operation of the alternator (see Section 10).

12 Starting system - general information and precautions

Refer to illustration 12.2

1 The starter motor assemblies used on 2.0L four-cylinder and V6 engines use a planetary gear reduction system. The starter

motor assembly on 2.4L four-cylinder engines uses an offset gear reduction system. The starter motor/solenoid for all models is not serviceable and is sold strictly as a complete assembly.
2 The starting system consists of the battery, the starter motor, the starter solenoid, the starter relay, clutch start switch (manual transaxles), PARK/NEUTRAL switch (automatic transaxles), ignition switch and the wires that connect the components **(see illustration)**. The solenoid is located on the starter motor which is located on the side of the engine mounted to the transaxle bellhousing towards the front of the vehicle.
3 When the ignition key is turned to the Start position, the starter solenoid is actuated through the starter control circuit which includes a starter relay located in the Power Distribution Center. The starter solenoid then connects the battery to the starter. The battery supplies the electrical energy to the starter motor, which does the actual work of cranking the engine.
4 Always observe the following precautions when working on the starting system:
a) *Excessive cranking of the starter motor can overheat it and cause serious damage. Never operate the starter motor for more than 15 seconds at a time without pausing for at least two minutes to allow it to cool.*

b) *The starter is connected directly to the battery and could arc or cause a fire if mishandled, overloaded or shorted out.*
c) *Always detach the negative battery cable from the ground stud on the left shock tower before working on the starting system.*

13 Starter motor - in-vehicle check

Refer to illustration 13.7

1 Make sure the battery is fully charged and all cable/connections - at the battery, starter solenoid terminals and remote terminals - are clean and secure.
2 If the starter motor does not function at all when the switch is operated, make sure the shift lever is in Neutral or Park (automatic transaxles) and check the operation of the PARK/NEUTRAL switch (see Chapter 7B). On vehicles equipped with manual transaxles, check the operation of the clutch start switch (see Chapter 8).
3 If the starter motor spins but the engine is not cranking, the overrunning clutch in the starter motor is slipping and the starter motor must be replaced. Also, the ring gear on the driveplate may be worn. Inspect it after removing the starter.
4 If, when the switch is actuated, the starter motor does not operate at all but the

5

13.7 The starter relay (arrow) is located in the Power Distribution Center inside the engine compartment

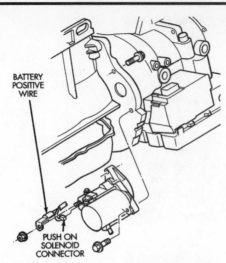

14.4 Starter motor electrical connections and mounting details - four-cylinder engine

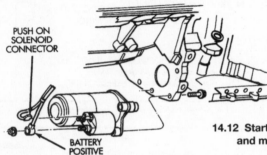

14.12 Starter motor electrical connections and mounting details - V6 engine

solenoid clicks, the problem lies with either the battery, the main solenoid contacts or the starter motor itself (or possibly the engine may be seized).

5   If the solenoid plunger cannot be heard when the switch is actuated, the battery may be faulty, the fusible link may be burned (the circuit is open), the starter relay may be faulty or the solenoid itself is defective.

6   To check the solenoid, connect a remote starter switch between the positive remote battery terminal and the ignition switch wire terminal (the small terminal) on the solenoid. If the starter motor operates when the remote switch is activated, the solenoid is OK and the problem is elsewhere in the circuit.

7   Locate the starter relay in the Power Distribution Center (PDC) **(see illustration)**. Remove the relay and perform the identical tests as for the Automatic Shutdown Relay (ASD) and the fuel pump relay in Chapter 4, Section 3. Replace the relay if it does not function as described.

8   If the starter motor still does not operate, remove the starter/solenoid assembly for replacement as a complete unit (see Section 14).

9   If the starter motor cranks the engine at an abnormally slow speed, first make sure that the battery is fully charged and that all electrical connections are clean and tight. If the engine is partially seized, or has the

wrong viscosity oil in it, it will crank slowly.

10   If the engine starts, run the engine until normal operating temperature is achieved, then turn off the engine. Remove the fuel pump relay to keep the engine from starting (see Chapter 4 if necessary).

11   Connect a voltmeter positive lead to the positive remote battery terminal and the negative lead to the negative remote battery terminal.

12   Crank the engine and take the voltmeter reading as soon as a steady figure is indicated. Do not allow the starter motor to turn for more than 15 seconds at a time. A reading of 9 volts or more, with the starter motor turning at normal cranking speed, is normal. If the reading is 9 volts or more but the cranking speed is slow, the motor, solenoid contacts or circuit connections are faulty. If the reading is less than 9 volts and the cranking speed is slow, the starter motor is probably bad.

14   Starter motor - removal and installation

Four-cylinder engines

Removal

Refer to illustration 14.4

1   Detach the negative battery cable from

the ground stud on the left shock tower (see Section 1).

2   Remove the air cleaner assembly (see Chapter 4).

3   On vehicles equipped with automatic transaxles, remove the Transmission Control Module (TCM) from its mounting and position it out of the way (see Chapter 7B). **Note:** *DO NOT disconnect the electrical connector from TCM.*

4   Remove the starter motor upper mounting bolt **(see illustration)**.

5   Raise the front of the vehicle and support it securely on jackstands.

6   Clearly label, then disconnect the wires from the terminals on the starter motor solenoid.

7   While supporting the starter motor, remove the lower mounting bolt and withdraw the starter motor from the vehicle.

Installation

8   Installation is the reverse of removal. Tighten the starter motor mounting bolts to the torque listed in this Chapter's Specifications.

V6 engine

Removal

Refer to illustrations 14.12 and 14.13

9   Detach the negative battery cable from the ground stud on the left shock tower (see Section 1).

10   Raise the front of the vehicle and support it securely on jackstands.

11   Remove the oil filter (see Chapter 1 if necessary).

12   Disconnect the wires from the terminals on the starter motor solenoid **(see illustration)**.

13   While supporting the starter motor, remove the three bolts securing it to the transaxle bellhousing **(see illustration)** and remove the starter motor from the vehicle.

Installation

14   Installation is the reverse of removal. Tighten the starter motor mounting bolts to the torque listed in this Chapter's Specifications.

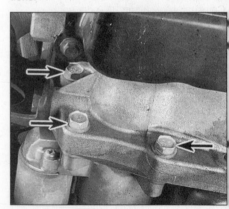

14.13 Starter motor mounting bolts (arrows) as viewed from under the vehicle - V6 engine

Chapter 6
Emissions and engine control systems

Contents

Specifications

Torque specifications

Ft-lbs (unless otherwise indicated)

Camshaft sensor (four-cylinder engines)	
Sensor bolts	105 in-lbs
Target magnet bolt	40 in-lbs
Crankshaft sensor retaining bolt	105 in-lbs
Engine Coolant Temperature sensor	
2.0L four-cylinder engine	60 in-lbs
2.4L four-cylinder and V6 engines	20
EGR tube bolts	95 in-lbs
EGR valve-to-cylinder head bolts	200 in-lbs
Intake Air Temperature sensor	
2.0L four-cylinder engine (1995 only)	60 in-lbs
2.4L four-cylinder and V6 engines	100 in-lbs
Intake Air Temperature/Manifold Absolute Pressure sensor (four-cylinder engines)	
Plastic intake manifold	20 in-lbs
Aluminum intake manifold	30 in-lbs
Knock sensor	90 in-lbs
Manifold Absolute Pressure sensor bolts (V6 engine)	30 in-lbs
Oxygen sensor	20

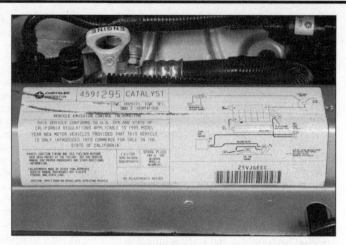

1.5 The Vehicle Emission Control Information (VECI) label is located in the engine compartment on the upper radiator support and contains information on engine type, tune-up specifications, type of emissions control devices used on your vehicle and a vacuum diagram

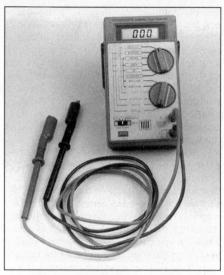

2.1 Digital multi-meters can be used for testing all types of circuits; because of their high impedance, they are much more accurate than analog type meters for measuring low voltage computer circuits

1   General information

Refer to illustration 1.5

1   To prevent pollution of the atmosphere from incompletely burned and evaporating fuel gases and to maintain good driveability and fuel economy, a number of emission control systems are incorporated. The major systems incorporated on the vehicles with which this manual is concerned include the:

Evaporative Emission Control (EVAP) system
Exhaust Gas Recirculation (EGR) system
Oxygen sensor (O2) system
Positive Crankcase Ventilation (PCV) system
Powertrain Control Module (PCM) (computer) and information sensors
Catalytic converter

2   The Sections in this Chapter include general descriptions, checking procedures within the scope of the home mechanic and component replacement procedures (when possible) for each of the systems listed above.

3   Before assuming an emissions control system is malfunctioning, check the fuel and ignition systems carefully. The diagnosis of some emission control devices requires specialized tools, equipment and training. If checking and servicing become too difficult or if a procedure is beyond your ability, consult a dealer service department or other qualified service facility. Remember, the most frequent cause of emissions problems is simply a loose or broken vacuum hose or wire, so always check the hose and electrical connections that interconnect the components within each system first.

4   This doesn't mean, however, that emission control systems are particularly difficult to maintain and repair. You can quickly and easily perform many checks and do most of the regular maintenance at home with common tune-up and hand tools. **Note:** *Because of a Federally mandated extended warranty which covers the emission control system components, check with your dealer about warranty coverage before working on any emissions-related systems. Once the war-*ranty *has expired, you may wish to perform some of the component checks and/or replacement procedures in this Chapter to save money.*

5   Pay close attention to any special precautions outlined in this Chapter. A Vehicle Emissions Control Information (VECI) label is located in the engine compartment **(see illustration)**. This label contains important emissions specifications and adjustment information. When servicing the engine or emissions systems, check the VECI label for information on your particular vehicle.

2   On Board Diagnosis (OBD-II) system - description and trouble code access

Diagnostic tool information

Refer to illustrations 2.1 and 2.2

1   A digital multi-meter is necessary for checking fuel injection and emission related components **(see illustration)**. A digital volt-ohmmeter is preferred over the older style analog multi-meter for several reasons. The analog multi-meter cannot display the volt, ohms or amps measurement in hundredths and thousandths increments. When working with electronic circuits which are often very low voltage, this accurate reading is most important. Another good reason for the digital multi-meter is the high impedance circuit. The digital multi-meter is equipped with a high resistance internal circuitry (10 million ohms). Because a voltmeter is hooked up in parallel with the circuit when testing, it is vital that none of the voltage being measured should be allowed to travel the parallel path set up by the meter itself. This dilemma does not show itself when measuring larger amounts of voltage (9 to 12 volt circuits) but if you are measuring a low voltage circuit such as the oxygen sensor signal voltage, a fraction of a volt may be a significant amount when diagnosing a problem.

2   Hand-held scanners are the most powerful and versatile tools for analyzing engine management systems used on later model vehicles **(see illustration)**. Each brand scan

2.2 Scanners like the Actron ScanTool and the AutoXray XP240 are powerful diagnostic aids - programmed with comprehensive diagnostic information, they can tell you just about anything you want to know about your electronic engine management system

tool must be examined carefully to match the year, make and model of the vehicle you are working on. Often interchangeable cartridges are available to access the particular manufacturer (Chrysler, Ford, GM, etc.). Some manufacturers will even specify by continent (Asia, Europe, USA, etc.).

OBD-II system general description

3   The OBD-II system consists of an on-board computer, known as the Powertrain Control Module (PCM) and information sensors which monitor various functions of the engine and then relay the data to the PCM. Based on the data received and the informa-

tion programmed into the computer's memory, the PCM then generates output signals to control various engine functions via control relays, solenoids and other output actuators.

4   The PCM, located in the engine compartment and mounted to a bracket between the air filter housing and the Power Distribution Center (PDC), is the "brain" of the OBD-II system. The PCM is specifically calibrated to optimize the emissions, fuel economy and driveability of the vehicle.

5   Because of a Federally mandated extended warranty which covers the OBD-II system components and because any owner-induced damage to the PCM, the sensors and/or the control devices may void the warranty, it is not recommended to attempt diagnosis of, or replace the PCM at home while the vehicle is under warranty. Take the vehicle to your local dealer service department if the PCM or a system component malfunctions.

Information sensors

6   The following is a list of the OBD-II system information sensors. For complete information and service procedures, refer to Section 3 (unless otherwise specified).

Brake switch
Camshaft Position sensor
Crankshaft Position sensor
Engine Coolant Temperature (ECT) sensor
Intake Air Temperature (IAT) sensor
Knock sensor
Leak Detection Pump (LDP) (see
   Section 7)
Manifold Absolute Pressure (MAP) sensor
Oxygen sensors
PARK/NEUTRAL switch (see Chapter 7B)
Power steering pressure switch
Throttle Position Sensor (TPS)
Vehicle Speed Sensor (VSS) (vehicles
   equipped with manual transaxle only)

Output actuators

7   The following is a list of the OBD-II system output actuators. For complete information and service procedures, refer to the Chapter or Section as specified.

Air conditioning clutch relay (see
   Section 3)
Automatic Shutdown relay (ASD) (see
   Chapter 4)
Canister purge control solenoid (see
   Section 7)
EGR solenoid (see Section 6)
Fuel injectors (see Chapter 4)
Fuel pump relay (see Chapter 4)
Idle Air Control (IAC) motor (see
   Chapter 4)

CHECK ENGINE light or Malfunction Indicator Light (MIL)

General description

8   The CHECK ENGINE light or Malfunction Indicator Light (MIL), is located in the instrument panel and should illuminate for

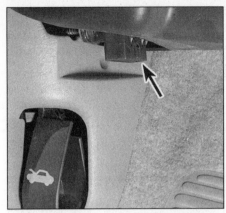

2.11 The OBD-II diagnostic connector (arrow) is located under the left (driver's) side of the instrument panel

three seconds as a bulb test each time the engine is started. When the Powertrain Control Module (PCM) detects a fault in the emissions or engine control system it sets a trouble code in the PCM's memory. If the PCM detects a fault related to vehicle emissions, it illuminates the CHECK ENGINE light which means an emissions component or system is in need of immediate service. In the event the PCM detects an active engine misfire, the CHECK ENGINE light will flash continuously. If this occurs, turn off the engine as soon as possible and diagnose/correct the problem or severe catalytic converter damage may occur.

9   The EVAP system (see Section 7), except on 1995 models, is pressurized by a Leak Detection Pump (LDP). If normal system pressure cannot be achieved by the LDP, which indicates a fuel vapor leak, the PCM will store the appropriate fault code and illuminate the CHECK ENGINE light on the instrument panel. The most common cause of CHECK ENGINE light illumination is EVAP system pressure loss due to a loose or poor sealing fuel filler cap. Before accessing the trouble codes and trying to determine the faulty component, make sure your gas cap seal is free from defects and is tightened securely. **Caution:** *Over-tightening the gas cap may cause the fuel tank filler neck to crack.*

10   In addition to notifying the driver when an emissions fault has occurred, the CHECK ENGINE light can be used to display the stored trouble codes from the PCM's memory (see below).

Trouble code access

Refer to illustration 2.11
Note: *All models covered by this manual are equipped with the OBD-II system. Generic trouble codes on 1997 and earlier models can be accessed using the ignition key method, but it is necessary to use a SCAN tool to read and interpret manufacturer-specific trouble codes (or any trouble codes on 1998 models). Before outputting the trouble codes, thoroughly inspect ALL electrical connectors and*

hoses. Make sure all electrical connections are tight, clean and free of corrosion; make sure all hoses are properly connected, fit tightly and are in good condition (no cracks or tears).

11   The self-diagnosis information contained in the PCM (computer) can be accessed either by the ignition key or by using a scan tool. This tool is attached to the diagnostic connector **(see illustration)** located under the left (driver's) side of the instrument panel in the passenger compartment and reads the codes and parameters on the digital display screen. The tool is expensive and most home mechanics prefer to use the alternate method. The drawback with the ignition key method is that it does not access all the available codes for display. Most problems can be solved or diagnosed quite easily and if the information cannot be obtained readily, have the vehicle's self-diagnosis system analyzed by a dealer service department or other qualified repair shop.

12   To obtain the codes using the ignition key method, first set the parking brake and put the shift lever in Park. Raise the engine speed to approximately 2,500 rpm and slowly let the speed down to idle. Also, if equipped, cycle the air conditioning system (on briefly, then off). Next, on models equipped with an automatic transaxle, apply the brakes and select each position on the transmission (Reverse, Drive, Low etc.), finally bring the shifter back to Park and turn off the engine. This will allow the computer to obtain any fault codes that might be linked to any of the sensors controlled by the transmission, engine speed or air conditioning system.

13   To display the codes on the instrument panel (CHECK ENGINE light or Malfunction Indicator Light), with the engine NOT running, turn the ignition key ON, OFF, ON, OFF and finally ON (must be done within 5 seconds). The codes will begin to flash. The light will blink the number of the first digit then pause and blink the number of the second digit. For example: Code 23, air temperature sensor circuit, would be indicated by two flashes, pause, three flashes.

14   Certain criteria must be met for a fault code to be entered into the PCM's memory. The criteria might be a specific range of engine rpm, engine temperature or input voltage to the PCM. It's possible that a fault code for a particular monitored circuit may not be entered into the memory despite a malfunction. This may happen because one of the fault code criteria has not been met. For example, the engine must be operating between 750 and 2,000 rpm in order to monitor the MAP sensor circuit correctly. If the engine speed is raised above 2,400 rpm, the MAP sensor output circuit shorts to ground and will not allow a fault code to be entered into the memory. Then again, the exact opposite could occur: A code is entered into the memory that suggests a malfunction within another component that is not monitored by the computer. For example, a fuel pressure problem cannot register a fault

6

directly but instead, it will cause a rich or lean fuel mixture problem. Consequently, this will cause an oxygen sensor malfunction resulting in a stored code in the computer for the oxygen sensor. Be aware of the interrelationship of the sensors and circuits and the overall relationship of the emissions control and fuel injection systems. A trouble code does not identify which component in a circuit is faulty, therefore the code should be treated as a symptom, not the direct cause of the problem.

15   The accompanying table is a list of the typical trouble codes which may be encountered while diagnosing the system. Also included are simplified troubleshooting procedures. If the problem persists after these checks have been made, more detailed service procedures will have to be performed by a dealer service department or other qualified repair shop.

Trouble codes - 1995 through 1997 models (using CHECK ENGINE light)

Note: *Not all trouble codes apply to all models.*

Code 11 .... Intermittent loss of crankshaft and/or camshaft position sensor signals to PCM.

Code 12 .... Problem with the battery connection. Direct battery input to PCM disconnected within the last 50 ignition key-on cycles.

Code 13** .... Problem with the MAP sensor circuit.

Code 14** .... MAP sensor voltage out of normal range.

Code 15** .... A problem with the Vehicle Speed Sensor signal. No Vehicle Speed Sensor signal detected during road load conditions.

Code 16 .... No input signal from knock sensor.

Code 17 .... Engine is cold too long. Engine coolant temperature remains below normal operating temperatures during initial operation (check the thermostat).

Code 21** .... Problem with oxygen sensor signal circuit. Sensor voltage to computer not fluctuating.

Code 22** .... Engine coolant temperature sensor voltage out of normal range.

Code 23** .... Intake air temperature sensor voltage out of normal range.

Code 24** .... Throttle position sensor voltage high or low. Test the throttle position sensor.

Code 25** .... Idle Air Control (IAC) valve circuits. A shorted condition is detected in one or more of the IAC valve circuits. Or a vacuum leak is detected.

Code 27 .... One of the injector control circuit output drivers does not respond properly to the control signal. Check the circuits.

Code 31** .... EVAP system fault.

Code 32** .... An open or shorted condition detected in the EGR solenoid circuit. Possible air/fuel ratio imbalance not detected during diagnosis.

Code 33 .... Air conditioning clutch relay circuit. An open or shorted condition detected in the compressor clutch relay circuit.

Code 34 .... Open or shorted condition detected in the speed control vacuum or vent solenoid circuits.

Code 35 .... Open or shorted condition detected in the radiator fan high or low speed relay circuits.

Code 37** .... Transaxle PARK/NEUTRAL switch failure.

Code 41*** .... Problem with the charging system. An open or shorted condition detected in the alternator field control circuit.

Code 42 .... Fuel pump relay or auto shutdown relay (ASD) control circuit indicates an open or shorted circuit condition.

Code 43** .... Multiple cylinder misfire detected. Peak primary circuit current not achieved with the maximum dwell time.

Code 44** .... Battery temperature sensor voltage circuit.

Code 45 .... Transaxle fault present in transmission control module - automatic transaxles.

Code 46*** .... Charging system voltage too high. Computer indicates that the battery voltage is not properly regulated.

Code 47*** .... Charging system voltage too low. Battery voltage sensor input below target charging voltage during engine operation and no significant change in voltage detected during active test of alternator output.

Code 51** .... Oxygen sensor signal input indicates lean fuel/air ratio condition during engine operation.

Code 52** .... Oxygen sensor signal input indicates rich fuel/air ratio condition during engine operation.

Code 53** .... Internal PCM failure detected.

Code 54** .... No camshaft position sensor signal from distributor. Problem with the distributor synchronization circuit.

Code 55 .... Completion of fault code display on CHECK ENGINE light. This is the end of stored codes.

Code 61 .... MAP sensor out of range.

Code 62 .... Unsuccessful attempt to update EMR mileage in the controller EEPROM.

Code 63** .... Controller failure. EEPROM write denied. Check the PCM.

Code 64** .... Catalytic converter efficiency below required level.

Code 65** .... Power steering switch failure or no release of brake switch detected.

Code 66 .... Transmission control module (TCM) or body control module (BCM) not sensed by PCM.

Code 71 .... PCM output voltage low.

Code 72** .... Catalytic converter efficiency below required level.

Code 77 .... Speed Control relay fault.

** These codes illuminate the CHECK ENGINE light on the instrument panel during engine operation once the trouble code has been recorded.

*** These codes illuminate the charging system light (battery) on the instrument panel during engine operation once the trouble code has been recorded.

Trouble codes - using scan tool

Note: *These are "generic" trouble codes and pertain to all models covered by this manual.*

Code	Probable cause
P0102	Mass Airflow (MAF) sensor circuit low input
P0103	Mass Airflow (MAF) sensor circuit high input
P0106	Barometric pressure out of range
P0107	Manifold Absolute Pressure (MAP) sensor voltage too low
P0108	Manifold Absolute Pressure (MAP) sensor voltage too high
P0112	Intake Air Temperature (IAT) sensor circuit low input
P0113	Intake Air Temperature (IAT) sensor circuit high input
P0117	Electronic Coolant Temperature (ECT) sensor circuit low input
P0118	Electronic Coolant Temperature (ECT) sensor circuit high input
P0121	In range Throttle Position Sensor (TPS) fault
P0122	Throttle Position Sensor (TPS) circuit low input
P0123	Throttle Position Sensor (TPS) circuit high input
P0131	Upstream heated O2 sensor circuit low voltage (Bank 1)
P0132	Upstream heated 02 sensor shorted to voltage
P0133	Upstream heated O2 sensor circuit slow response (Bank 1)
P0135	Upstream heated O2 sensor heater circuit fault (Bank 1)
P0136	Downstream heated O2 sensor fault (Bank 1)
P0138	Downstream heated 02 sensor shorted to voltage
P0140	Downstream heated 02 sensor - neither rich nor lean condition detected
P0141	Downstream heated O2 sensor heater circuit fault (Bank 1)
P0151	Upstream heated O2 sensor circuit low voltage (Bank 2)
P0153	Upstream heated O2 sensor circuit slow response (Bank 2)
P0155	Upstream heated O2 sensor heater circuit fault (Bank 2)
P0156	Downstream heated O2 sensor fault (Bank 2)
P0161	Downstream heated O2 sensor heater circuit fault (Bank 2)
P0171	System Adaptive fuel too lean (Bank 1)
P0172	System Adaptive fuel too rich (Bank 1)
P0174	System Adaptive fuel too lean (Bank 2)
P0172	System Adaptive fuel too rich (Bank 2)
P0191	Injector Pressure sensor system performance
P0192	Injector Pressure sensor circuit low input
P0193	Injector Pressure sensor circuit high input
P0201	Injector no. 1 output driver not responding properly
P0202	Injector no. 2 output driver not responding properly
P0203	Injector no. 3 output driver not responding properly
P0204	Injector no. 4 output driver not responding properly
P0205	Injector no. 5 output driver not responding properly
P0206	Injector no. 6 output driver not responding properly
P0300	Multiple cylinder misfiring detected
P0301	Cylinder no. 1 misfire detected
P0302	Cylinder no. 2 misfire detected
P0303	Cylinder no. 3 misfire detected
P0304	Cylinder no. 4 misfire detected
P0305	Cylinder no. 5 misfire detected
P0306	Cylinder no. 6 misfire detected
P0325	Knock sensor circuit fault
P0326	Knock sensor circuit performance
P0351	Ignition coil no. 1 primary circuit fault
P0352	Ignition coil no. 2 primary circuit fault
P0353	Ignition coil no. 3 primary circuit fault
P0354	Ignition coil no. 4 primary circuit fault
P0355	Ignition coil no. 5 primary circuit fault

Trouble codes - using scan tool (continued)

Note: *These are "generic" trouble codes and pertain to all models covered by this manual.*

Code	Probable cause
P0356	Ignition coil no. 6 primary circuit fault
P0400	EGR flow fault
P0401	EGR insufficient flow detected
P0402	EGR excessive flow detected
P0403	EGR transducer circuit open or shorted
P0420	Catalyst system efficiency below threshold (Bank 1)
P0421	Catalyst system efficiency below threshold (Bank 1)
P0430	Catalyst system efficiency below threshold (Bank 2)
P0431	Catalyst system efficiency below threshold (Bank 2)
P0442	EVAP small leak detected
P0443	EVAP VMV circuit fault
P0452	EVAP fuel tank pressure sensor low input
P0453	EVAP fuel tank pressure sensor high input
P0455	Leak in EVAP system detected
P0462	Fuel level sending unit - low voltage indicated
P0463	Fuel level sending unit - high voltage indicated
P0460	Fuel level sending unit - no movement detected
P0500	VSS fault
P0505	IAC valve system fault
P0600	PCM internal fault
P0601	PCM internal fault
P0603	PCM Keep Alive Memory test error
P0605	PCM Read Only Memory test error
P0622	Alternator field circuit open or shorted
P0645	A/C clutch relay circuit open or shorted
P0700	Automatic transmission fault detected
P0703	Brake switch stuck open or closed

3   Information sensors and output actuators - description, check and replacement

Note 1: *All models covered by this manual are equipped with the OBD-II system. The engine codes on 1997 and earlier models can be accessed using the ignition key, but it is necessary to use a special factory SCAN tool (DRB-II) to read and interpret all the various levels of diagnostic information (or any trouble codes on 1998 models). Have the vehicle diagnosed by a dealer service department or other qualified repair shop if the following component checking procedures fail to identify and correct a problem.*

Note 2: *After performing checking procedures on any of the OBD-II components, be sure to clear the PCM of all trouble codes by disconnecting the negative cable from the remote battery terminal for at least ten seconds.*

Air conditioning clutch relay

General description

1   If the vehicle is equipped with air conditioning, the PCM controls the application of the air conditioning compressor clutch. The PCM uses the air conditioning clutch relay to delay clutch engagement when the air conditioning is turned ON to allow the IAC motor to adjust the engine idle speed to compensate for the additional load. The PCM will also disengage the A/C compressor clutch if the refrigerant pressure is too high or too low, the engine coolant temperature is too hot, when the throttle is placed in the wide-open position or the PCM senses a part-throttle launch condition.

Check and replacement

Refer to illustration 3.3

2   First check for battery voltage to the air conditioning clutch with the engine running and the air conditioning turned ON. Detach the electrical connector from the air conditioning compressor and using a test light or a voltmeter check for battery voltage at the connector dark blue/black wire.

3   If voltage is not present at the connector, check for voltage to the air conditioning compressor clutch relay, which is located under the rectangular cover of the Power Distribution Center (PDC). Remove the relay from the PDC. With the engine running and the air conditioning ON, check for battery voltage to terminals 39 and 19 **(see illustration)**. If voltage is present, replace the relay. If voltage is not present at the connector, refer to Chapter 3 for more information on trou-

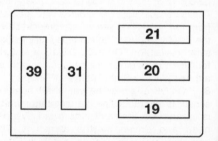

3.3 Terminal guide for the air conditioning compressor clutch relay socket

bleshooting the air conditioning system. In most cases, if the air conditioning system does not operate, a problem exists with the air conditioning pressure switches or controls and not the PCM.

4   To replace the air conditioning clutch relay, remove the cover from the PDC and pull the relay out of its socket. Installation is the reverse of removal.

Brake switch

General description

5   When the brakes are applied, the brake switch sends a signal to the PCM. After receiving this input, the PCM maintains idle speed to a scheduled rpm via the IAC motor.

3.7a Camshaft position sensor - 2.0L SOHC engines

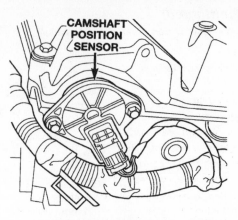

3.7b Camshaft position sensor - 2.0L DOHC and 2.4L engines

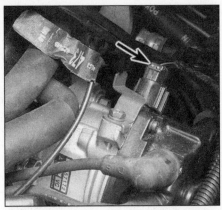

3.9 On V6 engines, the camshaft position sensor is located inside the distributor. The 6-pin electrical connector (arrow) contains the sensor wires - the 2-pin electrical connector is for the ignition coil circuit

Check and replacement

6   Refer to Chapter 9 for service procedures.

Camshaft position sensor

General description

Refer to illustrations 3.7a and 3.7b

7   On four-cylinder engines, the camshaft position sensor, located at the rear of the cylinder head **(see illustrations)**, provides cylinder identification to the PCM to synchronize the fuel system with the ignition system. The synchronizing signal is generated from a rotating target magnet attached to the rear of the camshaft. The target magnet has four different poles arranged in a symmetrical pattern. As the target magnet rotates, the sensor senses the changes in polarity and generates pulses from high (5 volts) to low (0.30 volts). These voltage pulses combined with the data from the crankshaft sensor are processed by the PCM which then determines fuel injection synchronization. On 2.0L DOHC and 2.4L four-cylinder engines, the sensor also acts as a thrust plate to control camshaft endplay.

8   On V6 engines the camshaft position sensor is located inside the distributor which is located on the right side (rear) cylinder head and driven by the camshaft. The camshaft position sensor is a Hall Effect device which detects a rotating ring (shutter) mounted to the distributor shaft. When the leading edge of the shutter enters the Hall Effect device, the interruption of the magnetic field causes a signal of approximately 5 volts to be sent to the PCM. As the trailing edge of the shutter leaves the device, the voltage signal is turned off. These voltage pulses combined with the data from the crankshaft sensor are processed by the PCM which then determines fuel injection synchronization.

Check

Refer to illustration 3.9

Note: *To backprobe an electrical connector, use pins or paper clips inserted into the rear of the connector (or wire) to facilitate meter attachment. Be careful not to short the probes during this process.*

9   With the ignition key in the ON position (engine OFF), check for supply voltage at the ORANGE/WHITE wire (1995 to 1997 vehicles) or the ORANGE wire (1998 vehicles) at the camshaft position sensor connector (four-cylinder engines) and the distributor connector (V6 engines) **(see illustration)**. The supply voltage should be approximately 8 volts. If no voltage is present, check the circuit for a broken wire or short (see Chapter 12). If the circuit checks out OK, have the PCM checked out by your local dealer service department or other qualified repair shop.

10   Next, disconnect the spark plug wires from the ignition coil (four-cylinder engines) or the distributor cap (V6 engine) (see Chapter 1 if necessary). With the connector attached to the sensor, use a voltmeter to backprobe the tan/yellow signal wire (positive) and the black/light blue ground wire and crank the engine. The voltmeter should fluctuate from approximately 0.3 to 5 volts for four-cylinder engines and 0 to 5 volts for V6 engines. If supply voltage is detected but there is no signal voltage, replace the camshaft sensor. After testing, replace the spark plug wires in their proper positions.

Replacement

Four-cylinder engines

11   Disconnect the negative battery cable from the ground stud on the left shock tower (see Chapter 5, Section 1).

12   Remove the air cleaner assembly (see Chapter 4).

13   On 2.0L SOHC engines, disconnect the electrical connectors from the engine coolant sensor and camshaft position sensor. Remove the brake booster hose and electrical connectors from the holders on the end of the valve cover.

14   Remove the bolts from the camshaft sensor and withdraw the sensor from the rear of the cylinder head.

15   If necessary, remove the target magnet mounting screw and remove the magnet.

16   Installation is the reverse of removal. If removed, align the locating pins on the back-side of the target magnet with the locating

holes in the rear of the camshaft. Tighten the fasteners to the torques listed in this Chapter's Specifications.

V6 engines

17   If the camshaft position sensor is determined to be defective, replace the distributor assembly (see Chapter 5).

Crankshaft position sensor

General description

Refer to illustrations 3.18a and 3.18b

18   The PCM uses the crankshaft position sensor to determine fuel injector sequence, ignition timing and engine rpm. The crankshaft position sensor is a Hall-Effect device which uses cut-outs in the crankshaft (four-cylinder engines) or slots is the drive-plate (V6 engine) to send voltage pulses to the PCM. The fuel injection and ignition systems will not operate if the PCM does not receive a signal from the crankshaft position sensor. On four-cylinder engines, the crankshaft position sensor is located on the side of the engine block between the main bearing cap/bedplate and engine block near the oil filter **(see illustration)**. On V6 engines,

3.18a Crankshaft position sensor - four-cylinder engines

6

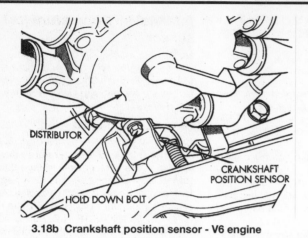

3.18b Crankshaft position sensor - V6 engine

3.33a On 2.0L four-cylinder engines, the Engine Coolant Temperature (ECT) sensor (arrow) is located at the rear of the cylinder head

the crankshaft position sensor is located on the transaxle bellhousing and below the distributor **(see illustration).**

Check

Note 1: *To perform this check on four-cylinder engines, it is necessary to raise the front of the vehicle and place it securely on jackstands. On V6 engines, it will be necessary to detach the speed control servo from the left shock tower, if equipped.*

Note 2: *To backprobe an electrical connector, use pins or paper clips inserted into the rear of the connector (or wire) to facilitate meter attachment. Be careful not to short the probes during this process.*

19 Check the supply voltage to the crankshaft sensor from the PCM. Locate the crankshaft sensor electrical connector. With the ignition key ON (engine OFF) backprobe the orange/white wire (positive) using a voltmeter. There should be approximately 8.0 volts present. If no voltage is present, check the circuit for a broken wire or short (see Chapter 12). If the circuit checks out OK, have the PCM checked out by your local dealer service department or other qualified repair shop.

20 Next, disconnect the spark plug wires from the ignition coil (four-cylinder engines) or the distributor cap (V6 engine) (see Chapter 1 if necessary). With the connector attached to the sensor, use a voltmeter to backprobe the gray/black signal wire (positive) and the black/light blue ground wire and crank the engine. The voltmeter should fluctuate from approximately 0.3 to 5 volts. If supply voltage is detected but there is no signal voltage, replace the crankshaft sensor. After testing, replace the spark plug wires in their proper positions.

Replacement

Four-cylinder engines

21 Raise the front of the vehicle and support it securely on jackstands.
22 Disconnect the crankshaft sensor wiring harness connector.
23 Remove the mounting bolt and withdraw the crankshaft sensor from the engine block.

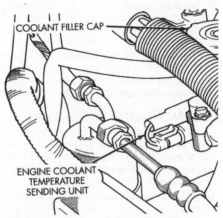

3.33b On 2.4L four-cylinder engines, the Engine Coolant Temperature (ECT) sensor is located at the front of the cylinder head

24 Installation is the reverse of removal. Tighten the bolt to the torque listed in this Chapter's Specifications and lower the vehicle.

V6 engine

25 If equipped, detach the speed control servo from the left shock tower and position it out of the way.
26 Detach the crankshaft sensor wiring harness connector from the heater tube bracket and disconnect the electrical connector.
27 Remove the mounting bolt and withdraw the crankshaft sensor from the transaxle bellhousing.
28 If the old sensor is to be re-installed, remove the paper spacer from the sensor face and install a new spacer. If installing a new sensor, verify the paper spacer is installed on the face.
29 Place the sensor in the bellhousing and install the mounting bolt loosely.
30 If the crankshaft sensor mounting hole is elongated, push the sensor down into the bellhousing until contact is made with the driveplate. Tighten the mounting bolt to the torque listed in this Chapter's Specifications (the paper spacer locates the sensor in the

proper position and will rub off during operation).
31 If the sensor does not have an elongated hole, simply install the sensor and tighten the mounting bolt to the torque listed in this Chapter's Specifications.
32 The remaining installation steps are the reverse of removal.

Engine Coolant Temperature (ECT) sensor

General description

Refer to illustrations 3.33a, 3.33b and 3.33c

33 The ECT sensor is a thermistor (a resistor which varies the value of its resistance in accordance with temperature changes) **(see illustrations).** The change in the resistance values will directly affect the voltage signal from the coolant thermosensor. As the sensor temperature DECREASES, the resistance values will INCREASE. As the sensor temperature INCREASES, the resistance values will DECREASE.

Check

Note: *On V6 engines it will be necessary to remove the air cleaner assembly (see Chapter 4) before performing this test.*

3.37 If you're re-installing the old ECT sensor, wrap the threads with Teflon tape to prevent leakage

34   To check the ECT sensor, release the locking tab and disconnect the electrical connector. Using an ohmmeter across the sensor terminals, measure the resistance of the ECT sensor with the engine cold (approximately 70-degrees F). The ECT resistance value should be between 7,000 and 13,000 ohms. Next, start the engine and allow it to reach operating temperature (approximately 200-degrees F), then turn off the engine. Measure the ECT resistance again, the resistance should be between 700 and 1,000 ohms. **Note:** *Since the coolant sensor is difficult to access on some vehicles, it may be easier to* remove the sensor and perform the tests in a pan of heated water where the water temperature can be controlled.

Replacement

Refer to illustration 3.37
Warning: *Wait until the engine is completely cool before beginning this procedure.*
35   Drain the cooling system until the coolant level is below the sensor (see Chapter 1).
36   Release the locking tab and disconnect the electrical connector, then carefully unscrew the sensor. **Caution:** *Handle the coolant sensor with care. Damage to this sensor will affect the operation of the entire fuel injection system.*
37   If you are re-installing the old sensor, clean the threads and then wrap them with Teflon tape to prevent leakage and thread corrosion **(see illustration)**. **Note:** *New ECT sensors have sealant already applied to the threads.*
38   Installation is the reverse of removal. Tighten the ECT sensor to the torque listed in this Chapter's Specifications. Refill the cooling system after installation (see Chapter 1).

Idle Air Control (IAC) motor

39   This output actuator controls the engine idle speed. For service procedures on the IAC motor, refer to Chapter 4. A failure in the IAC motor circuit will set a code 25 in the PCM memory.

Intake Air Temperature (IAT) sensor

Note: *1995 models with 2.0L SOHC engines came equipped with an IAT sensor and a MAP sensor. On 1996 and later models, the IAT sensor is combined with the MAP sensor into a single unit.*

General information

Refer to illustrations 3.40a, 3.40b and 3.40c
40   The Intake Air Temperature sensor is located in the intake manifold **(see illustrations)**. This sensor operates as a negative temperature coefficient (NTC) device. As the sensor temperature DECREASES, the resistance values will INCREASE. As the sensor temperature INCREASES, the resistance values will DECREASE. Most cases, the appropriate solution to the problem will be either repair of a wire or replacement of the sensor.

Check

Refer to illustration 3.41
Note: *On 2.4L four-cylinder engines, the air cleaner assembly must be removed (see Chapter 4) before this check can be performed. Since the IAT sensor is difficult to access on 2.4L models, it may be easier to remove the sensor and perform the check on a workbench and heat the sensor using a heat gun or hair dryer.*
41   To check the sensor, release the locking tab and disconnect the electrical connector

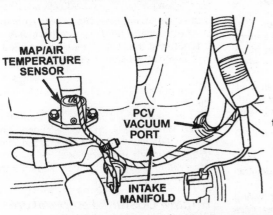

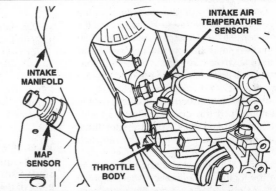

3.40a On 1996 and later 2.0L SOHC engines, the IAT and MAP sensors are combined into one unit

3.40b On 2.4L and 2.0L DOHC engines, the IAT sensor is located on the intake manifold on the cylinder head side

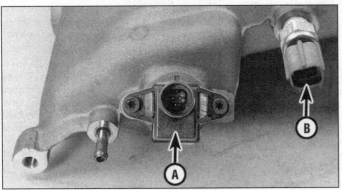

3.40c On V6 engines, the MAP (A) and IAT (B) sensors are located on the right (passenger) side of the upper intake manifold - manifold removed for clarity

3.41 Disconnecting the electrical connector from the IAT sensor - V6 engine shown

6

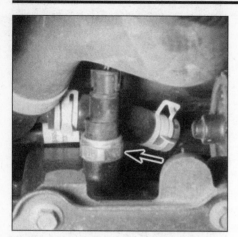

3.47 Knock sensor (four-cylinder engines) as viewed from under the vehicle

3.57 Typical MAP sensor electrical connector - inset shows 1996 and later 2.0L engine MAP/IAT sensor connector

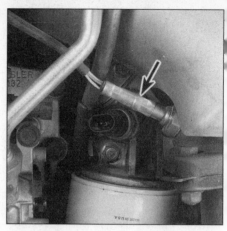

3.62a Upstream oxygen sensor (arrow) - V6 engine (front exhaust manifold) shown

(see illustration). Using an ohmmeter across the sensor terminals, measure the resistance of the sensor at ambient temperature (approximately 70-degrees F). The resistance should be between 7,000 and 13,000 ohms. Next, start the engine and allow it to reach operating temperature (approximately 200-degrees F). Measure the resistance again - it should be between 700 and 1,000 ohms.

Replacement

42   On 1996 and later models with 2.0L four-cylinder engines, refer to the MAP sensor removal procedure in this Section.

43   On 2.4L four-cylinder engines, remove the air cleaner assembly (see Chapter 4). To gain access to the IAT sensor, reach between the intake manifold and the cylinder head inserting your hand at the throttle body end. Perform this operation when the engine temperature is cold to avoid burning yourself.

44   Release the locking tab and disconnect the electrical connector from the sensor.

45   Unscrew and remove the sensor from the intake manifold.

46   Installation is the reverse of removal. Tighten the IAT sensor to the torque given in this Chapter's Specifications.

Knock sensor - four-cylinder engines

General information

Refer to illustration 3.47

47   Four-cylinder engines are equipped with a knock sensor mounted on the side of the engine block near the starter motor **(see illustration)**. The knock sensor is a piezo-electric crystal that oscillates with engine vibration. When knock is detected, the PCM retards the ignition timing until the knocking stops.

Check

Note 1: *1995 to 1997 models operate on direct current (dc), 1998 models use alternating current (ac).*

Note 2: *To backprobe an electrical connector, use pins or paper clips inserted into the*

rear of the connector (or wire) to facilitate meter attachment. Be careful not to short the probes during this process.

48   Raise the front of the vehicle and support it securely on jackstands.

49   Disconnect the sensor electrical connector.

50   Using a voltmeter (switched to the proper setting - see Note above), connect the negative probe to ground, and the positive probe to the knock sensor electrical connector black/light green wire. Turn the ignition switch ON (engine off). The voltmeter should indicate approximately 4 volts (dc) for 1995 to 1997 models and 600 mV (ac) for 1998 models. Turn OFF the ignition. If no voltage is indicated, check for a blown fuse and examine the wires for obvious damage. If the circuit looks OK, have the PCM checked out at your local dealer service department or other qualified repair shop.

51   Install the sensor electrical connector onto the sensor. Using a voltmeter, backprobe the knock sensor electrical terminals (positive probe to black/light green wire). Turn the ignition key ON (engine off).

52   While watching the voltmeter, lightly tap the metal part of the sensor body with a wrench. The voltmeter should start to jump as the sensor is triggered. Turn OFF the ignition. If the voltage doesn't fluctuate, replace the sensor.

Replacement

53   Raise the front of the vehicle and support it securely on jackstands.

54   Disconnect the electrical connector and unscrew the knock sensor from the engine block.

55   Installation is the reverse of removal. Tighten the knock sensor to the torque listed in this Chapter's Specifications.

Manifold Absolute Pressure (MAP) sensor

Note: *1995 models with 2.0L SOHC engines came equipped with an IAT sensor and a MAP sensor. On 1996 and later models, the*

IAT sensor is combined with the MAP sensor into a single unit.

General description

56   The MAP sensor monitors the intake manifold pressure changes resulting from changes in engine load and speed and converts the information into a voltage output. The PCM uses the MAP sensor to control fuel delivery and ignition timing. The PCM will receive the information as a voltage signal that will vary from approximately 1.5 to 2.1 volts at closed throttle (high vacuum) and 4.0 to 4.5 volts at wide open throttle (low vacuum). The MAP sensor is located on the intake manifold **(see illustrations 3.40a, 3.40b, and 3.40c)**.

Check

Refer to illustration 3.57

Note: *To backprobe an electrical connector, use pins or paper clips inserted into the rear of the connector (or wire) to facilitate meter attachment. Be careful not to let the probes touch each other during this process.*

57   First, check the MAP sensor supply voltage; disconnect the electrical connector and turn the ignition key ON (engine OFF). Using a voltmeter, check for voltage between the violet/white wire (positive) and the black/light blue wire (sensor ground) at the sensor connector **(see illustration)**. There should be approximately 4 to 5 volts present. If no voltage is indicated, check for a blown fuse and examine the wires for obvious damage. If the circuit looks OK, have the PCM checked out at your local dealer service department or other qualified repair shop.

58   Next check the MAP sensor output voltage; reconnect the electrical connector to the sensor and turn the ignition key ON (engine OFF). Using a voltmeter, backprobe the black/light blue wire (sensor ground) and the dark green/red wire (MAP signal output - positive) at the sensor connector. There should be approximately 4 to 5 volts present. If supply voltage is detected but there is no signal voltage, replace the MAP sensor. Start

3.62b Downstream oxygen sensor (arrow)

the engine, the voltage should drop to approximately 1.5 to 2.1 volts with the engine idling. If the MAP sensor voltage readings are incorrect, replace the MAP sensor.

Replacement

59   Disconnect the electrical connector from the MAP sensor.
60   Remove the MAP sensor mounting bolts and detach the sensor from the intake manifold.
61   Installation is the reverse of removal. Tighten the sensor bolts to the torque given in this Chapter's Specifications.

Oxygen sensor

General description

Refer to illustrations 3.62a and 3.62b

62   Four-cylinder engines are equipped with two oxygen sensors, an upstream oxygen sensor, which is located in the exhaust manifold and a downstream oxygen sensor, which is located at the outlet pipe of the catalytic converter **(see illustrations)**. On V6 engines, there are three oxygen sensors, two upstream sensors - one located in each exhaust manifold (front and rear) and one located at the outlet pipe of the catalytic converter. The upstream oxygen sensor(s) act as a rich/lean switch indicating the air/fuel mixture to the PCM which then adjusts the injector pulse width to obtain the ideal mixture ratio of 14.7 parts of air to 1 part fuel. The downstream oxygen sensor provides the PCM with the same information as the upstream sensor, but by comparing the data from both sensors, the PCM can monitor catalytic converter efficiency. The oxygen content in the exhaust reacts with the oxygen sensor to produce a voltage output which varies from 0.1 volt (high oxygen, lean mixture) to 1.0 volts (low oxygen, rich mixture). The sensors are equipped with a heating element that keeps the them at proper operating temperature during all operating modes.
63   The oxygen sensor produces no voltage when it is below its normal operating temperature of about 600 degrees F. During this initial period before warm-up, the PCM oper-

ates in the OPEN LOOP mode.
64   When there is a problem with the oxygen sensor or its circuit, the PCM operates in the open loop mode - that is, it controls fuel delivery in accordance with a programmed default value instead of feedback information from the oxygen sensors.
65   The proper operation of the oxygen sensors depends on four conditions:

a)   *Electrical - The low voltages generated by the sensors depend upon good, clean connections which should be checked whenever a malfunction of the sensor(s) is suspected or indicated.*

b)   *Outside air supply - The sensors are designed to allow air circulation to the internal portion of the sensor. Whenever the sensor is removed and installed or replaced, make sure the air passages are not restricted.*

c)   *Proper operating temperature - The PCM will not react to the sensor signal until the sensor reaches approximately 600-degrees F. This factor must be taken into consideration when evaluating the performance of the sensor.*

d)   *Unleaded fuel - The use of unleaded fuel is essential for proper operation of the sensors. Make sure the fuel you are using is of this type.*

66   In addition to observing the above conditions, special care must be taken whenever the sensor(s) is serviced.

a)   *The oxygen sensors have a permanently attached pigtail and electrical connector which should not be removed from the sensor. Damage or removal of the pigtail or electrical connector can adversely affect operation of the sensor(s) and engine.*

b)   *Grease, dirt and other contaminants should be kept away from the electrical connector and the louvered end of the sensor(s).*

c)   *Do not use cleaning solvents of any kind on the oxygen sensors.*

d)   *Do not drop or roughly handle the sensors.*

Check

67   Raise the vehicle and support it securely on jackstands.
68   Locate the oxygen sensor electrical connector and disconnect it. Using a voltmeter, check for battery supply voltage; connect the positive probe to the dark green/orange wire (or orange/dark green wire depending on engine/year) and the black wire at the connector terminal. Because the battery voltage is supplied to the sensor through the ASD relay, voltage will only be supplied for a very short time, approximately 4 seconds. Have an assistant turn the ignition key to the ON position (engine OFF) several times while you observe the voltmeter. The voltmeter should jump up to battery voltage each time the ignition is turned ON. If no voltage is indicated, check for a blown fuse and examine the wires for obvious damage. If the

circuit looks OK, check the ASD relay (see Chapter 4) and if necessary, have the PCM checked out at your local dealer service department or other qualified repair shop.
69   Next, check the sensor heater resistance; using an ohmmeter, measure the resistance between the two white wire terminals of the sensor electrical connector. The resistance should be approximately 4 to 7 ohms. If the resistance is not as specified, replace the sensor.

Replacement

Refer to illustration 3.71

Note: *Because they are installed in the exhaust manifold and catalytic converter, which contracts when cool, the oxygen sensors may be very difficult to loosen when the engine is cold. Rather than risk damage to the sensor (assuming you are planning to reuse it in another manifold or pipe), start and run the engine for a minute or two, then shut it off. Be careful not to burn yourself during the following procedure.*

70   Raise the vehicle and place it securely on jackstands.
71   Carefully disconnect the electrical connector from the sensor and unscrew the sensor from the exhaust manifold or catalytic converter **(see illustration)**.
72   If the sensor is to be re-installed, apply an anti-seize compound to the threads to facilitate future removal. The threads of new sensors are already coated with this compound.
73   Install the sensor and tighten it to the torque given in this Chapter's Specifications.
74   Reconnect the electrical connector of the sensor lead to the engine wiring harness and lower the vehicle.

PARK/NEUTRAL position switch

75   Refer to Chapter 7 for the Park/Neutral position switch service procedures. A failure in the PARK/NEUTRAL sensor circuit will set a code 37 in the PCM memory.

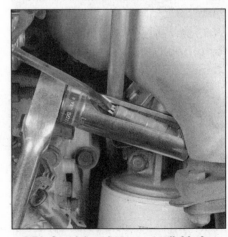

3.71 Special sockets are available for oxygen sensor removal; however, a flare-nut wrench or crows foot works just as well

Power steering pressure switch

76   Turning the steering wheel increases the power steering fluid pressure and the load placed upon the engine by the power steering pump. The pressure switch will close before the load causes an idle problem.

77   A pressure switch that will not open or an open circuit from the PCM will cause the ignition timing to retard at idle and this will affect idle quality.

78   A pressure switch that will not close or an open circuit may cause the engine to die when the power steering system is used heavily.

79   Any problems with the power steering pressure switch or circuit should be diagnosed and repaired by a dealer service department or other qualified repair shop.

Throttle Position Sensor (TPS)

General description

Refer to illustrations 3.80a and 3.80b

80   The Throttle Position Sensor (TPS) is located on the end of the throttle shaft on the throttle body **(see illustrations)**. By monitoring the output voltage from the TPS, the PCM can determine fuel delivery based on throttle valve angle (driver demand). A broken or loose TPS can cause intermittent bursts of fuel from the injectors and an unstable idle because the PCM senses the throttle is moving.

Check

Note: *To backprobe an electrical connector, use pins or paper clips inserted into the rear of the connector (or wire) to facilitate meter attachment. Be careful not to short the probes during this process.*

81   First, check the TPS supply voltage; disconnect the electrical connector and turn the ignition key ON (engine OFF). Using a voltmeter, check for voltage between the violet/white wire (positive) and the black/light blue wire (ground) at the sensor connector. There should be approximately 5 volts pre-

3.80a The throttle Position Sensor (TPS) (arrow) is mounted on the throttle body - 2.0L four-cylinder engine shown, 2.4L similar

sent. If no voltage is indicated, check for a blown fuse and examine the wires for obvious damage. If the circuit looks OK, have the PCM checked out at your local dealer service department or other qualified repair shop.

82   Next, connect the electrical connector to the TPS. Using a voltmeter, backprobe the orange/light blue wire (TPS signal - positive) and the black/light blue wire (ground). Turn the ignition key to the ON position (engine OFF). With the throttle valve fully closed, the voltmeter should indicate approximately 0.5 volts. Slowly open the throttle valve and watch for a smooth increase in voltage as the sensor travels from the closed to full position. The voltage should increase to approximately 4 volts. If the readings are not as specified, replace the TPS.

Replacement

Refer to illustration 3.85

83   Remove the throttle body from the intake manifold (see Chapter 4).

84   Unscrew the mounting screws and remove the TPS from the throttle body.

3.80b Throttle Position Sensor (TPS) (arrow) - V6 engines

85   When installing the TPS, be sure to align the socket locating tangs on the TPS with the throttle shaft in the throttle body **(see illustration)**. When the TPS is installed correctly, it must be rotated slightly clockwise to align the screw holes. After installing the screws, the throttle valve should be fully closed. If it's open, remove the TPS and reposition it on the shaft tangs.

86   Tighten the TPS screws securely.

87   The remaining installation steps are the reverse of removal.

Vehicle Speed Sensor (VSS) - manual transaxles only

General description

Refer to illustration 3.88

88   The Vehicle Speed Sensor (VSS) is located on the transaxle near the left engine mount **(see illustration)**. This sensor is a permanent magnetic variable reluctance sensor that produces a pulsing voltage whenever vehicle speed is over 3 mph. These pulses are translated by the PCM to determine vehicle speed, distance traveled and, on models equipped with cruise control, it governs the speed control servo.

3.85 When installing the TPS onto the throttle body, make sure the socket tangs are on the proper side of the throttle valve shaft blade (arrows). When installed correctly, the TPS must be rotated slightly clockwise to align the screw holes

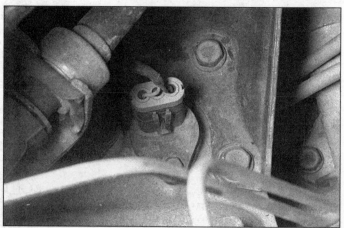

3.88 The Vehicle Speed Sensor (VSS) is located on the transaxle near the left engine mount - manual transaxles only

Check

Note: *To backprobe an electrical connector, use pins or paper clips inserted into the rear of the connector (or wire) to facilitate meter attachment. Be careful not to short the probes during this process.*

89   Raise the vehicle and support it securely on jackstands.

90   First, check the VSS sensor supply voltage; place the transaxle in Neutral and turn the ignition key ON (engine OFF). Using a voltmeter, backprobe the orange/white wire (1995 models) or orange wire (all other models) (positive) and ground the other probe to the transaxle. There should be approximately 8 volts present. If no voltage is indicated, check for a blown fuse and examine the wires for obvious damage. If the circuit looks OK, have the PCM checked out at your local dealer service department or other qualified repair shop.

91   Next check the VSS sensor output voltage; backprobe the black/light blue wire (sensor ground) and the white/orange wire (VSS signal output - positive) at the sensor connector. The voltage should fluctuate between 0 and 8 volts. If supply voltage is detected but there is no signal voltage, replace the VSS sensor.

Replacement

92   Raise the vehicle and support it securely on jackstands.

93   Clean the area around the VSS to prevent contaminating the transaxle.

94   Disconnect the electrical connector from the VSS.

95   Remove the retaining bolt and lift the VSS from the transaxle. **Note:** *When removing the VSS make sure the drive gear comes out along with the VSS. Should the drive gear fall into the transaxle, retrieve it and install it back onto the VSS.*

96   Installation is the reverse of removal. Tighten the VSS retaining bolt securely.

4   Powertrain Control Module (PCM) - check and replacement

Caution: *The PCM is an Electro-Static Discharge (ESD) sensitive electronic device, meaning a static electricity discharge from your body could possibly damage internal electrical components. Make sure to properly ground yourself and the PCM before handling it. Avoid touching the electrical terminals of the PCM unless absolutely necessary.*

Check

Note: *Because of a Federally mandated extended warranty which covers the OBD-II system components and because any owner-induced damage to the PCM, the sensors and/or the control devices may void the warranty, it is not recommended to attempt diagnosis of, or replace the PCM at home while the vehicle is under warranty.*

1   The PCM requires special test equip-

4.3 Disconnecting one of the two Powertrain Control Module (PCM) 40-pin connectors

ment to verify its integrity. Therefore, if the PCM is suspected to be faulty, the vehicle should be taken to your local dealer service department or other qualified repair shop for testing or repair.

Replacement

Refer to illustrations 4.3 and 4.4

2   Disconnect the negative battery cable from the ground stud on the left shock tower (see Chapter 5, Section 1).

3   The PCM is mounted to a bracket between the air filter housing and the Power Distribution Center (PDC). Disconnect both 40-pin connectors from the PCM **(see illustration)**.

4   Remove the PCM mounting screws **(see illustration)** and withdraw it from the vehicle.

5   Installation is the reverse of removal.

5   Positive Crankcase Ventilation (PCV) system - general description

1   The Positive Crankcase Ventilation (PCV) system reduces hydrocarbon exhaust emissions by scavenging crankcase vapors. This is accomplished by circulating fresh air from the air cleaner through the crankcase, where it mixes with blow-by gases and is then re-routed through the PCV valve to the intake manifold to be burned in the combus-

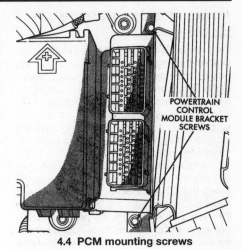

4.4 PCM mounting screws

tion process.

2   The main components of the PCV system are the PCV valve and the vacuum hoses that connect it to the manifold.

3   To maintain idle quality, the PCV valve restricts the flow when the intake manifold vacuum is high. If abnormal operating conditions (such as piston ring problems) arise, the system is designed to allow excessive amounts of blow-by gases to flow back through the crankcase vent tube into the air cleaner to be consumed by normal combustion.

4   Check and replacement of the PCV valve is performed in Chapter 1.

6   Exhaust Gas Recirculation (EGR) system - description, check and component replacement

Note: *If the EGR valve control solenoid becomes disconnected or damaged, the electrical signal will be lost and the EGR valve will be open at all times during warm-up and driving conditions. The symptoms will be poor performance, rough idle and driveability problems.*

General description

Refer to illustrations 6.1a and 6.1b

1   The EGR system reduces oxides of nitrogen (NOx) by recirculating exhaust gases

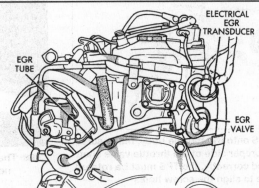

6.1a Typical four-cylinder engine EGR valve, tube and solenoid/transducer locations - 2.0L engine shown, as viewed from rear of engine

6

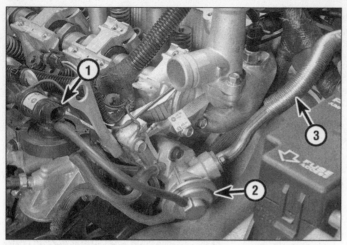

6.1b EGR system component location - V6 engine

1 *Solenoid/transducer*	2 *EGR valve*	3 *Tube*

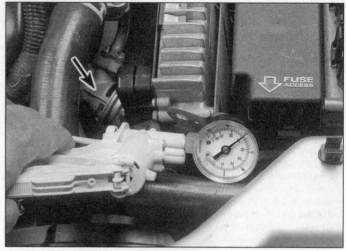

6.5 Checking the EGR valve (arrow) using a hand-operated vacuum pump

from the exhaust ports through the EGR valve and back into the intake manifold for ingestion into the engine which lowers the peak flame temperature during combustion **(see illustrations)**.

2   The EGR system consists of the EGR valve, the EGR solenoid/transducer assembly, the Powertrain Control Module (PCM) and various related sensors. The PCM uses the solenoid to control vacuum to the transducer. The transducer is controlled by exhaust system back-pressure which in turn regulates the amount of vacuum applied to the EGR valve. When exhaust system back-pressure becomes high enough, it fully closes a bleed valve in the transducer. Then the PCM de-energizes the solenoid and allows vacuum to flow through the transducer to operate the EGR valve. Turning the solenoid ON-and-OFF provides the correct amount of exhaust gas to be introduced into the engine for combustion.

Check

EGR valve

Refer to illustration 6.5

3   Check the condition of all the EGR system hoses and tubes for leaks, cracks, kinks or hardening of the rubber hoses. Make sure all the hoses are intact before proceeding with the EGR check.

4   Check the Vehicle Emission Control Information (VECI) label (see Section 1) for the correct EGR system hose routing. Reroute the hoses if necessary.

5   Detach the vacuum hose from the top of the EGR valve and attach a hand-operated vacuum pump to the valve **(see illustration)**.

6   Start the engine and warm it to its normal operating temperature.

7   Apply approximately 5 in-Hg of vacuum to the EGR valve with the engine at idle speed. The idle speed should drop considerably or even stall as vacuum is applied. This indicates that the EGR system is operating properly. If the engine speed does not

change, this indicates a possible faulty EGR valve, blocked or plugged EGR tube or passages in the intake and exhaust manifolds that may be plugged with carbon build-up. Turn off the engine.

8   Next, apply approximately 15 in-Hg of vacuum to the EGR valve and see if the stem on the EGR valve moves. If the valve opens and closes (apply and release the vacuum pressure as required) the EGR valve is operating correctly. The problem is either a plugged EGR tube or plugged passageways at the intake or exhaust manifold. Remove the EGR valve and clean the passages as required. **Note:** *If the EGR valve is severely plugged with carbon deposits, do not attempt to scrape them out, replace it with a new one.* If the stem did not move, replace the EGR valve.

9   Apply approximately 15 in-Hg of vacuum to the EGR valve and see if the vacuum pressure holds steady for at least three minutes. If you are unable to pull a vacuum on the EGR valve or the vacuum pressure doesn't remain constant, the diaphragm inside the EGR valve is faulty and the EGR valve and solenoid/transducer assembly must be replaced.

Solenoid/transducer assembly

Refer to illustration 6.10

10   Disconnect the electrical connector from the solenoid **(see illustration)**. Detach the vacuum hose connecting the solenoid/transducer to the intake manifold and attach a hand-held vacuum pump.

11   Attempt to apply approximately 15 in-Hg of vacuum to the solenoid. No vacuum should be produced. If vacuum develops, replace the EGR valve and solenoid/transducer assembly as a unit.

12   Next, connect one of the solenoid electrical terminals to the positive remote battery terminal using a fused jumper wire. Using another jumper wire, connect the other terminal to a good ground (this will energize the

6.10 EGR solenoid/transducer (arrow) - V6 engine shown

solenoid - be careful not to short them together). With battery voltage applied to the solenoid, try to pull approximately 15 in-Hg of vacuum on the solenoid. Vacuum should develop and hold steady. If vacuum is not produced or the pressure does not remain constant, replace the EGR valve and solenoid/transducer assembly as a unit. Reattach the vacuum hose and the electrical connector.

13   Check the transducer diaphragm; detach the back-pressure hose from the transducer and attach a hand-operated vacuum pump. Apply approximately 10 in-Hg of vacuum to the fitting. Vacuum should be produced and hold steady. If vacuum does not develop or remain constant, replace the EGR valve and solenoid/transducer assembly.

Replacement

Note: *Because the EGR valve and solenoid/transducer are a calibrated unit, they must be replaced as an assembly.*

14   Disconnect the electrical connector and vacuum hoses from the solenoid/transducer assembly **(see illustration 6.10)**.

15 Remove the mounting bolts and withdraw the solenoid/transducer assembly from it's mounting.

16 On V6 engines, remove the Transmission Control Module from it's mounting and position it out of the way (see Chapter 7B if necessary). **Note:** *Do not disconnect the electrical connector from the TCM.*

17 Remove the EGR tube mounting bolts from the EGR valve and intake manifold flanges.

18 Remove the EGR valve mounting bolts and then remove the EGR valve and tube.

19 Clean the gasket surfaces of the EGR valve, tube and intake manifold. If the EGR valve is to be re-installed, clean the gasket surfaces and, if necessary, remove any carbon build-up that may be present. If carbon build-up is excessive, replace the EGR valve and solenoid/transducer assembly.

20 Loosely assemble the EGR valve and tube, using new gaskets. Then hand tighten the all the bolts. Next, tighten the tube bolts to the torque listed in this Chapter's Specifications. Finish by tightening the EGR valve bolts to the torque listed in this Chapter's Specifications.

21 On V6 engines, place the TCM in it's proper position and secure it with the mounting screws.

22 Install the solenoid/transducer and tighten the mounting bolts.

23 Connect the vacuum hoses and electrical connector to the solenoid/transducer assembly.

7 Evaporative emissions control (EVAP) system - description, check and component replacement

General description

1 The function of the evaporative emissions control system is to prevent fuel vapors from escaping the fuel system and being released into the atmosphere. Vapors are trapped inside the fuel tank until the pressure overcomes the pressure-relief/rollover valve and is then routed to a charcoal canister via hoses for temporary storage. The Powertrain Control Module (PCM) monitors the engine operating parameters and then activates the EVAP purge control solenoid according to a programmed schedule which allows the fuel vapors from the canister to be drawn into the intake manifold and burned in the combustion process.

2 The charcoal canister on 1995 through 1997 models is mounted to a bracket behind the right front bumper fascia adjacent to the windshield washer reservoir. On 1998 models, it's located on top of the fuel tank. The canisters are maintenance-free and should last the life of the vehicle.

3 The most common symptom of a fault in the evaporative emissions system is a strong fuel odor in the engine compartment or raw fuel leaking from the canister. These indications are usually more prevalent during hot temperatures. All systems except for those installed on 1995 models are pressurized by a Leak Detection Pump (LDP). The LDP on all vehicles is located next to the charcoal canister. If normal system pressure cannot be achieved by the LDP, which indicates a leak, the PCM will store the appropriate fault code and illuminate the CHECK ENGINE light on the instrument panel. The most common cause of system pressure loss is a loose or poor sealing fuel filler cap. If the CHECK ENGINE light is illuminated, check the fuel filler cap first!

4 The fuel filler cap is equipped with a two-way pressure-vacuum relief valve as a safety device. If the pressure inside the tank exceeds approximately 1.5 to 2 psi, the relief valve vents the fuel vapors to the atmosphere. If the vacuum pressure inside the tank becomes greater than approximately 0.14 psi, the relief valve allows fresh air to be drawn into the tank.

5 All models are equipped with two rollover valves, which are mounted on the top of the fuel tank. The rollover valves are designed to close the fuel vapor vent ports in case the vehicle should flip upside down. The rollover valves are not serviceable.

6 1998 models are equipped with the Onboard Refueling Vapor Recovery (ORVR) system which incorporates a one-way check valve in the fuel tank filler neck and a control valve on top of the fuel tank. On models not equipped with ORVR, the fuel vapor displaced by the incoming fuel is allowed to vent to atmosphere during refueling. The ORVR system uses the control valve to vent the displaced vapors to the charcoal canister for storage. Vapor is absorbed in the canister until the fuel flow stops, either following fuel shut-off or by having the fuel rise high enough to raise the float located in the control valve which closes the valve. This feature combined with the LDP, will not allow the vehicle to be refueled with the engine running. If the vehicle will not accept fuel, cycle the ignition key ON and OFF a few times to allow the EVAP purge control solenoid to vent the pressure inside the tank.

Check

Note: *The evaporative control system, like all emission control systems, is protected by a Federally mandated extended warranty (5 years or 50,000 miles at the time this manual was written). The EVAP system probably won't fail during the service life of the vehicle; however, if it does, the hoses, gas cap or charcoal canister are usually to blame.*

7 If the CHECK ENGINE light is illuminated, check the gas cap first. A loose or bad sealing gas cap will cause the LDP to register a leak in the system. Then check the system hoses. A disconnected, damaged or missing hose is the next most likely cause of a malfunctioning EVAP system. Refer to the Vacuum Hose Routing Diagram (located on the

7.12 On 1995 models, the EVAP system charcoal canister (arrow) is located behind the right front bumper fascia (removed for clarity)

under side of the hood) to determine whether the hoses are correctly routed and attached. Repair any damaged hoses or replace any missing hoses as necessary. **Note:** *Be sure to replace with approved fuel resistant hoses.* Finally, check the purge control solenoid and LDP electrical connections and wires for corrosion and damage. Repair as necessary.

8 Because of the special equipment required, further diagnosis of the EVAP system must be performed by your local dealer service department or other qualified repair shop.

Component replacement
Charcoal canister
1995 models
Refer to illustration 7.12

9 Remove the fuel filler cap to relieve the pressure inside the fuel tank.

10 Loosen the right front wheel lug nuts. Raise the vehicle and place it securely on jackstands.

11 Remove the right front wheel inner and lower splash shields.

12 Label and disconnect the vacuum hoses, remove the nut and bolt securing the canister to the support bracket and then withdraw it from the vehicle **(see illustration)**.

13 Installation is the reverse of removal.

Charcoal canister and Leak Detection Pump
1996 and 1997 models
Refer to illustrations 7.17 and 7.19

14 Remove the fuel filler cap to relieve the pressure inside the fuel tank.

15 Remove the right headlight assembly (see Chapter 12).

16 Label and disconnect the hoses from the LDP and charcoal canister.

17 Remove the three nuts securing the

6

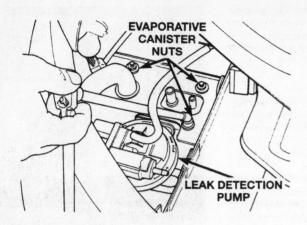

7.17 Remove the three nuts securing the canister to the LDP bracket (1996 and 1997 models)

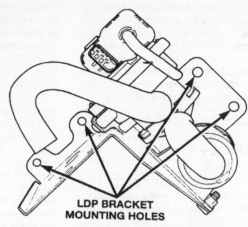

7.19 The LDP bracket on 1996 and 1997 models is secured at these four locations

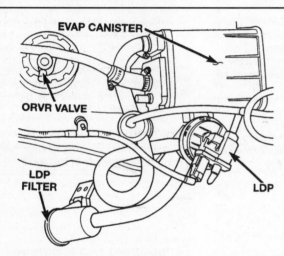

7.23 1998 EVAP system components - as viewed from the top of the fuel tank

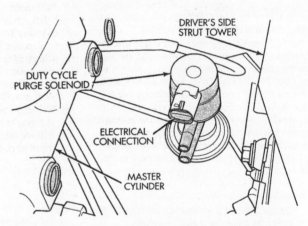

7.32 On 1995 to 1997 models, the purge control solenoid is located in the engine compartment on the driver's side shock tower

canister to the LDP bracket **(see illustration)** and let the canister rest on the lower front fascia.

18   Disconnect the electrical connector from the LDP.

19   Remove the four bolts securing the LDP bracket to the vehicle **(see illustration)**.

20   Remove the LDP (with bracket attached) from the vehicle.

21   Remove the charcoal canister.

22   Installation is the reverse of removal.

1998 models

Refer to illustration 7.23

23   The charcoal canister and LDP on these models mount to a bracket located on top of the fuel tank **(see illustration)**.

24   Remove the fuel filler cap to relieve the pressure inside the fuel tank.

25   Perform the fuel pressure relief procedure (see Chapter 4).

26   Drain and remove the fuel tank (see Chapter 4).

27   Label and disconnect the vapor hoses connected to the canister.

28   Withdraw the push-pin securing the

canister to the bracket and remove it from the fuel tank.

29   Remove the bracket and LDP, then remove the LDP from the bracket.

30   Since they are accessible, check the condition of all EVAP system hoses and electrical connections at this time and repair/replace as necessary.

31   Installation is the reverse of removal. Tighten the fuel tank strap bolts to the torque listed in the Chapter 4 Specifications.

Canister purge control solenoid

Refer to illustrations 7.32 and 7.33
Note: *The EVAP purge control solenoid must be installed with the solenoid electrical connector UP in order to operate properly.*

32   On 1995 to 1997 models, the purge control solenoid is mounted on the left (driver's) side of the engine compartment on the shock tower near the brake master cylinder **(see illustration)**.

33   On 1998 models, the purge control solenoid is mounted on the right (passenger) side of the engine compartment on the fender panel near the windshield washer fluid

7.33 On 1998 models, the purge control solenoid (arrow) is located in the engine compartment near the windshield washer fluid reservoir

reservoir **(see illustration)**.

34   Remove the fuel filler cap to relieve the pressure inside the fuel tank.

35   On 1995 to 1997 models, if equipped,

remove the cruise control servo from it's mounting and position it out of the way.

36   Label and disconnect the purge control solenoid vacuum hoses and electrical connector.

37   Unscrew the mounting bolt and remove the solenoid and bracket assembly.

38   Installation is the reverse of removal.

---

8   Catalytic converter system - description, check and replacement

Note: *Because of a Federally mandated extended warranty which covers emissions related components such as the catalytic converter, check with a dealer service department before replacing the converter at your own expense.*

General description

Refer to illustration 8.1

1   The catalytic converter **(see illustration)** is an emission control device added to the exhaust system to reduce pollutants from the exhaust gas stream. There are two types of converters. The conventional oxidation catalyst reduces the levels of hydrocarbon (HC) and carbon monoxide (CO). The three-way catalyst lowers the levels of oxides of nitrogen (NOx) as well as hydrocarbons (HC) and

carbon monoxide (CO). **Caution:** *Because the two types of catalytic converters are extremely similar looking, make sure you are purchasing the correct part for your particular vehicle.*

Check

2   The test equipment for a catalytic converter is very expensive and highly sophisticated. If you suspect that the converter on your vehicle is malfunctioning, take it to a dealer or authorized emissions inspection facility for diagnosis and repair.

3   Whenever the vehicle is raised for servicing of underbody components, check the converter for leaks, corrosion, dents and other damage. Check the welds/flange bolts that attach the front and rear ends of the converter to the exhaust system. If damage is discovered, the converter should be replaced.

4   Although catalytic converters don't often fail, they can become plugged. The easiest way to check for a restricted converter is to use a vacuum gauge to diagnose the effect of a blocked exhaust based on intake vacuum.

a) *Open the throttle until the engine speed is about 2000 rpm.*

b) *Release the throttle quickly.*

c) *If there is no restriction, the gauge will quickly drop to not more than 2 in-Hg or more above its normal reading.*

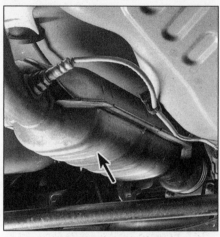

8.1 Catalytic converter (arrow)

d) *If the gauge does not show 5 in-Hg or more above its normal reading, or seems to momentarily hover around its highest reading for a moment before it returns, the exhaust system, or the converter, is plugged (or an exhaust pipe is bent or dented, or the core inside the muffler has shifted).*

Replacement

5   Refer to the exhaust system removal and installation Section in Chapter 4.

6

Notes

Chapter 7 Part A
Manual transaxle

Contents

Specifications

General

Transaxle type	NV T350 (A-578)
Fluid type and capacity	See Chapter 1

Torque specifications
Ft-lbs (unless otherwise indicated)

Back-up light switch	18
Clutch housing-to-engine bolts	70
Clutch housing lower cover bolts	105 in-lbs
Crossover cable adjusting bolt	70 in-lbs
Drain plug	67 in-lbs
Lateral strut fasteners	40
Shift cable bracket-to-transaxle bolts	250 in-lbs

1 General information

The vehicles covered by this manual are equipped with either the NV T350 (A-578) 5-speed manual or the 41TE 4-speed automatic transaxle. Information on the manual transaxle is included in this part of Chapter 7. Service procedures for the automatic transaxle are contained in Chapter 7, Part B.

Both the manual transaxle and the differential are housed in a compact, light-weight, two-piece aluminum alloy housing.

The Sections in this Chapter tell you how to replace and adjust those parts of the transaxle that can be serviced at home, as well as how to remove and install the transaxle itself. Because of the complexity of the transaxle rotating machinery, the difficulty of obtaining replacement parts and the special tools required to service those parts, we don't recommend repairing the transaxle at home. Before assuming that the transaxle is faulty, read through the *Troubleshooting* Section at the beginning of this manual for steps to help pin-point the problem. For service and repairs outside the scope of this manual, take the vehicle to a dealer service department or other qualified transmission repair shop.

2 Shift cables - removal, installation and adjustment

Warning: *These vehicles are equipped with air bags. Always disable the airbag system before working in the vicinity of the impact sensors, steering column or instrument panel to avoid the possibility of accidental deployment of the airbag(s), which could cause personal injury (see Chapter 12).*

Removal

Refer to illustrations 2.5a, 2.5b, 2.6, 2.9a, 2.9b and 2.10

1   In the event of hard shifting, disconnect both cables at the transaxle and operate the shifter. If the shift lever moves smoothly through all positions with the cables disconnected, the crossover cable should be adjusted as described at the end of this Section. To remove and install the shift cables, perform the following.

2   Raise the hood and place a blanket over the left (driver's) fender to protect it.

3   Disconnect the negative battery cable from the ground stud on the left shock tower (see Chapter 5, Section 1).

4   Remove the air cleaner assembly (see Chapter 4).

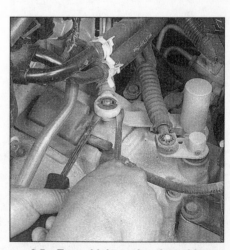

2.5a To avoid damaging the cable bushings, use two flat blade screwdrivers to evenly pry the selector cable . . .

5   Using two flat blade screwdrivers, carefully pry the selector cable and crossover cable from the select lever **(see illustrations)**. **Caution:** *To avoid damaging the cable isolator bushings, pry up with equal force on both sides of the shift cable end. Discard the cable retaining clips.*

7A

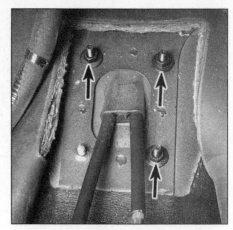

2.5b . . . and the crossover cable from their levers

2.6 Use pliers to remove the shift cable retaining clips (arrow) securing the cables to the bracket - the selector cable clip is hidden behind the EGR valve in this view

2.9a Remove the shift cable floorpan grommet mounting nuts from inside the vehicle . . .

6   Remove the cable retaining clips on the transaxle and remove the cables from the bracket **(see illustration)**. Discard the retaining clips.

7   Working inside the vehicle, remove the center console (see Chapter 11).

8   Raise the front of the vehicle and place it

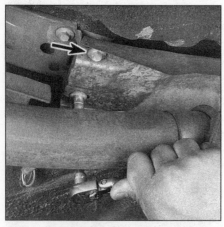

2.9b . . . then remove the bolts from under the vehicle and separate the plate/grommet from the floorpan

securely on jackstands.

9   Remove the shifter cable grommet plate and pry the grommet from the floorpan **(see illustrations)**.

10   Remove the cable retaining clips at the shifter and detach the cables from the bracket **(see illustration)**. Discard the retaining clips.

11   Using two flat blade screwdrivers, carefully pry the selector cable and the crossover cable from the shift lever assembly. Discard the cable retaining clips. **Caution:** *To avoid damaging the cable isolator bushings, pry up with equal force on both sides of the shift cable end.*

12   Detach both cables from the support clips on the tunnel above the catalytic converter.

13   Remove the cable assembly from the vehicle.

Installation

Refer to illustrations 2.18 and 2.19

14   Installation is the reverse of removal. Install new cable retaining clips at all locations and make sure they are properly seated

in the cable grooves.

15   Before installing the air cleaner assembly and center console, adjust the crossover cable (see below).

Adjustment

Note: *Only the crossover cable can be adjusted. There is no adjustment for the selector cable.*

16   Remove the air cleaner assembly (see Chapter 4).

17   Working inside the vehicle, remove the center console (see Chapter 11).

18   Loosen the crossover cable adjusting bolt located at the shifter end of the cable **(see illustration)**.

19   Working in the engine compartment, position the crossover lever on the transaxle so the hole in the crossover lever aligns with the hole in the transaxle raised boss. Insert a 1/4 inch drill bit through the crossover lever and into the raised boss **(see illustration)**. Make sure the drill bit penetrates into the transaxle hole at least 1/2 inch.

20   Place the gear shift lever in the neutral position (allow the shifter to self-center in it's proper location).

21   Without moving the gear shift lever from

2.10 Use needle-nose pliers to remove the cable retaining clips from the shift lever assembly brackets

2.18 Loosen the crossover cable adjusting bolt

2.19 Align the hole in the crossover lever with the hole in the transaxle raised boss. Insert a 1/4-inch drill bit (arrow) through the lever and into the raised boss at least 1/2-inch

3.4 Remove all four of the shift lever assembly mounting nuts (arrows) (only the two forward nuts are visible in this view), then remove the shift lever assembly

its neutral position, tighten the crossover cable adjusting bolt to the torque listed in this Chapter's Specifications.

22   Remove the 1/4 inch drill bit securing the crossover lever to the transaxle.

23   Shift the transaxle into all gear positions to make sure the cable is functioning properly. Readjust if necessary.

24   Install the center console (see Chapter 11).

25   Install the air cleaner assembly (see Chapter 4).

3   Shift lever assembly - removal and installation

Warning: *These vehicles are equipped with air bags. Always disable the airbag system before working in the vicinity of the impact sensors, steering column or instrument panel to avoid the possibility of accidental deployment of the airbag(s), which could cause personal injury (see Chapter 12).*

Removal

Refer to illustration 3.4

1   Disconnect the negative battery cable from the ground stud on the left shock tower (see Chapter 5, Section 1).

2   Remove the center console (see Chapter 11).

3   Disconnect the shift cables from the shift lever assembly (see Section 2).

4   Remove the shift lever bracket nuts **(see illustration)** and remove the shift lever assembly.

Installation

5   Install the shift lever assembly and tighten the nuts securely.

6   Attach the shift cables to the shift lever assembly and adjust the crossover cable (see Section 2).

7   Install the center console (see Chapter 11).

8   Attach the negative battery cable to the ground stud on the left shock tower.

4   Back-up light switch - check and replacement

Check

Refer to illustration 4.1

1   The back-up light switch **(see illustration)** is located on top of the transaxle, near the left (driver's side) front corner of the housing. However, access is gained from under the vehicle.

2   Turn the ignition key to the ON position and move the gear shift lever to the Reverse position. The back-up lights should illuminate.

3   If the back-up lights don't come on, first verify that each light bulb is in working condition. If the bulbs are OK, check the back-up light fuse located in the fuse box at the end of the instrument panel on the driver's side (see Chapter 12).

If the fuse has blown, replace it. If it blows again, look for a short in the back-up light circuit.

4   If the fuse is okay, raise the vehicle and support it securely on jackstands. Turn the ignition switch ON (engine off) and make sure the gear shift lever is in reverse. Using a test light or voltmeter, verify there is voltage present at the back-up light switch. If there's no voltage to the switch, look for an open or short in the power wire to the switch. Repair as necessary.

5   If the back-up lights still don't illuminate, unplug the electrical connector from the back-up light switch and, using an ohmmeter, verify that there is continuity between the switch terminals (with gear shift lever in reverse), i.e. when the switch is closed. If continuity is not detected, replace the back-up light switch.

6   If there is continuity between the switch terminals, (it opens and closes the circuit relative to the gear shift position), but the back-up lights don't come on when the gear shift lever is in the reverse position, check the wiring between the switch and the back-up lights for an open circuit and repair as necessary.

4.1 The back-up light switch is located on top of the transaxle case, near the left (driver's side) front corner

Replacement

7   Raise the vehicle and support it securely on jackstands.

8   Detach the electrical connector from the back-up light switch and unscrew the switch from the transaxle.

9   Wrap the threads of the replacement switch with Teflon tape, or equivalent, install the switch and tighten it to the torque listed in this Chapter's Specifications.

10   Attach the switch electrical connector and lower the vehicle.

11   Check the operation of the back-up lights to be sure the switch is working correctly.

5   Driveaxle oil seal replacement

Refer to illustrations 5.4 and 5.6

1   Oil leaks frequently occur at the driveaxle seals. Replacing these seals is relatively easy, since you don't have to remove the transaxle to access them.

2   The driveaxle oil seals are located in the sides of the transaxle, where the splined

7A

5.4 Using a large screwdriver or prybar, carefully pry the oil seal out of the transaxle (if you can't remove the oil seal with a screwdriver or prybar, you may need to obtain a special seal removal tool, available at most auto parts stores, to do the job)

5.6 Using a seal driver, large section of pipe or a large deep socket as a drift, drive the new seal squarely into the bore and make sure that it's completely seated

6.8 Remove the intake manifold support bracket

6.9 Remove the upper clutch housing fasteners (arrows)

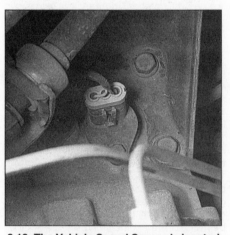

6.10 The Vehicle Speed Sensor is located on the transaxle next to the rear engine mount

inner ends of the driveaxles mate with the differential side gears. If you suspect that one of these seals is leaking, raise the vehicle and support it securely on jackstands. If a seal is in fact leaking, you'll see a trail of wet lubricant on the side of the transaxle below the seal.

3   Remove the driveaxle (see Chapter 8).

4   Using a large screwdriver or prybar, carefully pry the oil seal out of the transaxle **(see illustration)**.

5   If you can't remove the oil seal with a screwdriver or pry bar, you may need to obtain a special seal removal tool (available at most auto parts stores) to do the job.

6   Using a seal driver, large section of pipe or a large deep socket as a drift, install the new oil seal **(see illustration)**. Drive it into the bore squarely and make sure that it's completely seated. Lubricate the driveaxle oil seal, tripod joint splines and sealing surface with the appropriate transmission fluid (see Chapter 1).

7   Install the driveaxle (see Chapter 8). Be careful not to damage the lip of the new seal during installation.

---

6   Manual transaxle - removal and installation

Note 1: *This procedure requires the removal of all engine mounts except for the right side engine mount. If the vehicle must be moved after the transaxle has been removed, make sure the engine is supported at all times and the appropriate sized bolts and nuts are installed in the front wheel hub/bearings (refer to Chapter 8).*

Note 2: *There are four different gear ratios available with this transaxle. If you are going to replace this transaxle or obtain a rebuilt unit, check the metal identification tag*

mounted to the rear cover before purchasing a new or rebuilt transaxle to ensure you're getting the correct gear ratio for your particular application.

Removal

Refer to illustrations 6.8, 6.9, 6.10, 6.16, 6.17, 6.18, 6.19, 6.28 and 6.31

1   Open the hood and place protective covers on the front fenders and cowl. Special fender covers are available, but an old bedspread or blankets will also work.

2   Disconnect the negative battery cable from the ground stud on the left shock tower (see Chapter 5, Section 1).

3   Remove the air cleaner assembly (see Chapter 4).

4   Disconnect the clutch cable from the release lever (see Chapter 8).

5   Disconnect the shift cables from the transaxle and detach the cable bracket (with cables attached) from the transaxle (see Section 2). Position the cables out of the way.

6   Detach the accelerator cable and cruise control cable (if equipped) from the throttle

lever (see Chapter 4 if necessary).

7   Detach the accelerator/cruise control cable bracket from the throttle body (with cables attached) and position it out of the way.

8   Remove the intake manifold support bracket **(see illustration)**.

9   Remove the upper clutch housing bolts **(see illustration)**.

10   Disconnect the electrical connectors from the vehicle speed sensor **(see illustration)** and back-up light switch **(see illustration 4.1)**.

11   Loosen the driveaxle hub nuts (see Chapter 8) and front wheel lug nuts. Raise the vehicle and place it securely on jackstands. Remove both front wheels.

12   Drain the transaxle fluid (see Chapter 1).

13   Remove the driveaxles (see Chapter 8).

14   Remove the starter motor (see Chapter 5).

15   Remove the splash shield/battery cover from the left front wheel well (see Chapter 5). Extract the push-in fasteners and remove the transaxle splash shield.

16   On 1998 models, remove the oil pan-to-

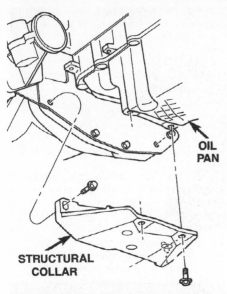

6.16 Oil pan-to-transaxle structural collar assembly details - 1998 models only

6.17 Remove the lateral strut (lower arrow) and clutch housing lower cover (upper arrow) - all except 1998 models

6.18 Match-mark the modular clutch assembly to the driveplate

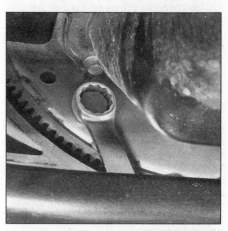

6.19 Rotate the engine clockwise using the crankshaft damper/pulley bolt and remove the four flywheel-to-clutch assembly bolts

transaxle structural collar and transaxle clutch housing lower cover **(see illustration)**.

17 On all models except 1998, remove the transaxle lateral strut and clutch housing lower cover **(see illustration)**.

18 If the modular clutch assembly is to be reinstalled, match-mark the clutch assembly to the driveplate **(see illustration)**.

19 Remove the four modular clutch assembly-to-driveplate bolts **(see illustration)**. To gain access to each bolt, rotate the engine clockwise (ONLY) as viewed from the drivebelt end of the engine using the crankshaft damper/pulley bolt. Remove all four bolts and discard them. Use a screwdriver placed in the ring gear of the driveplate to keep the crankshaft from turning during removal of the bolts.

20 After removing the clutch module mounting bolts, push the modular clutch assembly into the transaxle clutch housing as far as possible.

21 Remove any exhaust components

which will interfere with transaxle removal (see Chapter 4).

22 Remove any remaining chassis or suspension components which will interfere with transaxle removal. **Caution:** *If the front suspension crossmember has to be repositioned to facilitate transaxle removal, it must be match-marked to the body and frame (see Chapter 10) to maintain proper wheel alignment at reassembly.*

23 Support the engine from above with a hoist, or place a floor jack under the oil pan. Place a wood block on the jack head to spread the load on the oil pan.

24 Remove the left engine mounting bracket from the transaxle (see Chapter 2A).

25 Remove the front engine mounting bracket and strut (see Chapter 2A).

26 Remove the rear engine mounting bracket (see Chapter 2A).

27 Remove the engine support module (1995 through 1997 models) or front and rear lower engine mounts (1998 models) as applicable (see Chapter 2A). **Note:** *The engine support module is attached to the lower radiator support. When removing the engine support module, the radiator and air conditioning condenser (if equipped) must be supported.*

28 Support the transaxle with a transmission jack, if available, or use a floor jack **(see illustration)**. Secure the transaxle to the jack using straps or chains so it doesn't fall off during removal.

29 Remove the lower transaxle clutch housing-to-engine bolts. Make sure all clutch

7A

6.28 Place a jack under the transaxle (transmission jack shown) and secure the transaxle to the jack using chains or straps

6.31 While removing the transaxle from the engine, make sure to keep it level so the modular clutch assembly doesn't fall off the transaxle input shaft

housing-to-engine bolts are removed.

30   Make a final check that all wires, hoses and brackets have been disconnected from the transaxle, then with the engine properly supported, separate the transaxle from the engine.

31   Carefully lower the transaxle and remove it from under the vehicle **(see illustration)**. Make sure you keep the transaxle level as you maneuver it or the modular clutch assembly may fall out. **Note:** *Reinstalling the clutch housing lower cover after the transaxle clears the flywheel will help hold the clutch assembly in place.*

32   Remove the modular clutch assembly from the transaxle. Handle it carefully to avoid contaminating the friction surfaces. Inspect it for excessive wear or contamination (see Chapter 8). In most cases, because of the time and labor involved in gaining access to the clutch assembly, it should be replaced whenever the transaxle is removed or replaced unless its in new or near-perfect condition.

33   Check the crankshaft rear main seal for evidence of leakage. If replacement is necessary, refer to Chapter 2A.

Installation

34   Install the modular clutch assembly onto the transaxle input shaft. Handle it carefully to avoid contaminating the friction surfaces.

35   With the transaxle secured to the jack, raise it into position and carefully slide it forward until the clutch housing seats against the engine. Do not use excessive force to install the transaxle - if it doesn't slide into place easily, readjust the angle of the transaxle and try again. Make sure you keep the transaxle level as you maneuver it or the modular clutch assembly may fall out. Do not force it or use the clutch housing bolts to pull it together. Make sure the dowel pins on the engine are aligned with their respective holes in the transaxle. If you are experiencing difficulty, solicit the aid of an assistant.

37   Install the clutch housing-to-engine bolts with brackets and clamps where required and tighten them to the torque listed in this Chapter's Specifications.

38   Install the engine support module (1995 through 1997 models) or front and rear lower engine mounts (1998 models) as applicable (see Chapter 2A).

39   Install the rear engine mounting bracket to the transaxle and secure it to the engine support module (1995 through 1997 models) or rear lower engine mount (1998 models) as applicable (see Chapter 2A). Tighten the bracket-to-engine bolts (ONLY) to the torque listed in the Specification Section of Chapter 2A. Leave the through-bolt loose for now.

40   Install the front engine mounting bracket and strut (see Chapter 2A). Secure the bracket to the engine support module (1995 through 1997 models) or front lower engine mount (1998 models) as applicable (see Chapter 2A). Tighten the mounting bracket and strut-to-engine/transaxle bolts (ONLY) to

the torque listed in the Specification Section of Chapter 2A. Leave the through-bolt loose for now.

41   Install the left engine mounting bracket onto the transaxle and secure it to the support assembly on the frame rail (see Chapter 2A). Tighten the bolts to the torque listed in the Specification Section of Chapter 2A.

42   Tighten the front and rear engine mount through-bolts to the torque listed in the Specification Section in Chapter 2A.

43   Remove the engine and transaxle support jacks.

44   If you're reinstalling the old modular clutch assembly, align the driveplate-to-modular clutch assembly match-marks applied in Step 18. Install four new driveplate-to-modular clutch bolts. DO NOT install the old bolts - they are one-time use only. To gain access to each bolt hole, rotate the engine clockwise (ONLY) as viewed from the drivebelt end of the engine using the crankshaft damper/pulley bolt. Tighten the driveplate-to-modular clutch assembly bolts in a criss-cross pattern to the torque listed in the Specification Section of Chapter 8. Use a screwdriver placed in the ring gear of the driveplate to keep the crankshaft from turning during installation of the bolts.

45   Install the clutch housing lower cover. Tighten the bolts to the torque listed in this Chapter's Specifications.

46   On all models except 1998, install the lateral strut bracket **(see illustration 6.17)**. Tighten the bolts to the torque listed in this Chapter's Specifications.

47   On 1998 models, install the oil pan-to-transaxle structural collar. Tighten the bolts to the torque listed in the Specification Section of Chapter 2A.

48   Attach the electrical connectors to the vehicle speed sensor and back-up light switch.

49   Install the transaxle splash shield and secure it with the push-in fasteners. Install the splash shield/battery cover into the left front wheel well (see Chapter 5).

50   Install the starter motor (see Chapter 5). Tighten the bolts to the torque listed in the Specification Section of Chapter 5.

51   Install any chassis or suspension components that were removed. **Caution:** *If the front suspension crossmember was repositioned to facilitate transaxle removal, it must be aligned with the previously applied match-marks on the body and frame* (see Chapter 10) *to maintain proper wheel alignment.*

52   Install any exhaust components that were removed (see Chapter 4).

53   Install the driveaxles, hub nuts and front wheels (see Chapter 8).

54   Install the intake manifold support bracket **(see illustration 6.8)**.

55   Install the accelerator and cruise control (if equipped) cable bracket onto the throttle body and tighten the bolts securely.

56   Install the accelerator and cruise control (if equipped) cable ends into the throttle lever.

57   Install the shift cables and mounting

bracket onto the transaxle (see Section 2). Tighten the shift cable bracket bolts to the to the torque listed in this Chapter's Specifications.

58   Attach the clutch cable onto the clutch release lever and install the inspection cover (see Chapter 8).

59   Attach the negative battery cable to the ground stud on the left shock tower.

60   Adjust the shift crossover cable (see Section 2).

61   Install the air cleaner assembly (see Chapter 4).

62   Fill the transaxle with the appropriate fluid (see Chapter 1). Road test the vehicle and check for proper transaxle operation and fluid leaks. Shutoff the engine and recheck the transaxle fluid level.

7   Manual transaxle overhaul - general information

1   Overhauling a manual transaxle is a difficult job for the do-it-yourselfer. It involves the disassembly and reassembly of many small components. Numerous clearances must be precisely measured and, if necessary, changed with select fit spacers and snaprings. As a result, if transaxle problems arise, it can be removed and installed by a competent do-it-yourselfer, but overhaul should be left to a dealer service department or other qualified transmission repair shop. Rebuilt transaxles may be available - check with your dealer parts department or local auto parts stores. At any rate, the time and money involved in an overhaul is almost sure to exceed the cost of a rebuilt unit.

2   Nevertheless, it's not impossible for an inexperienced mechanic to rebuild a transaxle if the special tools are available and the job is done in a deliberate step-by-step manner so nothing is overlooked.

3   The tools necessary for an overhaul include internal and external snap-ring pliers, a bearing puller, a slide hammer, a set of pin punches, a dial indicator and possibly a hydraulic press. In addition, a large, sturdy workbench and a vise or transaxle stand will be required.

4   During disassembly of the transaxle, make careful notes of how each piece comes off, where it fits in relation to other pieces and what holds it in place - actually noting how they are installed when you remove the parts will make it much easier to put it back together. If necessary take photographs during disassembly. **Note:** *The output shaft cannot be disassembled.*

5   Before taking the transaxle apart for repair, it will help if you have some idea what area of the transaxle is malfunctioning. Certain problems can be closely tied to specific areas in the transaxle, which can make component examination and replacement easier. Refer to the *Troubleshooting* Section at the beginning of this manual for information regarding possible sources of trouble.

Chapter 7 Part B
Automatic transaxle

Contents

Specifications

General

Transaxle type	41TE
Fluid type and capacity	See Chapter 1

Torque specifications

Ft-lbs (unless otherwise indicated)

Cooler line fittings	105 in-lbs
Bellhousing lower cover bolts	105 in-lbs
Driveplate-to-torque converter bolts	55
Park/Neutral/Back-up light switch	25
Transaxle bellhousing-to-engine bolts	70

1 General information

The vehicles covered by this manual are equipped with either the NV T350 (A-578) 5-speed manual or the 41TE 4-speed automatic transaxle. Information on the automatic transaxle is included in this part of Chapter 7. Service procedures for the manual transaxle are contained in Chapter 7, Part B.

The automatic transaxle and the differential are housed in a compact, lightweight, two-piece aluminum alloy housing. Operation of the transaxle is controlled electronically by the Transmission Control Module (TCM) which is the "brain" of the transaxle. The TCM monitors engine and transaxle operating parameters through numerous sensors and then generates output signals to various relays and solenoids to regulate hydraulic

pressures, optimize driveability, provide efficient torque management and maintain maximum fuel economy. The TCM is part of the On-Board Diagnostic system OBD-II. For more information see Chapter 6. **Note:** *If the power has been interrupted (battery disconnected or has failed) the transaxle will shift roughly for the first few gear progressions while the TCM relearns the engine and transaxle parameters.*

The Sections in this Chapter instruct you on how to replace and adjust those parts of the transaxle that can be easily serviced at home, as well as how to remove and install the transaxle itself. Because of the complexity of the transaxle rotating machinery, electronic operating system and the special tools required to diagnose and service it properly, we don't recommend repairing the transaxle at home. For service and repairs outside the

scope of this manual, take the vehicle to a dealer service department or other qualified transmission repair shop.

Some models came equipped with a driver-interactive option called "Autostick." This system allows the transaxle to be shifted manually. When the shift lever is placed in the Autostick position, the transaxle will remain in whatever gear it was using before Autostick was activated. Moving the shift lever to the left (towards the driver) causes the transaxle to downshift and moving it to the right (towards the passenger seat) causes it to upshift. The instrument cluster displays the gear you have selected by illuminating a box around the gear currently engaged. In the Autostick mode the vehicle can be driven away in 1st, 2nd or 3rd gear. The speed (cruise) control system can be used while in the Autostick mode as long as the shift lever is in 3rd or 4th gear. However, when the shift lever is moved to 2nd gear the speed control system is disengaged. Shifting into Overdrive cancels the Autostick mode and the TCM resumes controlling transaxle operation.

2   Diagnosis - general

1   Automatic transaxle malfunctions may be caused by five general conditions:

 a) *Poor engine performance*
 b) *Improper adjustments*
 c) *Hydraulic malfunctions*
 d) *Mechanical malfunctions*
 e) *Malfunctions in the computer or its signal network*

2   Diagnosis of these problems should always begin with a check of the easily repaired items: fluid level and condition (see Chapter 1), shift cable adjustment and shift lever installation. Next, perform a road test to determine if the problem has been corrected or if more diagnosis is necessary. If the problem persists after the preliminary tests and corrections are completed, additional diagnosis should be performed by a dealer service department or other qualified transmission repair shop. Refer to the *Troubleshooting* section at the front of this manual for information on symptoms of transaxle problems.

Preliminary checks

3   Drive the vehicle to warm the transaxle to normal operating temperature.
4   Check the fluid level as described in Chapter 1:

 a) *If the fluid level is unusually low, add enough fluid to bring the level within the designated area of the dipstick, then check for external leaks (see following).*
 b) *If the fluid level is abnormally high, drain off the excess, then check the drained fluid for contamination by coolant. The presence of engine coolant in the automatic transmission fluid indicates that a failure has occurred in the internal radiator oil cooler walls that separate the coolant from the transmission fluid (see Chapter 3).*
 c) *If the fluid is foaming, drain it and refill the transaxle, then check for coolant in the fluid, or a high fluid level.*

5   Check the engine idle speed. **Note:** *If the engine is malfunctioning, do not proceed with the preliminary checks until it has been repaired and runs normally.*
6   Check and adjust the shift cable, if necessary (see Section 4).
7   If hard shifting is experienced, inspect the shift cable under the center console and at the manual lever on the transaxle (see Section 4).

Fluid leak diagnosis

8   Most fluid leaks are easy to locate visually. Repair usually consists of replacing a seal or gasket. If a leak is difficult to find, the following procedure may help.

9   Identify the fluid. Make sure it's transmission fluid and not engine oil or brake fluid (automatic transmission fluid is a deep red color).
10   Try to pinpoint the source of the leak. Drive the vehicle several miles, then park it over a large sheet of cardboard. After a minute or two, you should be able to locate the leak by determining the source of the fluid dripping onto the cardboard.
11   Make a careful visual inspection of the suspected component and the area immediately around it. Pay particular attention to gasket mating surfaces. A mirror is often helpful for finding leaks in areas that are hard to see.
12   If the leak still cannot be found, clean the suspected area thoroughly with a degreaser or solvent, then dry it thoroughly.
13   Drive the vehicle for several miles at normal operating temperature and varying speeds. After driving the vehicle, visually inspect the suspected component again.
14   Once the leak has been located, the cause must be determined before it can be properly repaired. If a gasket is replaced but the sealing flange is bent, the new gasket will not stop the leak. The bent flange must be straightened.
15   Before attempting to repair a leak, check to make sure that the following conditions are corrected or they may cause another leak. **Note:** *Some of the following conditions cannot be fixed without highly specialized tools and expertise. Such problems must be referred to a qualified transmission shop or a dealer service department.*

Gasket leaks

16   Check the pan periodically. Make sure the bolts are tight, no bolts are missing, the gasket is in good condition and the pan is flat (dents in the pan may indicate damage to the valve body inside).
17   If the pan gasket is leaking, the fluid level or the fluid pressure may be too high, the vent may be plugged, the pan bolts may be too tight, the pan sealing flange may be warped, the sealing surface of the transaxle housing may be damaged, the gasket may be damaged or the transaxle casting may be cracked or porous. If sealant instead of gasket material has been used to form a seal between the pan and the transaxle housing, it may be the wrong type of sealant.

Seal leaks

18   If a transaxle seal is leaking, the fluid level or pressure may be too high, the vent may be plugged, the seal bore may be damaged, the seal itself may be damaged or improperly installed, the surface of the shaft protruding through the seal may be damaged or a loose bearing may be causing excessive shaft movement.
19   Make sure the dipstick tube seal is in good condition and the tube is properly seated. Periodically check the area around the sensors for leakage. If transmission fluid is evident, check the seals for damage.

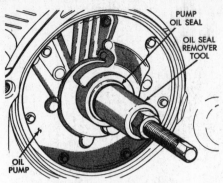

3.2 Oil pump seal removal tool

Case leaks

20   If the case itself appears to be leaking, the casting is porous and will have to be repaired or replaced.
21   Make sure the oil cooler hose fittings are tight and in good condition.

Fluid comes out vent pipe or fill tube

22   If this condition occurs the possible causes are, the transaxle is overfilled, there is coolant in the fluid, the case is porous, the dipstick is incorrect, the vent is plugged or the drain-back holes are plugged.

3   Oil seal - replacement

Oil pump seal

Refer to illustrations 3.2 and 3.3
Note: *The transaxle oil pump seal (front seal) can be replaced without removing the oil pump from the housing*

1   To replace the oil pump seal the transaxle and torque converter must be removed. Remove the transaxle from the vehicle and withdraw the torque converter from the bellhousing (see Section 9).
2   If available, use the factory seal removal tool (# C-3981). Thread the seal remover into the seal, then while holding the outer part of the tool, tighten the center bolt to pull the seal from its bore **(see illustration)**. If the factory tool is not available, use a hook-type seal removal tool or a screwdriver to carefully pry the seal out. Be extremely careful not to damage the input shaft or the seal bore.
3   If available, use the factory installation tools (# C-4193 installer and C-4171 handle) to install the oil pump seal **(see illustration)**. Apply a light coating of the appropriate transmission fluid (see Chapter 1) to the seal lip and input shaft outer diameter. Place the seal in the bore (lip side facing in), then using a hammer drive the seal in squarely until it bottoms. If the factory tools are not available, start the seal into the bore evenly by hand then using an appropriate sized section of pipe placed over the seal, drive it into place.
4   Carefully place the torque converter onto the transaxle input shaft and install the

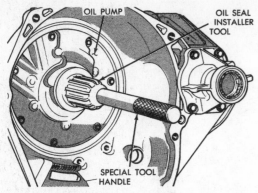

3.3 Oil pump seal installation tool

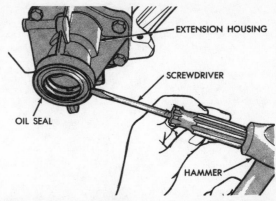

3.8 Remove the right side driveaxle oil seal using a screwdriver

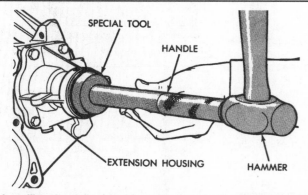

3.9 Installing the right side driveaxle oil seal using the factory tool

4.9 Transaxle shift cable end at manual shift lever (arrow "A") and attaching bracket (arrow "B")

transaxle (see Section 9).

5   Check the transaxle fluid level (see Chapter 1), test drive the vehicle and check for leaks.

Driveaxle oil seal - right side only

Refer to illustrations 3.8 and 3.9

Note: *Replacing the left side driveaxle oil seal requires the removal of the differential bearing retainer. This procedure is beyond the scope of the home mechanic and therefore not included in this manual. If the left side driveaxle seal requires replacement, take the vehicle to your local dealer service department or other qualified transmission repair shop for service.*

6   The right side driveaxle oil seal is located in the outer part of the extension housing which is bolted onto the right side of the transaxle.

7   Remove the right driveaxle (see Chapter 8).

8   Using a screwdriver, pry the driveaxle oil seal from its bore in the extension housing **(see illustration)**.

9   If available, use the factory installation tools (# L-4520 installer and C-4171 handle) to install the seal **(see illustration)**. Apply a light coating of the appropriate transmission fluid (see Chapter 1) to the seal lip and place the seal into the bore (lip side facing in), then using a hammer drive the seal in squarely

until it bottoms. If the factory tools are not available, start the seal into the bore evenly by hand then using an appropriate sized section of pipe placed over the seal, drive it into place.

10   Install the right driveaxle (see Chapter 8).

4   Shift cable - removal, installation and adjustment

Warning: *These vehicles are equipped with air bags. Always disconnect the negative battery cable and wait two minutes before working in the vicinity of the impact sensors, steering column or instrument panel to avoid the possibility of accidental deployment of the airbag(s), which could cause personal injury (see Chapter 12).*

Check

1   The easiest way to check the cable adjustment is to check the operation of the Park/Neutral/Back-up light switch. Apply the brakes and try to start the vehicle in all gear positions. The starter motor should only engage when the gearshift is in the PARK or NEUTRAL positions. If the engine starts in any other gears than PARK or NEUTRAL, adjust the shift cable as noted below and/or check operation of the Park/Neutral/Back-up light switch (see Section 6).

2   Verify that the NEUTRAL and DRIVE detents are within the limits of the gearshift gate stops. Adjust the shift cable as necessary, see below.

Removal

Refer to illustrations 4.9, 4.12 and 4.13

3   Raise the hood and place a blanket over the left (driver's) fender to protect it.

4   Disconnect the negative cable from the remote battery terminal.

5   Remove the air cleaner assembly (see Chapter 4).

6   Disconnect the positive cable from the remote battery terminal.

7   Remove the Transmission Control Module (see Section 8).

8   Remove the Power Distribution Center from its mounting and position it out of the way.

9   Using two flat blade screwdrivers, carefully pry the shift cable from the manual lever on the transaxle **(see illustration)**. To avoid damaging the cable isolator bushing, pry up with equal force on both sides of the shift cable end.

10   Remove the bolt securing the shift cable bracket to the transaxle and detach the cable from the transaxle **(see illustration 4.9)**.

11   Working inside the vehicle, remove the center console (see Chapter 11).

12   Using a flat blade screwdriver, carefully pry the shift cable from the gearshift lever pin

7B

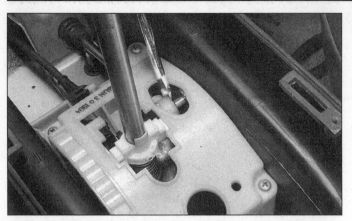

4.12 Position the gearshift lever so the shift cable end is in the access window and then pry the cable from the shift lever pin

4.13 Use pliers to remove the shift cable retaining clip

(see illustration).

13   Using pliers, remove the shift cable retaining clip **(see illustration)** and remove the cable from the bracket.

14   Raise the vehicle and support it securely on jackstands.

15   Working under the vehicle, remove the shift cable grommet from the floorpan.

16   Carefully remove the shift cable through the floorpan opening while unfolding the cable retainer clips.

17   Remove the shift cable assembly from the vehicle.

Installation

Refer to illustration 4.28

18   Route the shift cable into the engine compartment and through the opening in the floorpan.

19   Install the shift cable into the floorpan bracket at the gearshift lever assembly and secure it with the retaining clip **(see illustration 4.13)**.

20   Install the shift cable end onto the gearshift lever pin. Make sure it snaps into place.

21   Working in the engine compartment, connect the shift cable end onto the manual shift lever at the transaxle. Make sure it snaps into place.

22   Place the shift cable bracket into position and tighten the bolt securely **(see illus-**

tration 4.9).

23   Adjust the shift cable as described below.

24   The remaining installation steps are the reverse of removal.

Adjustment

25   Disconnect the negative cable from the remote battery terminal.

26   Remove the center console (see Chapter 11).

27   Place the gearshift lever in the PARK position.

28   Loosen the gearshift cable adjusting nut at the gearshift lever **(see illustration)**.

29   Working in the engine compartment, place the manual shift lever at the transaxle in the PARK position. The PARK sprag must be engaged when adjusting the cable. Rock the vehicle back and forth to ensure PARK sprag engagement. The vehicle should not be able to move.

30   Tighten the shift cable adjusting nut securely.

31   Check the shift lever for proper operation. It should operate smoothly without binding. Perform the cable check as noted above (see Steps 1 and 2). Readjust if necessary.

32   Install the center console (see Chapter 11).

33   Attach the negative cable to the remote battery terminal.

5   Gearshift assembly - replacement

Refer to illustration 5.6

Warning: *These vehicles are equipped with air bags. Always disconnect the negative battery cable and wait two minutes before working in the vicinity of the impact sensors, steering column or instrument panel to avoid the possibility of accidental deployment of the airbag(s), which could cause personal injury (see Chapter 12).*

1   Disconnect the negative cable from the remote battery terminal.

2   Remove the center console (see Chapter 11).

3   Disconnect the shift cable from the gearshift lever pin and floorpan bracket (see Section 4).

4   Disconnect the shifter/ignition interlock cable from the gearshift assembly (see Section 7).

5   On models equipped with Autostick, detach the electrical connector from the base of the gearshift assembly.

6   Remove the 4 attaching nuts and remove the gearshift assembly **(see illustration)**.

7   Installation is the reverse of removal, except adjust the shift cable (see Section 4) prior to installing the center console.

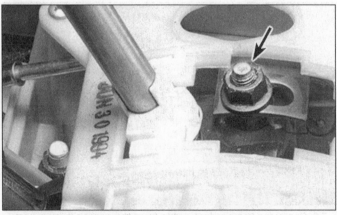

4.28 Shift cable adjusting nut (arrow)

5.6 Gearshift assembly mounting nuts (arrows)

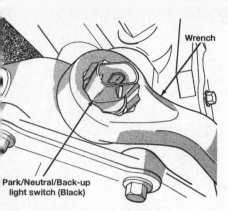

6.10 Removing the Park/Neutral/Back-up light switch

6   Park/Neutral/Back-up light switch - check and replacement

Check

1   The Park/Neutral/Back-up light switch has a black colored insulator and is located at the lower left hand side of the transaxle near the oil pan. The switch inhibits starter motor engagement unless the gearshift lever is in the PARK or NEUTRAL position and completes the back-up light circuit when the gearshift lever is placed in REVERSE.

2   Prior to checking the switch, first make sure the shift cable is adjusted properly (see Section 4).

3   Raise the vehicle and support it securely on jackstands. Extract the 2 push-in fasteners and remove the transaxle splash shield.

4   Disconnect the electrical connector from the Park/Neutral/Back-up light switch.

5   Using an ohmmeter, check for continuity between the center terminal of the switch and the switch body. Continuity should only be present with the gearshift lever in PARK and NEUTRAL. If continuity is detected with the gearshift lever in any other position, replace the switch.

6   Next, check for continuity between the two outer terminals. Continuity should only exist with the gearshift lever in the Reverse

position. Check the for continuity between each of the outer terminals and the switch body. No continuity should be present. Replace the switch if it fails any of these checks.

7   Install the transaxle splash shield and secure it with the 2 push-in fasteners. Lower the vehicle.

Replacement

Refer to illustration 6.10

8   Raise the vehicle and support it securely on jackstands. Extract the 2 push-in fasteners and remove the transaxle splash shield.

9   Working under the vehicle, disconnect the electrical connector from the switch. Place a drain container under the transaxle as some fluid loss will occur.

10   Unscrew the switch from the transaxle using a box-end wrench **(see illustration)**. Discard the switch seal.

11   Look into the switch opening in the transaxle. Have an assistant shift the transaxle from PARK to NEUTRAL. Check that the internal operating fingers are centered in the switch opening.

12   Install the new switch and seal into the transaxle and tighten the switch to the torque listed in this Chapter's Specification Section.

13   Recheck the switch operation (see Steps 1 through 6).

14   Attach the switch electrical connector, install the transaxle splash shield and lower the vehicle.

15   Check the transaxle fluid level and add more, if necessary (see Chapter 1).

7   Shifter/ignition interlock system - description, check and cable replacement

Warning: *These vehicles are equipped with air bags. Always disconnect the negative battery cable and wait two minutes before working in the vicinity of the impact sensors, steering column or instrument panel to avoid the possibility of accidental deployment of the airbag(s), which could cause personal injury (see Chapter 12).*

Description

1   The shift/ignition interlock system connects the automatic transaxle gearshift lever and the ignition lock system. With the ignition switch in the LOCK or ACCESSORY position, the interlock system holds the transmission shift lever in PARK. When the key is in the OFF or RUN position, the shift lever is unlocked and can be moved to any position. And if the shift lever is not in the PARK position, the system prevents the operator from turning the ignition switch to the LOCK or ACCESSORY position.

Check

Refer to illustrations 7.7, 7.8, 7.10a and 7.10b

2   Place the gearshift lever in the PARK position. The ignition switch should rotate freely from the OFF to the LOCK position. Next, move the gearshift lever to the DRIVE position. The ignition switch should not be able to rotate from the OFF to the LOCK position.

3   With the ignition switch in the OFF or RUN position, you should be able to move the gearshift lever out of the PARK position. With the ignition switch in the LOCK or ACCESSORY position, you should not be able to move the gearshift lever from the PARK position.

4   If you are able to move the shift lever in any way other than previously described, the interlock system requires service.

Cable replacement

5   Disconnect the negative cable from the remote battery terminal.

6   Remove the center console (see Chapter 11).

7   Detach the interlock cable housing from the gearshift assembly base **(see illustration)**.

8   Remove the interlock cable end from the gearshift lever cam **(see illustration)**.

9   Remove the steering column covers (see Chapter 11).

10   At the ignition key lock cylinder, squeeze the interlock cable retaining clip then pull the cable from the ignition lock

7B

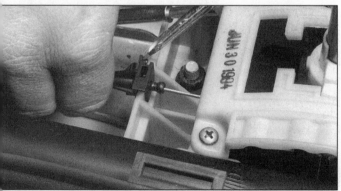

7.7 Use a screwdriver to disengage the shifter/interlock cable housing retainer, then slide the cable from the groove in the gearshift assembly base

7.8 Removing the interlock cable from the gearshift lever cam

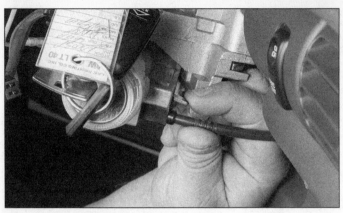

7.10a Depress the interlock cable retaining clip . . .

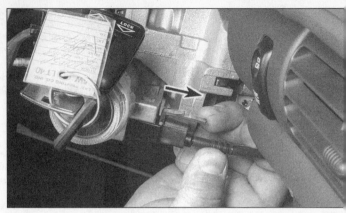

7.10b . . . then withdraw it from the ignition lock cylinder housing

cylinder housing **(see illustrations)**.

11   Detach the interlock cable from the routing clip and remove it from the vehicle.

12   To install the interlock cable, turn the ignition switch to the RUN position and insert the cable end into the ignition lock cylinder and make sure it snaps into place.

13   Then, route it down the steering column, secure it with the retaining clip and continue down to the gearshift assembly.

14   Attach the interlock cable to the gearshift lever cam **(see illustration 7.8)**.

15   Next, push the cable housing into the groove in the gearshift assembly base. The cable housing is fully seated when it snaps into place **(see illustration 7.7)**.

16   Adjust the interlock cable (see below).

17   Install the steering column covers and the center console (see Chapter 11).

Adjustment

Refer to illustration 7.21

18   Disconnect the negative cable from the remote battery terminal.

19   Remove the center console (see Chapter 11).

20   Remove the ignition key from the lock cylinder with the switch in the Lock position. Make sure the gearshift lever is in the PARK position.

21   When the adjustment nut on the interlock lever is loosened, the cable automatically indexes itself to the correct position. Loosen the adjustment nut and allow the cable to index itself **(see illustration)**. After the cable has found its position, tighten the adjusting nut.

22   With the ignition in the OFF (locked) position, the gearshift lever should be locked in the PARK position. If the gearshift lever can be moved to select another gear position, inspect the cable for binding, proper installation and repeat the adjustment procedure.

23   Next, place the ignition key in the RUN position (engine OFF). Move the gearshift lever to the REVERSE position. You should be unable to remove the key from the ignition lock cylinder. If the key can be removed, inspect the cable for binding, proper installation and repeat the adjustment procedure.

24   After adjustment, install the center con-

sole (see Chapter 11) and attach the negative cable to the remote battery terminal.

---

8   Transmission Control Module (TCM) - removal and installation

---

Note: *Do not interchange TCM's from different year vehicles. After replacing a TCM take the vehicle to your local dealer service department or other qualified transmission shop to have the TCM calibrated for your vehicle.*

Caution: *The TCM is an Electro-Static Discharge (ESD) sensitive electronic device, meaning a static electricity discharge from your body could possibly damage electrical components. Make sure to properly ground yourself and the TCM before handling it. Avoid touching the electrical terminals of the TCM unless absolutely necessary.*

Removal

Refer to illustration 8.3

1   Disconnect the negative cable from the remote battery terminal.

2   On 2.4L engines, remove the air cleaner assembly (see Chapter 4).

3   Detach the electrical connector from the TCM **(see illustration)**.

7.21 Loosening the interlock cable adjusting nut (arrow)

4   Remove the 3 mounting screws and withdraw the TCM from the vehicle.

Installation

5   Installation is the reverse of removal.

---

9   Automatic transaxle - removal and installation

Removal

Refer to illustrations 9.18, 9.19, 9.20, 9.21, 9.24 and 9.34

1   Open the hood and place protective covers on the front fenders and cowl. Special fender covers are available, but an old bedspread or blankets will also work.

2   Disconnect the negative cable from the remote battery terminal.

3   Remove the air cleaner assembly (see Chapter 4).

4   Remove the Transmission Control Module (see Section 8).

5   Remove the shift cable and bracket from the transaxle (see Section 4).

6   Disconnect and plug the transaxle oil cooler lines and position them out of the way.

7   Loosen the driveaxle hub nuts (see Chapter 8) and front wheel lug nuts. Raise the vehicle and place it securely on jackstands.

8.3 Transmission Control Module (TCM) (arrow)

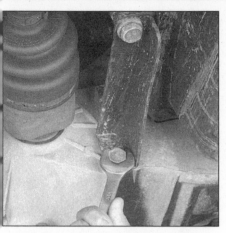

9.18 Removing a lateral strut bracket

9.19 Removing the bellhousing lower cover

9.20 Before removing the driveplate-to-torque converter bolts, find a hole in the drive plate and match-mark the torque converter to the driveplate

9.21 Removing the driveplate-to-torque converter bolts

Remove both front wheels.
8 Drain the transaxle fluid (see Chapter 1).
9 Remove the driveaxles (see Chapter 8).
10 Remove the splash shield/battery cover from the left front wheel well (see Chapter 5 if necessary).
11 Remove the accessory drivebelt splash shield from the right front wheel well (see Chapter 1 if necessary).
12 Remove the transaxle dipstick tube. To prevent foreign debris from entering the transaxle, cover the dipstick tube hole in the transaxle with duct tape or equivalent.
13 On 2.5L engines, remove the exhaust manifold cross-over pipe (see Chapter 2B if necessary).
14 Remove the engine oil filter (see Chapter 1 if necessary).
15 Remove the starter motor (see Chapter 5).
16 Disconnect the exhaust system from the rear exhaust manifold and position it out of the way (see Chapter 4). **Note:** *It may be necessary to remove, or partially remove, the exhaust system to accomplish this.*
17 On 1997 and 1998 models equipped with 2.4L engines, remove the oil pan-to-transaxle structural collar (see Chapter 2A, Section 13).
18 Remove the lateral strut brackets connecting the engine to transaxle **(see illustration)**.
19 Remove the bellhousing lower cover **(see illustration)**.
20 If the torque converter is to be reinstalled, match-mark it to the driveplate **(see illustration)**.
21 Remove the four torque converter-to-driveplate bolts **(see illustration)**. To gain access to each bolt, rotate the engine clockwise (ONLY) as viewed from the drivebelt end of the engine using the crankshaft damper/pulley bolt. Use a screwdriver placed in the ring gear of the driveplate to keep the crankshaft from turning during removal of the bolts.
22 After removing the torque converter-to-driveplate bolts, push the torque converter into the transaxle bellhousing as far as possible.

23 On 2.5L engines, remove the crankshaft position sensor (see Chapter 6).
24 Clearly label and detach the electrical connectors from the transaxle and position them out of the way **(see illustration)**.
25 Match-mark the front suspension cross-member to the body and frame so it can be reinstalled in the same position to maintain proper wheel alignment (see Chapter 10, Section 17).
26 Remove the front stabilizer-to-frame clamps.
27 Support the engine from above with a hoist, or place a floor jack under the oil pan. Place a wood block on the jack head to spread the load on the oil pan.
28 Loosen (ONLY) the right side steering gear bolts and front suspension crossmember bolts (see Chapter 10 if necessary).
29 Remove the left side steering gear and front suspension crossmember bolts (see Chapter 10 if necessary).
30 Remove the left engine mounting bracket from the transaxle (see the appropriate Part of Chapter 2).
31 Remove the front engine mounting bracket and strut (see the appropriate Part of Chapter 2).
32 Remove the rear engine mounting bracket (see the appropriate Part of Chapter 2).
33 Remove the engine support module

(1995 to 1997 models) or front and rear lower engine mounts (1998 models) as applicable (see the appropriate Part of Chapter 2). **Note:** *The engine support module is attached to the lower radiator support. When removing the engine support module, the radiator and air conditioning condenser (if equipped) must be supported.*
34 Support the transaxle with a transmis-

7B

9.24 41TE transaxle electrical connections

1 Solenoid pack connector
2 Input speed sensor
3 Transmission range sensor (white)
4 Park/Neutral/Back-up light switch (black)
5 Output speed sensor

sion jack, if available, or use a floor jack **(see illustration)**. Secure the transaxle to the jack using straps or chains so it doesn't fall off during removal.

35   Remove the transaxle bellhousing-to-engine bolts. Make sure all bellhousing-to-engine bolts are removed.

36   Make a final check that all wires, hoses and brackets have been disconnected from the transaxle, then with the engine properly supported, move the front suspension crossmember rearward and carefully lower the transaxle from the vehicle.

37   Make sure you keep the transaxle level as you maneuver it or the torque converter may fall out. **Note:** *Reinstalling the bellhousing lower cover after the transaxle clears the driveplate will help hold the torque converter in place.*

38   Remove the torque converter from the transaxle.

39   With the transaxle removed, now it a good time to inspect the engine rear main oil seal for leakage and replace if necessary (see the appropriate Part of Chapter 2). Also inspect the transaxle oil pump seal and replace if necessary (see Section 3).

Installation

40   Install the torque converter onto the transaxle input shaft. Handle it carefully to avoid damaging the transaxle input shaft seal. Make sure the torque converter hub splines are properly engaged with the splines on the transaxle input shaft. **Note:** *If reinstalling the old torque converter, position it so that match-mark applied in* Step 20 *will correspond with the mark on the driveplate.*

41   With the transaxle secured to the jack, raise it into position and carefully slide it forward until the transaxle bellhousing seats against the engine. Do not use excessive force to install the transaxle - if it doesn't slide into place easily, readjust the angle of the transaxle and try again. Make sure you keep the transaxle level as you maneuver it or the torque converter may fall out. Do not force it or use the bellhousing bolts to pull it together. Make sure the dowel pins on the engine are aligned with their respective holes in the transaxle. If you are experiencing difficulty, solicit the aid of an assistant.

42   Install the bellhousing-to-engine bolts with brackets and clamps where required and tighten them to the torque listed in this Chapter's Specification Section.

43   Install the engine support module (1995 to 1997 models) or front and rear lower engine mounts (1998 models) as applicable (see the appropriate Part of Chapter 2).

44   Install the left side steering gear and front suspension crossmember attaching bolts. Align the front suspension crossmember with the match-marks applied in Step 25 (see Chapter 10 if necessary). Tighten the steering gear and crossmember bolts to their respective torque values given in the Specifi-

cation Section of Chapter 10.

45   Position the front stabilizer bar against the front suspension crossmember and secure it with the retaining clamps. Tighten the stabilizer bar clamp bolts to the torque given in the Specification Section of Chapter 10.

46   Install the rear engine mounting bracket to the transaxle and secure it to the engine support module (1995 to 1997 models) or rear lower engine mount (1998 models) as applicable (see the appropriate Part of Chapter 2). Tighten the bracket-to-engine bolts (ONLY) to the torque listed in the Specification Section in the appropriate Part of Chapter 2. Leave the through-bolt loose for now.

47   Install the front engine mounting bracket and strut (see the appropriate Part of Chapter 2). **Note:** *On 1998 models equipped with 2.4L engines, the front engine mounting bracket and strut are tightened in sequence with the oil pan-to-transaxle structural collar, refer to Chapter 2A, Section 13.* Secure the bracket to the engine support module (1995 to 1997 models) or front lower engine mount (1998 models) as applicable (see the appropriate Part of Chapter 2). Tighten the mounting bracket and strut-to-engine/transaxle bolts (ONLY) to the torque listed in the Specification Section in the appropriate Part of Chapter 2. Leave the through-bolt loose for now.

48   Install the left engine mounting bracket onto the transaxle and secure it to the support assembly on the frame rail (see the appropriate Part of Chapter 2). Tighten the bolts to the torque listed in the Specification Section in the appropriate Part of Chapter 2.

49   Tighten the front and rear engine mount through-bolts to the torque listed in the Specification Section in the appropriate Part of Chapter 2.

50   Remove the engine and transaxle support jacks.

51   If you're reinstalling the old torque converter, align the driveplate-to-torque converter match-marks applied in Step 20. Install the four driveplate-to-torque converter bolts. To gain access to each bolt hole, rotate the engine clockwise (ONLY) as viewed from the drivebelt end of the engine using the crankshaft damper/pulley bolt. Tighten the driveplate-to-torque converter bolts to the torque listed in this Chapter's Specification Section. Use a screwdriver placed in the ring gear of the driveplate to keep the crankshaft from turning during installation of the bolts.

52   Install the bellhousing lower cover. Tighten the bolts to the torque listed in this Chapter's Specification Section.

53   Install the lateral strut brackets **(see illustration 9.18)**. Tighten the bolts to the torque listed in this Chapter's Specification Section.

54   On 1997 and 1998 models equipped with 2.4L engines, install the oil pan-to-transaxle structural collar. Tighten the bolts to the torque listed in the Specification Sec-

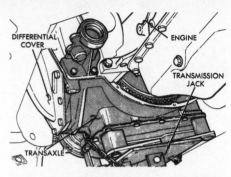

9.34 Using a transmission jack to remove the transaxle

tion of Chapter 2A.

55   Attach the electrical connectors to the transaxle **(see illustration 9.24)**.

56   On 2.5L engines, install the crankshaft position sensor, attach the electrical connector and tighten the retaining bolt to the torque given in the Specification Section of Chapter 6.

57   On 2.5L engines, install the exhaust manifold cross-over pipe. Tighten the nuts to the torque given in the Specification Section of Chapter 2B.

58   Attach the exhaust system to the exhaust manifold (see Chapter 4). Tighten the nuts to the torque given in the Specification Section of Chapter 4.

59   Install the transaxle dipstick tube.

60   Install the transaxle splash shield and secure it with the 2 push-in fasteners.

61   Install the splash shield/battery cover into the left front wheel well (see Chapter 5 if necessary).

62   Install the starter motor (see Chapter 5). Tighten the bolts to the torque listed in the Specification Section of Chapter 5.

63   Install the engine oil filter (see Chapter 1).

64   Install the driveaxles, hub nuts and front wheels (see Chapter 8). Tighten all fasteners to the torque values given in the Specification Section of Chapter 8.

65   Install the shift cable and mounting bracket onto the transaxle (see Section 4).

66   Install the transaxle oil cooler lines onto the fittings and tighten the clamps securely.

67   Install the Transmission Control Module (see Section 8).

68   Attach the negative cable to the remote battery terminal.

69   Install the air cleaner assembly (see Chapter 4).

70   Fill the transaxle with the appropriate fluid (see Chapter 1).

71   Check the shift cable operation and adjust if necessary (see Section 4).

72   Road test the vehicle and check for proper transaxle operation and fluid leaks. Shutoff the engine and recheck the transaxle fluid level.

Chapter 8
Clutch and driveaxles

Contents

Specifications

Torque specifications

	Ft-lbs
Driveplate-to-modular clutch assembly bolts	55
Driveplate-to-crankshaft bolts	See Chapter 2
Driveaxle/hub nut	180
Wheel lug nuts	110

1 General information

The information in this Chapter deals with the components from the rear of the engine to the front wheels, except for the transaxle, which is covered with in Chapter 7. For the purposes of this Chapter, these components are grouped into two categories: Clutch and driveaxles. Separate Sections within this Chapter offer general descriptions and checking procedures for both groups.

Since nearly all the procedures covered in this Chapter involve working under the vehicle, make sure it's securely supported on sturdy jackstands or a hoist where the vehicle can be easily raised and lowered.

2 Clutch - description and check

1   All vehicles with a manual transaxle use a single dry plate, diaphragm spring type modular clutch assembly. The modular clutch assembly works like a traditional clutch except that it has no serviceable parts. The flywheel, clutch friction disc and pressure plate are all in one unit which mounts to the driveplate at the rear of the engine. When a clutch failure occurs, the modular clutch assembly must be replaced with a new unit.

2   The clutch friction disc is compressed between two plates inside the modular clutch assembly by an internal one-piece diaphragm spring with multiple release fingers.

3   The clutch release system is cable-actuated. The system consists of the clutch pedal, the cable, a clutch release lever and the clutch release (or throw-out) bearing. The clutch cable on these models is self-adjusting and requires no routine maintenance or adjustment.

4   When pressure is applied to the clutch pedal to release the clutch, the cable moves the release lever, which pivots, moving the release bearing. The bearing pushes against the fingers of the diaphragm spring of the modular clutch assembly, which in turn allows the clutch friction disc to spin independently of the engine.

5   Here are some preliminary checks to help diagnose a clutch system failure:

a) *To check "clutch spin down time," run the engine at normal idle speed with the transaxle in Neutral (clutch pedal up - engaged). Disengage the clutch (pedal down), wait several seconds and shift the transaxle into Reverse. No grinding noise should be heard. A grinding noise would most likely indicate a problem with the clutch release system.*

b) *To check for complete clutch release, run the engine (with the parking brake applied to prevent movement) and hold the clutch pedal approximately 1/2-inch from the floor. Shift the transaxle between 1st gear and Reverse several times. If the shift is not smooth, clutch component failure is indicated.*

c) *Visually inspect the clutch pedal bushings at the top of the clutch pedal to make sure there is no sticking or excessive wear.*

6   For more information on clutch related problems see the *Troubleshooting* section at the beginning of this manual.

8

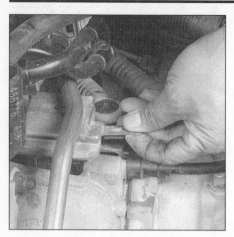

3.3 Remove the clutch cable inspection cover

3.4 Grab onto the clutch cable housing, pull it back and pass the clutch cable through the slot in the bellhousing, then disconnect it from the release lever

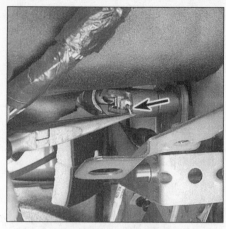

3.5a Working inside the vehicle, slightly depress the clutch pedal for access to the clutch cable, then remove the clip (arrow) securing the up-stop/spacer to the clutch pedal pivot pin . . .

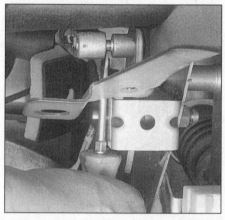

3.5b . . . next, wedge a narrow flat-blade screwdriver between the up-stop/spacer retainer and the clutch pedal pivot pin, then slide the up-stop/spacer off the pivot pin . . .

3   Clutch cable - removal and installation

Removal

Refer to illustrations 3.3, 3.4, 3.5a, 3.5b, 3.5c and 3.6

1   Raise the hood and place a blanket over the left (driver's) fender to protect it.
2   Remove the air cleaner assembly (see Chapter 4).
3   Remove the clutch cable inspection cover from the bellhousing **(see illustration)**.
4   Pull back on the clutch cable housing and disengage it from the slot in the bellhousing, then disconnect it from the release lever **(see illustration)**.
5   Working inside the vehicle, slightly depress the clutch pedal to allow access to the clutch cable up-stop/spacer. Remove the retaining clip securing the up-stop/spacer to the clutch pedal pivot pin **(see illustration)**. Wedge a narrow flat-blade screwdriver between the clutch pedal pivot pin and the up-stop/spacer retaining tab, then remove the up-stop/spacer from the pivot pin **(see illustration)**. Remove the up-stop/spacer from the clutch cable end **(see illustration)**.

6   **Caution:** *Do not pull on the clutch cable while removing it from the dash panel as the cable self-adjuster may be damaged.* Working inside the engine compartment, hold onto the grommet and, using a slight twisting motion, carefully remove the clutch cable grommet from the firewall and clutch bracket **(see illustration)**. If necessary, carefully use a screwdriver to free the grommet from the firewall opening. Remove the clutch cable assembly from the vehicle.

Installation

7   To help ease installation, apply a little petroleum jelly to the clutch cable grommet.
8   Working inside the engine compartment, insert the self-adjusting end of the clutch cable through the firewall and into the clutch bracket using a slight twisting motion. Make sure the cable grommet is fully seated in the firewall.
9   Working inside the vehicle, seat the cylindrical part of the grommet into the firewall opening and clutch bracket. Make sure the self-adjuster is firmly seated against the clutch bracket to ensure the adjuster will function properly.

10   Install the up-stop/spacer onto the clutch cable end, then install the up-stop/spacer onto the clutch pedal pivot pin.

3.5c . . . and remove the up-stop/spacer from the clutch cable end

3.6 Working in the engine compartment, carefully remove the clutch cable and grommet from the firewall

NORMAL FINGER WEAR

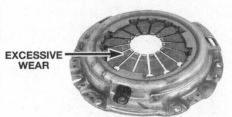
EXCESSIVE WEAR

EXCESSIVE FINGER WEAR

BROKEN OR BENT FINGERS

4.7 Typical diaphragm spring release finger defects

Install the retaining clip and make sure it is properly seated.

11 Working inside the engine compartment, using slight pressure, pull the clutch cable end to draw the cable taut. Push the cable housing toward the firewall with less than 25 lbs of pressure. The cable housing should move about 1 to 2 inches - this indicates proper adjuster operation. If the cable does not adjust (move), make sure the adjuster mechanism is properly seated in the bracket.

12 Connect the cable to the release lever making sure the cupped washer seats securely on the release lever tangs.

13 Pull back on the clutch cable housing and insert it into the bellhousing **(see illustration 3.4)**.

14 Install the clutch cable inspection cover onto the bellhousing **(see illustration 3.3)**.

4 Modular clutch assembly - removal, inspection and installation

Warning: *Dust produced by clutch wear and deposited on clutch components may contain asbestos, which is hazardous to your health. DO NOT blow it out with compressed air and DO NOT inhale it. DO NOT use gasoline or other petroleum-based solvents to remove the dust. Brake system cleaner should be used to flush the dust into a drain pan. After the clutch components are wiped clean with a rag, dispose of the contaminated rags and cleaner in a labeled, covered container.*

Removal

1 Access to the clutch components is normally accomplished by removing the transaxle, leaving the engine in the vehicle. If the engine is being removed for major overhaul, then the opportunity should always be taken to check the clutch for wear and replace worn components as necessary. However, the relatively low cost of the clutch components compared to the time and labor involved in gaining access to them warrants

their replacement any time the engine or transaxle is removed, unless they are new or in near-perfect condition. The following procedure assumes that the engine will remain in the vehicle.

2 Remove the transaxle from the vehicle (see Chapter 7, Part A). **Note:** *The modular clutch assembly remains on the transaxle input shaft during the removal process.*

3 Remove the modular clutch assembly from the transaxle. Handle it carefully to avoid contaminating the friction surfaces.

4 To remove the clutch release bearing and lever refer to Section 5.

Inspection

Refer to illustration 4.7

5 While they're accessible, inspect the engine rear main oil seal and transaxle input shaft seal for evidence of leakage. Replace seals if necessary.

6 Inspect the modular clutch for oil or grease contamination. Replace if contamination is present.

7 Inspect the clutch diaphragm spring release fingers for excessive wear or damage **(see illustration)**. Replace the modular clutch assembly if excessive wear or damage is observed.

Installation

8 If removed, install the clutch release bearing and lever (see Section 5).

9 Install the new modular clutch assembly onto the transaxle input shaft.

10 Install the transaxle (see Chapter 7, Part A). **Note:** *Be sure to install new clutch assembly-to-driveplate bolts.* Tighten the clutch assembly-to-driveplate bolts in a criss-cross pattern to the torque listed in this Chapter's Specifications.

5 Clutch release bearing and lever - removal, inspection and installation

Warning: *Dust produced by clutch wear and deposited on clutch components may contain asbestos, which is hazardous to your*

health. DO NOT blow it out with compressed air and DO NOT inhale it. DO NOT use gasoline or petroleum-based solvents to remove the dust. Brake system cleaner should be used to flush it into a drain pan. After the clutch components are wiped clean with a rag, dispose of the contaminated rags and cleaner in a labeled, covered container.*

Removal

Refer to illustration 5.4

1 Disconnect the negative battery cable from the ground stud on the left shock tower.

2 Remove the modular clutch assembly (see Section 4). Handle it carefully to avoid contaminating the friction surfaces.

3 Working on the transaxle, position the release lever and bearing so the lever is at a right angle to the input shaft. Grasp the release lever on each side of the pivot ball socket and pull; the release lever will pop off the pivot stud. **Caution:** *Do not use a screwdriver or pry bar to disengage the lever as the spring clips on the underside of the release lever will be damaged.*

4 Slide the release bearing and lever off the bearing sleeve **(see illustration)**.

5 Separate the fork from the bearing, being careful not to damage the retention tabs on the bearing.

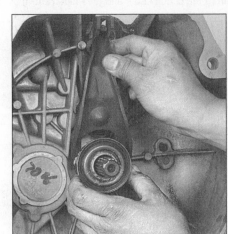

5.4 Removing the release bearing and lever

8

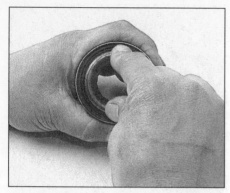

5.6 Hold the release bearing outer race and rotate the inner race while applying pressure. It should turn smoothly and quietly - if it feels rough or makes noise, replace it

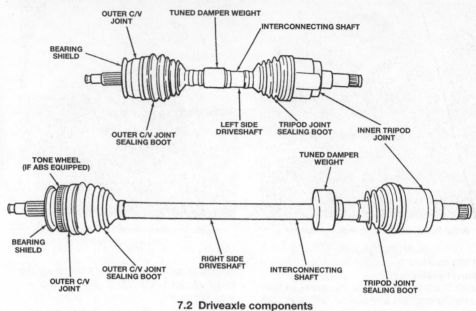

7.2 Driveaxle components

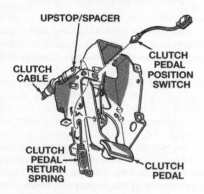

6.3 Clutch pedal details

Inspection

Refer to illustration 5.6

6   Hold the bearing by the outer race and rotate the inner race while applying pressure **(see illustration)**. If the bearing doesn't turn smoothly or if it's noisy, replace the bearing assembly with a new one. Wipe the bearing with a clean rag and inspect it for damage, wear and cracks. Don't immerse the bearing in solvent - it's sealed for life and to do so would ruin it. **Note:** *Because of the difficulty involved in removing the transaxle for release bearing replacement, we recommend routinely replacing the release bearing when the modular clutch assembly is replaced.*

7   Check the release lever fork for cracks or distortion. Replace if necessary.

8   Inspect the pivot ball spring clips on the back side of the lever. If they're cracked or broken, replace the lever.

9   Clean any dirt off the pivot ball and pocket in the release fork. Examine them for damage or excessive wear. Replace if necessary.

Installation

10   Lightly lubricate the release lever ends, the inner diameter of the release bearing and the input shaft with hi-temperature grease. **Caution:** *The pivot stud ball is Teflon coated - don't apply any lubrication to it or it's pocket*

in the release fork as this would break down the Teflon coating.

11   Install the release lever onto the bearing. **Note:** *The small pegs on the bearing must go over the fork arms.*

12   Install the release bearing and lever onto the input shaft sleeve. Snap the lever into place on the pivot ball. Make sure it is properly seated.

13   Install the modular clutch assembly (see Section 4).

6   Clutch start switch - check and replacement

Check

Refer to illustration 6.3

1   Verify that the engine will NOT start when the clutch pedal is released (up).

2   Verify that the engine WILL start when the clutch pedal is depressed (down).

3   If the engine won't start with the pedal depressed, or starts with the pedal released, unplug the electrical connector to the switch (located near the top of the clutch pedal) **(see illustration)** and check continuity between the connector terminals with the clutch pedal depressed.

4   If there's continuity between the terminals with the pedal depressed, the switch is okay; if there's no continuity between the terminals with the pedal depressed, replace the switch. If there's continuity between the terminals when the clutch pedal is released, replace the switch.

Replacement

5   The non-adjustable switch is mounted vertically at the upper end of the clutch pedal lever.

6   Unplug the switch electrical connector from the wiring harness.

7   Depress the wing tabs on the switch and push the switch out of the mounting bracket.

8   Remove the switch and slide the wires out of the slot in the bracket.

9   Installation is the reverse of removal.

7   Driveaxles - general information and inspection

Refer to illustration 7.2

1   Power is transmitted from the transaxle to the wheels through a pair of driveaxles. The inner end of each driveaxle is splined to the differential side gears. The driveaxles must be removed to replace the driveaxle oil seals located in the transaxle (see Chapter 7A). The outer ends of the driveaxles are splined to the front wheel hubs and secured by a large nut.

2   Each driveaxle assembly consists of an inner and outer constant velocity (CV) joint connected together by an axle shaft **(see illustration)**. The inner ends of the driveaxles are equipped with a tripod type CV joint on all models. This design is capable of both angular and axial motion. In other words, the inner CV joints are free to slide in-and-out according to the travel limits of the front suspension. The inner CV joint (tripod joint) can be disassembled and cleaned in the event of a sealing boot failure, but if any parts are damaged, the entire driveaxle assembly must be replaced as a unit (see Section 8).

3   The outer CV joint on all models, is a ball-and-cage design (Rzeppa joint), and is capable of angular - but not axial - movement. The outer CV joint is not serviceable. The only serviceable part on the outer CV joint is the hub/bearing shield (all models) and the sealing boot (1998 models only). In the event of bearing or sealing boot failure on

8.2a Remove the hub nut cotter pin . . .

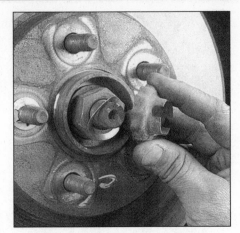

8.2b . . . then remove the lock and spring washer

8.3 Loosen the driveaxle/hub nut - DO NOT remove the nut - it holds the wheel hub/bearing assembly together!

1995 to 1997 models, the entire driveaxle must be replaced.

4   The boots should be inspected periodically for damage and leaking lubricant (see Chapter 1). Torn CV joint boots should be replaced immediately or the CV joints can become damaged due to lack of lubrication or the ingress of water. Boot replacement requires removal of the driveaxle (see Section 8). **Note:** *Some auto parts stores carry "split" type replacement boots, which can be installed without removing the driveaxle from the vehicle. This is a convenient alternative; however, the driveaxle should be removed and the CV joint disassembled and cleaned to ensure the joint is free from contaminants such as moisture and dirt which will accelerate CV joint wear.* The most common symptom of worn or damaged CV joints, besides lubricant leaks, is a clicking noise in turns, a clunk when accelerating after coasting and vibration at highway speeds. To check for wear in the CV joints and driveaxle shafts, grasp each axle (one at a time) and rotate it in both directions while holding the CV joint housings, feeling for play indicating worn

splines or sloppy CV joints. Also check the axleshafts for cracks, dents and distortion.

8   Driveaxle - removal and installation

Removal

Refer to illustrations 8.2a, 8.2b, 8.3, 8.8a, 8.8b, 8.8c, 8.10 and 8.11

1   Disconnect the negative cable from the remote battery terminal.
2   Remove the hub nut cotter pin, lock and spring washer **(see illustrations)**. Discard the old cotter pin - you'll need a new one for reassembly.
3   Set the parking brake, place the transmission in gear (or Park as applicable) and have an assistant apply the brakes firmly, then loosen the driveaxle/hub nut with a large socket and breaker bar **(see illustration)**. DO NOT remove the nut at this time - only loosen it - the driveaxle shaft/nut serves to maintain the required load on the hub/wheel bearings.

4   Loosen the front wheel lug nuts, raise the vehicle and support it securely on jackstands. Remove the wheel and driveaxle/hub nut.
5   Remove the front brake caliper and hang it from the upper control arm with a piece of wire (see Chapter 9). **Note:** *It is not necessary to remove the brake pads for this procedure.*
6   It's not absolutely necessary that you drain the transaxle lubricant prior to removing a driveaxle, but if the mileage on the odometer indicates that the transaxle is nearing the lubricant-change interval prescribed in Chapter 1 or the vehicle is at an angle that will allow the fluid to run out of the driveaxle hole - drain the transaxle lubricant (see Chapter 1).
7   Detach the lower control arm from the steering knuckle at the lower balljoint (see Chapter 10).
8   Angle the steering knuckle as required and remove the driveaxle from the hub **(see illustration)**. Suspend the outer end of the driveaxle with a piece of wire. DO NOT let it

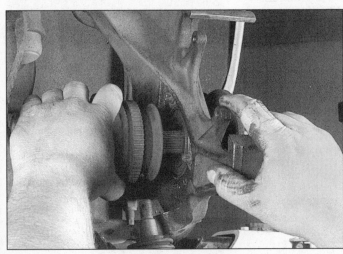

8.8a Angle the steering knuckle as required and pull the driveaxle from the wheel hub

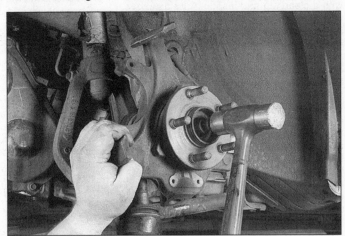

8.8b If the driveaxle is stuck in the wheel hub, apply some penetrating oil to the hub splines then install the hub nut onto the driveaxle a few turns (to protect the threads) and strike the end of the driveaxle with a soft-faced hammer to break it loose - DO NOT attempt to drive the driveaxle out of the hub using a hammer!

8

8.8c If the penetrating oil and hammer technique prove unsuccessful, use a two-jaw puller to push the driveaxle from the wheel hub

8.10 Insert a prybar between the tripod joint housing and the transaxle. Pry on the driveaxle until you feel the retaining circlip on the driveaxle disengage from the differential side gear

hang from the inner CV joint! If the driveaxle is stuck in the wheel hub, apply some penetrating oil to the hub splines, install the hub nut on a few turns and strike the end of the driveaxle with a soft-faced hammer to break it loose **(see illustration)**. DO NOT attempt to drive the driveaxle stub out of the wheel hub using a hammer! In some cases it may be necessary to push the driveaxle stub out of the hub using a two-jaw puller **(see illustration)**.

9   Before you remove the driveaxle from the transaxle, check for lubricant leakage in the area around the driveaxle oil seal. If there's evidence of a leak, you'll want to replace the seal after removing the driveaxle (see Chapter 7, Part A).

10   To remove the driveaxle from the transaxle, position a prybar against the inner tripod joint housing and carefully pry it out until the retaining snap-ring on the driveaxle is disengaged from the transaxle side gear **(see illustration)**.

11   While supporting the driveaxle, pull straight out on the tripod joint housing to

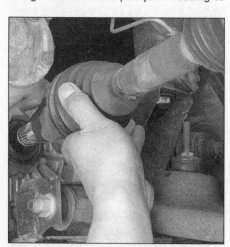

8.11 To avoid damaging the transaxle oil seal, support the ends of the driveaxle and pull it straight out

avoid damaging the driveaxle seal located in the transaxle **(see illustration)**. **Caution:** *Pull on the tripod housing only! DO NOT pull on the axleshaft - the only thing keeping the axleshaft and tripod housing together is the sealing boot - pulling on the axleshaft might separate the tripod joint and result in component damage.* Remove the driveaxle assembly from the vehicle.

12   Should it become necessary to move the vehicle while the driveaxle is removed, before installing the wheel, place a large bolt (approximately the same size as the driveaxle splined shaft) with two large washers (one on each side of the hub) through the hub and tighten the nut to 180 ft-lbs. This will prevent the hub/wheel bearing from separating when the vehicle weight is placed on the wheel hub/bearing assembly.

13   If you noted evidence of a leaking driveaxle seal, refer to Chapter 7A for the seal replacement procedure.

Installation

14   Installation is the reverse of removal, but with the following additional points:

a) *Thoroughly clean the driveaxle splines and hub/bearing shield. Clean the respective areas around the driveaxle oil seal and the steering knuckle/hub splines.*

b) *Install a new snap-ring on the inner driveaxle splines.*

c) *Lubricate the driveaxle oil seal, tripod joint splines and sealing surface with the appropriate transmission lubricant (see Chapter 1).*

d) *When installing the driveaxle into the transaxle, hold it straight out and push it in sharply to seat the driveaxle snap-ring into the groove in the transaxle side gear. To make sure the circlip is properly seated, grasp the tripod joint housing (not the driveaxle) and attempt to pull it out of the transaxle by hand.*

e) *Before installing the driveaxle into the hub/steering knuckle, lubricate the driveaxle outer splines with a light coat*

of multi-purpose grease. After installing the driveaxle, install the driveaxle/hub nut and tighten the nut securely but not to the specified torque at this time.

f) *Tighten the lower control arm balljoint nut (see Chapter 10) and brake caliper guide pins (see Chapter 9) to the torque listed in the Specification Section in their respective Chapters.*

g) *Install the wheel and lug nuts then lower the vehicle.*

h) *Tighten the driveaxle/hub nut to the torque listed in this Chapter's Specifications. Install the spring washer, lock and a new cotter pin. Bend the ends around the nut - not over it.*

i) *Tighten the wheel lug nuts to the torque listed in the Chapter 1 Specifications.*

j) *Check and add transaxle/differential lubricant as applicable (see Chapter 1).*

9   Driveaxle boot replacement

Note 1: *If the CV joints are damaged (usually due to torn boots), individual replacement parts are not available. The complete driveaxle, new or rebuilt, must be replaced as an assembly and are available on an exchange basis.*

Note: 2: *On 1995 to 1997 models, the only serviceable part on the outer CV joint is the hub/bearing shield which is pressed onto the outer CV joint housing splined shaft. The outer CV joint cannot be removed from the axleshaft. In the event of bearing or sealing boot failure on these models, the entire driveaxle must be replaced.*

Outer joint boot (1998 models only)

Disassembly

Refer to illustrations 9.2, 9.4, 9.5a and 9.5b

1   Remove the driveaxle from the vehicle (see Section 8).

2   Mount the driveaxle in a vise with soft

9.2 Cut the boot clamps and remove them from the driveaxle

9.4 Remove the boot from the CV joint housing

9.5a Use a soft-faced hammer to disengage the outer CV joint from the axleshaft retaining circlip . . .

jaws (to prevent damage to the axleshaft). Check the CV joint for excessive play in the radial direction, which indicates worn components. Check for smooth operation throughout the full range of motion for the CV joint. Using diagonal cutters, cut the boot clamps and remove them **(see illustration)**.

3   Before separating the outer CV joint from the axleshaft assembly, mark the CV joint housing to the axleshaft so they may be reinstalled in the same position.

4   Pry up on the edge of the boot and pull it off the outer CV joint housing **(see illustration)**.

5   Using a soft-faced hammer, carefully drive the outer CV joint off the axleshaft by striking the outer housing (only) - be careful not to damage the splines or the cage **(see illustrations)**.

6   Remove the large retaining circlip from the axleshaft then slide off the sealing boot.

Check

7   Clean the CV joint thoroughly with solvent to remove all grease. Blow the solvent out of the joint with compressed air, if available. **Warning:** *Wear eye protection!* Check

for cracks, pitting, scoring and other signs of wear.

8   If there's any evidence of damage or excessive wear, replace the outer CV joint as an assembly. The outer CV joint is not serviceable.

Installation

Refer to illustrations 9.10, 9.12 and 9.14

9   Pack the CV joint with half of the special CV joint grease included in the boot kit.

10   Wrap the splined end of the axleshaft with tape to protect the new boot from damage during installation **(see illustration)**. Install the new small clamp and new boot onto the axleshaft.

11   Remove the tape from the splines and install the large retaining circlip. Place the remaining CV joint grease into the sealing boot.

12   Install the CV joint assembly onto the axleshaft aligning the previously applied match-marks. Using a brass hammer, seat the joint onto the shaft **(see illustration)**. Make sure the CV joint assembly is locked into position on the axleshaft by trying to pull it off by hand.

9.5b . . . and remove the outer CV joint from the axleshaft

13   Wipe any excess grease from the axle boot groove on the CV joint housing. Seat the small diameter of the boot in the recessed area on the axleshaft. Push the other end of the boot onto the CV joint housing and move

8

9.10 Before installing the boot, wrap the axleshaft splines with tape to prevent damaging the boot

9.12 Install the outer CV joint onto the axleshaft, then use a brass drift and a hammer to seat the CV joint on the axleshaft

9.14 Tighten the boot clamps using special plier-type crimpers, which are available at most auto parts stores

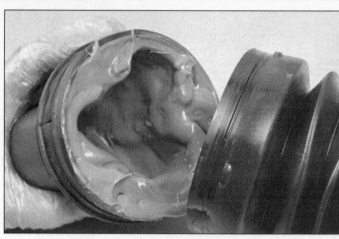

9.24 Once the boot is detached from the tripod housing, the joint can be separated

the race in or out until there's no deformation (distortion or dents) in the boot.

14 Install the large clamp onto the sealing boot. Secure the sealing boot to the axleshaft and CV joint housing using a special clamp crimping tool as shown **(see illustration)**. These special plier-type crimpers are available at most auto parts stores. Place the crimping tool over the bridge of the clamp and squeeze it together until the tool is fully closed.

15 Install the driveaxle (see Section 8).

Outer CV joint hub/bearing shield

Replacement

16 Remove the driveaxle from the vehicle (see Section 8).

17 Mount the driveaxle in a vise with soft jaws (to prevent damage to the axleshaft).

18 Using a drift and hammer, carefully and evenly drive the hub/bearing shield off the outer CV joint shaft.

19 Place the shield onto the axleshaft with the large diameter facing up. Using an appropriate size section of pipe and a hammer, drive the shield onto the axleshaft. Be careful

not to cock the hub/bearing shield. Drive it onto the shaft until it is fully seated.

20 Install the driveaxle onto the vehicle (see Section 8).

Inner joint boot

Disassembly

Refer to illustrations 9.24, 9.25, 9.26 and 9.27

21 Remove the driveaxle from the vehicle (see Section 8).

22 Mount the driveaxle in a vise with soft jaws (to prevent damage to the axleshaft). Check the CV joint for excessive play in the radial direction, which indicates worn components. Check for smooth operation throughout the full range of motion for the CV joint.

23 Before separating the tripod housing from the axleshaft assembly, use a centerpunch or equivalent to match-mark the housing to the axleshaft so they may be reinstalled in the same position.

24 After removing the boot clamps **(see illustration 9.2)**, pull the boot back from the tripod housing and slide the it off the spider assembly **(see illustration)**. **Caution:** *Hold onto the spider assembly bearings as you remove the housing to prevent them from*

falling off. If necessary, wrap some tape around them to secure them in position.

25 Use a centerpunch to mark the spider to the axleshaft so that they can be reassembled in the same position **(see illustration)**.

26 Remove the snap-ring from the end of the axleshaft with a pair of snap-ring pliers **(see illustration)**.

27 Use a hammer and a brass drift to drive the spider assembly from the driveaxle and then remove the old sealing boot **(see illustration)**. Be careful not to strike the spider assembly bearings.

Check

28 Clean all components with solvent to remove the grease, and check for cracks, pitting, scoring and other signs of wear. Replacement parts for these driveaxles are not available, so if any component exhibits damage, the entire driveaxle must be replaced.

Reassembly

Refer to illustration 9.34

Caution: *The inner tripod joint sealing boots on the vehicles covered in this manual are constructed from different materials for differ-*

9.25 Use a centerpunch to mark (arrows) the tripod spider to the axleshaft

9.26 Remove the spider retaining snap-ring from the end of the axleshaft

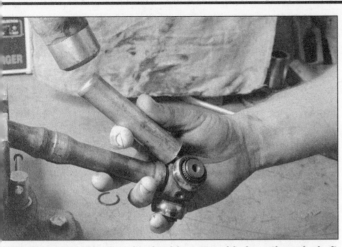

9.27 Carefully drive the tripod spider assembly from the axleshaft using a brass drift and hammer - make sure you don't damage the bearing surfaces or the splines on the axleshaft

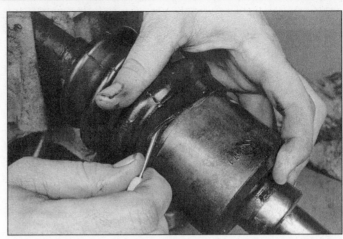

9.34 Equalize the pressure in the boot by inserting a small, dull screwdriver between the boot and the joint housing

ent temperature applications. High-temperature applications use silicone rubber that is soft and pliable. Standard temperature applications use Hytrel plastic that is stiff and rigid. The replacement boots must be the same type of material as the sealing boot that was removed.

29   Wrap the splined end of the axleshaft with tape to protect the new boot from damage during installation **(see illustration 9.10)**. Install the new small clamp and new sealing boot onto the axleshaft. Remove the tape from the splines.

30   Install the spider assembly onto the axleshaft aligning the centerpunch match-marks **(see illustration 9.25)**. Install the snap-ring onto the axleshaft. **Note:** *The snap-ring must be fully seated in it's groove. If necessary, use a hammer and brass drift to fully*

seat the spider assembly on the axleshaft. Be careful not to strike the spider assembly bearings.

31   Pack the tripod joint housing with half of the special CV joint grease included in the boot kit. Place the remaining CV joint grease into the sealing boot.

32   Place the tripod housing onto the axleshaft assembly aligning the previously applied match-marks.

33   Slide the sealing boot into place, making sure both ends seat in their grooves.

34   Next, insert a small DULL screwdriver or other small blunt object between the tripod housing and the sealing boot **(see illustration)**. This will equalize the pressure in the boot during positioning of the axleshaft in the tripod outer housing. **Caution:** *DO NOT damage the sealing boot during this procedure!*

35   With the sealing boot vented using the screwdriver (or equivalent), position the axleshaft so it is in the middle of it's axial travel within the tripod housing. Make sure there are no creases or dents in the sealing boot after positioning the axleshaft. Remove the screwdriver from between the housing and sealing boot.

36   Install the large clamp onto the sealing boot. Secure the sealing boot to the axleshaft and CV joint housing using a special clamp crimping tool as shown **(see illustration 9.14)**. These special plier-type crimpers are available at most auto parts stores. Place the crimping tool over the bridge of the clamp and squeeze it together until the tool is fully closed.

37   Install the driveaxle (see Section 8).

8

Notes

Chapter 9 Brakes

Contents

Specifications

General
Brake fluid type .... See Chapter 1

Disc brakes
Brake pad minimum thickness (metal backing plus lining)	3/8 inch
Disc lateral runout limit	0.005 inch
Disc minimum thickness	Cast into disc
Thickness variation	0.0005 inch

Drum brakes
Minimum brake lining thickness	1/8 inch
Maximum drum diameter	Cast into drum

Torque specifications
Ft-lbs (unless otherwise indicated)

Brake booster mounting nuts	250 in-lbs
Brake hose banjo bolt-to-caliper	35
Caliper guide pin bolts	16
Master cylinder-to-brake booster mounting nuts	250 in-lbs
Wheel cylinder-to-backing plate mounting nuts	97 in-lbs
Wheel lug nuts	See Chapter 1

9

1 General information

General

All models covered by this manual are equipped with a hydraulically operated brake system. The front brakes are disc type and the rear brakes are drum type. Both brake types are self-adjusting. Disc brakes automatically compensate for pad wear, while drum brakes incorporate an adjustment mechanism which is activated as the brakes are applied.

The hydraulic system is split diagonally - the left front and right rear brakes are on one circuit; the right front and left rear on the other. If one circuit fails, the other circuit will remain functional and a warning indicator will illuminate on the dashboard when a substantial amount of brake fluid is lost, showing that a failure has occurred.

Before disconnecting any electrical connector from a vehicle equipped with an Antilock Brake System (ABS), make sure the ignition is in the OFF position and the negative battery cable has been disconnected from the ground stud on the left shock tower (see Chapter 5, Section 1). If any weld repair is going to be performed on a vehicle equipped with an ABS system, disconnect the CAB or ICU electrical connector (see Section 2) or damage to the electronics may occur.

Calipers

All disc brakes used by the vehicles covered in this manual are equipped with a double-pin floating caliper, a single-piston design that "floats" on two steel guide pins. When the brake pedal is depressed, hydraulic pressure pushing on the piston is transmitted to the inner brake pad and against the inner surface of the brake disc. As the force against the disc from the inner pad is increased, the caliper assembly moves in, sliding on the guide pins and pulling the outer pad against the disc, exerting a pinching force on the disc.

Master cylinder

The master cylinder is located in the engine compartment on the power brake booster, and can be identified by the large fluid reservoir on top. The master cylinder has two separate circuits to accommodate the diagonally split system.

Power brake booster

The power brake booster uses engine manifold vacuum to provide assistance to the brakes. It is mounted on the firewall in the engine compartment, directly behind the master cylinder.

Parking brake system

The parking brake actuates the rear brakes via two cables. The parking brake cables pull on a lever attached to the brake shoe assembly, causing the shoes to expand against the drum.

Precautions

There are some general precautions and warnings related to the hydraulic brake system:

a) *Use only brake fluid conforming to DOT 3 specifications.*

b) *The brake pads and linings may contain asbestos fibers which are hazardous to your health if inhaled. Whenever you work on brake system components, DO NOT blow it out with compressed air and DO NOT inhale it. DO NOT use gasoline or petroleum-based solvents to clean components. Brake system cleaner should be used to flush the dust into a drain pan. After the brake components are cleaned, dispose of the contaminated rags and cleaner in a labeled, covered container. Do not allow the fine dust to become airborne.*

c) *Safety should be paramount whenever any servicing of the brake components is performed. Do not use parts or fasteners which are not in perfect condition, and be sure all clearances and torque specifications are adhered to. If you are at all unsure about a certain procedure, seek professional advice. Upon completion of any brake system work, test the brakes carefully in a controlled area before driving the vehicle in traffic.*

d) *If a problem is suspected in the brake system, don't drive the vehicle until it's been corrected.*

2 Anti-lock Brake System (ABS) - general information

Description

1   The Anti-lock Brake System (ABS) prevents wheel lock-up on virtually any road surface. Preventing the wheels from locking up maintains vehicle maneuverability, preserves directional stability, and allows optimal deceleration on all surfaces. How does ABS work? Basically, by monitoring the rotational speed of the wheels and controlling the brake line pressure to the calipers/wheel cylinders at each wheel.

Components

Controller Anti-lock Brake (CAB)

Refer to illustration 2.2

2   The CAB consists of a pair of microprocessors which monitor wheel speeds and control the anti-lock and traction control functions. The CAB receives two identical signals and process the information independently of one another. The results are compared to make sure that they agree. If they don't, the CAB turns off the ABS and traction control functions, and turns on the warning lights. The CAB is located in the engine compartment on the right hand side and mounted near the windshield washer fluid and coolant reservoirs **(see illustration)**.

2.2 The Controller Anti-lock Brake (arrow) is the brain of the ABS system (1997 and earlier style shown; on 1998 models, the CAB is mounted on the HCU

Hydraulic Control Unit (HCU)

Refer to illustration 2.3

3   The Hydraulic Control Unit (HCU) is located in the engine compartment on the right hand side and mounted to the front suspension crossmember **(see illustration)**. The HCU contains the valve block assembly, fluid accumulators, the pump/motor assembly and relay box.

Integrated Control Unit (ICU) - 1998 models only

4   On 1998 models a new ABS brake system was introduced which functions very much like the previous ABS system except it combines the HCU and CAB into one unit, called the Integrated Control Unit (ICU). The ICU is located in the same location as the HCU on previous models (see above).

Valve block assembly

5   The valve block assembly contains eight valve/solenoids: four inlet valves and four outlet valves. The inlet valves are spring-loaded in the open position and the outlet valves are spring-loaded in the closed position. During ABS operation, these valves are cycled to maintain the proper slip ratio for each channel. If a wheel locks, the inlet valve is closed to prevent a further increase in pressure. Simultaneously, the outlet valve is opened to release the pressure back to the accumulators until the wheel is no longer slipping. Once the wheel no longer slips, the outlet valve closes and the inlet valve opens to allow pressure to the wheel caliper or wheel cylinder.

Pump/motor assembly

6   The pump/motor assembly consists of an electric motor and a dual-piston pump. The pump provides high-pressure brake fluid to the hydraulic control unit when the ABS system is activated.

Fluid accumulators

7   The two fluid accumulators located inside the HCU are for the primary and secondary hydraulic circuits. The accumulators

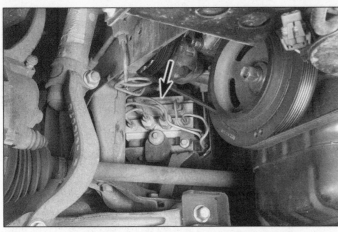

2.3 The Hydraulic Control Unit (arrow) is located below the power steering pump

2.9 Wheel Speed Sensor (arrow)

temporarily store brake fluid that is blocked during ABS operation. This fluid is re-routed to the pump.

Proportioning valves

8   Refer to Section 9 for a description of the proportioning valves.

Wheel Speed Sensors (WSS)

Refer to illustration 2.9

9   A speed sensor is mounted at each wheel **(see illustration)**. The speed sensors send variable voltage signals to the HCU. These analog voltage outputs are proportional to the speed of rotation of each wheel.

Diagnosis and repair

10   The ABS system has self-diagnostic capabilities. Each time the ignition key is turned to ON, the system runs a self-test. If it finds a problem, the ABS and traction control warning lights come on and remain on. If there's no problem with the system, the lights go out after a second or two.

11   If the ABS and traction control warning lights come on and stay on during vehicle operation, there is a problem in the ABS

system. Two things now happen: The controller stores a diagnostic trouble code (which can be displayed with a DRB II scanner at the dealer) and the ABS system is shut down. Once the ABS system is disabled, it will remain disabled until the problem is corrected and the trouble code is erased. However, the regular brake system will continue to function normally.

12   Although a DRB II scan tool (a special electronic tester) is necessary to properly diagnose the system, you can make a few preliminary checks before taking the vehicle to a dealer or other shop for service:

   a) *Make sure the brake calipers and wheel cylinders are in good condition.*

   b) *Check the electrical connector at the CAB, HCU or ICU as applicable.*

   c) *Check the fuses.*

   d) *Follow the wiring harness to the wheel speed sensors and brake light switch and make sure all connections are clean, secure and the wiring isn't damaged.*

   If the above preliminary checks don't rectify the problem, the vehicle should be diagnosed by a dealer service department or other qualified repair shop.

3   Disc brake pads - replacement

Refer to illustrations 3.2, 3.3, 3.4a through 3.4l
Warning: *Disc brake pads must be replaced on both front wheels at the same time - never replace the pads on only one wheel. Also, the dust created by the brake system may contain asbestos, which is harmful to your health. Never blow it out with compressed air and don't inhale any of it. An approved filtering mask should be worn when working on the brakes. Do not, under any circumstances, use petroleum-based solvents to clean brake parts. Use brake system cleaner only!*

1   Loosen the front wheel lug nuts 1/4-turn, raise the front of the vehicle and support it securely on jackstands. Apply the parking brake. Remove the front wheels.

2   Using a syringe or equivalent, siphon approximately two-thirds of the fluid from the master cylinder reservoir and discard it. Position a drain pan under the brake assembly and clean the caliper and surrounding area with brake system cleaner **(see illustration)**.

3   Push the piston back into its bore using a C-clamp **(see illustration)**. As the piston is

9

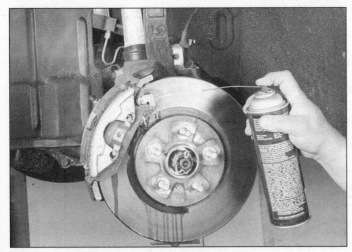

3.2 Always wash the brakes with brake system cleaner before working on them

3.3 Use a C-clamp to press the caliper piston into its bore

3.4a To remove the front brake caliper, remove the two guide pin bolts (arrows)

3.4b Lift the caliper off the steering knuckle and remove the outer pad from the caliper

3.4c Remove the inner pad from the caliper

3.4d If you're not going to reinstall the caliper any time soon, hang it from the upper control arm with a piece of wire or equivalent - don't let it hang by the brake hose

3.4e Remove the guide pin bushings

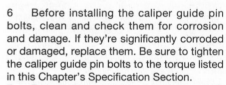

3.4f Remove the bushing boots, inspect them for damage and replace if necessary

depressed to the bottom of the caliper bore, the fluid in the master cylinder will rise as the brake fluid is displaced. Make sure it doesn't overflow. If necessary, siphon off more of the fluid. **Warning:** *Never siphon brake fluid by mouth!*

4   To replace the brake pads, follow the accompanying photos, beginning with illustration 3.4a. Be sure to stay in order and read the caption under each illustration.

5   While the pads are removed, inspect the caliper for brake fluid leaks and ruptures of the piston dust boot. Replace the caliper if necessary (see Section 4). Also inspect the brake disc carefully (see Section 5). If machining is necessary, follow the information in that Section to remove the disc. Inspect the brake hoses for damage and replace if necessary (see Section 10).

6   Before installing the caliper guide pin bolts, clean and check them for corrosion and damage. If they're significantly corroded or damaged, replace them. Be sure to tighten the caliper guide pin bolts to the torque listed in this Chapter's Specification Section.

7   Repeat the procedure for the opposite wheel, then install the wheels, lug nuts and lower the vehicle. Tighten the lug nuts to the torque listed in the Chapter 1 Specification Section. Add the appropriate brake fluid to

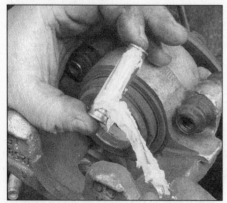

3.4g Lubricate the guide pin bushings with multi-purpose grease before installing them

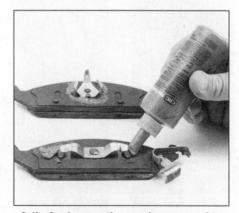

3.4h Apply an anti-squeal compound to the backs of the pads where they mate with the caliper and piston

3.4i Install the inner brake pad - make sure the retaining spring is fully seated into the piston bore

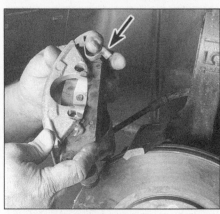

3.4j Install the outer brake pad - make sure the retaining spring is properly engaged with the caliper body and the wear indicator (arrow) on the pad is positioned at the top of the caliper as shown

3.4k Place the caliper/brake pad assembly onto the steering knuckle (make sure the upper ends of the pads seat properly)

3.4l Install the guide pin bolts and tighten them to the torque listed in this Chapter's Specifications

the reservoir until it's full (see Chapter 1 if necessary).

8   Pump the brakes several times to seat the pads against the disc, then check the brake fluid level in the reservoir again. Top it up as necessary.

9   Carefully test the operation of the brakes before resuming normal operation. Try to avoid heavy brake applications until the brakes have been applied lightly several times to seat the pads.

4   Disc brake caliper - removal and installation

Warning: *Dust created by the brake system may contain asbestos, which is harmful to your health. Never blow it out with compressed air and don't inhale any of it. An approved filtering mask should be worn when working on the brakes. Do not, under any circumstances, use petroleum-based solvents to clean brake parts. Use brake system cleaner only.*

Note: *If replacement is indicated (usually because of fluid leaks, a stuck piston or broken bleed screw) explore all options before beginning this procedure. New and factory rebuilt calipers are available on an exchange basis, which makes this job quite easy. Always replace the calipers in pairs - never replace just one of them.*

Removal

1   Loosen the front wheel lug nuts, raise the vehicle and support it securely on jackstands. Remove the front wheels.

2   Unscrew the banjo bolt from the caliper and detach the hose. **Note:** *If you're just removing the caliper for access to other components, don't disconnect the hose.* Discard the sealing washers on each side of the fitting and use new ones during installation. Plug the hose to prevent fluid loss and contamination.

3   Refer to the first few steps in Section 3 (caliper removal is the first part of the brake

pad replacement procedure). Clean the caliper assembly with brake system cleaner. **Warning:** *DO NOT, under any circumstances, use kerosene, gasoline or petroleum-based solvents to clean brake parts!* Be sure to check the pads as well and replace them if necessary (see Section 3).

Installation

4   Install the brake pads and caliper (see Section 3). Tighten the caliper guide pin bolts to the torque listed in this Chapter's Specification Section.

5   Connect the brake hose to the caliper using new sealing washers. Tighten the banjo bolt to the torque listed in this Chapter's Specification Section.

6   Firmly depress the brake pedal a few times to bring the pads into contact with the disc. Check the fluid level in the master cylinder reservoir and add more if necessary.

7   Bleed the brakes (see Section 11).

8   Install the wheels and lug nuts. Lower the vehicle and tighten the lug nuts to the torque listed in the Chapter 1 Specifications.

9   Carefully check for fluid leaks and test the operation of the brakes before resuming normal operation.

5.2 The brake pads on this vehicle were obviously neglected, as they wore down to the rivets, then cut deep grooves into the disc, which must now be replaced

5   Brake disc - inspection, removal and installation

Inspection

Refer to illustrations 5.2, 5.3, 5.4a and 5.4b

1   Loosen the wheel lug nuts 1/4-turn, raise the front of the vehicle and support it securely on jackstands. Apply the parking brake. Remove the front wheels. Reinstall the lug nuts to hold the disc firmly against the hub. **Note:** *Washers may be required.*

2   Remove the brake caliper (see Section 4). Visually inspect the disc surface for score marks and other damage **(see illustration)**. Light scratches and shallow grooves are normal after use and won't affect brake operation. Deep grooves - over 0.015-inch deep - require disc removal and refinishing by an automotive machine shop. Be sure to check both sides of the disc.

3   To check the disc runout, place a dial indicator at a point about 1/2-inch from the outer edge of the disc **(see illustration)**. Rotate the disc until you find the lowest point on the disc. Set the dial indicator to zero and turn the disc again. The indicator reading should not exceed the runout limit listed in this Chapter's Specification Section. Check

5.3 Use a dial indicator to check disc runout - if the reading exceeds the specified runout limit, the disc will have to be machined or replaced

the runout on both sides of the disc. If the runout exceeds specification, the disc must be refinished by an automotive machine shop. **Note:** *Professionals recommend resurfacing the brake discs regardless of the dial indicator reading (to produce a smooth, flat surface that will eliminate brake pedal pulsations and other undesirable symptoms related to questionable discs). At the very least, if you elect not to have the discs resurfaced, deglaze them with sandpaper or emery cloth.*

4   The disc must not be machined to a thickness less than the specified minimum thickness. The minimum (or discard) thickness is cast into the disc **(see illustration)**. The disc thickness should be checked with a micrometer **(see illustration)**.

Removal

Refer to illustration 5.7

5   Loosen the wheel lug nuts 1/4-turn, raise the vehicle and place it securely on jackstands. Remove the wheel.

6   Remove the caliper (see Section 4).

7   Remove the retaining clips, if present, from the wheel studs **(see illustration)**.

8   Pull the disc off the hub.

Installation

9   Installation is the reverse of removal. Make sure you tighten the caliper guide pin bolts to the torque listed in this Chapter's Specification Section. Tighten the lug nuts to the torque listed in the Chapter 1 Specifications.

---

6   Drum brake shoes - replacement

Refer to illustrations 6.2, 6.4a through 6.4v and 6.5

Warning: *Drum brake shoes must be replaced on both wheels at the same time - never replace the shoes on only one wheel. Also, the dust created by the brake system may contain asbestos, which is harmful to your health. Never blow it out with compressed air and don't inhale any of it. An*

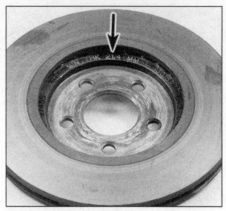

5.4a The minimum thickness is cast into the inside of the disc

approved filtering mask should be worn when *working on the brakes. Do not, under any circumstances, use petroleum-based solvents to clean brake parts. Use brake system cleaner only!*

Caution: *Whenever the brake shoes are replaced, the hold-down springs should also be replaced. Due to the continuous heating/cooling cycle that the springs are subjected to, they lose their tension over a period of time and may allow the shoes to drag on the drum and wear at a much faster rate than normal.*

1   Loosen the wheel lug nuts 1/4-turn, raise the rear of the vehicle and support it securely on jackstands. Block the front wheels to keep the vehicle from rolling. Release the parking brake. Remove the wheel. **Note:** *The brake shoes on both wheels must be replaced at the same time. The drum brake assemblies on these models are unique for each side of the vehicle (left hand only - right hand only) so to avoid mixing up parts, service one brake assembly at a time.*

2   Remove the brake drum. If the drum won't come off, the brake shoes must be retracted from their fully adjusted position by inserting a screwdriver through the adjuster hole in the backing plate. Locate the adjuster

5.4b Use a micrometer to measure the thickness of the disc at several locations

5.7 Cut off and discard the disc retaining washers, if present (it isn't necessary to reinstall them)

access hole and remove the plug. Insert a screwdriver through the access hole and engage the adjuster quadrant teeth. Using the screwdriver, move the adjuster quadrant teeth fully toward the FRONT of the vehicle. The drum should now come off. Wash the brake assembly with brake system cleaner **(see illustration)**.

6.2 Before disassembling the brake shoe assembly, spray it with brake cleaner to remove brake dust; DO NOT blow brake dust off with compressed air

6.4a Using locking pliers, grasp the lower return spring and detach it from the leading brake shoe (left hand brake assembly shown

6.4b Remove the lower return spring -
note that the shorter spring end is
towards the trailing brake shoe

6.4c Using locking pliers, grasp the upper
return spring and detach it from the
trailing brake shoe

6.4d Unhook the upper return spring from
the leading brake shoe

6.4e Using locking pliers, detach the
automatic self-adjuster spring
from the adjuster

6.4f Compress the retaining clip,
remove the pin . . .

6.4g . . . and separate the leading brake
shoe and the automatic self-adjuster
from the backing plate

3   Remove the wheel hub/bearing assembly (see Chapter 10). **Note:** *Removal of the wheel hub/bearing assembly is not mandatory, but it makes the job a lot easier.*

4   Follow **illustrations 6.4a through 6.4v** for inspection and replacement of the brake

shoes. Be sure to stay in order and read the caption under each illustration.

5   Before reinstalling the drum, carefully examine it for cracks, score marks, deep scratches and hard spots, which will appear as small discolored areas. If the hard spots

cannot be removed with fine emery cloth or if any of the other conditions listed above exist, the drum must be taken to an automotive machine shop to have it resurfaced. **Note:** *Professionals recommend resurfacing the drums whenever a brake job is performed.*

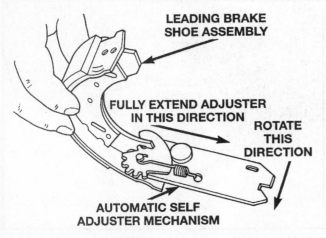

6.4h To remove the adjuster from the shoe, pull it outward, then
rotate it toward the reinforced side of the shoe

6.4i Compress the retaining clip, then remove the pin
and clip from the trailing shoe

9

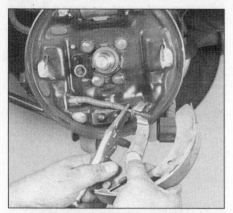

6.4j Detach the parking brake cable from the actuating lever - **DO NOT** try to separate the actuating lever from the brake shoe

6.4k Before installing the brake shoes, apply a small amount of high-temperature grease to all areas where the brake shoes make contact with the backing plate

6.4l Obtain the correct replacement trailing brake shoe (they are unique for each side of the vehicle, RH or LH and the parking brake actuating lever should be permanently attached) and install the parking brake cable onto the actuating lever

6.4m Correctly position the trailing shoe in place on the backing plate (parking brake actuating lever toward the inside) and secure it with a new pin and retaining clip

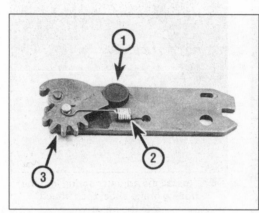

6.4n Inspect the automatic self-adjuster for damage and replace if necessary

1   *Knurled pin* - check to see it is firmly attached and the teeth are not damaged or excessively worn
2   *Quadrant spring* - inspect for damage and verify it hasn't lost it's tension
3   *Quadrant* - verify the quadrant is free to slide within its mounting slot and can rotate through the entire tooth range

Resurfacing will eliminate the possibility of out-of-round drums. If the drums are worn so much that they can't be resurfaced without exceeding the maximum allowable diameter (stamped into the drum) **(see illustration)**, *then new ones will be required. At the very least, if you elect not to have the drums resurfaced, remove the glazing from the surface with emery cloth or sandpaper using a swirling motion.*

6   Install the wheel hub/bearing assembly (with a new hub nut), if removed (see Chapter 10).

7   Install the brake drum, mount the wheel and install the lug nuts.

8   Repeat the procedure for the opposite wheel.

9   Lower the vehicle and tighten the lug

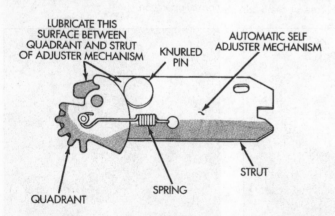

6.4o Before installing the adjuster on the leading brake shoe, lubricate the area between the quadrant and the adjuster strut with a small amount of multi-purpose grease

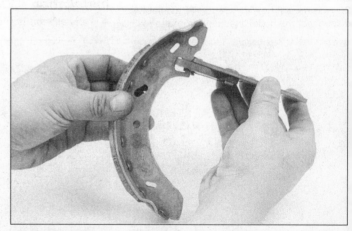

6.4p Install the automatic self-adjuster onto the proper leading brake shoe (they are unique for each side of the vehicle, RH or LH and are marked on the reinforcement plate) - after installation the quadrant teeth should be on the reinforced side of the brake shoe

6.4q Place the leading brake shoe (with adjuster installed) in position on the backing plate, making sure to match up the notch in the adjuster strut with the notch in the trailing brake shoe

6.4r Install the new pin and retaining clip

6.4s Compress the retaining clip and turn the pin 90-degrees to retain the brake shoe

nuts to the torque listed in the Chapter 1 Specifications.

10   To adjust the brakes, start the engine and fully depress the brake pedal two or three times to activate the automatic adjusters.

11   Carefully test brake operation before driving the vehicle in traffic.

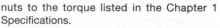

7   Wheel cylinder - removal and installation

Note: *If replacement is warranted (usually because of fluid leakage or sticky operation) explore all options before beginning the job. New wheel cylinders are available, which makes this job quite easy. Never replace only one wheel cylinder. Always replace both of them at the same time.*

Removal

Refer to illustration 7.2

1   Remove the rear brake shoes (see Section 6).

2   Using a flare-nut wrench (if available) disconnect the brake line fitting from the rear

6.4t Install the adjuster spring into the trailing brake shoe, then attach it to the adjuster

of the wheel cylinder (**see illustration**). Plug the end of the brake line to prevent fluid loss and contamination.

3   Remove the two bolts securing the wheel cylinder to the backing plate and remove the wheel cylinder.

Installation

4   Installation is the reverse of removal.

6.4u Install the upper return spring

Tighten the wheel cylinder mounting bolts to the torque listed in this Chapter's Specifications. Tighten the line fitting securely.

5   Install the brake shoes, wheel hub/bearing assembly, if removed (with a new hub nut) and brake drum (see Section 6).

6   Bleed the brakes (see Section 11). Carefully test brake operation before resuming normal operation.

6.4v Install the lower return spring, positioned as shown

6.5 The maximum allowable diameter is stamped into the drum (arrow)

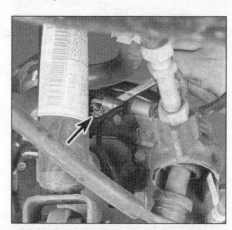

7.2 Disconnecting the brake hose fitting (arrow) from the wheel cylinder

8.2 Cruise control servo mounting nuts (arrows)

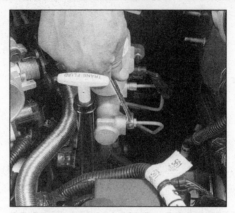

8.5 Disconnect the brake line fittings with a flare-nut wrench (ABS-equipped models have two line fittings, while non-ABS models have four)

8.6 Unhook the retaining clip and unplug the electrical connector from the brake fluid level sensor

8   Master cylinder - removal, installation and fluid reservoir replacement

Note: *The master cylinder used on these vehicles is not serviceable and must be replaced as a unit. However, you can replace the fluid reservoir and/or reservoir sealing grommets.*

Removal

Refer to illustrations 8.2, 8.5, 8.6 and 8.8

1   Disconnect the negative battery cable from the ground stud on the left shock tower (see Chapter 5, Section 1). With the ignition switch in the OFF position, pump the brake pedal until a firm pedal is achieved.

2   If equipped, disconnect the cruise control electrical connector and detach the cruise control servo from its mounting on the shock tower and position it out of the way **(see illustration)**.

3   Using a syringe or equivalent, siphon the brake fluid from the master cylinder reservoir and dispose of it properly. **Caution:** *Brake fluid will damage paint. Cover all painted surfaces and avoid spilling fluid during this procedure.*

4   Place rags under the brake line fittings and prepare caps or plastic bags to cover the ends of the lines once they're disconnected.

5   Loosen the tube nuts at the ends of the brake lines where they enter the master cylinder **(see illustration)**. To prevent rounding off the corners of these fittings, a flare-nut wrench, which wraps around the nut, should be used. Pull the brake lines away from the master cylinder slightly and plug the ends to prevent leakage and contamination. Also plug the openings in the master cylinder to prevent fluid spillage.

6   Unhook the clip and unplug the electrical connector from the brake fluid level sensor **(see illustration)**.

7   Clean the area where the master cylinder attaches to the vacuum booster using brake system cleaner.

8   Remove the two master cylinder mounting nuts **(see illustration)** and any brackets that may be attached. Slide the master

cylinder off the studs and remove it from the vehicle.

Installation

Note: *Read this entire procedure before beginning this operation.*

9   Install the master cylinder onto the power brake booster making sure to engage the operating rod. Install any brackets as necessary and tighten the mounting nuts securely.

10   Before installing the brake lines to the master cylinder, it should be bled. Since you'll have to apply pressure to the master cylinder piston and at the same time, control flow from the brake line outlets, the aid of an assistant will be required.

11   Insert threaded plugs into the brake line outlet holes and snug them down so no air will leak past them, but not so tight that they can't be easily loosened.

12   Fill the reservoir with the recommended brake fluid (see Chapter 1).

13   Place a suitable container under one of the plugs and remove the plug. Have your assistant SLOWLY depress the brake pedal to expel the air from the master cylinder. Use a rag to catch any brake fluid that squirts out. A clear plastic bag placed over the master cylinder will help you guide the expelled fluid for collection and prevent it from squirting in unwanted areas.

14   To prevent air from being drawn back into the master cylinder, place your finger tightly over the hole to keep air from being drawn back into the master cylinder before releasing the brake pedal. Wait several seconds for brake fluid to be drawn from the reservoir into the bore, then depress the brake pedal again, removing your finger as brake fluid is expelled. Be sure to put your finger firmly back over the hole each time before releasing the piston, and when the bleeding procedure is complete for that outlet, install the plug (with the pedal depressed) and tighten it before going on to the next port.

15   Repeat the procedure until only brake fluid is expelled from the brake line outlet

hole. When only brake fluid is expelled, repeat the procedure at the other outlets. Be sure to keep the master cylinder reservoir filled with brake fluid to prevent the introduction of air into the system.

16   Loosen the master cylinder mounting nuts and connect the brake lines into the master cylinder. Since the master cylinder is a bit loose, it can be moved slightly so the fittings can thread in easily.

17   Tighten the master cylinder mounting nuts to the torque given in this Chapter's Specification Section. Tighten the fitting nuts securely.

18   If equipped, install the cruise control servo onto the shock tower and plug in the electrical connector.

19   Fill the master cylinder reservoir with the recommended fluid (see Chapter 1), then bleed the brake hydraulic system (see Section 11).

Fluid reservoir replacement

Refer to illustration 8.22

20   Using a syringe or equivalent, siphon the brake fluid from the master cylinder reservoir and dispose of it properly.

8.8 To detach the master cylinder from the power brake booster, remove the mounting nuts (arrows), then pull the master cylinder assembly straight off the mounting studs

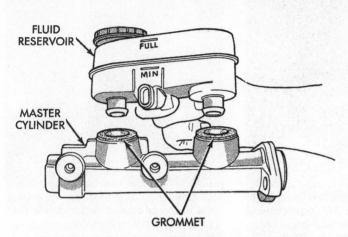

8.22 The brake fluid reservoir is secured and sealed
to the master cylinder by the grommets

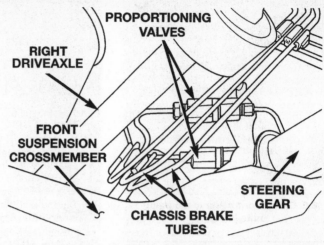

9.5 On non-ABS models, the proportioning valves are located on
the right side of the front suspension crossmember

21   Disconnect the brake fluid level sensor electrical connector from the reservoir **(see illustration 8.6)**.
22   To remove the reservoir, carefully rock it back-and-forth while gently pulling upward **(see illustration)**.
23   After removing the reservoir, carefully remove the grommets from the master cylinder. **Note:** *New grommets should be installed anytime the reservoir is detached from the master cylinder.*
24   Remove the brake fluid level sensor from the reservoir.
25   Installation is the reverse of removal. Coat the new grommets with clean brake fluid prior to installation.

9   Proportioning valves - check and replacement

Description

1   All models have two proportioning valves that balance front-to-rear braking by controlling the increase in rear system hydraulic pressure above a preset level. Under light pedal pressure, the valve allows full hydraulic pressure to the front and rear brakes. But above a certain pressure - known as the "split point" - the proportioning valve reduces the amount of pressure increase to the rear brakes in accordance with a predetermined ratio. This lessens the chance of rear wheel lock-up and skidding.

Check

2   If either rear wheel skids prematurely under hard braking, it could indicate a defective proportioning valve. If this occurs, have the system checked out by your local dealer service department. A pair of special pressure gauges and fittings are required for proper diagnosis of the proportioning valves. While diagnosis is beyond the scope of the home mechanic, you may still save money by replacing the valves yourself.

Replacement

Non-ABS models

Refer to illustration 9.5

3   Loosen the right front wheel lug nuts, raise the front of the vehicle and support it securely on jackstands. Remove the wheel.
4   Remove the accessory drivebelt splash shield (see Chapter 1).
5   Loosen the brake hydraulic fluid lines from the proportioning valve with a flare-nut wrench to prevent rounding off the corners of the fittings **(see illustration)**. Back off the fittings and remove the valve from the line. Plug the ends of the lines to prevent loss of brake fluid and the entry of dirt.
6   Installation is the reverse of removal.
7   Bleed the brakes (see Section 11). Carefully test the brakes before resuming normal operation.

1995 to 1997 models with ABS

Refer to illustration 9.8

8   If your vehicle was manufactured between 1995 and 1997 and equipped with

ABS, the proportioning valves are mounted to the HCU **(see illustration)** and upon removal, the ABS system will be required to be bled using a DRB scan tool. We recommend you let your local dealer service department or other qualified repair shop replace the proportioning valves on these models.

1998 models with ABS

Refer to illustration 9.10

9   Loosen the appropriate rear wheel lug nuts, raise the rear of the vehicle and support it securely on jackstands. Remove the wheel.
10   Loosen the line fitting from the proportioning valve with a flare-nut wrench to prevent rounding off the corners of the fittings **(see illustration)**. Be sure to hold the valve with another wrench to prevent the line from twisting.
11   Detach the brake hose bracket from the upper frame rail.
12   Unscrew the valve from the brake hose and plug the ends of the lines to prevent leakage and contamination.

9.8 On 1995 to 1997 models equipped with ABS, the proportioning valves (arrows) are threaded into the Hydraulic Control Unit which is mounted on the right side of the front suspension crossmember

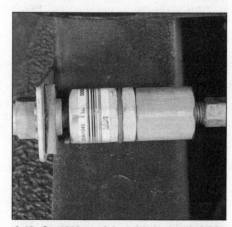

9.10 On 1998 models equipped with ABS, the proportioning valves are located in the rear wheel well and mounted on the upper frame rail between the metal brake line and the brake hose

9

13   Installation is the reverse of removal. Fit the metal line to the proportioning valve before attaching the brake hose bracket to the upper frame rail.

14   Bleed the brakes (see Section 11). Carefully test brake operation before resuming normal operation.

10   Brake hoses and lines - inspection and replacement

1   Whenever the vehicle is raised and supported securely on jackstands, the rubber hoses which connect the steel brake lines with the front and rear brake assemblies should be inspected for cracks, chafing of the outer cover, leaks, blisters and other damage. These are important and vulnerable parts of the brake system and inspection should be thorough. A light and mirror will be helpful for a complete check. If a hose exhibits any of the above conditions, renew it immediately.

Flexible hose replacement

Refer to illustration 10.3

2   Clean all dirt away from the hose fittings.

3   Using a flare-nut wrench, disconnect the metal brake line from the hose fitting **(see illustration)**. Be careful not to bend the frame bracket or line. If the threaded fitting is corroded, spray it with penetrating oil and allow it to soak in for about 10 minutes, then try again. If you try to break loose a fitting nut that's frozen, you will kink the metal line, which will then have to be replaced.

4   Remove the brake hose from the bracket (some are secured to a bracket with a retaining clip, others have an integral bracket/fitting). Detach the brake hose from the bracket or bracket from the vehicle as applicable. Immediately plug the metal line to prevent excessive leakage and contamination. **Note:** *On 1998 models with ABS, see Section 9 for rear brake hose-to-proportioning valve separation.*

5   On the rear brake hose(s), use a flare-nut wrench to loosen the hose fitting at the wheel cylinder and remove the hose.

6   On the front brake hose(s), unscrew the banjo bolt at the caliper and remove the hose, discarding the sealing washers on either side of the fitting.

7   Attach the new brake hose to the caliper or wheel cylinder as applicable. **Note:** *When replacing the front brake hoses, always use new sealing washers.* Tighten the banjo bolt or tube nut to the torque listed this Chapter's Specification Section.

8   Insert the other end of the new hose through the bracket or loosely attach the fitting/bracket to the vehicle as applicable making sure the hose isn't kinked or twisted. Then fit the metal line to the hose (or hose fitting), tighten the hose bracket (if applicable) and tighten the brake tube fitting nut to the torque listed this Chapter's Specifications.

10.3 Disconnecting the front brake hose from the metal brake line using a flare-nut wrench

9   Carefully check to make sure the suspension or steering components don't make contact with the hose. Have an assistant push down on the vehicle while you watch to see whether the hose interferes with suspension operation. If you're replacing a front hose, have your assistant turn the steering wheel lock-to-lock while you make sure the hose doesn't interfere with the steering linkage or the steering knuckle.

10   After installation, check the master cylinder fluid level and add fluid as necessary. Bleed the brakes (see Section 11). Carefully test brake operation before resuming normal operation.

Metal brake lines

11   When replacing brake lines, be sure to use the correct parts. Do not use copper tubing for any brake system components. Purchase steel brake lines from a dealer parts department or auto parts store.

12   Prefabricated brake line, with the tube ends already flared and fittings installed, is available at auto parts stores and dealer parts departments. These lines are also sometimes bent to the proper shapes. If it is necessary to bend a line, use a tubing bender to prevent kinking the line.

13   When installing the new line make sure it's well supported in the brackets and has plenty of clearance between moving or hot components. Make sure you tighten the fittings securely.

14   After installation, check the master cylinder fluid level and add fluid as necessary. Bleed the brakes (see Section 11). Carefully test brake operation before resuming normal operation.

11   Brake system - bleeding

Refer to illustration 11.9

Warning: *Wear eye protection when bleeding the brake system. If the fluid comes in con-*

11.9 When bleeding the brakes, a hose is connected to the bleed screw at the caliper or wheel cylinder and then submerged in clean brake fluid - air will be seen as bubbles exiting the tube (all air must be expelled before moving to the next wheel)

tact with your eyes, immediately rinse them with water and seek medical attention.
Note: *Bleeding the brake system is necessary to remove any air that's trapped in the system when it's opened during removal and installation of a hose, line, caliper, wheel cylinder or master cylinder.*

1   If a brake line was disconnected only at a wheel, then only that caliper or wheel cylinder must be bled.

2   On conventional (non-ABS) brake systems, if air has entered the system due to low fluid level or master cylinder replacement, all four brakes must be bled. **Warning:** *If this has occurred on a model with an Anti-lock Brake System (ABS), or if the lines to the Hydraulic Control Unit or Integrated Control Unit (1998 models) have been disconnected, the vehicle must be towed to a dealer service department or other repair shop equipped with a DRB II scan tool to have the system properly bled.*

3   If a brake line is disconnected at a fitting located between the master cylinder and any of the brakes, that part of the system served by the disconnected line must be bled.

4   Remove any residual vacuum from the brake power booster by applying the brake several times with the engine OFF.

5   Raise the vehicle and support it securely on jackstands. **Note:** *The wheels do not have to be removed for this process.*

6   Remove the master cylinder reservoir cover and fill the reservoir with brake fluid. Reinstall the cover. **Note:** *Check the fluid level often during the bleeding operation and add fluid as necessary to prevent the fluid level from falling low enough to allow air bubbles into the master cylinder.*

7   Have an assistant on hand, as well as a supply of new brake fluid, an empty clear container, a length of clear plastic or vinyl tubing to fit over the bleed screw and a box-

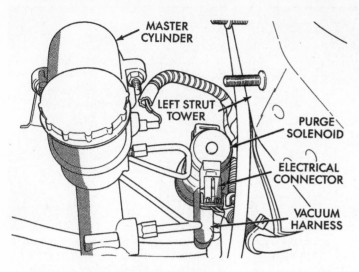

12.9 The purge solenoid is located on the left shock tower

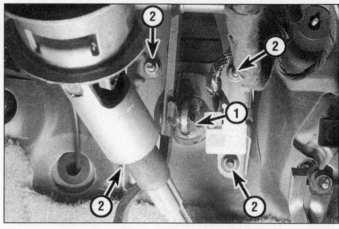

**12.16 Power brake booster mounting details
(as viewed from under the dash)**

1   Brake pedal-to-booster pushrod retaining clip (DO NOT reuse)
2   Power brake booster mounting nuts (the lower left nut is hidden behind steering intermediate shaft)

end wrench to open and close the bleed screw.

8   Beginning at the left rear wheel, remove the bleed screw dust cap. Loosen the bleed screw slightly, then tighten it to a point where it's snug but can still be loosened quickly and easily. Use the box-end wrench to avoid rounding off the bleed screw wrenching flats.

9   With the wrench in place on the bleed screw, attach one end of the tubing over the bleed screw fitting and submerge the other end in a clear container filled with about 1 inch of new brake fluid **(see illustration)**.

10   Have the assistant slowly push down on the brake pedal and hold it firmly depressed.

11   While the pedal is held depressed, open the bleed screw just enough to allow a flow of fluid to leave the valve. Watch for air bubbles to exit the submerged end of the tube. When the fluid flow slows after a couple of seconds, tighten the screw and have your assistant slowly release the pedal.

12   Repeat Steps 10 and 11 until no more air is seen leaving the tube, then tighten the bleed screw securely and proceed to the right front wheel, the right rear wheel and the left front wheel, in that order, and perform the same procedure. Be sure to check the fluid in the master cylinder reservoir frequently.

13   NEVER use old brake fluid. Brake fluid absorbs moisture from the atmosphere. When moisture is present in the hydraulic system, it will deteriorate the brake system components and lower the boiling point of the fluid which could lead to brake failure.

14   After bleeding the system, top up the brake fluid reservoir and reinstall the bleed screw dust caps.

15   Check the operation of the brakes. The pedal should feel solid when depressed, with no sponginess. If necessary, repeat the bleeding process. Check for leakage. **Warning:** *Do not operate the vehicle if the pedal feels low or spongy, if the ABS light on the dash won't go off, or if you are in doubt about the effectiveness of the brake system.*

12   Power brake booster - check, removal and installation

Operating check

1   Depress the brake pedal several times with the engine off and make sure that there is no change in the pedal reserve distance.

2   Depress the pedal and start the engine. If the pedal goes down slightly, operation is normal.

Airtightness check

3   Start the engine and turn it off after one or two minutes. Depress the brake pedal several times slowly. If the pedal goes down farther the first time but gradually rises after the second or third depression, the booster is airtight.

4   Depress the brake pedal while the engine is running, then stop the engine with the pedal depressed. If there is no change in the pedal reserve travel after holding the pedal for 30 seconds, the booster is airtight.

Removal

Refer to illustrations 12.9 and 12.16

5   The power brake booster unit requires no special maintenance apart from periodic inspection of the vacuum hoses and the case. The booster is not serviceable. If a problem develops, it must be replaced with a new one.

6   Disconnect the negative battery cable from the ground stud on the left shock tower (see Chapter 5, Section 1). Remove the air intake resonator and the related ducting between the throttle body and the air cleaner (see Chapter 4).

7   If equipped, unplug the cruise control servo electrical connector. Detach the unit from the shock tower and position it out of the way **(see illustration 8.2)**.

8   On models with a V6 engine, remove the throttle body from the intake manifold (see Chapter 4). Detach the accelerator cable bracket from the intake manifold and position it out of the way (the cable(s) may remain attached to bracket).

9   Label and detach the electrical connector and vacuum hose from the purge solenoid **(see illustration)**. Remove the purge solenoid from the vehicle.

10   Disconnect the vacuum hose(s) from the power brake booster vacuum fitting.

11   Label and disconnect the vacuum hoses and electrical connector from the EGR valve transducer (see Chapter 6). Remove the EGR valve transducer.

12   Disconnect the fluid level sensor connector from the master cylinder reservoir **(see illustration 8.6)**.

13   On models with a four-cylinder engine, it is not necessary to disconnect the brake lines from the master cylinder; simply remove the mounting nuts **(see illustration 8.8)** and slide the master cylinder off the studs and let it rest on the top of the transaxle (just make sure you don't kink the metal brake lines).

14   On models with a V6 engine, remove the master cylinder from the vehicle (see Section 8).

15   On V6 models equipped with an automatic transaxle, remove the transaxle fluid dipstick tube. Cover the dipstick tube hole in the transaxle with duct tape to prevent the entry of foreign debris.

16   Working inside the vehicle under the dash, disconnect the power brake pushrod from the top of the brake pedal by prying off the retaining clip **(see illustration)**. For safety reasons, discard the old pushrod retaining clip and buy a new clip for reassembly.

17   Remove the nuts attaching the booster to the firewall **(see illustration 12.16)**.

18   Working inside the engine compartment, carefully withdraw the power brake booster unit from the firewall and out of the engine compartment.

9

Installation

19   To install the booster, place it into position on the firewall and tighten the retaining nuts to the torque listed in this Chapter's Specifications. Connect the pushrod to the brake pedal. **Warning:** *Use a new retainer clip. DO NOT reuse the old clip.*

20   The remaining installation steps are the reverse of removal.

21   If the master cylinder was removed from the vehicle, bleed the brake hydraulic system (see Section 11).

22   Carefully test the operation of the brakes before placing the vehicle in normal operation.

13 Parking brake lever assembly - removal, installation and adjustment

Removal

Refer to illustrations 13.3 and 13.6

1   Remove the center console (see Chapter 11).

2   Place the parking brake lever in the fully released position (down).

3   Loosen the adjusting nut on the output cable **(see illustration)**.

4   Using a screwdriver, pry the output cable retaining clip **(see illustration 13.3)** from the rear cable tension equalizer and detach the output cable. Discard the old clip, it is not to be reused. **Note:** *If the parking brake lever assembly is going to be replaced, ignore this step.*

5   Disconnect both rear brake cables from the cable tension equalizer **(see illustration 13.3)**.

6   Unplug the electrical connector from the parking brake warning light switch **(see illustration)**.

7   Remove the fasteners attaching the parking brake lever assembly to the center console bracket.

8   Remove the parking brake lever and the front output cable as an assembly.

Installation

9   Installation is the reverse of removal. Install a new cable tension equalizer and output cable retaining clip. Be sure the output cable retaining clip is firmly attached after installation. Before installing the center console, perform the parking brake cable adjustment procedure below.

Adjustment

Refer to illustration 13.12

Note: *Anytime the parking brake cable requires adjustment, the cable tension equalizer must be replaced to ensure proper adjustment.*

10   Remove the center console (see Chapter 11).

11   Place the parking brake lever in the fully released position (down).

13.3 Parking brake lever details

1   *Output cable adjusting nut*
2   *Output cable retaining clip (DO NOT reuse)*
3   *Rear cable tension equalizer*

12   Tighten the output cable adjusting nut until 12 mm (approximately 7/16 to 1/2 inch) of threads are protruding from the nut **(see illustration)**.

13   Pull the lever back as far as it will travel - one time only. Fully actuating the lever in this manner stretches the portion of the cable tensioner which automatically provides the correct tension on the cables.

14   After adjustment, verify that the rear brakes are not dragging on the drums and the parking brake lever does not exhibit any freeplay. If either condition exists, tighten or loosen the output cable adjusting nut as required.

15   Install the center console (see Chapter 11).

14 Parking brake cables - replacement

Front cable

Note: *Anytime the parking brake cables are replaced or require adjustment, the cable tension equalizer must be replaced to ensure proper adjustment.*

Replacement

1   The front output cable is an integral part of the parking brake lever assembly and

cannot be replaced separately. If the output cable requires replacement, replace the parking brake lever assembly (see Section 13).

Rear cables

Removal

Refer to illustrations 14.8, 14.10, 14.11, 14.13, 14.14 and 14.15

2   Remove the center console (see Chapter 11).

3   Place the parking brake lever in the fully released position (down).

4   Loosen the adjusting nut on the output cable **(see illustration 13.3)**.

5   Using a screwdriver, pry the output cable retaining clip **(see illustration 13.3)** from the rear cable tension equalizer and detach the output cable. Discard the old clip - it is not to be reused.

6   Disconnect both rear brake cables from the cable tension equalizer **(see illustration 13.3)**.

7   Remove the rear seat assembly (see Chapter 11).

8   Remove the rear door sill scuff plate on each side **(see illustration)**.

9   Fold the rear carpeting forward to expose the parking brake cables.

10   Remove the parking brake cable routing clip from the floor pan **(see illustration)**.

11   Compress the retaining tabs of the

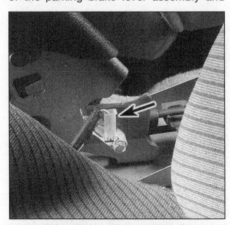

13.6 Parking brake warning light electrical connector

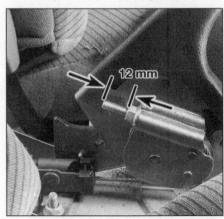

13.12 Tighten the output cable adjusting nut onto the cable until 12 mm of threads are exposed as shown

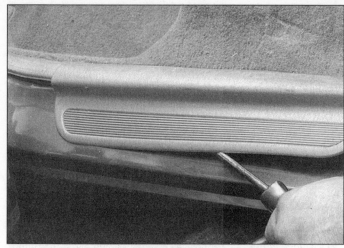

14.8 Carefully pry off the rear door sill plates from each rear door jam

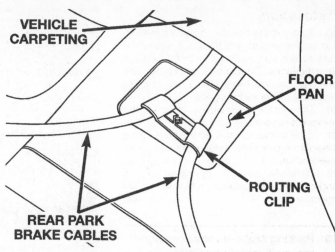

14.10 Parking brake cable routing clip

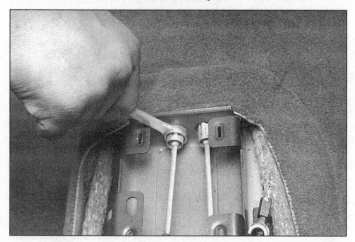

14.11 Sliding a 1/2 inch box-end wrench over the parking brake cable as shown will compress the retaining clip tabs so you can remove the cable from the bracket

14.13 If a 1/2 inch box-end wrench isn't available, use a small hose clamp to compress the parking brake cable retaining clip tabs

cable housing with a 1/2-inch box-end wrench or a small hose clamp **(see illustration)**. Pull the cable through the opening in the center console bracket. **Note:** *On some models, the center console rear bracket may have to be removed.*

12   Remove the rear drum brake shoes (see Section 6).
13   Compress the retaining tabs of the cable housing with a 1/2-inch box-end wrench or a small hose clamp and pull the cable through the brake backing plate **(see illustration)**.
14   Remove the cable brackets from the frame rail **(see illustration)**.
15   Remove the cable sealing grommet from the floor pan **(see illustration)**.
16   Remove the cable assembly from the vehicle.

Installation

17   Insert the front end of the cable through the hole in the floor pan and guide the cable grommet into place.
18   Insert the rear of the cable through the hole in the brake assembly backing plate. Make sure the cable is pulled through the hole far enough to allow the retaining tabs to expand all the way, locking the cable to the backing plate.
19   Install the cable brackets onto the appropriate cable (brackets are unique for left hand and right hand applications). Install the brackets onto the frame rail and tighten the bolts securely.
20   Connect the cable end to the parking brake lever on the trailing brake shoe and reassemble the rear brake assembly (see

9

14.14 Parking brake cable brackets (left side shown)

14.15 Parking brake cable sealing grommet as viewed from under the vehicle

Section 6). **Note:** *If the wheel hub/bearing assembly was removed, a new hub nut must be installed.*

21   Working inside the vehicle, grasp the parking brake cable grommet at the floor pan and pull hard to make sure the grommet is fully seated to the floor pan. **Note:** *If you're concerned about the quality of the grommet-to-floor pan seal, apply some RTV sealant around the grommet sealing areas.*

22   Install the cable into its appropriate position in the center console bracket and make sure the cable retainers have expanded to hold the cable firmly in place. If removed, install the center console rear bracket.

23   Secure the cables to the floor pan with the routing clip.

24   Place the carpet back into position and install both rear door opening sill scuff plates.

25   Install the rear seat assembly (see Chapter 11).

26   Connect both rear brake cables to the new cable tension equalizer **(see illustration 13.3)**.

27   Install the parking brake lever output cable into the cable tension equalizer and secure with a new retaining clip **(see illustration 13.3)**. DO NOT reuse the old output cable retaining clip!

28   Before attempting to adjust the parking brake cables, start the engine and fully depress the brake pedal two or three times to adjust the rear brakes.

29   Adjust the parking brake cable (see Section 13).

15   Brake light switch - check, replacement and adjustment

Description

1   The brake light switch is a normally open switch that controls the operation of the brake lights. The switch is located near the top of the brake pedal and is attached to a bracket. When the brake pedal is applied, the pedal arm moves away from the switch and a spring-loaded plunger closes the circuit to the brake lights.

2   Models equipped with cruise control use a dual purpose brake light switch that also deactivates the cruise control system when the brake pedal is depressed.

Check

3   Check the brake light fuse (see Chapter 12). If the fuse has blown, replace it. If it blows again, look for a short in the brake light circuit.

4   If the fuse is okay, use a test light or voltmeter to verify that there's voltage to the switch. If there's no voltage to the switch, look for an open or short in the power wire to the switch. Repair as necessary.

5   If the brake lights still don't come on when the brake pedal is applied, unplug the electrical connector from the brake light switch and, using an ohmmeter, verify that there is continuity between the switch terminals when the brake pedal is applied, i.e. when the switch is closed. If continuity is not detected, replace the switch.

6   If there is continuity between the switch terminals when the brake is applied (it closes the circuit), but the brake lights don't come on when the brake pedal is applied, check for power to the brake light bulb sockets when the pedal is depressed. If voltage is present, replace the bulbs (it isn't very likely that all of them would fail simultaneously, but it is possible that they could be burned out). If voltage is not available, check the wiring between the switch and the brake lights for an open circuit and repair as necessary.

Replacement and adjustment

Refer to illustration 15.7

7   Depress and hold the brake pedal, then rotate the brake light switch about 30-degrees in a counterclockwise direction

15.7 The brake light switch (arrow) is located under the dash and mounted on a bracket near the brake pedal arm (dual-purpose brake light/cruise control switch shown)

(see illustration) and remove it from the mounting bracket.

8   Unplug the electrical connector from the switch and remove it from the vehicle.

9   Grasp the switch plunger and pull it outward until it has ratcheted to it's fully extended position.

10   Depress the brake pedal as far as it will go, then install the switch in the bracket by aligning the index key on the switch with the slot at the top of the square hole in the mounting bracket. When the switch is fully installed in the bracket, rotate the switch clockwise about 30-degrees to lock the switch into the bracket.

11   Gently pull back on the brake pedal until the pedal stops moving. The switch plunger will ratchet backward to the correct position. **Caution:** *Don't use excessive force when pulling back on the brake pedal to adjust the switch. If you use too much force, you will damage the switch or the striker.*

12   Plug the electrical connector into the switch.

Chapter 10
Suspension and steering systems

Contents

Specifications

Torque specifications

Front suspension

	Ft-lbs (unless otherwise indicated)
Driveaxle/hub nut	180
Lower control arm front pivot bolt	
1995	120
1996	85
1997 on	135
Lower control arm-to-crossmember rear bolt	
1995	120
1996 on	85
Shock absorber-to-shock tower bolts	
1995	23
1996	68
1997 on	70
Shock absorber damper rod nut	
1995	55
1996 on	40
Shock absorber-to-clevis pinch bolt	70
Shock absorber clevis-to-control arm bolt	
1995	120
1996	135
1997 on	68
Stabilizer bar attaching link nuts	
1995	21
1996	78
1997 on	75
Stabilizer bar bushing clamp bolts	
1995, 1996	21
1997 on	45
Lower balljoint-to-steering knuckle castle nut	
1995	70
1996 on	55

10

Torque specifications

Ft-lbs (unless otherwise indicated)

Front suspension (continued)

Upper balljoint-to-steering knuckle castle nut	
1995	70
1996	45
1997 on	40
Upper control arm-to-shock mount bolts	68
Wheel lug nuts	See Chapter 1

Rear suspension

Balljoint-to-knuckle castle nut	
1995	63
1996 on	50
Brake support plate mounting bolts	45
Crossmember-to-body bolts	70
Control arm pivot bar-to-crossmember	79
Hub and bearing assembly-to-knuckle retaining nut	185
Lateral link-to-knuckle bolts/nuts	70
Lateral link jam nuts	70
Lateral link-to-crossmember bolts	70
Shock absorber mounting bracket-to-body nuts	
1995 models	25
1996 and later models	40
Shock absorber-to-knuckle bolts/nuts	70
Shock absorber rod-to-upper mount nut	
1995 models	55
1996 and later models	40
Stabilizer bar bushing clamp bolts	20
Stabilizer-to-lateral link nuts	24
Trailing link shaft nuts - both ends	70
Trailing bracket-to-body bolts	
1995 models	70
1996 and later models	21

Steering system

Airbag module retaining nuts	90 in-lbs
Power steering pump mounting bolts	40
Power steering fluid pressure and return line fitting nuts	23
Power steering fluid pressure banjo	
fitting bolt (alternate-to-pressure fitting nut)	25
Steering gear mounting bolts	50
Power steering fluid line tube fittings	23
Tie-rod (outer)-to-inner jam lock nut	55
Tie-rod balljoint stud-to-steering knuckle nut	45
Steering column flex coupler pinch bolt	20
Steering wheel nut	45

1   General information

Refer to illustrations 1.1a, 1.1b, 1.2a and 1.2b

The front suspension **(see illustrations)** uses coil-over shock absorber assemblies and unequal length control arms. The upper end of the shock absorber/coil spring assembly is attached to an aluminum housing in the inside of the shock tower. The bottom of the shock absorber is attached to the lower control arm. The front and rear ends of the lower control arm are bolted to the front crossmember. The inner end of the upper control arm is attached to the aluminum housing in the shock tower. The steering knuckle is connected to both the upper and lower control arms through balljoints. The stabilizer bar is bolted to the suspension cradle and the underbody of the vehicle and attached to both lower control arms, which reduces body roll during cornering.

The rear suspension **(see illustrations)** also uses coil-over shock absorber assemblies. The coil spring is mounted on the shock absorber, and the upper end of the shock is attached to the vehicle body. The lower end of the shock is attached to the rear knuckle. The knuckle is located by a pair of lateral links on each side, and an upper control arm, plus a longitudinally mounted trailing link between the body and each knuckle.

The power-assisted rack-and-pinion steering gear is located on the front suspension crossmember, behind the engine and in front of the firewall. The steering gear actuates the tie-rods. The tie-rod ends are connected to steering arms on the steering knuckles. The steering column actuates the steering gear and is designed to collapse in the event of an accident.

When working on the suspension or steering system components, you may come across fasteners which seem impossible to loosen. Fasteners on the underside of the vehicle are continually subjected to water, road grime, mud, etc., and can become rusted or "frozen," making them extremely difficult to remove. To unscrew these fasteners without damaging them (or other components), be sure to use lots of penetrating oil and allow it to soak in for a while. Use a wire brush to clean exposed threads and ease removal of the nut or bolt and prevent damage to the threads. A sharp blow with a hammer and punch will sometimes break the bond between nut and bolt threads, but be careful to keep the punch from slipping off the fastener and ruining the threads. Heating the stuck fastener and surrounding area with

1.1a Front suspension and steering components

1	Stabilizer bar	4	Brake caliper	7	Steering knuckle
2	Lower control arm	5	Heat shield	8	Tie-rod
3	Brake disc	6	Stabilizer bar bushing retainers	9	Tie-rod end

1.1b Front suspension and steering details

1   Upper control arm
2   Coil spring
3   Steering knuckle
4   Shock absorber
5   Shock absorber clevis
6   Tie-rod end
7   Lower control arm
8   Steering gear boot

10

1.2a Rear suspension components

1	Crossmember	4	Forward lateral link	7	Rear knuckle
2	Upper control arm	5	Stabilizer bar attaching link	8	Trailing link
3	Rear lateral link	6	Stabilizer bar	9	Trailing link bracket

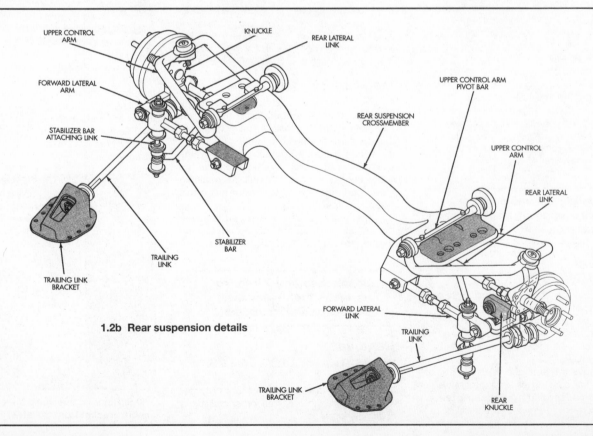

1.2b Rear suspension details

2.2a Remove the nuts (arrow) . . .

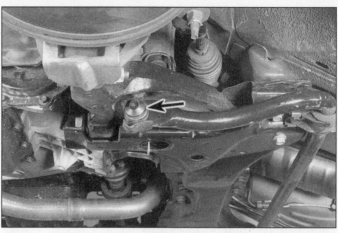

2.2b . . . and the attaching link assemblies from the lower control arm (arrow)

a torch sometimes helps too, but isn't recommended because of the obvious fire dangers. Long breaker bars and extension, or "cheater," pipes increase leverage, but never use an extension pipe on a ratchet - the ratcheting mechanism could be damaged. Tightening the nut or bolt first will sometimes help break it loose. Fasteners that require drastic measures to remove should always be replaced with new ones.

Most of the procedures in this Chapter involve jacking up the vehicle and working underneath it. A good pair of jackstands will be needed. A hydraulic floor jack is the preferred type of jack to lift the vehicle, and it can also be used to support certain components during various operations. **Warning:** *Never rely on a jack to support a vehicle while working on it. Whenever any of the suspension or steering fasteners are loosened or removed they must be inspected and, if necessary, replaced with new ones of the same part number or of original equipment quality and design. Torque specifications must be followed for proper reassembly and component retention. Never attempt to heat or straighten any suspension or steering components. Instead, replace any bent or damaged part with a new one.*

2 Stabilizer bar and bushings (front) - removal, inspection and installation

Removal

Refer to illustrations 2.2a, 2.2b and 2.3

1   Loosen the front wheel lug nuts, raise the front of the vehicle and support it securely on jackstands. Apply the parking brake and block the rear wheels to keep the vehicle from rolling off the stands. Remove the front wheels.
2   Remove the nuts and the stabilizer bar attaching link assemblies from the front lower control arms **(see Illustrations)**. **Note:** *Use an Allen wrench in the end of the lower con-*

trol arm stud to prevent the stud from moving when removing the attaching link nut.
3   Remove the four bolts attaching the stabilizer bar bushing clamps to the front suspension crossmember and body **(see illustration)**.
4   Remove the stabilizer bar from the vehicle.

Inspection

5   Inspect for cracked, torn, or distorted stabilizer bar bushings, bushing retainers, and worn or damaged stabilizer bar attaching links. Damaged stabilizer bar attaching links must be replaced before reinstalling the stabilizer bar.
6   To replace damaged stabilizer bar bushings, open the bushing slit and peel the bushing from the stabilizer bar. **Caution:** *Install the new bushings with the slits facing the same way that the original bushing slits faced.*

Installation

7   Position the stabilizer bar and bushings in the front crossmember. Install the clamps and bolts, tightening them to the torque listed in this Chapter's Specifications.
8   Align the stabilizer bar attaching link assemblies with the mounting holes in the lower control arms and install the retaining nuts. Tighten the nuts to the torque in this Chapter's Specifications.
9   Install the wheels and lug nuts. Lower the vehicle and tighten the lug nuts to the torque listed in the Chapter 1 Specifications.

3 Shock absorber/coil spring assembly (front) - removal, inspection and installation

Removal

Refer to illustrations 3.3, 3.4, 3.5, 3.6, 3.7 and 3.9
Warning: *Do not remove the shock absorber rod nut before the shock absorber coil spring is compressed.*

2.3 Remove the stabilizer bar bushing retainer bolts (arrows)

1   Loosen the wheel lug nuts, raise the front of the vehicle, support it securely on jackstands and remove the wheel.
2   Mark the shock absorbers with a R or L if they are both removed at the same time.
3   Remove the wheel speed sensor cable bracket from the steering knuckle **(see illustration)**.

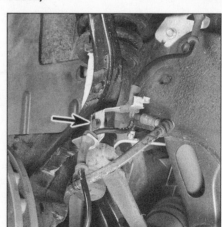

3.3 Remove the wheel speed sensor cable bracket from the steering knuckle

10

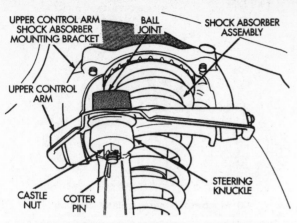

3.4 Upper balljoint stud cotter pin and castle nut

3.5 Push the upper balljoint stud out of the steering knuckle
with a puller

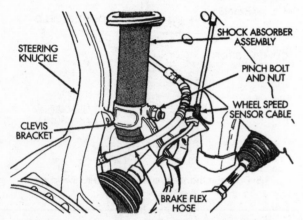

3.6 Remove the shock absorber clevis pinch bolt

3.7 Remove the bolt that attaches the shock absorber clevis to
the lower control arm

4   Remove the cotter pin and loosen the castle nut from the upper balljoint stud **(see illustration)**.
5   Detach the balljoint from the steering knuckle using a puller **(see illustration)**. Remove the nut and pull the steering knuckle outward and to the back of the front wheel opening. **Caution:** *Be careful not to strain the brake hose.*

6   Remove the shock absorber clevis pinch bolt and nut **(see illustration)**.
7   Remove the clevis bolt from the lower control arm **(see illustration)**.
8   Use a soft-faced hammer (brass) to tap the clevis from the shock absorber.
9   Remove the four bolts from the shock tower attaching the upper control arm/shock absorber **(see illustration)**.

10   Remove the upper control arm mounting bracket and shock absorber as an assembly.
11   Separate the upper control arm mounting bracket and the shock absorber.

Inspection

12   Check the shock absorber assembly for leaking fluid, dents, cracks and other obvious damage which would warrant replacement.

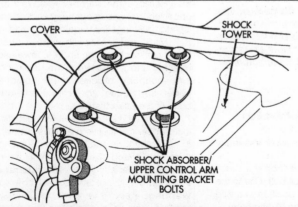

3.9 Remove the four upper control arm/shock absorber mount
bolts from the shock tower (arrows)

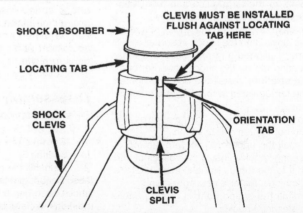

3.14 Proper positioning of the clevis on the shock absorber

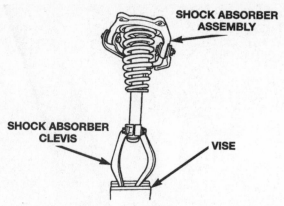

4.2 Clamp the shock absorber by the clevis in a vise

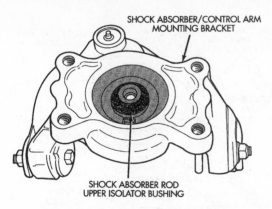

4.6 Remove the upper isolator bushing . . .

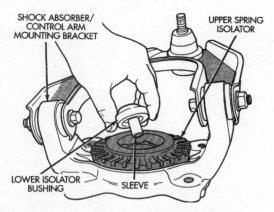

4.7 . . . and the lower isolator bushing and sleeve

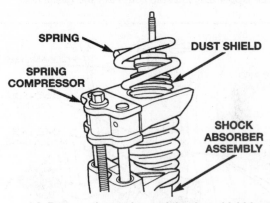

4.8 Remove the washer and the dust shield from the shock absorber

Check the coil spring for chips and corrosion. Replace it if any undesirable symptoms are found. See Section 4 for the shock absorber or coil spring replacement procedure.

Installation

Refer to illustration 3.14

13   Connect the shock absorber assembly to the upper control arm mount. Install the assembly (with the clevis removed) into the shock tower. Align the two locating pins and the four mounting holes on the upper control arm/shock absorber mount and tighten the four bolts to the torque listed in this Chapter's Specifications.

14   Install the clevis on the shock absorber. Tap the clevis onto the shock absorber until it is properly aligned and fully seated against the locating tab on the shock absorber body **(see illustration)**. Install the bolt and tighten it to the torque listed in this Chapter's Specifications.

15   Install the clevis-to-lower control arm bolt. Do not tighten it at this time.

16   Install the upper balljoint into the top of the steering knuckle. Install the castle nut and tighten it to the torque listed in this Chapter's Specifications. Install a new cotter pin.

17   Install the speed control routing cable on the steering knuckle.

18   Using a floor jack placed under the outer end of the lower control arm, raise the lower

control arm to simulate normal ride height. Tighten the shock absorber clevis-to-lower control arm bolt to the torque in this Chapter's Specifications. Remove the floor jack.

19   Install the wheel and lug nuts. Lower the vehicle and tighten the lug nuts to the torque listed in the Chapter 1 Specifications.

4   Shock absorber/coil spring - replacement

Warning: *Disassembling a shock absorber/coil spring assembly is dangerous. Use only a high-quality spring compressor, which can be rented at most auto parts stores or equipment yards. Carefully follow all instructions furnished by the tool manufacturer or serious injury could result.*

Disassembly

Refer to illustrations 4.2, 4.6, 4.7, 4.8 and 4.10

1   Remove the shock absorber assembly (see Section 3).

2   Reinstall the clevis bracket on the shock absorber and tighten the pinch bolt. Clamp the shock absorber in a vertical position in a vise holding the clevis bracket **(see illustration)**.

3   Compress the coil spring using a coil spring compressor (which can be obtained at

most auto parts stores or equipment yards). Follow the tool manufacturer's instructions, install the spring compressor on the spring, and compress it sufficiently to relieve all pressure from the upper spring seat. **Warning:** *Do not remove the shock absorber damper rod nut before the coil spring is compressed. Be sure to have the first full top and bottom coil of the coil spring captured by the coil spring compressor.*

4   Remove the shock absorber damper rod nut while holding the rod to prevent it from rotating.

5   Remove the damper rod washer, the upper control arm mounting bracket and the isolator bushings from the damper rod.

6   Mark and remove the shock absorber upper isolator bushing, and the lower isolator bushing and sleeve from the upper control arm mounting bracket. Then remove the upper spring isolator from the mounting bracket **(see illustration)**.

7   Remove the lower isolator bushing from the damper rod sleeve **(see illustration)**.

8   Remove the washer from the top of the dust shield and the dust shield from the shock absorber assembly **(see illustration)**.

9   Remove the compressed coil spring. **Warning:** *Keep the ends of the spring pointed away from your body. Set the spring aside in a safe, isolated location.* **Note:** *Mark the springs R or L for proper reinstallation.*

10

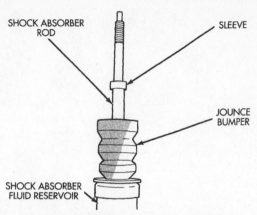

4.10 Remove the jounce bumper and sleeve from the shock absorber

4.14 Upper and lower shock absorber rod bushing identification

10   Remove the jounce bumper and sleeve from the shock absorber assembly **(see illustration)**.

11   Remove the coil spring isolator from the lower spring seat on the shock absorber.

Inspection

12   Inspect the shock absorber for rod binding, and the shock mount and upper spring seat/isolator for cracks/distortion, deterioration, rips and cracks. Check the coil spring for chips, cracks and corrosion.

13   Replace any components found to be worn or defective.

Assembly

Refer to illustration 4.14

14   Assembly is the reverse of disassembly. When installing the sleeve on the shock absorber rod, install it with the undercut side of the sleeve facing downward. **Caution:** *The top and bottom shock absorber rod bushings must be reinstalled on the rod exactly as they were when they were removed* **(see illustration)**.

15   Install the shock absorber/coil spring assembly (see Section 3).

5   Upper control arm (front) - removal, inspection and installation

Removal

1   Remove the shock absorber (see Section 3).

2   Remove the coil spring from the shock absorber (see Section 4).

3   Remove the nuts and bolts attaching the upper control arm to the mounting bracket.

4   Remove the upper control arm from the mounting bracket.

Inspection

5   Make sure the control arm is straight. If it is bent, replace it. Do not attempt to

straighten a bent control arm.

6   Inspect the bushings in the mounting bracket for cracks and tears. If any bushing is torn or worn out, replace the control arm mounting bracket.

Installation

7   Install the upper control arm on the mounting bracket. **Note:** *The bolt heads must face inward (towards the coil spring).* Tighten the nuts to the torque listed in this Chapter's Specifications.

8   Install the coil spring on the shock absorber (see Section 4). Install the upper shock mount/upper control arm assembly (see Section 4). Install the shock absorber (see Section 3).

9   Using a floor jack placed under the outer end of the lower control arm, raise the lower control arm to simulate normal ride height. Tighten the shock absorber clevis-to-lower control arm bolt to the torque in this Chapter's Specifications. Remove the floor jack.

10   Install the wheel and lug nuts. Lower the vehicle and tighten the lug nuts to the torque listed in the Chapter 1 Specifications.

6   Lower control arm - removal and installation

Removal

Refer to illustrations 6.4, 6.6, 6.12a and 6.12b

1   Loosen the wheel lug nuts, raise the front of the vehicle, support it securely on jackstands and remove the wheel.

2   Remove the brake caliper (see Chapter 9) and support it with a piece of wire - don't let it hang from the brake hose.

3   Remove the brake disc from the front hub/bearing assembly.

4   If the vehicle is equipped with 15-inch wheels, the balljoint heat shield must be removed from the steering knuckle. Remove the two bolts and the heat shield from the steering knuckle **(see illustration)**.

5   Remove the cotter pin and loosen the lower balljoint castle nut a few turns.

6   Use a hammer to strike the boss on the steering knuckle until it separates from the lower balljoint stud **(see illustration)**. **Cau-**tion: *Do not hit the lower control arm or the balljoint grease seal, be careful not to sepa-*

6.4 Remove the balljoint heat shield

6.6 Strike the boss on the steering knuckle until it separates from the lower balljoint stud

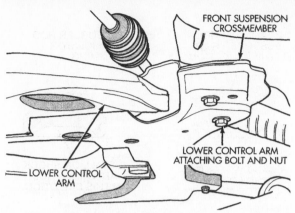

6.12a Remove the nut/bolt attaching the rear of the lower control arm to the front suspension crossmember . . .

6.12b . . . and the pivot bolt holding the front of the lower control arm to the front suspension crossmember

rate the inner CV joint and **do not** pry the lower balljoint from the steering knuckle. Once the balljoint stud has been released from the steering knuckle, remove the castle nut.

7   Remove the shock absorber clevis-to-lower control arm bolt and separate the clevis from the lower control arm **(see illustration 3.7)**.

8   Detach the stabilizer bar link from the lower control arm (see Section 2).

9   Remove the bolts attaching the stabilizer bar bushing clamp to the front suspension crossmember and the body of the vehicle.

10   Lower one side of the stabilizer bar away from the lower control arm.

11   Remove the nut and bolt attaching the lower control arm to the front suspension crossmember.

12   Remove the nuts and bolts attaching the lower control arm to the front suspension crossmember **(see illustrations)**.

13   Separate the front of the lower control arm from the front suspension crossmember. **Caution:** Be careful not to damage the balljoint seal against the steering knuckle when lowering it from the crossmember.

14   Remove the rear of the lower control arm from the front suspension crossmember. Be careful to keep the rear bushing from binding on the crossmember. Check the bushings in the lower control arm for cracking and other signs of deterioration. If necessary, take the control arm to an automotive machine shop to have the bushings replaced.

Installation

15   Install the rear, and then the front of the lower control arm into the front suspension cradle. Do not tighten the bolts at this time.

16   Connect the lower balljoint to the steering knuckle, tightening the castle nut to the torque listed in this Chapter's Specifications. Install a new cotter pin.

17   Installation of the remaining components is the reverse of removal. **Caution:** Be sure to install the balljoint heat shield. If the heat shield is not installed, the boot may fail due to excessive heat from the brake disc.

18   After installing the clevis on the lower control arm, place a floor jack under the lower control arm and raise the lower control arm to simulate normal ride height. Tighten the lower control arm-to-crossmember bolts and the shock absorber clevis-to-lower control arm bolt/nut to the values listed in this Chapter's Specifications.

19   Install the brake disc and caliper. Tighten the caliper mounting bolts to the torque listed in the Chapter 9 Specifications.

20   Install the wheel and lug nuts. Lower the vehicle and tighten the lug nuts to the torque listed in the Chapter 1 Specifications.

7   Balljoints (front) - check

1   With the vehicle on the ground, reach around the tire and try to wiggle the balljoint grease fitting. If any movement is felt, the balljoint is worn out.

2   Raise the vehicle and support it securely on jackstands. Make sure the tires are not contacting the ground.

3   Grasp the tire at top and bottom and try to rock it in and out. Have an assistant feel for play in the balljoints while you do this. The balljoints on these vehicles are not supposed to have any freeplay, so if any movement is evident, the balljoint must be replaced.

4   The balljoints on these vehicles are not

serviceable, nor can they be removed from the control arms. If a balljoint is bad, replace the control arm (see Section 5).

5   The balljoint seal, however, is replaceable. This is done by prying the old seal off and pressing a new one into place with a socket large enough to contact the outer circumference of the seal.

6   Remove the jackstands and lower the vehicle.

8   Hub and bearing assembly (front) - removal and installation

Removal

Refer to illustrations 8.1, 8.2 and 8.9

Warning: Dust created by the brake system may contain asbestos, which is harmful to your health. Never blow it out with compressed air and don't inhale any of it. Do not, under any circumstances, use petroleum-based solvents to clean brake parts. Use brake system cleaner only.

1   Remove the cotter pin, nut lock, and spring washer from the front stub axle **(see illustration)**.

2   Loosen the driveaxle/hub nut **(see illustration)**. **Note:** The hub and driveshaft are attached by splines through the steering knuckle and retained by the hub nut.

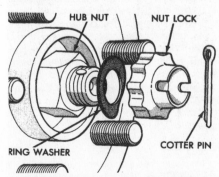

8.1 Remove the cotter pin, nut lock, and spring washer from the front stub axle

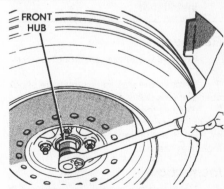

8.2 Loosen the front hub nut

10

8.9 Pull the steering knuckle away from the outer C/V joint

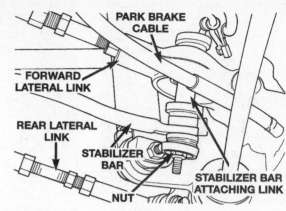

10.2 Remove the nuts attaching the stabilizer links and isolator bushings to the stabilizer

3   Loosen the wheel lug nuts, raise the vehicle and support it securely on jackstands. Remove the wheel.
4   Remove the brake caliper, support it with a piece of wire and remove the brake disc from the hub (see Chapter 9).
5   Remove the balljoint heat shield from the lower control arm on vehicles equipped with 15-inch wheels **(see illustration 6.4)**. **Note:** *The heat shield must be removed before separating the balljoint stud from the steering knuckle.*
6   Separate the tie-rod end from the steering knuckle arm (see Section 21).
7   Remove the speed sensor cable routing bracket from the steering knuckle on vehicles equipped with anti-lock brakes **(see illustration 3.3)**.
8   Separate the steering knuckle from the lower control arm balljoint (see Section 6).
9   Support the driveshaft and pull the steering knuckle away from the outer C/V joint **(see illustration)**. If the driveaxle splines stick in the hub, push the stub axle through the hub with a two-jaw puller.
10   Remove the cotter pin and the nut from the upper balljoint stud **(see illustration 3.4)**.
11   Separate the upper balljoint stud from the steering knuckle using a puller **(see illustration 3.5)**.
12   Mount the steering knuckle securely in a vise.
13   Remove the hub/bearing mounting bolts from the steering knuckle.
14   Remove the hub/bearing from the steering knuckle. It may be necessary to tap the assembly out with a hammer.

Installation

15   Clean all hub/bearing mounting surfaces on the steering knuckle.
16   Install the hub/bearing on the steering knuckle. Install the bolts and tighten them to the torque listed in this Chapter's Specifications.
17   Installation of the remaining components is the reverse of removal. **Caution:** *Be sure to install the tie-rod and balljoint heat shields. If the heat shields are not installed, the seals may fail due to excessive heat from*

the brake disc.
18   Tighten all nuts/bolts to the torque listed in this Chapter's Specifications.
19   Install the wheel and lug nuts. Lower the vehicle and tighten the lug nuts to the torque listed in the Chapter 1 Specifications.
20   Have an assistant apply the brakes, then tighten the driveaxle/hub nut to the torque listed in this Chapter's Specifications.

9   Steering knuckle - removal and installation

Removal and installation of the steering knuckle is covered as part of the sequence in Section 8.

10   Stabilizer bar and bushings (rear) - removal and installation

Refer to illustrations 10.2 and 10.3

Removal

1   Loosen the rear wheel lug nuts. Raise the rear of the vehicle and place it securely on jackstands. Block the front wheels and remove the rear wheels.
2   Remove the nuts attaching the stabilizer links and isolator bushings to the stabilizer **(see illustration)**.
3   Unbolt the stabilizer bar clamps from the crossmember **(see illustration)**.
4   Remove the stabilizer bar from the vehicle. **Note:** *Take note of the orientation of the stabilizer bar bend at the end of the bar before removal for proper installation later - the bend in the end of the bar is positioned upwards in the vehicle when viewed from the side. The stabilizer bar will come out of the vehicle between the exhaust pipe and the suspension crossmember.*

Inspection

5   Inspect the stabilizer bushings for cracks and tears. If the bushings are damaged, distorted or excessively worn, replace them.

10.3 The stabilizer bar bushing clamps are secured with two bolts (arrows)

Installation

6   Installation is the reverse of removal, first tightening the stabilizer bar ends to the torque listed in this Chapter's Specifications, then installing the bushing clamps. Make sure the rubber bushings are installed with the slits in the bushings positioned toward the front of the vehicle. Tighten the stabilizer bushing clamp bolts to the torque listed in this Chapter's Specifications.
7   Install the rear wheels and lug nuts. Lower the vehicle and tighten the lug nuts to the torque listed in the Chapter 1 Specifications.

11   Shock absorber/coil spring assembly (rear) - removal, inspection, component replacement and installation

Removal

Refer to illustrations 11.2 and 11.4

1   Inside the trunk, roll back the carpeting on the top of the rear shock absorber tower to access the upper shock mounting bolts. Remove the plastic cap.

11.2 Lift the carpeting and unsnap the plastic cover from the upper shock tower, then remove the two upper mounting bolts (arrows)

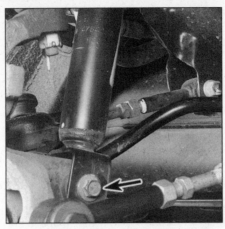

11.4 Remove the lower shock mount clevis bolt and nut (arrow)

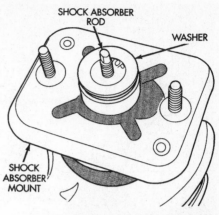

11.13 Remove the washer on the top of the shock absorber assembly

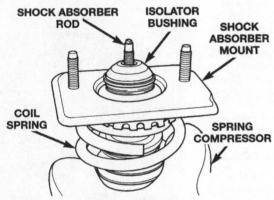

11.14a Remove the isolator bushing and shock absorber mount

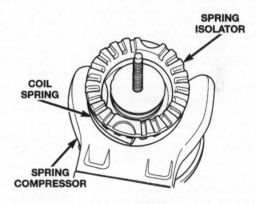

11.14b Remove the spring isolator from the coil spring

2   Inside the trunk, remove the two shock absorber upper mounting nuts **(see illustration)**. **Note:** *Do not remove the shock damper rod nut at the center of the upper mount.*

3   Loosen the rear wheel lug nuts, raise the rear of the vehicle and support it securely on jackstands. Block the front wheels and remove the rear wheels.

4   Remove the shock absorber lower mounting bolt from the rear knuckle **(see illustration)**.

5   Push down on the rear suspension and pull the shock away from the knuckle. Then guide the shock downward and remove the shock absorber.

Inspection

6   Check the shock absorber for leaking fluid, dents, cracks and other obvious damage which would require repair or replacement. To check for loss of gas charge, remove the coil spring (see Step 10) push the shaft of the shock in, then release - the shaft should return to its fully extended position.

7   Check the coil spring for chips or cracks in the spring coating (this can cause premature spring failure due to corrosion). Inspect the spring seat for general deterioration.

8   Inspect the rubber isolators and bushings in the upper mount bracket for cracks,

distortion, or any deterioration. Inspect the dust shield for rips or deterioration. Inspect the jounce bumper for cracks and deterioration.

9   Replace components as necessary.

Component replacement

Refer to illustrations 11.13, 11.14a, 11.14b, 11.15 and 11.18

Warning: *Disassembling a shock absorber/coil spring assembly is dangerous. Use only a high-quality spring compressor, which can be rented at most auto parts stores or equipment yards. Carefully follow all instructions furnished by the tool manufacturer or serious injury could result.*

10   Mount the shock assembly in a vise, clamping the bottom shock clevis bracket. Mark the shock absorber and the coil spring RIGHT or LEFT, depending on which side of the vehicle from which it was removed. **Warning:** *Do not remove the shock damper rod nut before the spring is compressed.*

11   Installing the spring compressor on the first full top and bottom coil of the spring, compress the spring until it can be wiggled, indicating that all pressure has been relieved from the upper mount.

12   Hold the damper rod from rotating using a wrench or locking pliers, then unscrew the

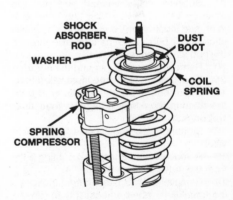

11.15 Remove the rod washer from the top of the shock absorber dust boot

10

damper rod nut.

13   Remove the washer from the shock mounting bracket **(see illustration)**.

14   Remove the isolator bushing, the shock absorber mount, and the spring isolator from the coil spring **(see illustrations)**.

15   Remove the rod washer from the top of the shock absorber dust boot **(see illustration)**.

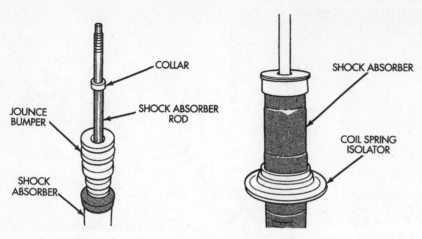

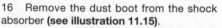

11.18 Slide off the shock absorber rod rubber jounce bumper, collar, and coil spring isolator

12.2 Use an open-end wrench to hold the trailing link from rotating while removing the nut and washer at the knuckle

16   Remove the dust boot from the shock absorber **(see illustration 11.15)**.

17   Lift the coil spring off of the shock absorber. **Warning:** *Keep the ends of the spring pointed away from your body. Set the spring aside in a safe, isolated location.*

18   Remove the rubber jounce bumper, collar, and coil spring isolator from the shock absorber **(see illustration)**.

19   Reassembly is the reverse of removal. When installing the sleeve on the shock absorber rod, install it with the undercut side of the sleeve facing downward. Push the sleeve tightly onto the rod step until the sleeve is seated firmly. Reinstall the top washer on the shock rod with the work TOP stamped on the washer facing upward **(see illustration 11.13)**. When reinstalling the spring, align the studs at the top of the mounting plate with the hole in the bottom clevis bracket *before* relieving the spring force.

Installation

20   Guide the shock absorber into place, inserting the upper mounting studs through the holes in the shock tower. Install the nuts, but don't tighten them yet.

21   Connect the lower end of the shock absorber to the knuckle, with the bolt head facing the rear of the vehicle. Tighten the bolt/nut to the torque listed in this Chapter's Specifications.

22   Install the wheel and lug nuts. Lower the vehicle and tighten the lug nuts to the torque listed in the Chapter 1 Specifications. Tighten the upper mounting nuts to the torque listed in this Chapter's Specifications. Install the cap.

12   Trailing link (rear) - removal and installation

Refer to illustrations 12.2 and 12.3

1   Loosen the rear wheel lug nuts, raise the vehicle and support it securely on jackstands.

Block the front wheels and remove the rear wheel.

2   At the rear knuckle, remove the nut, bushing retainer, and outer trailing link bushing from the trailing link **(see illustration)**.

3   Remove the four bolts from the trailing link bracket which attach the bracket to the body and frame rail **(see illustration)**.

4   Remove trailing link and mounting bracket as an assembly from the vehicle.

5   If separating the trailing link from the mounting bracket, note the location and positions of the bushings and retainer for correct reinstallation later.

6   Installation is the reverse of the removal procedure. Be sure to tighten the bolts and nuts to the torque listed in this Chapter's Specifications.

13   Lateral links (rear) - removal and installation

Refer to illustrations 13.2, 13.4, 13.6 and 13.7

1   Loosen the rear wheel lug nuts, raise the rear of the vehicle and support it securely on jackstands. Remove the rear wheel.

12.3 Unbolt the trailing link bracket bolts (arrow) to remove the forward end of the trailing link

Forward lateral link

2   Remove rear stabilizer bar attaching link from the forward lateral link **(see illustration)**.

3   Remove the nut, bolt and washer attaching the forward lateral link to the knuckle **(see illustration 11.2)**.

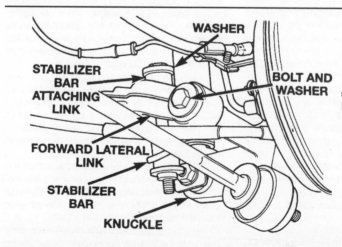

13.2 Remove the stabilizer bar attaching link bolt/nuts and front lateral link to knuckle bolt and washer

13.4 Remove the front lateral link-to-crossmember bolt (arrow) and nut

13.6 Remove the rear lateral link to knuckle bolt (arrow) and nut

4   Remove the nut, bolt and washer attaching the forward lateral link to the suspension crossmember **(see illustration)**.
5   Remove the forward lateral link from the vehicle. **Note:** *Lateral links are replaced as a unit - do not repair or straighten a lateral link. Do not apply heat to the lateral link adjusting screws or jam nuts to loosen them.*

Rear lateral link

6   Remove the nut, bolt and washer attaching the rear lateral link to the knuckle **(see illustration)**.
7   Remove the bolt and washer attaching the rear lateral link to the suspension crossmember **(see illustration)**.
8   Remove the rear lateral link from the vehicle. **Note:** *Lateral links are replaced as a unit - do not repair or straighten a lateral link. Do not apply heat to the lateral link adjusting screws or jam nuts to loosen them.*

Installation

9   Installation is the reverse of removal. Install the front lateral link crossmember bolt with the head of the bolts are toward the front of the vehicle. Install the rear lateral link crossmember bolt with the head of the bolts are toward the rear of the vehicle. For the forward lateral link, make sure the cup in the cast portion faces downward and toward the rear knuckle when installed. For the rear lateral link, install with the adjusting screw toward the knuckle, not toward the suspension crossmember **(see illustration 13.6)**. Tighten all fasteners to the torque listed in this Chapter's Specifications.
10   Install the wheel and lug nuts, then lower the vehicle to the ground. Tighten the wheel lug nuts to the torque listed in the Chapter 1 Specifications.

14   Rear suspension crossmember - removal and reinstallation

Refer to illustration 14.6
1   Loosen the rear wheel lug nuts, raise the

13.7 Remove the rear lateral link bolt/washer from the suspension crossmember

rear of the vehicle and support it securely on jackstands. Remove the rear wheels.
2   Remove the muffler support bracket from the rear frame rail.
3   Remove the rear exhaust pipe hanger from the suspension crossmember, then ease the exhaust system while it drops down as far as possible.
4   Support the suspension crossmember with a hydraulic jack and a wooden block on the jack. If the vehicle has ABS (Anti-lock Brake System), remove the routing clips for the wheel speed sensor cable from the brackets on the upper control arm.
5   Remove the nuts and bolts on each side of the vehicle which attach both rear lateral links and both front lateral links to the knuckles.
6   Remove the bolts attaching the suspension crossmember to the rear frame rails **(see illustration)**.
7   Lower the suspension crossmember using the hydraulic jack a sufficient distance to remove the upper control arm pivot bolts which attach the control arm pivot bar to the crossmember **(see illustration 1.2b)**.
8   Remove the four upper control arm mounting bolts from the suspension cross-

14.6 Remove the suspension crossmember mounting bolts (arrow)

member. Remove the upper control arms from the crossmember.
9   Lower the suspension crossmember, lateral arms, and stabilizer bar as far as possible and then remove the suspension crossmember.
10   Installation is the reverse of removal. Mount the lateral links, stabilizer bar bushing clamps and the stabilizer bar on the crossmember before installation. Align the crossmember as described in Section 15. Tighten the fasteners to the torque listed in this Chapter's Specifications.

15   Upper control arm (rear) - removal and installation

Refer to illustrations 15.6 and 15.13
1   Loosen the rear wheel lug nuts, raise the entire rear of the vehicle and support it securely on jackstands. Remove the rear wheels.
2   Remove the shock absorber clevis bracket bolt and nut from both sides of the vehicle **(see illustration 11.4)**.
3   Remove the muffler support bracket from the rear frame rail.

10

15.6 Use a puller to detach the upper control arm balljoint from the rear knuckle

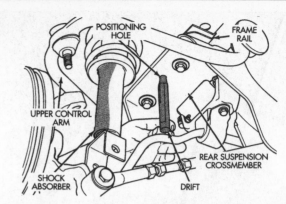

15.13 Position a temporary locating drift in the suspension crossmember to frame rail alignment hole - one drift on each side of the vehicle

4   Remove the rear exhaust pipe hangar from the suspension crossmember, then ease the exhaust system while it drops down as far as possible.

5   Remove the cotter pin and loosen the castle nut attaching the upper control arm balljoint to the knuckle.

6   With the castle nut loosened a few turns, detach the balljoint stud from the knuckle using a puller **(see illustration)**.

7   Support the suspension crossmember with a hydraulic jack and a wooden block on the jack. If the vehicle has ABS (Anti-lock Brake System), remove the routing clips for the wheel speed sensor cable from brackets on the upper control arm.

8   Remove the nuts and bolts on each side of the vehicle which attach both rear lateral links and both front lateral links to the knuckles.

9   Remove the bolts attaching the suspension crossmember to the rear frame rails **(see illustration 14.6)**.

10   Lower the suspension crossmember using the hydraulic jack a sufficient distance to remove the upper control arm pivot bolts which attach the control arm pivot bar to the crossmember **(see illustration 1.2b)**.

11   Remove the two upper control arm

mounting bolts from the suspension crossmember. Remove the upper control arm from the crossmember.

12   The upper control arm, bushings, and pivot bar are serviced as a complete assembly. Only the balljoint and balljoint seal are replaceable. Replace the balljoint and balljoint seal with the control arm removed from the vehicle.

13   Installation is the reverse of removal. When installing the suspension crossmember, install a drift **(see illustration)** into the positioning holes (one positioning hole in each side of the crossmember and frame rail) to properly locate the suspension in the vehicle body. Tighten fasteners to the torque listed in this Chapter's Specifications. Remove the drifts.

14   Drive the vehicle to an alignment shop to check rear wheel camber and toe and adjust as necessary.

16 Upper balljoint (rear) - replacement

The balljoint on the rear upper control arm is replaceable, but it is a press fit in the

arm and requires a hydraulic press and special adapters to remove and install. For this reason we recommend that you take the upper control arm to an automotive machine shop to have the balljoint replaced (refer to Section 15 for the removal and installation procedure). Many auto parts stores are also equipped to handle such work.

17 Hub and bearing assembly (rear) - removal and installation

Refer to illustrations 17.3, 17.4 and 17.5
Warning: *Dust created by the brake system may contain asbestos, which is harmful to your health. Never blow it out with compressed air and don't inhale any of it. Do not, under any circumstances, use petroleum-based solvents to clean brake parts. Use brake system cleaner only.*

1   Loosen the wheel lug nuts, raise the vehicle and support it securely on jackstands. Remove the wheel.

2   Remove the brake drum from the rear hub/bearing (see Chapter 9).

3   Remove the dust cap **(see illustration)**.

4   Remove the hub/bearing retaining nut

17.3 Tap off the rear hub/bearing dust cap with a hammer and chisel

17.4 Remove the rear spindle nut

17.5 Pull the rear hub/bearing assembly off of the knuckle spindle

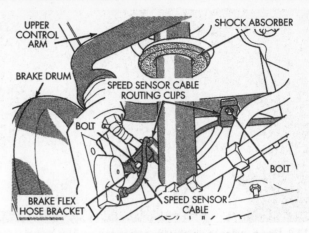

18.3 Detach the wheel speed sensor from the brake backing plate

(see illustration). Discard the nut - a new one must be used upon installation.

5   Pull the hub/bearing assembly off of the rear spindle (see illustration).

6   Installation is the reverse of removal. Use a new retaining nut - do not reuse the old nut. Tighten the nut to the torque listed in this Chapter's Specifications.

7   Install the wheel and hand tighten the wheel lug nuts. Remove the jackstands, lower the vehicle and tighten the lug nuts to the torque listed in the Chapter 1 Specifications.

18   Knuckle/spindle (rear) - removal and installation

Refer to illustrations 18.3, 18.5a and 18.5b

Warning: *Dust created by the brake system may contain asbestos, which is harmful to your health. Never blow it out with compressed air and don't inhale any of it. Do not, under any circumstances, use petroleum-based solvents to clean brake parts. Use brake system cleaner only.*

Removal

1   Loosen the rear wheel lug nuts, raise the vehicle and support it on jackstands. Block the front wheels and remove the rear wheel.

2   Remove the rear hub/bearing assembly (see Section 17).

3   On models with ABS, remove the wheel speed sensor from the brake backing plate (see illustrations).

4   Remove the parking brake cable from the parking brake actuator lever. Then remove the cable from the brake backing plate (see Chapter 9).

5   Remove the brake backing plate bolts. Using a length of wire, hang the brake assembly from the coil spring above the knuckle so that you do not need to remove the brake hose from the wheel cylinder (see illustrations).

6   Remove the nuts and bolts attaching the forward and rear lateral links (see Section 13).

18.5a Remove the brake backing plate bolts (arrows)

7   Separate the upper control arm balljoint from the rear knuckle (see Section 15).

10   Remove the nut and washer attaching the trailing link to the rear knuckle (see Section 12).

11   Remove the shock absorber-to-knuckle nut and bolt (see illustration 11.4).

12   Remove the knuckle assembly from the vehicle.

Installation

13   Installation is the reverse of removal. Make sure the shock absorber clevis bracket bolt is installed with the head of the bolt facing the rear of the vehicle. Reinstall the trailing link bushings in the same locations as when you removed them, and with the retainers installed with the cupped side of retainer facing away from the bushing and knuckle. Be sure to tighten all suspension fasteners to the torque listed in this Chapter's Specifications.

14   Install the wheel and lug nuts. Lower the vehicle and tighten the lug nuts to the torque listed in the Chapter 1 Specifications.

15   Drive the vehicle to an alignment shop

18.5b Hang the brake assembly on the coil spring using a length of wire

to have the rear wheel alignment checked and, if necessary, adjusted.

19   Steering system - general information

All models are equipped with power rack-and-pinion steering. The steering gear, which is located on the suspension crossmember behind the engine and in front of the firewall, operates the steering knuckles via tie-rods connected to steering arms on the steering knuckles. The tie-rod ends can be replaced by unscrewing them from the inner tie-rods.

The power assist system consists of a belt-driven pump and the associated lines and hoses. The fluid level in the power steering pump reservoir should be checked periodically (see Chapter 1).

The steering wheel operates the steering shaft, which actuates the steering gear through an intermediate shaft with a universal joint at the lower end of the steering column (referred to as the flex joint) and a lower inter-

10

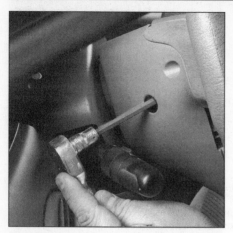

20.3 Remove the two screws retaining the steering wheel airbag module

20.5a Remove the lock from the airbag clockspring electrical connector

20.5b Disconnect the electrical connector from the back of the airbag module

mediate shaft coupler which connects to the steering gear input shaft. Looseness in the steering can be caused by wear in the flex joints, the shaft coupler, the steering gear, the tie-rod ends and loose retaining bolts. The steering gear is either a standard power steering rack-and-pinion unit or an optional speed-proportional/variable-assist type.

20 Steering wheel - removal and installation

Removal

Refer to illustrations 20.3, 20.5a, 20.5b and 20.7

Warning: *These models have airbags. Always disable the airbag system before working in the vicinity of the impact sensors, steering column or instrument panel to avoid the possibility of accidental deployment of the airbag, which could cause personal injury* (see Chapter 12).

1   Park the vehicle with the front wheels pointing straight ahead.

2   Disconnect the negative battery cable from the ground stud on the left shock tower (see Chapter 5, Section 1). Wait at least two minutes before proceeding (the system has a back-up capacitor that must fully discharge).

3   Remove the two screws, one on each side of the steering wheel, which retain the airbag module to the steering wheel **(see illustration)**.

4   Remove the airbag module from the steering wheel. **Warning:** *When handling the airbag module, make sure that at no time any source of electricity is allowed near the inflator on the back of the airbag module; when carrying the airbag module, the trim cover must be pointed away from your body or any other person; if the airbag module is placed on a workbench or any other surface, the trim cover must face upwards. When removing the airbag module, tag or mark all fasteners, screws, bolts, and other parts for the airbag module with their location as removed, for correct installation later.*

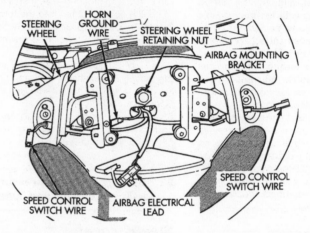

20.7 Remove the steering wheel retaining nut

5   Remove the lock from the airbag clockspring electrical connector and disconnect the electrical connector from the back of the airbag module **(see illustrations)**.

6   Remove the screws on the rear of the steering wheel attaching the speed control switches and remove the speed control switches from the steering wheel. Disconnect the clockspring and horn ground wire from the airbag mounting bracket.

7   Remove the steering wheel retaining nut **(see illustration)**. Mark the steering column shaft and the steering wheel for correct positioning when reinstalling later.

8   Remove the steering wheel with a steering wheel puller - do not bump or hammer on the steering wheel or steering column in an attempt to remove the wheel.

Installation

9   Before installing the steering wheel, make sure the airbag clockspring is centered. To do this, push in on the two locking pins to disengage the locking mechanism. While continuing to depress the pins, turn the clockspring rotor clockwise until it stops (don't turn it with too much force or you could damage it). Slowly turn the rotor counter-clockwise until yellow appears in the centering window. The arrow on the rotor of the

clockspring should now be pointing at the yellow window on the clockspring. Release the locking pins to engage the locking mechanism.

10   Lower the steering wheel into position, feeding the clockspring wiring harness through the opening in the wheel.

11   Place the steering wheel on the shaft, aligning the marks. Also, make sure the flats on the hub of the steering wheel engage with the flats on the inside of the clockspring. Install the nut and tighten it to the torque listed in this Chapter's Specifications.

12   Correctly route and reconnect electrical connectors such as the speed control switch electrical leads from the clockspring to switch openings in the steering wheel. Connect the clockspring electrical leads to the speed control switches. Install the speed control switches in the steering wheel. Then install and tighten the screws attaching the speed control switches.

13   Plug in the horn and airbag module electrical connectors. Press the speed control wires into the retaining channels on the steering wheel.

14   Install the airbag module electrical lead from the clockspring into the connector on the airbag module. Insert the locking tab in the back of the airbag module connector.

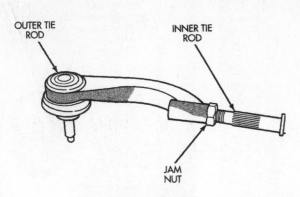

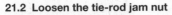

21.2 Loosen the tie-rod jam nut

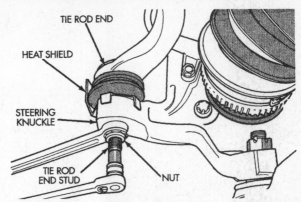

21.4a While holding the ballstud with a wrench to prevent it from turning, loosen the nut

15 Install the airbag module into the center of the steering wheel, aligning the airbag module alignment pins with the mating hole and slot in the steering wheel. Use the two original or factory replacement airbag module retaining bolts. Tighten the airbag module retaining bolts to the torque listed in this Chapter's Specifications. **Warning:** *Make sure the electrical connector from the clockspring is securely latched into the airbag module connector. The fasteners, screws, bolts, and other parts for the airbag module are specifically designed and must never be replaced with anything other than genuine factory part number replacements.*

16 Install the remote ground cable on the ground stud (at the underhood shock tower) to reapply battery power.

21 Tie-rod ends - removal and installation

Refer to illustrations 21.2, 21.4a and 21.4b

Removal

1 Loosen the wheel lug nuts, raise the front of the vehicle and support it securely on jackstands. Apply the parking brake and block the rear wheels to keep the vehicle from rolling off the jackstands. Remove the wheel.

2 Loosen the tie-rod end jam nut **(see illustration)**.

3 Mark the relationship of the tie-rod end to the threaded portion of the tie-rod. This will ensure the toe-in setting is restored when reassembled.

4 Loosen the nut from the tie-rod end ballstud a few turns, while holding the ballstud with a wrench **(see illustration)**. Disconnect the tie-rod end from the steering knuckle arm with a puller **(see illustration)**.

5 Remove the nut from the ballstud, separate the tie-rod end from the steering knuckle, then unscrew the tie-rod end from the tie-rod.

Installation

6 Thread the tie-rod end onto the tie-rod

to the marked position and connect the tie-rod end to the steering arm. Install the nut on the ballstud and tighten it to the torque listed in this Chapter's Specifications while holding the ballstud with a wrench to prevent it from turning.

7 Tighten the jam nut securely and install the wheel. Lower the vehicle and tighten the lug nuts to the torque listed in the Chapter 1 Specifications.

8 Drive the vehicle to an alignment shop and have the front end alignment checked and, if necessary, adjusted.

22 Steering gear and pressure switch - removal and installation

Steering gear

Removal

Refer to illustrations 22.3, 22.7a, 22.7b, 22.15, 22.16a and 22.16b

Warning: *These models are equipped with airbags. Make sure the steering shaft is not turned while the steering gear is removed or you could damage the airbag system. To prevent the shaft from turning, turn the ignition key to the lock position before beginning work or run the seat belt through the steering wheel and clip the seat belt into place. Due to the possible damage to the airbag system, we recommend only experienced mechanics attempt this procedure.*

1 Disconnect the negative battery cable from the ground stud on the left shock tower (see Chapter 5, Section 1).

2 Drain the power steering fluid from the remote power steering reservoir. This can be accomplished with a suction gun or large syringe, or by disconnecting the fluid hose and draining the fluid into a container.

3 From inside the vehicle under the dashboard, slide the steering shaft boot up from the floorboard area and remove the safety clip on the intermediate shaft pinch bolt. Then remove the pinch bolt **(see illustration)**.

4 Mark the intermediate shaft and the steering gear shaft with alignment markings for later installation. Then separate the inter-

21.4b Using a puller, separate the ballstud from the knuckle

mediate shaft coupler from the steering gear shaft.

5 Loosen the front wheel lug nuts. Raise the vehicle and place it securely on jackstands. Remove both front wheels.

6 Detach the tie-rod ends from the steering knuckles (see Section 21).

22.3 At the base of the steering column, slide the boot up and remove the retaining pin and pinch bolt (arrow)

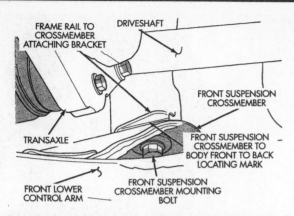

22.7a Scribe a locating mark from the front suspension crossmember to the attaching bracket (left side front shown)

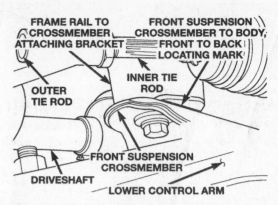

22.7b Also mark the rear position of the crossmember (left side rear shown)

7   Scribe marks showing the relationship of the front suspension crossmember to the crossmember attaching bracket **(see illustrations)**. Be sure to mark each side, at the front and at the rear.

8   Remove the front stabilizer bar mounting clamp to body bolts. It is not necessary to remove the stabilizer bar clamp-to-front sus-

22.15 If the vehicle is equipped with electronic module type speed-sensing/variable assist power steering, detach the electrical connectors (arrows)

pension crossmember bolts.

9   For ABS-equipped vehicles, remove the three bolts attaching the Anti-lock Brake System hydraulic control unit to the front suspension crossmember. Using a length of wire, hang the hydraulic control unit from the body/engine.

10   Remove the left and right side shock absorber clevis bolts from the lower control arms.

11   Remove the two bolts from the engine support bracket attaching to the front edge of the suspension crossmember, and the two bolts attaching the rear support bracket at the rear of the suspension crossmember.

12   Remove the bolt attaching the engine support bracket to the transaxle mounting bracket.

13   Using a transmission jack or two floor jacks, support the front suspension crossmember. Lower the crossmember sufficiently to allow the steering gear to be removed. **Note:** *Make sure you support the crossmember and do not allow it to hang from the lower control arms at any time.*

14   Place a drain pan under the steering gear and detach the power steering pressure and return lines. Cap the ends to prevent excessive fluid loss and contamination.

15   Disconnect the pressure switch wiring

harness connector from the steering gear. On models equipped with the electronic speed sensing/variable assist steering, disconnect the speed sensing/variable assist module and solenoid control valve electrical connectors **(see illustration)**.

16   Remove the two steering gear mounting bolts and isolators at the crossmember and then remove the two steering gear-to-crossmember clamp bolts **(see illustrations)**.

17   Remove the steering gear assembly from the vehicle.

Installation

18   If you're installing a new steering gear assembly, carefully grasp the steering gear in your left hand and rotate the shaft counterclockwise with your right hand until the steering gear is in the full-left position.

19   Installation is the reverse of removal. Make sure you align the marks on the steering gear shaft with the marks on the intermediate shaft. Gently tap the front suspension crossmember into place, aligning it with the marks scribed during removal. Make sure the electrical connector(s) are fully connected with the connector locking tabs securely latched. Use a new steering gear intermediate shaft coupler pinch bolt, and make sure the retention pin is installed in the bolt after

22.16a Steering gear-to-crossmember clamp bolts (lower arrow)

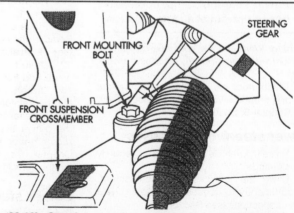

22.16b Steering gear-to-crossmember mounting bolt (front shown)

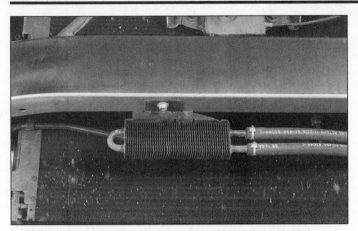

23.11 The power steering fluid cooler is bolted to the bumper reinforcement bar (1996 and later models)

23.20 Remove the bolt at the power steering pump adjustment slot (arrow)

tightening the pinch bolt to the torque listed in this Chapter's Specifications.

20   Refill the power steering with power steering fluid (see Chapter 1), and bleed the system (see Section 24).

21   Install the wheel and lug nuts. Lower the vehicle and tighten the lug nuts to the torque listed in the Chapter 1 Specifications. Drive the vehicle to an alignment shop to have the wheel alignment checked and, if necessary, adjusted.

Pressure switch

22   Raise the vehicle and support it securely on jackstands.

23   Remove the pressure switch electrical connector, located on the back side of the power steering gear.

24   Place a drain pan under the power steering gear. Using a crow foot wrench, remove the pressure switch from the power steering gear.

25   Installation is the reverse of removal. Tighten the switch to the torque listed in this Chapter's Specifications. Fill the power steering with the recommended power steering fluid (see Chapter 1), and bleed the system (see Section 24).

---

23 Power steering pump, cooler and hoses - removal and installation

Warning: *Wait until the engine is completely cool before beginning any of these procedures.*

1   Disconnect the negative battery cable from the ground stud on the left shock tower (see Chapter 5, Section 1).

Power steering fluid hoses

2   Raise the vehicle and support it securely on jackstands.

3   Lower the front suspension crossmember sufficiently to access the steering gear hose connections (see Section 22).

4   Place a drain pan under the power steering gear. Disconnect the hose from the power steering gear and let the fluid drain

into the drain pan. Cap the hose and the power steering gear port to prevent entry of foreign material.

5   Remove power steering fluid hose brackets or tie-straps as necessary to remove the hose(s).

6   Disconnect the power steering hose(s) from the power steering pump.

7   Remove the hose(s) from the bottom of the vehicle.

8   Installation is the reverse of removal. Use new O-rings on the pressure hose fittings, lubricated with clean power steering fluid. Before installing, wipe clean all hose fittings and power steering pump and gear ports. When installing, do not fully tighten the fittings until the suspension crossmember is re-installed. Tighten the fittings when the entire hose is in place with brackets and tie-strap attached. Fill the power steering reservoir with the recommended power steering fluid (see Chapter 1), and bleed the system (see Section 24).

Power steering oil cooler (1996 and later models)

Refer to illustration 23.11

9   Raise the vehicle and support it securely on jackstands.

10   Remove the front fascia and grill (see Chapter 11).

11   Place a drain pan under the oil cooler. Remove the hose clamps from the oil cooler **(see illustration).**

12   Drain the power steering fluid from the hoses and from the oil cooler.

13   Unbolt the oil cooler from the front bumper reinforcement bar.

14   Installation is the reverse of removal. Fill the power steering fluid reservoir with the recommended power steering fluid (see Chapter 1), and bleed the system after lowering the vehicle (see Section 24).

Power steering pump

Refer to illustrations 23.20, 23.23, 23.24, 23.26, 23.27a, 23.27b and 23.27c

15   Using a large syringe or suction gun,

suck as much fluid out of the power steering fluid reservoir as possible.

16   Loosen the right front wheel lug nuts. Raise the vehicle and support it securely on jackstands.

17   Remove the right front wheel. Also remove the right front wheel splash shield.

18   Place a drain pan under the vehicle to catch any fluid that spills out when the hoses are disconnected.

19   Disconnect the power steering pump hoses. Cap the hoses and the power steering pump ports.

20   Remove the bolt at the pump adjustment slot **(see illustration)**.

21   Remove the bolt attaching the back of the power steering pump to the cast aluminum mounting bracket.

22   Remove the ABS hydraulic control unit heat shield adjacent to the power steering pump.

23   On four-cylinder models with ABS, remove the wheel speed sensor cable bracket from the right front wheel well **(see illustration)**. Then remove the grommet from the right front inner fender, disconnect the wheel speed sensor connector, and push the wiring harness back through the hole in the

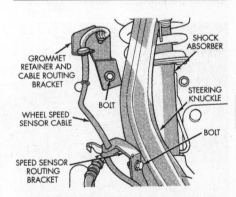

23.23 Remove the ABS speed sensor harness bracket from the right front wheel well and remove the grommet from the inner fender - four-cylinder models with ABS

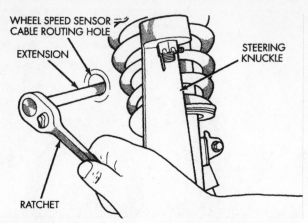

23.24 Use a 15mm flex socket with long extension inserted through the ABS sensor wiring harness hole in the inner fender to remove the bolt attaching the top of the power steering pump front bracket - four-cylinder models with ABS

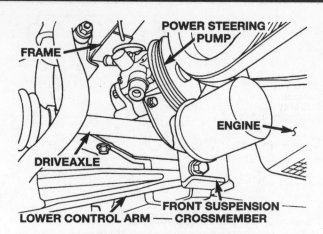

23.26 Remove the power steering pump/mounting bracket assembly through the area between the rear of the engine, driveaxle and front suspension crossmember

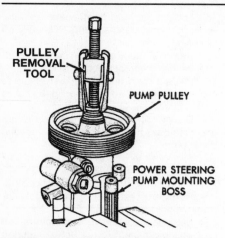

23.27a If you're installing a new pump, you'll need a special puller to remove the pulley from the old pump . . .

inner fender and unclip the wiring harness from the frame rail. If the vehicle does not have ABS brakes, just remove the grommet plug from the hole.

24   On four-cylinder models with ABS, insert a socket wrench with long extension and a 15mm flex socket through the ABS sensor wiring harness hole and remove the bolt attaching the top of the power steering pump front bracket to the cast aluminum mounting bracket **(see illustration)**.

25   Remove the power steering pump drivebelt from the pump pulley.

26   Carefully remove the power steering pump and mounting bracket as an assembly through the area between the rear of the engine, driveaxle and front suspension crossmember **(see illustration)**.

27   Installation is the reverse of removal. If you're installing a new pump, you'll need a special puller to remove the pulley from the old pump and another special tool **(see illustrations)** to install it on the new pump. These tools are available at most auto parts stores. First, loosely install mounting bolts and hose fittings. **Note:** *The power steering pump pressure hose must be installed between the front bracket of the pump and the pump pulley.* Mount the power steering drivebelt. Using a 1/2-inch drive breaker bar in the square adjustment hole of the pump, rotate the pump to the correct belt tension (see Chapter 1), hold the pump in position and tighten the bottom adjusting slot bolts and then tighten the top pivot bolt to the torque listed in this Chapter's Specifications.

28   Fill the power steering fluid reservoir with the recommended power steering fluid (see Chapter 1), and bleed the system (see Section 24).

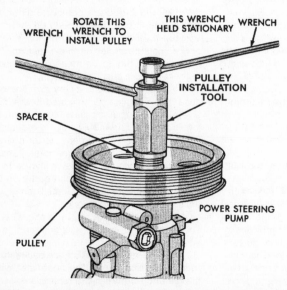

23.27b . . . and another special tool to install it on the new pump

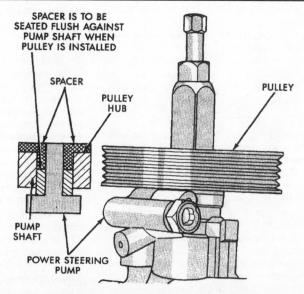

23.27c When installing the pulley on the new pump, make sure the spacer is fully seated as shown

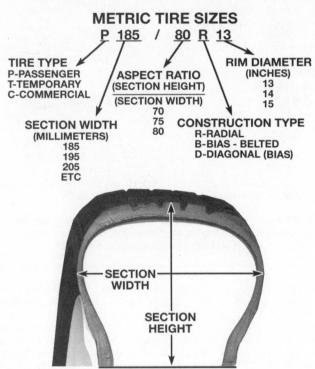

METRIC TIRE SIZES
P 185 / 80 R 13

TIRE TYPE
P-PASSENGER
T-TEMPORARY
C-COMMERCIAL

ASPECT RATIO
(SECTION HEIGHT)
―――――――
(SECTION WIDTH)
70
75
80

RIM DIAMETER
(INCHES)
13
14
15

SECTION WIDTH
(MILLIMETERS)
185
195
205
ETC

CONSTRUCTION TYPE
R-RADIAL
B-BIAS - BELTED
D-DIAGONAL (BIAS)

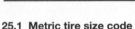

SECTION WIDTH

SECTION HEIGHT

25.1 Metric tire size code

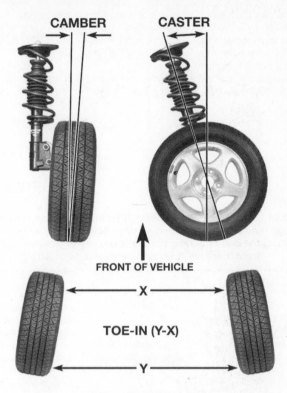

CAMBER   CASTER

FRONT OF VEHICLE

X

TOE-IN (Y-X)

Y

26.1 Camber, caster and toe-in angles

---

24 Power steering system - bleeding

1   Following any operation in which the power steering fluid lines have been disconnected, the power steering system must be bled to remove all air and obtain proper steering performance.

2   With the front wheels in the straight ahead position, check the power steering fluid level and, if low, add fluid until it reaches the Cold mark on the dipstick.

3   Start the engine and allow it to run at fast idle. Recheck the fluid level and add more if necessary to reach the Cold mark on the dipstick.

4   Bleed the system by running the engine for a few seconds, turning the steering wheel from side to side several times without hitting the stops, with the weight of the vehicle off of the wheels (vehicle front end raised and securely supported on jackstands), then stopping the engine and rechecking level. This will work the air out of the system. Keep the reservoir full of fluid as this is done.

5   When the air is worked out of the system, return the wheels to the straight ahead position and leave the vehicle running for several more minutes before shutting it off.

6   Road test the vehicle to be sure the steering system is functioning normally and noise free.

7   Recheck the fluid level to be sure it is up to the Hot mark on the dipstick while the engine is at normal operating temperature. Add fluid if necessary (see Chapter 1).

25 Wheels and tires - general information

Refer to illustration 25.1

All vehicles covered by this manual are equipped with metric-sized fiberglass or steel belted radial tires **(see illustration)**. Use of other size or type of tires may affect the ride and handling of the vehicle. Don't mix different types of tires, such as radials and bias belted, on the same vehicle as handling may be seriously affected. It's recommended that tires are replaced in pairs on the same axle, but if only one tire is being replaced, be sure it's the same size, structure and tread design as the other.

Because tire pressure has a substantial effect on handling and wear, the pressure on all tires should be checked at least once a month or before extended trips (see Chapter 1).

Wheels must be replaced if they are bent, dented, leak air, have elongated bolt holes, are heavily rusted, out of vertical symmetry or if the lug nuts won't stay tight. Wheel repairs that use welding or peening are not recommended.

Tire and wheel balance is important in the overall handling, braking and performance of the vehicle. Unbalanced wheels can adversely affect handling and ride characteristics as well as tire life. Whenever a tire is installed on a wheel, a shop with the proper equipment should balance the tire and wheel.

26 Wheel alignment - general information

Refer to illustration 26.1

A wheel alignment refers to the adjustments made to the wheels so they are in proper angular relationship to the suspension and the ground. Wheels that are out of proper alignment not only affect vehicle control, but also increase tire wear. The alignment angles normally measured are camber, caster and toe-in **(see illustration)**. Toe-in on the front, and toe-in and camber on the rear are the only adjustable angles on these vehicles. The other angles should be measured to check for bent or worn suspension parts.

Wheel alignment is a very exacting process, one in which complicated and expensive machines are necessary to perform the job properly. You should have a technician with the proper equipment perform these tasks. We will, however, use this space to give you a basic idea of what is involved with a wheel alignment so you can better understand the process and deal intelligently with the shop that does the work.

Toe-in is the turning in of the wheels. The purpose of a toe specification is to ensure parallel rolling of the wheels. In a vehicle with zero toe-in, the distance between the front edges of the wheels will be the same as the distance between the rear edges of the wheels. The actual amount of toe-in is normally only a fraction of an inch. On the front

10

end, toe-in is controlled by the tie-rod end position on the tie-rod. On the rear end, it's controlled by a threaded adjuster on the rear lateral link. Incorrect toe-in will cause the tires to wear improperly by making them scrub against the road surface.

Camber is the tilting of the wheels from vertical when viewed from one end of the vehicle. When the wheels tilt out at the top, the camber is said to be positive (+). When the wheels tilt in at the top the camber is negative (-). The amount of tilt is measured in degrees from vertical and this measurement is called the camber angle. This angle affects the amount of tire tread which contacts the road and compensates for changes in the suspension geometry when the vehicle is cornering or traveling over an undulating surface.

Caster is the tilting of the front steering axis from the vertical. A tilt toward the rear is positive caster and a tilt toward the front is negative caster.

Chapter 11   Body

Contents

1   General information

The models covered by this manual feature a "unibody" layout, using a floor pan with front and rear frame side rails which support the body components, front and rear suspension systems and other mechanical components. Certain components are particularly vulnerable to accident damage and can be unbolted and repaired or replaced. Among these parts are the body moldings, bumpers, front fenders, the hood and trunk lids and all glass. Only general body maintenance practices and body panel repair procedures within the scope of the do-it-yourselfer are included in this Chapter.

2   Body - maintenance

1   The condition of the vehicle's body is very important, because the resale value depends a great deal on it. It's much more difficult to repair a neglected or damaged body than it is to repair mechanical components. The hidden areas of the body, such as the wheel wells, the frame and the engine compartment, are equally important, although they don't require as frequent attention as the rest of the body.

2   Once a year, or every 12,000 miles, it's a good idea to have the underside of the body steam cleaned. All traces of dirt and oil will be removed and the area can then be inspected carefully for rust, damaged brake lines, frayed electrical wires, damaged cables and other problems. The front suspension components should be greased after completion of this job.

3   At the same time, clean the engine and the engine compartment with a steam cleaner or water-soluble degreaser.

4   The wheel wells should be given close attention, since undercoating can peel away and stones and dirt thrown up by the tires can cause the paint to chip and flake, allowing rust to set in. If rust is found, clean down to the bare metal and apply an anti-rust paint.

5   The body should be washed about once a week. Wet the vehicle thoroughly to soften the dirt, then wash it down with a soft sponge

11

and plenty of clean soapy water. If the surplus dirt is not washed off very carefully, it can wear down the paint.

6   Spots of tar or asphalt thrown up from the road should be removed with a cloth soaked in solvent.

7   Once every six months, wax the body and chrome trim. If a chrome cleaner is used to remove rust from any of the vehicle's plated parts, remember that the cleaner also removes part of the chrome, so use it sparingly.

3   Vinyl trim - maintenance

Don't clean vinyl trim with detergents, caustic soap or petroleum-based cleaners. Plain soap and water works just fine, with a soft brush to clean dirt that may be ingrained. Wash the vinyl as frequently as the rest of the vehicle. After cleaning, application of a high-quality rubber and vinyl protectant will help prevent oxidation and cracks. The protectant can also be applied to weatherstripping, vacuum lines and rubber hoses, which often fail as a result of chemical degradation, and to the tires.

4   Upholstery and carpets - maintenance

1   Every three months remove the floor mats and clean the interior of the vehicle (more frequently if necessary). Use a stiff whisk broom to brush the carpeting and loosen dirt and dust, then vacuum the upholstery and carpets thoroughly, especially along seams and crevices.

2   Dirt and stains can be removed from carpeting with basic household or automotive carpet shampoos available in spray cans. Follow the directions and vacuum again, then use a stiff brush to bring back the "nap" of the carpet.

3   Most interiors have cloth or vinyl upholstery, either of which can be cleaned and maintained with a number of material-specific cleaners or shampoos available in auto supply stores. Follow the directions on the product for usage, and always spot-test any upholstery cleaner on an inconspicuous area (like the bottom edge of a back seat cushion) to ensure that it doesn't cause a color shift in the material.

4   After cleaning, vinyl upholstery should be treated with a protectant. **Note:** *Make sure the protectant container indicates the product can be used on seats - some products make may a seat too slippery.* **Caution:** *Do not use a protectant on vinyl-covered steering wheels.*

5   Leather upholstery requires special care. It should be cleaned regularly with saddle soap or leather cleaner. Never use alcohol, gasoline, nail polish remover or thinner to clean leather upholstery.

6   After cleaning, regularly treat leather upholstery with a leather conditioner, rubbed in with a soft cotton cloth. Never use car wax on leather upholstery.

7   In areas where the interior of the vehicle is subject to bright sunlight, cover leather seating areas of the seats with a sheet if the vehicle is to be left out for any length of time.

5   Body repair - minor damage

Repair of scratches

1   If the scratch is superficial and does not penetrate to the metal of the body, repair is very simple. Lightly rub the scratched area with a fine rubbing compound to remove loose paint and built up wax. Rinse the area with clean water.

2   Apply touch-up paint to the scratch, using a small brush. Continue to apply thin layers of paint until the surface of the paint in the scratch is level with the surrounding paint. Allow the new paint at least two weeks to harden, then blend it into the surrounding paint by rubbing with a very fine rubbing compound. Finally, apply a coat of wax to the scratch area.

3   If the scratch has penetrated the paint and exposed the metal of the body, causing the metal to rust, a different repair technique is required. Remove all loose rust from the bottom of the scratch with a pocket knife, then apply rust inhibiting paint to prevent the formation of rust in the future. Using a rubber or nylon applicator, coat the scratched area with glaze-type filler. If required, the filler can be mixed with thinner to provide a very thin paste, which is ideal for filling narrow scratches. Before the glaze filler in the scratch hardens, wrap a piece of smooth cotton cloth around the tip of a finger. Dip the cloth in thinner and then quickly wipe it along the surface of the scratch. This will ensure that the surface of the filler is slightly hollow. The scratch can now be painted over as described earlier in this Section.

Repair of dents

See photo sequence

4   When repairing dents, the first job is to pull the dent out until the affected area is as close as possible to its original shape. There is no point in trying to restore the original shape completely as the metal in the damaged area will have stretched on impact and cannot be restored to its original contours. It is better to bring the level of the dent up to a point which is about 1/8-inch below the level of the surrounding metal. In cases where the dent is very shallow, it is not worth trying to pull it out at all.

5   If the back side of the dent is accessible, it can be hammered out gently from behind using a soft-face hammer. While doing this, hold a block of wood firmly against the opposite side of the metal to absorb the hammer blows and prevent the metal from being stretched.

6   If the dent is in a section of the body which has double layers, or some other factor makes it inaccessible from behind, a different technique is required. Drill several small holes through the metal inside the damaged area, particularly in the deeper sections. Screw long, self tapping screws into the holes just enough for them to get a good grip in the metal. Now the dent can be pulled out by pulling on the protruding heads of the screws with locking pliers.

7   The next stage of repair is the removal of paint from the damaged area and from an inch or so of the surrounding metal. This is easily done with a wire brush or sanding disk in a drill motor, although it can be done just as effectively by hand with sandpaper. To complete the preparation for filling, score the surface of the bare metal with a screwdriver or the tang of a file or drill small holes in the affected area. This will provide a good grip for the filler material. To complete the repair, see the subsection on *filling and painting*.

Repair of rust holes or gashes

8   Remove all paint from the affected area and from an inch or so of the surrounding metal using a sanding disk or wire brush mounted in a drill motor. If these are not available, a few sheets of sandpaper will do the job just as effectively.

9   With the paint removed, you will be able to determine the severity of the corrosion and decide whether to replace the whole panel, if possible, or repair the affected area. New body panels are not as expensive as most people think and it is often quicker to install a new panel than to repair large areas of rust.

10   Remove all trim pieces from the affected area except those which will act as a guide to the original shape of the damaged body, such as headlight shells, etc. Using metal snips or a hacksaw blade, remove all loose metal and any other metal that is badly affected by rust. Hammer the edges of the hole on the inside to create a slight depression for the filler material.

11   Wire brush the affected area to remove the powdery rust from the surface of the metal. If the back of the rusted area is accessible, treat it with rust inhibiting paint.

12   Before filling is done, block the hole in some way. This can be done with sheet metal riveted or screwed into place, or by stuffing the hole with wire mesh.

13   Once the hole is blocked off, the affected area can be filled and painted. See the following subsection on *filling and painting*.

Filling and painting

14   Many types of body fillers are available, but generally speaking, body repair kits which contain filler paste and a tube of resin hardener are best for this type of repair work. A wide, flexible plastic or nylon applicator will be necessary for imparting a smooth and contoured finish to the surface of the filler material. Mix up a small amount of filler on a clean piece of wood or cardboard (use the hardener sparingly). Follow the manufacturer's instructions on the package, otherwise the filler will set incorrectly.

15   Using the applicator, apply the filler paste to the prepared area. Draw the applicator across the surface of the filler to achieve the desired contour and to level the filler surface. As soon as a contour that approximates the original one is achieved, stop working the paste. If you continue, the paste will begin to stick to the applicator. Continue to add thin layers of paste at 20-minute intervals until the level of the filler is just above the surrounding metal.

16   Once the filler has hardened, the excess can be removed with a body file. From then on, progressively finer grades of sandpaper should be used, starting with a 180-grit paper and finishing with 600-grit wet-or-dry paper. Always wrap the sandpaper around a flat rubber or wooden block, otherwise the surface of the filler will not be completely flat. During the sanding of the filler surface, the wet-or-dry paper should be periodically rinsed in water. This will ensure that a very smooth finish is produced in the final stage.

17   At this point, the repair area should be surrounded by a ring of bare metal, which in turn should be encircled by the finely feathered edge of good paint. Rinse the repair area with clean water until all of the dust produced by the sanding operation is gone.

18   Spray the entire area with a light coat of primer. This will reveal any imperfections in the surface of the filler. Repair the imperfections with fresh filler paste or glaze filler and once more smooth the surface with sandpaper. Repeat this spray-and-repair procedure until you are satisfied that the surface of the filler and the feathered edge of the paint are perfect. Rinse the area with clean water and allow it to dry completely.

19   The repair area is now ready for painting. Spray painting must be carried out in a warm, dry, windless and dust free atmosphere. These conditions can be created if you have access to a large indoor work area, but if you are forced to work in the open, you will have to pick the day very carefully. If you are working indoors, dousing the floor in the work area with water will help settle the dust which would otherwise be in the air. If the repair area is confined to one body panel, mask off the surrounding panels. This will help minimize the effects of a slight mismatch in paint color. Trim pieces such as chrome strips, door handles, etc., will also need to be masked off or removed. Use masking tape and several thickness of newspaper for the masking operations.

20   Before spraying, shake the paint can thoroughly, then spray a test area until the spray painting technique is mastered. Cover the repair area with a thick coat of primer. The thickness should be built up using several thin layers of primer rather than one thick one. Using 600-grit wet-or-dry sandpaper, rub down the surface of the primer until it is very smooth. While doing this, the work area should be thoroughly rinsed with water and the wet-or-dry sandpaper periodically rinsed as well. Allow the primer to dry before spraying additional coats.

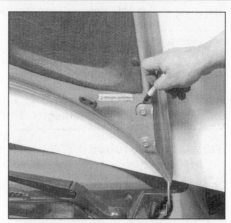

9.3 For a reference point at installation, outline the hinges on the hood with a felt tip marker

21   Spray on the top coat, again building up the thickness by using several thin layers of paint. Begin spraying in the center of the repair area and then, using a circular motion, work out until the whole repair area and about two inches of the surrounding original paint is covered. Remove all masking material 10 to 15 minutes after spraying on the final coat of paint. Allow the new paint at least two weeks to harden, then use a very fine rubbing compound to blend the edges of the new paint into the existing paint. Finally, apply a coat of wax.

6   Body repair - major damage

1   Major damage must be repaired by an auto body shop specifically equipped to perform unibody repairs. These shops have the specialized equipment required to do the job properly.

2   If the damage is extensive, the body must be checked for proper alignment or the vehicle's handling characteristics may be adversely affected and other components may wear at an accelerated rate.

3   Due to the fact that all of the major body components (hood, fenders, etc.) are separate and replaceable units, any seriously damaged components should be replaced rather than repaired. Sometimes the components can be found in a auto salvage or wrecking yard that specializes in used vehicle components, often at considerable savings over the cost of new parts.

7   Hinges and locks - maintenance

Once every 3000 miles, or every three months, the hinges and latch assemblies on the doors, hood and trunk should be given a few drops of light oil or lock lubricant. The door latch strikers should also be lubricated with a thin coat of grease to reduce wear and ensure free movement. Lubricate the door and trunk locks with spray-on graphite lubricant.

8   Windshield and fixed glass - replacement

Replacement of the windshield and fixed glass requires the use of special fast-setting adhesive/caulk materials and some specialized tools and techniques. These operations should be left to a dealer service department or a shop specializing in glass work.

9   Hood - removal, installation and adjustment

Note: *The hood is heavy and somewhat awkward to remove and install - at least two people should perform this procedure.*

Removal

Refer to illustration 9.3

1   Use blankets or pads to cover the cowl area of the body and both fenders. This will protect the body and paint as the hood is lifted off.

2   Open the hood and support it on the prop rod.

3   Scribe alignment marks around the bolt heads and hinges to aid alignment during installation (a permanent-type felt-tip marker also will work for this) **(see illustration)**.

4   Disconnect the under hood lamp electrical wire harness connector.

5   Have an assistant support one side of the hood while you support the other. Simultaneously remove the hinge-to-hood bolts.

6   Lift off the hood. **Note:** *A good place to store the hood is on the roof of the vehicle. Place blankets or pads on the roof first and lay the hood painted side down on the blankets.*

Installation

7   Installation is the reverse of removal. Align the marks around the hinges and bolts (one side at a time) and then check for proper clearance. Readjust as necessary (see below).

Adjustment

8   Fore-and-aft and side-to-side adjustment of the hood is done by moving the hood in relation to the hinge plate after loosening the bolts. The hood must be aligned so there is a 5/32-inch gap (approximate) to the front fenders and flush with the top surface.

9   Scribe or trace a line around the entire hinge plate so you can judge the amount of movement **(see illustration 9.3)**.

10   Loosen the bolts and move the hood into correct alignment. Move it only a little at a time. Tighten the hinge bolts and carefully lower the hood to check the alignment.

11   Adjust the hood bumpers on the radiator support so the hood is flush with the fenders when closed.

12   The hood latch assembly can also be adjusted up-and-down and side-to-side after loosening the nuts. Make sure you place

11

These photos illustrate a method of repairing simple dents. They are intended to supplement *Body repair - minor damage* in this Chapter and should not be used as the sole instructions for body repair on these vehicles.

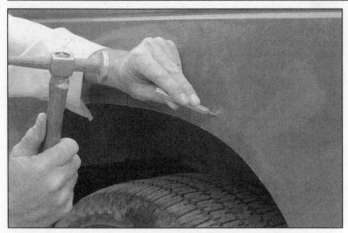

1   If you can't access the backside of the body panel to hammer out the dent, pull it out with a slide-hammer-type dent puller. In the deepest portion of the dent or along the crease line, drill or punch hole(s) at least one inch apart . . .

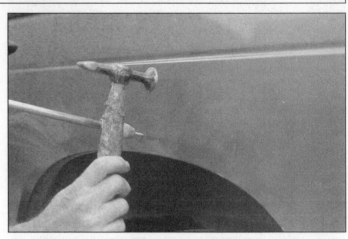

2   . . . then screw the slide-hammer into the hole and operate it. Tap with a hammer near the edge of the dent to help 'pop' the metal back to its original shape. When you're finished, the dent area should be close to its original contour and about 1/8-inch below the surface of the surrounding metal

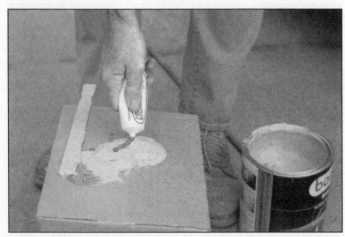

3   Using coarse-grit sandpaper, remove the paint down to the bare metal. Hand sanding works fine, but the disc sander shown here makes the job faster. Use finer (about 320-grit) sandpaper to feather-edge the paint at least one inch around the dent area

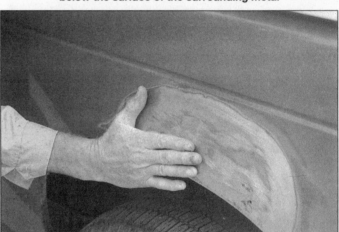

4   When the paint is removed, touch will probably be more helpful than sight for telling if the metal is straight. Hammer down the high spots or raise the low spots as necessary. Clean the repair area with wax/silicone remover

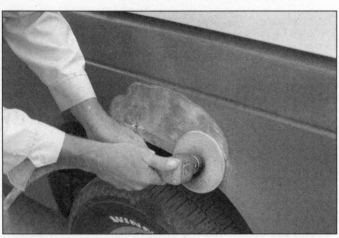

5   Following label instructions, mix up a batch of plastic filler and hardener. The ratio of filler to hardener is critical, and, if you mix it incorrectly, it will either not cure properly or cure too quickly (you won't have time to file and sand it into shape)

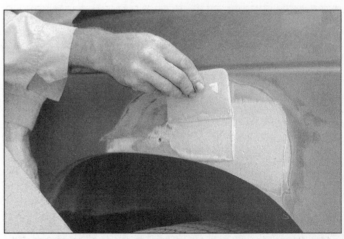

6   Working quickly so the filler doesn't harden, use a plastic applicator to press the body filler firmly into the metal, assuring it bonds completely. Work the filler until it matches the original contour and is slightly above the surrounding metal

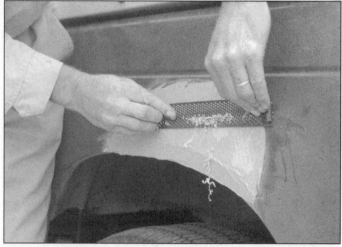

7   Let the filler harden until you can just dent it with your fingernail. Use a body file or Surform tool (shown here) to rough-shape the filler

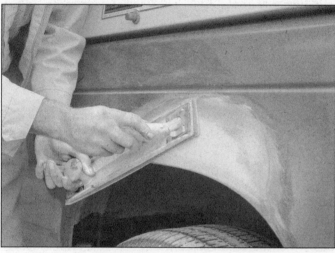

8   Use coarse-grit sandpaper and a sanding board or block to work the filler down until it's smooth and even. Work down to finer grits of sandpaper - always using a board or block - ending up with 360 or 400 grit

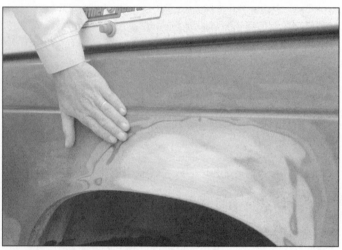

9   You shouldn't be able to feel any ridge at the transition from the filler to the bare metal or from the bare metal to the old paint. As soon as the repair is flat and uniform, remove the dust and mask off the adjacent panels or trim pieces

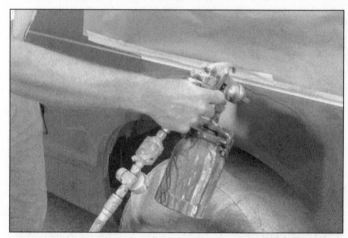

10   Apply several layers of primer to the area. Don't spray the primer on too heavy, so it sags or runs, and make sure each coat is dry before you spray on the next one. A professional-type spray gun is being used here, but aerosol spray primer is available inexpensively from auto parts stores

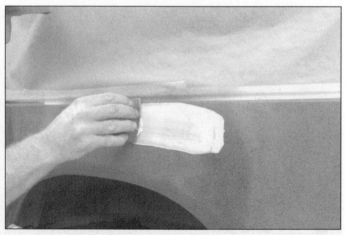

11   The primer will help reveal imperfections or scratches. Fill these with glazing compound. Follow the label instructions and sand it with 360 or 400-grit sandpaper until it's smooth. Repeat the glazing, sanding and respraying until the primer reveals a perfectly smooth surface

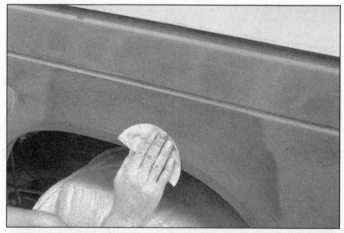

12   Finish sand the primer with very fine sandpaper (400 or 600-grit) to remove the primer overspray. Clean the area with water and allow it to dry. Use a tack rag to remove any dust, then apply the finish coat. Don't attempt to rub out or wax the repair area until the paint has dried completely (at least two weeks)

10.2 For a reference point at installation, mark the position of the hood latch on the radiator support

10.3 Slide the cable housing from the key-hole slot in the hood latch, then slide the cable through the slot (arrow) in the release arm and separate the cable from the hood latch assembly

8   Remove the bolts securing the hood release handle/cable assembly to the cowl panel **(see illustration)**.
9   Under the dash, locate and disengage the push-in retainer and cable grommet from the firewall.
10   Connect a piece of heavy string or flexible wire to the engine compartment end of the cable, then from inside the vehicle, pull the cable with string or wire attached through the firewall into the vehicle. Disconnect the string or wire from the old cable.

Installation

11   Connect the string or wire to the new cable and carefully pull it through the firewall into the engine compartment.
12   The remaining installation steps are the reverse of removal.

11   Radiator grille (Cirrus models) - removal and installation

Warning: *These models have airbags. Always disable the airbag system before working in the vicinity of the impact sensors, steering column or instrument panel to avoid the possibility of accidental deployment of the airbag, which could cause personal injury (see Chapter 12).*

Removal

1   Open the hood and support it on the prop rod.
2   Remove the front bumper with grille attached (see Section 12).
3   Using an appropriate size drill, remove the rivets securing the grille to the bumper and separate the grille from the bumper.

Installation

4   Installation is the reverse of removal. The grille can be reattached to the bumper using rivets (if available) or screws, nuts and washers. If threaded fasteners are used, apply thread locking compound to the screw threads.

---

alignment marks around the hood latch assembly before loosening the mounting nuts.
13   The hood latch assembly, as well as the hinges, should be periodically lubricated with white lithium-base grease to prevent sticking and wear.

10   Hood latch and cable - removal and installation

Warning: *These models have airbags. Always disable the airbag system before working in the vicinity of the impact sensors, steering column or instrument panel to avoid the possibility of accidental deployment of the airbag, which could cause personal injury (see Chapter 12).*

Latch

Removal

Refer to illustrations 10.2 and 10.3
1   Open the hood and support it on the prop rod.
2   Scribe alignment marks around the hood latch assembly to aid alignment during

installation (a permanent-type felt-tip marker or paint will also work for this) **(see illustration)**.
3   Remove the nuts and detach the latch assembly from the radiator support, then disconnect the release cable from the hood latch assembly **(see illustration)**.

Installation

4   Installation is the reverse of removal. Align the hood latch assembly with the marks on the radiator support and then tighten the nuts. Check hood latch operation. Readjust as necessary.

Cable

Removal

Refer to illustration 10.8
5   Disconnect the release cable from the hood latch (see Steps 1 through 3).
6   Detach the cable from the clips securing it to the radiator support.
7   Inside the vehicle, remove the left front kick panel to gain access to the hood release handle bolts.

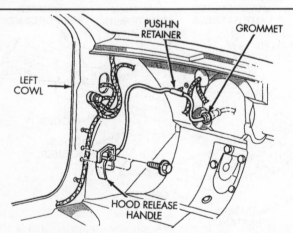

10.8 Hood release cable and handle details as viewed from inside the vehicle

12.5 Remove the five push-in fasteners (arrows) securing the bottom of the front bumper to the radiator lower support

12.7 To remove the push-in fasteners, pry out the center stud and then remove the outer housing

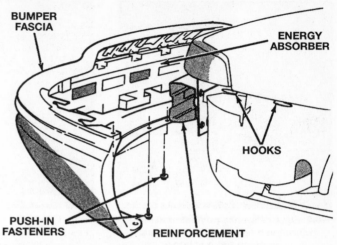

12.8 Front bumper assembly details

12 Bumpers - removal and installation

Warning: *These models have airbags. Always disable the airbag system before working in the vicinity of the impact sensors, steering column or instrument panel to avoid the possibility of accidental deployment of the airbag, which could cause personal injury* (see Chapter 12).

Front bumper

Removal

Refer to illustrations 12.5, 12.7, 12.8 and 12.9

1   Open the hood and support it on the prop rod.
2   Disconnect the negative battery cable from the ground stud on the left shock tower (see Chapter 5, Section 1).
3   Remove the fasteners securing the front fender inner splash shields to the lower section of the bumper.

4   Pull the splash shields away from the fender well as necessary to remove the bolts securing the bumper to the front fender.
5   Remove the push-in fasteners securing the bottom of the bumper to the radiator lower support **(see illustration)**.
6   If equipped, disconnect the foglight wiring harness connectors.
7   Remove the push-in fasteners securing the bumper (and grille on Cirrus models) to the radiator upper support **(see illustration)**.
8   Disengage the bumper from the hooks on the front fenders (both sides) and remove the bumper from the vehicle **(see illustration)**. **Note:** *If you are performing this job alone, place some blankets or other suitable padding on the ground below the bumper to protect the paint should the bumper fall during removal.*
9   If required, the bumper reinforcement bar can be removed at this time **(see illustration)**.

Installation

10   Installation is the reverse of removal.

Rear bumper

Removal

Refer to illustration 12.13

11   Open the trunk lid.
12   Remove the left rear tail lamp and disconnect the license plate light wiring from the tail lamp assembly.
13   On Cirrus models, remove the right rear tail lamp. Working inside the tail lamp cavities, remove the push-in fasteners securing the bumper to each rear quarter panel **(see illustration)**.
14   Remove the push-in fasteners securing the trunk lid slam pads to the rear bumper and the center of the bumper to the rear closure panel.
15   Remove the screws holding bumper to each rear wheel well splash shield.
16   Remove the bolts securing the bumper to the rear quarter panel in each wheel well.
17   Slide the bumper rearward to disengage the hooks securing it to the bottom of each quarter panel and remove it from the vehicle.

12.9 To detach the front bumper bar, disconnect the battery temperature sensor electrical connector and remove the three bolts (arrows) at each end of the bar

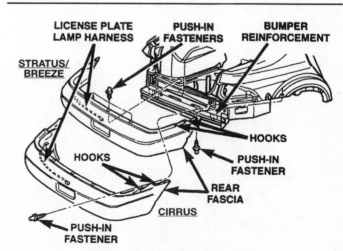

12.13 Rear bumper assembly details

11

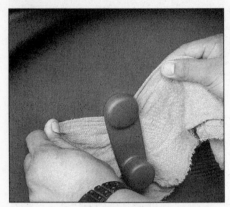

13.2 If you don't have a window crank removal tool (which is available at most auto parts stores and relatively inexpensive), place a shop cloth behind the window crank handle and work it back-and-forth to dislodge the retaining clip

Note: *If you are performing this job alone, place some blankets or other suitable padding on the ground below the bumper to protect the paint should the bumper fall during removal.*

18   If required, the bumper reinforcement bar can be remove at this time, however, before removal use a felt tip pen to mark the position of the nuts on the bar to aid with installation.

Installation

19   Installation is the reverse of removal.

13   Door trim panel - removal and installation

Removal

Refer to illustrations 13.2, 13.3, 13.4, 13.5a, 13.5b, 13.6, 13.7, 13.8, 13.9 and 13.11
Note: *This procedure applies to both the front and rear doors.*
1   Open door and completely lower window glass.
2   On manual window models, remove the window crank using a special tool (available

13.3 Carefully pry off the speaker grille

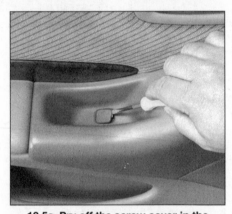

13.5a Pry off the screw cover in the pull handle area . . .

at most auto parts stores) or by working a cloth back-and-forth behind the handle to dislodge the retaining clip **(see illustration)**.
3   Carefully pry off the speaker grille **(see illustration)**.
4   Inside the speaker opening, remove the three screws securing the trim panel to the door **(see illustration)**.
5   On the pull handle, pry off the screw cover and remove the screw **(see illustrations)**.
6   Pry the screw cover from the door handle latch trim and remove the screw **(see illustration)**.

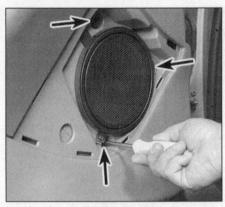

13.4 Remove the 3 screws (arrows) that secure the panel to the door

13.5b . . . and remove the screw

7   Remove the screw securing the door trim panel near the upper door hinge **(see illustration)**.
8   Carefully pry around the door trim panel to disengage it from the retaining clips **(see illustration)**.
9   Grasp the trim panel and pull up sharply to detach it from the retainer channel in window sill **(see illustration)**.
10   Position the trim panel slightly away from the door and disengage the clip holding the door latch linkage to the door handle.
11   On models so equipped, disconnect the electrical connectors from the speaker,

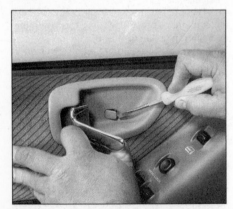

13.6 Pry off the screw cover in the door latch handle trim and remove the screw

13.7 Remove the door trim panel screw near the upper door hinge

13.8 Carefully pry around the door panel to disengage it from the retaining clips

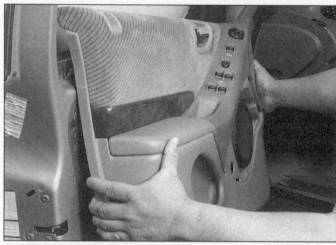

13.9 Grasp the door trim panel and lift it up sharply to detach it from the retainer channel in the window sill, then separate it from the door just far enough to disconnect the electrical connectors

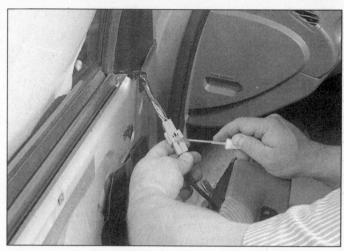

13.11 Disconnect the outside mirror electrical connector from the door trim panel

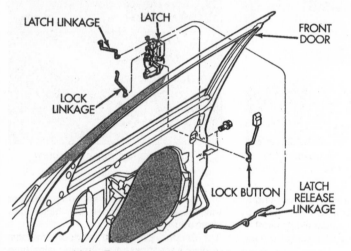

14.4a Front door latch assembly details

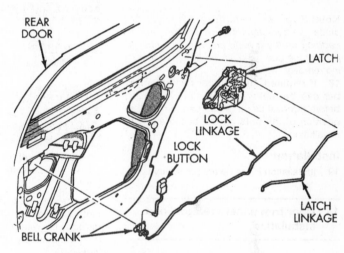

14.4b Rear door latch assembly details

power door lock switch, the mirror switch and power window switch **(see illustration)** and then remove the trim panel. **Caution:** *Do not allow the trim panel to hang from the electrical wires.*

14.6 Door latch mounting screws (arrows) - "A" indicates the latch adjustment slot (front door shown)

Installation

12   Reconnect any electrical connectors and install the latch linkage into the door handle. Secure it with the retaining clip.

13   Engage the top of the trim panel into the window sill retainer channel and press it into place and seating all clip fasteners.

14   The remaining installation steps are the reverse of removal.

14   Door latch, outside handle and lock cylinder - removal, installation and adjustment

Note: *This procedure applies to both the front and rear doors.*

Latch

Removal

Refer to illustrations 14.4a, 14.4b and 14.6

1   Remove the door trim panel (see Section 13), except on vehicles equipped with electric windows, close the window before

disconnecting the door trim panel electrical connectors.

2   On vehicles with manual windows, install the window crank (without the retaining clip) and roll up the window.

3   If you are removing a rear door latch, remove the window glass lower rear run channel.

4   Disconnect the lock cylinder, lock button and latch release operating rods from the door latch **(see illustrations)**.

5   On vehicles equipped with power door locks, disconnect the electrical connector from door lock motor.

6   Remove the three mounting screws from the end of the door and remove the door latch **(see illustration)**.

Installation

7   Place the latch in position, install the screws and tighten them securely.

8   Connect the operating rods to the latch and secure with retaining clips. **Caution:** *Do not close the door until the latch has been properly adjusted* (see below) *it may not reopen.*

11

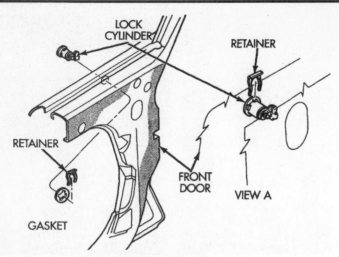

14.21 Door lock assembly details

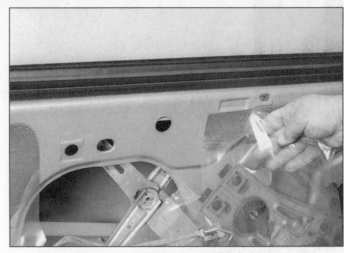

15.2 Remove the plastic water shield from the door

Adjustment

9   Insert a hex-wrench through the elongated hole in the end of the door near the latch **(see illustration 14.6)**.

10   Engage the wrench in the socket head screw located on the side of the door latch linkage and loosen it a couple of turns.

11   Lift the outside door handle all the way up and then release it.

12   Tighten the socket head screw on the door latch linkage and check door operation.

Outside handle

Removal

13   Remove the door trim panel (see Section 13), except on vehicles equipped with electric windows, close the window before disconnecting the door trim panel electrical connectors.

14   On vehicles with manual windows, install the window crank (without the retaining clip) and roll up the window.

15   On vehicles equipped with the Vehicle Theft Security System (VTSS), remove the disarming switch from the door handle.

16   Disconnect the operating rod, remove the mounting nuts and withdraw the handle from the door.

Installation

17   Installation is the reverse of removal.

Lock cylinder

Removal

Refer to illustration 14.21

18   Remove the outside door handle (see Steps 13 through 16).

19   Detach the operating rod retaining clip and operating rod from the lock cylinder.

20   On vehicles equipped with the Vehicle Theft Security System (VTSS), remove the illuminated entry switch wiring clip and disconnect the electrical connector.

21   Using a screwdriver, pry the lock cylinder retainer off and withdraw it from the door **(see illustration)**.

Installation

22   Installation is the reverse of removal.

15   Door window glass - removal and installation

Note: *This procedure applies to both the front and rear doors.*

Removal

Refer to illustrations 15.2, 15.3, 15.4 and 15.9

1   Remove the door trim panel (see Section 13).

2   Carefully remove the plastic water shield from the door **(see illustration)**.

3   Remove the inner belt weatherstrip from the window sill **(see illustration)**.

4   If you are removing the rear door glass, remove the window glass lower rear run channel **(see illustration)**.

5   On vehicles equipped with power windows, remove the switch from the door trim panel and connect it to the wiring harness. This will allow you to move the window as necessary.

6   On vehicles with manual windows, install the window crank (without the retaining clip). This will allow you to move the window

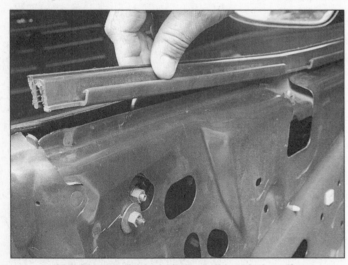

15.3 Remove the inner belt weatherstrip from the door window sill

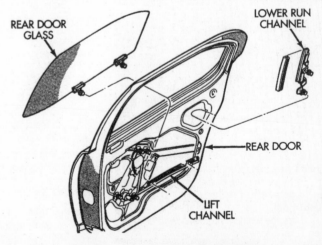

15.4 Rear door glass assembly details

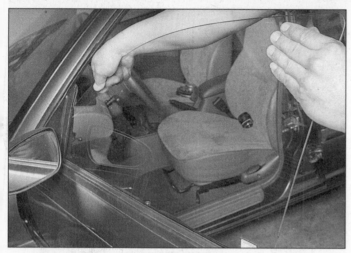

15.9 Carefully maneuver the glass out of the opening in the top of the door

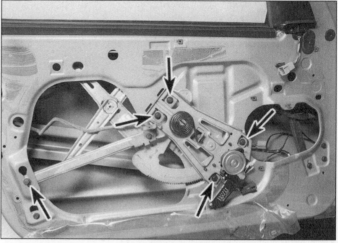

16.4 To remove the window regulator, remove these five bolts (arrows)

as necessary.

7   Place the window approximately two inches from the bottom of its travel.

8   Loosen the screws that secure the glass to the regulator roller channel.

9   While supporting the glass, slide the roller channel rearward and pass the screw heads through the key-hole slots in the channel, then maneuver the glass out of the opening in the top of the door **(see illustration).**

Installation

10   Installation is the reverse of removal. Make sure there is enough adhesive remaining on the water shield to seal properly, replace adhesive if necessary.

16   Door window regulator - removal and installation

Note: *This procedure applies to both the front and rear doors and both manual and power operated windows.*

Removal

Refer to illustration 16.4

Warning: *On power window models, do not remove the motor from the regulator assembly without first clamping the sector gear to the mounting plate or serious personal injury may result.*

1   Remove the door trim panel (see Section 13).

2   Remove the door window glass (see Section 15), except do not remove the glass from the door, let it rest at the bottom of its travel.

3   On power window models, disconnect window motor electrical connector.

4   Remove the five bolts securing the window regulator to the inner door panel **(see illustration).**

5   Slide the window regulator rearward and then rotate forward end of the lower roller channel through the access hole in the door and remove the regulator.

Installation

6   Installation is the reverse of removal.

17   Door - removal and installation

Note 1: *This procedure applies to both the front and rear doors.*

Note 2: *The door is heavy and somewhat awkward to remove and install - at least two people should perform this procedure.*

Removal

Refer to illustration 17.1

1   Open the door and disconnect the wiring harness connector at the door pillar **(see illustration).**

2   Remove the bolts and detach the check strap from the door pillar.

3   Place a jack or jackstands under the door or have an assistant on hand to support it when the hinge pins are removed. **Note:** *If a jack is used, place a rag and a piece of wood between it and the door to protect the door's painted surfaces.*

4   Remove the E-clip from the lower hinge

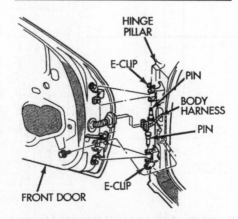

17.1 Door hinge assembly details

pin, then remove the lower hinge pin **(see illustration 17.1).**

5   Remove E-clip from the upper hinge pin, make sure door is properly supported then remove upper hinge pin and remove the door.

Installation

6   Installation is the reverse of removal. Make sure both hinge pin E-clips are properly secured in the hinge pins. Check door fit and adjust if necessary by loosening the hinge bolts. **Note:** *Place scribe marks around the hinges before loosening the bolts to maintain a reference point.*

18   Trunk lid, support strut, latch striker and release cable - removal, installation and adjustment

Trunk lid

Note: *The trunk lid is heavy and somewhat awkward to remove and install - at least two people should perform this procedure.*

Removal

Refer to illustration 18.3

1   Open the trunk lid and cover the edges of the trunk compartment with pads or cloths to protect the painted surfaces when the lid is removed.

2   Disconnect the electrical connectors attached to the trunk latch and center brake light. To aid with installation, attach a length of flexible wire to the connector end of the harness and then carefully pull it out of the trunk lid. **Note:** *If difficulty is experienced removing the wiring harness, another alternative is to cut the harness at a convenient place and install insulated crimp type connectors. Disconnect the guide wire from the harness and secure it at both openings of the trunk lid.*

11

3   Use a permanent type marking pen to make alignment marks around the hinge bolt heads and hinges **(see illustration)**.

4   Have an assistant support one side of the trunk lid while you support the other. Simultaneously remove the hinge-to-trunk lid bolts.

5   Lift off the trunk lid.

Installation

6   Installation is the reverse of removal. **Note:** *When reinstalling the trunk lid, align the hinge bolt heads with the marks made during removal.* After installation, close the lid and see if it's in proper alignment with the surrounding panels and adjust if necessary.

Adjustment

Refer to illustration 18.8

7   Fore-and-aft and side-to-side adjustments of the lid are controlled by the position of the hinge bolts in the holes. To adjust it, loosen the hinge bolts, reposition the lid and retighten the bolts. Make sure to mark the position of the hinges before loosening the bolts.

8   The height of the lid in relation to the surrounding body panels when closed can be adjusted by loosening the lock striker bolts, repositioning the striker and retightening the bolts. Make sure to mark the position of the striker before loosening the bolts **(see illustration)**.

Support strut

Removal

Refer to illustration 18.10

9   Open the trunk.

10   Remove the lock caps from the support

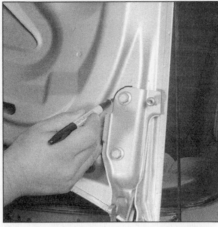

18.3 For a reference point at installation, outline the hinges on the trunk lid with a felt tip marker

18.8 For a reference point at installation, outline the trunk latch striker with a felt tip marker

struts **(see illustration)**.

11   Remove support strut from mounting studs.

Installation

12   Installation is the reverse of removal.

Latch striker and release cable

Removal

Refer to illustration 18.16

13   Using a screwdriver, pry the sill plates from the left front and rear doors.

14   Partially detach the lower B-pillar to access the trunk release cable.

15   Disengage the retainers securing the carpet to the door opening sills.

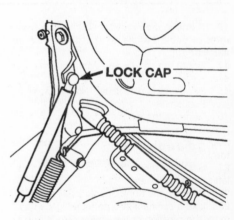

18.10 To remove the trunk lid support strut, pry off the lock caps at each end and withdraw it from the mounting studs

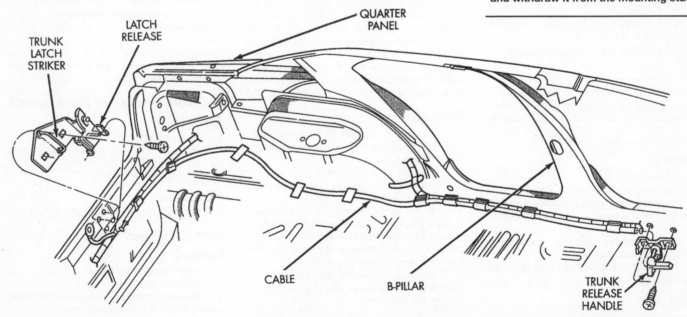

18.16 Trunk lid release cable assembly details

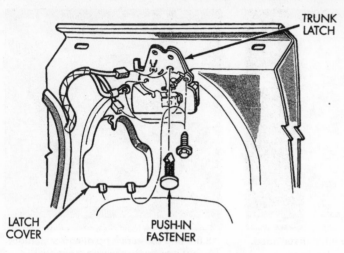

19.2 Trunk latch assembly details

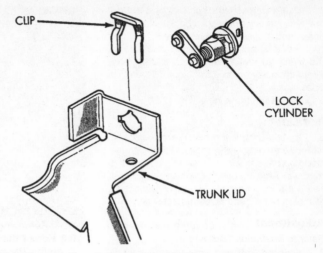

19.7 Remove the retaining clip and withdraw the lock cylinder from the trunk lid

16   Remove the screws securing the trunk release cable handle to the floorpan **(see illustration)**.

17   Route the handle and cable into the rear seat area.

18   Remove the rear seat cushion and back (see Section 29).

19   Remove the left side lower quarter trim panel.

20   Route the handle and cable into the trunk.

21   Separate the trunk lining away from the left rear quarter panel.

22   Remove the trunk opening sill plate.

23   Use a permanent type marking pen and mark the position of the striker **(see illustration 18.8)**.

24   Remove the bolts attaching the striker/cable assembly to the trunk closure panel and remove it from the vehicle.

Installation

25   Installation is the reverse of removal.

19   Trunk latch and lock cylinder - removal and installation

Latch

Removal

Refer to illustration 19.2

1   Open the trunk.

2   Remove the push-in fasteners securing the latch cover and remove it **(see illustration)**.

3   Disconnect the electrical connectors from the latch assembly.

4   Remove the latch bolts and separate the latch from the trunk.

Installation

5   Installation is the reverse of removal, making sure the lock cylinder linkage properly engages with the latch assembly.

Lock cylinder

Removal

Refer to illustration 19.7

6   Remove the trunk latch (see above).

7   Using pliers, remove the lock retaining clip and withdraw the lock from the trunk lid **(see illustration)**.

Installation

8   Installation is the reverse of removal.

20   Instrument panel top cover - removal and installation

Warning: *These models have airbags. Always disable the airbag system before working in the vicinity of the impact sensors, steering column or instrument panel to avoid the possibility of accidental deployment of the airbag, which could cause personal injury (see Chapter 12).*
Caution: *The cover can be easily scratched or bent, take care in removing the top cover to avoid damage.*

Removal

1   Disconnect the negative battery cable from the ground stud on the left shock tower (see Chapter 5, Section 1).

2   Open the glove box door.

3   Remove the right end cap and remove the screw.

4   Lift the right rear edge of the top cover to disengage the clips along the rear edge, starting from the right side and proceeding to the left. To avoid damage, do not pry on the top cover during removal.

5   Lift the rear edge and slide the top cover rearward to disengage the clips and then remove the top cover.

Installation

6   Installation is the reverse of removal,

except engage the top cover into the two center clips first. Place your thumb in the Vehicle Identification Number (VIN) slot and pull the top cover towards pad to ensure VIN alignment. If a gap exists between the top cover and the pad after installation, check for a damaged retaining clip and replace as necessary.

21   Dashboard trim panels, glove box door handle and lock cylinder - removal and installation

Warning: *These models have airbags. Always disable the airbag system before working in the vicinity of the impact sensors, steering column or instrument panel to avoid the possibility of accidental deployment of the airbag, which could cause personal injury (see Chapter 12).*
Caution: *The following trim covers can be easily scratched, take care in removing them to avoid damage.*

Left side end cover (fuse cover)

Removal

1   Open the left front door.

2   Pull on the access handle and pivoting around the A-pillar, detach the end cover clips and remove the cover.

Installation

3   Installation is the reverse of removal.

Right side end cover

Removal

4   Open the right front door.

5   Open the glove box door.

6   Remove the end cover by pulling rearward to disengage it from the clips.

Installation

7   Installation is the reverse of removal.

21.8 To remove the center bezel, simply pull it out evenly

22.3 Removing the screw securing the left side of the instrument cluster hood

22.6 Remove the three screws (arrows) holding the instrument cluster hood to the instrument panel

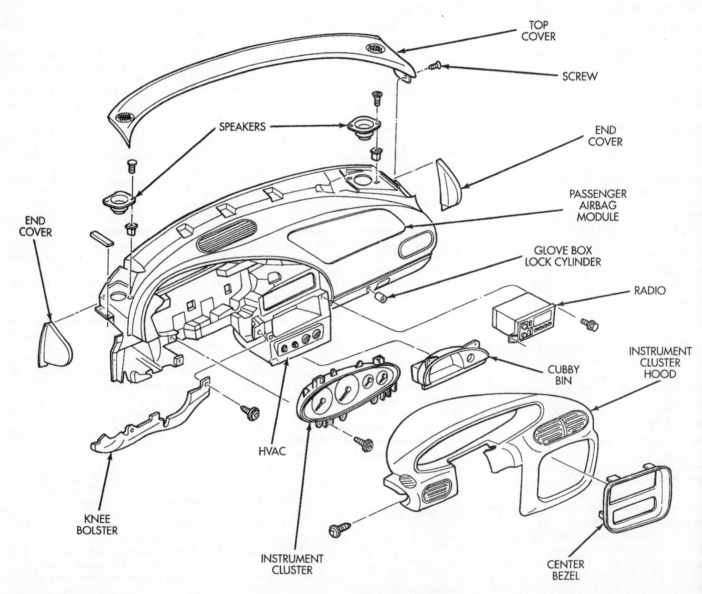

23.2 Instrument panel assembly details

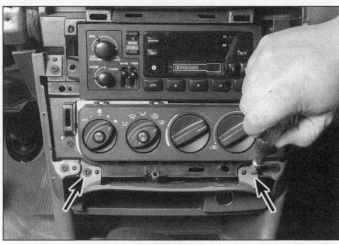

23.6 Cubby bin screw locations (arrows)

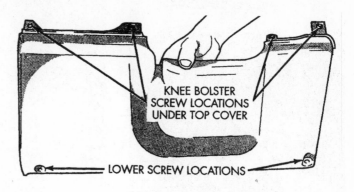

KNEE BOLSTER
SCREW LOCATIONS
UNDER TOP COVER

LOWER SCREW LOCATIONS

23.7 Knee bolster screw locations

Center bezel

Removal

Refer to illustration 21.8

8   Grasp the bezel on each side and pull out evenly to remove it **(see illustration)**.

Installation

9   Installation is the reverse of removal.

Glove box door handle

Removal

10   Open the glove box door.
11   Remove the four screws securing the handle to the door and remove handle.

Installation

12   Installation is the reverse of removal.

Glove box door lock cylinder

Removal

13   Remove the glove box door handle (see above).
14   Insert the proper key into the glove box lock.
15   Depress the gray locking tab on the backside of the lock housing at the three o'clock position.
16   While depressing the tab, rotate the key clockwise to remove the cylinder from the housing.

Installation

17   Installation is the reverse of removal.

22   Instrument cluster hood - removal and installation

Warning: *These models have airbags. Always disable the airbag system before working in the vicinity of the impact sensors, steering column or instrument panel to avoid the possibility of accidental deployment of the airbag, which could cause personal injury (see Chapter 12).*

Removal

Refer to illustrations 22.3 and 22.6

1   Disconnect the negative battery cable from the ground stud on the left shock tower (see Chapter 5, Section 1).
2   Remove the dashboard left end cover (see Section 21).
3   At the left end of the hood, remove the screw securing the hood to the instrument panel **(see illustration)**.
4   Position the tilt steering wheel to its lowest position.
5   Remove the dashboard center bezel (see Section 21).
6   Remove the three screws attaching the hood to the instrument panel **(see illustration)**.
7   Pull the hood straight back to disengage the eight clips. If the vehicle is equipped with a Compass/Temperature Mini-Trip Computer (CMTC), pull the hood rearward about three inches and stop. Reach through the radio opening and disconnect the CMTC wire connector.
8   Remove the instrument cluster hood.

Installation

9   Installation is the reverse of removal. Keep the forward edge of the hood down on the instrument panel while sliding the hood forward to engage the retaining clips.

23   Instrument panel - removal and installation

Warning: *These models have airbags. Always disable the airbag system before working in the vicinity of the impact sensors, steering column or instrument panel to avoid the possibility of accidental deployment of the airbag, which could cause personal injury (see Chapter 12).*
Note: *It is not necessary, but it is suggested to remove both front seats to allow additional working space and lessen the chance of damage to the seats during this procedure.*

Removal

Refer to illustrations 23.2, 23.6, 23.7, 23.17, 23.18 and 23.19

1   Disconnect the negative battery cable from the ground stud on the left shock tower (see Chapter 5, Section 1).
2   Remove the dashboard right and left end trim panels (see Section 21) **(see illustration)**.
3   Remove the floor console (see Section 26).
4   Disconnect the Airbag Control Module (ACM).
5   Remove the instrument cluster hood (see Section 22).
6   Remove the two screws securing the cubby bin and withdraw it from the forward console **(see illustration)**.
7   Remove the five knee bolster mounting screws and remove the knee bolster **(see illustration)**.
8   Open the glove box, squeeze the sidewalls in and hinge the glove box door all the way down. Remove the passenger airbag module (see Section 24). **Warning:** *Carry the airbag with the trim cover side FACING AWAY from your body to minimize injury if the airbag module accidentally deploys. Store the airbag module aside in a safe, isolated location with the trim cover side facing UP.*
9   Remove the nine forward floor console attaching screws and one push-in fastener at forward driver's side.
10   Remove the forward floor console (see Section 26).
11   Pull the driver's side under panel silencer outboard off the distribution duct.
12   Remove the instrument panel top cover (see Section 20).
13   Remove the heating and air conditioning control module (see Chapter 11). Remove the radio (see Chapter 12).
14   Remove the center distribution duct screws from behind the radio and duct.
15   Locate and remove the three heating and air conditioning unit attaching screws securing the duct and instrument panel. Remove the three screws securing the heat-

11

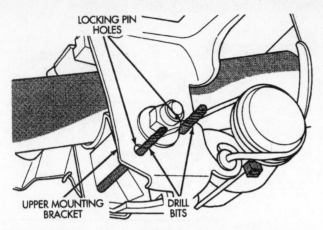

23.17 Before loosening the steering column mounting bolts, on models equipped with a tilt steering wheel, insert two drill bits into the locking pin holes

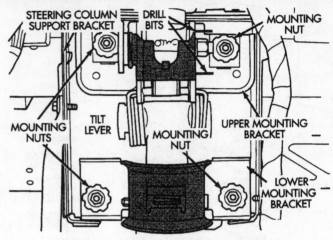

23.18 Steering column mounting nut locations

ing and air conditioning unit to the cross-car beam.

16 Remove the five screws attaching the instrument panel frame to the air distribution duct and the two fasteners at the air duct below the steering column.

17 The steering column must be lowered, but before loosening the steering column mounting nuts on a model equipped with a tilt steering wheel, use the following procedure to lock the tilt mechanism or it will not operate correctly when installed **(see illustration)**.

a) Place the steering wheel straight ahead and ensure the tilt mechanism is fully locked.

b) Insert two 7/32-inch drill bits into the two locking pin holes on the steering column mounting bracket.

c) Loosen the two upper steering column mounting nuts.

d) Loosen the two lower steering column mounting nuts.

18 Remove the steering column mounting

nuts **(see illustration)**. Lower and support the column securely.

19 Disconnect the engine and body wiring harness from the junction block/Body Control Module **(see illustration)**.

20 Remove the seven fasteners securing the instrument panel to the cross-car beam.

21 Remove the fastener at the glove box hinge to cowl area.

22 Remove the two fasteners at the center support-to-floorpan bracket.

23 Remove the screw attaching the rear of the heating and air conditioning unit to the center support bracket.

24 Lift up the instrument panel and pull rearward and withdraw it from the vehicle.

Installation

Refer to illustration 23.25

25 Installation is the reverse of removal noting the following points **(see illustration)**:

a) *Raise the steering column onto the support bracket and loosely install the four nuts.*

b) *Snugly tighten the lower nuts and ensure the plastic capsules are seated in the slots in the upper mounting bracket and the studs are centered in the plastic capsules.*

c) *Tighten the upper mounting nuts until the upper mounting bracket is seated.*

d) *Tighten the four steering column mounting nuts to 105 in-lbs.*

e) *On models equipped with a tilt steering wheel, remove the drill bits from the locking pin holes.*

f) *Turn the ignition switch to the Off position, then turn it to the On position. Check that the instrument cluster AIRBAG lamp illuminates for six to eight seconds and then goes out indicating the airbag system is functioning properly. If the lamp fails to light, blinks on and off or stays on, there is a malfunction in the airbag system. If any of these conditions exist, the vehicle should be diagnosed by a dealer service department or other qualified repair shop.*

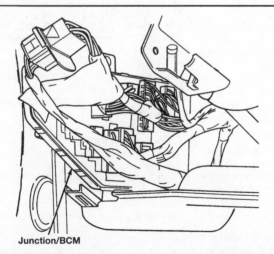

Junction/BCM

23.19 The junction block/Body Control Module is located behind the instrument panel on the driver's side

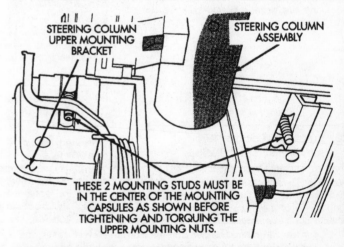

23.25 When installing the steering column, ensure that the two upper mounting studs are centered before tightening the nuts

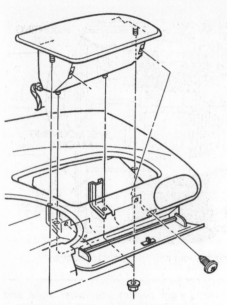

24.3 Passenger airbag assembly details

24 Passenger airbag module - removal and installation

Warning: *Always disable the airbag system before working in the vicinity of the impact sensors, steering column or instrument panel to avoid the possibility of accidental deployment of the airbag, which could cause personal injury (see Chapter 12).*
Note: *Refer to Chapter 10, steering wheel removal, for driver's side airbag service procedures.*

Removal

Refer to illustration 24.3

1   Disconnect the negative battery cable from the ground stud on the left shock tower (see Chapter 5, Section 1).
2   Open the glove box, squeeze the side-walls in and hinge the glove box door all the way down.
3   Remove the four nuts securing the airbag to the top of the instrument panel **(see illustration)**.
4   Remove the two screws securing the airbag to the support structure.
5   Lift the airbag module up and disconnect module electrical connector and remove the airbag module. **Warning:** *Carry the airbag with the trim cover side FACING AWAY from your body to minimize injury if the airbag module accidentally deploys. Store the airbag module aside in a safe, isolated location with the trim cover side facing UP.*

Installation

6   Installation is the reverse of removal. Ensure that the electrical connector is joined securely. Tighten the screws and nuts securely.
7   Turn the ignition switch to the Off position, then turn it to the On position. Check that the instrument cluster AIRBAG lamp illuminates for six to eight seconds and then goes out indicating the airbag system is functioning properly. If the lamp fails to light, blinks on and off or stays on, there is a malfunction in the airbag system. If any of these conditions exist, the vehicle should be diagnosed by a dealer service department or other qualified repair shop.

25 Steering column covers - removal and installation

Warning: *These models have airbags. Always disable the airbag system before working in the vicinity of the impact sensors, steering column or instrument panel to avoid the possibility of accidental deployment of the airbag, which could cause personal injury (see Chapter 12).*
Caution: *These covers can be easily scratched, take care when removing them to avoid damage.*

Removal

Refer to illustration 25.4

1   Disconnect the negative battery cable from the ground stud on the left shock tower (see Chapter 5, Section 1).
2   Remove the instrument cluster hood (see Section 22).
3   Remove the knee bolster **(see illustration 23.7)**.
4   Remove the two screws from the lower steering column cover and separate the covers **(see illustration)**.

Installation

5   Installation is the reverse of removal.

26 Center console - removal and installation

Warning: *These models have airbags. Always disable the airbag system before working in the vicinity of the impact sensors, steering column or instrument panel to avoid the possibility of accidental deployment of the airbag, which could cause personal injury (see Chapter 12).*
Caution: *The center console can be easily scratched, take care in removing the assembly to avoid damage.*
Note: *The center console on these vehicles is composed of two separate sections.*

Floor console

Removal

Refer to illustrations 26.3a, 26.3b, 26.4, 26.5 and 26.6

1   Disconnect the negative battery cable from the ground stud on the left shock tower (see Chapter 5, Section 1).
2   Completely raise the parking brake lever.
3   On vehicles equipped with a manual transaxle, pull the gear shift boot down away from the knob to expose the knob retaining clips. Pry the clips away from the shift lever

25.4 After removing the two screws from the lower cover, the covers can then be separated from the steering column

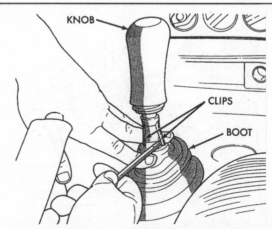

26.3a To remove the gearshift knob on vehicles equipped with a manual transaxle, pull the boot down to expose the knob retaining clips, pry the clips off the gearshift tangs and pull the knob off the gearshift lever

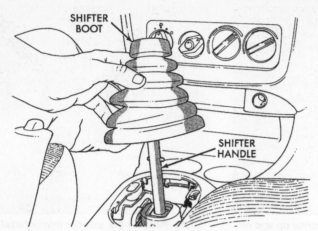

26.3b Squeeze the base of the gearshift boot to disengage it from the floor console and then pull it off the gearshift lever

26.4 To remove the shift lever handle on vehicles equipped with an automatic transaxle, remove the set screw (arrow) and pull the handle off the shift lever

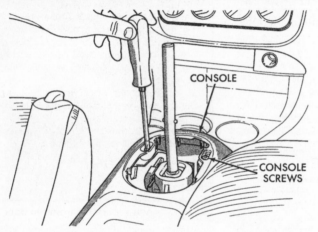

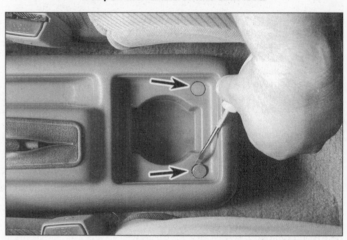

26.5 Floor console forward attaching screw locations

26.6 Pry off the trim plugs (arrows) to access the console rear attaching screws

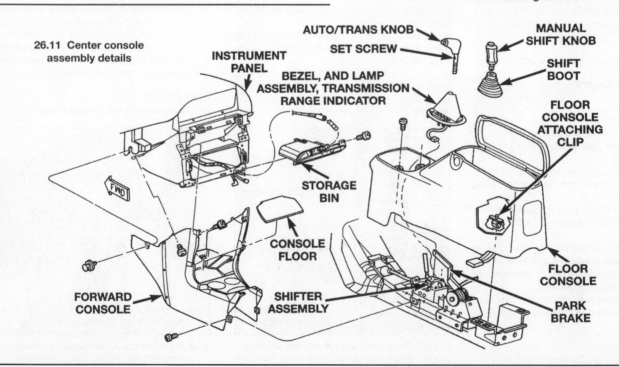

26.11 Center console assembly details

27.1a The interior mirror mounts to a button which is bonded to the windshield and is held in place by a set screw - loosen this screw . . .

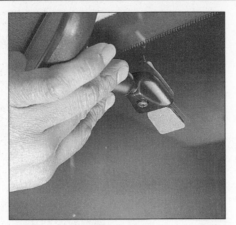

27.1b . . . and slide the mirror up and off the button

27.4a Remove the exterior mirror bezel mounting screws (arrows) . . .

and remove the gear shift knob **(see illustration)**. Grasp the base of the boot at the floor console and squeeze it together, then remove it from the gear shift lever **(see illustration)**.

4   On vehicles equipped with an automatic transaxle, remove the shift lever set screw and lift the handle assembly off the shift lever **(see illustration)**. Using a screwdriver, carefully pry the shift position indicator bezel from the floor console and disconnect the electrical connector.

5   Remove the two screws securing the front of the console **(see illustration)**.

6   At the rear of the floor console, pry off the trim plugs and remove the two screws from the console **(see illustration)**. Note: *On vehicles equipped with a storage box/arm rest type console, the rear attaching screws are located inside the storage area.*

7   Maneuver the floor console up and over the shift lever and parking brake handle and remove it from vehicle.

Installation

8   Installation is the reverse of removal.

Forward console
Removal

Refer to illustration 26.11

9   Remove the floor console (see above).

10   Remove the dashboard center bezel (see Section 21).

11   Unscrew the screws securing the storage bin and remove it from the console **(see illustration)**.

12   Remove the two screws securing the forward console to the gear selector mount bracket.

13   Remove the screws holding the console to the instrument panel at each side of the heater/air conditioning controls, storage bin area and panel support braces.

14   With all fasteners removed, carefully withdraw the forward console from the vehicle.

Installation

15   Installation is the reverse of removal.

27   Mirrors - removal and installation

Interior
Removal

Refer to illustrations 27.1a and 27.1b

1   Use a Phillips head screwdriver to remove the set screw, then slide the mirror up off the button on the windshield **(see illustrations)**.

Installation

2   Installation is the reverse of removal.

Exterior
Removal

Refer to illustrations 27.4a, 27.4b, 27.7 and 27.8

3   Remove the door trim panel (see Section 13).

4   Remove the two screws securing the mirror bezel and remove it from the door **(see illustrations)**.

5   On vehicles equipped with standard mirrors, loosen the set screw holding the mirror adjuster cable to bezel and separate the adjuster from the bezel.

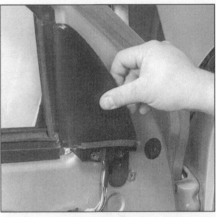

27.4b . . . then separate it from the door

6   On vehicles equipped with power mirrors, detach the mirror electrical connector from it's mounting on the door.

7   Using a screwdriver, pry the caps from the mirror nut access holes **(see illustration)**.

8   Remove the three nuts **(see illustration)** and detach the mirror from the door.

Installation

9   Installation is the reverse of removal.

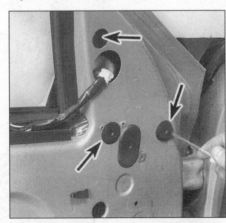

27.7 Pry off the caps from the exterior mirror mounting nut access holes (arrows)

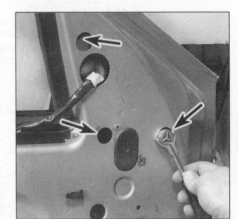

27.8 Remove the exterior mirror mounting nuts through these holes (arrows)

28 Cowl cover - removal and installation

Removal

Refer to illustrations 28.1a, 28.1b, 28.2 and 28.3

1   Lift up the plastic trim cap on the windshield wiper arms, then detach the wiper arm retaining nuts and remove the wiper arms **(see illustrations)**.
2   Peel off the hood rubber sealing strip from the cowl edge **(see illustration)**.
3   Remove the two retaining screws on each side of the cowl cover and carefully lift it from the vehicle **(see illustration)**.

Installation

4   Installation is the reverse of removal.

29 Seats - removal and installation

Front

Removal

Refer to illustrations 29.1 and 29.2

1   Move the seat fully rearward and

28.1a Lift the plastic trim cap on the windshield wiper arms . . .

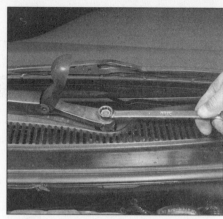

28.1b . . . remove the retaining nuts and remove the wiper arms from the vehicle

remove the seat track front bolts **(see illustration)**.
2   Move the seat fully forward and remove the seat track rear bolts **(see illustration)**.
3   If the vehicle is equipped with power seats, disconnect the electrical connector and lift the seat out of the vehicle.

Installation

4   Installation is the reverse of removal.

Rear

Lower seat cushion

Removal

Refer to illustration 29.5

5   Remove the seat cushion by grasping the front edge securely, then pulling up sharply to detach the cushion from the retainer cups in the floorpan **(see illustration)**.

28.2 Carefully remove the hood rubber sealing strip from the edge of the cowl cover

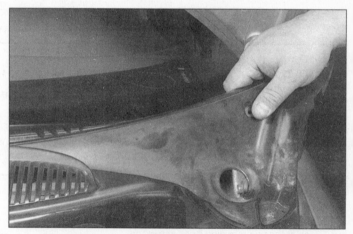

28.3 After removing the four attaching screws, lift off the cowl cover

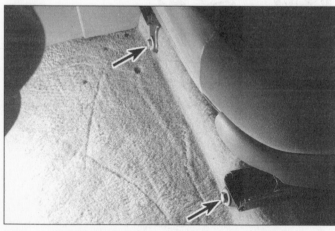

29.1 Front seat - front mounting bolts (arrows)

29.2 Front seat - rear mounting bolts (arrows)

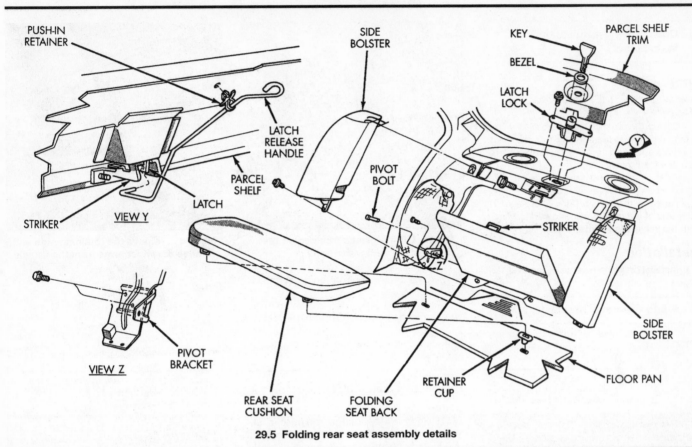

29.5 Folding rear seat assembly details

Installation

6   Installation is the reverse of removal. Press down firmly over the seat retainers to ensure they are fully engaged in the floorpan.

Seat back - child restraint models

Removal

Refer to illustration 29.8

7   Remove the lower seat cushion.
8   Remove the bolts holding the seat backs and belts to the floorpan **(see illustration)**.
9   Open the child seat and remove the lining. Remove the two retaining bolts within the lining area.
10   Lift up the seat back to disengage the hooks from the slots and remove the seat back from the vehicle.

Installation

11   Installation is the reverse of removal.

Seat back - folding models

Removal

12   Remove the lower seat cushion (see above).
13   Remove the bolts securing the bottoms of the each side bolster to the floorpan. Lift each bolster up to detach it from the retaining hook and remove it from the vehicle **(see illustration 29.5)**.
14   Remove the seat back-to-pivot bracket bolts.
15   Release the folding seat latch and remove the seat back from the vehicle.

Installation

16   Installation is the reverse of removal.

Rear seat back latch/lock

Removal

Refer to illustrations 29.22 and 29.23

17   Remove the lower seat cushion (see above).

18   Remove the seat back (see above).
19   Remove the bolts securing the rear seat belt anchors to the floorpan.
20   Disengage the clips holding the left and right upper quarter trim pieces to the inner quarter panels.
21   Route the seat belt webbing through the access hole in each upper quarter trim piece and remove them from the vehicle.

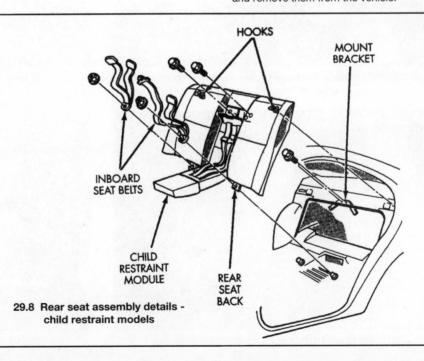

29.8 Rear seat assembly details - child restraint models

11

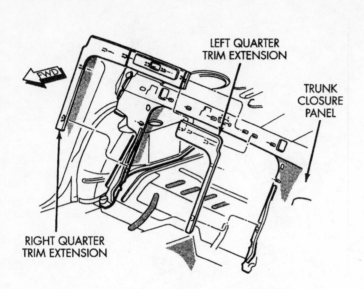

29.22 Quarter trim extension assembly details

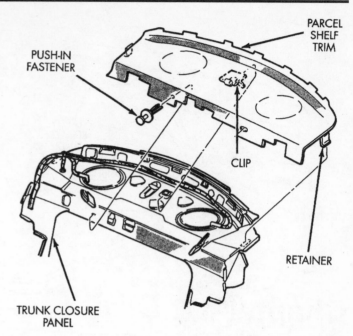

29.23 Parcel shelf assembly details

22   Using a screwdriver, pry off the left and right quarter panel extensions **(see illustration)**.
23   Remove the push-in fasteners securing the parcel shelf to the trunk closure panel **(see illustration)**.
24   Pull the parcel shelf forward to disengage the clip securing parcel shelf to the trunk closure panel and remove it from the vehicle.
25   Remove the two bolts securing the seat back latch/lock to the trunk closure panel and remove it from the vehicle.

Installation
26   Installation is the reverse of removal.

Rear seat back latch handle

Removal
27   Inside the trunk, remove the push-in fastener securing the latch handle to the bottom of the parcel shelf.
28   Detach the handle from the folding rear seat latch **(see illustration 29.5)**.

Installation
29   Installation is the reverse of removal.

30   Seat belt check

1   Check the seat belts, buckles, latch plates and guide loops for obvious damage and signs of wear.
2   See if the seat belt reminder light comes on when the ignition key is turned to the RUN or START positions. A warning chime should also sound.
3   The seat belts are designed to lock up during a sudden stop or impact, yet allow free movement during normal driving. Make sure the retractors return the belt against your chest while driving and rewind the belt fully when the buckle is unlatched.
4   If any of the above checks reveal problems with the seat belt system, replace parts as necessary.

Chapter 12
Chassis electrical system

Contents

1   General information

The electrical system is a 12-volt, negative ground type. Power for the lights and all electrical accessories is supplied by a lead/acid-type battery which is charged by the alternator.

This Chapter covers repair and service procedures for the various electrical components not associated with the engine. Information on the battery, alternator, distributor and starter motor can be found in Chapter 5. **Warning:** *When working on the electrical system, disconnect the negative battery cable from the ground stud on the left shock tower (see Chapter 5, Section 1) to prevent electrical shorts and/or fires.*

2   Electrical troubleshooting

A typical electrical circuit consists of an electrical component, any switches, relays, motors, fuses, fusible links or circuit breakers related to the component and the wiring and connectors that link the component to both the battery and the chassis. To help pinpoint an electrical circuit problem, wiring diagrams are included at the end of this Chapter.

Before tackling any troublesome electrical circuit, first study the appropriate wiring diagrams to get a complete understanding of what makes up that individual circuit. Trouble spots, for instance, can often be narrowed down by noting if other components related to the circuit are operating properly. If several components or circuits fail at one time, chances are the problem is in a fuse or ground connection, because several circuits are often routed through the same fuse and ground connections.

Electrical problems usually stem from simple causes, such as loose or corroded connections, a blown fuse, a melted fusible link or a bad relay. Visually inspect the condition of all fuses, wires and connections in a problem circuit before troubleshooting it.
If testing instruments are going to be utilized, plan ahead of time where to make the necessary connections to accurately pinpoint the trouble spot.

The basic tools needed for electrical troubleshooting include a circuit tester or voltmeter (a 12-volt bulb with a set of test leads can also be used), a continuity tester (which includes a bulb, battery and set of test leads) and a jumper wire, preferably with a fuse or circuit breaker incorporated, which can be used to bypass electrical components. Before attempting to locate a problem with test instruments, use the wiring diagram(s) to decide where to make the connections.

Voltage checks

Voltage checks should be performed if a circuit isn't functioning properly. Connect one lead of a circuit tester to either the negative battery terminal or a known good ground. Connect the other lead to a connector in the circuit being tested, preferably nearest to the battery or fuse. If the bulb of the tester lights, voltage is present, which means the part of the circuit between the connector and the battery is problem free. Continue checking the rest of the circuit in the same fashion. When you reach a point where no voltage is present, the problem lies between that point and the last test point with voltage. Most of the time the problem can be traced to a loose connection. **Note:** *Keep in mind that some circuits receive voltage only when the ignition key is in the Accessory or Run position.*

Finding a short

One method of finding a short in a circuit is to remove the fuse and connect a test light or voltmeter in its place to the fuse terminals. There should be no voltage present in the circuit. Move the wiring harness from side-to-side while watching the test light. If the bulb lights, there's a short to ground somewhere in that area, probably where the insulation has rubbed through. The same test can be performed on each component in the circuit, even a switch.

"Short finders" are also commonly available. These reasonably priced tools connect in place of a fuse and pulse voltage through the circuit. An inductive meter (included with the kit) is then run along the wiring for the circuit. When the needle on the meter stops moving, you've located the short.

Ground check

Perform a ground test to check whether a component is properly grounded. Disconnect the negative battery cable from the ground stud on the left shock tower and connect one lead of a self-powered test light, known as a continuity tester, to a known good ground. Connect the other lead to the wire or ground connection being tested. If the bulb lights, the ground is good. If the bulb doesn't light, the ground is faulty.

Continuity check

A continuity check is done to determine if there are breaks in a circuit - if it's capable of passing electricity properly. With the circuit off (no power in the circuit), a self-powered continuity tester can be used to check it. Connect the test leads to both ends of the circuit (or to the "power" end and a good ground) - if the test light comes on the circuit is passing current properly. If the light doesn't come on, there's a break (open) somewhere in the circuit. The same procedure can be used to test a switch by connecting the continuity tester to the switch terminals. With the switch on, the test light should come on.

Finding an open circuit

When diagnosing for possible open circuits, it's often difficult to locate them by sight because oxidation or terminal misalignment are hidden by the connectors. Merely wiggling a connector on a sensor or in the wiring harness may correct the open circuit condition. Remember this when an open is indicated when troubleshooting a circuit. Intermittent problems may also be caused by oxidized or loose connections. Electrical troubleshooting is simple if you keep in mind that all electrical circuits are basically electricity running from the battery, through the wires, switches, relays, fuses and fusible links to each electrical component (light bulb, motor, etc.) and to ground, where it's passed back to the battery. Any electrical problem is an interruption in the flow of electricity to and from the battery.

3 Fuses - general information

Refer to illustrations 3.1a, 3.1b and 3.3

1 The electrical circuits of the vehicle are protected by a combination of fuses, circuit breakers and fusible links. One fuse block is located under a cover on the end of the instrument panel on the left (driver's) side, easily accessible by opening the driver's door **(see illustration)**. A fuse and relay block, called the Power Distribution Center (PDC) is located on the left side of the engine compartment near the radiator upper support **(see illustration)**.

2 Each fuse, relay or circuit breaker is designed to protect a specific circuit. The various circuits and fuses are identified on the underside of the PDC or fuse block covers.

3 Miniaturized fuses are employed in the fuse block. These compact fuses, with blade terminal design, allow fingertip removal and replacement. If an electrical component fails, always check the fuse first. A blown fuse is

3.1a The interior fuse block is located at the left end of the instrument panel - open the driver's door and pull off the cover. Fuse identification is located on the underside of the cover

3.1b The Power Distribution Center is located in the engine compartment and contains both fuses and relays (additional relays are under the square cover directly above the PDC)

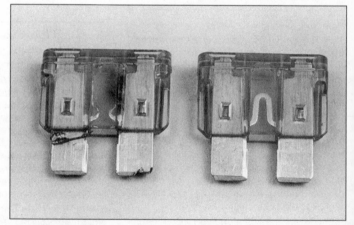

3.3 The fuses used on these models can be checked visually to determine if they are blown (good fuse on right, blown fuse on left)

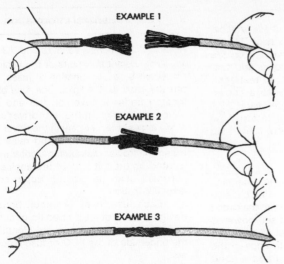

4.2 Strip about 1 inch of insulation off both wires, then spread the strands, push them together and twist them in place

7.1 The turn signal/hazard flasher unit is located in the steering column and mounted behind multi-function switch

easily identified through the clear plastic body. Visually inspect the element for evidence of damage **(see illustration)**. If a continuity check is called for, the blade terminal tips are exposed in the fuse body.

4   Be sure to replace blown fuses with the correct type and rating. Fuses of different ratings are physically interchangeable, but only fuses of the proper rating should be used. Replacing a fuse with one of a higher or lower value than specified is not recommended. Each electrical circuit needs a specific amount of protection. The amperage value of each fuse is molded into the fuse body.

5   If the replacement fuse immediately fails, don't replace it again until the cause of the problem is isolated and corrected. In most cases, the cause will be a short circuit in the wiring caused by a broken or deteriorated wire.

4   Fusible links - general information

Refer to illustration 4.2

1   The circuit from the output terminal of the Power Distribution Center to the alternator and the starter motor (1995 and 1996 vehicles with manual transaxles only) is protected by a wire called a fusible link. Fusible links are used in circuits which are not ordinarily fused, such as the starting or ignition circuit(s).

2   Although the fusible links appear to be a heavier gauge than the wires they're protecting, the appearance is due to the thick insulation. All fusible links are four wire gauges smaller than the wire they're designed to protect. Fusible links cannot be repaired, but a new link of the same amperage rating can be installed. The procedure is as follows:

a) *Disconnect the negative cable from the remote battery terminal.*

b) *Disconnect the fusible link from the component at the eyelet terminal connection.*

c) *Cut the damaged fusible link out of the wiring just behind the crimp connector.*

d) *Strip the insulation back approximately 1-inch.*

e) *Spread the strands of the exposed wire apart, push them together and twist them in place* **(see illustration)**. **Note:** *If available, this connection may be made using another crimp type connector.*

f) *Use rosin core type solder and solder the wires together to obtain a good connection.*

g) *Use plenty of electrical tape around the soldered joint. No wires should be exposed.*

h) *Connect the new fusible link eyelet terminal to the component and tighten the screw securely.*

i) *Connect the negative cable to the remote battery terminal. Test the circuit for proper operation.*

5   Circuit breakers - general information

Circuit breakers protect components such as power windows, power door locks, power seats and sunroof (if equipped). The circuit breakers are located in the fuse block. On some models the circuit breaker resets itself automatically, so an electrical overload in the circuit will cause it to fail momentarily, then come back on. If the circuit doesn't come back on, check the circuit breaker immediately (some circuit breakers must be reset manually). If the circuit breaker blows again, check the circuit for a short and correct it as soon as possible. Once the condition is corrected, the circuit breaker should resume its normal function.

6   Relays - general information

Several electrical circuits in the vehicle that draw heavy amperage utilize relays to transmit current to the component. If the relay is defective, the component won't operate properly. Relays are located in the fuse block and the Power Distribution Center **(see illustrations 3.1a and 3.1b)**.

If a faulty relay is suspected, it can be removed and tested by a dealer service department or other qualified repair shop. Defective relays are not serviceable and must be replaced as a unit. **Note:** *Checks for the starter, automatic shutdown and fuel pump relays are located in Chapter 4.*

7   Turn signal/hazard flasher - check, removal and installation

Warning: *These models have airbags. Always disable the airbag system before working in the vicinity of the impact sensor, steering column or instrument panel to avoid the possibility of accidental deployment of the airbag, which could cause personal injury (see Section 29).*

Check

Refer to illustration 7.1

1   The turn signal/hazard flasher is a small unit located behind the multi-function switch inside the steering column **(see illustration)**.

2   When the flasher unit is functioning properly, an audible click can be heard during its operation. An inoperative or incomplete turn signal circuit will result in an increased flasher speed.

3   If both turn signals fail to blink, the problem may be due to a blown fuse, a faulty flasher unit, a broken switch or a loose or

12

open connection. If a quick check of the fuse box indicates the turn signal fuse has blown, check the wiring for a short before installing a new fuse.

4   If the fuse is OK, remove the turn signal light bulbs and make sure they are operational by attaching them to a 12 volt power source.

5   If the bulbs check out OK, check the turn signal section of the multi-function switch (see Section 8). Also check the wiring harness continuity.

Removal

6   To replace the flasher, remove the steering wheel column covers (see Chapter 11).

7   Locate the turn signal/hazard combo-flasher (black relay) behind the multi-function switch **(see illustration 7.1)**.

8   Pull the flasher unit out of the multi-function switch.

Installation

9   Make sure the replacement flasher unit is identical to the original. Compare the old one to the new one before installing it.

10   Install the flasher unit into the multi-function switch making sure it is fully seated.

11   Install the steering wheel column covers (see Chapter 11).

8   Multi-function switch - check and replacement

Warning: *These models have airbags. Always disable the airbag system before working in the vicinity of the impact sensor, steering column or instrument panel to avoid the possibility of accidental deployment of the airbag, which could cause personal injury (see Section 29).*

1   The multi-function switch is located on the steering column. It incorporates the turn signals, hazard warning, headlights, headlight beam select (HI/LO), headlight flasher, instrument panel dimmer switch, fog lights, windshield wiper and windshield washer functions. There are two levers on the multi-function switch, the left side controls the signaling and lighting, the right side controls the wipers and washer system.

Check

Refer to illustration 8.3

2   Remove the multi-function switch from the steering column and remove the flasher unit from the switch (see below).

3   Using an ohmmeter or a continuity tester, refer to the accompanying chart and check for continuity between the switch terminals with the switch in each position **(see illustration)**. If any portion of the switch is faulty, the entire multi-function switch assembly must be replaced.

4   After the check is complete, replace the flasher unit and install the multi-function switch onto the steering column (see below).

SWITCH POSITION	MODE	CONTINUITY BETWEEN
TURN SIGNAL with HAZARD WARNING SWITCH OFF	RIGHT	A-1 and B-6
	LEFT	A-1 and B-7
TURN SIGNAL with HAZARD WARNING SWITCH ON	RIGHT or OFF or LEFT	A-1 and B-6 A-2 and A-5 A-1 and B-7 B-6 and B-7
HEADLAMP BEAM ON	PARK	C-2 and C-1
	LOW	C-2 and C-1 C-4 and C-7
	HIGH	C-2 and C-1 C-4 and C-8
PANEL DIMMER DETENT	1 2 3 to 8 9	A-2 and C-6 <100 Ω 300 to 2630 Ω LINEAR 4.99k to 10.5k Ω
OPTICAL HORN	ON	C-4 and C-8
FRONT FOG	ON	C-9 and C-10
WIPER	INT DETENT	B-3 and B2
	1	11.87k Ω
	2	9.87k Ω
	3	7.87k Ω
	4	5.87k Ω
	5	3.87k Ω
	6	1.87k Ω
	LOW	B-3 and B-2 1.25k Ω
	HIGH	B-3 and B-2 1.82k Ω
MIST	ON	B-3 and B-2 1.25k Ω
WASHER	ON	B-3 and B-1

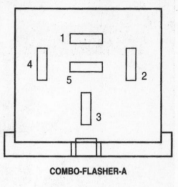

COMBO-FLASHER-A

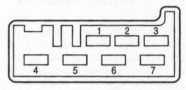

7-WAY CONNECTOR-B

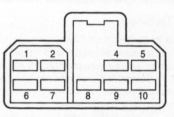

10-WAY CONNECTOR-C

8.3 Multi-function switch terminal guide and continuity chart

8.7 Multi-function switch mounting screws (arrows)

Replacement

Refer to illustration 8.7

5   Remove the steering column covers (see Chapter 11).

6   Disconnect the electrical connectors from the back side of the switch.

7   Remove the 2 mounting screws and detach the switch from the steering column **(see illustration)**. Installation is the reverse of removal.

8   Installation is the reverse of removal.

9   Windshield wiper/washer switch - check and replacement

Warning: *These models have airbags. Always disable the airbag system before working in the vicinity of the impact sensor, steering column or instrument panel to avoid the possibility of accidental deployment of the airbag, which could cause personal injury (see Section 29).*

10.7 Windshield washer pump (arrow) is located in the reservoir

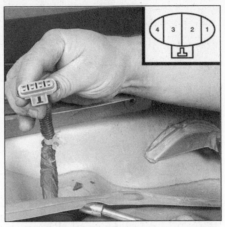

11.3 Windshield wiper motor electrical connector terminal identification

1   *Wiper park switch*
2   *Ground*
3   *Wiper switch low speed*
4   *Wiper switch high speed*

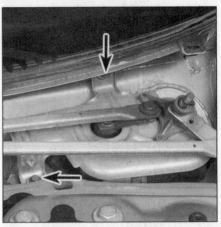

11.8a Wiper motor/linkage mounting bolts (arrows) - left side

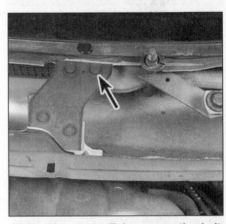

11.8b Wiper motor/linkage mounting bolt (arrow) - right side

1   The wiper/washer switch is part of the multi-function switch, refer to Section 8 for check, removal and installation procedures.
2   If the wipers do not operate, check the windshield wiper motor (see Section 11).

10   Windshield washer fluid pump - removal and installation

Removal

Refer to illustration 10.7

1   If the washer reservoir contains fluid, siphon it into a suitable container.
2   Detach the washer fluid hose at the in-line connector on top of the right shock tower.
3   Remove the front bumper (see Chapter 11).
4   Remove the EVAP carbon canister (see Chapter 6).
5   Disconnect the electrical connector from the washer pump.
6   Detach the washer hose from the reservoir.
7   Remove the mounting screws and maneuver the reservoir (with pump attached) from the vehicle **(see illustration)**.
8   To remove the washer pump, simply grasp the pump and using a twisting motion pull the pump out of the reservoir grommet.

Installation

9   Installation is the reverse of removal. If the pump was removed, install a new grommet.

11   Windshield wiper motor - check and replacement

Check

Refer to illustration 11.3

1   If the wipers do not operate at all, check the fuses (see Section 3).
2   If the fuses are OK, remove the cowl

cover (see Chapter 11) to access the wiper motor electrical connector. Make sure the terminals are clean and tight. Turn the ignition switch and wiper switch on. Recheck the wiper operation.
3   If the wipers still do not operate, disconnect the electrical connector and connect a voltmeter to terminal no. 2 (-) and 4 (+) **(see illustration)**. Turn the ignition switch On and the wiper switch to the HI position - voltage should be indicated. Connect the voltmeter to terminal no. 2 (-) and 3 (+), place the wiper switch in the LO position - voltage should be indicated. If no voltage is indicated in either position, check for continuity between terminal no. 2 and ground, if no continuity is indicated, repair the ground connection.
4   If voltage is present in the HI and LO positions, remove the motor and check it off the vehicle with fused jumper wires connected to the battery remote terminals. If the motor now operates, check for binding linkage. If the motor still does not operate, replace it.
5   If there's no voltage at the motor electrical connector, the problem is in the switch, the wiper relays, the Body Control Module (BCM) or the related wiring. Check the wiper switch (see Section 9) and, if necessary, perform continuity tests on the wiring. Have the BCM checked by a dealer service department or other properly equipped repair shop.

Replacement

Refer to illustrations 11.8a, 11.8b and 11.11

6   Disconnect the negative battery cable from the ground stud on the left shock tower (see Chapter 5, Section 1).
7   Remove the cowl cover (see Chapter 11).
8   Remove the wiper motor/linkage assembly mounting bolts **(see illustrations)**. Remove the wiper motor/linkage assembly.
9   Disconnect the wiper motor electrical connector and harness clip from the forward

mounting leg.
10   To remove the linkage from the motor crank, insert a screwdriver between the crank and the linkage, then twist the screwdriver and lift straight up on the linkage to separate the ball cap from the ball.
11   Remove the motor retaining nuts **(see illustration)** and separate the motor from the linkage assembly.
12   Installation is the reverse of removal.

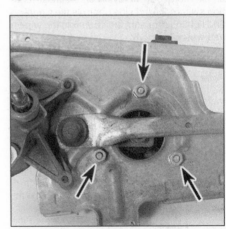

11.11 Wiper motor mounting nuts (arrows)

12

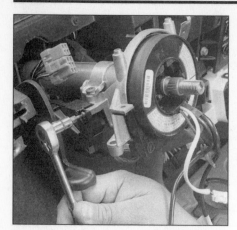

12.6 Remove the ignition switch mounting screw

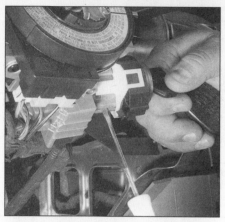

12.14 To remove the lock cylinder, place the ignition key in the RUN position and use a small screwdriver to depress the spring loaded retaining tab, then pull the lock/key out of the housing

12.15 Make sure the ignition switch mating slot located inside the housing (arrow) is in the RUN position before installing the lock cylinder

12   Ignition switch and lock cylinder - removal and installation

Warning: *These models have airbags. Always disable the airbag system before working in the vicinity of the impact sensor, steering column or instrument panel to avoid the possibility of accidental deployment of the airbag, which could cause personal injury (see Section 29).*

1   When the ignition switch is in the RUN/START position, it connects power from the Power Distribution Center (PDC) to the fuel pump relay, starter motor relay, Powertrain Control Module, ABS control module and distributor (V6 engine).

Ignition switch

Removal

Refer to illustration 12.6

2   The ignition switch is located inside the steering column and is activated by, and attached to, the key lock cylinder.
3   Disconnect the negative battery cable from the ground stud on the left shock tower (see Chapter 5, Section 1).
4   Remove the steering column covers (see Chapter 11).
5   Remove the key lock cylinder (see below).
6   Remove the screw securing the switch to the steering column **(see illustration)**.
7   Depress the retaining tabs, then detach the switch and lower it from the steering column.
8   Disconnect the electrical connector from the ignition switch.

Installation

9   Installation is the reverse of removal. Make sure the switch and lock cylinder are in the RUN position before installation. Tighten the switch mounting screw securely.

Lock cylinder

Removal

Refer to illustration 12.14

10   The ignition key lock cylinder is located

on the right side of the steering column.
11   Disconnect the negative battery cable from the ground stud on the left shock tower (see Chapter 5, Section 1).
12   Remove the steering column covers (see Chapter 11).
13   Insert the ignition key and turn the switch to the RUN position.
14   Depress the retaining tab with a small screwdriver and then withdraw the lock cylinder from the housing **(see illustration)**.

Installation

Refer to illustration 12.15

15   Make sure the slot in the ignition switch is in the RUN position **(see illustration)** and insert the lock cylinder into the housing until the retaining tab locates the housing. Check key operation.
16   The remaining installation steps are the reverse of removal.

13   Headlight switch - check and replacement

Warning: *These models have airbags. Always disable the airbag system before working in the vicinity of the impact sensor, steering column or instrument panel to avoid the possibility of accidental deployment of the airbag,*

which could cause personal injury (see Section 29).
1   The headlight switch is part of the multi-function switch, refer to Section 8 for check, removal and installation procedures.

14   Headlight assembly - removal and installation

Warning: *The headlight bulbs are gas-filled halogen type and under pressure. If the surface is scratched or the bulb is dropped it may shatter. Wear eye protection and handle the bulbs carefully, grasping only the base whenever possible. Don't touch the surface of the bulb with your fingers because the oil from your skin could cause it to overheat and fail prematurely. If you happen to touch the bulb surface, clean it with rubbing alcohol.*

Removal

Refer to illustrations 14.1 and 14.3

1   Open the hood and remove the headlight mounting screws **(see illustration)**.
2   To protect the body paint, place a soft piece of thin material such as a credit card or cardboard between the headlight assembly and the front fender.
3   Using a screwdriver applied between the cardboard (or equivalent) and the head-

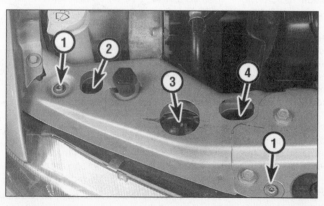

14.1 Headlight mounting and adjustment details

1   *Headlight assembly mounting screws*
2   *Vertical position adjusting screw*
3   *Vertical position indicator (bubble level)*
4   *Horizontal position indicator/adjuster*

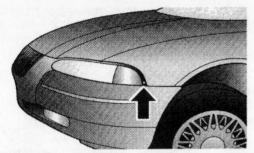

14.3 While protecting the body paint with padding placed between the screwdriver and the fender, use a screwdriver to carefully pry the headlight assembly from the ball socket (arrow)

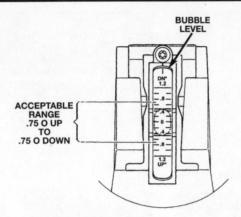

15.4 Headlight vertical position indicator - Do not tamper with the screw located on the indicator or calibration will be lost. When properly adjusted, the bubble should be in the range shown

light assembly, carefully pry the headlight assembly away from the fender to disengage it from the ball socket **(see illustration)**.

4   Disconnect the electrical connectors from the headlight and park/turn signal bulb holders and remove the headlight assembly from the vehicle.

Installation

5   Installation is the reverse of removal. Make sure the electrical connectors are securely attached. Adjust the headlights if necessary (see Section 15).

15   Headlight and fog light - adjustment

Warning: *The headlights must be aimed correctly. If adjusted incorrectly, they could temporarily blind the driver on an oncoming vehicle and cause an accident or seriously reduce your ability to see the road. The headlights should be checked for proper aim every 12 months and any time a new headlight is installed or front end body work is performed. The following procedure is only an interim step to provide temporary adjustment until the headlights can be adjusted by a dealer service department or other properly equipped shop.*

Headlights

Using the built-in indicators

Refer to illustrations 15.4 and 15.6

1   The headlight assemblies have built-in horizontal and vertical position indicators which are calibrated at the factory.

2   Adjustment should be made with the vehicle on a level surface, with a full gas tank and a normal load in the vehicle.

3   Rock the vehicle side-to-side three times, then push down on the front bumper to jounce the front suspension up-and-down three times. This will allow the suspension to stabilize prior to adjustment.

4   Open the hood and check the vertical indicators on the headlight assemblies. The bubble in the vial should be centered over the zero **(see illustration)**. **Note:** *A bubble located anywhere between 0.75 degrees UP and 0.75 degrees DOWN is also acceptable.*

5   If the bubble is not within the 0.75 degrees UP to 0.75 degrees DOWN range, adjust the vertical aiming screw **(see illustration 15.1)** as required to bring the bubble back to the centered location. **Caution:** *Do not tamper with the screw on the vial itself or calibration will be lost.*

6   Next, check the horizontal indicators. The arrow on the adjuster should be pointing to the zero mark on the gauge wheel **(see illustration)**.

7   If the arrow is not pointing to the zero mark, adjust the horizontal aiming screw **(see illustration 15.6)** as required to align the horizontal marks.

Using an alignment screen

Refer to illustration 15.13

8   This procedure requires a level surface and a flat blank wall with room to park the vehicle 25 feet from the wall.

9   Position a masking tape line vertically on the wall in reference to the centerline of the vehicle and the headlights. **Note:** *It may be easier to position the tape on the wall with the vehicle parked only a few inches away, then move the vehicle directly backwards away from the wall.*

10   With the vehicle 25 feet away from the wall, rock the vehicle side-to-side three times, then push down on the front bumper to jounce the front suspension up-and-down three times. This will allow the suspension to stabilize.

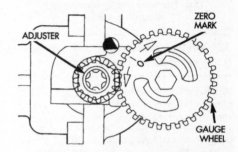

15.6 Headlight horizontal position indicator - When properly adjusted, the arrow on the adjuster should be pointing to the zero mark on the gauge wheel

11   Measure the distance from the floor to the centerline of each headlight lens. Transfer these dimensions to the wall and place another masking tape line horizontally at each location.

12   Measure the distance from the centerline of each headlight lens to the center of the vehicle. Transfer these dimensions to the flat wall on each side of the vertical centerline tape line and place a masking tape line vertically at each location.

13   On the wall at the left headlight location, place a 2 inch square piece of tape 8 inches below the horizontal line and 5 inches to the right of the vertical centerline. This is the target spot for the left headlight **(see illustration)**.

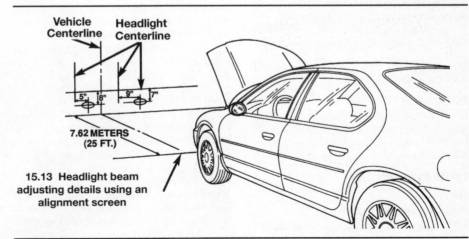

15.13 Headlight beam adjusting details using an alignment screen

15.20 Fog light adjusting screw (arrow)

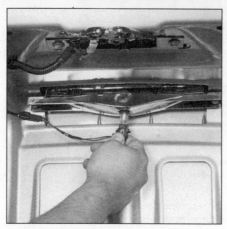

16.6 Removing the center mounted brake light from the trunk lid. This bulb is a halogen type. Don't touch it with your bare hands because the oil from your skin could cause the bulb to fail prematurely

14   On the wall at the right headlight location, place a 2 inch square piece of tape 7 inches below the horizontal line and 9 inches to the right of the vertical centerline. This is the target spot for the right headlight.

15   With the vehicle 25 feet from the wall and the headlights illuminated in the low beam position, turn the adjusting screws on each headlight **(see illustration 15.1)** until the hot spot of each headlight is centered on it's respective target spot (2 inch square piece of tape). **Note:** *The high beam pattern should be correct after proper alignment of the low beam.*

16   If you cannot align either headlight, or the light pattern on the road appears incorrect after adjustment, have the headlights adjusted by a dealer service department or other qualified repair shop at the earliest opportunity.

Fog light adjustment

Refer to illustration 15.20

17   This procedure requires a level surface and a flat blank wall with room to park the vehicle 25 feet from the wall.

18   With the vehicle 25 feet away from the wall, rock the vehicle side-to-side three times, then push down on the front bumper to jounce the front suspension up-and-down three times. This will allow the suspension to stabilize.

19   Measure the distance from the floor to the horizontal centerline of each fog light lens. Transfer these dimensions to the wall and place a 3 foot masking tape line horizontally at each location.

20   With the fog lights illuminated, turn the adjusting screws on each fog light **(see illustration)** until the top of each fog light beam pattern is approximately 4 inches below the horizontal tape line.

---

16   Bulb replacement

Ash tray/cup holder bulb

1   Insert a small screwdriver into the slot in

the light bezel and pry it from the cubby bin.

2   Pull the light socket from the light bezel.

3   Remove the bulb from the socket.

4   Installation is the reverse of removal.

Center mounted brake light

Refer to illustration 16.6

Warning: *Halogen bulbs are gas-filled and under pressure and may shatter if the surface is scratched or the bulb is dropped. Wear eye protection and handle the bulbs carefully, grasping only the base whenever possible. Don't touch the surface of the bulb with your fingers because the oil from your skin could cause it to overheat and fail prematurely. If you do touch the bulb surface, clean it with rubbing alcohol.*

5   Open the trunk lid.

6   Rotate the bulb holder 1/4-turn counterclockwise and withdraw it from the light bezel **(see illustration)**.

7   Grasp the bulb and pull it out of the holder.

8   Using gloves or a clean shop towel, insert the new bulb into the holder. **Note:** *This bulb is a halogen type. Don't touch the surface of the bulb with your fingers because the oil from your skin could cause it to overheat and fail prematurely. If you happen to touch the bulb surface, clean it with rubbing alcohol.*

9   Insert the holder into the light bezel and rotate it clockwise to lock it in place. Close the trunk.

Dome lamp

10   Using a small screwdriver, pry the dome light lens from the light assembly.

11   Remove the bulb from the socket.

12   Installation is the reverse of removal.

Fog light

Warning: *Halogen bulbs are gas-filled and under pressure and may shatter if the surface is scratched or the bulb is dropped. Wear eye*

protection and handle the bulbs carefully, grasping only the base whenever possible. Don't touch the surface of the bulb with your fingers because the oil from your skin could cause it to overheat and fail prematurely. If you do touch the bulb surface, clean it with rubbing alcohol.

13   Remove the screws securing the fog light assembly to the front bumper and withdraw it from the bumper.

14   Grasp the bulb holder and rotate it 1/4-turn counterclockwise and then remove it from the light bezel.

15   Grasp the bulb and pull it out of the holder.

16   Using gloves or a clean shop towel, insert the new bulb into the holder. **Note:** *This bulb is a halogen type. Don't touch the surface of the bulb with your fingers because the oil from your skin could cause it to overheat and fail prematurely. If you happen to touch the bulb surface, clean it with rubbing alcohol.*

17   Insert the holder into the light bezel and rotate it clockwise to lock it in place.

18   Install the light bezel into the bumper and secure it with the mounting screws.

19   Check and adjust the fog light beam (see Section 15).

Glove box light

20   Open the glove box.

21   Pull down on the light/switch assembly to disengage it from the instrument panel.

22   Pull bulb from socket.

23   Installation is the reverse of removal.

Headlight bulb

Refer to illustration 16.25

Warning: *Halogen bulbs are gas-filled and under pressure and may shatter if the surface is scratched or the bulb is dropped. Wear eye protection and handle the bulbs carefully, grasping only the base whenever possible. Don't touch the surface of the bulb with your fingers because the oil from your skin could cause it to overheat and fail prematurely. If you do touch the bulb surface, clean it with rubbing alcohol.*

24   Remove the headlight assembly (see Section 14).

25   Grasp the headlight bulb holder retaining ring and rotate it 1/4-turn counterclockwise and remove the bulb holder from the headlight assembly **(see illustration)**.

26   Grasp the bulb and pull it out of the holder.

27   Using gloves or a clean shop towel, insert the new bulb into the holder. **Note:** *Don't touch the surface of the bulb with your fingers because the oil from your skin could cause it to overheat and fail prematurely. If you happen to touch the bulb surface, clean it with rubbing alcohol.*

28   Install the bulb holder in the headlight assembly and rotate it clockwise to lock it in place. Attach the electrical connectors to the bulb holders.

29   Install the headlight assembly (see Sec-

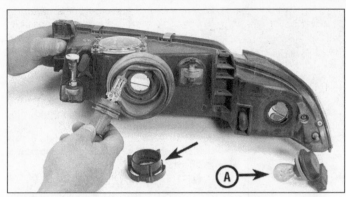

16.25 After removing the headlight bulb holder retaining ring (arrow), the bulb/holder can be withdrawn from the headlight assembly - (A) indicates the park/turn signal bulb/holder

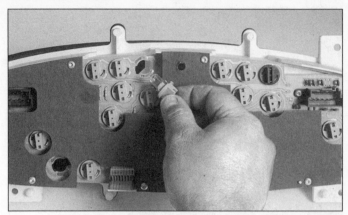

16.31 Replacing an instrument cluster bulb

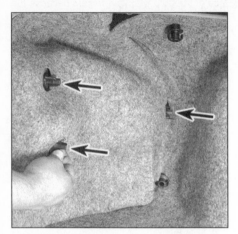

16.50 Inside the trunk, remove these plastic wing-nuts (arrows)

16.51 Withdraw the tail light assembly from the quarter panel and disconnect the electrical connector

16.52 Remove the tail/stop light from the tail light assembly

tion 14) and adjust if necessary (see Section 15).

Instrument panel bulbs

Refer to illustration 16.31

Note: *Depending on the location of the bulb being replaced, you may be able to access the bulb from under the dashboard.*

30   Remove the instrument cluster (see Section 20).
31   Grasp the bulb holder and rotate it 1/4-turn counterclockwise and then remove it from the instrument cluster **(see illustration)**.
32   Pull the bulb from the holder.
33   Install the new bulb into the holder.
34   Insert the holder into the instrument panel and rotate it clockwise to lock it in place.
35   Install the instrument cluster (see Section 20).

License plate light

36   Remove the license plate light assembly retaining screws and withdraw it from the rear bumper.
37   Grasp the bulb holder and rotate it 1/4-turn counterclockwise and then remove it from the light bezel.
38   Remove the bulb from the holder.
39   Install the new bulb into the holder.

40   Insert the holder into the light bezel and rotate it clockwise to lock it in place.
41   Install the light bezel into the bumper and secure it with the mounting screws.

Park/turn signal bulb

42   Remove the headlight assembly (see Section 14).
43   Grasp the bulb holder and rotate it 1/4-turn counterclockwise and remove the holder from the headlight assembly **(see illustration 16.25)**.
44   To remove the bulb from the holder, push it down slightly then rotate it 1/4-turn counterclockwise and withdraw it from the holder.
45   Install the new bulb into the holder.
46   Install the bulb holder in the headlight assembly and attach the electrical connectors to the bulb holders.
47   Install the headlight assembly (see Section 14) and adjust if necessary (see Section 15).

Tail, stop, back-up and turn signal bulbs

Refer to illustrations 16.50, 16.51 and 16.52

48   Open the trunk.
49   Separate the trunk lining from the rear

tail lamp assembly.
50   Unscrew and remove the plastic wing-nuts securing the tail light assembly to the quarter panel **(see illustration)**.
51   Withdraw the tail light assembly from the quarter panel and disconnect the wiring harness connector from the tail lamp assembly **(see illustration)**.
52   To replace a bulb, rotate the bulb holder 1/4-turn counterclockwise and withdraw it from the light bezel, then pull the bulb from the holder **(see illustration)**.
53   Installation is the reverse of removal.

Trunk light

54   Open the trunk.
55   Carefully insert a trim stick (plastic or wood) between the rear self reinforcement panel and cargo lamp lens. Carefully pry downward and remove it.
56   Grasp the bulb and remove it from the socket.
57   Installation is the reverse of removal.

Underhood lamp

58   Disconnect the wiring harness from the lamp assembly.
59   Rotate the bulb counterclockwise, then remove it.
60   Installation is the reverse of removal.

12

17.3 Radio mounting screws (arrows)

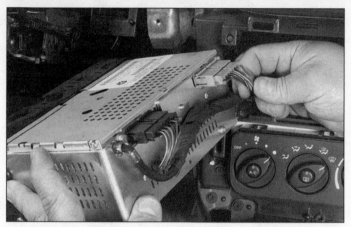

17.4 Disconnecting the electrical connectors and antenna lead from the rear of the radio

Visor vanity lamp

61   Lower the visor.
62   Carefully insert a trim stick (plastic or wood) between the visor and vanity lamp lens. Carefully pry outward and remove it.
63   Grasp the bulb and remove it from the socket.
64   Installation is the reverse of removal.

---

17   Radio, amplifier and speakers - removal and installation

---

Warning: *These models have airbags. Always disable the airbag system before working in the vicinity of the impact sensor, steering column or instrument panel to avoid the possibility of accidental deployment of the airbag, which could cause personal injury (see Section 29).*

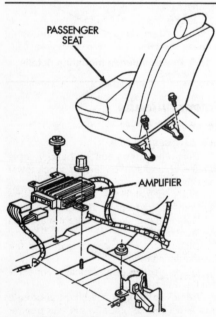

17.7 Amplifier mounting details

Caution: *Do not operate the radio without the speakers attached, damage to the amplifier may occur.*

Radio
Removal
Refer to illustrations 17.3 and 17.4

1   Disconnect the negative battery cable from the ground stud on the left shock tower (see Chapter 5, Section 1).
2   Remove the center bezel (see Chapter 11).
3   Remove the mounting screws **(see illustration)**.
4   Pull the radio out of the instrument panel. Release the clips and disconnect the electrical connectors and the antenna lead from the rear of the radio **(see illustration)** and remove it from the vehicle.

Installation
5   Installation is the reverse of removal.

Amplifier
Removal
Refer to illustration 17.7

6   Remove the left front (driver's) seat (see Chapter 11).
7   Remove the screws and nut securing the amplifier to the floorpan **(see illustration)**.
8   Disconnect the electrical connectors from the amplifier and remove it from the vehicle.

Installation
9   Installation is the reverse of removal.

Speakers
Door
Removal
Refer to illustration 17.12

10   On vehicles equipped with manual windows, remove the window crank using a special tool (available at most auto parts stores) or by working a cloth back-and-forth behind the handle to dislodge the retaining clip (see

Chapter 11).
11   Carefully, pry the speaker grille from the door trim panel.
12   Remove the speaker mounting screws and withdraw the speaker from the door trim panel **(see illustration)**.
13   Disconnect the electrical connector and remove the speaker from the vehicle.

Installation
14   Installation is the reverse of removal.

Instrument panel
Removal
15   Remove the instrument panel top cover (see Chapter 11).
16   Remove the mounting screws, lift the speaker out of the instrument panel, then disconnect the electrical connector and remove the speaker from the vehicle.

Installation
17   Installation is the reverse of removal.

Rear
Removal
Refer to illustration 17.24
18   Remove the rear lower seat cushion (see Chapter 11).

17.12 Front door speaker mounting screws (arrows)

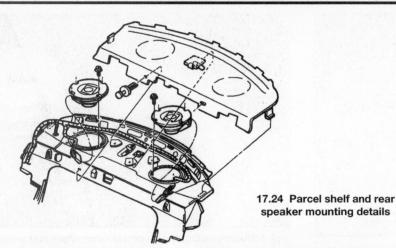

17.24 Parcel shelf and rear speaker mounting details

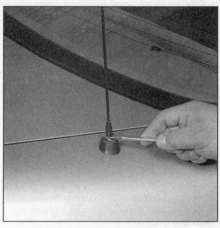

18.1 Use a small end-wrench to remove the antenna mast (fixed antenna)

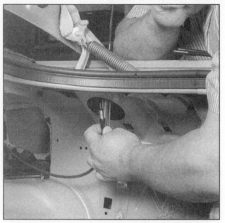

18.3 Disconnect the lead from the antenna body

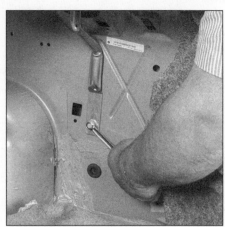

18.4 Remove the antenna mounting bolt

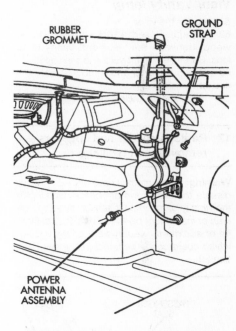

18.9 Power antenna mounting details

19   Remove the rear seat back (see Chapter 11).
20   Remove the bolts securing the rear seat belt anchors to the floorpan.
21   Disengage the clips holding the left and right upper quarter trim pieces to the inner quarter panels.
22   Route the seat belt webbing through the access hole in each upper quarter trim piece and remove them from the vehicle.
23   Using a screwdriver, pry off the left and right quarter panel trim extensions (see Chapter 11).
24   Remove the push-in fasteners securing the parcel shelf to the trunk closure panel (see illustration).
25   Pull the parcel shelf forward to disengage the clip securing parcel shelf to the trunk closure panel and remove it from the vehicle.
26   Remove the mounting screws, lift the speaker(s) out of the trunk closure, disconnect the electrical connector(s) and remove it from the vehicle.

Installation

27   Installation is the reverse of removal, making sure that the speaker wire connectors face outward (toward the rear wheels).

18   Antenna - removal and installation

Warning: *These models have airbags. Always disable the airbag system before working in the vicinity of the impact sensor, steering column or instrument panel to avoid the possibility of accidental deployment of the airbag, which could cause personal injury (see Section 29).*

Fixed antenna

Removal

Refer to illustrations 18.1, 18.3 and 18.4
1   Use a small open end wrench and unscrew the antenna mast from the antenna body (see illustration).
2   Working inside the trunk, detach the liner from the right side of the trunk.
3   Disconnect the antenna lead from the base of the antenna body (see illustration).
4   Remove the mounting bolt securing the antenna body to the rear quarter panel (see illustration).
5   Withdraw the antenna body from the rear quarter panel.

Installation

6   Installation is the reverse of removal.

Power antenna

Removal

Refer to illustration 18.9
7   Disconnect the negative battery cable from the ground stud on the left shock tower (see Chapter 5, Section 1).
8   Working inside the trunk, detach the liner from the right side of the trunk.
9   Detach the drain tube from the antenna (see illustration).
10   Disconnect the antenna lead from the power antenna harness.
11   Disconnect the electrical connector from the antenna motor.
12   Remove the bolts securing the ground strap and antenna brace to the rear quarter panel.
13   Withdraw the antenna from the rear quarter panel.

12

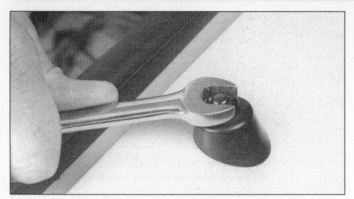

18.15 Remove the power antenna cap nut

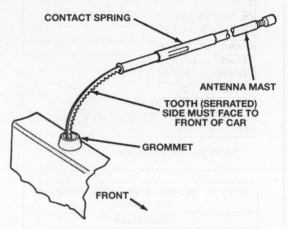

18.17 Power antenna mast, contact spring and drive rod assembly details

TACHOMETER …6000 rpm SPEEDOMETER …100mph (220 kmh) FUEL GAUGE pointer ON …F TEMPERATURE GAUGE pointer ON …H
TACHOMETER …3000 rpm SPEEDOMETER …75mph (120 kmh) FUEL GAUGE pointer ON …1/2 TEMPERATURE GAUGE pointer ON …midscale
TACHOMETER …3000 rpm SPEEDOMETER …55mph (100 kmh) FUEL GAUGE pointer ON …1/2 TEMPERATURE GAUGE pointer ON …midscale
TACHOMETER …1000 rpm SPEEDOMETER …20mph (40 kmh) FUEL GAUGE pointer ON …E TEMPERATURE GAUGE pointer ON …C

19.5a Instrument cluster CHEC 1 chart

CHECK ENGINE
SEAT BELT
AIRBAG
CHARGING SYSTEM
LOW FUEL
HIGH BEAM INDICATOR
ENGINE TEMPERATURE
CRUISE

19.5b Instrument cluster CHEC 2 chart

Installation

14   Installation is the reverse of removal. Make sure that the fender grommet locating tab is in line with the slot in the body before installing the antenna. Make sure the ball of the antenna body is fully seated in the grommet.

Power antenna mast

Removal

Refer to illustrations 18.15 and 18.17

15   Remove the cap nut **(see illustration)**.
16   Turn the ignition key to the ACCESSORY position.
17   Turn the radio ON and while the antenna is moving UP, grab the mast and pull it out of the antenna body. The antenna mast, contact spring and drive rod should all come out at this time **(see illustration)**.

Installation

18   Insert the new antenna mast, contact spring and drive rod into the body with the drive rod teeth facing toward the antenna motor (remove the trunk lining if necessary).
19   Turn the radio OFF and guide the drive rod into the body.
20   Install the cap nut. **Note:** *The antenna may not completely retract after initial installation. Turn the radio ON-and-OFF to cycle* the antenna up-and-down. The mast should completely retract after raising and lowering the antenna a few times.

---

19 Instrument cluster self-diagnosis

General description

1   The instrument cluster is equipped with a self-diagnosis feature. When activated, the electronic display, odometer/transmission range indicator and all indicator lamps will illuminate in a specific sequence.
2   If the instrument cluster is not receiving power from the CCD bus, the cluster will appear non-functional except the airbag indicator lamp will illuminate and a NO BUS message will be displayed. If this message is displayed, further diagnosis should be performed by a dealer service department or other qualified repair shop.

Starting the self-diagnosis

Refer to illustrations 19.5a, 19.5b, 19.5c, 19.5d, 19.5e and 19.5f

3   While depressing the odometer/trip reset button, turn the ignition key to the OFF/RUN/START position.
4   This will initiate an electronic display system check and the illumination (in sequence) of all CCD bus activated instrument cluster warning indicators. Due to the complexity of replacing the instrument cluster circuit board, gauges and transmission range indicator, the home mechanic should limit service to bulb replacement (see Section 16). If the instrument cluster circuit board, gauge or transmission range indicator replacement is indicated, take the vehicle to a dealer service department or other qualified repair shop.
5   There are four check (CHEC) functions **(see illustrations)**:

 a) *CHEC 1 - Gauges: If all gauges fail to move or do not indicate at the proper locations, the instrument cluster circuit board is faulty and should be replaced. If any one gauge fails to move or indicate properly, have it replaced.*

 b) *CHEC 2 - Warning lamps: If any lamp listed in Step 1 does not illuminate, check the bulb operation. If the bulb is OK, the instrument cluster circuit board is faulty and should be replaced.*

 c) *CHEC 3 - Odometer/trip meter: If any LED does not illuminate, have it replaced.*

 d) *CHEC 4 - Transmission range indicator/Autostick indicator: If any LED does not illuminate, have it replaced.*

TRIP
ODOMETER CENTER
ODOMETER LOWER RIGHT
ODOMETER BOTTOM
ODOMETER LOWER LEFT
ODOMETER UPPER LEFT
ODOMETER TOP
ODOMETER UPPER RIGHT
ALL ODOMETER V/F DISPLAY DIGIT SEGMENTS ON

19.5c Instrument cluster CHEC 3 chart

PRND3L
PRND3L AND BOX AROUND P
PRND3L AND BOX AROUND R
PRND3L AND BOX AROUND N
PRND3L AND BOX AROUND D
PRND3L AND BOX AROUND 3
PRND3L AND BOX AROUND L
PRND3L AND ALL BOXES
END

19.5d Instrument cluster CHEC 4 chart - automatic transaxle models without the Autostick option

CHEC 4 - TRANSMISSION RANGE INDICATOR LED DISPLAY
AUTOSTICK
PRND AS 1 AND AS BOX
PRND AS 2 AND AS BOX
PRND AS 3 AND AS BOX
PRND AS 4 AND AS BOX
PRND AS AND BOX AROUND P
PRND AS AND BOX AROUND R
PRND AS AND BOX AROUND N
PRND AS AND BOX AROUND D
PRND AS 1234 AND ALL BOXES
END

19.5e Instrument cluster CHEC 4 chart - 1997 and earlier automatic transaxle models with the Autostick option

CHEC 4 - TRANSMISSION RANGE INDICATOR LED DISPLAY
AUTOSTICK
PRND1234 AND BOX AROUND 1
PRND1234 AND BOX AROUND 2
PRND1234 AND BOX AROUND 3
PRND1234 AND BOX AROUND 4
PRND1234 AND BOX AROUND P
PRND1234 AND BOX AROUND R
PRND1234 AND BOX AROUND N
PRND1234 AND BOX AROUND D
PRND1234 AND ALL BOXES
END

19.5f Instrument cluster CHEC 4 chart - 1998 automatic transaxle models with the Autostick option

20 Instrument cluster - removal and installation

Warning: *These models have airbags. Always disable the airbag system before working in the vicinity of the impact sensor, steering column or instrument panel to avoid the possibility of accidental deployment of the airbag, which could cause personal injury (see Section 29).*

Removal

Refer to illustration 20.3

1 Disconnect the negative battery cable from the ground stud on the left shock tower (see Chapter 5, Section 1).

2 Remove instrument cluster hood (see Chapter 11).

3 Remove the 4 screws securing the cluster to the instrument panel **(see illustration)**.

4 Slightly withdraw the instrument cluster from the instrument panel, disconnect the electrical wiring harness connectors and remove the cluster from the vehicle.

Installation

5 Installation is the reverse of removal.

21 Horn - check, removal and installation

Warning: *These models have airbags. Always*

disable the airbag system before working in the vicinity of the impact sensor, steering column or instrument panel to avoid the possibility of accidental deployment of the airbag, which could cause personal injury (see Section 29).

Check

Refer to illustrations 21.2, 21.3 and 21.9

1 If the horn doesn't sound, check the horn fuses in the Power Distribution Center (PDC) and fuse block (see Section 3). If a fuse is blown, replace it and retest. If it blows again, there is a short circuit in the horn or wiring between the horn and fuse block.

2 Check the circuit to the horn relay; remove the cover from the interior fuse block.

20.3 Instrument cluster mounting screws (arrows)

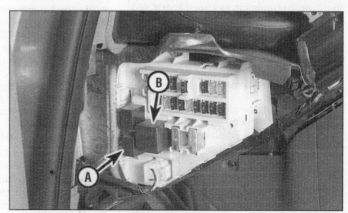

21.2 Horn relay (A) and rear window defogger relay (B)

12

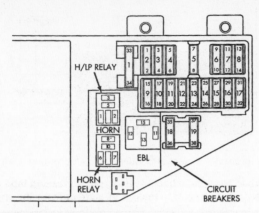

21.3 Interior fuse block relay terminal identification

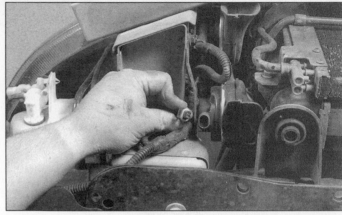

21.9 Lower horn electrical connector

Depress the horn pad on the steering wheel, a "click" should be heard as the horn relay activates. If the relay "clicks" proceed to Step 7. If the horn relay cannot be heard, remove it from the interior fuse block **(see illustration)**.

3   Using a fused jumper wire, connect terminals 8 and 10 in the fuse block **(see illustration)**. The horns should sound.

4   Using a voltmeter, check for battery voltage to terminals 6 and 8 in the fuse block. Battery voltage should be present. If voltage is not present, repair the circuit as required (see Section 31).

5   Connect a voltmeter between terminals 6 and 7 in the fuse block. No voltage should be present. While observing the voltmeter, press the horn pad on the steering wheel - battery voltage should be present when the horn pad is depressed and absent when released. If the voltage is not present with the horn pad depressed, the problem exists in the steering column wiring. If voltage is present, replace the relay.

6   Reinstall the relay into the fuse block.

7   Check for battery voltage at the horn; raise the front of the vehicle and support it securely on jackstands.

8   Remove the push-in fasteners and remove lower splash shield to access the horn(s) electrical connectors.

9   Disconnect the electrical connector from the discrepant horn **(see illustration)**. Connect a voltmeter to the wiring harness connector and depress the horn pad on the steering wheel. Battery voltage should be present when the horn pad is depressed. If no voltage is present, there is a fault in the wiring. If voltage is present, replace the horn.

10   If no voltage is present, connect the voltmeter positive probe to the DARK GREEN/PINK wire and the other probe to a good ground on the chassis. Depress the horn pad. If battery voltage is now present, the short exists in the ground circuit. Repair the circuit as required (see Section 31). If voltage is not present, the short exists in the power circuit. Remove the horn relay from the fuse block and using a fused jumper wire, connect terminals 8 and 10. Battery voltage

should be present at the horn connector. If it is, replace the relay. If no voltage is present, repair the circuit as required (see Section 31).

11   After testing is complete, reattach the horn electrical connector, install the splash shield and lower the vehicle.

Removal

Refer to illustration 21.12

12   Both horns are located behind the front bumper on the right side frame rail, one above the other **(see illustration)**.

13   Raise the front of the vehicle and support it securely on jackstands.

14   Remove the push-in fasteners and remove lower splash shield.

15   Disconnect the horn electrical connector, remove the mounting bolt and withdraw the horn from the vehicle.

Installation

16   Installation is the reverse of removal. Check horn operation after installation.

22   Rear window defogger switch - check and replacement

Warning: *These models have airbags. Always disable the airbag system before working in the vicinity of the impact sensor, steering column or instrument panel to avoid the possibility of accidental deployment of the airbag, which could cause personal injury (see Section 29).*

Check

1   With the ignition switch ON (engine OFF), depress the defogger switch. The indicator lamp should illuminate and remain on for approximately 10 minutes then go out. If the indicator illuminates, the relay is operational - check the rear window defogger heat grid (see Section 23). If the indicator lamp fails to illuminate, either the LED light in the switch is faulty, a short exists in the circuit or the rear window defogger relay is faulty.

Note: *The indicator will illuminate for 10 minutes the first time the switch is activated and*

21.12 The horns (arrows) are located behind the front bumper on the right side frame rail, one above the other

then will only remain on for 5 minutes each time the switch is depressed thereafter, unless the ignition switch is turned to the OFF position which resets the timer located inside the Body Control Module.

2   If the indicator light fails to illuminate, check the circuit to the rear window defogger relay; remove the cover from the interior fuse block. Depress the defogger switch, a "click" should be heard as the rear window defogger relay activates **(see illustration 21.2)**. If the relay "clicks" check the rear window defogger heat grid (see Section 23). If the rear window defogger relay cannot be heard, remove it from the fuse block and with the ignition key ON (engine OFF), check for battery voltage to the rear window defogger relay terminals 15 and 11 **(see illustration 21.3)**. Battery voltage should be present. If no voltage is present, repair the circuit (see Section 31).

3   Next, connect the voltmeter between relay terminals 13 and 15. With the defogger switch depressed, battery voltage should be present. If battery voltage is present, replace the relay. If no voltage is present, repair the circuit (see Section 31).

4   Remove the heater/air conditioning control assembly (see Chapter 3), but DO NOT disconnect the electrical connectors.

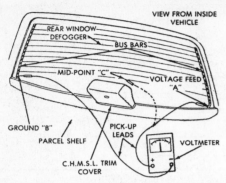

23.4   Rear window defogger testing locations

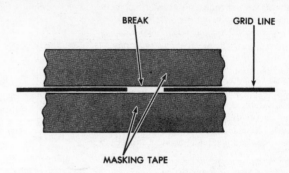

23.13   When repairing a heat element, place masking tape on both sides of the element to make a straight path for the epoxy

5   With the ignition switch OFF, use an ohmmeter to backprobe the 8-way electrical connector RED wire (+) and the BLACK/PINK (-) wire. **Note:** *To backprobe an electrical connector, use pins or paper clips inserted into the rear of the connector (or wire) to facilitate meter attachment. Be careful not to short the probes during this process.*

6   Depress the defogger switch, the resistance should be between 500 and 520 ohms. If the resistance is out of tolerance, replace the defogger switch.

7   Next, switch the multi-meter to the volts scale and turn the ignition key ON (engine OFF). Battery voltage should be present. If not, repair the circuit (see Section 31).

Replacement

8   The rear window defogger switch is incorporated into the heating/air conditioning control assembly, refer to Chapter 3 for replacement procedures.

23   Rear window defogger heat grid - check and repair

1   The rear window defogger consists of a number of horizontal elements baked onto the inner surface of the rear window glass.
2   Small breaks in the element can be repaired without removing the rear window.

Check

Refer to illustration 23.4

Note: *When measuring the voltage at the rear window defogger heat grid, wrap a piece of aluminum foil around the voltmeter probes and press the foil against the heating element with your finger.*

3   Turn the ignition switch and defogger system switches to the ON position.
4   Working within the back seat area, ground the negative lead of a voltmeter to terminal B (lower corner passengers side) and the positive lead to terminal A (lower corner drivers side) of the defogger grid **(see illustration)**.
5   The voltmeter should read between 10 and 12 volts. If the reading is lower, there is a poor ground connection. Check the ground connection at the right rear wheel well.

6   Next, connect the voltmeter negative probe to a good ground on the chassis. If the ground circuit is OK, the reading should stay the same. If not, repair the ground circuit (see Section 31).
7   Connect the negative lead to terminal B, then touch each grid line at the mid-point with the positive lead.
8   The reading should be approximately 5 to 6 volts. If the reading is 0, there is a break between mid-point C and terminal A.
9   A 10 to 12 volt reading is an indication of a break between terminal B and mid-point C. Move the lead toward the break; the voltage will change when the break is crossed.

Repair

Refer to illustration 23.13

10   Repair the break in the heating element using repair kit recommended specifically for this purpose, such as Mopar Repair Kit No. 4267922 (or equivalent). Included in this kit is plastic conductive epoxy.
11   Prior to repairing a break, turn off the system and allow it to de-energize for a few minutes.
12   Lightly buff the element area with fine

steel wool, then clean it thoroughly with rubbing alcohol.
13   Use masking tape to mask off the area of repair **(see illustration)**.
14   Mix the epoxy thoroughly, according to the instructions on the package. **Warning:** *Read the warning instructions included with the kit relating to the chemical component makeup of the kit (epoxy resin and amine type hardener) and protect yourself accordingly.*
15   Follow the instructions in the kit and apply the conductive epoxy material to the slit in the masking tape, overlapping the undamaged area about 3/4-inch on either end.
16   Allow the repair to cure for 24 hours (at room temperature) before removing the tape and using the system.

24   Cruise control system - description and check

General description

Refer to illustration 24.1

1   The cruise control system maintains

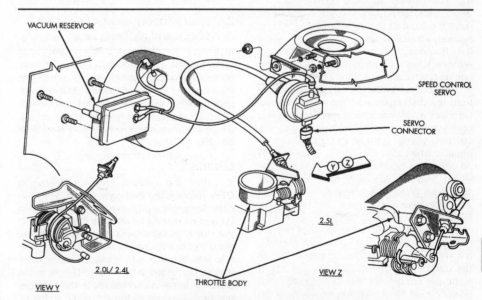

24.1   Cruise control system - mechanical components

vehicle speed with a vacuum-actuated servo motor located in the engine compartment, which is connected to the throttle linkage by a cable **(see illustration)**. The system consists of the Powertrain Control Module (PCM), brake switch, control switches, a relay, the vehicle speed sensor and associated wiring. Listed below are some general procedures that may be used to locate common cruise control problems.

Check

2   If the system does not operate, check the fuse (see Section 3). Also check the vacuum hose to the cruise control servo to make sure it's not plugged, cracked or soft (which will cause it to collapse in operation. With the engine off, check the servo by applying vacuum (with a hand-operated vacuum pump) to the vacuum fitting on the servo - the servo should move the throttle linkage and hold vacuum if it's working properly.

3   Have an assistant operate the brake lights while you check their operation (voltage from the brake light switch deactivates the cruise control).

4   If the brake lights don't come on or don't shut off the cruise control, correct the problem and recheck cruise control operation.

5   Inspect the cable linkage between the cruise control servo and the throttle linkage. The cruise control servo is located on the left (driver's) side of the vehicle.

6   Visually inspect the wires connected to the cruise control servo and check for damage and broken wires.

7   The cruise control on these vehicles use two types of Vehicle Speed Sensors (VSS). The VSS is located in the transaxle. **Note:** *Due to the complexity of diagnosing the Output speed sensor on automatic transaxles, this manual only addresses the VSS on manual transaxles. However, you can still make sure the electrical connector at the sensor is clean and tight. Refer to Chapter 6 for information on checking the VSS on manual transaxles.*

8   Test drive the vehicle to determine if the cruise control is now working properly. If it isn't, take it to a dealer service department or an automotive electrical specialist for further diagnosis and repair.

25   Electric rear view mirrors - description and check

General description

1   Electric rear view mirrors use two motors to move the glass; one for up-and-down adjustments and one for left-to-right adjustments. The motors are integral with the mirror assembly and not serviceable.

Check

2   The control switch, located in the driver's door panel, has a selector portion

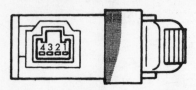

SWITCH POSITION	CONTINUITY BETWEEN	RESISTANCE VALUE
UNLOCK	1 and 4	2700 Ω ± 10%
LOCK	1 and 4	620 Ω ± 10%

26.5 Power door lock switch terminal guide and continuity chart

which sends voltage to the left or right side mirror. With the ignition ON but the engine OFF, roll down the windows and operate the mirror control switch through all functions (left-right and up-down) for both the left and right side mirrors.

3   Listen carefully for the sound of the electric motors running in the mirrors.

4   If the motors can be heard but the mirror glass doesn't move, there's probably a problem with the drive mechanism inside the mirror. Remove and disassemble the exterior mirror to locate the problem and correct if possible (see Chapter 11).

5   If the mirrors don't operate and no sound comes from the mirrors, check the fuses (see Section 3).

6   If the fuses are OK, remove the door trim panel (see Chapter 11).

7   Turn the ignition switch ON and check for battery voltage at the mirror switch electrical connector PINK wire terminal. Battery voltage should be present. If there's no voltage at the switch, check for an open or short in the wiring between the fuse panel and the switch and repair the circuit (see Section 31). **Note:** *It's common for wires to break in the portion of the harness between the body and door (opening and closing the door fatigues and eventually breaks the wires).*

8   If voltage is present, connect a jumper wire from the BLACK wire terminal to a good ground on the chassis. Use another fused jumper wire and connect the PINK wire terminal to each one of the other terminals with the ignition switch ON (engine OFF). If the mirror motor operates, replace the switch. If the mirror does not respond, replace the discrepant mirror assembly (see Chapter 11).

26   Power door lock system - description and check

General description

1   Power door lock systems are operated by bi-directional solenoids located in each door latch. The lock switches have two operating positions: Lock and Unlock. These switches connect voltage to the door latch solenoids. Depending on which way the switch is activated, it reverses polarity, allowing the two sides of the circuit to be used alternately as the feed (positive) and ground side.

Check

Refer to illustration 26.5

2   Check the fuses (see Section 3).

3   Operate the door lock switches in both directions (Lock and Unlock) with the ignition ON (engine OFF). Listen for the click of the solenoid operating.

4   If there's no click, check for voltage at the switches. If no voltage is present, check the wiring between the fuse panel and the switches for continuity.

5   If voltage is present but no click is heard, remove the door trim panel (see Chapter 11). Using an ohmmeter and the accompanying chart, check for continuity between the switch terminals with the switch in each position **(see illustration)**. Replace the switch if the resistance value is not as specified.

6   With the ignition ON (engine OFF), use a voltmeter to check for battery voltage to the switch electrical connector at the PINK wire terminal. Repair the wiring if voltage is not present.

7   If the switch is OK and voltage is present but the solenoid still doesn't click, check the wiring between the switch and solenoid for continuity. Repair the wiring if there's no continuity.

8   Using a voltmeter, check for battery voltage at the solenoid electrical connector; with the ignition switch ON (engine OFF) operate the lock switch. One of the wires should have voltage in the Lock position; the other should have voltage in the Unlock position. If voltage is present, replace the door latch assembly (see Chapter 11). If the inoperative solenoid isn't receiving voltage, check for an open or short in the wire between the switch and the solenoid. **Note:** *It's common for wires to break in the portion of the harness between the body and door (opening and closing the door fatigues and eventually breaks the wires).*

27   Power window system - description, check and window motor replacement

General description

1   The power window system consists of the circuit breaker, control switches, the motors, glass mechanisms (regulators), and

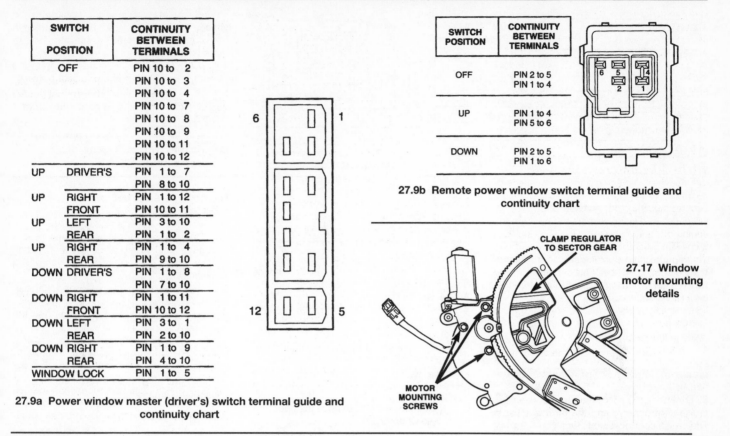

SWITCH POSITION		CONTINUITY BETWEEN TERMINALS
OFF		PIN 10 to 2
		PIN 10 to 3
		PIN 10 to 4
		PIN 10 to 7
		PIN 10 to 8
		PIN 10 to 9
		PIN 10 to 11
		PIN 10 to 12
UP	DRIVER'S	PIN 1 to 7
		PIN 8 to 10
UP	RIGHT FRONT	PIN 1 to 12
		PIN 10 to 11
UP	LEFT REAR	PIN 3 to 10
		PIN 1 to 2
UP	RIGHT REAR	PIN 1 to 4
		PIN 9 to 10
DOWN	DRIVER'S	PIN 1 to 8
		PIN 7 to 10
DOWN	RIGHT FRONT	PIN 1 to 11
		PIN 10 to 12
DOWN	LEFT REAR	PIN 3 to 1
		PIN 2 to 10
DOWN	RIGHT REAR	PIN 1 to 9
		PIN 4 to 10
WINDOW LOCK		PIN 1 to 5

27.9a Power window master (driver's) switch terminal guide and continuity chart

SWITCH POSITION	CONTINUITY BETWEEN TERMINALS
OFF	PIN 2 to 5
	PIN 1 to 4
UP	PIN 1 to 4
	PIN 5 to 6
DOWN	PIN 2 to 5
	PIN 1 to 6

27.9b Remote power window switch terminal guide and continuity chart

27.17 Window motor mounting details

CLAMP REGULATOR TO SECTOR GEAR

MOTOR MOUNTING SCREWS

associated wiring.

2   Power windows are wired so they can be lowered and raised from the master control switch by the driver or by remote switches located at the individual windows. Each window has a separate motor which is reversible. The position of the control switch determines the polarity and therefore the direction of operation.

3   The power window system will operate only when the ignition switch is in the ON position.

Check

Refer to illustrations 27.9a and 27.9b

4   These procedures are general in nature, so if you can't find the problem after performing them, take the vehicle to a dealer service department or other qualified repair shop for further diagnosis and/or repair.

5   If the power windows don't work at all, check the circuit breaker continuity (see Section 3).

6   If the circuit breaker is OK, remove the door trim panel from the driver's door (see Chapter 11).

7   With the ignition ON (engine OFF), use a voltmeter to check for battery voltage to the master switch electrical connector at the TAN wire terminal. **Note:** *Battery voltage should also be present at one terminal on each remote switch. Repair the wiring if voltage is not present.*

8   If one window is inoperative from the master control switch, try the control switch

located at that window. **Note:** *This doesn't apply to the driver's door window.*

9   If a window works from one switch, but not the other, remove the door trim panel (see Chapter 11) and check the switch for continuity. Use an ohmmeter and the accompanying chart to check for continuity between the switch terminals with the switch in each position **(see illustrations)**. Replace the switch if continuity is not as specified.

10   If the switch tests OK, check for a short or open circuit in the wiring between the affected switch and the window motor.

11   If one window is inoperative from both switches, remove the trim panel from the affected door (see Chapter 11) and check for voltage at the motor while the switch is operated.

12   If voltage is reaching the motor, disconnect the glass from the regulator (see Chapter 11). Move the window up and down by hand while checking for binding and damage. Also check for binding and damage to the regulator. If the regulator is not damaged and the window moves up and down smoothly, replace the motor (see below). If there's binding or damage, lubricate, repair or replace parts, as necessary.

13   If voltage isn't reaching the motor and switch continuity is OK, check the wiring in the circuit for continuity between the interior fuse block and the switch, master switch to remote switch, and local switch to the window motor. **Note:** *It's common for wires to break in the portion of the harness between the body and door (opening and closing the*

door fatigues and eventually breaks the wires).

14   Test window operation after you are finished to confirm proper repairs.

Window motor - replacement

Refer to illustration 27.17

Warning: *Do not remove the window motor from the regulator assembly without first clamping the sector gear to the mounting plate or serious personal injury may result. The sector gear is spring loaded.*

15   Remove the window regulator (see Chapter 11).

16   Using a C-clamp or locking pliers, clamp the sector gear to the mounting plate.

17   Remove the bolts securing the motor and remove it from the regulator **(see illustration)**.

18   Installation is the reverse of removal.

28   Power seats - description and check

General description

1   Power seats allow you to adjust the position of the seat with little effort. The optional power seats on these vehicles adjust 8 ways; forward and backward, up and down, tilt forward and backward, and recline up and down.

2   The power seat system consists of four individual electric motors, the seat switch, a

12

SWITCH POSITION	CONTINUITY BETWEEN
OFF	1-2, 1-3, 1-4, 1-6, 1-7, 1-8, 1-9, 1-10
SEATBACK RECLINER UP	5-2, 1-4
SEATBACK RECLINER DOWN	5-4, 1-2
SEAT BACKWARD	5-3, 1-6
SEAT FORWARD	5-6, 1-3
FRONT RISER UP	5-4, 1-10
FRONT RISER DOWN	5-10, 1-7
REAR RISER UP	5-8, 1-9
REAR RISER DOWN	5-9, 1-8

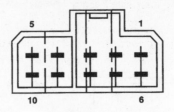

28.8 Power seat switch terminal guide and continuity chart

20 amp circuit breaker (located in the interior fuse block), a 40 amp fuse located in the Power Distribution Center and the wires that connect them.

Check

Refer to illustration 28.8

3   These procedures are general in nature,

29.1a The driver's side airbag (arrow) is located in the steering column horn pad

so if you can't find the problem after performing them, take the vehicle to a dealer service department or other qualified repair shop for further diagnosis and/or repair.

4   First, look under the seat for any objects which may be caught in the seat mechanism preventing the seat from moving.

5   Check the circuit breaker continuity (see Section 3).

6   In a quiet place, operate the seat switch and listen for motor actuation. If you can hear the motors, but the seat doesn't move, something is jammed in the mechanism or the mechanism itself is damaged. Repair or replace parts as necessary.

7   If the motors don't make any sound, check for battery voltage at the seat switch connector RED wire. Battery voltage should be present, if it isn't, repair the wiring.

8   If voltage is present at the RED wire, remove the seat switch and check it for continuity in all operating positions **(see illustration)**. Replace the switch if any position does not have continuity as specified.

9   If the switch is OK, check the operation of each individual motor. Disconnect the electrical connector from the motor. Using fused jumper wires, apply battery voltage to the motor electrical connector. The motor

should operate. Reverse the polarity of the voltage applied. The motor should operate in the opposite direction. If the motor fails to respond as noted, replace the motor(s).

10   If the switch is OK and the motors are operational, an open circuit exists between the switch and the motor(s). Repair the wiring as required.

29   Airbag system - general information

General description

Refer to illustrations 29.1a, 29.1b and 29.1c

These models are equipped with a Supplemental Restraint System (SRS), more commonly called an airbag system. This system is designed to protect the driver and front seat passenger from serious injury in the event of a collision. It consists of airbag modules in the center of the steering wheel and the right side top surface of the dashboard **(see illustrations)**. The Airbag Control Module (ACM), which is mounted on the floorpan between the shift lever and the parking brake lever under the center console, controls the system and also incorporates the impact sensor **(see illustration)**.

Airbag modules

Each airbag module contains a housing incorporating the cushion (airbag) and inflator unit. The inflator assembly is mounted on the back of the housing over a hole through which gas is expelled, inflating the bag almost instantaneously when an electrical signal is sent from the system. The steering column incorporates a specially wound wire called a clockspring that carries this signal to the module regardless of the steering wheel position. The clockspring is a flat, ribbon-like electrically conductive tape which is wound so that the steering wheel can be rotated to any position without ever loosing electrical contact.

29.1b The passenger's airbag (arrow) is located on the dashboard above the glove box

29.1c The Airbag Control Module is located under the center console and mounted to the floorpan

Impact sensor

The system has one impact sensor located inside the Airbag Control Module (ACM). The impact sensor acts as a threshold sensitive switch that completes an electrical circuit during an impact of sufficient G-force. When the circuit is completed, the airbags inflate.

Airbag Control Module (ACM)

The ACM also contains the safing sensor, a capacitor that maintains an electrical charge strong enough to deploy the airbags which lasts approximately two minutes after the battery power has been disconnected. Additionally, the ACM incorporates an on-board microprocessor which monitors the operation of the system. It checks this system every time the vehicle is started, causing the AIRBAG light to go on, then off, if the system is operating properly. If there is a fault in the system, the light will go on and stay on, or the light will fail to go on, and the ACM will store fault codes indicating the nature of the fault. If the AIRBAG light does go on and stay on, the vehicle should be taken to your dealer immediately for service.

Disabling the airbag system

Whenever working in the vicinity of the center console, steering column or instrument panel the airbags must be disarmed. To disable the airbag system, perform the following steps:

a) *Make sure the steering wheel is in the straight-ahead position, turn the ignition key to the Lock position and remove the key.*

b) *Disconnect and isolate the negative bat-*

tery cable from the ground stud on the left shock tower (see Chapter 5, Section 1).

c) *Wait at least two minutes for the backup power supply to be depleted before beginning work.*

Enabling the system

To enable the airbag system, perform the following steps:

a) *Make sure the steering wheel is in the straight-ahead position, the ignition switch is in the Lock position and the key is removed.*

b) *Connect the negative battery cable to the ground stud on the left shock tower.*

c) *Turn the ignition switch to the On position. Observe the airbag warning light, it should glow for approximately 6 to 8 seconds then go out, indicating the system is functioning properly*

---

30   Compass/temperature Mini-Trip Computer self diagnosis (if equipped)

General description

1   The Compass/temperature Mini-Trip Computer (CMTC) is capable of performing a self-check on it's internal functions. When activated, the CMTC will illuminate all segments of the vacuum florescent (VF) display and indicate it's status. Upon completion of the internal check, the CMTC will display one of the following: PASS, FAIL or CCD. Due to the complexity of diagnosing and replacing the CMTC or related components, this check

should be used for indication purposes only. If anything but PASS is displayed after the test is performed, have the vehicle diagnosed/repaired at a dealer service department or other qualified repair shop.

Starting the self-diagnosis

2   With the ignition switch in the OFF position, simultaneously depress the US/M and STEP buttons.

3   While holding the buttons down, turn the ignition switch to the ON position. The CMTC will begin diagnosis and display one of the following:

a) *PASS: All functions operational - system OK*

b) *FAIL: The CMTC module is faulty and should be replaced*

c) *CCD: A CCD bus connection or the Body Control Module is faulty*

---

31   Wiring diagrams

---

1   Since it isn't possible to include all wiring diagrams for every year covered by this manual, the following diagrams are those that are typical and most commonly needed.

2   Prior to troubleshooting any circuits, check the fuse and circuit breakers (if equipped) to make sure they're in good condition. Make sure the battery is properly charged and check the cable connections (see Chapter 1).

3   When checking a circuit, make sure that all connectors are clean, with no broken or loose terminals. When unplugging a connector, do not pull on the wires. Pull only on the connector housings themselves.

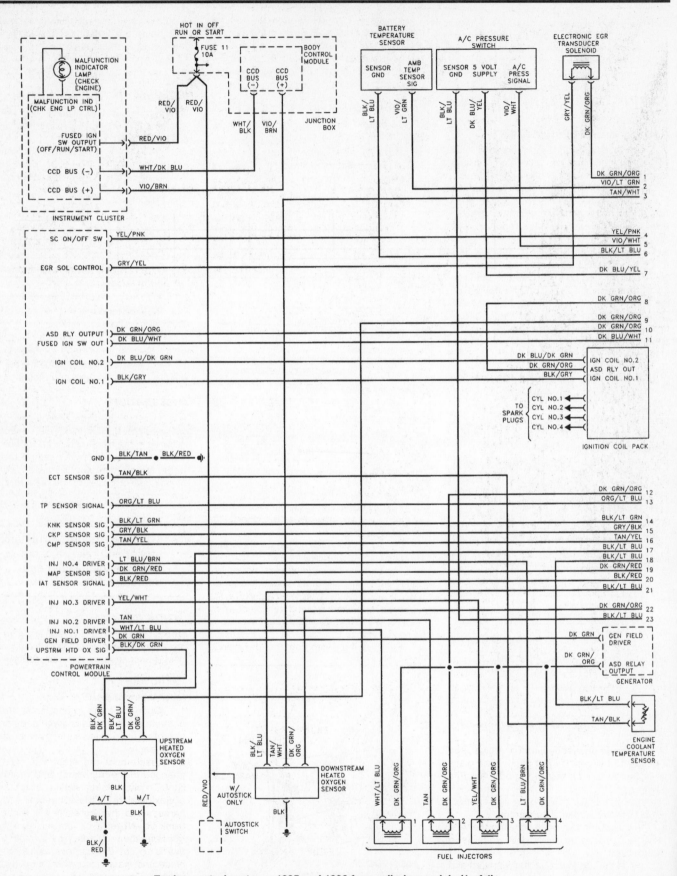

Engine control system - 1995 and 1996 four-cylinder models (1 of 4)

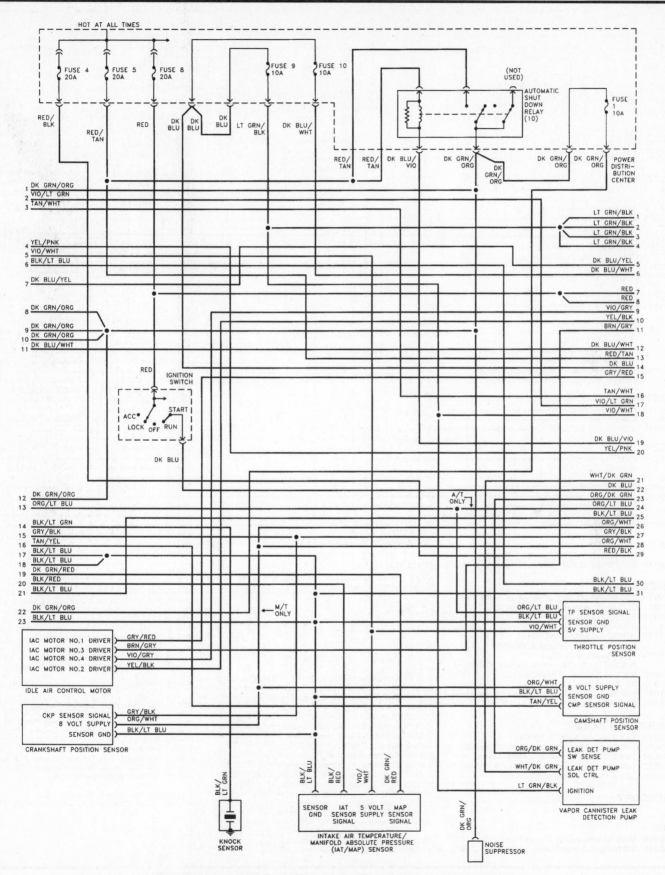

Engine control system - 1995 and 1996 four-cylinder models (2 of 4)

12

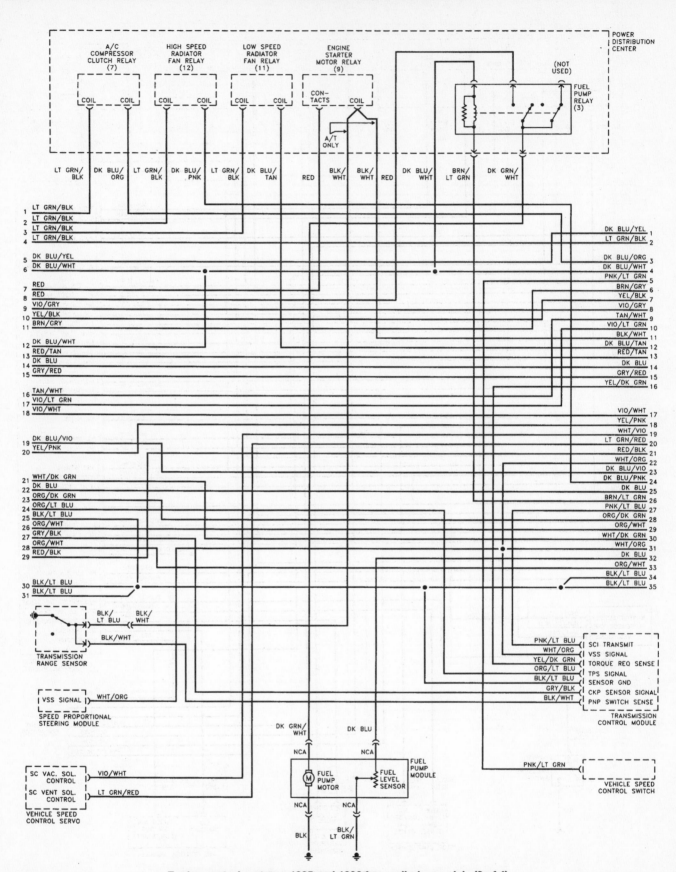

Engine control system - 1995 and 1996 four-cylinder models (3 of 4)

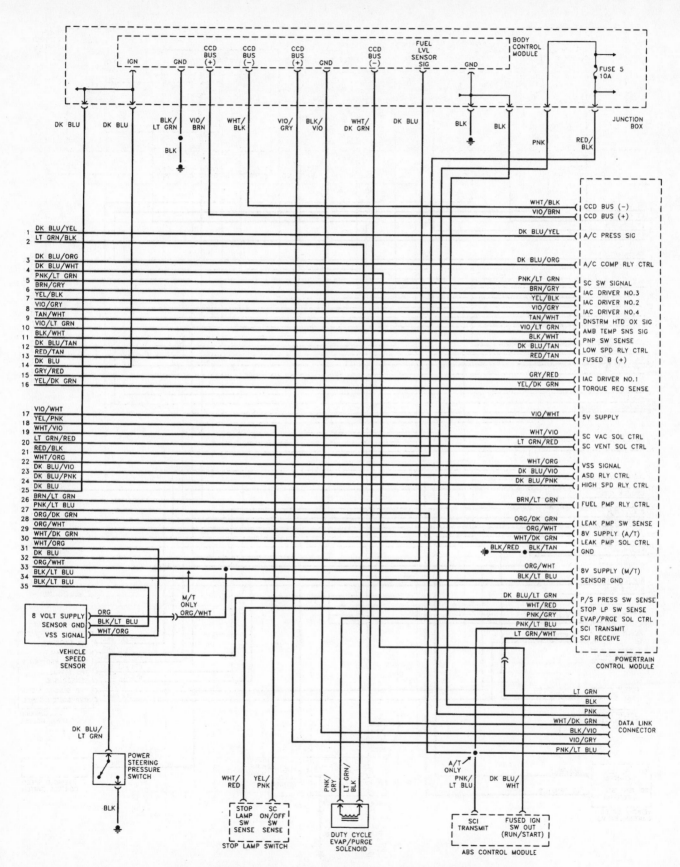

Engine control system - 1995 and 1996 four-cylinder models (4 of 4)

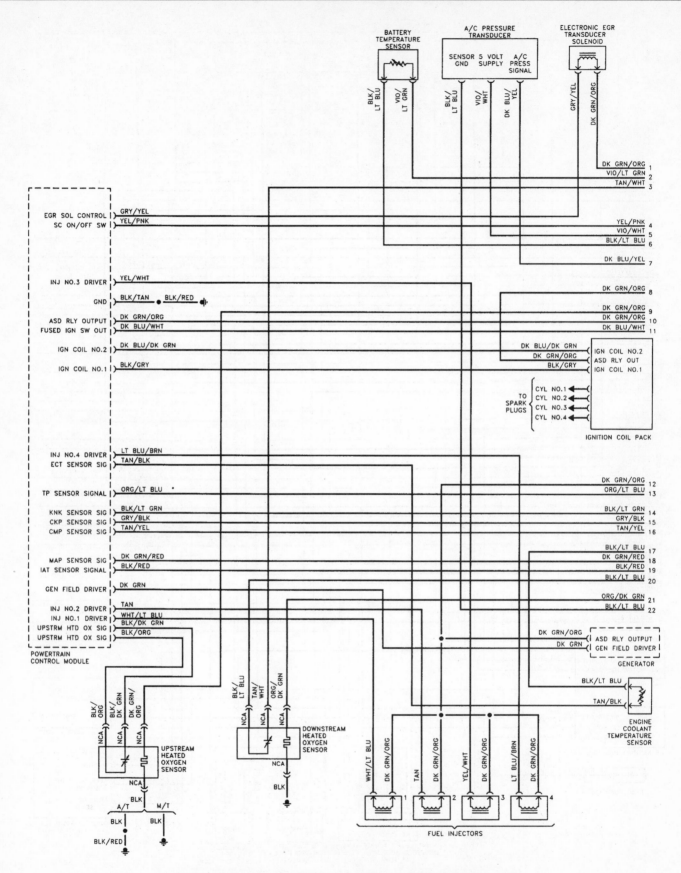

Engine control system - 1997 and later four-cylinder models (1 of 3)

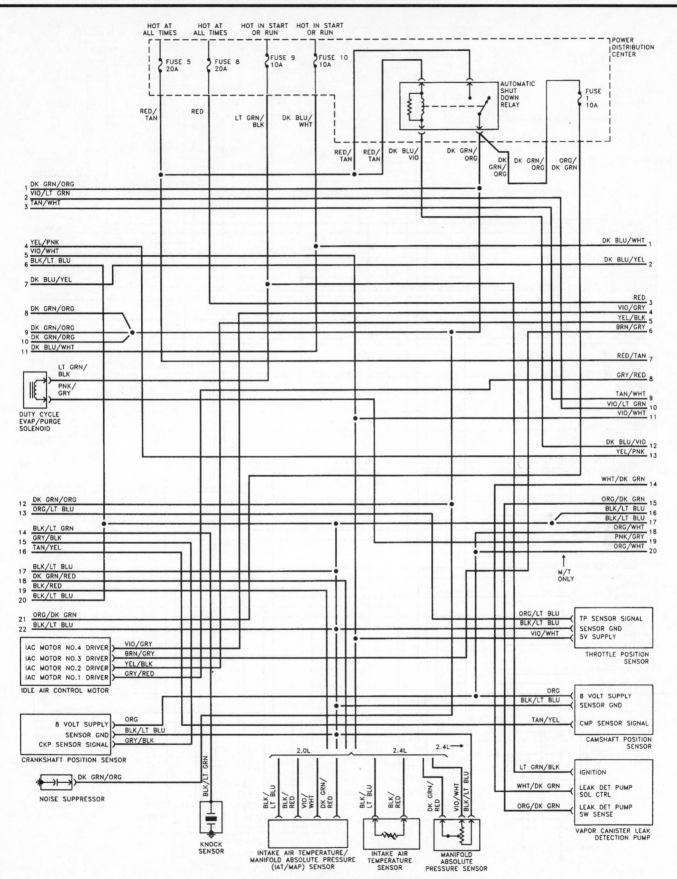

Engine control system - 1997 and later four-cylinder models (2 of 3)

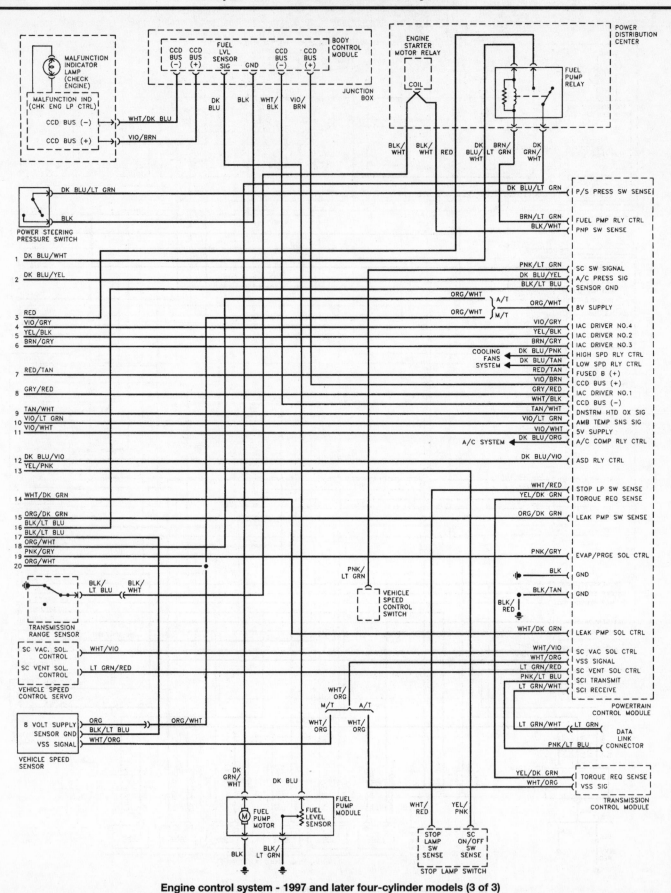

Engine control system - 1997 and later four-cylinder models (3 of 3)

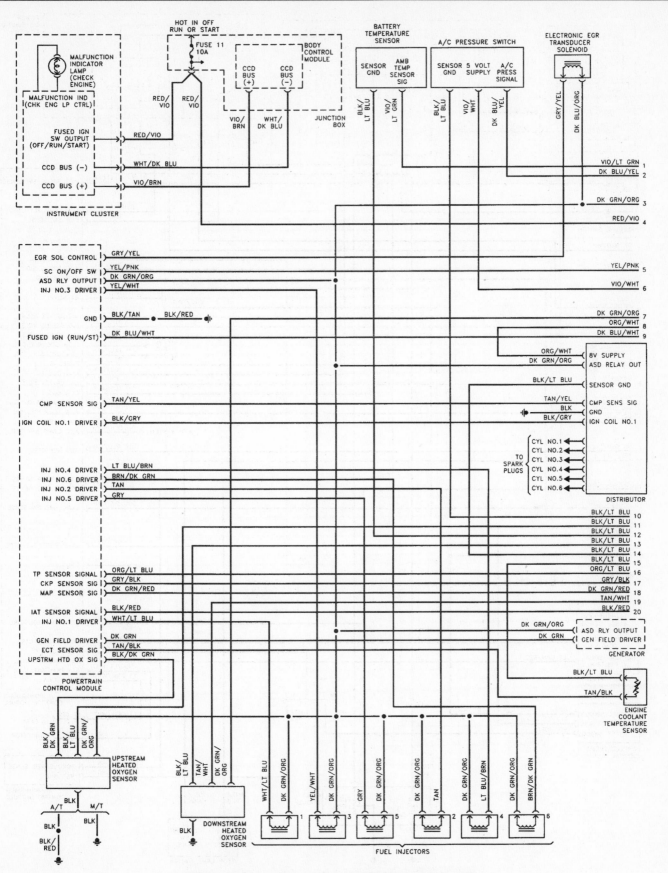

Engine control system - 1995 and 1996 V6 models (1 of 4)

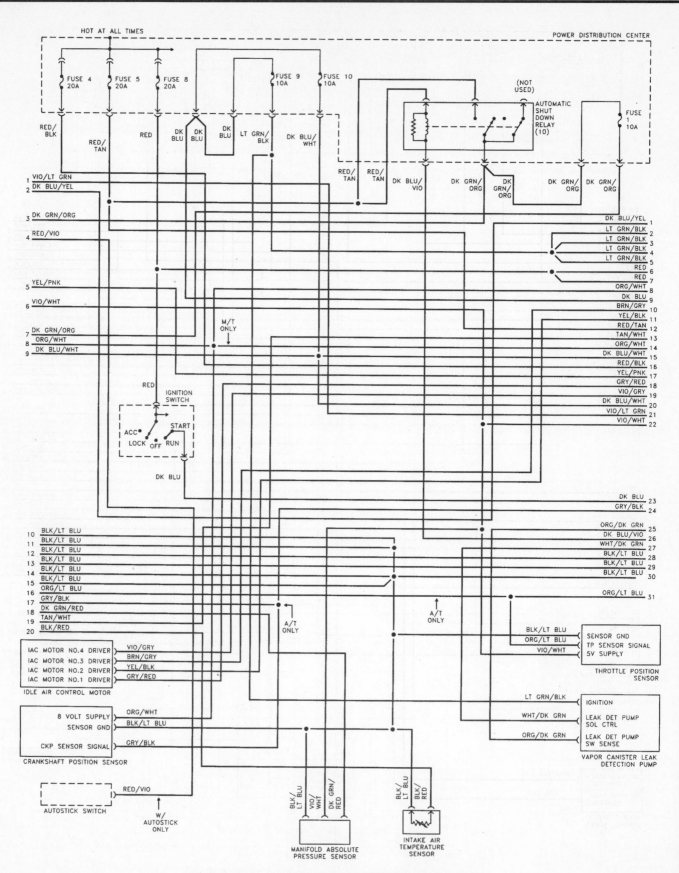

Engine control system - 1995 and 1996 V6 models (2 of 4)

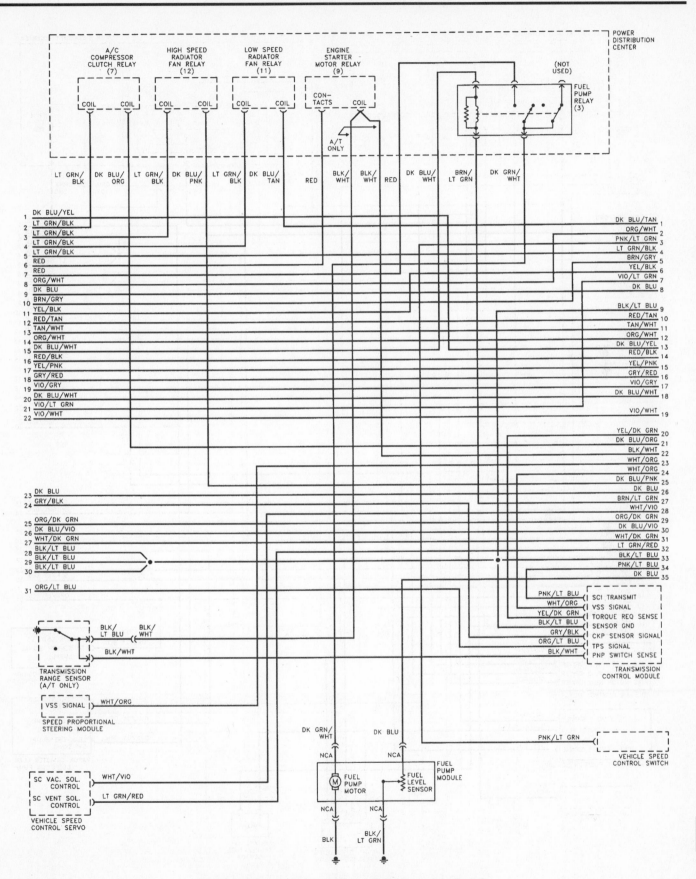

Engine control system - 1995 and 1996 V6 models (3 of 4)

12

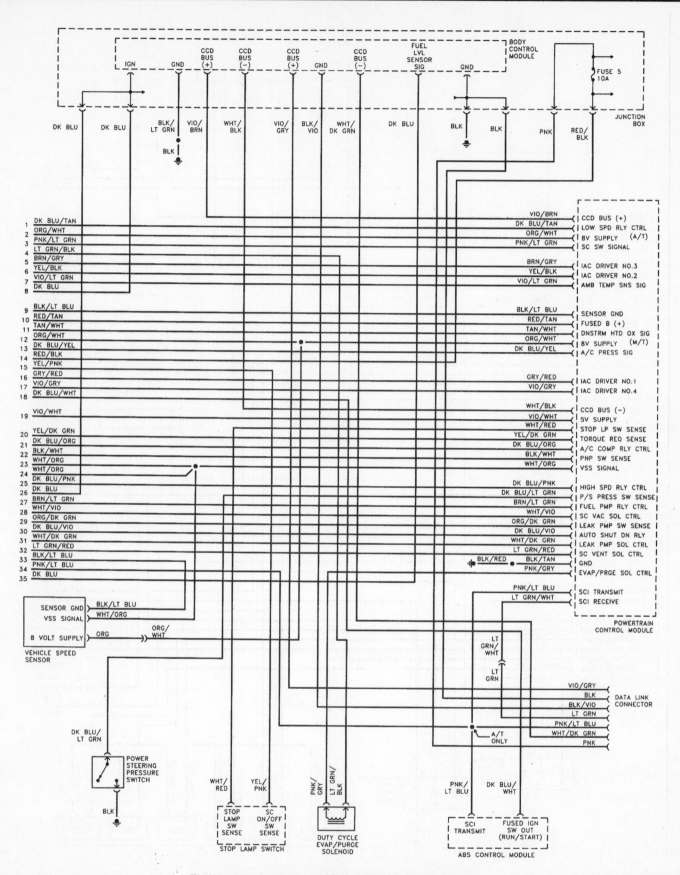

Engine control system - 1995 and 1996 V6 models (4 of 4)

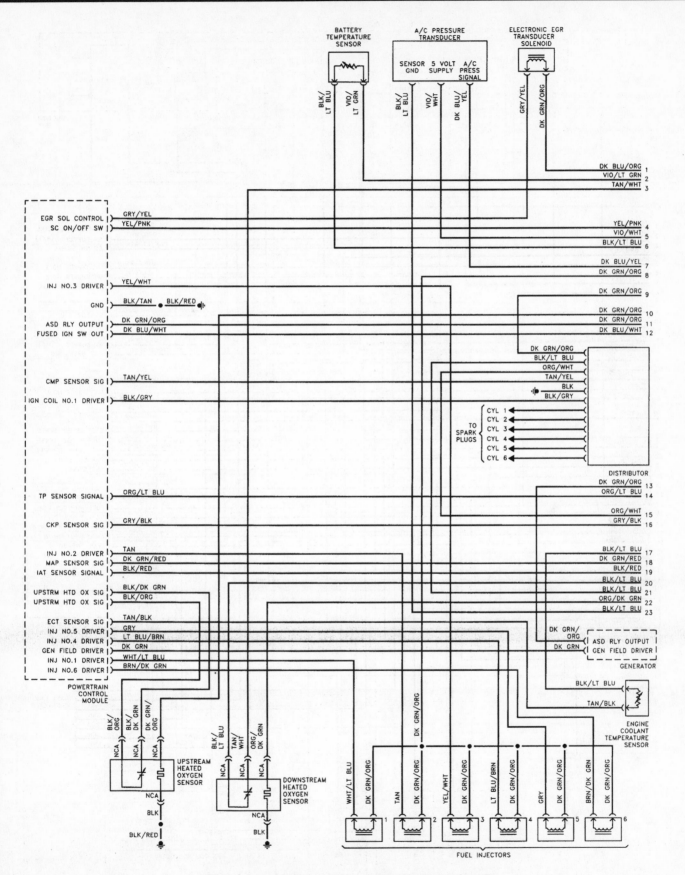

Engine control system - 1997 and later V6 models (1 of 3)

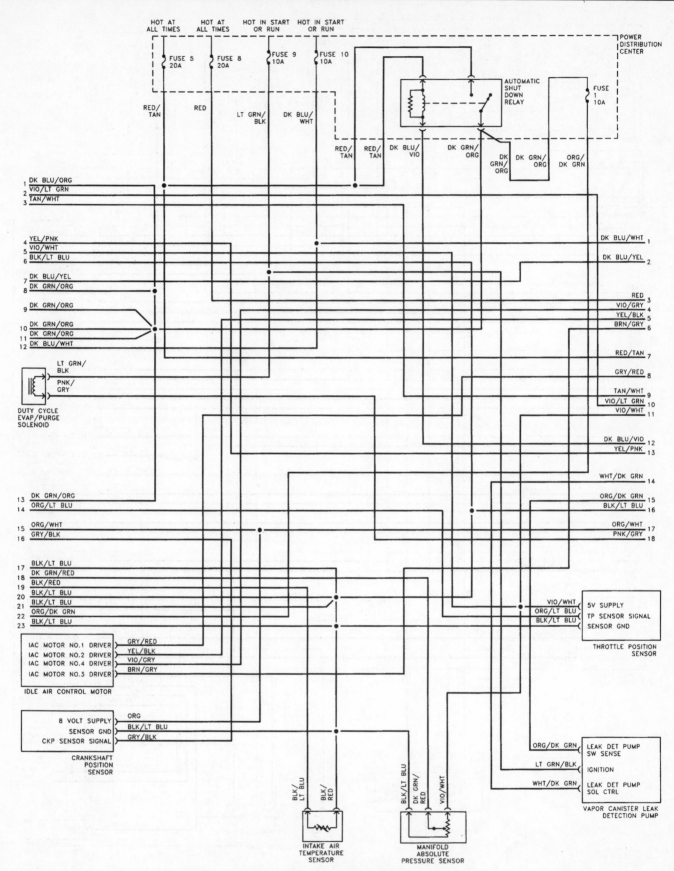

Engine control system - 1997 and later V6 models (2 of 3)

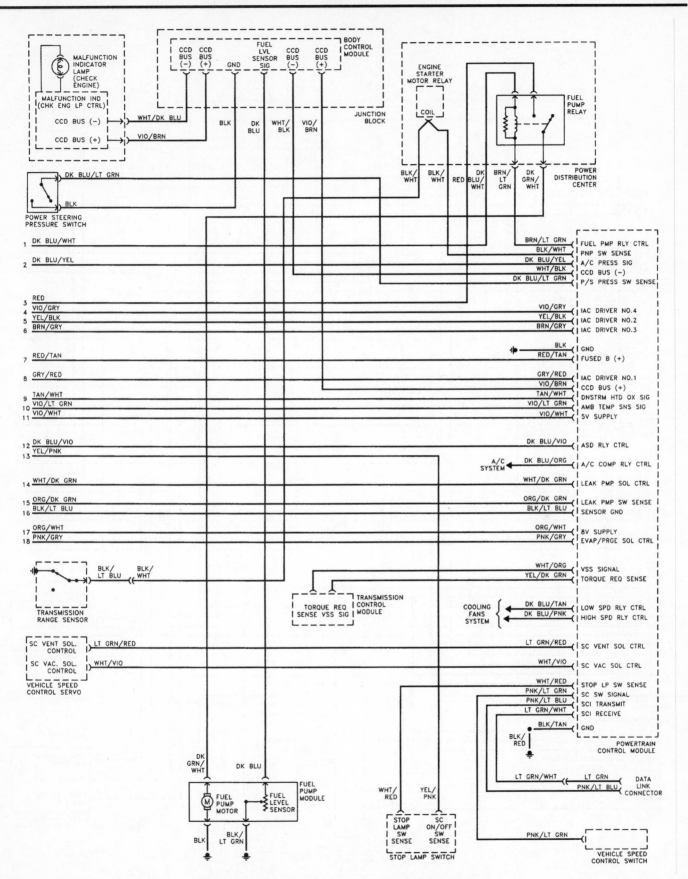

Engine control system - 1997 and later V6 models (3 of 3)

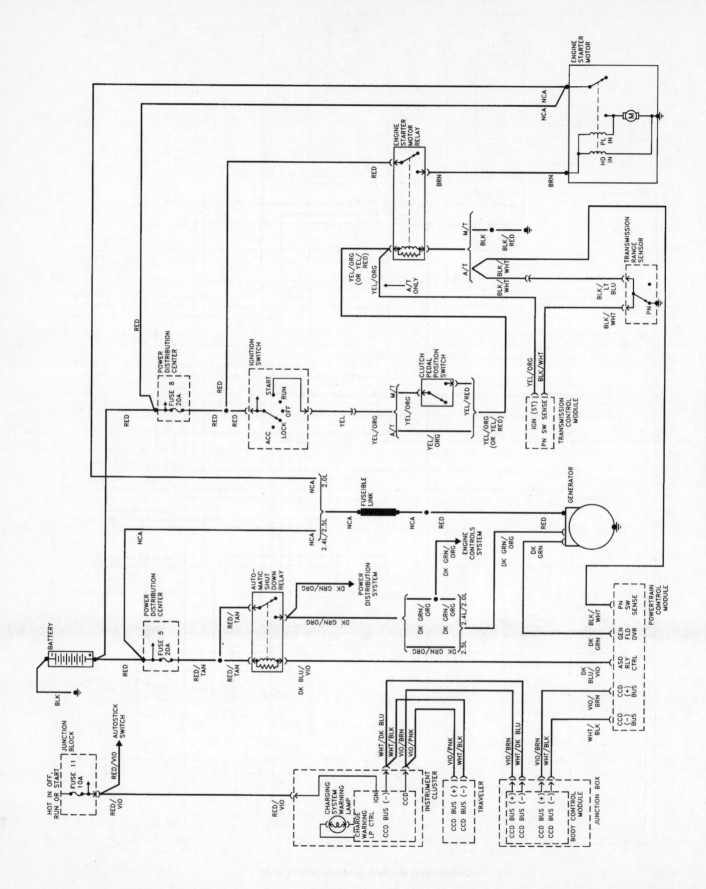

Starting and charging systems

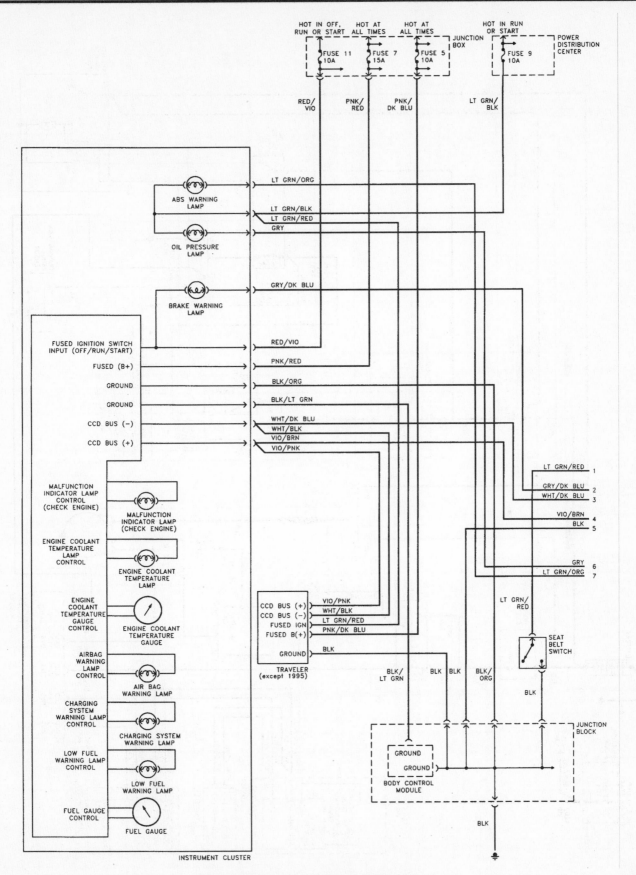

Gauges and warning lights system (1 of 2)

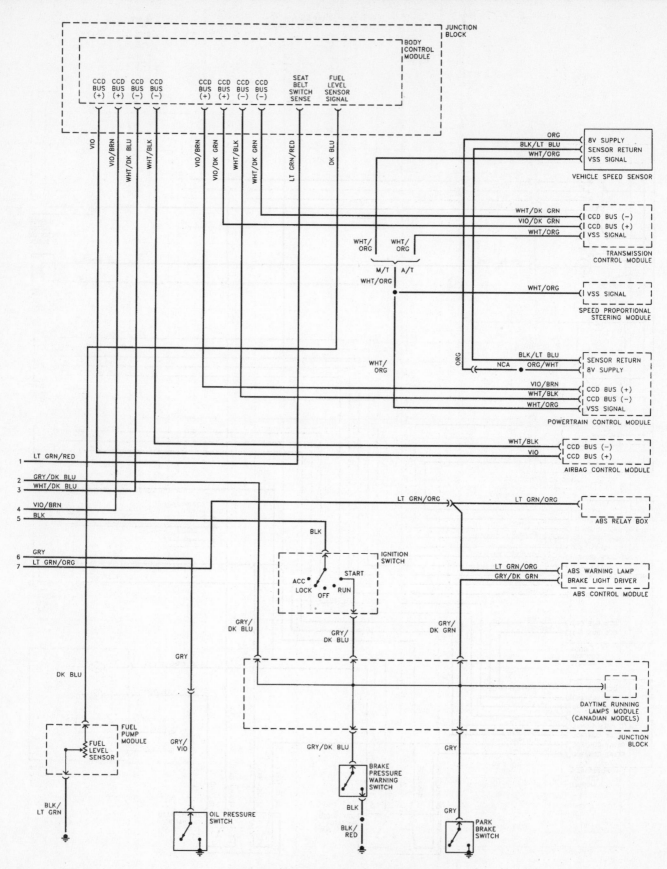

Gauges and warning lights system (2 of 2)

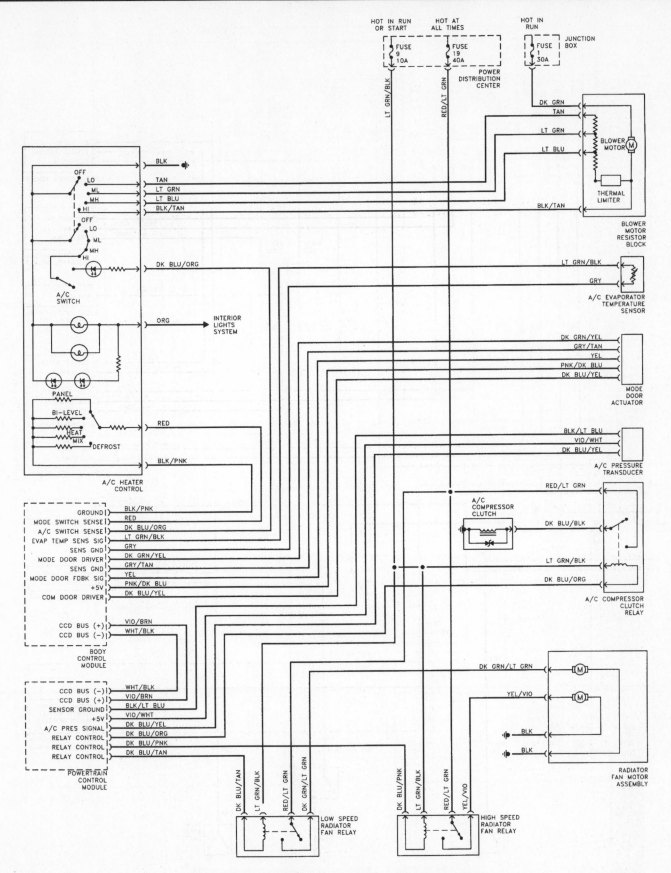

Heating, air conditioning and engine cooling fan systems

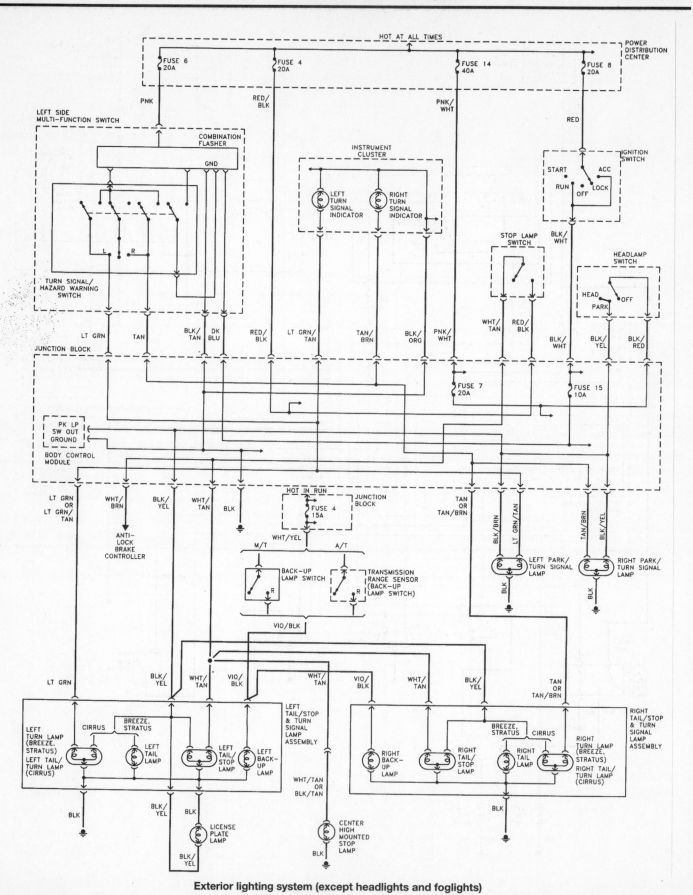

Exterior lighting system (except headlights and foglights)

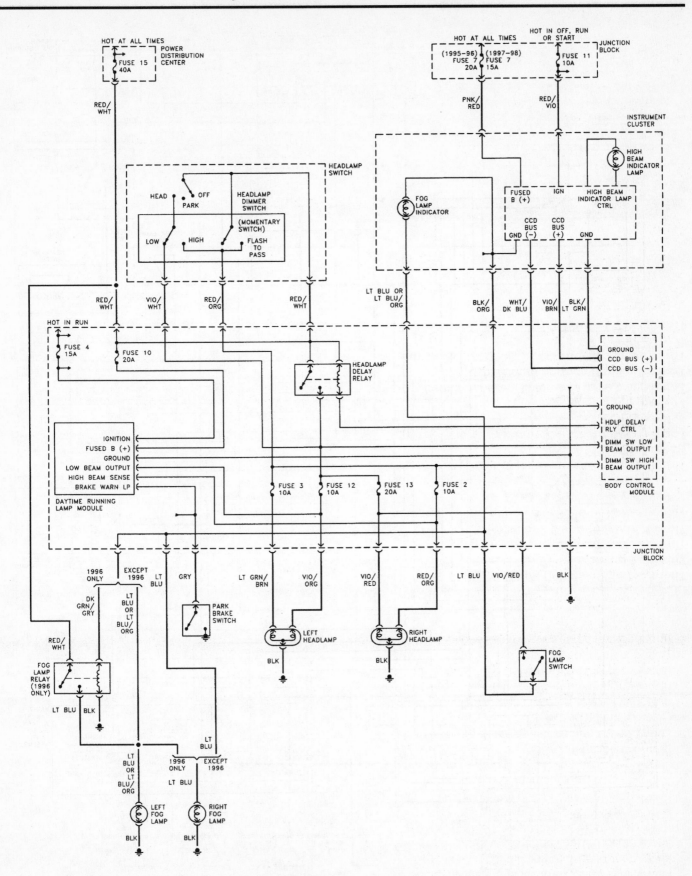

Headlight and foglight systems

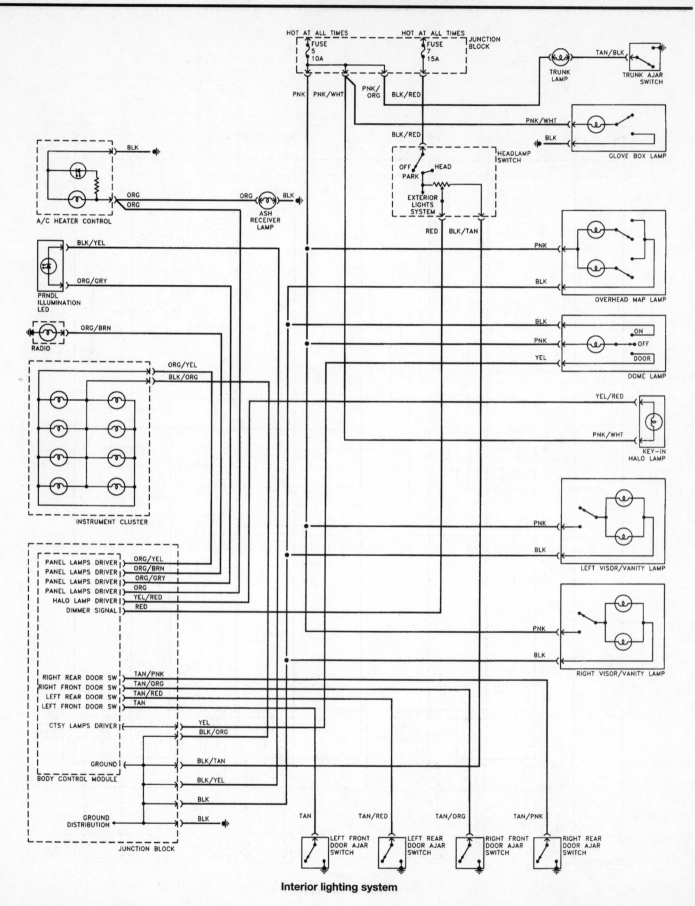

Interior lighting system

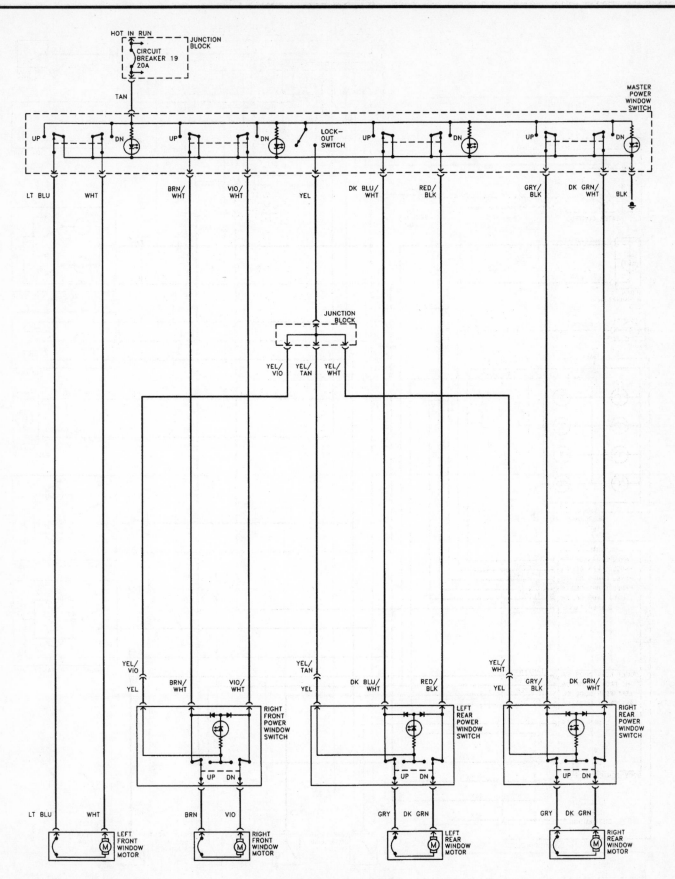

Power window system

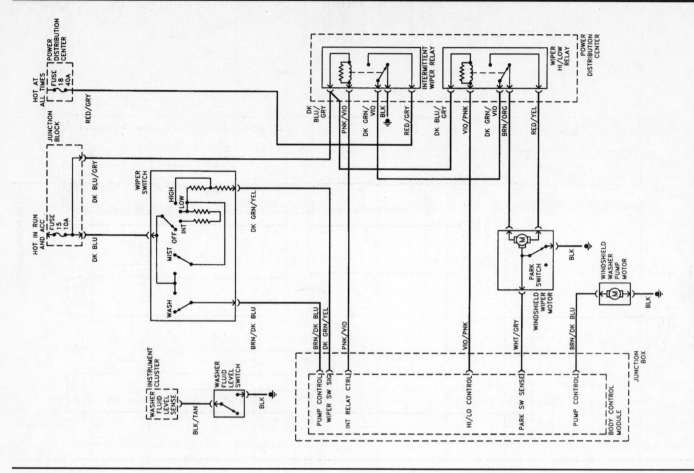

Windshield wiper and washer system

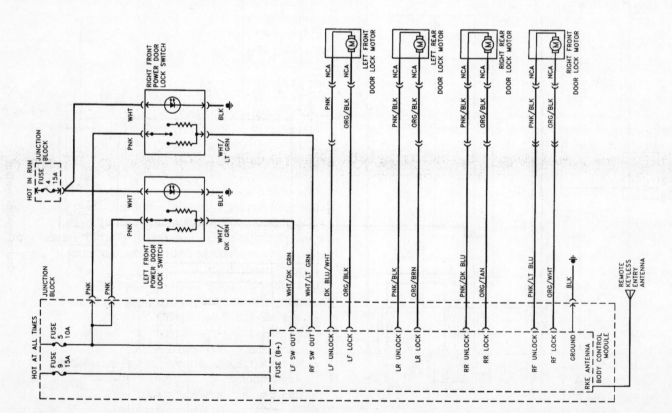

Power door lock system

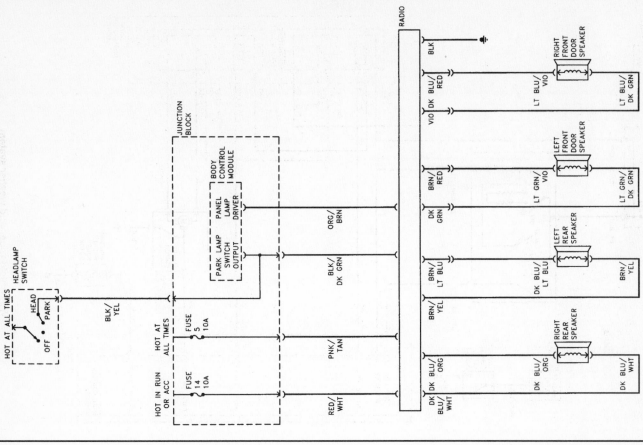

Typical audio system

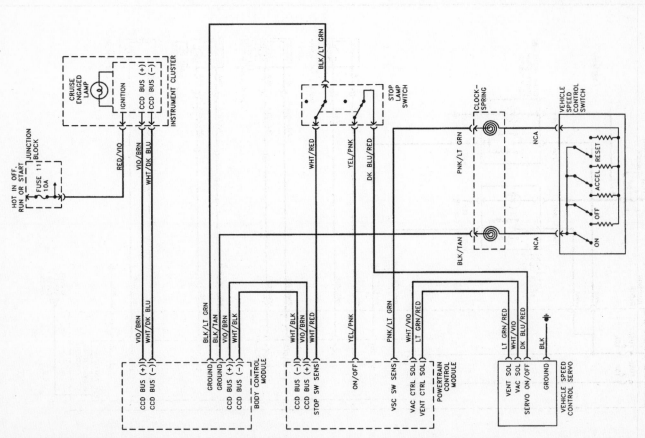

Cruise control system

Notes

Index

Haynes Automotive Manuals

NOTE: New manuals are added to this list on a periodic basis. If you do not see a listing for your vehicle, consult your local Haynes dealer for the latest product information.

ACURA
*12020 Integra '86 thru '89 **& Legend** '86 thru '90

AMC
Jeep CJ - *see JEEP (50020)*
14020 Mid-size models, Concord, Hornet, Gremlin & Spirit '70 thru '83
14025 (Renault) Alliance & Encore '83 thru '87

AUDI
15020 4000 all models '80 thru '87
15025 5000 all models '77 thru '83
15026 5000 all models '84 thru '88

AUSTIN-HEALEY
Sprite - *see MG Midget (66015)*

BMW
*18020 3/5 Series not including diesel or all-wheel drive models '82 thru '92
*18021 3 Series except 325iX models '92 thru '97
18025 320i all 4 cyl models '75 thru '83
18035 528i & 530i all models '75 thru '80
18050 1500 thru 2002 except Turbo '59 thru '77

BUICK
Century (front wheel drive) - *see GM (829)*
*19020 Buick, Oldsmobile & Pontiac Full-size (Front wheel drive) all models '85 thru '98
Buick Electra, LeSabre and Park Avenue; **Oldsmobile** Delta 88 Royale, Ninety Eight and Regency; **Pontiac** Bonneville
19025 Buick Oldsmobile & Pontiac Full-size (Rear wheel drive)
Buick Estate '70 thru '90, Electra '70 thru '84, LeSabre '70 thru '85, Limited '74 thru '79
Oldsmobile Custom Cruiser '70 thru '90, Delta 88 '70 thru '85,Ninety-eight '70 thru '84
Pontiac Bonneville '70 thru '81, Catalina '70 thru '81, Grandville '70 thru '75, Parisienne '83 thru '86
19030 Mid-size Regal & Century all rear-drive models with V6, V8 and Turbo '74 thru '87
Regal - *see GENERAL MOTORS (38010)*
Riviera - *see GENERAL MOTORS (38030)*
Roadmaster - *see CHEVROLET (24046)*
Skyhawk - *see GENERAL MOTORS (38015)*
Skylark '80 thru '85 - *see GM (38020)*
Skylark '86 on - *see GM (38025)*
Somerset - *see GENERAL MOTORS (38025)*

CADILLAC
*21030 Cadillac Rear Wheel Drive all gasoline models '70 thru '93
Cimarron - *see GENERAL MOTORS (38015)*
Eldorado - *see GENERAL MOTORS (38030)*
Seville '80 thru '85 - *see GM (38030)*

CHEVROLET
*24010 Astro & GMC Safari Mini-vans '85 thru '93
24015 Camaro V8 all models '70 thru '81
24016 Camaro all models '82 thru '92
Cavalier - *see GENERAL MOTORS (38015)*
Celebrity - *see GENERAL MOTORS (38005)*
24017 Camaro & Firebird '93 thru '97
24020 Chevelle, Malibu & El Camino '69 thru '87
24024 Chevette & Pontiac T1000 '76 thru '87
Citation - *see GENERAL MOTORS (38020)*
*24032 Corsica/Beretta all models '87 thru '96
24040 Corvette all V8 models '68 thru '82
*24041 Corvette all models '84 thru '96
10305 Chevrolet Engine Overhaul Manual
24045 Full-size Sedans Caprice, Impala, Biscayne, Bel Air & Wagons '69 thru '90
24046 Impala SS & Caprice and Buick Roadmaster '91 thru '96
Lumina - *see GENERAL MOTORS (38010)*

24048 Lumina & Monte Carlo '95 thru '98
Lumina APV - *see GM (38035)*
24050 Luv Pick-up all 2WD & 4WD '72 thru '82
*24055 Monte Carlo all models '70 thru '88
Monte Carlo '95 thru '98 - *see LUMINA (24048)*
24059 Nova all V8 models '69 thru '79
*24060 Nova and Geo Prizm '85 thru '92
24064 Pick-ups '67 thru '87 - Chevrolet & GMC, all V8 & in-line 6 cyl, 2WD & 4WD '67 thru '87; Suburbans, Blazers & Jimmys '67 thru '91
*24065 Pick-ups '88 thru '98 - Chevrolet & GMC, all full-size pick-ups, '88 thru '98; Blazer & Jimmy '92 thru '94; Suburban '92 thru '98; Tahoe & Yukon '98
24070 S-10 & S-15 Pick-ups '82 thru '93, Blazer & Jimmy '83 thru '94,
*24071 S-10 & S-15 Pick-ups '94 thru '96 Blazer & Jimmy '95 thru '96
*24075 Sprint & Geo Metro '85 thru '94
*24080 Vans - Chevrolet & GMC, V8 & in-line 6 cylinder models '68 thru '96

CHRYSLER
25015 Chrysler Cirrus, Dodge Stratus, Plymouth Breeze '95 thru '98
25025 Chrysler Concorde, New Yorker & LHS, Dodge Intrepid, **Eagle** Vision, '93 thru '97
10310 Chrysler Engine Overhaul Manual
*25020 Full-size Front-Wheel Drive '88 thru '93
K-Cars - *see DODGE Aries (30008)*
Laser - *see DODGE Daytona (30030)*
*25030 Chrysler & Plymouth Mid-size front wheel drive '82 thru '95
Rear-wheel Drive - *see Dodge (30050)*

DATSUN
28005 200SX all models '80 thru '83
28007 B-210 all models '73 thru '78
28009 210 all models '79 thru '82
28012 240Z, 260Z & 280Z Coupe '70 thru '78
28014 280ZX Coupe & 2+2 '79 thru '83
300ZX - *see NISSAN (72010)*
28016 310 all models '78 thru '82
28018 510 & PL521 Pick-up '68 thru '73
28020 510 all models '78 thru '81
28022 620 Series Pick-up all models '73 thru '79
720 Series Pick-up - *see NISSAN (72030)*
28025 810/Maxima all gasoline models, '77 thru '84

DODGE
400 & 600 - *see CHRYSLER (25030)*
*30008 Aries & Plymouth Reliant '81 thru '89
30010 Caravan & Plymouth Voyager Mini-Vans all models '84 thru '95
*30011 Caravan & Plymouth Voyager Mini-Vans all models '96 thru '98
30012 Challenger/Plymouth Saporro '78 thru '83
30016 Colt & Plymouth Champ (front wheel drive) all models '78 thru '87
*30020 Dakota Pick-ups all models '87 thru '96
30025 Dart, Demon, Plymouth Barracuda, Duster & Valiant 6 cyl models '67 thru '76
*30030 Daytona & Chrysler Laser '84 thru '89
Intrepid - *see CHRYSLER (25025)*
*30034 Neon all models '95 thru '97
*30035 Omni & Plymouth Horizon '78 thru '90
*30040 Pick-ups all full-size models '74 thru '93
*30041 Pick-ups all full-size models '94 thru '96
*30045 Ram 50/D50 Pick-ups & Raider and Plymouth Arrow Pick-ups '79 thru '93
30050 Dodge/Plymouth/Chrysler rear wheel drive '71 thru '89
*30055 Shadow & Plymouth Sundance '87 thru '94
*30060 Spirit & Plymouth Acclaim '89 thru '95
*30065 Vans - Dodge & Plymouth '71 thru '96

EAGLE
Talon - *see Mitsubishi Eclipse (68030)*
Vision - *see CHRYSLER (25025)*

FIAT
34010 124 Sport Coupe & Spider '68 thru '78
34025 X1/9 all models '74 thru '80

FORD
10355 Ford Automatic Transmission Overhaul
*36004 Aerostar Mini-vans all models '86 thru '96
*36006 Contour & Mercury Mystique '95 thru '98
36008 Courier Pick-up all models '72 thru '82
36012 Crown Victoria & Mercury Grand Marquis '88 thru '96
10320 Ford Engine Overhaul Manual
36016 Escort/Mercury Lynx all models '81 thru '90
*36020 Escort/Mercury Tracer '91 thru '96
*36024 Explorer & Mazda Navajo '91 thru '95
36028 Fairmont & Mercury Zephyr '78 thru '83
36030 Festiva & Aspire '88 thru '97
36032 Fiesta all models '77 thru '80
36036 Ford & Mercury Full-size,
Ford LTD & Mercury Marquis ('75 thru '82); Ford Custom 500,Country Squire, Crown Victoria & Mercury Colony Park ('75 thru '87); Ford LTD Crown Victoria & Mercury Gran Marquis ('83 thru '87)
36040 Granada & Mercury Monarch '75 thru '80
36044 Ford & Mercury Mid-size,
Ford Thunderbird & Mercury Cougar ('75 thru '82); Ford LTD & Mercury Marquis ('83 thru '86); Ford Torino,Gran Torino, Elite, Ranchero pick-up, LTD II, Mercury Montego, Comet, XR-7 & Lincoln Versailles ('75 thru '86)
36048 Mustang V8 all models '64-1/2 thru '73
36049 Mustang II 4 cyl, V6 & V8 models '74 thru '78
36050 Mustang & Mercury Capri all models Mustang '79 thru '93; Capri '79 thru '86
*36051 Mustang all models '94 thru '97
36054 Pick-ups & Bronco '73 thru '79
36058 Pick-ups & Bronco '80 thru '96
36059 Pick-ups, Expedition & Mercury Navigator '97 thru '98
36062 Pinto & Mercury Bobcat '75 thru '80
36066 Probe all models '89 thru '92
36070 Ranger/Bronco II gasoline models '83 thru '92
*36071 Ranger '93 thru '97 & Mazda Pick-ups '94 thru '97
36074 Taurus & Mercury Sable '86 thru '95
*36075 Taurus & Mercury Sable '96 thru '98
*36078 Tempo & Mercury Topaz '84 thru '94
36082 Thunderbird/Mercury Cougar '83 thru '88
*36086 Thunderbird/Mercury Cougar '89 and '97
36090 Vans all V8 Econoline models '69 thru '91
*36094 Vans full size '92-'95
*36097 Windstar Mini-van '95-'98

GENERAL MOTORS
*10360 GM Automatic Transmission Overhaul
*38005 Buick Century, Chevrolet Celebrity, Oldsmobile Cutlass Ciera & Pontiac 6000 all models '82 thru '96
*38010 Buick Regal, Chevrolet Lumina, Oldsmobile Cutlass Supreme & Pontiac Grand Prix front-wheel drive models '88 thru '95
*38015 Buick Skyhawk, Cadillac Cimarron, Chevrolet Cavalier, Oldsmobile Firenza & Pontiac J-2000 & Sunbird '82 thru '94
*38016 Chevrolet Cavalier & Pontiac Sunfire '95 thru '98
38020 Buick Skylark, Chevrolet Citation, Olds Omega, Pontiac Phoenix '80 thru '85
38025 Buick Skylark & Somerset, Oldsmobile Achieva & Calais and Pontiac Grand Am all models '85 thru '95
38030 Cadillac Eldorado '71 thru '85, **Seville** '80 thru '85, **Oldsmobile Toronado** '71 thru '85 **& Buick Riviera** '79 thru '85
*38035 Chevrolet Lumina APV, Olds Silhouette & Pontiac Trans Sport all models '90 thru '95
General Motors Full-size Rear-wheel Drive - *see BUICK (19025)*

(Continued on other side)

Haynes North America, Inc., 861 Lawrence Drive, Newbury Park, CA 91320-1514 • (805) 498-6703

Haynes Automotive Manuals (continued)

NOTE: New manuals are added to this list on a periodic basis. If you do not see a listing for your vehicle, consult your local Haynes dealer for the latest product information.

GEO

Metro - *see CHEVROLET Sprint (24075)*
Prizm - *'85 thru '92 see CHEVY (24060), '93 thru '96 see TOYOTA Corolla (92036)*
*40030 **Storm** all models '90 thru '93
Tracker - *see SUZUKI Samurai (90010)*

GMC

Safari - *see CHEVROLET ASTRO (24010)*
Vans & Pick-ups - *see CHEVROLET*

HONDA

42010 **Accord CVCC** all models '76 thru '83
42011 **Accord** all models '84 thru '89
42012 **Accord** all models '90 thru '93
42013 **Accord** all models '94 thru '95
42020 **Civic 1200** all models '73 thru '79
42021 **Civic 1300 & 1500 CVCC** '80 thru '83
42022 **Civic 1500 CVCC** all models '75 thru '79
42023 **Civic** all models '84 thru '91
*42024 **Civic & del Sol** '92 thru '95
*42040 **Prelude CVCC** all models '79 thru '89

HYUNDAI

*43015 **Excel** all models '86 thru '94

ISUZU

Hombre - *see CHEVROLET S-10 (24071)*
*47017 **Rodeo** '91 thru '97; **Amigo** '89 thru '94; **Honda Passport** '95 thru '97
*47020 **Trooper & Pick-up**, all gasoline models Pick-up, '81 thru '93; Trooper, '84 thru '91

JAGUAR

*49010 **XJ6** all 6 cyl models '68 thru '86
*49011 **XJ6** all models '88 thru '94
*49015 **XJ12 & XJS** all 12 cyl models '72 thru '85

JEEP

*50010 **Cherokee, Comanche & Wagoneer Limited** all models '84 thru '96
50020 **CJ** all models '49 thru '86
*50025 **Grand Cherokee** all models '93 thru '98
50029 **Grand Wagoneer & Pick-up** '72 thru '91 Grand Wagoneer '84 thru '91, Cherokee & Wagoneer '72 thru '83, Pick-up '72 thru '88
*50030 **Wrangler** all models '87 thru '95

LINCOLN

Navigator - *see FORD Pick-up (36059)*
59010 **Rear Wheel Drive** all models '70 thru '96

MAZDA

61010 **GLC Hatchback (rear wheel drive)** '77 thru '83
61011 **GLC (front wheel drive)** '81 thru '85
*61015 **323 & Protegé** '90 thru '97
*61016 **MX-5 Miata** '90 thru '97
*61020 **MPV** all models '89 thru '94
Navajo - *see Ford Explorer (36024)*
61030 **Pick-ups** '72 thru '93
Pick-ups '94 thru '96 - *see Ford Ranger (36071)*
61035 **RX-7** all models '79 thru '85
*61036 **RX-7** all models '86 thru '91
61040 **626 (rear wheel drive)** all models '79 thru '82
*61041 **626/MX-6 (front wheel drive)** '83 thru '91

MERCEDES-BENZ

63012 **123 Series Diesel** '76 thru '85
*63015 **190 Series four-cyl gas models**, '84 thru '88
63020 **230/250/280** 6 cyl sohc models '68 thru '72
63025 **280 123 Series** gasoline models '77 thru '81
63030 **350 & 450** all models '71 thru '80

MERCURY

See FORD Listing.

MG

66010 **MGB** Roadster & GT Coupe '62 thru '80
66015 **MG Midget, Austin Healey Sprite** '58 thru '80

MITSUBISHI

*68020 **Cordia, Tredia, Galant, Precis & Mirage** '83 thru '93
*68030 **Eclipse, Eagle Talon & Ply. Laser** '90 thru '94
*68040 **Pick-up** '83 thru '96 & **Montero** '83 thru '93

NISSAN

72010 **300ZX** all models including Turbo '84 thru '89
*72015 **Altima** all models '93 thru '97
*72020 **Maxima** all models '85 thru '91
*72030 **Pick-ups** '80 thru '96 **Pathfinder** '87 thru '95
72040 **Pulsar** all models '83 thru '86
*72050 **Sentra** all models '82 thru '94
*72051 **Sentra & 200SX** all models '95 thru '98
*72060 **Stanza** all models '82 thru '90

OLDSMOBILE

*73015 **Cutlass** V6 & V8 gas models '74 thru '88

For other OLDSMOBILE titles, see BUICK, CHEVROLET or GENERAL MOTORS listing.

PLYMOUTH

For PLYMOUTH titles, see DODGE listing.

PONTIAC

79008 **Fiero** all models '84 thru '88
79018 **Firebird** V8 models except Turbo '70 thru '81
79019 **Firebird** all models '82 thru '92

For other PONTIAC titles, see BUICK, CHEVROLET or GENERAL MOTORS listing.

PORSCHE

*80020 **911** except Turbo & Carrera 4 '65 thru '89
80025 **914** all 4 cyl models '69 thru '76
80030 **924** all models including Turbo '76 thru '82
*80035 **944** all models including Turbo '83 thru '89

RENAULT

Alliance & Encore - *see AMC (14020)*

SAAB

*84010 **900** all models including Turbo '79 thru '88

SATURN

87010 **Saturn** all models '91 thru '96

SUBARU

89002 **1100, 1300, 1400 & 1600** '71 thru '79
*89003 **1600 & 1800** 2WD & 4WD '80 thru '94

SUZUKI

*90010 **Samurai/Sidekick & Geo Tracker** '86 thru '96

TOYOTA

92005 **Camry** all models '83 thru '91
92006 **Camry** all models '92 thru '96
92015 **Celica Rear Wheel Drive** '71 thru '85
*92020 **Celica Front Wheel Drive** '86 thru '93
92025 **Celica Supra** all models '79 thru '92
92030 **Corolla** all models '75 thru '79
92032 **Corolla** all rear wheel drive models '80 thru '87
92035 **Corolla** all front wheel drive models '84 thru '92
*92036 **Corolla & Geo Prizm** '93 thru '97
92040 **Corolla Tercel** all models '80 thru '82
92045 **Corona** all models '74 thru '82
92050 **Cressida** all models '78 thru '82
92055 **Land Cruiser** FJ40, 43, 45, 55 '68 thru '82
92056 **Land Cruiser** FJ60, 62, 80, FZJ80 '80 thru '96
*92065 **MR2** all models '85 thru '87
92070 **Pick-up** all models '69 thru '78
*92075 **Pick-up** all models '79 thru '95
*92076 **Tacoma** '95 thru '98, **4Runner** '96 thru '98, & **T100** '93 thru '98
*92080 **Previa** all models '91 thru '95
92085 **Tercel** all models '87 thru '94

TRIUMPH

94007 **Spitfire** all models '62 thru '81
94010 **TR7** all models '75 thru '81

VW

96008 **Beetle & Karmann Ghia** '54 thru '79
96012 **Dasher** all gasoline models '74 thru '81
*96016 **Rabbit, Jetta, Scirocco, & Pick-up** gas models '74 thru '91 & Convertible '80 thru '92
96017 **Golf & Jetta** all models '93 thru '97
96020 **Rabbit, Jetta & Pick-up** diesel '77 thru '84
96030 **Transporter 1600** all models '68 thru '79
96035 **Transporter 1700, 1800 & 2000** '72 thru '79
96040 **Type 3 1500 & 1600** all models '63 thru '73
96045 **Vanagon** all air-cooled models '80 thru '83

VOLVO

97010 **120, 130 Series & 1800 Sports** '61 thru '73
97015 **140 Series** all models '66 thru '74
*97020 **240 Series** all models '76 thru '93
97025 **260 Series** all models '75 thru '82
*97040 **740 & 760 Series** all models '82 thru '88

TECHBOOK MANUALS

10205 **Automotive Computer Codes**
10210 **Automotive Emissions Control Manual**
10215 **Fuel Injection Manual, 1978 thru 1985**
10220 **Fuel Injection Manual, 1986 thru 1996**
10225 **Holley Carburetor Manual**
10230 **Rochester Carburetor Manual**
10240 **Weber/Zenith/Stromberg/SU Carburetors**
10305 **Chevrolet Engine Overhaul Manual**
10310 **Chrysler Engine Overhaul Manual**
10320 **Ford Engine Overhaul Manual**
10330 **GM and Ford Diesel Engine Repair Manual**
10340 **Small Engine Repair Manual**
10345 **Suspension, Steering & Driveline Manual**
10355 **Ford Automatic Transmission Overhaul**
10360 **GM Automatic Transmission Overhaul**
10405 **Automotive Body Repair & Painting**
10410 **Automotive Brake Manual**
10415 **Automotive Detailing Manual**
10420 **Automotive Eelectrical Manual**
10425 **Automotive Heating & Air Conditioning**
10430 **Automotive Reference Manual & Dictionary**
10435 **Automotive Tools Manual**
10440 **Used Car Buying Guide**
10445 **Welding Manual**
10450 **ATV Basics**

SPANISH MANUALS

98903 **Reparación de Carrocería & Pintura**
98905 **Códigos Automotrices de la Computadora**
98910 **Frenos Automotriz**
98915 **Inyección de Combustible 1986 al 1994**
99040 **Chevrolet & GMC Camionetas** '67 al '87 Incluye Suburban, Blazer & Jimmy '67 al '91
99041 **Chevrolet & GMC Camionetas** '88 al '95 Incluye Suburban '92 al '95, Blazer & Jimmy '92 al '94, Tahoe y Yukon '95
99042 **Chevrolet & GMC Camionetas Cerradas** '68 al '95
99055 **Dodge Caravan & Plymouth Voyager** '84 al '95
99075 **Ford Camionetas y Bronco** '80 al '94
99077 **Ford Camionetas Cerradas** '69 al '91
99083 **Ford Modelos de Tamaño Grande** '75 al '87
99088 **Ford Modelos de Tamaño Mediano** '75 al '86
99091 **Ford Taurus & Mercury Sable** '86 al '95
99095 **GM Modelos de Tamaño Grande** '70 al '90
99100 **GM Modelos de Tamaño Mediano** '70 al '88
99110 **Nissan Camionetas** '80 al '96, **Pathfinder** '87 al '95
99118 **Nissan Sentra** '82 al '94
99125 **Toyota Camionetas y 4Runner** '79 al '95

---

* Listings shown with an asterisk (*) indicate model coverage as of this printing. These titles will be periodically updated to include later model years - consult your Haynes dealer for more information.

Over 100 Haynes motorcycle manuals also available

5-98

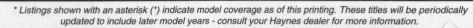